POLITICS IN THE AMERICAN STATES

A COMPARATIVE ANALYSIS

Authors

RICHARD E. DAWSON   *Washington University of St. Louis*

THOMAS R. DYE   *University of Georgia*

DANIEL J. ELAZAR   *Temple University*

ROBERT S. FRIEDMAN   *University of Michigan*

HERBERT JACOB   *University of Wisconsin*

LESTER W. MILBRATH   *Northwestern University*

CLARA PENNIMAN   *University of Wisconsin*

AUSTIN RANNEY   *University of Wisconsin*

JAMES A. ROBINSON   *Ohio State University*

ROBERT H. SALISBURY   *Washington University of St. Louis*

JOSEPH A. SCHLESINGER   *Michigan State University*

KENNETH N. VINES   *Tulane University*

HARMON ZEIGLER   *University of Oregon*

POLITICS IN THE AMERICAN STATES

A COMPARATIVE ANALYSIS

HERBERT JACOB
and
KENNETH N. VINES
Editors

Boston   *Toronto*

LITTLE, BROWN AND COMPANY

FIRST PRINTING

Published simultaneously in Canada
by Little, Brown & Company (Canada) Limited

PRINTED IN THE UNITED STATES OF AMERICA

FOREWORD

THIS TEXT SEEKS TO BRING contemporary political science concepts and techniques to the general study of state politics. It examines the states comparatively; it is systematically empirical; it limits itself to state politics. Each of these features is incorporated through the experience of leading experts.

The principal feature of this volume is that it undertakes a comparative analysis of politics in the fifty states. It has always seemed anomalous to us that "comparative government" is a phrase used to describe the study of foreign governments. Comparative analysis is even more appropriate to the study of domestic institutions like the states since they are enough alike to make comparative analysis plausible, but different enough to produce valuable insights into the conditions which affect political institutions and the behavior of citizens and officials. Furthermore, comparative analysis of state politics reveals those features of the political process which are common not only to the states but also to political phenomena in general. It emphasizes the extent to which the study of state politics is not an insulated specialization, but in the mainstream of political science.

A second characteristic of this book is that it is empirical and analytic. Our collaborators have sought to describe by keeping close to the facts, and to analyze by examining those empirical relationships they actually found. As there are only fifty states, they have always sought to account for each of them. All too often in the literature of state politics one or another state has been selected to illustrate a point; this allows colorful description but it introduces biases into the analysis, for such casual selections can hardly serve as a valid basis for generalizations. Either the whole "universe" must be described, or the limits of generalization must be carefully specified. We have examined political practices in all

v

fifty states wherever possible; where this was not feasible, we have tried to limit our conclusions accordingly.

Empirical analysis has been enriched in the last decade by the development of new political science techniques. Our authors make frequent use of these advances. Their data, for example, are sometimes based on sample surveys, as well as upon official government sources. Quantitative techniques that have been employed include percentage distributions, averages, cross tabulations, and correlation coefficients. These are used when appropriate to describe, analyze, and simplify the complexities of state politics. In addition, measurements are used because some features of state politics lend themselves to quite precise measurement — for example, voter turnout. Other concepts are less precise. The degree of party competition, the amount of interest group activity, the degree of legislative cohesion, and the power of a governor do not allow the same degree of precision as the number of votes cast at an election. Yet each of these important phenomena are measurable and have been tabulated by our authors. For instance, the degree of party competition can yield an ordinal scale which shows where each state stands in relation to every other state. It enables us to say that New York is less competitive than Wyoming and more competitive than Wisconsin (see Table 1 in Chapter 3), although it does not allow us to say that New York is twice as competitive as any other state.

The third distinctive feature of this book is that it limits its attention to state politics. Most texts combine state politics with local politics. We have not done so because we felt that local political systems cannot be examined thoroughly when combined with state politics. Local political systems involve different participants, different institutions, and different stakes. Moreover, local politics flourishes in many forms; no simple generalizations do justice to the variety of local political systems which exist in the United States. As a consequence, we felt it unwise to attempt an analysis of local politics here.

Emphasis on comparative analysis of empirical data about state politics has yielded a text rich in description and explicit in its analysis. Rather than summarize and digest the process of analysis for the student, we allow him to see for himself the methods by which conclusions are reached and the process by which the descriptions and analyses are made.

The idea for this book originated in correspondence between the Editors concerning the possibility of a more effective text for teaching state politics. Given the increase in information about the states and the important advances in the methodology and theory of political studies in recent years, we felt the time had come to depart from traditional ways of presenting the subject.

The conception of a comparative study of state politics is not new. The Social Science Research Council encouraged this type of state study through its publications and fellowship programs after World War II. V. O. Key,

Jr., in his pioneering *Southern Politics* and *American State Politics* undertook the comparative examination of several aspects of state political experience; a few others have also looked at different geographical regions along these lines. Yet, after hopeful beginnings, no systematic treatment of state politics emerged.

The character of state politics indicated that successful study could best by achieved by a collaborative project. The amount of literature and the effort required for research and analysis make it difficult for one or two scholars, no matter how experienced, to cope with the variety of phenomena and the complexities encompassed. On the other hand, a team of scholars — each highly qualified in some area of state politics — could command the resources necessary for a thorough treatment. Therefore, the Editors invited scholars who had published in various fields to participate, and found them enthusiastic about the idea.

Although written by separate experts, the chapters form a unified study for each is set within a common frame of reference. Each encompasses:

1. A comparative analysis in which variations and similarities of state politics are systematically described, examined, and then related to other features of the political and social environment of the states;

2. An analysis that utilizes modern methods and theoretical conceptions to clarify the operation and functions of state political systems.

Through correspondence and conversations, the Editors and authors discussed the problems of comparison, and in some cases worked together toward the solution of difficulties in data collection and analysis. The Editors commented on rough drafts of the texts. Each chapter, however, is the product of its author.

Although this volume is as definitive as present available knowledge allows us to make it, throughout the book our authors point to gaps in the data — areas about which we do not know enough to make even tentative generalizations. This is part of the challenge of state politics. We hope this volume does not lull the reader into complacence; on the contrary, we hope it generates disagreement, controversy, and productive new research.

We are more than usually indebted to several members of the staff of Little, Brown and Company. Donald R. Hammonds gave us his enthusiastic support and made the project financially possible. Ronald Q. Lewton, Freda Alexander, and their assistants rounded off many rough edges which inevitably appear in such a collaborative work.

We dedicate this volume to the memory of V. O. Key, Jr., whose research in state politics marked the path we have tried to follow.

Madison, Wisconsin   HERBERT JACOB
New Orleans, Louisiana   KENNETH N. VINES
October 25, 1964

CONTENTS

Part One: Introduction

Part Two: Participation in State Politics

Part Three: The Policy-Making Arenas

Part Four: Policies and Programs

Part Five: The Bounds of State Politics

LIST OF
TABLES AND FIGURES

TABLES

FIGURES

PART ONE

INTRODUCTION

EACH OF THE FIFTY STATES that comprise the United States has its own governmental structure and political system. Therefore, we need to specify what state political systems comprise in order to outline what we shall include in this volume. We begin with an examination of the nature of state political systems and some of their general characteristics. Next, we shall look at the manner in which private citizens by themselves, in groups, or in political parties prod their government into action or keep it out of certain areas. We shall consider the policy-making institutions of government — the legislature, the executive, and the judiciary — and the manner in which each makes decisions. The programs and policies of government will be analyzed for insight into the results of political struggles. Finally, we shall define the boundaries within which the states may act.

STATE
POLITICAL
SYSTEMS

CHAPTER 1
by
HERBERT JACOB*

THE HIGH INTENSITY AND BROAD SCOPE of politics at the state level is one of the peculiar characteristics of American government. In most other countries, political affairs are concentrated at the national capital. In the United States, most political decisions are made outside Washington — in the Albanys, Columbias and Sacramentos which house their state's government.

The fate of most domestic programs and policies is settled in state capitals. Most of them are supervised in whole or in part by state governments. Even when the program is a national one, states must often decide whether to participate or what local policies to adopt for administering the program. Education, public health, regulation of businesses and professions, and policing are functions that are primarily under the control of state governments and their subdivisions. Most decisions with respect to such programs are made in the states.

States are also significant innovators. They develop novel programs and new policies far more frequently than the national government does. The first statutes regulating business practices to control monopolies were developed by the states; the first maximum-hours, minimum-wage legislation was state legislation. Long before the federal government enacted effective anti-discrimination legislation with respect to employment and public accommodations, many states had such legislation and were enforcing it. Even in technological areas, initiative is often exercised by state governments. Thus, in the late 1950's when the federal government refused to measure the fall-out resulting from atmospheric nuclear explosions, state governments did so in order to warn their populations if a danger should arise.

The broad scope of state governmental services is matched by the intensity of politics in many state capitals. Each year when the state

*The author is much indebted to his colleague, Professor Jack Dennis, for helpful comments on an earlier draft.

legislature convenes, the atmosphere in the capital city becomes charged with conflict. Campaigns for state office are unmatched in their bitterness. It is hard to imagine more caustic campaigns than those staged by such figures as "Happy" Chandler of Kentucky, the late Earl Long of Louisiana, or Richardson Dilworth of Pennsylvania.

Moreover, most political careers are made and broken within the states. Except for the President and Vice-President, every elected official in the United States is elected by a state or subdivision of one. Senators are representatives of their states; Congressmen come from smaller districts within their states. Both must often campaign on purely local issues and bargain with local party organizations for their survival.

Politics at the state level possesses many of the characteristics of national politics. It involves elections and the struggle to control the governmental machinery. It involves conflict over resources controlled by government. It is the process by which the demands for services are met or balanced off against the desire to minimize taxation. Yet, unlike national politics, the states are scarcely involved in the world at large. They do not contribute substantially to securing the nation's defense. State politics is entirely focused on domestic affairs.

Outwardly state politics appears very much the same throughout the United States. Each state has much the same set of governmental institutions. The states grapple with many of the same problems. The states operate in the same national environment.

Such appearances are entirely misleading, for state politics varies tremendously from state to state. Contrast the sedate campaigns of Vermont with the swashbuckling campaigns replete with hillbilly bands in Texas. Compare the $41 million that Massachusetts spent in 1963 on state colleges and universities with the $127 million the smaller, less wealthy state of Wisconsin spent.[1] In a state like Louisiana, the state collects three-fourths of all state-local taxes; in another like South Dakota, the state collects less than two-fifths of the total.[2] A state like Mississippi spares no resources in maintaining Negroes in a segregated status; a state like California expends great energy to eliminate inequality. The list of differences could be expanded a hundred times.

Why do such differences occur? Why do Vermont and Texas politicians campaign so differently? Why does Massachusetts spend so little on its public colleges and Wisconsin so much? Why are some state governments relatively powerful while others remain relatively weak?

The following chapters seek to describe in detail the differences between the states and explain their occurrence. Before going into such details, it is necessary to understand the environment in which state politics takes place and what state politics involves, for both the nature of the environment and the specific features of state political systems can help us understand the puzzling variety that confronts the student of American state politics.

THE PHYSICAL AND SOCIAL ENVIRONMENT OF STATE POLITICS

The milieu in which state politicians operate conditions their behavior in many ways. It leads to the development of some demands and the absence of others. It provides resources which help some states meet their problems; in other states, the resources are missing. It provides social conditions to which the political system must adapt or which it must seek to change.

Physical features make a difference to the political system. States which have great mineral or oil resources are able to tax them heavily without bearing the burden of the taxation themselves, since such taxes become part of the price paid for oil, gas, iron, or coal by other industries in other states. Thus, a state can export its tax burden; it can impose high taxes which are not heavily felt by its own citizens.[3] Mountains, deserts, and plains may affect the cost of providing governmental services. It is clear that it is more expensive to build highways through mountains than across plains and that a physical environment which leads to a widely dispersed population makes many other governmental services expensive to maintain. The distribution of water may become vital to a political system as in California. Northern California has more water than it can use; the problem there is to dam it up so it does not cause floods. Southern California suffers from a perennial shortage of water. This physical condition has made the distribution of water a central issue in California politics and the main bone of contention between California and its neighboring states which also have water that Southern Californians want.

The social environment — the manner in which people live in their physical surroundings — has an even greater impact on state politics. To a large degree, the social environment is the same for all American states. All Americans speak the same language. No state is marked by special racial distinctions or nationality groupings as is the case in Canada or Switzerland. Minority groups exist in every state and members of such groups identify themselves as Americans first and only secondarily as members of minority groups. Moreover, familial and other personal relationships bind Americans in one state to those living in another.

These uniformities are reflected in a host of ways. People across the nation wear the same kinds of clothes. The same churches and clubs exist throughout the land. The same stores, products, and prices can be seen in the East or West, North or South. Homes are built in much the same architectural style and public buildings all look alike. The people look equally healthy; they suffer from the same illnesses in New York as in California and receive the same quality medical care. Although school systems differ, the amount of schooling Americans receive in one state is much the same as they get in others.

Yet there are striking differences in social conditions of the several states. The states differ markedly in their size. The largest state (Alaska) is more than five hundred times the size of the smallest (Rhode Island); even the states which rank in the middle of the fifty states in size (Iowa and Wisconsin) are fifty times larger than Rhode Island.[4]

There is a like variation in the population of the states. The most populous, New York, has 16 million people living within its borders. Nevada, the least populous state, has only 285,000 people — fewer than the forty-five largest cities in the United States in 1960.[5]

Neither area alone nor people alone raises particular problems for government. The characteristics of the people and the conditions under which they live are more important. Here, too, there are large differences among the states. The very largest state, Alaska, has a small population that is thinly spread throughout its territory. It has the lowest number of persons per square mile (0.4) and not a single city with as many as 50,000 people. The smallest state (Rhode Island), on the other hand, has the most densely packed population: 812.4 persons per square mile.[6] Such variations in the density of population may make a lot of difference in the manner in which states face political problems. Thinly scattered populations place different demands on their governments. There is less need, for instance, for strict water and air pollution controls or land use regulations, but it may be more expensive to provide adequate services. In densely populated areas governmental services may be less expensive to provide, but demands are likely to be more varied.

Four states — Vermont, Idaho, Wyoming, and Alaska — had no large cities in 1960.[7] They were predominantly rural even though a large part of their population lived in small towns of less than 50,000. Other states had most of their population in metropolitan centers. Eighty per cent of all Californians lived in urbanized metropolitan areas; in another three states, more than 75 per cent of the population lived in cities over 50,000 or in urban areas surrounding such cities. On the other hand, fifteen states had less than one-quarter of their population living in such heavily urbanized areas.[8]

In those states where most people live in metropolitan or urban centers, we might expect different demands for government services than in those where few lived in cities. People in cities demand more education, better sanitation facilities, parks, and playgrounds; they need redevelopment projects for slums and assistance for the multitude of needy people who are concentrated in slum areas. Although many of these programs are primarily the responsibility of city governments, the state and federal governments increasingly assist cities in financing such programs. Furthermore, states in which most people live in large cities are more likely to be responsive to the needs of urban residents than those where most people live outside the metropolis. Even where state legislatures are malapportioned to give an advantage to the small town and rural voter, the big cities are large enough to elect the governor who will make at least part of the state government responsive to city needs.

Still other differences among the states are likely to be reflected on the political scene. The people of some states are rich, whereas those of others are poor. In 1959, the median family income in the United States was $5,660. In fourteen states it was more than $6,000 with the highest occurring in Alaska where the median family income that year was $7,326. But in six states, the median family income was below $4,000; Mississippians earned the least in the nation, for in that state the median income for families was only $2,884. Another way to describe the variation in the fortunes of state residents is to examine the proportion of poor people in each state. In the United States as a whole, 21.4 per cent of all families earned less than $3,000 annually in 1959. In Mississippi more than half of all families earned less than $3,000; in another seven states, one-third of all families had such a low income. In Connecticut, on the other hand, only 9.7 per cent of the state's families earned less than $3,000. Thus, a few states are mostly populated by poor people; some have a very large proportion of their population on the verge of poverty; in others, poverty is a marginal problem.[9]

The impact of these conditions on state politics is great. The poor states have the greatest need (though not necessarily the greatest demand) for public education, public health programs, and welfare facilities. They are poor and their populations are ill-educated. More of their people require public welfare services — food allowances, medical services, housing. Although the need for governmental services may be greater than in richer states, the resources of the poorer states do not allow state governments to provide the level of services which might be desirable. The poorest state, Mississippi, uses its tax resources even more than some wealthier ones, but its resources remain insufficient.

The states also vary in what people do to earn their living. There are still thirteen states where agriculture engages more people than manufacturing.[10] In all the remainder, agriculture has faded to secondary importance. But manufacturing is not equally important in all the non-agricultural states. In the United States as a whole, an average of 30.8 per cent of the non-agricultural labor force was engaged in manufacturing;

the heaviest concentration occurred in Connecticut where 44.4 per cent were so engaged. In Hawaii, on the other hand, only 14 per cent of those not engaged in agriculture earned their living by working in a factory; almost half were employed by the government or in wholesale or retail trade. Nine states had more than 40 per cent of their non-agricultural labor force in manufacturing; five states had less than 10 per cent. The states varied much less in the distribution of other occupations; about the same proportion of people worked in sales jobs, at service occupations, and other pursuits.[11]

These differences set the stage for some differences in politics among the states. But, as we shall see in the following chapters, only some political phenomena are closely related to differences in social conditions. Many others are not. The reason they are not related is that the degree of variation in social conditions remains relatively small among American states. The difference in the standards of living in Mississippi and Connecticut is great, but not nearly as great as the difference between the Mississippi standard of living and that of Kivu Province in the Congo. Where social conditions differ only within a narrow range, such differences are not likely to be systematically reflected in political affairs.

We must, therefore, search for other factors which might explain the great differences that exist in American state politics. The most important differences lie in the characteristics of state political systems.

STATE POLITICAL SYSTEMS

In each of the fifty states, numerous individuals and organizations are drawn into the political process. Politics revolves about governmental agencies but it involves much more than government. Every person and organization that makes demands on the government becomes involved in politics; every person or organization that is consulted about governmental decisions becomes involved in politics. Every voter who casts a ballot becomes involved in politics.

The relationships which characterize the political process can be referred to as "the political system." We use the word "system" because we want to refer to networks of relationships. By "political system" we refer to relationships which exist between branches of government, individual citizens, political parties, interest groups (lobbies), the press, and other social institutions when they seek to influence governmental decisions.[12]

Each of the fifty states has its own political system. The political systems of the states are somewhat similar to each other for many reasons. They operate within the same nation and national political system; they possess similar governmental institutions. They face similar problems; they have similar resources. They work to achieve similar ends. But state political systems are not *identical.* Although they share some common characteristics, they differ on others.

As is true of all complex institutions, we may describe political systems by examining many characteristics. The ones we shall focus on are the participants who bring demands and support to the political system, the rules which govern political conflict and the attitudes on which the rules are founded, the programs and policies which result from the interactions taking place within the state political system, and the boundaries which circumscribe state politics.

PARTICIPANTS, DEMANDS, AND SUPPORT. The participants who take part in the political process distinguish one political system from another. All of the states have a democratic system and allow a high degree of participation by the general populace. Yet some states are more restrictive than others. In Mississippi — to take the extreme case — democracy has existed only for whites; Negroes have been systematically excluded from political life. Some states make it easy for new residents to vote; others make it difficult. In no states except Mississippi, South Carolina, and Alabama is any single group of citizens systematically and successfully excluded from the franchise.[13]

The channels used to participate in politics differ from state to state. In some states, citizens group themselves into competing political parties; election campaigns focus on party differences and governmental decisions follow party platforms. In most states, however, party competition is much less keen; in many it is entirely absent. In these states, interest groups are much more effective instruments in conveying the desires of citizens to state government agencies. Thus, some states have party-oriented political systems while other states have interest-group-oriented political systems.

In every state, the news media become important participants in the political system. Newspapers have no mandate to represent a constituency, but they often take positions on controversial matters. Together with radio and television, the press provides a communications channel through which groups of politically interested persons signal each other and communicate with the general public.[14] Some states have competing media which communicate opposing views of controversial issues and expose the weaknesses of competing groups of politicians. In other states the media are dominated by a single point of view. In the South, for instance, it is difficult for Negroes to communicate their viewpoint to each other or to the general population; the press censors stories of interracial significance. In many Southern cities, citizens may not even know that a major race riot occurred in their midst, since there is no mention of it in the local newspapers.[15] When the press plays the role of censor in the political process, it isolates other participants in the political process; when the press facilitates communication and debate, it promotes the entry of others into the political arena.

Finally, each state has the same set of governmental institutions which are not only the focus of other participants but which also become participants in the political process. In the first instance, these agencies provide the forum in which other participants seek to obtain a governmental decision either in the form of a legislative enactment, an executive decision, or a court decree. Frequently, different participants control the several branches of government so that decisions made by them conflict. Rural conservatives may control the legislature, while urban liberals have the ear of the governor. Such conflicts sometimes transcend the original participants in the dispute and become struggles over legislative power, executive superiority, or judicial review. On such occasions, the governmental branches themselves become conspicuous participants in the political process.

Of itself, whether one group or another participates in the political system is not terribly important. What makes participation significant are the demands and supports which it brings to the political system.[16] A high level of participation which marks a broad concensus has quite different consequences for the system than a high level of participation which reflects basic dissatisfaction with the system. The contrast is between high voter turnout which generally signifies agreement on fundamentals and mass riots which signify alienation from the political system.

Different groups characteristically (although not always) make quite different demands. Labor and management often make conflicting claims on government: the one for more extensive welfare services and regulation of business, the other for more extensive commercial services and the regulation of unions. Unions typically demand better educational systems, while management groups want the harbor dredged or a bigger airport built.

As subsequent chapters show, different participants are active in the several states. Some states are dominated by a single interest, as Montana was for a long time by Anaconda mining interests. Other states are dominated by a pair of competing interests, as is Michigan where the auto workers compete with automobile manufacturers for control of state government. In Southern states, racial differences are more significant than economic interests; since 1954, both whites and Negroes have openly organized to make explicit claims for one racial policy or another. However, it is important to note that those who participate in politics to make certain claims do not commit themselves to a lifetime of political activity. As issues change and new problems become more salient to people, new participants replace old ones in the political system. The system is like a Broadway show which runs forever but whose cast and lines, as well as audiences, constantly change.

RULES OF THE POLITICAL PROCESS AND THEIR ATTITUDINAL BASIS.
The manner in which the participants make demands and give support
is as important as the demands and supports themselves in characterizing
a political system. In one system demands may be made by riots, rebellion,
and revolution; in another they may be made by voting, lobbying, and
public debates. In one system support is provided by apathetic compliance;
in another it is delivered by enthusiastic participation in mass ceremonies.
Moreover, the manner in which demands are met may be strikingly different.
In one system, demands are met with police and military suppression; in
another, they are the subject of negotiations and bargaining.

The manner in which demands are stated, support given, and response
to demands made is a function of the rules of the political process. Rules
consist of expectations about behavior. A rule specifies behavior which is
expected. When the rules are widely understood, each participant in the
political system can operate with a high degree of certainty about the responses of others to his actions; when the rules are not widely understood
or followed, political life is fraught with uncertainty.

Various kinds of rules exist in a political system. Some are formal;
others are informal. The formal rules are often embodied in documents
like a constitution or in laws. Informal rules are not written down but are
part of the political culture which operates within the system. Such rules
include political customs and taboos; they are generally known, widely observed, and publicly acknowledged. In many systems the informal rules
are more significant than the formal ones, for they govern broader spheres
of political behavior.

Some rules (formal and informal) govern only the behavior of political
leaders. Others prescribe the behavior of the mass citizenry. That different
rules apply to leaders and the masses follows from the fact that the two
groups engage in quite different behavior. In a democracy like America's,
the masses principally participate by voting and making demands through
group actions. The leaders are constantly engaged in making decisions, in
negotiating and bargaining, in obtaining the support necessary to carry out
what they believe to be their mandate.

The values which support informal rules also vary widely between
political actives and inactives and between those who live in one region of
the country and those who live in another. One recent study showed that
more general principles of democratic politics, such as the right to free
speech, are more widely accepted than a particular application of that principle — granting free speech to Communists. Moreover, there was a broader
concensus on democratic values in a Northern community than in a similar
Southern community.[17] Like differences exist between those who are active
in politics and those who are not. Delegates to national party conventions

showed more agreement with democratic values than a sample of the general population.[18]

Because American states are part of the same national political system, they share many rules of the political game. This is particularly true of the formal rules specified by state constitutions which govern decision-making by government agencies.[19] Every state has a constitution. Although state constitutions vary greatly in length and detail, almost all have certain common features. One rule common to all states is that which specifies a division of powers in the governmental structure. Every constitution establishes separate but equal legislative, executive, and judicial branches. Many of the same checks and balances which exist in the national government also operate within the states. Like the national government, state governmental power is fragmented.

Moreover, every state constitution has a Bill of Rights which confirms certain guarantees of freedom to citizens of that state. Most of these guarantees are more detailed than those found in the federal constitution.

Every state constitution specifies permissible political action by the mass citizenry. Constitutions assert the conditions under which people may vote; they state the requirements which must be met by those who seek to hold public office. Most state constitutions guarantee free speech and freedom of assembly and petition and thereby provide channels through which the public may make demands of its government.

Important differences exist between states regarding the informal rules that political leaders follow. The differences in part come from the varying social background of state political leaders. In some states political leaders come from the social and economic elite of the state because political leadership is perceived as a respectable and responsible task; moreover, political leadership in these states often affords opportunities for national or world leadership. For instance, in New York the gubernatorial office has attracted the scions of such families as the Roosevelts, the Harrimans, the Lehmans, and the Rockefellers. In Pennsylvania the Dilworths and the Scrantons agree to run for public office. In Michigan the Williams' and Romneys have controlled the State House for a decade and a half. Contrast this to the record in Missouri where the governor's office falls to professional politicians who have labored long in the service of their party and have accumulated experience in minor offices. Missouri governors are often able and intelligent men but they come from families of modest background; they rarely have any connection with the social and economic elite of the state. Or consider Louisiana. The families who still make New Orleans' social season one of the most splendid in the nation rarely enter politics. The political arena is monopolized by demagogues: the Huey Longs, the Leander Perez', and the Jimmy Davis'. Much of the difference in the flavor of New York and Louisiana politics can be directly attributed to the nature of the

Table 1

ATTITUDES OF AMERICANS TOWARD GOVERNMENT

QUESTION NO.	ITEM	Miss., Ala., Ky. & Tenn.	Remainder of United States	Diff.
		PER CENT OF SAMPLE		
11a	Regularly follow politics and government affairs.	10.7	28.2	17.5
15	Don't understand national and international issues at all.	39.3	13.1	26.2
16	Don't at all understand local issues.	26.8	9.2	17.6
23	Impossible to change local regulation which you considered unjust or harmful.	58.9	23.1	35.8
24	Would not try to change such a regulation.	62.5	24.5	38.0
25	Never have done anything to influence a local decision.	85.7	70.0	15.7
30a	Political party is most effective vehicle for changing governmental decision.	8.9	24.0	15.1
32a	Local governments greatly affect your life.	23.2	35.5	12.3
32b	Local governments tend to improve conditions.	44.6	70.2	25.6
34	Would be treated equally at government office.	62.5	84.6	22.1
35	Your point of view would be seriously considered at government office.	23.2	49.4	26.2
37a	Police would treat you equally.	64.3	86.8	22.5
37b	Police would give your view serious consideration.	30.3	57.3	27.0
72b	Agree that people will take advantage of you.	83.9	66.5	17.4
72d	Agree that candidates sound good but are undependable.	89.3	78.5	10.8
72e	Agree that human nature is cooperative.	53.6	81.6	28.0
72f	Agree that people like me don't have any say.	50.0	36.5	14.5
72h	Agree that no one cares about you.	58.9	36.7	22.2
72a	Agree that voting is the main thing that decides how things are run in this country.	87.5	70.5	17.0
82	Economic situation of my family will go up in next ten years.	33.9	50.9	17.0
	Number of respondents	56	914	

Source: Almond and Verba Study, American respondents. See footnote 20. The question numbers refer to the questionnaire reprinted in Almond and Verba, pp. 526–536.

political leadership in these states. New York governors are urbane; they concern themselves with national and international issues almost as often as local issues. Louisiana governors are folksy and provincial. Political campaigns usually take the "high road" in New York and the "low road" in Louisiana.

The attitude of the general population toward politics on which informal rules of the game are based also differs among the states.[20] In most of the United States, citizens feel that politics and government play a useful role in their community life; they trust their government and feel able to influence it when the occasion arises. In other areas, exactly the opposite is true; citizens indicate alienation, distrust, and inefficacy. This is particularly true of some of the Southern states. A recent study of the attitudes of Americans toward public life indicates that the most alienated citizens are concentrated in the region consisting of Mississippi, Alabama, Kentucky, and Tennessee. Their attitudes toward public life stand in sharp contrast to those of people living in other sections of the nation — as can be seen in Table 1. The alienation of these Southerners is indicated by the extraordinarily small proportion (10.7 per cent) who regularly follow political and governmental affairs as well as by the relatively small proportion (44.6 per cent as compared to 70.2 per cent in the rest of the country) who feel that local governments tend to improve local conditions. Their distrust of government is illustrated by the comparatively small proportions who felt that government officials or the police would treat them equally or give their point of view serious consideration. Their sense of inefficacy or inability to influence government decisions is shown by the large proportion who felt it impossible to change an unfair local regulation, who would not *try* to change it, and who have *never* tried to influence local decisions.

These attitudes are associated with the acceptance or rejection of certain rules of the game. In this region, many Negroes are disfranchised and many people perceive such disfranchisement as perfectly proper. The Negro is especially alienated from the political system. He consequently has turned to sit-ins, demonstrations, and rioting as his mode of political expression. Moreover, these attitudes breed demagoguery. Where people are alienated and distrustful of government, they are more responsive to emotional appeals and scapegoat politics. It seems no accident, therefore, that three of these four states have been governed by political demagogues. Of course, demagogues have existed in other states as well, yet rarely have they been prominent for so long as in these states where public attitudes reinforce their appeal. Moreover, the states in this region rank among the lowest in the nation in the proportion of people who vote in state and national elections.

Other differences in informal rules of the game are more difficult to document but are evident to every careful observer. In some states political corruption is so evident that it has almost become the norm rather than the exception. Louisiana politics was once described in the following terms:

> Few would contest the proposition that among its professional politicians of the past two decades Louisiana has had more men who have been in jail, or who should have been, than any other American state. Extortion, bribery, peculation, thievery are not rare in the annals of politics, but in the scale, variety, and thoroughness of its operations, the Long gang established after the death of the Kingfish a record unparalleled in our times.[21]

Massachusetts during the 1950's seemed to share Louisiana's penchant for corruption. In contrast, Wisconsin and Minnesota governments are rarely shaken by scandal.

OUTPUTS AND THEIR FEEDBACK. A political system consists of more than people making demands and acting according to formal and informal rules. Politicking leads to the establishment of programs; through political processes, public policies are adopted which govern the lives of many citizens. The characteristics of these outputs are another hallmark of a political system.

American states can be characterized as "welfare" systems. They do more than simply police and enforce law and order. They do not simply promote private enterprise through the granting of corporate charters. The states sponsor many programs which actively cultivate the welfare of their citizens; these programs consume the largest part of state budgets. In 1963, for instance, states spent 34.8 per cent of their funds on education, 25.7 per cent of their money on highways, and 25.3 per cent on public welfare programs.[22] Simple police and regulatory functions consumed much smaller portions of state budgets. Many of the basic programs are similar among the states. Each state, for instance, provides a system of colleges and a university which provide post-high school education for the young people. Each state has built a far-flung highway system that connects every city and town within the state. Every state has welfare programs to assist the indigent, aged, and sick.

The states differ, however, in the quality and variety of programs offered. State universities, for instance, differ widely in their reputation and the educational programs they offer. Some are little more than large liberal arts colleges; others equal Harvard and Yale in the quality of education they offer. The same is true for state mental hospitals with a few states providing first-class institutions and many having only marginal programs.

Moreover, states differ markedly from one another in their adoption of certain policies. Some states have so-called right-to-work laws which restrict union contracts; some do not. Some states have and enforce fair-employment-practice laws; many do not. Some are active in water and air pollution control; others do nothing.[23]

The initiative of some states sometimes leads to changes in all the others. The fact that a few states required the installation of seat-belts in all new cars led Detroit manufacturers to offer the belts as standard equipment; even in states without the law new cars are delivered with such seat belts. States are slow to pioneer but quick to copy. Once one or two states have adopted a new insurance code, a novel criminal statute, or a different tax levy, many others rapidly follow suit.

The policies and programs which result from the political process eventually feed back into the political system. They generate new demands or, satisfying old ones, they lay to rest a problem on which the political process focused for years. The establishment of state colleges and universities may lead to demands for the establishment of junior colleges. Regulation of one profession by the state may lead another to seek the same protection. On the other hand, when a state finally solves a perennial problem such as imposing a major new tax which will provide adequate financing for many years, attention is turned to new problems. Different participants with different demands may arise as a result of the feedback process. Those who are disadvantaged by a new policy may arise to protest even though they remained inactive while the program was being considered. Construction companies, for instance, may not realize that state regulation of engineers will eventually impinge on them until the State Board of Engineers declares the work they are doing as belonging to engineers.[24] Realtors may remain unperturbed by regulations affecting lawyers until the courts declare activities they have customarily engaged in (like making out sales contracts) as the proper business only of lawyers.[25] Engineers in the first case and realtors in the second may then become active in the political process to reverse the policy that is adverse to their interest or seek a new accommodation with it. In this way, the political system must face new demands and adapt to them as old ones are met or compromised.

BOUNDARIES OF STATE POLITICAL SYSTEMS. State political systems are bounded in a variety of ways. The boundaries restrict the activities which the system may undertake.

One of the bounds is the geographic boundary of a state. Like the border of nations, the state line denotes the limit of a state's political action. A state may not tax beyond its boundary; its police may not arrest someone on the other side; its programs halt at the line. In some states the borders follow natural and social boundaries; in others they cross over them and create grave difficulties. The boundary which sets off New York from

Connecticut on one side and New Jersey on the other does not follow the border of community life in the New York metropolitan area. Many people who live in Connecticut or New Jersey work in New York; they are not subject to all the programs of New York's government. For instance, the commuters require New York to build expensive highways leading into the city, but as commuters are likely to buy their gasoline where they live, they pay their highway taxes to Connecticut or New Jersey rather than New York. The same is true for many other metropolitan areas. Kansas City spills over from Missouri to Kansas. The Chicago metropolitan area includes parts of Wisconsin and Indiana as well as Illinois. St. Louis consists of East St. Louis, Illinois, and St. Louis, Missouri. Missouri officials cannot control the vice occurring in East St. Louis even though it affects Missouri citizens; Illinois cannot take a hand in the racial problems facing the Missouri part of the city.

Constitutions set legal limits to the scope of state politics. Under the federal Constitution, states may not conduct foreign affairs, coin money, raise armies, or interfere with interstate commerce. Each state has its own constitution which erects other limits on state actions. Some state constitutions prohibit state governments from becoming substantially indebted; others prohibit the levying of an income tax.

State governments are not the only governments operating within the boundaries of their states; counties, cities, school districts, and others operate within a state's boundaries as well. According to legal doctrine, all local governments are subordinate to the state. In fact, however, most of them operate independent of daily state control. When they directly oppose a state government's program, the state may be strong enough to impose its will, but direct confrontations and the imposition of a state's iron fist rarely occur. Normally, local governments cooperate with their state government; they bargain with the state. Because forcing its will on local governments is costly in terms of the effort involved and the ill will created, state governments seldom use their power in this way. They prefer to bargain and cooperate. Thus, the presence and activity of these local governments constitute a real limit on the activities of the state governments.

State political systems are thus bounded in a number of different ways. The geographic limits of the state constitute one boundary. The legal relationships between state and federal governments on the one hand and state and local governments on the other constitute a second boundary. A third boundary consists of the functions which are performed by other governmental levels and which either deprive states of an opportunity to be active or present them with an occasion to expand services to a waiting clientele.

The pressures exerted on state political systems as the result of the impinging activities of federal and local governments pose a grave threat to state political systems. To survive, states must maintain their identity, their functions, and a measure of autonomy. They are threatened by federal activities because many federal programs either regulate, supervise, or take over existing state programs. Local policies threaten the autonomy of state governments, for local programs may also supplant state activities and local agencies may win the loyalty of city dwellers to the detriment of the state government.

State political systems are constantly engaged in the struggle to maintain their boundaries and thus insure their survival. In some instances, boundary maintenance may be attained through direct resistance to the encroachment of federal or local intruders. This is the stance of Mississippi with regard to federal pressure on civil rights matters and the stance of many states when they refuse their cities authority to undertake a program the city desires. At the same time, state systems may seek to adapt themselves to new situations and thereby maintain their boundaries. By reforming their governmental structure, they may seek to become more efficient and better able to administer important programs than either federal or local agencies. By reapportioning legislatures, states may make themselves more responsive to urban demands so that local governments need not seek help from Washington. By initiating new programs, states may carve out new areas of responsibility before they are seized upon by the federal government or municipalities.

In some instances, however, states are not able to maintain their boundaries; they succumb to pressures from either the federal or local governments. A state like Mississippi cannot resist federal pressures which threaten to cut off federal funds to the state, for Mississippi depends on federal grants-in-aid for about one-third of its total revenues. States like New York and Illinois are much less able to withstand pressures from their largest cities than are Alaska or South Dakota, for New York City and Chicago are too influential in the political system to be ignored.[26]

The political significance of the boundaries of state systems and their struggle to maintain the boundaries varies with the problems that are involved. Southern states, for instance, became militant when seeking to maintain their autonomy against the encroachment of the federal government where race relations policy is concerned; they are not very hesitant, however, to accept federal grants and federal policy controls for welfare programs. As a Mississippian told a reporter, "You know, when it comes to the handouts, we are the first ones up to the trough."[27] Some states do not object to local initiative in correcting slum conditions within their boundaries, but they insist on enforcing state laws against vice by sending the state patrol to raid local establishments. The boundaries constantly shift so that it is impossible to describe with absolute certainty what states may or may not do. However, it is clear that the boundaries themselves and the struggle to maintain them are central characteristics of state political systems.

CONCLUSIONS

Which elements of a political system are most important for determining political outcomes? Is the crucial element the struggle to maintain boundaries? . . . the nature of participants and the demands and supports they deliver? . . . the rules of the game? . . . or the policies and programs that are adopted?

Political systems are so complex and our understanding of them still so rudimentary that it is necessary to examine all elements of the system that we have outlined. For instance, it might seem strange that, at one and the same time, Mississippi fiercely resists the encroachment of the federal government in civil rights matters but actively courts federal financial aid for welfare, highway, and river improvement programs. This seemingly contradictory behavior is consistent in terms of the struggle to maintain boundaries and the participants active in the Mississippi political system. Whites who are dedicated to the preservation of segregation are the dominant participants in politics. They direct all their efforts to avoiding the objective of the federal government — the ending of segregation in Mississippi. But such efforts do not prevent other participants from pursuing different goals. For instance, merchants who need good roads and industries which depend on river transportation court federal aid for their projects because such aid does not endanger segregation and is essential to the successful enactment of the program they desire. Thus, the political system permits seemingly inconsistent political actions.

In other situations the rules of the game seem to be the major difference among states. It is hard to explain the difference between Wisconsin and Missouri politics in any other way. In both, farming is still relatively important. Both states have large metropolitan areas. Neither is particularly wealthy. The climate is rather similar. Missouri more often goes Democratic and Wisconsin, Republican, but both have active minority parties. Missouri has been quite conservative in its adoption of novel policies and the expenditure of funds; it has often been rocked by scandals. Wisconsin has been among the most progressive of states and is a large spender of funds; it is rarely tarnished by chicanery. The difference — so it seems, at least — lies in the political tradition, the political culture, and the rules governing political behavior in the two states. Wisconsin has become accustomed to clean, progressive government; Missouri has become accustomed to a conservative, occasionally corrupt, do-little regime.

In the following chapters, we shall examine in detail the participants in state political systems, the manner in which political decisions are made, the characteristics of state policies and programs, and the boundaries setting state systems apart from the national system. Through this examination the nature of the differences which exist and the reasons for them will become more evident.

NOTES

1. U.S. Bureau of the Census, *Summary of State Government Finances in 1963* (Washington: U.S. Government Printing Office, April 1963) p. 12.
2. *Ibid.,* p. 18.
3. See p. 320 for a fuller discussion.
4. U.S. Bureau of the Census, *Statistical Abstract of the United States, 1963* (Washington: U.S. Government Printing Office, 1963) p. 173.
5. *Ibid.,* pp. 11, 22–23.
6. *Ibid.,* p. 11.
7. *Ibid.,* p. 19.
8. *Ibid.*
9. All of the above income figures come from *ibid.,* p. 340.
10. *Ibid.,* pp. 227, 642.
11. *Ibid.,* p. 228.
12. The following discussion has been much influenced by David Easton, "An Approach to the Analysis of Political Systems," *World Politics IX* (1957) 383–400.
13. For a detailed discussion, see pp. 45–49.
14. For a general discussion of the theoretical significance of communications in a political system, see Gabriel Almond and James S. Coleman, *The Politics of the Developing Areas* (Princeton: Princeton University Press, 1960) pp. 45–52.
15. George McMillan, "Georgia Unchronicled," *Columbia Journalism Review I* (Summer 1962) 39–42; James Boylan, "Birmingham Newspapers in Crisis," *ibid., II* (Summer 1963) 29–32.
16. Cf. Easton, pp. 387–400.
17. James W. Prothro and Charles M. Grigg, "Fundamental Principles of Democracy: Bases of Agreement and Disagreement," *Journal of Politics XXII* (1960) 276–294.
18. Herbert McClosky, "Concensus and Ideology in American Politics," *American Political Science Review LVIII* (1964) 364–373.
19. A handy reference source for the provisions of state constitutions is the loose-leaf collection, *Constitutions of the United States: National and State,* Legislative Drafting Research Fund of Columbia University (Dobbs Ferry, N.Y.: Oceana Publications).
20. The following data are drawn from a study by Gabriel Almond and Sidney Verba which was reported in *The Civic Culture* (Princeton: Princeton University Press, 1963). The analysis was made possible by the services of the Inter-University Consortium for Political Research (Ann Arbor, Michigan) which made the data available to the author. However, neither Messrs. Almond and Verba nor the Consortium bear any responsibility for the results of the analysis.
21. V. O. Key, Jr., *Southern Politics in State and Nation* (New York: Alfred A. Knopf, 1949) p. 156. For Massachusetts, see James Reichly, *States in Crisis* (Chapel Hill: University of North Carolina Press, 1964) pp. 142–162.
22. U.S. Bureau of the Census, *Summary of State Government Finances in 1963,* p. 6. Hospital and health expenditures are included under "welfare."

23. For a summary of these matters, see the most recent edition of Council of State Governments, *Book of the States.*
24. See Milwaukee *Journal,* August 16, 1964, Part 7, p. 9, for an example of this.
25. Merton E. Marks, "The Lawyers and the Realtors: Arizona's Experience," *American Bar Association Journal XLIX* (1963) 139–141.
26. The role of Chicago in Illinois politics is clearly shown in Gilbert Y. Steiner and Samuel K. Gove, *Legislative Politics in Illinois* (Urbana: University of Illinois Press, 1960). For New York, the best study is still Warren Moscow, *Politics in the Empire State* (New York: Alfred A. Knopf, 1948).
27. *The New York Times,* August 17, 1964, p. 18.

PART TWO

PARTICIPATION
IN STATE POLITICS

ALTHOUGH VOTING IS THE MOST CHARACTERISTIC FORM of participation in a popular democracy, it is not the only way in which people can participate in their government. In fact, some citizens may not vote but may be allied to political parties or involved in pressure groups. Others may take an active part on all levels — as faithful voters, party workers, and members of interest groups.

Participation in state politics can thus occur in a number of different areas and in a number of different forms. There are distinctive variations in the resultant patterns. Some states have low voter participation but more activity in other forms of participation. People in other states place more emphasis on party politics than interest group activity; in some states the reverse occurs. Some states are characterized by high levels of all forms of participation.

Therefore, the manner in which people take part in the political struggles of their state becomes an important feature of the state's political system. It leads to further differences in the demands made of state governments and the manner in which the demands are met.

POLITICAL
PARTICIPATION
IN THE
STATES

CHAPTER 2
by
LESTER W. MILBRATH

IF WE ARE TO UNDERSTAND how American state politics functions, it is necessary to learn as much as we can about the manner and the extent of participation in politics. Citizens relate quite differently to their political system. Some persons take the system for granted and are only concerned about adjusting their behavior to its demands; others want to improve or transform it. Some persons have only a passive relationship to the system while others are very actively involved. To some the system is frightening and confusing; to others it is an object to be explored and conquered. Some focus their attention on what the system demands from them while others focus on the benefits they derive.

Some of the differences in the ways persons relate to the political system find their origin in the political setting. In this chapter we shall be especially concerned with systematic variations in participation from state to state. The political cultures of some states such as Idaho and Utah facilitate the involvement of citizens in political activity. Public servants go out of their way to help citizens become registered to vote. The political cultures of other states, especially those in the deep South, place barriers to participation in politics. In addition to outright intimidation frightening Negroes so they do not vote, white citizens as well in many of these states must pass elaborate and difficult literacy tests before they are allowed to participate. Before examining these materials closely, however, we must first learn how to think about political participation.

DIMENSIONS OF PARTICIPATION

Taking any political action generally requires two decisions: a person decides to act or not to act; an individual must also decide the direction of his action. For example, a person not only decides to vote or not to vote, but also decides whom he favors. Usually the decision to perform an action like voting precedes the decision about the direction the action will take, but the time sequence could be reversed. Somtimes a person decides that he likes a candidate or a party before making up his mind to cast a vote. Certain actions do not involve a directional choice: we cannot choose the government to which we pay taxes (without changing residence).

Decisions to act in a particular way often are accompanied by a third decision as to the intensity, duration, and/or extremity of the action. Citizens may lend political support mildly or vigorously, in a single instance or repeatedly. This third choice is intimately related to the other two. A person who takes vigorous and sustained political action very likely is strongly attracted in a certain direction. The very fact that he feels intensely makes it more likely that he will participate. This chapter will focus mainly on decisions to act or not to act and on decisions about the intensity and duration of action. Decisions about the direction of action, such as preferring Republicans or Democrats, will be handled in other chapters, especially Chapter 3.

THE ACTIVE–INACTIVE DIMENSION. Acting politically seems to have two types of contrasts: inactive and passive. Most citizens have both active and passive postures toward politics. Every person participates at least passively in the political system in which he lives. Mere compliance gives support to the existing regime and, therefore, is a type of political behavior. There are other essentially passive responses to the political system: obeying laws, paying taxes, experiencing order and security. These passive behaviors are to be distinguished from the inactive counterparts to political action: non-voting vs. voting, non-contributing vs. contributing, non-attending vs. attending, and so forth.

A refined analysis of the dimensions of political participation would examine certain sub-dimensions of activity. For example, some political action is avoiding in contrast to approaching. A person who does not make a political contribution because he is unaware that anyone wants him to contribute is not avoiding; but an individual who does not contribute when he is requested to do so is avoiding. Some actions, like making a speech, are overt in contrast to a covert action like casting a secret ballot. Some actions are episodic (voting on election day) while others are more or less continuous (exposing oneself to political communication). Some actions contribute inputs to the system (voting, campaigning) in contrast to others which withdraw services from it (justice, public order, education). Some actions are largely expressive (shouting a protest, engaging in political argument) while others are largely instrumental (collecting information, canvassing door-to-door). Most political actions are verbal but some (making speeches) are more so than others (stuffing envelopes). Some political actions require a great deal of social interaction (campaigning door-to-door) compared to others requiring little (voting, making a monetary contribution).[1] Unfortunately, most of the research to date has gathered information only on whether a given act took place or not; therefore, little data can be brought to bear on the more subtle sub-dimensions just mentioned. Bearing this data limitation in mind, we shall concentrate on the more general active–inactive dimension.

CLUSTERING

Activity generally can be graded into quantities: some persons do more of a given thing than others. They may engage in an activity with greater frequency or regularity; they may give more hours or money at a time; they may participate in a wider repertoire of activities. Some persons are almost totally inactive; some are active in one political behavior but inactive in others; some are active in a wide variety of political behaviors. Inactivity may be thought of as a zero base point from which quantities of action can be measured.

Political activity seems to have a patterning or clustering characteristic. This seems to be true in two senses: (1) *Variables associated with a specific political act are associated with other political acts as well.* (2) *There seems to be a hierarchy of political involvement* in that persons at a given level of involvement tend to perform many of the same acts as persons at lower levels of involvement. Each of these points will be discussed in turn.

A broad generalization about political participation, which is widely supported in research findings, is that the same independent variables are related to a variety of political acts.[2] For example, higher socio-economic-status (SES) is positively associated with increased likelihood of participation in many different political acts such as voting, attending meetings, joining a political party, campaigning, and so forth. There are some minor exceptions to this generalization, but the repetitiveness with which a given variable relates significantly with different political acts is impressive.

In addition to the above, research findings show that variables which are associated with political activity also are associated with non-political community activity. Furthermore, those who participate in political activities also often participate in non-political community activities.[3] This finding suggests that political participation can be thought of as a special case of general activity in social and community activities. Not everyone who is active socially becomes active in politics, but it is probably easier for a person who enjoys social activity to enter politics than it is for a person who shuns social and community participation.

Political participation is cumulative in another way: persons who engage in one political action often engage in others as well. Figure 1 shows a hierarchical ranking of behaviors; those most often engaged in are at the bottom while those least engaged in are at the top. The cumulative characteristic arises from the fact that persons who engage in the topmost behaviors also perform those lower in rank. The hierarchy includes most, but not all, common political activities that fit into the normal process of a democracy.

Figure 1

HIERARCHY OF POLITICAL INVOLVEMENT

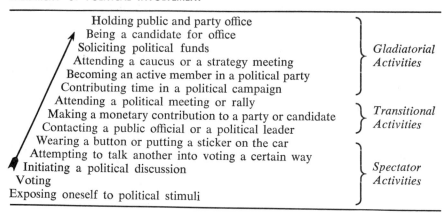

Holding public and party office
Being a candidate for office
Soliciting political funds   *Gladiatorial*
Attending a caucus or a strategy meeting   *Activities*
Becoming an active member in a political party
Contributing time in a political campaign

Attending a political meeting or rally
Making a monetary contribution to a party or candidate   *Transitional*
Contacting a public official or a political leader   *Activities*

Wearing a button or putting a sticker on the car
Attempting to talk another into voting a certain way
Initiating a political discussion   *Spectator*
Voting   *Activities*
Exposing oneself to political stimuli

Although political demonstrations are considered a legitimate expression of political feeling in a democracy, this type of behavior does not fit into the hierarchy in the United States because wide segments of the population frown on the activity as undignified. The hierarchy also does not apply to behavior that is designed to disrupt the normal operation of political processes or to dislodge a regime from office by violent means: a general strike is an example of the former, and a palace revolt or a coup d'état are examples of the latter.

LEVELS OF PARTICIPATION. Another general characteristic of the levels of participation shown in Figure 1 is that they constitute a hierarchy of costs. Time and energy costs are least for behaviors at the bottom of the hierarchy. Behaviors higher in the hierarchy obviously require a greater expenditure of energy and probably require a greater personal commitment. The particular ranking shown in the figure is based on percentages of Americans who engage in the behavior. Probably less than 1 per cent of the American adult population engage in the top two or three behaviors. Only about 4 or 5 per cent are active in a party, campaign, and attend meetings. About 10 per cent make monetary contributions, about 13 per cent contact public officials, and about 15 per cent display a button or a sticker. Around 25 or 30 per cent try to proselyte others to vote a certain way, and from

40 to 70 per cent perceive political messages and vote in any given election.[4]

The ranking of a given item in the hierarchy may vary from state to state, from election to election, from decade to decade, and from country to country. Since it is a hierarchy of costs, however, we would not expect the variation to be more than a shift of a rank or two. The hierarchy seems to have a kind of internal logic, a natural progression of involvement. Persons engaging in the topmost behaviors are likely also to engage in those behaviors ranking lower. The obverse does not hold, however; minimally involved persons confine their actions to those acts ranking low in the hierarchy. As a person becomes more involved in politics, he engages in a wider repertoire of political acts and he moves upward in the hierarchy from the more frequent to the less frequent behaviors.

Although the statement above suggests a smooth progression from less to more involvement, data on the American citizenry suggest that persons cluster into three general types or roles along the active-inactive dimension. One group participates only passively in the political process; it does not engage in any of the political acts shown in Figure 1. The second group is minimally active in some or all of the first five activities shown in the hierarchy: seeking information, voting, discussing, proselyting, and displaying preference. A small group not only participates in the above activities but also is drawn into the political fray: these persons attend meetings, campaign, become active in a party, solicit money, run for and hold public and party office.

This division into three roles is reminiscent of the roles played at a Roman gladiatorial contest. A small band of gladiators battles fiercely to please the spectators who have the power to decide their fate. The spectators in the stands cheer, transmit messages of advice and encouragement, and at given periods vote to decide who has won a particular battle (election). The apathetics do not bother to come to the stadium to watch the show. Taking a cue from the roles played in the gladiatorial contest, the three political participation roles will be called apathetics, spectators, and gladiators.

About one-third of the American adult population can be characterized as politically apathetic or passive; in most cases they are unaware, literally, of the political part of the world around them. Another 60 per cent play largely spectator roles in the political process; they watch, they cheer, they vote, but they do not do battle. Only about 5 to 7 per cent can be characterized as political gladiators. These proportions apply mainly to elections at which a President is chosen in the United States. The apathetic ranks probably are even larger in strictly state and local elections. As we shall see later in the chapter, the apathetic ranks also are larger in the American South.

One of the striking things about these roles is their stability. From time to time a gladiator who no longer enjoys the contest may withdraw to the role of spectator or apathetic. Occasionally a spectator jumps into the political fray. But, by and large, personality and environmental factors seem to encourage persons to stay in their roles. There seems to be a kind of threshold that must be crossed before a person changes roles; this seems especially characteristic of the transition from spectator to gladiator. He seems to need an extra strong push from the environment (e.g., earnest solicitation from a friend) or needs to feel very strongly about an issue or a candidate before he will cross the threshold and become a political combatant. Once the threshold is crossed and the new team member becomes integrated to his role, he usually participates in a wide repertoire of political acts.

Transitions between the roles seem to occur at two points of the hierarchy shown in Figure 1. A person in transition from apathetic to spectator likely would seek information as a way of orienting himself as spectator and voter. Similarly, the man who chooses to lend more support than a cheer for his side in a political contest is likely to contact public officials, attend meetings, and make a monetary political contribution as first transitional steps toward becoming a full-fledged gladiator.

An additional role differentiation might be made within the gladiatorial category. Just as the political participation of spectators is nearly always leisure (non-work) time participation, leisure time participation characterizes a certain proportion of gladiators. Some gladiators, however, make politics their profession. In most settings we should think of the professional politician as the most involved of all political roles.

CHARACTERISTICS OF SPECIFIC POLITICAL ACTS

The political acts shown in Figure 1 involve quite different degrees of commitment to politics and occur at different occasions. This may be shown by discussing each of them separately.

EXPOSURE TO STIMULI PERCEIVED AS POLITICAL. The person who hopes to deal effectively with his political environment must devote some energy to collecting information about it. This activity is elemental and fundamental to all other political activity, but people still vary a great deal in the extent of their exposure to stimuli about politics. Despite the great flood of political stimuli available through the mass media, some persons are remarkably effective in exposing themselves to little or none of it. Variation in exposure to political stimuli is a function of an individual's predispositions and of the environment in which he lives. The senses of some persons are tuned to political stimuli and pick up large amounts, whereas others seem to tune out all political stimuli. The environments of some are filled with political talk and political events, sometimes to the point where they could not avoid politics even if they tried. Other environments have so few political stimuli that citizens must deliberately seek them. Generally, the more political stimuli received by a person, the more likely he is to be active in politics.

VOTING. This most thoroughly researched of all political behaviors requires two decisions: first, the decision to engage in the act or not; and second, the decision as to which candidate or party to support. It is episodic behavior in that it can occur only on days specified by law. These days are known well in advance so that a person can gather relevant data and make a preliminary decision. Voting research also investigates the time of this decision and the frequency, regularity, and stability (in terms of direction) of the voting act.

DISCUSSION AND OPINION LEADERSHIP. Of all the stimuli about politics which an individual may encounter, those that come via personal discussions are probably most influential. Nearly everyone gets caught in a political discussion once in a while; some persons studiously avoid them while others enjoy them and seek them out. Therefore, in thinking about discussions, it is important to distinguish initiator and recipient, leader and follower, missionary and the unconvinced. A certain proportion of the population (about 20 per cent in the United States) regularly exercises political leadership in face-to-face interactions. This group may be called opinion leaders. Opinion leadership may not be directed toward support of a party or candidate and, therefore, is more a spectator than a gladiatorial activity. Opinion leaders, however, are much more likely to become gladiators than followers are.

WEARING A BUTTON OR PUTTING A STICKER ON THE CAR. Displaying a partisan or candidate preference with a button or a sticker is another, but relatively weak, form of opinion leadership. Those doing this generally do not engage in additional proselyting activity to bring home their point. In many communities children make a game of wearing buttons displaying the candidate preference of their parents. The desire of children to conform to the button-wearing pattern and to have some preference to display instills party identification at an early age and helps make the adoption of partisan preference an accepted thing.

PETITIONING POLITICAL LEADERS. Only a relatively small proportion of citizens take the step of contacting political leaders and public officials.[5]

This may be done via letter, telegram, telephone, or direct personal contact. A few persons, as a function of their position in the social or political structure, have normal daily interaction with political leaders and find it natural and useful to communicate their views to these men. This may constitute an easy transitional step toward becoming a gladiator. Most individuals, however, feel they must take special pains to communicate with political leaders; seemingly a large majority of them do not wish to take the trouble or may feel uncomfortable in attempting to do so. This barrier partially can be overcome by institutional intervention; a larger proportion of citizens[6] belong to special interest groups which represent them before government. Many of these organizations hire lobbyists to devote their full time to represent these groups at the seat of government.

MAKING A MONETARY CONTRIBUTION. As mentioned above, this act may be the first transitional step toward becoming a gladiator. It also may be the extreme spectator activity beyond which a citizen refuses to go. Like voting, it requires a decision to perform the act or not and a second decision as to the direction of the act. Some busy and wealthy persons look upon monetary contributions as a substitute for their personal participation in gladiatorial activity. Most contributions, however, come from gladiators themselves; they see political money as another weapon in their battle with the opposition.[7]

ATTENDING A POLITICAL MEETING. This is a spectator activity for some members; they merely come to watch the show. No commitment of support is implied by their presence. For others, however, attending meetings is a gladiatorial activity, especially if they attend them oftener than once or twice a year. Perhaps they are officials and have responsibility for organizing or participating in the meetings; perhaps they wish to show their partisan support by helping to swell the crowd. Highly involved partisans also regularly attend caucuses and strategy meetings.

CAMPAIGNING. Political campaigns are episodic, but working in them can be continuous for several weeks. Some campaign work, like typing letters or stuffing envelopes, can be routine and boring. Most campaign work, however, requires considerable social interaction with other people, some of it in a pleading or salesman-like posture. This is especially true of canvassing door-to-door or of making speeches. Research evidence shows that self-confidence and a feeling of social ease are important prerequisites to participation in the social, interactive phase of campaigning.[8]

ACTIVE PARTY MEMBERSHIP. There are three ways by which a person could be said to be a party affiliate or member: (1) psychological identification with a party; (2) formal membership via payment of dues; and (3) active participation in party affairs. A fairly large proportion of citizens (about 75 per cent) in the United States psychologically identify with a political party.[9] When a person says he "thinks of himself as" a Democrat or a Republican, however, he very likely does not mean that he is a member of the party. He means only that he is inclined to support the party at election time.

Formal membership means that an individual's name is entered on the party rolls and that possibly he has been issued a membership card. Even this formal membership is loosely and variously defined. Some parties require only a declaration of support as a membership requirement, but more commonly dues or a monetary contribution are required. In many instances, formal membership is not a very active commitment and little is done to engage the "member" in party affairs. At the state and local levels in the United States there are party clubs to which citizens can belong and which constitute the effective working organizations of the parties. National parties, per se, have no provision for formal membership; a citizen can belong to a national party only through a state party.

The most meaningful kind of party membership (and the kind we are primarily concerned with in this chapter) is active party work. Party actives participate in meetings, caucuses and conventions, they hold precinct, township, or ward offices, they do the multitude of chores required around party or campaign headquarters, they canvass voters at election time, and so forth. Many party actives are leaders or aspire to be leaders, but, as in all organizations, there also are many followers. Active followers and leaders, taken together, constitute a relatively small cadre; usually less than 5 per cent of the citizenry are active party members.

SOLICITING POLITICAL FUNDS. Relatively few persons have the position or the talent for soliciting money for parties or candidates. Some soliciting takes the form of canvassing door-to-door, usually for small contributions. Solicitors responsible for raising large sums of money not only need a talent for soliciting but also must be in a position (social, professional, commercial, etc.) which enables them to approach persons of wealth and prominence to request money. Any kind of soliciting requires social interaction, and a sociable personality trait is an important prerequisite to taking the action. Solicitors are important middlemen in politics who have ready access to decision-makers and transmit the desires of persons giving money.[10]

OFFICE SEEKING AND HOLDING. At the center of the political structure are the party and public officeholders. Generally, a special set of talents is required just to seek office. In certain party structures, where party discipline is strong and many jobs are filled by patronage, the main talent required for holding lesser office is the ability to carry out orders effectively. In other structures, or for holding higher office, it is important to have strong initiative and great ego strength. These differences in talent requirements for different kinds of offices point up the analytical importance of distinguishing party and public office, appointive and elective office, lesser and higher office.

PROTESTS AND DEMONSTRATIONS. Whether or not protest demonstrations are used seems to be affected more by political setting than most other political acts. Almost by definition they are extraordinary rather than normal and, thus, are difficult to place on Figure 1. Citizens with ready access to officials and whose needs are handled routinely within the political system tend to look upon demonstrations as undignified and not very effective. Persons in certain minorities who do not have ready access to decision-makers or who feel that the system does not respond to their demands have quite a different perspective on protest demonstrations. The very extraordinary character of the demonstrations helps to get their message of dissatisfaction across to the public as well as to officials. Demonstrations also provide an important expressive outlet for pent-up feelings of resentment and dissatisfaction. Certain states with deprived minorities are more likely to experience protest demonstrations than states with a more homogeneous population; this is especially true of minorities in the South and in states with large metropolitan centers.

AMOUNTS OF PARTICIPATION

It is impossible to obtain state-by-state figures on the percentage of persons who participate in each of the types of political activities discussed above, although states do have figures on turnout at elections as part of their official election records. Turnout comparisons will be used in this chapter insofar as they inform our inquiry. We lack data on other types of participation, such as working for a party or attending meetings, for they are likely to be gathered only by survey research organizations. No national polling or survey research organization draws random samples state-by-state. This data gap is not likely to be corrected in the near future because state-by-state samples would require about five hundred respondents per state. This would make a total national sample of 25,000, more than ten times as large as most national polling samples today. Some national survey organizations, however, to draw regional samples; we can obtain region-by-region figures for several types of political participation.

The 1956 election study conducted by the Survey Research Center of the University of Michigan gathered regional figures for the seven political acts shown in Table 1. The behaviors are arranged in order from the most popular spectator activities to the least popular gladiatorial activities. One is struck immediately by the similarities across the regions in percentages participating in each activity. The South shows a somewhat lower than average participation rate for spectator activities (voting, proselyting, displaying preference, and contributing money). For the three gladiatorial activities, however, participation rates in the South are not significantly different from rates in the other regions.

Table 1

PERCENTAGES OF RESPONDENTS IN 1956 NATIONWIDE ELECTION STUDY
WHO PERFORMED EACH TYPE OF POLITICAL ACT — BY REGION

	Northeast	*Midwest*	*Far West*	*South*
Vote	85	81	80	57
Talk others into voting a certain way	28	30	30	25
Wear a button or put sticker on car	18	17	17	10
Give money to candidate or party	13	10	10	6
Attend political meetings	7	8	5	6
Join political club	4	3	2	1.7
Work for a party	3	4	1.7	2.5

Source: Data drawn from the 1956 election study of the Survey Research Center, University of Michigan. Percentages total more than 100 because some individuals performed more than one act.

The data in Table 1 demonstrate the point made earlier that gladiators constitute a very small proportion of the population. If anything, the figures in Table 1 are inflated estimates of the true percentages. Voting turnout is the only behavior in the table for which we can get reliable official figures to compare with percentages obtained from sample surveys. Nationwide turnout figures for eleven recent Presidential elections are shown in Table 2. The nationwide percentage in 1956 was 60.1, yet Table 1 shows turnout percentages in three regions of 80 per cent and above. As another check, we can examine Table 3 which shows Presidential voting turnout percentages state by state for the same eleven elections. Looking down the column for the 1956 election, we see that in none of the states does the turnout percentage reach 80 per cent.

Table 2

U.S. VOTER PARTICIPATION FIGURES

Turnout in elections for President and House of Representatives (*Vote as a percentage of the civilian population of voting age*)

1920–1962

Year	President	Representatives
1962.	....	48.9
1960.	63.8	59.4
1958.	....	43.4
1956.	60.1	56.6
1954.	....	42.2
1952.	62.0	58.2
1950.	....	41.6
1948.	51.5	48.6
1946.	....	37.6
1944.	56.3	53.0
1942.	....	32.7
1940.	59.7	56.2
1938.	....	44.5
1936.	57.5	54.0
1934.	....	41.8
1932.	52.9	50.2
1930.	....	34.1
1928.	52.3	48.2
1926.	....	30.1
1924.	44.3	41.0
1922.	....	32.4
1920.	44.2	41.4

Source: U.S. Bureau of the Census, *Statistical Abstract of the U.S.: 1962,* eighty-third edition, Washington: 1962. Reproduced from the Report of the President's Commission on Registration and Voting Participation, November 1963.

There are several reasons why the turnout figures for the sample survey are somewhat inflated. The most important one is that it is extremely difficult to include certain groupings (mostly non-participants in politics) in random samples: persons living in institutions, non-citizens, the "floating population," and mental incompetents. The Survey Research Center estimates these non-included persons account for 6 per cent of the difference between their figures and the national percentage. A second factor is that about 2 per cent of the ballots cast are invalidated and not counted in the turnout totals, but respondents still report having voted. A third factor is that those who faithfully turn out and vote are somewhat easier to locate and to get to consent to an interview than persons disinclined to vote. A final factor derives from the tendency for some to report that they have voted to an interviewer when, in fact, they have not. This percentage is not large, but it may be as high as 3 or 4 per cent.[11]

Because of these factors we can be confident that the percentages shown for the seven types of political acts in Table 1 are a slight exaggeration of the true figures. Thus, the percentage of political gladiators in the population may be as low as 3 or 4 per cent. If we study Tables 2, 3, and 4, we see that the percentage of non-voters in some elections is as high as 70 or 80 per cent. The inescapable conclusion is that a very large percentage of citizens are almost completely unconcerned with political action.

Certain other patterns emerge from a study of the tables. Table 2 demonstrates that invariably the percentage of votes cast in representative elections is less than the percentage cast in Presidential elections. Turnout in state elections is closely comparable to turnout in Representative elections. If the state or Representative election occurs in a non-Presidential year, the turnout is likely to be significantly lower. Table 4 shows state-by-state average percentage turnout in non-Presidential election years from 1952–1960 for elections for governor and Senator. If the percentage turnout in these state elections is compared with Presidential turnouts for comparable years (1952, 1956, 1960) shown in Table 3, we note consistently lower turnout figures for the state elections (averaging 15 to 20 per cent below the Presidential turnout figures).

Study of Table 3 suggests that turning out to vote is a habitual or patterned behavior. The percentage turning out in each state is fairly constant across the eleven elections; drastic shifts in percentage turnout from election to election are extremely rare. The 1948 election, generally considered an unexciting election, is the major exception (Figure 2). Most states show a slight gradual rise in turnout from the 1920's up to the present. (The over-all trend can be seen in Tables 2 and 3 and in Figure 2.) The cause of this trend is not known for certain. We can speculate that it is due to improvements in economic well-being, in education, in transportation, and in communication. We know from other studies that improvements in these conditions are associated with increasing political participation. This interpretation is given credence by the figures in Table 3 and the slope of the

Table 3

TURNOUT IN PRESIDENTIAL ELECTIONS 1920–1960

(VOTE AS A PERCENTAGE OF THE CIVILIAN POPULATION OF VOTING AGE.)

State	1960	1956	1952	1948	1944	1940	1936	1932	1928	1924	1920
Idaho	80.7	77.6	82.2	65.3	76.3	75.1	71.3	73.4	62.7	63.1	57.9
Utah	80.1	75.2	81.4	74.7	76.2	80.3	75.2	75.1	68.2	64.3	63.8
N.H.	79.4	75.2	78.9	67.3	78.1	72.4	70.1	68.5	66.9	57.4	56.6
N.Dak.	78.5	70.6	75.2	64.0	71.0	75.2	74.8	71.4	69.7	61.4	63.7
S.Dak.	78.3	73.5	75.1	66.7	70.8	79.5	75.6	73.4	69.5	55.9	52.8
W.Va.	77.3	75.2	75.9	67.5	74.1	81.4	81.2	78.5	73.5	72.4	67.8
Minn.	77.0	67.7	72.3	65.5	70.2	69.6	66.5	62.7	63.3	56.1	53.3
Ind.	76.9	71.8	74.4	65.3	76.2	79.8	76.5	76.4	72.3	68.1	71.0
Conn.	76.8	76.6	79.6	63.7	70.2	67.4	63.8	58.3	57.7	44.8	43.6
Iowa	76.5	73.2	75.7	62.8	72.0	74.1	72.3	67.8	68.3	67.9	62.7
Mass.	76.1	75.7	77.8	65.9	73.0	69.5	63.1	58.0	59.7	44.3	41.2
Ill.	75.7	73.2	76.0	68.1	79.4	78.4	76.3	68.6	65.5	55.8	53.1
R.I.	75.1	73.7	81.6	62.3	65.3	67.4	70.1	62.9	58.9	52.0	47.3
Wyo.	74.0	67.8	75.1	62.2	75.6	72.2	71.3	71.3	65.5	63.4	45.4
Del.	73.6	72.1	79.8	66.9	68.9	76.8	77.3	72.8	73.5	67.8	69.5
Wis.	73.4	67.4	73.3	59.2	71.2	69.6	65.3	60.7	58.6	50.9	45.9
Maine	72.6	62.8	62.5	47.6	60.5	60.2	58.8	60.2	54.1	40.1	41.6
Vt.	72.5	67.4	66.2	54.1	63.6	62.7	64.1	62.0	62.0	47.6	41.4
Mich.	72.4	68.1	67.0	52.4	63.7	61.8	58.5	56.6	48.8	46.0	47.3
Wash.	72.3	70.8	71.9	61.4	65.6	66.5	63.3	59.9	50.4	45.4	46.5
Oreg.	72.3	68.2	67.5	55.9	59.7	64.3	59.9	57.5	53.1	51.5	48.2
N.J.	71.8	69.0	71.1	59.2	70.9	69.6	67.4	62.3	63.6	50.4	48.0
Mo.	71.8	67.8	72.2	61.2	68.9	73.3	75.4	68.7	67.6	61.7	65.4
Colo.	71.4	67.6	75.1	64.4	76.2	76.9	73.3	71.5	64.6	56.5	51.7
Nebr.	71.4	67.1	73.4	59.6	75.9	73.6	72.9	69.1	68.6	60.9	51.8
Mont.	71.4	71.0	72.6	65.4	70.8	69.6	68.0	67.4	61.0	55.7	55.8
Ohio	71.3	65.0	70.0	55.8	69.5	72.4	67.7	61.3	61.6	52.1	56.8
Pa.	70.5	65.7	66.3	54.6	64.1	64.2	68.3	48.8	55.3	39.7	36.7
Kans.	70.3	67.2	72.0	64.1	68.3	74.0	73.4	68.9	65.0	63.0	55.7
Calif.	67.4	63.8	68.0	58.9	62.9	66.9	59.6	55.9	49.7	41.9	40.7
N.Y.	67.0	66.0	68.3	60.8	74.1	67.4	61.7	56.0	60.2	47.2	44.5

curves in Figure 2. They show the rise in turnout in the Southern region coinciding very closely with the postwar period of swift industrialization of the South.

The consistency of state-by-state voting turnout can be demonstrated another way. If the states are ranked by turnout for different years and for different types of elections, the similarities in the rankings for the several

Table 3, continued

State	1960	1956	1952	1948	1944	1940	1936	1932	1928	1924	1920
Okla.	63.8	63.6	71.8	56.2	62.0	60.3	55.6	53.7	50.1	47.4	47.6
N.Mex.	62.1	59.6	61.0	57.1	59.0	64.4	65.2	66.2	55.9	57.3	56.9
Nev.	61.2	62.8	71.5	59.2	62.3	70.6	63.5	63.7	54.9	48.1	52.1
Ky.	59.2	58.8	59.2	49.8	59.7	59.3	60.2	67.4	68.1	60.6	71.2
Md.	57.2	54.5	58.8	40.7	47.5	55.7	56.2	49.1	54.2	39.2	49.7
Ariz.	54.5	50.8	54.4	44.0	43.4	52.0	45.6	46.6	38.8	34.9	35.4
N.C.	53.5	48.2	52.8	36.7	43.1	42.6	47.3	43.7	43.0	36.1	44.5
Hawaii	51.3	....	....	....	....	....	....	....	....	....	....
Tenn.	50.3	46.3	44.8	28.5	31.0	30.6	29.9	26.1	25.9	23.0	35.3
Fla.	50.0	45.9	50.3	34.5	36.3	39.8	31.8	30.2	30.5	16.7	36.0
Alaska	45.5	....	....	....	....	....	....	....	....	....	....
La.	44.8	36.4	39.9	27.1	26.3	27.1	25.4	22.5	19.7	12.1	13.6
Tex.	41.8	37.9	42.3	24.7	30.5	27.0	23.4	25.8	23.0	23.9	19.8
Ark.	41.1	39.9	37.6	22.8	22.0	18.2	17.1	22.5	20.9	15.4	21.2
Va.	33.4	33.5	31.7	22.1	23.9	22.0	22.3	21.7	23.6	17.7	19.1
Ala.	31.1	28.3	24.6	12.7	16.4	18.9	18.4	17.6	18.8	13.6	20.8
S.C.	30.5	25.2	29.4	13.4	11.0	10.1	12.4	12.1	8.5	6.5	8.6
Ga.	30.4	29.7	30.1	20.4	18.2	17.6	17.7	16.4	15.6	11.5	10.4
Miss.	25.5	21.7	24.1	16.7	16.8	14.7	14.4	13.8	15.2	12.1	9.4
Average for U.S.	63.8	60.1	62.0	51.5	56.3	59.7	57.5	52.9	52.3	44.3	44.2

Sources: U.S. Bureau of the Census, *Statistical Abstract of the U.S.: 1962,* eighty-third edition, Washington: 1962 (for civilian population of voting age figures, 1920, 1940, 1960); Population Division, U.S. Bureau of the Census (for estimates of civilian population of voting age, 1924–1936, 1944–1956); Richard M. Scammon (ed.), *America Votes, Vol. IV* (Pittsburgh: University of Pittsburgh Press), 1962 (for votes cast in Presidential elections, 1948–1960); *Statistics of Presidential and Congressional Elections, 1920–1958,* compiled under direction of Clerk of House of Representatives (for votes cast in Presidential elections, 1920–1944). Reproduced from the Report of the President's Commission on Registration and Voting Participation, November 1963.

years and elections is striking. Table 5 shows a correlation matrix for five different types of turnout rankings; the very high correlation coefficients shown indicate how very similar those rankings are. We can also note in Table 5 that the correlations with the turnout ranking which does not include Presidential elections (the same as that shown in Table 4) are a bit lower than the other correlations in the matrix. This difference suggests that some-

Table 4

FORTY-EIGHT STATES RANKED BY THEIR AVERAGE TURNOUT IN GUBERNATORIAL AND SENATORIAL ELECTIONS IN NON-PRESIDENTIAL YEARS 1952–60, AND PERCENTAGE TURNOUT

Rank	*State*	*Average Percentage Turnout**		*Rank*	*State*	*Average Percentage Turnout**
1	Idaho	64.6		25	Michigan	51.2
2	Utah	64.3		26	Vermont	51.0
3	Connecticut	63.4		27.5	Iowa	50.9
4	Indiana	63.1		27.5	New York	50.9
5	Rhode Island	62.7		29	New Jersey	49.9
6	South Dakota	62.5		30	Nebraska	48.7
7	Delaware	61.4		31	Maine	45.7
8	Wyoming	60.5	Border States	32	New Mexico	44.4
9	Montana	59.6		33	Kentucky	44.0
10.5	Minnesota	58.8		34	Missouri	43.7
10.5	Massachusetts	58.8		35	Arizona	43.5
12	North Dakota	56.5		36	Maryland	42.6
13	Oregon	55.9		37	Oklahoma	40.9
14	Nevada	55.7	Middle South	38	Arkansas	29.0
15.5	Illinois	55.3		39	North Carolina	25.1
15.5	West Virginia	55.3		40	Virginia	21.4
17	New Hampshire	55.0		41	Tennessee	18.5
18	Pennsylvania	54.6		42	Florida	17.4
19	Colorado	54.3	Deep South	43	Alabama	16.7
20	California	53.4		44	Texas	13.6
21	Kansas	52.7		45	Louisiana	12.3
22	Washington	52.6		46	South Carolina	11.9
23	Ohio	52.3		47	Georgia	10.7
24	Wisconsin	51.3		48	Mississippi	4.2

*Alaska and Hawaii did not become the 49th and 50th states of the union until after the 1956 election and thus could not be included in the table.

what different factors are operating to get people to turn out and vote in Presidential elections than the factors operating in purely state or local elections.

The strikingly lower turnout figures shown for the South have been alluded to above. What causes this behavior difference? We can seek an answer by examining several social and economic factors which are likely to be related to political participation.

First, it is important to note how consistently the South ranks lower in turnout than the other regions of the country. The data in Table 3 and the curves in Figure 2 demonstrate that the low turnout characteristic of the South goes back three or four decades, at least. Tables 1 and 4 carry supporting data for recent years. Close study of Table 4 shows that the state-by-state ranking on turnout assumes a North-South gradient pattern. The states with the lowest turnout ranking are the deep South states; next lowest are the middle South states; and next lowest to them are the border states. Among states ranking high on turnout are a preponderance of northern plains and mountain states. These are sparsely populated, largely agricultural states. There are a few exceptions to this generalization (Connecticut, Indiana, Rhode Island, Delaware) which suggests that region is not the sole explanatory factor. The heavily industrialized states, with large metropolitan complexes, tend to cluster toward the middle of the distribution.

Figure 2

AVERAGE VOTING TURNOUT IN PRESIDENTIAL ELECTIONS BY REGIONS FROM 1920 TO 1960

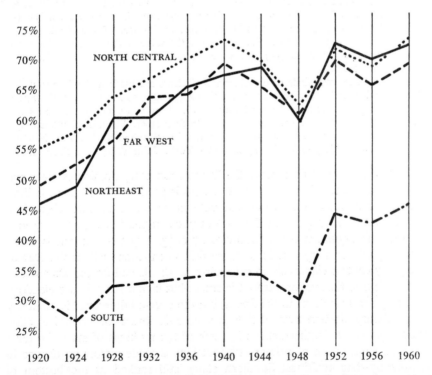

Source: The data were derived from Table 3. For each election the turnout percentages for states in a given region were averaged. Regional definitions are those used by the U.S. Bureau of the Census; see *Statistical Abstract, 1963*, p. xii, for details.

Table 5

RANK-ORDER CORRELATION* MATRIX FOR FIVE DIFFERENT MEASURES OF VOTING TURNOUT

	Average Presidential Turnout 1940–1948	Average Presidential Turnout 1952–1960	Presidential Turnout 1960	Average Gubernatorial Turnout 1952–1960
Average Presidential Turnout 1952–1960	.93			
Presidential Turnout 1960	.88	.96		
Average Gubernatorial Turnout 1952–1960	.89	.92	.89	
Average Turnout for Governor or Senator in Non-Presidential Years 1952–1960	.84	.88	.86	.87

*A correlation coefficient — as used in this table and others in this book — is a numerical index of the strength of the relationship between two variables. Its value ranges from 0 to 1. The closer the coefficient is to + or − 1, the stronger the relationship; the closer the coefficient is to 0, the weaker the relationship. The sign before the coefficient (+ or −) indicates whether the relationship is direct or inverse. If the relationship is direct (+), as the value of one variable increases, the value of the other also increases. If the relationship is inverse (−), the value of one variable *decreases* as the value of the other increases.

In this volume, two kinds of correlation coefficients are used: a simple correlation coefficient and a rank-order correlation coefficient (usually, as in this table, the Spearman coefficient which is named after its inventor). They accommodate data in somewhat different forms but are roughly equivalent to each other. For a detailed discussion of how such coefficients are calculated, see Mordacai Ezekiel and Karl A. Fox, *Methods of Correlation and Regression Analysis* (New York: John Wiley and Sons, 1959).

It is often argued that, since the Democratic party dominates state and local elections in the South and the outcome is predetermined, there is little incentive for citizens to turn out and vote in general elections. There is a grain of truth to the argument; the turnout percentages, indeed, are very low. However, the argument often continues by suggesting that turnout is much higher in party primary elections where different factions within the Democratic party contest vigorously to get their man nominated on the Democratic ticket. It is true that voting turnout is somewhat higher for primary elections than for general elections in the South, but the over-all difference is relatively slight. Primary election turnout figures were substituted for general election turnout figures for Southern states in some of the rankings of states by turnout. This substitution of primary turnout figures made almost no change in the state-by-state rankings; Southern states still ranked at the bottom of the list. The pattern of low voting turnout seems to be a general cultural factor in the South which holds true no matter what the type of election is. This finding lends additional credence to the point made above, that turning out to vote (or not turning out) is patterned or habitual behavior. What are the cultural factors that depress turnout in the South? Some of them are social, some are economic, and some are political. Perhaps the most important factor is political: the lack of inter-party competition in the South. Other studies have shown that the more vigorous the competition between parties, the greater the interest of citizens in the election, and the larger the turnout.[12] Dawson and Robinson developed a rank order of the states on party competition.[13] Their measure included: (1) percentage of popular vote for governor; (2) percentage of seats in the senate held by the major party; (3) percentage of seats in the house held by the major party. It covered the years from 1938 to 1958. This measure showed a Spearman rank-order correlation of .807 with the ranking on turnout reported in Table 4: the more vigorous the party competition the greater the turnout. This measure showed a positive correlation with all the other rankings of turnout we developed. Furthermore, six other measures of party competition were developed, some of them based on competition in Presidential elections, some based on competition in both Presidential and state elections, some based on evaluations of the party system in the state. For five of these measures there was a positive, significant correlation with each of the measures of turnout (forty-six correlations in all).

The exception among these measures of party competition was a measure based on the extent to which the two-party vote differed from 50 per cent in recent Presidential elections. In these Presidential elections there has been much more competition between the parties in the South than formerly. Some Southern states have moved up to the middle competitive ranks and others have moved up to be some of the most competitive. For example, in 1960 Arkansas ranked 6th in competition whereas in the 1940–48 period she ranked 44th; Louisiana ranked 8th in 1960 but 45.5 in 1940–48; Texas ranked 9th in 1960 but tied with Louisiana at 45.5 in 1940–48; South Carolina ranked 3rd in 1952–60 but 47th in 1940–48; North Carolina ranked 6.5 in 1952–60 but 43rd in 1940–48; Tennessee ranked 1.5 in 1952–60 but 40.5 in 1940–48; Mississippi ranked 6.5 in 1952–60 but 48th in 1940–48. The tendency is clear: the South has become more competitive in *Presidential elections*. Despite this, Southern states have much less party competition for state and local elections. Interestingly, the increase in party competition for Presidential elections has had only a minor impact on turnout (see Table 3); Southern states continue to rank lowest on turnout, even in Presidential elections. This suggests that other factors as well as party competition contribute to low Southern turnout.

The racial composition of the South is another contributing factor to low turnout there. Generally, the higher the percentage of Negroes in an area, the lower the turnout. A ranking of states by percentage Negro shows a negative ($-.67$) correlation with the turnout ranking shown in Table 4. Several studies of political participation show that Negroes generally are less likely to vote than whites.[14] More important than that, however, are the systematic pressures, both social and political, in the South to keep Negroes from voting.[15] Generally, the higher the percentage of Negroes in an area, the greater the pressure to keep them from voting; this generalization holds especially true in the rural South. Some of these pressures are legal regulations, such as stringent registration requirements. Some are social pressures, such as ostracism and verbal abuse. Some take the form of economic reprisals, such as being fired from a job or being evicted from rented quarters. Some pressures are unabashedly violent, such as beatings and killings.[16] It is inescapable that these pressures depress turnout. Beware of the interpretation that there is some biological characteristic of race that depresses Negro turnout; some studies show that in certain cities where the Negro is given free opportunity and encouragement to participate he is as likely, or even more likely, to turn out than white persons.[17]

Another factor that may contribute to low turnout in the South is its depressed economic condition in comparison to other sections of the country. The impact of this factor is difficult to assess. Ranking of the states for several economic variables for 1960 show a positive correlation with turnout rankings: average weekly unemployment benefits .55; median family income .52; per capita tax revenue .55; median school years completed .52; per pupil expenditures on education .51. On all of these variables the South ranks lower than the rest of the nation. Is the correlation between turnout and these economic variables mere coincidence of the rankings or is there some causative relationship? A variety of other studies (in at least six countries) have shown that persons of lower socio-economic-status (SES) are less likely to participate in politics than those of higher SES.[18] But socio-economic-status, per se, cannot cause any social behavior. Rather, it is only as someone's life situation affects his personality, beliefs, and attitudes and, through these factors, affects behavior that we can speak of SES causing behavior.

West Virginia presents an interesting contrast to the deep South on economic and turnout factors. For several decades West Virginia had been a highly industrialized and reasonably prosperous state. In recent years, however, some of her industries have become obsolete, and currently the state has a very high rate of unemployment and considerable poverty. If we look at West Virginia's turnout in Table 3 we can see that her turnout rate has been consistently high from the early 1920's (sometimes the highest in the nation). With her recent decline in prosperity there has been no accompanying decline in turnout. In contrast, in recent years the deep South has shown the greatest percentage rise on several prosperity indices: percentage increase in per capita income 1950–60, percentage increase in median family income 1949–59, percentage increase in urban population 1950–60. Yet, although the South is growing more prosperous yearly, the turnout habits of its citizens are changing more slowly. The rankings of states on prosperity increase are negatively related to turnout rankings for the years 1950–60: the greater the percentage rise in prosperity, the more likelihood of a low ranking on turnout.

Other possible factors producing lower turnout in the South are legal restrictions on the franchise. Many of these were adopted to make it more difficult for Negroes to vote, but they have the side effect of making it slightly more difficult for some whites to vote, too. These factors are discussed more fully in the next section of the chapter.

PARTICIPATION AS A FUNCTION OF POLITICO/LEGAL SETTING

Political and legal characteristics of the environment may confine or depress participation, but they also may facilitate participation. Under the United States Constitution the states, rather than the national government, are given the power to legally define who is eligible to participate in elections. However, certain limitations are set on that power: persons shall be eligible to vote in federal elections who are eligible to vote for members of the most numerous house of the state legislature; they shall not be denied the franchise because of sex, race, color, or previous condition of servitude. Because of these and other conventions, general suffrage requirements are quite uniform across the states. Nearly all the states grant the vote at age twenty-one (exceptions: Georgia and Kentucky at eighteen, Alaska at nineteen, and Hawaii at twenty). The Twenty-Fourth Amendment to the Constitution forbids the poll tax in elections for national office.

Beyond these uniformities, however, there are important state differences in election laws, some of which have a significant impact on turnout. Table 6 presents a state-by-state summary of the more important of these laws vis-à-vis their impact on turnout. Note that the states are ranked in order of their average turnout in the Presidential election of 1960. The presence of a star in a column means that the election law tends to facilitate turnout. A quick study of the patterning of the table shows that states ranking high in turnout tend to have more facilitative laws than states ranking low in turnout. The clustering of Southern states at the bottom of the ranking and the relative infrequency of facilitative laws for those states is also evident.

Table 6

VOTING TURNOUT AND ELECTION LAW

Vote in Presidential Elections as a Percentage of Civilian Population of Voting Age, by State, with Provisions of Election Laws Facilitating Participation. Key: ★ = statewide, ☆ = some areas only.*

1920	1940	1960	State	Residence in state under 1 year	No literacy test	Permanent registration	General civilian absentee registration permitted	Precinct registration	Registration closes within 1 month of election	Civilian absentee vote	Mere absence a ground for absentee vote	Absentee ballot application by mail	Polls open 12 hours or longer	Presidential voting by new residents	Presidential voting by former residents
57.9	75.1	80.7	Idaho	★	★	★	★	★	★	★	★	★	★	★	
63.8	80.3	80.1	Utah		★	★	★	★	★	★	★	★	★	★	
56.6	72.4	79.4	N.H.	★		★				★	★	★	★	★	
63.7	75.2	78.5	N.Dak		★		No registration		★	★	★	★	☆		
52.8	79.5	78.3	S.Dak		★	★			★	★	★	★	★		
67.8	81.4	77.3	W.Va.		★	★	★	★	★		★	★	★	★	
53.3	69.6	77.0	Minn.	★	★	☆	★			★	★	★	★	★	
71.0	79.8	76.9	Ind.	★	★	★			★	★	★	★	★	★	
43.6	67.4	76.8	Conn.			★			★	★	★	★	★		
62.7	74.1	76.5	Iowa		★	★			★	★	★	★	★	★	★
41.2	69.5	76.1	Mass.	★	★	☆	★	★	★	★	★	★	☆	★	
53.1	78.4	75.7	Ill.		★	★			★	★	★	★	★	★	
47.3	67.4	75.1	R.I.		★	★		☆		★	★	★	★	☆	★
45.4	72.2	74.0	Wyo.			☆	★	★	★	★	★	★	★		★
69.5	76.8	73.6	Del.			★		★	★	★	★	★	★		
45.9	69.6	73.4	Wis.		★	☆	★	★		★	★	★	★	☆	
41.6	60.2	72.6	Maine	★		★	★			★	★	★	★	★	★
41.4	62.7	72.5	Vt.		★	★				★	★	★	★	☆	★
47.3	61.8	72.4	Mich.	★	★	★	★		★	★	★	★	★		★
46.5	66.5	72.3	Wash.			★	★		★	★	★	★	★		
48.2	64.3	72.3	Oreg.	★		★	★	★	★	★	★	★	★		
48.0	69.6	71.8	N.J.	★	★	★				★	★	★	★	★	★
65.4	73.3	71.8	Mo.		★	☆				★	★	★	★	★	
51.7	76.9	71.4	Colo.		★	★	☆	★	☆	★	★	★	★		
51.8	73.6	71.4	Nebr.	★	★	★	☆	★		★	★	★	★	★	
55.8	69.6	71.4	Mont.		★	☆	★	★		★	★	★	★	☆	★
56.8	72.4	71.3	Ohio		★	☆	★	★		★		★	★	★	
36.7	64.2	70.5	Pa.		★	★		★		★		★	★	★	
55.7	74.0	70.3	Kans.	★	★	☆	★		★	★	★	★	☆	★	
40.7	66.9	67.4	Calif.			★		★		★	★	★	★	☆	★
44.5	67.4	67.0	N.Y.			★			★	★	★	★	★		
47.6	60.3	63.8	Okla.		★	★	☆	☆	☆	★	★	★	☆		
56.9	64.4	62.1	N.Mex.		★	★	★	★		★	★				
52.1	70.6	61.2	Nev.	★	★	★			★	★	★	★	★	☆	
71.2	59.3	59.2	Ky.		★	★			★	★	★	★			
49.7	55.7	57.2	Md.		★	☆		★		★	★	★	★	★	★
35.4	52.0	54.5	Ariz.		★	★		★		★	★	★	☆	☆	
44.5	42.6	53.5	N.C.		★	★		☆		★	★	★	★	★	★
		51.3	Hawaii		★	★	★		★	★	★	★			
35.3	30.6	50.3	Tenn.	★	★	★			★	★	★	★			
36.0	39.8	50.0	Fla.		☆	★		☆	★	★	★	★	★		
		45.5	Alaska		★	No registration		☆	★	★	★	★	★		
13.6	27.1	44.8	La.		☆		★	★	★	★	★			
19.8	27.0	41.8	Tex.		★	No registration			★	★	★	☆		
21.2	18.2	41.1	Ark.		★	No registration		★	★	★	★			
19.1	22.0	33.4	Va.	★	★			★	★	★	★	★	★	
20.8	18.9	31.1	Ala.		★			★	★	★				
8.6	10.1	30.5	S.C.					★	★					
10.4	17.6	30.4	Ga.		★			★	★	★	★	★		
9.4	14.7	25.5	Miss.		★			★						

*The information in this chart has been checked with responsible officials in every state. In certain instances, it has not been feasible to show in detail specific exceptions to general provisions.

Source: Reproduced from the Report of the President's Commission on Registration and Voting Participation, November 1963. The states are ranked by percentage turnout in the 1960 Presidential election.

REGISTRATION REQUIREMENTS. Registration can be administered to facilitate as well as to hinder voting. Many countries have what is called official or automatic registration. In this system no initiative by the potential voter is required to get his name on the list of eligibles; the responsibility for keeping the list up to date is with the registration officials. Some studies suggest that turnout for voting is higher under such automatic registration.[19] Certain states in the United States use a registration system that is akin to automatic registration. Idaho selects and pays a deputy registrar in each precinct to canvass door-to-door and keep registration rolls up to date (Idaho is the top-ranking state in turnout in both Tables 4 and 6). California law authorizes the appointment of deputy registrars and door-to-door canvassing.[20] Canada uses teams of enumerators, two to each electoral district, to canvass each residence prior to each parliamentary election.

In many localities the act of registration is much more inconvenient than the act of voting. Some states require a trip to the county court house, usually during working hours. To alleviate this inconvenience, somewhat more than half of the states have adopted precinct or mobile registration on designated days preceding elections (Table 6). On these days the voter makes only a short trip in his immediate neighborhood. There does not seem to be any pattern, however, for states permitting precinct registration to rank high or low on turnout.

In some states, again mainly in the South, registration is more than inconvenient, it is downright difficult. Registration forms are deliberately made complicated. Some jurisdictions require witnesses to testify to the identity and residence of the applicant. Literacy tests in many jurisdictions are extremely difficult and, if the applicant is Negro, letter-perfect accuracy often is required to pass. Such a literacy test was administered by a political science professor at a good Southern university to his class of white students; a large majority of the class would have failed to qualify to vote under the test.

Nearly all states permit some type of permanent registration so that the citizen does not need to re-register prior to each election. Seventeen states also permit absentee registration. Having absentee registration in a state does show a significant, positive relationship with turnout ranking. It also facilitates registration if the registration books can be kept open reasonably close to the election. This objective must be balanced against the practical task of the registrar to prepare precinct lists of eligibles by election day. Most states close registration within one month of the election (Table 6). Finally, it should be noted that four states have no registration system. This arrangement seems to be practical only in sparsely populated areas. All in all, registration can be a nuisance, but it does not seem to be a significant barrier preventing persons from voting, except in the South.

RESIDENCE REQUIREMENTS. The United States Census Bureau revealed that twenty million American adults changed residence in 1961. In a society with a highly mobile population, requiring lengthy periods of residence before a citizen is allowed to vote can be a significant barrier to turnout. Using census data for 1960, states were ranked by the percentage of their citizens who changed residence after 1958; this ranking was correlated against the state-by-state turnout rankings. It shows a negative correlation with all of the turnout measures: the greater the mobility the lower the turnout. As we might expect, since the ranking is for persons who moved after 1958, it shows the highest negative correlation ($-.515$) with turnout in the 1960 Presidential election.

Ralph Goldman found that the most general residence requirements were two years in the state (for two-thirds of the states) and thirty days in the precinct.[21] He estimated that 5 per cent of adults who normally would have been eligible to vote in 1952 were made ineligible by residence requirements. Table 6 shows that only twelve states have residence requirements of less than one year. The lowest turnout states uniformly require a year or more of residence. The President's Commission on Registration and Voting Participation (hereafter called the President's Commission) estimated that four million persons were disfranchised by residence requirements in 1950, five million in 1954, and eight million in 1960. The Commission recommended that state residence requirements should not exceed six months, and that the local residence requirements should not exceed a period of thirty days.

The Commission also recommended that new state residents should be allowed to vote for President even if not for state and local offices. Fifteen states now grant this privilege (Table 6). This characteristic was correlated with the turnout rankings; the correlation was not significant for turnout in state elections but was significant for turnout in Presidential elections. We note also in Table 6 that seven states allow former residents to vote for President.

LITERACY TEST REQUIREMENT. Table 6 shows that nineteen states require some sort of demonstration of literacy before a person is allowed to vote. There is a slight tendency for states not requiring a literacy test to rank higher on turnout, but there are enough exceptions to the trend to suggest that this requirement is not a significant depressant of turnout. It is not so much the presence of the test but the manner in which it is administered that can disfranchise potential voters. The test has become infamous for the manner in which it was used to deprive Negroes of their vote in some Southern states. The President's Commission recommended abandonment of the requirement in all states.

ABSENTEE BALLOT. All states except Mississippi, New Mexico, and South Carolina provide some form of absentee balloting for their non-military citizens. Thirty-four states provide absentee privileges for anyone who expects to be away from home on election day (Table 6). In the other states, a person must be unavoidably absent or have special status, such as a businessman on a regular trip or a student at an accredited college or university. There is a slight trend in the data for states making it easy to vote absentee to rank high in turnout but there are enough exceptions to suggest that the trend is not significant.

POLLS OPEN LONG. The President's Commission recommended that polling places should be kept open all day and remain open until 9 P.M. Ten states have their polls open for less than twelve hours. Six of these ten states are Southern and rank low in turnout, so there is a significant correlation between length of time the polls are open and state rank on turnout. The original justification for closing polls early was to give election officials time to count the ballots. Widespread use of voting machines makes this plea seem less and less valid.

The Survey Research Center examined several of the above legal requirements and grouped states into a two-category measure as having restrictive suffrage laws or moderate suffrage laws.[22] They conclude from their analysis that restrictive suffrage requirements inhibit turnout the most in the South. This inhibition was most pronounced among Southern Negroes and was highest in areas where the percentage of Negroes living there was close enough to the percentage of whites as to constitute a threat to white political dominance. They also conclude that informal, extralegal barriers — not state legislation — account for much of the variability in turnout of Southern Negroes.

The SRC research team found that restrictive suffrage requirements inhibited Negro turnout more than white turnout in Northern states as well as in Southern states. This relates to a general finding, noted above, that Negroes participate less than whites in all types of routine political acts — this holds in both North and South. As a corollary of these findings, survey research generally has shown that Negroes feel less intensely about elections than do whites. This pattern suggests that there are important differences between the white and Negro sub-cultures. Given the differences in intensity about politics between the two sub-cultures, the differential impact of legal codes on the turnout of the races is more understandable. "Formal political institutions have their greatest impact on behavior when the attitudes relevant to that behavior are least intense."[23] The additional depression of turnout found for Southern Negroes is attributable to the informal, extralegal sanctions that also are applied there.[24]

THE POLITICAL PARTY SETTING. The finding reported above, that states with vigorous party competition tend to rank higher in turnout, also is relevant here. Several related mechanisms are operating. When parties and candidates compete vigorously, they make news and are given a large play via the mass media. Thus, a setting of competitive politics tends to have a greater amount of political stimuli available in the environment than does a setting with weak competition. Persons living in an environment containing a high level of politically relevant stimuli are a bit more likely to become active in politics than those living where there are relatively few political stimuli.[25] Political interest tends to rise in an environment with competitive parties, not only because more stimuli are available for consumption, but also because interest rises with increasing conflict. People tend to follow a close contest with more interest. Furthermore, in a close contest they are more likely to perceive that their votes count and, thus, they are more likely to cast them. An additional factor is that, when parties are fighting in a close contest, their workers tend to spend more time and energy campaigning and getting out the vote. To summarize, strongly competitive political contests produce more news, more stimuli, more interest in the contest, more sense of importance to the vote, and more activity by party workers.[26]

A similar kind of point was made by Campbell as he classified elections into high stimulus and low stimulus elections.[27] In a high stimulus election persons generally perceive that the vote will be close and, therefore, that their votes will count; they feel that the office being decided is an important one; they tend to perceive a clear choice between alternative candidates or parties; the candidates tend to be attractive, and there is a high flow of campaign propaganda. High stimulus elections bring out a comparatively high turnout. It is easy to see that persons living in a state with vigorous party competition are more likely to experience high stimulus elections than those living in states dominated by one party.

In connection with this discussion of political party setting and turnout, two other correlations might be mentioned. Turnout was negatively correlated ($-.32$) with the strength of pressure groups in the state (Committee on American State Legislatures' measure):[28] the stronger the pressure groups the greater the likelihood of low turnout. Turnout was positively correlated (.38) with strength of party cohesion (another Committee on State Legislatures' measure): the greater the cohesion the greater the likelihood of high turnout.

These party and pressure group characteristics are associated with one another. At one extreme, or perfect type, are states that have vigorous party competition, cohesive parties in the legislature, high turnout at elections, and relatively weak pressure groups. At the opposite extreme are states that have one dominant party, low party cohesion in the legislature, strong pressure groups, and low turnout at the polls. Between these extremes the combination of these factors is less pronounced and we would expect departures from the pattern on one or two variables.

PARTICIPATION AS A FUNCTION OF SOCIAL AND ECONOMIC SETTING

Economic and social factors are important determinants of political participation patterns; this is as true of other types of participation as it is of voting. It has repeatedly been found that persons who rank high on socioeconomic-status are more likely to participate in politics. In an attempt to relate state-by-state differences on voting turnout to state-by-state differences on social and economic characteristics, the states were ranked on twenty-six different social and economic characteristics; these variables were then included in a factor analysis along with the turnout and party competition rankings mentioned above.

Turnout loaded heavily on only one of the factors extracted in the analysis. Close study showed that it was essentially a North-South factor, the one we have already discussed. The rankings shown in Table 4 and Table 6 are close approximations of how the states were ranked by their scores on that factor. Any social or economic variable on which the North and South differed tended to load on that factor and correlated with turnout. Several of these factors were mentioned above in the discussion of regional differences: (1) income differences as reflected in per capita income, medium family income, weekly unemployment benefits, per pupil expenditure on education, and per capita tax revenue; (2) education differences as reflected in median school years completed and per pupil expenditure on education; (3) rate-of-change differences as reflected in faster prosperity increases in the South, faster urbanization in the South, faster non-white migration in the North; and (4) racial composition differences as reflected in the percentage of Negroes in the state. (Figure 3 gives a summary of the social and economic variables discussed here as well as above.)

Several social and economic variables did not relate to turnout. For example, several studies have shown that persons living in the cities are more likely to participate in politics than persons living in the country.[29] Yet, ranking the states on per cent urban showed no relationship with the turnout rankings. Type of employment as primary (agriculture, forestry, fishing), secondary (manufacturing), or tertiary (service, clerical, professional) often has turned out to be a significant social variable. Generally, it has been shown that persons employed in the primary sector are less likely to participate actively in politics than persons in the secondary sector who, in turn, are less active than persons in the tertiary sector. However, ranking the states on primary employment and on secondary employment showed no relationship with the turnout rankings.

Figure 3

THE RELATIONSHIP OF SOCIAL AND ECONOMIC VARIABLES TO VOTING TURNOUT

Positively Related to Turnout (states high on turnout tended to rank high on
            the variable)
    per capita personal income 1960
    median family income 1960
    average weekly unemployment benefits 1960
    per capita tax revenue 1960
    per pupil expenditure on education 1960
    median school years completed — persons 25 and over — 1960
    net non-white migration 1950–60 (also 1940–50)
    per cent of total population foreign born or of foreign or mixed parentage
        1960

Negatively Related to Turnout (states high on turnout tended to rank low on
            the variable)
    per cent increase in personal income 1950–60
    per cent increase in median family income 1949–59
    per cent increase in urban population 1950–60
    per cent Negro population 1960
    per cent moved into their house after 1958 (question put in 1960 census)

Unrelated to Turnout
    total population 1960 (also 1950)
    population density 1960 (also 1950)
    per cent increase in population 1950–60 (also 1940–50)
    per cent urban 1960 (also 1950)
    primary employment — per cent employed in agriculture, forestry, and
        fishing 1960
    secondary employment — per cent employed in manufacturing 1960
    per cent of state budget spent on higher education 1957–58
    state and local tax revenue in relation to personal income 1960

Source: Data were drawn from United States Census materials. The states were then
ranked on each variable. These measures were then correlated with several measures
of voting turnout, also ranked by states. Factor analysis was then used to indicate the
relationship of the social and economic variables to the general turnout factor.

The percentage of the total state budget spent on higher education was
unrelated to turnout. Total population, population density, and percentage
increase in population all showed no relationship to turnout. The percentage
of the population in the state that was foreign born or of foreign or mixed
parentage showed a slight positive association with turnout which is probably
only a function of the fact that most immigrants went to Northern large
cities and not to the South. We certainly would not expect the presence of
a large percentage of immigrants to lead to or cause a high turnout.
    Lack of association between rankings on economic and social variables

and rankings on turnout does not necessarily mean that these social and economic factors have no influence on turnout. Economic factors, such as income, characterize individuals and a behavior like turning out to vote can only be carried out by individuals. Correlational procedures which do not use individuals as units (as a rank correlation of states does not) inevitably do not account for a sizeable portion of the variance between the variables. Judgment about the relationship between these socio-economic factors and political participation must ultimately be based upon better quality data derived from and standing for individuals.

Some state differences on economic and social factors may correlate more highly with gladiatorial activity than with turnout. Unfortunately, without state-by-state data on gladiatorial activity that notion cannot be checked out. We might hypothesize, for example, that, although rural and urban areas do not differ significantly on turnout, persons living in large cities are more likely to be drawn into gladiatorial activity than persons living in the country. Similarly, we know from other studies that persons belonging to labor unions are more likely to become involved in politics than similar types of workers not belonging to unions. State-by-state figures on percentage of workers in unions could be correlated with state-by-state figures on participation in gladiatorial activities (if they were available) to see if the union membership factor affects participation in state politics.

Survey studies generally have shown that persons of the Jewish religion are more active in politics than Catholics who, in turn, are more active than Protestants. The SRC 1956 election survey showed Catholics more likely to vote than Protestants, but not more likely to engage in gladiatorial activities. Jews were more likely than either to engage in both spectator and gladiatorial activities. Since Jews and Catholics tend to concentrate in large Northern cities and Protestants are more likely to live in small towns and rural areas (also the South is solidly Protestant) we do not know if the religious differences create the impact on participation or whether locational differences, and all their attendant correlates, create the impact on participation.

PARTICIPATION AS A FUNCTION OF PERSONAL FACTORS

Political participation is related to quite a number of personal factors, such as personality, attitudes, and beliefs. It is difficult, however, to relate these personal factors to state-by-state differences. While we might expect state agencies to keep records on voting turnout and on economic variables, such as unemployment, we do not expect these agencies to keep records of the percentage of people who feel cynical about politics, for example. Data on personal factors would be gathered only by sample survey and there are no state-by-state samples covering the United States.

Two bits of research suggest locational differences for political attitudes. Several studies have shown that persons who feel very cynical about politics are less likely to participate actively in politics.[30] Litt conducted a study of the effect of cynicism on the political participation patterns of people living in Boston and its suburbs.[31] With various socio-economic variables (such as education) held constant he found that persons living in Boston were more cynical than similar types of individuals living in the suburbs. He speculated that long experience with the political machine in Boston may have produced the more cynical attitudes of the big city dweller. If the pattern Litt found should be upheld by replicative studies in other big cities, we could expect cynicism to be higher, and participation to be lower, in large cities dominated by a political machine (e.g., Chicago). Since city dwellers generally partici- pate more in politics than rural dwellers, the inquiry could be controlled to confine it to participation differences between large cities, some of which are dominated by machines and others not.

The Survey Research Center (University of Michigan) has found that persons with efficacious attitudes toward politics are more likely to become active in politics; this has been confirmed in many studies.[32] A person feels efficacious if he believes he can have or does have some effect on the political process. A sense of efficacy correlates very significantly with participation in spectator activities, but there is a significant positive trend also for participa- tion in gladiatorial activities. How do people develop a feeling of efficacy in politics? At this point we have only a partial answer to that question. Persons of upper socio-economic-status, especially the better educated, more likely develop efficacious feelings. Males, white persons, and city dwellers also are more likely to score high on efficacy. Persons living in the South are less likely to develop a sense of efficacy.[33]

The pattern of correlations just discussed suggests some interesting loca- tional characteristics. Persons growing up in the South not only participate less in politics (as we saw above), but they are less likely to feel that their personal efforts influence the political process. Both factors probably grow out of a general cultural milieu in the South which discourages open political combat. How this culture arose and the nature of its dynamics are only dimly understood at this point. The less efficacious feelings of Negroes (North and South) very likely are traceable to the Negro sub-culture. The efficacy scale, by the way, is oriented mainly to "normal" patterns of political action, such as voting; it is, perhaps, despair with these normal patterns that has driven the Negro to street demonstrations and protests to achieve his political objec- tives.

The tendency for city dwellers to feel more efficacious about politics than rural dwellers may be counteracted in some large cities by the cynicism engendered by machine politics. Normally, there is a negative relationship between the cynicism scale and the efficacy scale; efficacious persons are less likely to feel cynical. Litt found in Boston, however, that attitudes on cynicism and efficacy were unrelated; yet, the normal correlation pattern held in the suburbs.

In evaluating the pattern of correlations relevant to political participation it is baffling to try and sort out cause from effect because of widespread covariance. Does a person participate in politics because he feels efficacious politically, or does he feel efficacious because he participates in politics? Is there a circularity of effect so that minimal successful participation leads to increased efficacy which, in turn, leads to increased participation? Both factors correlate with SES. Does SES affect participation through developing a sense of efficacy or is the effect direct (without the intervention of efficacy)? Dahl found no significant correlation between SES and political participation when efficacy was held constant.[34] It is possible that feelings of efficacy and participating actively in politics tend to raise social and economic standing, especially across generations; in such a situation, does efficacy and participation cause or produce SES rank or does SES rank produce or cause efficacy and participation?

The data used in this chapter have two kinds of deficiencies: (1) there is lack of coverage (witness the point made above lack of state-by-state data on participation); and (2) there is lack of precision or quality. The student of social science must be content with a good deal of ambiguity about cause and effect as he tries to understand the world he lives in. Evidence of a relationship between factors is important and useful information, even if it does not make clear which is cause and which is effect. Sometimes, clear knowledge of the time at which certain factors occur enables us to distinguish cause and effect. As we improve our measurement techniques and gather additional and more reliable data, we can examine differences in strength of correlation and arrive at more valid inferences about cause and effect than are possible today.

THE MEANING OF CONTEMPORARY PATTERNS OF PARTICIPATION

Do differences in patterns and levels of political participation produce differences in the conduct of politics from state to state? The problems in sorting out cause from effect, just discussed, make it difficult to say whether differences in participation produce differences in the conduct of politics or vice versa. For example, we noted that weak party competition is associated with low levels of participation, but which is cause and which is effect is more difficult to say. This entire book deals with differences in the conduct of politics from state to state; the reader can speculate as he goes along whether some of those differences are related to the differences in participation set forth in this chapter.

An important aspect of politics in any society is the competition between groups for preference in the decisions made by government. We can readily generalize that groups which participate vigorously are more likely to see their preferences fulfilled than groups which participate weakly or not at all. While this generalization is valid for the most part, it is a little too simple and should not be pushed too far. Some groups, especially those with few members, may participate very vigorously and still not achieve the policies they hope for. On the other hand, the needs of completely inactive groups may partially be met. Sometimes the needs of the apathetic are cared for out of simple justice or compassion. More frequently, public leaders operate according to the law of anticipated reactions; they try to anticipate the demands of the inactive public in order to prevent their rising up in wrath and throwing them out of office. Public leaders often are motivated to keep the mass of the public from becoming active.

For the law of anticipated reactions to function properly it is important that politics be kept open for a large influx of new participants should they desire it. Persons who cannot enter the competition for public office, even if they should wish to, can more safely be ignored. Keeping politics open is one of the best guarantees that governmental decisions will serve all the people. We have seen that there are important state differences in the openness of politics. Some of these differences are regulational as shown, for example, in Table 6; registration and voting are much easier in some states than in others. Differences in openness derive also from environmental differences. Citizens who are well educated and know the political system find it easier to enter and participate than those who do not know what to do. Persons growing up in a community where participation is normal and expected have fewer inhibitions toward participation than those reared in an environment where participation is almost unknown. Some political parties are more open to new recruits than are other parties. It is the openness or "closedness" of the system, rather than the mere fact of participation or non-participation, that most affects the likelihood that the government will serve all the people.

What do groups do when they find the ordinary channels of participation and political redress closed to them? History suggests that for a time they wait patiently to see if the system will open and respond to their wishes. But history also suggests that eventually they lose patience and use extraordinary methods of participation to get around the barriers thrown up by the dominant political group. There are several contemporary examples in state politics. Negroes who were systematically excluded from participation in politics in the American South used several extraordinary methods. First, they took

their grievances to the federal government, thus by-passing the state governments which were closed to them. Second, they took their grievances to the
federal courts rather than to the presumably more responsive Congress which
could not act because it was hamstrung by antiquated rules. Finally, they
took their grievances to the streets in mass demonstrations, sit-ins, boycotts,
and even riots. Until these people are admitted openly and equally to the use
of normal channels of electoral politics we can expect extraordinary means
to be used.

Although the fight of the Negro for access to the political and social system is the most dramatic of our time, there are other examples of the use of
extraordinary methods to by-pass closed channels in state politics. For a half
century urban elements in many states had tried to get reapportionment of
state legislatures in order to reflect better the growing population of urban
centers. Rural elements which controlled most state legislatures steadfastly
refused to reapportion despite, in many cases, specific constitutional provisions to the contrary. Normal political access in the form of equality of the
vote was blocked. The first attempts to use the extraordinary method of
appeal to the Supreme Court failed; the Court declared reapportionment was
a political not a justiciable question.[35] Redress of grievance was to be sought
by political action. Repeated political efforts (election of legislators) produced no substantial change, however, and the problem was brought again to
the Supreme Court (now having several new Justices). This time the Court
decided the problem was justiciable and in a series of cases has ordered reapportionment of both the house and the senate in states on the basis of population.[36]

Another example goes back a way in history. Labor unions had been
frustrated in their attempts in many states to achieve collective bargaining
rights. Anti-labor elements dominated most state legislatures, and urban
under-representation prevented removal of these elements by normal channels
of electoral state politics. Labor groups then shifted their drive to the federal
government where urban elements were not seriously under-represented.
Political action aimed at the Congress, the Presidency, and the Supreme Court
finally produced the passage of the Wagner Act in 1935 and a favorable
verdict on its constitutionality in 1937.[37]

A major consequence for state politics, then, of differences in the openness of political systems to influence through normal electoral channels is
that extraordinary means and alternative political arenas may be sought by
those shut out of normal electoral participation in their home state. The fact
that the percentages of persons participating generally is low does not mean,
in and of itself, that democracy is in danger. Governments can function quite
adequately and responsibly, even if the mass of people give it very little

attention and take very little political action. A much more critical consideration is whether or not the system is open to all the elements of the society that seek to enter it.[38]

NOTES

1. For a discussion of these sub-dimensions, see Lester W. Milbrath, *Political Participation* (Chicago: Rand McNally & Co., 1965) chapter 1.
2. At least twelve studies in three or more countries support this generalization. *Ibid.,* chapter 1.
3. At least twenty-five studies in five or more countries support this generalization. *Ibid.,* fn. 5, chapter 1.
4. Figures are drawn from Angus Campbell, *et al., The American Voter* (New York: John Wiley and Sons, 1960); Robert E. Lane, *Political Life* (Glencoe: The Free Press, 1959); and Julian L. Woodward and Elmo Roper, "Political Activity of American Citizens," *American Political Science Review XLIV* (1950) 872–885.
5. Woodward and Roper (1950) found 21 per cent in the United States.
6. Woodward and Roper (1950) found 38 per cent in the United States.
7. Alexander Heard, *The Costs of Democracy* (Chapel Hill: University of North Carolina Press, 1960) chapter 3; Lester W. Milbrath, *The Motivations and Characteristics of Political Contributors: North Carolina General Election, 1952,* Ph.D. dissertation, University of North Carolina, 1956.
8. Lester W. Milbrath, "Predispositions Toward Political Contention," *Western Political Quarterly XIII* (1960) 5–18; Lester Milbrath and Walter Klein, "Personality Correlates of Political Participation," *Acta Sociologica VI* (1962) 53–66.
9. Campbell, *et al.,* chapters 6–7.
10. Heard, chapter 10.
11. See Campbell, *et al.,* pp. 94–96, for a more complete discussion of these factors.
12. For a summary of findings on this point consult Milbrath, *Political Participation,* chapter 4.
13. Richard E. Dawson and James A. Robinson, "Inter-Party Competition, Economic Variables, and Welfare Policies in the American States," *Journal of Politics XXV* (1963) 265–289.
14. See the studies cited in fn. 4.
15. See V. O. Key, Jr., *Southern Politics* (New York: Alfred A. Knopf, 1949) Part 5, "Restrictions on Voting."
16. For information on a variety of impediments to voting, see the Hearings of the United States Commission on Civil Rights, New Orleans, Louisiana, 1960–1961 (Washington: U.S. Government Printing Office, 1961).
17. Robert A. Dahl, *Who Governs? Democracy and Power in an American City* (New Haven: Yale University Press, 1961); Jack Jensen, *Political Participation: A Survey in Evanston, Illinois,* M.A. thesis, Northwestern University, 1960.
18. See Milbrath, *Political Participation,* chapter 5, for a summary of these findings.
19. Harold F. Gosnell, *Why Europe Votes* (Chicago: University of Chicago Press, 1930); Stein Rokkan, "The Comparative Study of Political Participation: Notes toward a Perspective on Current Research," in Austin Ranney (ed.), *Essays on the Behavioral Study of Politics* (Urbana: University of Illinois Press, 1962) 47–90.
20. The detailed information on states presented in this section is drawn from the *Report of the President's Commission on Registration and Voting Participation,* November 1963.

21. Ralph Goldman, "Move—Lose Your Vote," *National Municipal Review XLV* (1956) 6–10.
22. Campbell, *et al.,* chapter 11.
23. *Ibid.,* p. 283.
24. *Ibid.,* p. 282.
25. For an expanded discussion and citation of findings, see Milbrath, *Political Participation,* chapter 2.
26. See *ibid.,* chapter 4, for an expanded discussion of these points.
27. Angus Campbell, "Surge and Decline: A Study of Electoral Change," *Public Opinion Quarterly XXIV* (1960) 397–418.
28. Belle Zeller (ed.), *American State Legislatures* (New York: Thomas Y. Crowell Co., 1954) pp. 190–191.
29. For a summary of pertinent research on this and other variables discussed in this section, see Milbrath, *Political Participation,* chapter 5.
30. See *ibid.,* chapter 3, for a summary of recent research.
31. Edgar Litt, "Political Cynicism and Political Futility," *The Journal of Politics XXV* (1963) 312–323.
32. For a summary of findings, see Milbrath, *Political Participation,* chapter 3.
33. Angus Campbell, Gerald Gurin, and Warren Miller, *The Voter Decides* (Evanston: Row Peterson, 1954) pp. 189–191.
34. Dahl, pp. 291–292.
35. *Colegrove* vs. *Green,* 328 U.S. 549 (1946).
36. *Baker* vs. *Carr,* 369 U.S. 186 (1962); *Reynolds* vs. *Sims,* 12 Lawyers ed. 2d 506 (June 15, 1964).
37. *NLRB* vs. *Jones & Laughlin Steel Corp.,* 301 U.S. 1 (1937).
38. For a development of the point made in this paragraph, see Milbrath, *Political Participation,* chapter 6.

SELECTED BIBLIOGRAPHY

Almond, Gabriel, and Sidney Verba. *The Civic Culture.* Princeton: Princeton University Press, 1963. This is a report of a cross-national survey conducted in the United States, Mexico, Great Britain, Germany, and Italy. A good deal of attention is devoted to explaining political participation, especially as it varies from nation to nation.

Campbell, Angus, Phillip Converse, Warren Miller, and Donald Stokes. *The American Voter.* New York: John Wiley and Sons, 1960. This report of the 1956 Presidential election in the United States is the best and most comprehensive book on American voting behavior. Chapter V deals with voting turnout.

Davies, James. *Human Nature in Politics.* New York: John Wiley and Sons, 1963. This book focuses on individual political behavior; much of the explanation uses psychological factors. It is not a report of an original study but is based on many previous studies.

Key, V. O., Jr. *Southern Politics in State and Nation.* New York: Alfred A. Knopf, 1949. This book, a recognized classic in political science, is based on empirical studies of politics in eleven Southern states. It is especially good on the problems of Negro participation in politics.

————. *Public Opinion and American Democracy.* New York: Alfred A. Knopf, 1961. This leading text on public opinion does a good job of relating public opinion to the functioning of the political system. Much of the empirical evidence presented is drawn from the voting studies conducted by the Survey Research Center of the University of Michigan. (See Campbell, *et al.,* above.)

Lane, Robert E. *Political Life: Why People Get Involved in Politics.* Glencoe: The Free Press, 1959. This is the most comprehensive book dealing strictly with political participation. It is not a research report but is based on many previous studies.

Lipset, Seymour Martin. *Political Man: The Social Bases of Politics.* Garden City, N.Y.: Doubleday and Co., 1960. This book takes a sociological perspective on political behavior. It is not a report of original research, but materials are drawn from many countries in addition to the United States.

Milbrath, Lester W. *Political Participation.* Chicago: Rand McNally & Co., 1965. This is a short book summarizing all that is known at this point about why individuals become involved in politics. Findings are drawn from many studies and linked together in a theoretical structure.

President's Commission on Registration and Voting Participation, Report of, U.S. Government Printing Office, November 1963. This report focuses on participation in Presidential elections. In addition to reporting state-by-state data, it argues for reforms to stimulate voting turnout.

Rokkan, Stein. "The Comparative Study of Political Participation: Notes Toward a Perspective on Current Research," in Austin Ranney (ed.), *Essays on the Behavioral Study of Politics.* Urbana: University of Illinois Press, 1962. This article by a leading scholar of political participation discusses problems of studying participation cross-culturally. He argues for the use of historical and ecological data as well as survey findings.

Woodward, Julian L., and Elmo Roper. "The Political Activity of American Citizens," *American Political Science Review XLIV* (December 1950) 872–885. This article is based on a nationwide sample of 8,000 cases. It was the first article to give nationwide percentages for participation in a variety of political activities.

PARTIES IN STATE POLITICS

CHAPTER 3
by
AUSTIN RANNEY

"THE RISE OF POLITICAL PARTIES is indubitably one of the principal distinguishing marks of modern government . . . modern democracy is unthinkable save in terms of the parties. As a matter of fact, *the condition of the parties is the best possible evidence of the nature of any regime.*"[1] So begins one of the most influential books in modern political science; and the italicized affirmation will serve as the major premise of this chapter.

In all democratic polities, political parties are, first and foremost, organizations formed to make nominations and contest elections. Consequently, wherever the constitutional-legal structure decrees that important elections be held — parliamentary constituencies, congressional districts, cities, and the like — political parties organize to win those elections.

In the United States elections are regulated and administered mainly by the fifty states, not by the national government. The national Constitution and Congress, to be sure, exercise some control over their timing and conduct. But, for the most part, the questions of who can get on the ballot and how, who can and cannot vote, and how the votes shall be cast and counted and the winners identified are determined by the states.

Accordingly, the Democratic and Republican parties in each of the states are in no sense merely local representatives of national firms. Many commentators, indeed, regard the national parties as little more than coalitions of state parties formed intermittently to capture the Presidency. However that may be, we can be sure that in the governments of the states — as in any modern democracy — parties, in Schattschneider's words, "are not merely appendages of modern government; they are in the center of it and play a determinative and creative role in it."[2]

LEGAL FORMS AND POLITICAL REALITIES

In most democratic countries political parties are largely or wholly outside the law. Written constitutions and statutes do not mention them, and no governmental agency has the legal power to regulate their recruitment of members, organization, or selection of leaders so long as they do not transgress general prohibitions against conspiracy, subversion, and the like. Hence most political parties are considered to be purely private associations, like Freemasons or Rotarians, and they transact their internal business privately.

So it was in the United States until after the Civil War. However, the steady parade of political scandals, bribery, and "boss rule" in the post-war decades convinced respectable people that the parties had become dangerously corrupt. Acting in the characteristic American conviction that the best way to prevent an evil is to pass a law against it, one state legislature after another wrote statutes regulating the parties. Consequently, in our time each of the states fences its parties about with elaborate legal rules intended to keep them within proper bounds. The principal matters regulated are:[3]

1. *Access to the Ballot.* Each state specifies the conditions an organization must meet to qualify as a political party and thus get its candidates' names printed on election ballots.

2. *Membership.* Each state stipulates the qualifications for membership in a party — that is, how one acquires the right to vote in the party's primary elections.

3. *Organization.* Each state prescribes the number, composition, selection, and functions of the various officials, committees, and conventions that constitute the parties' legal organizations.

4. *Nominating Procedures.* The state, not the parties, decides how the latters' official candidates for public office shall be selected. As we shall note later, most states require that most nominations be made publicly by direct primaries rather than privately by party caucuses or conventions.

5. *Party Finance.* All the states except Delaware, Illinois, and Rhode Island regulate one or more aspect of party finance: how much a party may spend in election campaigns, who may and may not contribute to party funds, what public reports of receipts and expenditures should be filed, and so on.

In each of the states, in short, political parties are legally defined public organizations required to transact their most important business in public. Their high legal visibility may well elicit the often-heard remark that the United States has not two major parties but one hundred and two: the national Democrats and Republicans and their namesakes in each of the states. It may also underlie the view of some political scientists that our national parties are "loose alliances to win the stakes of power embodied in the presidency" or "ghost parties" with neither the commanders nor the discipline of *real* parties, and that the loci of effective party power and discipline are in the state and local parties.[4]

Whether or not these are accurate characterizations of the national parties, the most casual glance at state politics shows that the orderly structures erected by the statutes mask a wide variety of political realities. For example, in Florida the legal structure of the Democratic party is no more than a neutral arena for a kaleidoscopic interplay of forming and re-forming factions and appearing and disappearing personalities striving for place and perquisites.[5] In Wisconsin, the legal Democratic organization is a shell inhabited and animated by an entirely extralegal band of dues-paying enthusiasts.[6] In Connecticut the legal Democratic committees and conventions come close to matching the unity, discipline, and "responsibility" some commentators insist our national parties should have.[7]

In short, by no means all state political parties are highly organized, well disciplined, and strongly led political "armies."[8] Like most other aspects of state government discussed in this book they vary widely from one state to the next. The present chapter is intended to describe some of the principal variations and their causes and consequences for state politics.

INTER-PARTY COMPETITION

Of all the variables studied in the analysis of state party politics, the one receiving the most attention from political scientists has been "inter-party competition": that is, the usual or "normal" distribution of popular votes and public offices between Republicans and Democrats. Most writers on the subject of state politics believe that a state's competitiveness is significantly related to other characteristics of its parties and politics. Taking their lead from the pioneering works of V. O. Key, they generalize that the state parties facing the closest competition are likely to have the most centralized control of nominations, and the highest cohesion in state legislatures and in gubernatorial-legislative relations. Consequently, they are likely to be the most effective and responsible governing agencies.[9] Thus we begin our analysis by categorizing the states according to degree of inter-party competition.

DIMENSIONS AND MEASUREMENT. In recent years a number of political scientists have developed various ways of measuring inter-party competition in the states.[10] Each measure differs somewhat from the others in time period covered, offices for which elections are tabulated, and definitions of categories. All who try to measure inter-party competition, however, agree with Richard Dawson and James Robinson that it has three basic dimensions:

Proportion of Success: the per cent of the votes won by each party for statewide offices and the per cent of seats in the legislature held by each.

Duration of Success: the length of time each party has controlled the statewide offices and/or the legislature.

Frequency of Divided Control: the proportion of time in which control of the governorship and legislature has been divided between the parties.

The purposes of this chapter seem best served by an adaptation of the Dawson-Robinson measure, which we have used as follows: *

For each state we first tabulated the percentages of the two-party popular vote for governor received by each party in each election, and the percentages of the seats in each house of the legislature held by each party in each legislative session.† From these tables we computed four basic figures: (1) the average per cent of the popular vote won by Democratic gubernatorial candidates; (2) the average per cent of the seats in the state senate held by the Democrats; (3) the average per cent of the seats in the state house of representatives held by the Democrats; and (4) the per cent of all terms for governor, senate, and house in which the Democrats had control.

For each state we then averaged together all four percentages to produce an "index of competitiveness" carried to four decimal places. It has a possible range of .0000 (total Republican success) to 1.0000 (total Democratic success), with .5000 representing absolutely even two-party competition.

Finally, we listed the states in descending order of index numbers, and the resulting clusters suggested the following categories and definitions:

.9000 or higher: one-party Democratic
.7000 to .8999: modified one-party Democratic
.3000 to .6999: two-party
.1000 to .2999: modified one-party Republican
.0000 to .0999: one-party Republican

No state qualified as one-party Republican by these criteria. The states' distribution among the other four categories is given in Table 1, and their geographical distribution is shown in the map in Figure 1.

SOME WARNINGS. The classifications in Table 1 and Figure 1 are likely to hold some surprises for most readers: for example, Arizona, the home of

---

*Since this book is concerned exclusively with state government and politics, we have examined only state offices; and the governors and state legislators have been chosen because they are the states' most powerful elected officers. The period from 1946 to 1963 takes account of the fact that post-war state politics have differed significantly from pre-war, yet still gives a long enough period in which to absorb temporary surges or declines for particular parties in particular states (for obvious reasons, Alaska and Hawaii were covered only from 1958 to 1963).

†Since Minnesota and Nebraska have formally nonpartisan legislatures, only their gubernatorial elections have been used to measure inter-party competition.

Table 1

THE FIFTY STATES CLASSIFIED ACCORDING TO DEGREE OF INTER-PARTY COMPETITION

One-Party Democratic	Modified One-Party Democratic	Two-Party		Modified One-Party Republican
South Carolina (1.0000)	Virginia (.8795)	Alaska (.6767)	Pennsylvania (.4050)	Wisconsin (.2997)
Georgia (.9915)	North Carolina (.8793)	Missouri (.6603)	California (.3930)	New Hampshire (.2680)
Louisiana (.9867)	Tennessee (.8715)	Rhode Island (.6327)	Nebraska (.3875)	Iowa (.2495)
Mississippi (.9805)	Oklahoma (.8193)	Washington (.5647)	Illinois (.3847)	Kansas (.2415)
Texas (.9590)	Kentucky (.7650)	Delaware (.5420)	Idaho (.3780)	Maine (.2405)
Alabama (.9565)	Arizona (.7490)	Nevada (.5263)	Michigan (.3770)	South Dakota (.2320)
Arkansas (.9427)	West Virginia (.7223)	Massachusetts (.5227)	New Jersey (.3605)	North Dakota (.1860)
Florida (.9220)	Maryland (.7137)	Hawaii (.4897)	Indiana (.3545)	Vermont (.1760)
	New Mexico (.7023)	Colorado (.4827)	Oregon (.3545)	
		Montana (.4695)	Ohio (.3523)	
		Minnesota (.4610)	Wyoming (.3470)	
		Utah (.4605)	New York (.3173)	
		Connecticut (.4420)		

Barry Goldwater, is classified as modified one-party Democratic; Nebraska, on the other hand, is labeled two-party, while Wisconsin is called modified one-party Republican. Our classifications will raise fewer eyebrows if we bear in mind two warnings about what they mean.

First, they are based wholly on state offices. Hence while Arizona twice elected Goldwater Senator and voted for the Republican candidate for President in three of the four elections from 1948 to 1960, the Republicans never held more than 25 per cent of the seats in the upper house or over 31 per cent of the seats in the lower house of the state legislature. Wisconsin, which

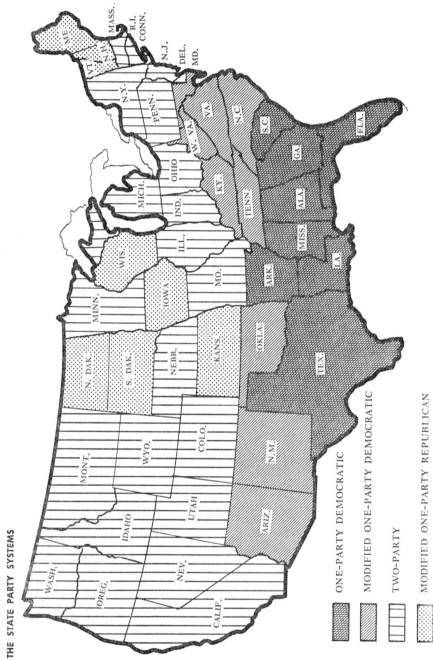

Figure 1
THE STATE PARTY SYSTEMS

ONE-PARTY DEMOCRATIC

MODIFIED ONE-PARTY DEMOCRATIC

TWO-PARTY

MODIFIED ONE-PARTY REPUBLICAN

at the present writing has a Democratic governor and two Democratic U.S. Senators, has seen Democratic control of either legislative house only once in eighteen opportunities in this period, and Democratic governors only three of nine terms. Florida voted for the Republican Presidential candidate in 1952, 1956, and 1960 and elected two Republican U.S. Representatives in 1962; but the Republicans never won the governorship or more than 7 per cent of the seats in either house of the legislature. These examples show that a state which has been highly competitive for some national offices may have been much less so for state offices; and the latter are our primary concern here.

Second, any measurement such as ours is a snapshot of an object moving in time and hence does not always capture changes that may be occurring when the measurement is taken. Thus, Wisconsin and South Dakota are becoming more Democratic and Arizona and Florida more Republican; another measurement taken a decade hence may well change the classifications of all four states. All our present classification does is to indicate the relative competitiveness of the fifty states in the two decades after World War II.

Our next task, then, is to see whether the differences shown in Table 1 are significantly related to any other characteristics of the states in each category.

CORRELATES OF COMPETITIVENESS. Most of the one-party and modified one-party states of both parties have had their present political colorations ever since the Civil War. All eight Democratic one-party states were members of the Confederacy; and, of the nine modified Democratic one-party states, North Carolina, Tennessee, and Virginia were Confederate, West Virginia was the Unionist rump of Virginia, Kentucky and Maryland were border states (i.e., states which allowed slavery but remained in the Union), and Arizona, New Mexico, and Oklahoma were originally settled mainly by immigrants from the South. Of the eight Republican modified one-party states, on the other hand, Iowa, Kansas, Maine, New Hampshire, Vermont, and Wisconsin all fought on the Union side, and the two Dakotas were settled mainly by immigrants from Union states.

It is not surprising that the deepest political trauma of American history left its mark on state politics. The Republican party, after all, was founded in 1854 specifically to resist the further spread of slavery and to secure its eventual abolition. A Republican President wrote the Emancipation Proclamation and led the Union to victory over the Confederacy. A Republican Congress launched the Thirteenth, Fourteenth, and Fifteenth Amendments to the national Constitution and adopted the Reconstruction Acts. Most leading Confederates were Democrats before the war, and Southern resistance to

Reconstruction was led by Democrats. For both sides, accordingly, party identification and patriotism were closely intertwined, and for a long time after Appomattox a familiar electioneering slogan for both parties was, "Vote as You Shot!" And when the federal occupation troops left the South after 1876, the Southern whites determined to restore and maintain racial segregation and white supremacy by the one-party system and by excluding Negroes from participation in that one party.[11]

But the Civil War ended a century ago; how can it influence the party loyalties of so many voters in the 1960's? The answer seems to lie in the essential nature of party identification. The leading studies of voting behavior emphasize that the typical American acquires his party preference early in life, and it grows stronger the longer he holds it. Moreover, it is reinforced and activated by the similar preferences of his parents, his wife, and his friends and work associates, and living in a one-party atmosphere tends to corrode the loyalties of the few who identify with the minority party.[12] Although a few individuals switch parties, perhaps because they move to new communities and/or change their socio-economic positions, *massive* switches take place only under such apocalyptic circumstances as the Civil War or the Great Depression of the early 1930's.[13]

Given, then, the self-renewing and self-intensifying nature of party identification, it is not surprising that the deepest political cleavage in our history remains the basic source of party predominance in half our states. It is more surprising that the other half have two-party systems. After all, no fewer than seventeen fought for the Union in the war, one (Missouri) was a border state, and most of the others were settled by immigrants from the North. Why are they not also one-party or modified one-party Republican? Some of the answers are suggested by the data in Table 2.

The most striking contrast evident in Table 2 is the fact that the two-party states are substantially more urbanized than the states in the other three categories; and we may add that all the nation's cities with populations of over one million (New York, Chicago, Los Angeles, Philadelphia, and Detroit) are located in these states. The two-party states also have to a higher degree than the others the characteristics usually associated with urbanization: they have the highest median income, the highest percentage of labor force engaged in manufacturing and the lowest in agriculture, and the highest proportion of "foreign stock" (i.e., immigrants or children of immigrants).

When we compare the two-party states with the two groups of Democratic-dominated states we see that the former have a much smaller proportion of Negroes,* and a larger proportion of foreign stock and Roman Catholics.

*Note that the per cent of Negroes declines sharply as we pass from the most Democratic to the least Democratic groups of states.

Table 2

SOCIAL AND ECONOMIC CHARACTERISTICS OF STATES BY DEGREE OF COMPETITIVENESS

Characteristic	One-Party Democratic	Modified One-Party Democratic	Two-Party	Modified One-Party Republican
Number of States	8	9	25	8
Per cent of population urban	55%	56%	69%	50%
Per cent of population living in cities over 100,000	18%	21%	21%	7%
Per cent of Negroes in population	27%	11%	5%	1%
Per cent of foreign stock in population	5%	6%	23%	21%
Per cent of Roman Catholics in population	18%	11%	23%	25%
Median income	$3982	$4814	$6034	$5060
Per cent of labor force in agriculture	9%	8%	7%	15%
Per cent of labor force in manufacturing	20%	19%	22%	20%

Source: *Congressional District Data Book* (Washington: Bureau of the Census, 1963).

A more suggestive comparison, however, is that between the two-party states and the modified one-party Republican states; for if the Civil War were the sole source of present-day political loyalties, the two groups of states should be very similar. However, in certain respects they are at opposite extremes: the two-party states are the most urban and the Republican states the least; the two-party states are the least agricultural and the Republican states, the most.

All these comparisons are consistent with the general pattern of distribution of party strength *outside the South* noted by most commentators. Democratic support generally tends to be concentrated in big cities, for the minority ethnic groups and trade unionists who vote predominantly Democratic constitute the bulk of the big cities' populations. Republican voting strength tends to be concentrated in smaller towns and cities (i.e., those with populations from 2,500 to 100,000), for the "WASPs" (white, Anglo-Saxon Protestants) who vote predominantly Republican constitute the bulk of the small town populations.* And the Northern rural farm areas are the most

*The "WASPs" also constitute the bulk of the small town populations in the South, of course, but for the reasons noted earlier they vote Democratic.

likely to switch back and forth between the two parties depending upon whether farms are prosperous (vote Republican) or depressed (vote Democratic).[14]

The states' differences in inter-party competition, then, are related to their differences in certain social and economic traits and in historical experiences and traditions. But what does it matter? In what, if any, significant respects do parties in the one-party states differ from those in the two-party states? Let us see.

PARTY ORGANIZATION

LEGAL STRUCTURE. We noted earlier that in most states political parties are elaborately regulated by statute. Significantly, the only major exceptions are six Southern states: five (Alabama, Arkansas, Georgia, North Carolina, and Virginia) in which the laws affecting parties have always been substantially looser than elsewhere; and South Carolina which, after the U.S. Supreme Court outlawed the "white primary" in 1944,[15] repealed all laws regulating parties so as to give its Democrats the best possible chance of evading regulation by the federal courts.[16]

Statutes in each of the other forty-four states prescribe the number, composition, powers, and duties of the committees, conventions, and caucuses that constitute the parties' legal skeletons. They vary widely in detail, of course, but most state legislatures evidently regard parties as primarily agencies for making nominations and contesting elections; hence they have established party organizations at every level significant for the conduct of elections. Every state has precinct or ward "committeemen" or "captains," county "central committees" and county chairmen, and state "central committees" and state chairmen. Many states also prescribe party committees and/or conventions for congressional districts, state senatorial districts, state representative districts, state judicial districts, and cities.

The committees' members are officially selected in various ways, but the most common are: selection by party activists in local caucuses, election by party registrants in direct primaries, election by delegates to party conventions, or ex officio membership by virtue of holding posts in lower party committees.[17]

It is difficult to generalize about the number, composition, and selection of legal party committees, caucuses, and conventions in all the states, but it is easy to generalize about the legal allocation of authority among them. In no state are the legal party units organized as a true hierarchy, with the lower levels legally controlled and removable by the upper. Most commonly the officers and committees at each level are chosen locally and cannot be removed by any higher party authority. In Illinois, for example, each precinct committeeman is elected by the registered party voters in his precinct and holds office for four years; he cannot be removed by the county or state central committees even if he campaigns for the opposition party (which some have actually done).[18] In Washington, as another example, each county central committee consists of all the precinct committeemen in the county and elects its own chairman; he, in turn, cannot be removed by his party's state central committee or even its national committee no matter what he does.[19]

So it is in most states. The result is that authority is not legally concentrated in any single statewide party agency; rather the law chops it into many small bundles and scatters them among the precinct, county, and district committeemen and committees.

INFORMAL ALLOCATION OF AUTHORITY. In most states most of the time informal or "actual" authority is quite as decentralized as legal authority. To be sure, there have been a few statewide "machines" headed by state "bosses" who by effective use of patronage and persuasion controlled the selection and commanded the loyalties of most county and district committees and chairmen. Some, like the Huey Long organization in Louisiana in the 1920's and 1930's and the Harry Byrd organization in Virginia from the 1930's to the 1960's,[20] appeared in solid one-party states. Others, like the Thomas Dewey organization in New York in the 1940's and the Hubert Humphrey organization in Minnesota in the 1950's and 1960's,[21] have operated in two-party states. However, these few instances are highly exceptional, and the powerful sub-national "machines" which have received so much attention (and tongue-clucking) from political commentators and civic reformers have mostly been confined to particular metropolitan areas *within* states: e.g., Tammany Hall in New York City, the William Green "machine" in Philadelphia, and Mayor Daley's "machine" in Chicago.[22]

Some political scientists have the impression that state party organizations tend to have more centralized authority where two-party competition is keenest.[23] But the tendency is slight at best, and both Republicans and Democrats are highly decentralized in many of our most competitive two-party states: e.g., Washington (with a competitiveness index of .5647), California (.3930), Illinois (.3847), and Indiana (.3545).

The most distinguished scholar of state parties summed it up thus:

> The party organization is sometimes regarded as a hierarchy based on the precinct executive and capped by the national committee, but it may be more accurately described as a system of layers of organization. Each successive layer — county or city, state, national — has an independent concern about elections in its geographical jurisdiction. Yet each higher level of organization, to accomplish its ends, must obtain the collaboration of the lower layer or layers of organization. That collabo-

ration comes about, to the extent that it does come about, through a
sense of common cause rather than by the exercise of command.[24]

In a few states the legal organizations' feebleness and/or concentration
upon dispensing patronage rather than advancing programs has led some
party activists to form "clubs" to ginger or take over or by-pass the official
structures.[25] The earliest instance was "The Republican Party of Wisconsin,"
an extralegal organization founded by Conservative Republican activists in
1925 to take the party's machinery and nominations away from the La Follette progressive wing. They were so successful that in the 1930's the La
Follette faction broke away entirely to form a third party. In 1948 Democratic activists formed "The Democratic Party of Wisconsin" to breathe some
life into their moribund formal organization. Since then both parties' legal
structures have been controlled entirely by their extralegal "clubs."[26]

In 1934 a progressive faction among California Republicans created
"The California Republican Assembly" to revive the party after its disastrous
defeat of 1932. California Democratic enthusiasts established "The California Democratic Council" in 1953, and since then both organizations have
played key roles in their parties' affairs, although neither has dominated the
regular organization to quite the same degree as in Wisconsin.[27]

In New York City after 1952 a number of local anti-Tammany Democratic "reform clubs" were formed under the leadership of such distinguished
party activists as Mrs. Eleanor Roosevelt, former Governor and Senator
Herbert Lehman, and former Secretary of the Air Force Thomas Finletter.
These clubs have, with varying degrees of success, fought Tammany's domination of the party's official organization and nominations.[28]

Despite differences in ideology and partisan affiliation, these extralegal
activist organizations have several features in common. Their members,
like party members in western European nations, pay regular dues. They
consist mainly of middle-class business and professional people who have
no interest in patronage jobs and go into politics primarily to advance the
political programs they believe in. They are usually organized into local
clubs which federate for county and state purposes. One of their main objectives is getting the right kind of candidates nominated (all but the Wisconsin Democrats publicly endorse particular candidates in primaries). They
do most of their parties' grass-roots campaigning and fund raising. And they
have generally had considerable success in rebuilding and invigorating moribund legal organizations (as in Wisconsin and California) or in weakening the
hold of patronage-oriented professionals over the official structures (as in
New York City).

Only a few comparable movements have been launched elsewhere, however, and most of them have failed.[29] There is as yet no reason to believe

that the "clubs" are the wave of the future in American state politics. Accordingly, it seems likely that for some time to come the party organizations in most states — legal *and* informal — will remain congeries of sporadically active state and local caucuses, committees, and conventions supplemented by *ad hoc* organizations formed to support particular candidates. In a word, *decentralization* is likely to continue to be as characteristic of American state parties as national.

NOMINATIONS

LEGAL PROCEDURES. Every state except Connecticut* legally requires that party candidates for some or all public offices be nominated by "direct primaries." Thirty-eight states require it for both parties for all major offices; three Southern states (Alabama, Georgia, and South Carolina) require it for the Democrats, but allow the Republicans to use conventions if they wish (as they usually do); and eight states require it for some offices and allow party conventions to choose nominees for others.[30]

All direct primaries have several features in common: they require that nominations be made directly by ordinary voters rather than indirectly by the voters' representatives in party conventions; they are regulated by state law, not by party rules; they are administered by state-appointed officials, not by extralegal party officers; and, as in general elections, the secrecy of the ballot is legally protected.

However, a few variations deserve brief notice. Seven states (Alaska, Hawaii, Michigan, Minnesota, Montana, Utah, and Wisconsin) use some version of the "open primary," in which the person may vote in whichever party's primary he chooses without public disclosure of his choice; Washington uses the "blanket primary," in which a voter may indicate preferences in both parties, but not two preferences for one office; and the remaining forty-two states use some version of the "closed primary," in which the voter must declare his party affiliation and vote only in that party's primary until he publicly changes his affiliation.

In addition, all eight Southern one-party states and three modified one-party Democratic states (North Carolina, Oklahoma, and Virginia) provide for second or "run-off" primaries: if no candidate receives at least 50-per-cent-

*Under its unique "challenge primary" law adopted in 1955, Connecticut provides that all party candidates be nominated by party conventions. However, anyone who receives at least 20 per cent of a convention's votes but loses the nomination may petition the authorities to hold a primary election in which he "challenges" the convention-nominated candidate. A regular closed primary is then held, and whoever wins a majority of the votes becomes the official nominee. If no person challenges the convention's choice within fourteen days after the convention, he automatically becomes the official party nominee: see Duane Lockard, *Connecticut's Challenge Primary: a Study in Legislative Politics* (New York: Henry Holt and Co., 1959).

plus-one of the votes in the first primary, a second may be held in which only the two top candidates compete. This, of course, is a device to ensure that the Democratic nominee, who is in effect the elected official, has majority support.

COMPETITION AND PARTICIPATION IN PRIMARY ELECTIONS. The direct primary was generally adopted in the "progressive era" from the early 1900's to the late 1920's with the avowed purpose of taking control of nominations away from the party "bosses," who were thought to manipulate party conventions in a disgracefully undemocratic manner, and restoring it to the party "rank-and-file."[31] But has it done the job?

A number of studies have been made of the degree of competition and voting turnout in primary elections,[32] and their findings generally agree on the following observations:

First, there are fewer contestants in primaries in which incumbents are seeking renomination than in those in which no incumbents are running. The reason for this is, of course, that an incumbent is hard to beat: he is usually far better known than his opponent(s); he usually has the best campaign organization and the best stocked war chest; and the local party leaders are usually reluctant to surrender the benefits his legislative seniority brings the district. Thus, Key's study of primaries from 1920 to 1954 in which incumbent U.S. Senators ran for renomination found that only 10 per cent were defeated. Significantly, however, only 2 per cent were defeated in the non-Southern states, while 30 per cent lost in the Southern states.[33] Evidently, voters are more likely to defeat an incumbent in the primary if that is their only real shot at him than if they have another in the general election.

Second, the better a party's chances of winning the election, the more probable are its primaries to be contested, especially if no incumbent is running. Thus, at the Democratic extreme of our scale of competitiveness, South Carolina (1.0000) and Georgia (.9915) are likely to have two or three contestants in Democratic primaries for most offices where there is no incumbent running, while the Republicans not only hold no primaries but are likely not to put up any candidate at all. At the Republican extreme, Vermont (.1760) and North Dakota (.1860) will usually have their Republican primaries contested and their Democratic primaries uncontested, although the Democrats will usually put up candidates. And in the middle, Nevada (.5263) and Colorado (.4827) are likely to have only one or two contestants in each party's primary, for each party knows it will have to have a united front to beat the opposition party in the general election. So, if at all possible, they will avoid intra-party primary fights that might leave bitterness and division.

Thirdly, outside the South voting turnout is markedly lower in primaries than in general elections. The figures are given in Table 3.

Table 3

MEAN VOTING TURNOUT IN PRIMARY AND GENERAL ELECTIONS
FOR GOVERNOR AND U.S. SENATOR, 1956-60

STATE GROUPS	PER CENT VOTING FOR GOVERNOR			PER CENT VOTING FOR U.S. SENATOR		
	Prim. Elect.	Gen. Elect.	Difference	Prim. Elect.	Gen. Elect.	Difference
One-Party Democratic	32.5%	17.0%	+15.5%	22.8%	19.2%	+ 3.7%
Modified One-Party Democratic	28.5%	41.3%	−12.8%	25.7%	40.7%	−15.0%
Two-Party	25.4%	59.2%	−23.8%	21.5%	58.3%	−36.8%
Modified One-Party Republican	21.9%	56.9%	−35.0%	22.7%	55.3%	−32.6%

Source: Richard Scammon (ed.), *America Votes* (New York: Macmillan Co., 1956–57; and Pittsburgh: University of Pittsburgh Press, 1958–60).

The data in Table 3 show that only in the Southern one-party Democratic states have turnouts for primary elections generally been higher than turnouts for general elections. Moreover, this appears to result from extremely low turnouts in general elections rather than unusually high turnouts in primaries. In the other three types of states, primary turnouts have averaged around 25 per cent while turnouts in general elections have averaged from 13 to 37 points higher.

Unfortunately, we lack reliable sample-survey data to tell us *why* turnouts in primaries should generally be so much lower than in general elections. The general discussion of political participation in Chapter 2, however, gives us several clues. We know that in general elections the turnout rate is highest among the most "involved" voters — that is, those who care most who wins. This kind of involvement usually stems from strong party identification: persons who are deeply attached to the Democratic or Republican party are likely to vote in November to make sure *their* side wins.[34] But a primary election is not a contest between one's own party and its opponents; it is a disagreement among different members of the same party. Hence, the party identification basis for involvement in general elections does not operate for primaries. Moreover, the newspapers, television, and other mass media usually give less attention to campaigns in primaries than those in general elections, and so the non-party stimuli making for high involvement and large voting turnouts are also weaker in primaries.

CONTROL OF NOMINATIONS FOR STATEWIDE OFFICES. The direct primary, in short, gives "the people" power to control the parties' nominations;

but usually only about a quarter of those busy and bored worthies bother to use it. If they do not control the nominations, who does?

The only accurate answer is that the patterns of control of nominations vary widely from one state to another and from one time to another within most states. The principal patterns appear to be the following:

Candidates for state senators and representatives are everywhere nominated by primaries or conventions in senatorial and representative districts. In almost all states almost all of the time these nominations are controlled locally. It is as rare for a statewide party "machine" to reach into a local district and determine its nominee as for the President or the National Chairman to reach into a state or Congressional district and control the nomination for U.S. Senator or Representative. It has happened on a few occasions, but in the overwhelming bulk of instances legislative nominations are locally controlled.[35]

In the few states in which nominations for statewide offices are made by state party conventions rather than primaries, the nominees are usually selected by negotiation among the leaders of the parties' principal factions; rarely does an "outsider" sweep the convention delegates against the leaders' wishes.

In Colorado and Massachusetts the law stipulates that state party conventions must meet before the primaries and ballot on nominees. In Colorado the winners are listed first for their respective offices on the primary ballots and, while anyone who receives over 20 per cent of the convention votes also goes on the ballot, the candidate preferred by the convention majority usually wins the primary.[36] In Massachusetts the same system is used, except that the convention winners are designated as such on the primary ballots and they, too, usually win the primaries.[37] In California and Wisconsin state conventions of the extralegal party activists meet before the primaries and (except for Wisconsin's Democrats) endorse candidates. No evidence of the endorsements appears on the primary ballots, and occasionally their choices lose (as when Glenn Davis lost the Wisconsin Senatorial primary to incumbent Senator Alexander Wiley in 1956 despite having been endorsed by the Republican activists' convention); but usually they win.

In some states strong leaders of powerful statewide factions publicly endorse and support certain candidates in the primaries and regularly muster enough votes in the primaries to win. One well-known case in point is Mayor Daley's Cook County organization, which has played a decisive role in Illinois's statewide Democratic primaries since the mid-1950's.[38] In some Southern one-party states, notably Louisiana and Virginia, the Democratic party is divided into two well organized and durable factions, each of which regularly presents and supports slates of candidates for all statewide offices in primary elections, and the result resembles — but is not identical with — two-party competition in general elections.[39]

In such Southern states as Alabama and Florida and in some Northern states as well, primary elections are usually contested by temporary, *ad hoc* factions which arise to support particular candidates and disappear when the primary is over. At the next primary some old factions try again, some drop out, and some new ones emerge. Thus, personalities, issues, and factions come and go so rapidly that the conflict over nominations is truly "patternless."[40]

For the most part, then, the control of nominations is not noticeably more centralized in American state politics than in national politics. And in the states as in the nation this has a profound impact upon the conduct of elections and government.

ELECTIONS

CAMPAIGN ORGANIZATION AND TECHNIQUES. Professors Daniel Ogden and Hugh Bone describe campaign organization in the state of Washington thus:

> Candidates are on their own in political campaigns in the state of Washington. Because of the independence of regular local party organizations, no candidate can be sure they will put forth the effort necessary to elect him. Thus every candidate, to some degree, creates his own campaign organization. . . . Candidates further illustrate their independence of party organization by running alone, rather than as part of a team. Their advertising is individual. Each candidate pictures himself as making the state stronger or doing a great job. Rarely will a popular candidate permit his name to appear on an ad or billboard with that of a much less known figure.[41]

This description fits most other two-party states as well. The decentralization it portrays results in part from the general decentralization of party organization reviewed earlier. It also stems in part from the fact that most states still retain the Jacksonian long ballot — that is, they select most major executive officers by independent election rather than by appointment by the governor.[42] Maine, New Hampshire, New Jersey, and Tennessee elect only the governor, who, like the President, appoints the other top executives. Alaska and Hawaii elect the governor and one other executive. The remaining 42 states elect not only the governor and lieutenant governor, but also four to ten other executives — the most common being the secretary of state, treasurer, auditor, and attorney general.*

*The champion is Oklahoma, which elects a governor, lieutenant governor, secretary of state, attorney general, treasurer, auditor, state examiner and inspector, superintendent of public instruction, chief mine inspector, commissioner of labor, commissioner of charities and corrections, commissioner of insurance, clerk of the supreme court, and corporation commissioner!

Not only are these officials elected independently, but it is by no means uncommon for a particularly popular incumbent to win re-election even when his fellow partisans are being defeated.* Such a man has every reason to play up his own experience and qualifications and play down his party connections with other candidates on the ticket. So usually only weak or little-known candidates talk much about the party ticket or seek joint campaign appearances with their fellow candidates. Thus does the long ballot contribute to the general decentralization of state parties and campaigns.

The years since 1945 have seen three main innovations in campaign techniques. First, parties and candidates have made increasing use of professional public relations firms to plan and conduct their campaigns rather than relying on regular party committees and workers in the traditional manner. Since such firms charge fees averaging 15 per cent of the total outlay and range in amount from $5,000 to $75,000, using them adds considerably to campaign costs. Nevertheless, more and more candidates seem to feel that the professionals do a far better job of "projecting the right image" than the old-line party faithful, and so they use them.[43]

Second, candidates and campaign managers are increasing use of privately-hired and secretly-reported public opinion polls to measure the impact of their appeals and the most effective allocation of their resources. This, too, has added considerably to campaign costs.

Thirdly, while most candidates still devote considerable time and energy to personal appearances at party rallies and shaking hands (and eating cheese blintzes) on street corners, more and more — particularly those running for governor and other major offices — are placing their main reliance on televised spot announcements and speeches, "telethons," and the like. Some die-hards still dispute the prevailing view that television provides the most effective exposure to the most voters, but no one disputes that the "televisation" of campaigns has, like the other two innovations, greatly increased campaign costs.

CAMPAIGN COSTS. The leading student of money in American elections gives some sample costs of state campaigns, as shown in Table 4.

Table 4 shows that the costs in primaries in the one-party states are as high or higher than those in general elections in the two-party states. The

---

*Among the better-known of many examples are "Pat" Brown, whose success in winning the attorney generalship in California while the Republicans were sweeping the other offices in the early 1950's led to his nomination and election as governor in 1958; Republican Charles Carpentier, who won re-election as Illinois's secretary of state in 1960 while the rest of the state ticket went down to defeat; and Democrat Edward J. Barrett, who won the same office during Republican state sweeps in 1940 and 1944.

Table 4

REPRESENTATIVE CENTRAL CAMPAIGN COSTS, PER VOTE CAST IN ELECTION:
SELECTED STATEWIDE CONTESTS, 1952–1956

Type of Campaign	Approximate Costs, Central Campaign Responsibility	Approximate No. of Votes Cast	Cents per Vote Cast
California, statewide election	$300,000–500,000	4,000,000	8–13
Connecticut, statewide election	150,000–250,000	950,000	16–26
Illinois, statewide primary	100,000–200,000	850,000	12–24
Illinois, statewide election	400,000–600,000	3,500,000	11–17
Montana, statewide election	40,000–60,000	250,000	16–24
New York, statewide election	800,000–1,000,000	5,000,000	16–20
Virginia, statewide primary	40,000–80,000	350,000	11–22
Oregon, statewide election	100,000–150,000	550,000	18–27
Kentucky, statewide primary	400,000–600,000	500,000	18–20
Kentucky, statewide election	200,000–400,000	1,000,000	20–40
Tennessee, statewide primary	150,000–300,000	650,000	23–46
Texas, statewide primary, 1st	500,000–1,000,000	1,500,000	33–66
Texas, statewide primary, 2nd	500,000–1,000,000	1,500,000	33–66

Source: Adapted from Alexander Heard, *The Costs of Democracy* (Chapel Hill: University of North Carolina Press, 1960) Table 56, p. 425.

Illinois example shows that primaries in the two-party states increase the total costs by a third or more. Other observers have estimated that in a large state like California it costs over $2,000,000 to win a gubernatorial primary and fight for a gubernatorial election; and running for mayor of a great metropolis like Chicago costs from $500,000 to $1,500,000.[44] Moreover, the nation's general inflationary trend, the decreasing incidence of joint campaigning, and the increasing use of public relations firms, private polling, and television are likely to make costs continue to mount.

The foregoing facts of life mean that persons or factions wishing to make serious tries for statewide office must be able to lay their hands on a great deal of money. Where do they get it? The general rule emphasized by students of campaign finance is this: however many individuals or groups may make contributions, the great bulk of campaign funds for both parties comes from large donations by a few donors. In the two-party states the Republicans are financed mainly by businessmen and the Democrats by labor unions, although it is not unknown for both to contribute to both parties.[45] There have also undoubtedly been substantial contributions by underworld "syndicates" as rewards for past favors and insurance against future prosecutions. Just how much no one can say, though most would agree that any is too much.[46]

What campaign contributors *expect* to get for their contributions ranges from a "generally favorable climate" for their interests to such specific rewards as public works contracts, liquor licenses, utility franchises, and tax favors. What they actually *get* is a topic discussed at several points in this book.

A surprising number of people believe that money is an absolute weapon in state politics — that whoever mounts the most lavish campaign wins. If this were true, the Democrats, who rarely get or spend as much as the Republicans, would rarely win; yet, as we have seen, the Democrats have won more often than they have lost in twenty-four states, and only eight states are classified as modified one-party Republican. The leading students of the subject suggest a more balanced view: money, they say, is only one of a number of factors affecting the outcome of elections. If most of these — e.g., traditional party identifications, recent political events, the candidates' personalities, and the level of prosperity — favor a particular party, the opposing one cannot win no matter how much more it may spend. But, if the other factors are evenly balanced, the party which outspends and outcampaigns the other is likely to win.

Less widely discussed but probably more significant is the impact of money on nominations. Direct primaries make getting a nomination almost as expensive as winning an election; and there is little doubt that even an aspirant for nomination by a convention will receive substantial support if he has convinced the party's leaders that he and/or his backers are able and willing to contribute heavily to the party's war chest. It is these considerations rather than any ability to "buy" elections that increasingly favor the well-to-do and/or the well-backed in state politics.[47]

LEGAL REGULATIONS OF CAMPAIGN FINANCE. We noted earlier that all states except Delaware, Illinois, and Rhode Island have laws regulating one or more aspects of party finance. As in so many other matters, the details vary widely from state to state, but the principal forms of regulation are the following: limitations on total expenditures *by* a candidate (thirty-two states) or, more stringently, on expenditures *in behalf of* a candidate (twenty states); prohibitions against contributions by corporations (thirty-three states), labor unions (five states), and persons or firms holding state franchises, liquor licenses, and the like (ten states); compulsory filing of public statements of receipts (thirty-three states); and compulsory filing of public statements of expenditures (forty-five states).[48]

However, most commentators agree that most of these regulations are not only ineffective but actually damaging. The limits on expenditures, for example, were generally adopted decades ago and are far too low for the demands of modern campaigns. As a consequence, they are regularly evaded by such subterfuges as the proliferation of special campaign committees, each spending the legal limit, or the filing of reports containing something less than full accounts of receipts and expenditures. The prohibitions against contributions by corporations are evaded by "private" contributions by corporation executives and members of their families, and those against contributions by labor unions by the formation of "political education" organizations like the A.F.L.-C.I.O.'s Committee on Political Education. The campaign finance laws have not controlled the role of money in state politics; they have only forced it to be collected and spent in an atmosphere of evasion, misrepresentation, and hypocrisy.

Accordingly, most political scientists now contend that the most the law can do is publicize the getting and spending of campaign money somewhat more effectively than at present, and that the real problem is finding ways of broadening the base of support by encouraging small contributors, perhaps by making political contributions tax deductible, and by instituting some form of direct public subsidy of campaigns.[49] To date, few steps have been taken in these directions by state legislatures, so it seems probable that the role of money in state politics will remain substantially the same for some time to come.

THE INFLUENCE OF NATIONAL POLITICS ON STATE ELECTIONS. Many commentators contend that state elections should be as independent as possible of influence by national issues, personalities, and party loyalties. The states and the nation, they argue, are separate sovereignties with distinct powers and different problems. They feel it makes no sense that elections for state officials should largely reflect the voters' feelings about national issues and parties.

One way of insulating state elections from national influences which some civic reformers have urged is to hold state elections at times other than the dates of national elections. It is particularly important, they argue, to avoid holding state elections at the same time as Presidential elections, when popular concentration on national affairs is at its highest. The following review of the scheduling of state gubernatorial elections shows that they have won their point in some states, but not all.

At present, only five states (Kentucky, Mississippi, New Jersey, Virginia, and Louisiana) have complete separation. Each of the first four elects its governor for a four-year term in odd-numbered years (i.e., 1959, 1963, 1967) and its legislators for two- or four-year terms also in odd-numbered years; Louisiana elects its governor in the spring of every Presidential year. Note that four of the five states are one-party or modified one-party Democratic.

Next closest to the separation ideal are the nineteen states which elect their governors for four-year terms in off-years (i.e., even-numbered years in which no Presidential election is held). Of these, three (Alabama, Georgia, and South Carolina) are one-party Democratic, three (Maryland, Oklahoma, and Tennessee) are modified one-party Democratic, and the remaining thirteen are two-party.

Still further from the separation model are the fourteen states which elect their governors for two-year terms in even-numbered years and, therefore, alternate between Presidential and off-years. Seven of the eight modified one-party Republican states are in this group, together with four two-party states, two one-party Democratic (Arkansas and Texas), and one modified one-party Democratic (Arizona).

Furthest away from separation are the twelve states which elect their governors for four-year terms in Presidential years. They include nine two-party states (Alaska, Hawaii, Illinois, Indiana, Michigan, Missouri, Montana, Utah, and Washington), one-party Democratic Florida, and two modified one-party Democratic (North Carolina and West Virginia).[50]

Thus the device of formal separation of state elections from national has been fully adopted by only four states and largely rejected by ten. Does this mean that state elections are unduly influenced by national factors? V. O. Key attempted to answer this question for the period 1932–1950, which was dominated by an unusually popular Democratic Presidential candidate, Franklin D. Roosevelt. Key took the states electing governors every two years and compared the gubernatorial results in Presidential years with those in off-years. He found that the better the Democrats did in Presidential elections, the more likely they were to win governorships in Presidential years but not in off-years, and he ascribed this to the power of Mr. Roosevelt's "coattails" in state politics.

Table 5

SUCCESS OF REPUBLICAN GUBERNATORIAL CANDIDATES IN PRESIDENTIAL YEARS
AND OFF-YEARS ACCORDING TO SUCCESS OF DEMOCRATIC PRESIDENTIAL CANDIDATES
(FOR STATES WITH TWO-YEAR GUBERNATORIAL TERMS, 1932–1962)

	PER CENT OF GOVERNORS REPUBLICAN			
DEMOCRATIC	*1932–1950*		*1952–1962*	
PRESIDENTIAL	*Presidential*	*Following*	*Presidential*	*Following*
PERCENTAGE	*Years*	*Off-Years*	*Years*	*Off-Years*
Under 45	80.0%	80.0%	74.5%	51.5%
45–49	70.6	82.4	41.7	8.3
50–54	45.0	75.0	22.3	22.0
55–59	9.5	42.9	*	*
60 or more	6.7	20.0	*	*

*No states in these categories.

The present writer has extended Key's study to the period 1952–1962, which was dominated by an unusually popular Republican candidate, Dwight D. Eisenhower. The results, presented in Table 5, generally confirm Key's findings.[51]

Table 5 shows that in the period 1952–1962 the Republicans generally did better in gubernatorial elections in Presidential years than in off-years, which is consistent with Key's findings. However, it also shows that the general disparity between Presidential and gubernatorial voting in the Eisenhower years was substantially greater than in the Roosevelt years. This is largely a result of the fact that in the period from 1948 to 1960 there were a number of Southern and border state defections from Democratic Presidential candidates. These defections are summarized in Table 6.

Table 6

SOUTHERN AND BORDER STATES IN POST-WAR PRESIDENTIAL ELECTIONS

STATE	Democrat	ELECTIONS CARRIED BY Republican	Third Party	Other
One-Party Democratic				
Alabama	1952, 1956		1948	1960*
Arkansas	1948, 1952, 1956, 1960			
Florida	1948	1952, 1956, 1960		
Georgia	1948, 1952, 1956, 1960			
Louisiana	1952, 1960	1956	1948	
Mississippi	1952, 1956		1948	1960*
South Carolina	1952, 1956, 1960		1948	
Texas	1948, 1960	1952, 1956		
Modified One-Party Democratic				
Kentucky	1948, 1952	1956, 1960		
North Carolina	1948, 1952, 1956, 1960			
Oklahoma	1948	1952, 1956, 1960		
Tennessee	1948	1952, 1956, 1960		
Virginia	1948	1952, 1956, 1960		

*In 1960, all of Mississippi's Electors and six of Alabama's eleven voted for Senator Harry Byrd for President.

Table 6 shows that the Southern states classified as one-party for state purposes defected from the Democratic Presidential candidate twelve times out of thirty-two chances. The Southern and border states classified as modified one-party defected eleven times out of twenty opportunities. Consequently, however "solid" the South may be in state and local elections, it has become much more competitive for national offices. We shall return to this development and its significance at the end of this chapter.

PARTY GOVERNMENT IN THE STATES

For almost a century now a number of eminent political scientists, from Woodrow Wilson and Frank Goodnow in the 1890's to E. E. Schattschneider and James MacGregor Burns in the 1960's, have argued that the only way a modern mass society can have a government that is both effective and democratic is by establishing "responsible party government."[52] By this they mean a situation in which two (and preferably only two) parties regularly present alternative programs in election campaigns, and a majority of the voters chooses one or the other to rule. The party winning a majority of the votes wins a majority of the public offices and all the governmental power it needs to write its program into law. During their terms in office the majority party's public officials act cohesively as a unit, not as isolated individuals. As a result, their party is *collectively* responsible for whether affairs have gone well or badly. At the end of its term the voters decide whether they approve of how the governing party has managed affairs; if a majority approve, they return it to power for another term; if they disapprove, they replace it with the opposition party.

Other political scientists believe that the responsible-parties model is neither practicable nor desirable for the special requirements of American society.[53] Without weighing the merits of either position, we need to know what role political parties actually do play in the governing processes of the states.

STRUCTURAL DIFFICULTIES: DIVIDED PARTY CONTROL BETWEEN GOVERNOR AND LEGISLATURE. Two essential prerequisites for responsible party government in the states are: (1) the majority party must control both the governorship and the legislature at any given time, or else it cannot be collectively responsible for how the government is run; and (2) there must be strong two-party competition so that the majority party may be turned out at any time when the voters decide it is time for a change.

However, the separate elections of the governor and the legislature endanger the first prerequisite, for they make it possible for the governor to be of one party and one or both houses of the legislature to be controlled by the other. This possibility, moreover, often becomes reality: from 1952 to 1962 in only sixteen states were the governor and both houses of the legislature controlled at all times by the same party. These were the Southern one-party and modified one-party states, and the Republican modified one-party states of Vermont and New Hampshire.[54] The two-party states, on the other hand, had united party control only 50 per cent of the time. The result: the states most likely to satisfy the second prerequisite of party government are *least* likely to fulfill the first!

V. O. Key found the same pattern of divided control in the period from 1931 to 1952, and suggested several reasons for it.[55] One is the apportionment of state legislatures, which, by overrepresenting rural areas and small towns and underrepresenting metropolitan areas, typically exaggerates Republican strength and understates Democratic. Dramatic evidence of this is provided by the fact that since World War II the Democrats have never controlled the upper house of the legislature in such highly competitive states as Connecticut, Illinois, Indiana, Michigan, Nevada, New Jersey, and Wyoming. Therefore, if responsible party government were ever to operate in these states, the Republicans had to operate it, for the very structure of the state governments made it impossible for the Democrats to do so. The "apportionment revolution" growing from *Baker* vs. *Carr*[56] may alter this situation somewhat in the Democrats' favor in the years ahead; but the concentration of Democratic votes in the metropolitan areas will probably sustain this anti-Democratic bias for a long time, and the resulting tendency to divided party control will persist.

A governor facing a legislature controlled by the opposition party does not invariably mean angry partisan wrangling and deadlock. If the governor carefully cultivates the opposition's legislative leaders, proposes a moderate program to which they have agreed, and in general plays down party politics and the independence of his office, the government may proceed about as smoothly as if all concerned were members of the same party. Such was the case with Democratic Governors Abraham Ribicoff of Connecticut and Robert Meyner of New Jersey in the 1950's. But men are not angels and politicians have to fight elections, so such cross-partisan harmony is rare. A more common story has been the bitter partisan conflict and resultant near-total deadlock between Democratic governors and Republican legislators that marked such administrations as those of G. Mennen Williams in Michigan in the 1950's, and Otto Kerner in Illinois and John Reynolds in Wisconsin in the early 1960's. All resulted in deadlocks over such basic matters as taxation, legislative apportionment, and executive appointments; and for a good part of the time the governments of all three states were brought to nearly complete standstills. In short, separation of powers, rural overrepresentation in legislatures, and close statewide two-party competition sometimes make for inter-party deadlock rather than responsible party government.

STRUCTURAL DIFFICULTIES: DIVIDED PARTY CONTROL WITHIN THE EXECUTIVE. We noted earlier that forty-two states retain the "long ballot" by which from four to twelve executive officers in addition to the governor are independently elected. Not only does this encourage the decentralization of parties in campaigns, as we have seen, but it also enables divided party control *within* the executive branch to complicate the divisions between the executive and the legislature. How often does this actually happen and in what kinds of states? Key has given us our most complete answer in his study of the outcome of all executive elections in nine Northern states from 1900 to 1952, with results summarized in Table 7.

Table 7

RELATION BETWEEN SIZE OF GUBERNATORIAL PLURALITIES AND OUTCOMES OF SIMULTANEOUS ELECTIONS OF MINOR STATE OFFICIALS IN NINE STATES, 1900–1952

		RESULTS OF SIMULTANEOUS ELECTIONS OF MINOR OFFICERS					
PER CENT 2-PARTY VOTE FOR GOVERNOR	NUMBER OF GUBERNATORIAL ELECTIONS	*All from governor's party*		*All from opposition party*		*Divided between parties*	
		No.	%	No.	%	No.	%
50.1–52.4	58	32	55.2	12	20.7	14	24.1
52.5–54.9	49	30	61.2	5	10.2	14	28.6
55.0–57.4	40	35	87.5	0	0.0	5	12.5
57.5–59.9	23	23	100.0	0	0.0	0	0.0
60.0–62.4	18	18	100.0	0	0.0	0	0.0
62.5–64.9	8	8	100.0	0	0.0	0	0.0

Source: V. O. Key, Jr., *American State Politics,* Table 27, p. 200. (The nine states were: Illinois, Indiana, Iowa, Massachusetts, Michigan, Missouri, Ohio, Rhode Island, and Wisconsin.)

Table 7 shows that divided control within the executive follows the same general pattern as divided control between the governor and the legislature: the closer the competition for governor, the more likely it is that the governor and some other elected executives will be of different parties. When the governor was elected by less than 52 per cent of the vote the chances were one in two that some of his fellow executives would be of the opposition party. When he won by less than 55 per cent the chances were two in five. Only when he won by 57.5 per cent of the vote or more were his fellow executives always of his own party.

Here again, where political conditions make for the keen inter-party competition responsible party government requires, constitutional structures and ticket-splitting voters combine to work powerfully against the majority-party control the model also requires.

PARTY ORGANIZATION IN STATE LEGISLATURES. Both parties in both houses of the United States Congress have elaborate arrays of caucuses, steering committees, floor leaders, whips, committees on committees, and other organizations purporting — though by no means always succeeding — to mobilize their legislators for coordinated action. In any legislative body such agencies would seem to be indispensable if the parties are to play significant roles; yet they are by no means universal in state legislatures.

The basic party organ in most legislatures is the "caucus" or "conference" — an assembly of all the party's members in the particular house. However, a survey of state legislatures conducted by the Committee on American Legislatures of the American Political Science Association in the early 1950's reported that the majority parties had no caucuses of any kind in fifteen senates and fourteen houses. Most of these, to be sure, were in the one-party states in which caucuses would simply be meetings of all or nearly all of the members of the entire assembly, and would therefore seem pointless. But, the Committee's Report adds, "in only thirteen states do majority caucuses meet frequently and exert or attempt to exert any significant control over their members or the program of the legislature."[57] Significantly, all thirteen (Colorado, Connecticut, Delaware, Idaho, Indiana, Massachusetts, Nevada, New Jersey, New York, Pennsylvania, Rhode Island, Washington, and Wyoming) are two-party states. However, factional caucuses within the majority party were reported for three one-party states (Arkansas, Florida, and Georgia) and four modified one-party states (Arizona, Kansas, New Mexico, and North Dakota).

Each party in each house of Congress has a "steering" or "policy" committee — a small group of leaders selected by the caucus to act as a sort of board of directors. These bodies have little influence and less power in Congress, and the Committee on Legislatures reported that their counterparts exist and operate regularly in only eleven states.[58]

The dominant figures of party organization in Congress are the Speaker of the House and the Minority Leader, and the Majority and Minority Leaders in the Senate. The counterparts of the latter three offices exist in thirty-seven states, but the legislatures' proceedings are more widely dominated by the presiding officers than by the floor leaders: for example, the members of standing committees are selected by the presiding officers in twenty senates and thirty-three houses.[59]

In general, then, only some of the states have the full paraphernalia of legislative party organization. How effective is it?

PARTY COHESION IN STATE LEGISLATURES. Another prerequisite of responsible party government is that the parties' legislators maintain high cohesion in their votes on legislative issues, for only in this way can the voters meaningfully hold the majority party — as opposed to individual legislators — responsible for what the legislature does or fails to do. The varying degrees and conditions of party cohesion in state legislatures are discussed at length in Chapter 5. For present purposes the essential points to grasp are: first, party cohesion is generally very low in the one-party and modified one-party states, and tends to be higher in the two-party states. Its general relation to party competitiveness is illustrated in Table 8, which classifies the states in each of the categories of competitiveness according to their degree of party cohesion as reported by the Committee on Legislatures.

Table 8

LEGISLATIVE PARTY COHESION AND INTER-PARTY COMPETITION

COHESION IN THE TWO-PARTY STATES			COHESION IN THE MODIFIED ONE-PARTY STATES			COHESION IN THE ONE-PARTY STATES		
Strong	*Moderate*	*Weak*	*Strong*	*Moderate*	*Weak*	*Strong*	*Moderate*	*Weak*
Colo.	Ill.	Calif.	Iowa	N.H.	Ariz.			Ala.
Conn.	Mont.	Neb.†	Kans.	S.Dak.	Ky.			Ark.
Dela.	Nev.	Ore.	Md.	Vt.	Me.			Fla.
Ida.	Ohio		N.C.	Wis.	N.Dak.**			Ga.
Ind.	Utah		W.Va.		N.M.			La.
Mass.	Wash.				Okla.			Miss.
Mich.	Wyo.				Tenn.			S.C.
Minn.*					Va.			Tex.
Mo.								
N.J.								
N.Y.								
Pa.								
R.I.								

*Strong factional cohesion in nonpartisan legislature.
†Weak factional cohesion in nonpartisan legislature.
**Strong factional cohesion in dominant party.

Source: Adapted from Belle Zeller (ed.), *American State Legislatures,* Table 9, pp. 190–191 (Alaska and Hawaii not included).

Table 8 shows that more two-party states have strong cohesion than weak or moderate; more modified one-party states have weak cohesion than strong or moderate; and all eight one-party states have weak cohesion. So the degree of party competition is clearly one, but only one, factor affecting legislative cohesion.

Chapter 5 shows that the other factors have to do with the degree to which party divisions correspond with socio-economic divisions. Generally speaking, where the basic political conflict is that between metropolitan areas and small towns, and where most Democratic legislators are elected from the former and most Republicans from the latter, cohesion in both legislative parties tends to be high.[60] Where party divisions do not coincide with metropolitan–small town conflict, however, party cohesion tends to be lower even where party competition is close. Thus in some state legislatures cohesion comes very close to the responsible-parties model, while in others it is considerably further away.

THE GOVERNOR AS PARTY LEADER. Chapter 6 describes the general position of the governor as a legislative, executive, and administrative leader. Here we are concerned with his position as leader of his party and the extent to which it helps him in his other roles. We should begin by distinguishing between his "outside" and "inside" roles.

In most states, whether one-party or two-party, the governor is usually (though not invariably) the principal leader and spokesman for his party in its relations with other state parties and with the national party. One evidence of this is the fact that the dominant figures in state delegations to national party conventions are usually governors rather than U.S. Senators, mayors, state chairmen, or other rivals.[61] The reason is plain enough: most state parties see many advantages in presenting a united front in their operations in national party affairs, for this is the way to maximize their power. The governor is usually the logical person to act as their spokesman and chief strategist. This fact has sometimes misled outsiders to assume that the governor must be just as much in charge back home as he is at national conventions. But this is rarely the case.

We observed earlier that in some one-party and modified one-party states (e.g., Virginia, Louisiana, Vermont, and North Dakota) the dominant party is divided into two well organized, relatively cohesive and durable factions. Where this is the case, the governor can usually count upon regular support only from his fellow factionalists in the legislature; and, while he cannot be said to be the leader of the whole party for state purposes, he certainly has as much control over the machinery of government as any governor of a two-party state. In other one-party states (e.g., Florida, Oklahoma, and Mississippi) there are no durable factions, and the coalition that elects the governor usually has little carry-over in the legislature. As a result, the governor of such a state is the leader of his party in only the most nominal sense, and he must negotiate with factions in the legislature on an issue-by-issue basis to accomplish whatever he wishes to accomplish.[62]

However, whether in a bifactional or multifactional state, the leadership of most governors in the one-party states is materially weakened by the fact that they are constitutionally prohibited from succeeding themselves: six of the eight one-party Democratic states have such prohibitions (only Arkansas and Texas do not), as well as six of the nine modified one-party Democratic states (only Arizona, Maryland, and New Mexico do not). By contrast, only three two-party states (Indiana, Missouri, and Pennsylvania) have comparable prohibitions, and only four more (Alaska, Delaware, New Jersey, and Oregon) limit their governors to two terms.[63]

Where the governor's term is limited, as it is in most of the Democratic states, whatever leadership he may have had over his party when first elected is likely to dissipate as he nears the end of his term; for legislators and party chairmen alike know that he will soon be in a position where he can neither help nor hurt them very much.

A leading student of American governorship, Professor Coleman Ransone, sums up the party leadership of governors in the two-party states thus:

> It is primarily because we do not really have party government at the state level that the governor must continue to play the role of the politician even after his election. . . . The idea of disciplined parties in the legislature who work with the governor to execute a party program is largely a none-too-effective myth at the state level. The governor is elected in an atmosphere of factional politics and he continues to operate in that atmosphere in his dealings with the legislature, with his department heads, and with the other members of the executive branch.[64]

The principal reasons for this relative weakness of gubernatorial party leadership in the two-party states include: (1) the general decentralization of the state parties, which means that most county leaders and state legislators hold their positions by their own efforts and owe the governor nothing; (2) the frequency with which divided party control forces the governor to bargain with factions in the opposition party in the legislature and within the executive branch; (3) the fact that the use of his patronage and item-veto powers may well make at least as many enemies as friends. The upshot, Ransone concludes, is this:

> There are situations in the two-party states in which the governorship and the legislature are controlled by the same party and where, given some party discipline, the governor may be able to make an appeal to the legislators on the basis of a party program. These situations, however, tend to be infrequent. . . . The American governor must concern himself with building legislative support from among clusters of legislative factions. In only a few states does the party actually play its traditional role.[65]

THE NEW VULNERABILITY OF THE GOVERNOR. Traditionally the governorships of large Northern two-party states like New York, Ohio, Pennsylvania, and Illinois, have been ideal stepping-stones to the major parties'

Presidential nominations. However, in both 1960 and 1964 none of the Presidential and Vice-Presidential candidates of either party had ever been a governor. Why this sudden downgrading of gubernatorial office? Undoubtedly, part of the reason lies in the increasing importance of foreign policy issues and the need of a Presidential candidate to have some experience and reputation in foreign affairs. But part also lies in the increasing political vulnerability of governors. In 1960, for example, twenty-nine incumbent U.S. Senators ran for re-election and only one was defeated; but of the fourteen incumbent governors running in the same year, six were beaten. In 1962, thirty incumbent Senators ran, and only five lost; but of the twenty-six incumbent governors running, ten lost. So in these two elections 90 per cent of the incumbent Senators survived, compared with only 60 per cent of the incumbent governors.

The reason for the new political vulnerability of governors is plain: most state governments, as this volume makes abundantly clear, now face enormously increased demands for more and better schools, highways, welfare, recreational facilities, and so on — but most face them armed with very inadequate revenue sources. Consequently, most large two-party states are in perpetual financial crisis. The governor is to a great extent the most visible state official and therefore the logical scapegoat for the state's apparent inability to solve its problems. It is he who must press for new taxes or announce the curtailment of services — neither of which makes for political popularity. Thus, when the voters wish to express their annoyance with high taxes or inadequate services, the governor is the natural target.

Most state politicians know this, and many are reluctant to tie their own fortunes to a man who might well be thrown out at the next election. Accordingly, the governors in the two-party states, as Ransone points out, are rarely both strong *and* durable party leaders. To get things done they must rely mainly on weapons other than their leadership of their parties; they must often enlist the cooperation of at least some of the opposition party. As this becomes more and more common, governorships may well lose their traditional place as ideal stepping-stones to higher office.

CHANGING ELECTORAL PATTERNS IN STATE POLITICS

THE GROWTH OF INTER-PARTY COMPETITION. We noted earlier that the Civil War hammered most states' party alignments into forms that long seemed permanent. Since 1945, however, a number of hitherto one-party states have seen their second parties mount major challenges to the dominant parties. As a result, the nation's political landscape has come to look much different since V-J Day from the way it appeared before Pearl Harbor.

Perhaps the most dramatic instances have been the rise of Republican strength in a number of Southern and border states. We have already observed its effects on Presidential voting, but in some states it has operated in elections for other offices as well.

For example, in 1962 veteran Alabama Senator Lister Hill barely won re-election over Republican James D. Martin; Florida elected two Republican U.S. Representatives out of twelve; South Carolina gave over 40 per cent of its popular vote to a Republican candidate for the U.S. Senate for the first time since Reconstruction; Texas elected a second Republican U.S. Representative, and in 1961 Texas voters made John Tower the first Republican U.S. Senator from the state since Reconstruction; and Tennessee elected Republicans in three of its nine Congressional Districts. In all, 11 of 105 Southern U.S. Representatives were Republicans in the 88th Congress, the highest number since the 1870's.

Only Oklahoma, to be sure, elected a Republican to any high *state* office — when it elected Henry Bellmon the first Republican governor in the state's history — so full two-party competition is still some distance off in most Southern and border states. Nevertheless, Southern Republicans are stronger today than they have been for a century, and they are likely to grow stronger.[66]

Less dramatic but equally significant has been the rise of Democratic strength for state offices in a number of formerly solid Republican states. For example: Iowa elected Democratic governors in 1956, 1958, and 1962; Kansas did the same in 1956 and 1958; Maine elected Democratic governors in 1954, 1956, and 1958, and a Democratic U.S. Senator in 1958; New Hampshire elected both a Democratic governor and U.S. Senator in 1962; North Dakota returned a Democratic governor in 1960 and 1962, and a Democratic U.S. Senator in 1960;[67] in South Dakota the Democrats not only won the governorship in 1958 and a U.S. Senatorship in 1962 but actually controlled one house of the legislature in 1958; Vermont elected a Democratic Congressman-at-Large in 1958 and a Democratic governor in 1962, the first Democrats elected to statewide office since 1854; and Wisconsin elected Democratic governors in 1958, 1960, and 1962, and Democratic U.S. Senators in 1958 and 1962.[68] What the Democrats have lost in the South they have regained in the rural Midwest and Northeast.

We cannot now provide a complete and definitive explanation for these changes from traditional state political alignments. However, a major part of any such explanation will surely be interstate migration.[69] Americans have always moved about within their country frequently and in large numbers, and the post-1945 era has witnessed one of the greatest migrations since the Civil War: the Bureau of the Census found that 12 per cent of the population over five years of age in 1960 had moved from one state to another since 1955![70]

Perhaps the most significant movement politically has been the parallel immigration of Northern whites into the South and emigration of Southern Negroes out of the South. One effect has been to reduce the proportion of Negroes in the Southern states' populations: in the decade from 1950 to 1960 the proportion of Negroes declined in all eight Democratic one-party states, the largest drops being from 27 to 18 per cent in Florida and from 43 to 35 per cent in South Carolina; the average drop for the eight states was 5.6 per cent.[71] This Negro exodus has "lightened" many of the South's "black belts," which, according to Key, have always constituted the nucleus of Southern one-party politics.[72] At the same time the influx of Northern whites, about half of whom were Republicans in the North and have remained so after moving to the South, has not only given Southern Republicans more votes; more significantly, it has greatly enlarged the pool of well-educated and active party supporters from which they can draw candidates for office and leaders of party organization. Both movements, accordingly, have encouraged a higher degree of inter-party competition in the South.

The other main post-war interstate migration has been the massive movement to the far West. The most spectacular instance, of course, is the growth of California from a population of 6,907,000 in 1940 to 15,717,000 in 1960, and a position as the most populous state in the Union by the mid-1960's. The Survey Research Center of the University of Michigan studied a sample of 588 western adults in 1956, and its findings tell us much about the post-war western immigrants and their impact on western politics. Slightly over twice as many came from the North as from the South. Those from the North were closely split between Democratic identifiers (39 per cent) and Republican (34 per cent), while those from the South were heavily Democratic (57 per cent to 20 per cent Republican). From one point of view, the net effect has been to make the West somewhat more Democratic than before; from another, it has sustained two-party competition, for the Northern immigrants have supplied large numbers of Republicans, enough indeed to keep the region from the two-to-one lead the Democrats would probably have if the western electorate consisted entirely of persons born in the region and immigrants from the South.[73]

CONCLUSIONS

We end where we began: in every state most elections are fought and most public offices are held by persons bearing the labels "Democratic" and "Republican"; but the meaning of the term "political parties" as applied to these aggregates varies considerably from one state to another. In the eight Southern one-party states "the Democratic party" is almost coterminous with the state itself; everyone is a Democrat; elections are not inter-party contests;

and the Democratic party has as much "cohesion" and "responsibility" as the whole government, for they are one and the same.[74]

In the seventeen modified one-party states, the "political parties" are somewhat more meaningful entities. Although most voters identify with the dominant party, a noticeable minority identifies with the other. Both parties nominate candidates in most elections, which thereby become genuine choices between parties; and occasionally a candidate of the second party wins. Much political conflict is fought out in the primaries and committees of the dominant party, but the presence of an organized party opposition ready to take over in case of schism or scandal makes the context of intra-party conflict substantially different from that in the one-party states.[75]

In the two-party states each party musters a large segment of the population as its identifiers. Almost every election is contested by a Republican and a Democrat. In some two-party states there is high cohesion among both parties in the legislature and close cooperation between the governor and his fellow partisans. Such states, indeed, come closer than the national government to the responsible-party-government model. In other two-party states, however, the parties are a little, if any, more cohesive than in the modified one-party states. And we are as yet unable to say why two-party competition produces unified parties in some states but not in others.

Therefore, relatively even party competition seems to be a necessary — but not sufficient — condition for state parties to operate as unified governing agencies. Its post-war increase in many American states may help bring some of them nearer the responsible-parties ideal. But in other two-party states, two-party competition may, because of its combination with separation of powers and malapportionment of the legislatures, serve instead to intensify the partisan political deadlock and governmental paralysis which constitutes one of the principal barriers to making states into more effective units of government. Inter-party competition, in short, does make a difference; but the kind of difference it makes depends upon the context in which it operates.

Whatever may be the future of inter-party competition, however, political parties will continue to be the states' principal agencies for making nominations, contesting elections, recruiting governmental leaders from the general population, and so providing the vital link between the people and their government that democracy demands. What Clinton Rossiter has said of the nation applies with equal force to each of the states:

> Our party system will continue to serve us well as long as we keep the old definition firmly in mind: Politics is the art of the possible. Whatever America finds necessary to do in the years to come, the politics of American democracy will surely make possible.[76]

NOTES

1. E. E. Schattschneider, *Party Government* (New York: Farrar and Rinehart, 1942) p. 1, emphasis added.
2. *Loc. cit.*
3. For more detailed summaries, see Joseph R. Starr, "The Legal Status of American Political Parties," *American Political Science Review XXXIV* (1940) 439–455, 685–699; and Austin Ranney and Willmoore Kendall, *Democracy and the American Party System* (New York: Harcourt, Brace and Co., 1956) pp. 217–222.
4. Cf. Arthur W. Macmahon, *Encyclopaedia of the Social Sciences* (New York: Macmillan Co., 1937) Vol. XI, p. 596; and Schattschneider, pp. 66–67.
5. V. O. Key, Jr., *Southern Politics in State and Nation* (New York: Alfred A. Knopf, 1949) chapter 5.
6. See p. 72.
7. Duane Lockard, *New England State Politics* (Princeton: Princeton University Press, 1959) chapters 9–10.
8. As is recognized by at least one prominent advocate of more disciplined national parties: cf. James MacGregor Burns, *The Deadlock of Democracy* (Englewood Cliffs, N.J.: Prentice-Hall, 1963) pp. 236–241.
9. Cf. V. O. Key, Jr., *American State Politics: An Introduction* (New York: Alfred A. Knopf, 1956) p. 201; Key, *Southern Politics,* chapter 14; Ranney and Kendall, pp. 190–191; and Robert T. Golembiewski, "A Taxonomic Approach to State Political Party Strength," *Western Political Quarterly XI* (1958) 494–513.
10. The principal measures are in Key, *American State Politics,* pp. 97–104; Austin Ranney and Willmoore Kendall, "The American Party Systems," *American Political Science Review XLVIII* (1954) 477–485; Joseph A. Schlesinger, "A Two-Dimensional Scheme for Classifying the States According to Degree of Inter-Party Competition," *American Political Science Review XLIX* (1955) 1120–1128; Belle Zeller (ed.), *American State Legislatures* (New York: Thomas Y. Crowell Co., 1954) pp. 199–211; Golembiewski, "A Taxonomic Approach to State Political Party Strength"; and Richard E. Dawson and James A. Robinson, "Inter-Party Competition, Economic Variables, and Welfare Policies in the American States," *Journal of Politics XXV* (1963) 265–289.
11. The story is well told in Key, *Southern Politics,* pp. 551ff; and in Alexander Heard, *A Two-Party South?* (Chapel Hill: University of North Carolina Press, 1952).
12. Warren E. Miller, "One-Party Politics and the Voter," *American Political Science Review L* (1956) 707–725.
13. Cf. Angus Campbell, Philip E. Converse, Warren E. Miller, and Donald E. Stokes, *The American Voter* (New York and London: John Wiley and Sons, 1960) chapters 6–7, and p. 555; Herbert Hyman, *Political Socialization* (Glencoe: The Free Press, 1959) chapters 3–6; and V. O. Key, Jr., *Public Opinion and American Democracy* (New York: Alfred A. Knopf, 1961) chapters 5, 12–13, 17–18.
14. For the general pattern, see Campbell, *et al.,* chapters 15–17; and Key, *American State Politics,* chapter 8. For instances of the general pattern in particular states, see Leon D. Epstein, *Politics in Wisconsin* (Madison: University of Wisconsin Press, 1958) chapter 4; Frank J. Sorauf, *Party and Representation: Legislative Politics in Pennsylvania* (New York: Atherton Press, 1963) chapter 2; and Heinz Eulau, "The Ecological Basis of Party Systems: The Case of Ohio," *Midwest Journal of Political Science I* (1957) 125–135. Iowa is apparently an exception:

see David Gold and John R. Schmidhauser, "Urbanization and Party Competition: The Case of Iowa," *Midwest Journal of Political Science IV* (1960) 62–75.

15. In *Smith* vs. *Allwright,* 321 U.S. 649 (1944), in which the Court held that when the primary election of one party is, in effect, the final election, the executive committee of the dominant party becomes an agent of the state, and any rules it makes barring Negroes from voting in its primaries are just as much violations of the Fifteenth Amendment as if they were laws adopted by the state legislature.

16. Key, *Southern Politics,* pp. 395–396; Howard R. Penniman, *Sait's American Parties and Elections* (4th ed.; New York: Appleton-Century-Crofts, 1948) p. 341.

17. For more detailed summaries, see Ranney and Kendall, pp. 223–230; and John E. Reeves and W. C. Bradford, "Methods of Choosing Delegates and Officials of Political Parties," *Kentucky Law Journal XLV* (1957) 459–477.

18. Cf. Austin Ranney, *Illinois Politics* (New York: New York University Press, 1960) pp. 9–11.

19. Daniel M. Ogden, Jr., and Hugh A. Bone, *Washington Politics* (New York: New York University Press, 1960) pp. 26–28.

20. See Key, *Southern Politics,* chapters 2, 8; Allan P. Sindler, *Huey Long's Louisiana: State Politics, 1920–1952* (Baltimore: The Johns Hopkins Press, 1956); and William Manchester, "The Byrd Machine," *Harper's Magazine CCV* (November 1952) 80–87.

21. See Ralph A. Straetz and Frank J. Munger, *New York Politics* (New York: New York University Press, 1960) pp. 27, 62–63, 65; Warren Moscow, *Politics in the Empire State* (New York: Alfred A. Knopf, 1948); and G. Theodore Mitau, *Politics in Minnesota* (Minneapolis: University of Minnesota Press, 1960) pp. 24–26.

22. See Justin N. Feldman, "How Tammany Holds Power," *National Civic Review XXXIX* (1950) 330–334; James Reichley, *The Art of Government: Reform and Organization Politics in Philadelphia* (New York: Fund for the Republic, 1959); and Edward Banfield, *Political Influence* (Glencoe: The Free Press, 1960).

23. Cf. Lockard, chapter 12; and V. O. Key, Jr., *Politics, Parties, and Pressure Groups* (5th ed.; New York: Thomas Y. Crowell Co., 1964) p. 336.

24. Key, *Politics, Parties, and Pressure Groups,* p. 316.

25. The best general discussion is James Q. Wilson, *The Amateur Democrats* (Chicago: University of Chicago Press, 1962).

26. See Epstein, chapter 5; and Frank J. Sorauf, "Extra-Legal Parties in Wisconsin," *American Political Science Review XLVIII* (1954) 692–704.

27. See Francis M. Carney, *The Rise of the Democratic Clubs in California* (New York: Henry Holt and Company, 1958); and Hugh A. Bone, "New Party Associations in the West," *American Political Science Review XLV* (1951) 1115–1120.

28. See Donald C. Blaisdell, "The Riverside Democrats," in Paul Tillett (ed.), *Cases on Party Organization* (New York: McGraw-Hill Book Co., 1963) pp. 64–92; Robert S. Hirschfield, *et al.,* "A Profile of Political Activists in Manhattan," *Atlantic Monthly CCVI* (October 1960) 65–70; and Daniel P. Moynihan, " 'Bosses' and 'Reforms': A Profile of New York Democrats," *Commentary XXXI* (June 1961) 461–470.

29. As, for example, the Democratic Federation of Illinois: see Ranney, *Illinois Politics,* pp. 29–30.

30. For example, in New York nominees for statewide offices are selected by state party conventions, while nominees for other offices are chosen by direct primaries. For a summary of the systems used in the various states, see *The Book of the States, 1962–1963* (Chicago: Council of State Governments, 1962) p. 22.

31. See the arguments reviewed in Charles E. Merriam and Louise Overacker, *Primary Elections* (rev. ed.; Chicago: University of Chicago Press, 1928).

32. Among the more notable are: Key, *American State Politics*, chapter 5, pp. 97–118; Cortez A. M. Ewing, *Primary Elections in the South* (Norman: University of Oklahoma Press, 1953); Julius Turner, "Primary Elections as the Alternative to Party Competition in 'Safe' Districts," *Journal of Politics XV* (1953) 197–210; Allan P. Sindler, "Bifactional Rivalry as an Alternative to Two-Party Competition in Louisiana," *American Political Science Review XLIX* (1955) 641–662; James A. Robinson, "Inter-Party Competition and Primary Contesting: The Case of Indiana," *American Political Science Review LII* (1958) 1066–1077; Malcolm E. Jewell, "Party and Primary Competition in Kentucky State Legislative Races," *Kentucky Law Journal XLVIII* (1960) 517–535.

33. Key, *Politics, Parties, and Pressure Groups*, p. 441.

34. Cf. Campbell, *et al.*, pp. 96–99.

35. Key, *Politics, Parties, and Pressure Groups*, pp. 381–383; Ranney and Kendall, pp. 284–289.

36. Curtis Martin, *Colorado Politics* (2nd ed.; Denver: Big Mountain Press, 1962) pp. 50–51, 60–61.

37. Key, *Politics, Parties, and Pressure Groups*, pp. 387–388.

38. Ranney, *Illinois Politics*, pp. 24–26.

39. For Louisiana, see Sindler; for Virginia, see Key, *Southern Politics*, chapter 2.

40. For Alabama, see Key, *Southern Politics*, chapter 5; and William J. Keefe, "Southern Politics Revisited," *Public Opinion Quarterly XX* (1956) 405–412. For Florida, see Key, *Southern Politics*, chapter 3; and Herbert J. Doherty, Jr., "Liberal and Conservative Voting Patterns in Florida," *Journal of Politics XIV* (1952) 403–417.

41. Ogden and Bone, p. 47.

42. *The Book of the States, 1962–1963*, pp. 23–25.

43. Cf. Stanley Kelley, Jr., *Professional Public Relations and Political Power* (Baltimore: The Johns Hopkins Press, 1956).

44. Cf. Joseph P. Harris, *California Politics* (3rd ed.; Stanford: Stanford University Press, 1963) p. 48; and Ranney, *Illinois Politics*, p. 38.

45. Alexander Heard, *The Costs of Democracy* (Chapel Hill: University of North Carolina Press, 1960) chapters 5, 7, especially Table 7, pp. 100–102.

46. *Ibid.*, pp. 162–168.

47. Cf. *ibid.*, chapter 2; and Jasper B. Shannon, *Money and Politics* (New York: Random House, 1959).

48. The states using each form of regulation are given in *The Book of the States, 1962–1963*, pp. 26–29.

49. See Heard, chapter 16; and Herbert Alexander, *Money, Politics, and Public Reporting* (Princeton: Citizens' Research Foundation, 1960).

50. Election calendars for each state are given in *The Book of the States, 1962–1963*, pp. 23–25.

51. The figures for 1932–1950 in Table 5 are taken from Key, *State Politics*, Table 2, p. 38.

52. The argument is summarized and evaluated in Austin Ranney, *The Doctrine of Responsible Party Government* (Urbana: University of Illinois Press, 1954, 1962).

53. See Pendleton Herring, *The Politics of Democracy* (New York: Rinehart & Company, 1940); Herbert Agar, *The Price of Union* (Boston: Houghton Mifflin Co., 1959); and Ranney and Kendall, pp. 527–532.

54. See p. 65.

55. Key, *American State Politics*, chapter 3.

56. See pp. 160–162.
57. Zeller, p. 194, and Table 12, p. 196.
58. *Ibid.,* Table 11, p. 195.
59. *Ibid.,* Table 13, p. 197.
60. For a detailed analysis of just such a situation in Pennsylvania, see Sorauf, *Party and Representation.*
61. Paul T. David, Ralph M. Goldman, and Richard C. Bain, *The Politics of National Party Conventions* (Washington: The Brookings Institution, 1960) chapter 5, especially p. 357.
62. Coleman B. Ransone, Jr., *The Office of Governor in the United States* (University, Ala.: University of Alabama Press, 1956) chapters 2, 7.
63. *The Book of the States, 1962–1963,* p. 139. Maryland and New Mexico limit their governors to two consecutive terms.
64. Ransone, p. 94.
65. *Ibid.,* p. 193.
66. For a more detailed discussion of Southern Republican resurgence, see: Virginius Dabney, "What the GOP is Doing in the South," *Harper's Magazine* (May 1963) 86–94; Keefe, "Southern Politics Revisited"; and Kenneth N. Vines, "Republicanism in New Orleans," *Tulane Studies in Political Science II* (1955) 89–134.
67. For details of the North Dakota story, see Henry J. Tomasek, "North Dakota's Advent as a Two-Party System," *North Dakota Quarterly XXX* (1960) 57–66; and Ross B. Talbot, "North Dakota — a Two-Party State," *North Dakota Quarterly XXV* (1957) 93–104.
68. Epstein, chapter 3, portrays the background for these Democratic successes.
69. An illuminating analysis is given in Campbell, *et al.,* chapter 16.
70. *Congressional District Data Book* (Washington: Bureau of the Census, 1963) p. 2.
71. *Statistical Abstract of the United States, 1962* (Washington: Bureau of the Census, 1962) Table 24, p. 30.
72. Key, *Southern Politics,* chapter 31.
73. Campbell, *et al.,* pp. 446–449.
74. Cf. Key, *Southern Politics,* chapters 18–22; and Malcolm B. Parsons, "Quasi-Partisan Conflict in a One-Party Legislative System: The Florida Senate, 1947–1961," *American Political Science Review LVI* (1962) 605–614.
75. Cf. Samuel C. Patterson, "Dimensions of Voting Behavior in a One-Party State Legislature [Oklahoma]," *Public Opinion Quarterly XXVI* (1962) 185–200.
76. Clinton Rossiter, *Parties and Politics in America* (Ithaca: Cornell University Press, 1960) p. 188.

SELECTED BIBLIOGRAPHY

Epstein, Leon D. *Politics in Wisconsin.* Madison: University of Wisconsin Press, 1958. An application of Key's hypotheses and techniques to Wisconsin, supplemented by the author's interviews with state party leaders.

Fenton, John R. *Politics in the Border States.* New Orleans: The Hauser Press, 1957. Descriptions of politics in Kentucky, Maryland, Missouri, and West Virginia.

Herndon, James, Charles Press, and Oliver P. Williams (eds.). *A Selected Bibliography of Materials in State Government and Politics.* Lexington: Bureau of Government Research, University of Kentucky, 1963. The most complete, recent state-by-state bibliography of state politics.

Key, V. O., Jr. *American State Politics: An Introduction.* New York: Alfred A. Knopf, 1956. A pioneering and influential study of non-Southern state politics resting almost entirely upon statistical analysis of aggregate data.

——. *Southern Politics in State and Nation.* New York: Alfred A. Knopf, 1949. A classic of contemporary political science, somewhat outdated in detail but still the most comprehensive and authoritative general analysis.

Lockard, Duane. *New England State Politics.* Princeton: Princeton University Press, 1959. Useful analysis concentrating on inter-party competition and legislative politics.

National Center for Education in Politics, Series on State Politics. Useful short paperback studies, by various authors, of politics in California, Colorado, Illinois, Massachusetts, Michigan, Minnesota, New York, Pennsylvania, and Washington.

Ransone, Coleman B., Jr. *The Office of Governor in the United States.* University, Ala.: University of Alabama Press, 1956. Comprehensive analysis of state politics focused on the office of governor.

Sindler, Allan P. *Huey Long's Louisiana: 1920–1952.* Baltimore: The Johns Hopkins Press, 1956. The most scholarly account of a significant case in Southern state politics.

Sorauf, Frank J. *Party and Representation: Legislative Politics in Pennsylvania.* New York: Atherton Press, 1963. A stimulating study of the selection of candidates and conduct of elections for the Pennsylvania legislature in 1958, used as a base for generalizing about interrelations among constituencies, local party organizations and leaders, and state organizations and leaders.

Wilson, James Q. *The Amateur Democrat.* Chicago: University of Chicago Press, 1956. The most complete account of the "club" movements.

INTEREST GROUPS IN THE STATES

CHAPTER 4

by

HARMON ZEIGLER

As POLITICAL PARTIES ARE INEFFECTIVE in many states, we may ask how political demands are communicated and translated into policies. Since the pioneering studies of Arthur F. Bentley,[1] interest groups have been regarded as the principal alternative to parties or the major supplement to their activity.[2]

Interest groups are abundant and visible in the American states. Heterogeneous populations have given rise to varied social groupings which make demands on the states' rich and varied resources. The fifty states with their various histories and traditions have created bureaucracies that themselves generate demands.

This chapter will examine the role of interest groups in state politics. As with political parties, we must examine the composition and structure of interest groups and their influence in the several states. To do this, we must also examine the manner in which groups gain access to policy makers. The background of lobbyists and the manner in which they communicate demands will complete our analysis of the role of interest groups in state political systems.

ORGANIZATIONAL MEMBERSHIP AND POLITICAL LIFE

Much has been written about the alleged evils of pressure groups. James Madison's famous warning about the "dangerous vice" of what he termed factions has been echoed by critics through the years by such phrases as "group organization is one of the perils of our times."[3] However damning the criticism of selected writers, it tells us little of the beliefs of the American people, few of whom ever express their ideas in writing. Explorations into these beliefs have recently been undertaken by Gabriel Almond and Sidney Verba.[4] Their data will form the basis of the remainder of this section.

ATTITUDES TOWARD ORGANIZED GROUP ACTIVITY. Leaving aside for the moment the actual participation of Americans in formal organizations, we inquire first into their perceptions of the role of such organizations in the political process. Few people prefer to spend their free time in organizational activities. When asked to indicate what sorts of activities interested them most, the respondents in the Almond-Verba study rarely specified politics. In fact, participation in organizations such as unions, business associations, and professional associations received less mention than any other type of activity. Thus the types of activity of greatest interest to us rank at the bottom of the scale. If most people prefer to spend their leisure time in nonpolitical (or more specifically non-organizational) activities, this does not necessarily mean that they would not join an organization if their style of life appeared to be threatened. Indeed, one aspect of group theory deals with the idea of "potential" groups.[5] People who are normally unconcerned about politics may become active if threatened. Does this mean that the formal organization would be their choice of an instrument?

The evidence indicates that taking action through an organized group would be just about the last choice of those who would undertake any effort at achieving a satisfactory solution. When asked what they would do if a law were being considered by Congress which they believed to be unjust or harmful, the sample indicated the following choices: (1) contact elected leaders as an individual; (2) work through informal, unorganized groups; (3) do nothing; (4) vote; (5) work through a formal group; and (6) work through a political party. Clearly the individual and informal method is preferred, perhaps reflecting the distrust of organized activity mentioned previously. However, some reservations to these findings must be made. First, the hypothetical nature of the question can only simulate imperfectly the reaction of a person who has actually been in a position of believing himself to be damaged by a governmental decision. Second, the preference for informal, unorganized groups certainly leaves open the possibility that a more formal organization might emerge if the threat continued to be severe. In fact, the evolution from informal to formal organizations is a typical pattern. With these reservations, we can still assert that organized groups are not the main device for the settling of grievances when they arise.

A final aspect of the perception of group activity may be gleaned from perceptions of the most *effective* method of influencing a governmental decision. People apparently believe that group activity is very effective when considered in impersonal terms. By asking a question with no reference to personal reactions it was learned that the formation of a group was believed to be the best way to achieve success, followed by writing to government officials, working through a political party, working through personal and family connections, and forming a protest demonstration. It seems that group activity is perceived as a more effective device when undertaken by *others*. Does this reinforce suspicions about the questionable legitimacy of organized activity? The data do not provide an explicit answer to this question, but we can infer that the average person would not want to engage in "pressure politics" but believes that the "others" who do so are successful. Further clarification of this idea is given by the fact that 58 per cent of the sample indicated agreement with the statement that there are some people or groups having so much influence on the way government is run that the interests of the majority are ignored. What kinds of groups have this influence? According to the sample, big business or "the rich" rank first, followed by political parties and labor unions. When we examine these beliefs by income, we find that the high income groups think labor is more powerful than business and the low income groups think business is more powerful than labor.

Table 1

PERCEPTIONS OF POWERFUL GROUPS BY INCOME OF RESPONDENTS

	PER CENT WHO PERCEIVE LABOR OR BUSINESS AS POWERFUL	
INCOME OF RESPONDENTS	*Labor*	*Business*
$ 2,000–2,999 (99)*	16%	13%
3,000–4,999 (217)	10	15
5,000–7,499 (265)	13	21
7,500–9,999 (98)	13	21
10,000–14,999 (75)	18	15
15,000 or more (28)	22	16

*Number in parentheses indicates total number of respondents in each income group.

Here again we see evidence of the belief that the other fellow is the one with power. If we examine the literature of organized groups we find that, with rare exceptions, the description of a particular group conflict is phrased in terms of power opponents with unlimited funds — an enemy whose defeat will require unusual loyalty and devotion among the members of the organization.

THE BELIEF THAT STATE LOBBYING IS "DIRTIER" THAN NATIONAL LOBBYING. A popular conception of lobbying is that, for the most part, lobbyists engage in providing elaborate entertainment for legislators, offering bribes and, if all else fails, threatening retaliation by defeating the recalcitrant legislator in his next effort at re-election. Insofar as the national legislative process is concerned, recent research has fairly well dispelled this notion.[6] However, there does seem to be some evidence of the belief that at the state level the highhanded methods of yesteryear still persist. For instance, Robert Engler in discussing the techniques of oil lobbyists before state legislatures says, "The crude and more obvious practices commonly identified with lobbying are still familiar here." Engler refers to a remark by a Standard Oil executive to Rockefeller in the early days of the growth of refining companies that he had "arranged to kill two bills in the Maryland legislature at comparatively small expense."[7] Conceding that it is difficult to document such activity today, Engler gives the impression that unscrupulous lobbying is the order of the day.

Further evidence of the belief in the crude nature of state lobbying techniques is provided by Lester Milbrath. In interviewing lobbyists and legislators in Washington, he found that their perception of state lobbying was that it was considerably more corrupt than national lobbying. Some of the comments of his respondents illustrate this belief:

> Lobbying is very different before state legislatures; it is much more individualistic. Maybe this is the reason they have more bribery in state legislatures than in Congress.
> In the state legislatures, lobbying is definitely on a lower plane. The lobbyists are loose and hand out money and favors quite freely.
> Lobbying at the state level is cruder, more basic, and more obvious.
> . . . Lobbying at the state level is faster and more freewheeling and less visible; that is why it is more open to corruption.[8]

Whether or not state legislatures are subjected to such crass techniques remains to be established. However, we should want to know what characteristics of state legislatures and legislators would (theoretically) contribute to more corrupt lobbying techniques. Some of the more apparent contributing factors come readily to mind. State legislators meet less often and for shorter durations of time than does the national Congress. Therefore, an internalized set of formal and informal rules such as those of the U.S. Senate would be more difficult to develop. Such a system of internalized expectations of behavior would, perhaps, impose limits upon individual legislative behavior and thus restrict the operating limits of interest groups. Contributing to the lack of internal systems of authority is the rapid turnover of state legislators. Since about half of these legislators are first-term members of their respective houses, the unfamiliarity of the situation improves the general access of lobbyists. The amateur status of state legislative politics also means that legislators are less likely to be "professionals" and more likely to regard the legislative career as a secondary aspect of their lives. Finally, state legislators make less money than national legislators; they usually do not reside in the state capital and incur more expenses in relation to their incomes than national legislators.

THE EXTENT OF ORGANIZATIONAL MEMBERSHIP. Having given a brief description of the attitudinal environment in which state interest groups operate, we turn our attention to the problem of finding out what kinds of people belong to organizations. The folk saying that "Americans are joiners" is supported by the findings of Almond and Verba. Of the five nations in which interviews were conducted, the American respondents indicated the highest degree of organizational membership (57 per cent).[9] However, only 24 per cent of the respondents believed the organizations to which they belonged were engaged in politics. As Almond and Verba themselves point out, this does not mean that the perception is in accordance with the reality. Organizations engaging in political activities may be perceived as non-political by their members. Further, organizations should not be categorized as political or non-political as though this were a static definition. Robert Lane, for example, is unwilling to categorize organizations as either political or non-political and prefers the term "quasi-political." In his study of the Connecticut Manufacturers Association, he found that the political involvement of the organization varied through time. By analyzing the content of its journal from 1937 to 1946 he found that attention to government-business relationships decreased while attention to problems of production increased. During the same period there was a steady rise in the political interest of unions.[10] Thus, the perception of the member of the political nature of the organization could change from year to year. At the particular moment in time when the interviews were conducted for the Almond-Verba study, we find that members of certain types of organizations had differing perceptions of their extent of political involvement. The following table illustrates these differences:

Table 2
PERCEPTIONS OF POLITICAL INVOLVEMENT

Type of Organization	Per Cent of Membership Perceiving the Organization As Politically Involved	Total Number of Members in Sample
Farm	71	29
Civic-Political	62	111
Professional	60	41
Business	55	40
Labor	50	136
Religious	35	180

Whether these perceptions reflect the actual extent of participation can be determined only by observation of the behavior of the particular organization at a given moment in history. It would be expected that during periods of organizational crisis (labor during the Taft-Hartley or Landrum-Griffith episodes and doctors during struggles over medical insurance) political involvement and corresponding perceptions of this involvement would increase.

Laying aside for the moment the categorizing of organizations according to perceptions of political activity, what do we know about *participation* in voluntary associations? Virtually no sample of national or local populations has failed to conclude that membership in voluntary organizations is greater among the upper socio-economic strata. Membership in organizations is positively correlated with high income and high educational attainment.[11] Here we are concerned more with describing environmental factors which influence group membership. Specifically, what characteristics of a state can be said to be related to a relatively large organizational membership?

The Almond-Verba data do not indicate any clear regional pattern in group membership. The firmest conclusion which emerges when we distribute organizational membership by region is that the South is well below the national average. It is also true that, of the four major regions (Northeast, Midwest, South, and West), the South ranks last in urban population, per capita income, and industrialization. Another way of reaching a similar conclusion is to distribute organizational membership by size of city, as is done in Table 3. The table indicates that people who live in cities of more than 100,000 population are more likely to belong to organizations than people who live in smaller towns. The main thrust of this evidence is that states with an urban, industrial economy are more likely to be characterized by an organization-oriented population than the more rural states whose population is more individualistic.

Table 3

URBANISM AND ORGANIZATIONAL MEMBERSHIP; VARIATIONS ACCORDING TO SIZE OF TOWN

SIZE OF TOWN	PER CENT BELONGING TO:		Number of Respondents
	No *Organizations*	*One or More* *Organizations*	
Less than 5,000	45.7	54.3	297
5,000 to 100,000	41.7	58.3	247
100,000 or more	40.8	59.2	423

Returning to the perceived distinction between political and non-political organizations, we find the urban dominance remains. More of the members of perceived political organizations live in large towns than do the members of perceived non-political organizations.

CHARACTERISTICS OF STATE INTEREST GROUPS. The survey data outlined above, while providing a general profile of the group affiliations of the American people, tells us nothing about the extent to which the organizations try to influence the state political process. This information must come from material provided by various states which require that lobbying organizations register with an agency of the state government. Before examining this material, some theoretical comments about the extent to which the formal institutions of American government influence the nature of state interest groups are in order. Clearly, the most significant institution of this type is the federal system.

The American federal system has contributed to the proliferation of interest groups at the state level. By creating numerous points of decision-making, federalism contributes to a diffusion of the political process. The federal system gives interest groups opportunities for their activities by increasing the number of points at which decisions are made. It does not follow, however, that all groups are equally concerned with state politics. The degree to which a group concerns itself with state politics may be understood to be a function of two factors: (1) the degree to which it has access to state decision-makers; and (2) the extent to which the decisions of state governments seem to affect the well-being of the group.

Successful access depends, in the first instance, on the ability of a group or its leaders to get a favorable response from those officials in a position to make a crucial decision. Access or lack of access cannot be linked directly to any set of circumstances or characteristics. However, it is likely that access is determined less by the skill or "pressure" of organized groups and more by the structure of the situation. To illustrate, the access of labor in Idaho is less than it is in Massachusetts. The pathetic lament of the Idaho State Federation of Labor makes this point succinctly: "It is fitting and proper that this page is set aside as an acknowledgement to those few legislators who . . . fought their and our battle for legislation which will benefit the common people of the state of Idaho. Organized labor . . . could not afford to have a paid lobbyist at the legislative session."[12] This was written during the 1930's — a period in which labor legislation was faring rather well at the national level.

As to the decisions of state governments and their impact on interest groups, one point ought to be made clear. As the federal government has expanded its role, the states have followed suit. Since the end of World War II, expenditures of state and local governments have increased more rapidly than the non-war expenditures of the federal government. Naturally, there are interest groups which are concerned about how this money is to be spent.

Those groups with resources at the state level and a clear stake in state politics are most likely to concentrate their efforts in state legislatures. Several examples will illustrate this point. In the South, segregationist groups have functioned almost as semi-official arms of the state government while Negro groups have been subjected to vigorous legal attacks and legislative investigation. In Louisiana, for example, Negroes believe that no legislators can be depended upon to initiate measures favorable to the Negro community when such a measure might come into conflict with the policy aims of whites.[13] Access to the national legislature is more easily achieved by Negroes. On the other hand, independent retailers anxious to prevent the growing dominance of chain stores were much more successful in persuading state legislatures to adopt restrictive taxes than they were in convincing Congress to adopt a national fair-trade law. The same general conclusion might be reached about oil companies who have fought against federal regulation on the assumption that their access to the various state legislatures was superior to their access to Congress.

Turning to the national government is not the only strategy available to those groups which are denied access to the state legislature. Within the state governments themselves there is the possibility of success. It has been suggested that the Supreme Court is the most effective arena for the presentation of claims by groups whose access to the Congress is restricted. Groups which are unable to influence the electoral, legislative, or administrative process may turn to the courts and, in the case of the Supreme Court, enjoy considerable success. This is especially true of the organizations representing minority groups such as the National Association for the Advancement of Colored People.[14] Is it true that groups disadvantaged through state legislation will perceive the state courts as accessible as they do national courts, or will the difference in values of state and national judges channel minority groups away from state courts? Neither of the questions can be answered with certainty. Stuart Nagel's study of the off-the-bench attitudes of state supreme court justices has called our attention to the essentially conservative values of these men. His correlation of attitudes and the content of decisions leads him to conclude that their conservatism is reflected in their decisions.[15]

In view of these findings, especially the expected discovery that Southern state supreme court justices are more conservative than their Northern brethren, is it likely that minority groups would turn to the state courts? Vines's study of Southern state courts and race relations sheds some light upon these questions.[16] He finds that Negroes prefer to avoid the state courts if possible since the Southern supreme court judges are elected officials with strong functional links to the state political system. The state supreme courts render decisions favorable to Negroes about one-third of the time, substantially less than the percentage of favorable dispositions by federal district courts in the South. Vines's research indicates that the state courts do not play the same role in the state political systems (at least in the South) as does the Supreme Court in the national political system. However, during the same period that the state supreme courts were deciding against Negroes two-thirds of the time, Southern state legislatures failed to pass a single bill favorable to Negroes. Further, state supreme court reversals of lower court decisions are, in over 90 per cent of the cases, favorable to Negroes. It may be suggested, therefore, that, relative to the other political institutions in the Southern states, the supreme courts have to some extent played the same role as does the Supreme Court in national politics.

A final point to be made has bearing on lobbying strategy. To what extent are the groups concerned with state policies coordinated by a national association? There appear to be relatively few examples of interstate coordination. Most groups probably operate without much national direction. Exceptions to the rule are, of course, available. The American Petroleum Industries Committee has branches in most state capitals and operates in a rather unitary fashion. The same can be said of the National Association of Real Estate Boards which worked through state legislatures to defeat rent control after the war, or the American Truckers Association which provides information to state truckers' associations in their opposition to taxes or length and weight limitations.[17] However, few groups have a large enough membership or treasury to allow very much planning. For example, there was no national coordination of the campaign against chain stores, as revealed by the fact that the restrictive tax varied so extremely from state to state.[18] Even the right-to-work controversy, which has attracted national organizational involvement from such groups as the Chamber of Commerce, National Association of Manufacturers, and National Right to Work Committee, seems primarily a state by state affair.[19]

Is there any appreciable difference in the types of groups which appear before the legislatures of differing types of states? Information for all states is not available but the following table, which presents information on the types of organizations which register to lobby before selected state legislatures, is suggestive.[20]

Notice that, while the percentages vary considerably, in every state the registrations are dominated by business associations or single businesses or corporations. No matter what kind of economy enjoyed by the state, the businesses dominate the *numerical* structure of lobbying. For example, 30.6 per cent of the population of South Dakota is employed in non-industrial occupations while 1.8 per cent of the population of Connecticut is so employed. Yet 63 per cent of the South Dakota interests are either business associations or single businesses and 71 per cent of the Connecticut interests are in this category.

Does this mean that business generally has more access to state legislatures than to the national legislature? While many people believe this to be the case, it cannot be established solely from the magnitude of business lobby-

Table 4

CLASSIFICATION OF INTEREST GROUPS IN SELECTED STATES, 1964

State	Business %	Single Bus. Corp. %	Labor %	Farm %	Prof. %	Reform %	Public Agency %	Religious and Ethnic %	Veteran %	Other %
California (432)*	28.8	23.1	10.7	1.9	4.7	4.4	11.2	1.1	0	14.1
Florida (439)	18.7	28.2	20.1	2.3	5.7	1.1	10.3	1.0	0	12.6
Iowa (204)	36.3	10.8	8.8	2.9	5.3	6.9	7.4	7.8	1.5	12.3
Kentucky (59)	49.2	6.8	16.8	1.7	10.2	1.7	6.8	0	0	6.8
Maine (165)	40.0	16.4	8.5	3.0	5.4	2.4	14.6	.6	.6	8.5
Michigan (322)	19.9	35.4	8.1	2.1	12.1	5.0	11.2	1.6	1.2	3.4
Montana (180)	27.2	27.2	13.9	4.4	4.4	3.0	8.9	1.0	1.7	8.3
Nebraska (150)	35.3	13.3	4.7	5.3	9.1	4.7	11.3	1.3	1.0	14.0
South Dakota (92)	41.5	21.7	5.4	5.4	8.7	4.3	5.4	0	3.3	4.3
Kansas (41)	9.5	39.4	9.5	2.8	5.2	3.8	13.7	1.9	0	14.2
New York (174)	47.1	27.0	8.1	1.0	7.5	1.0	3.5	1.0	0	3.8
Ohio (173)	35.8	23.9	15.0	1.2	12.1	1.0	4.6	1.0	1.0	4.4
Pennsylvania (243)	32.8	30.8	10.3	1.0	12.4	1.2	7.8	1.6	0	2.1
Virginia (107)	18.7	62.6	8.4	3.7	1.9	0	1.0	0	0	3.7
Connecticut (175)	44.6	26.3	4.6	1.1	6.3	1.7	6.3	1.1	1.1	6.9
Indiana (136)	38.2	11.8	10.3	1.5	7.4	9.4	3.7	2.9	0	14.8
Rhode Island (60)	33.3	21.7	16.7	1.7	8.3	0	0	1.7	5.0	11.6

*Numbers in parentheses indicate total number of interest groups registered with the state.

ing. We could hardly justify a conclusion based upon the relation between magnitude of lobbying and power of lobbying units. Many of the registrations before the state legislatures are "one shot" affairs, and the lobbyist is not in attendance more than a few days during the session. However, evidence drawn from interviews with legislators also indicates that business groups are the most important contributors to the pressure system. This was true of states with such differing economic structures as Ohio, California, Tennessee, New Jersey, Michigan, and North Carolina.[21] Business associations are the most numerous group in Washington, as Schattschneider and Milbrath have established by different methods.[22] This means that "the business character of the pressure system," which Schattschneider discovered in examining groups engaged in lobbying before Congress, can also be extended to the states.

One basic difference between the representation of business in Washington and at the various state capitals is the extent to which businesses work directly with their own lobbyist rather than through an intermediary organization. In Washington, there are relatively few corporations functioning independently and most of their energy is directed toward securing defense contracts — an endeavor in which they are quite successful.[23] At the state level, an examination of the lobby registration will reveal that — with the exception of giants such as Anaconda and General Motors — most of these businesses are rather small and have only a local economic impact. In four of the states included in Table 4 (Florida, Kansas, Michigan, and Virginia) unaffiliated businesses outnumber associations, and in Montana and Pennsylvania the two categories are about equal.

It is probable that most of these businesses are interested only in specific legislation that occurs during a particular legislative session and do not look upon lobbying as a continuing function. An examination of the registrations of selected states indicates that relatively few businesses are represented for more than a single session. Those that send representatives for more than one session are usually large companies with a continuing interest in state policy. Of course, a more rigorous examination of this thesis is not available since employment figures are available only in rare instances. We can surmise, however, that McPherson's Drug Store or the Sanitary Laundry are not very permanent features of the pressure system of their respective states.

These data on the scope of state lobbying tell us nothing about the relative power of specific groups which might be numerically insignificant, but quite influential. The less than 3 per cent representation of farm groups in the Iowa legislature surely does not reflect the influence they might have. Indeed, the existence of relatively few groups interested in a particular policy area may actually indicate substantial cohesion and agreement among the group membership as opposed to the possible fragmentation of the membership of the more numerically significant groups. Also, it is impossible to know how many people are actually members of the various organizations. We would suspect that most of the organizations are rather small in membership, if the organizations listed in *National Associations of the United States* can be considered typical. Most of these organizations have a membership of less than one hundred.

To summarize the ideas of this section we may note the following conclusions:

1. Organized group activity is not the choice of people who might undertake an effort to influence government.
2. Organized group activity is perceived as an effective method of influence.
3. Membership in formal organizations is characteristic of urban populations.
4. Business associations are the most frequent participants in the influence process in state politics.

Schattschneider has examined data similar to that presented above and concluded that "pressure politics is essentially the politics of small groups" and that "probably 90 per cent of the people do not get into the pressure system."[24] It is probably correct that few people are actually personally involved in the pressure system and it is certainly true that very few people spend their leisure time in interest group affairs. Membership in a perceived political organization, which is even rarer than membership in a perceived non-political organization, is characteristic of a small but active minority. For instance, on the question of preferred methods of influencing government, only 1 per cent of the members of political organizations select individual efforts, whereas 16 per cent of the members of non-political organizations prefer this method. These active participants are more likely to live in large cities. For the purpose of a comparative state politics, therefore, we should expect greater group activity (as well as group membership) in the urban, industrial states which contain more people of this type than do the more rural states. Yet, while we can expect more organizational efforts in the industrial states we should not expect that group politics will necessarily be more prominent in actually influencing a government decision. We may suggest that a more open and competitive group politics would reduce the chances of the success of any given group. Organization for political action will produce counter-organization and, if the resources in the struggle approach equality, stalemate or compromise rather than total dominance may result.

THE POLITICO-ECONOMIC SETTING

The speculation which ended the previous section can be stated as an explicit hypothesis and tested. The argument is that within the states in which voluntary association membership should be the greatest the impact of interest groups on public policy is estimated to be the least. The greater participation in organizations in the urban states means that more group-anchored conflicts will come to the attention of the governmental decision-makers. The greater the number of demands which come to the attention of any single decision-making agency, the less likely will be the probability that any one set of demands will be able to maintain control over the content of policy.

THE LINK BETWEEN ECONOMIC AND POLITICAL VARIABLES. It is not difficult to establish the fact that the economic and social systems of a society structure its political system. It is more difficult to establish the manner in which these systems interact with each other. If we maintain that the socio-economic structure of a state structures the behavior and importance of interest groups, is it not likely that other components of the political system, such as political parties, are influenced too? Also, it is probable that the strength of the party system itself may inhibit or encourage interest groups. To illustrate, it has long been suggested that strong party cohesion in legislative voting contributes to a weakness of interest groups. However, if we examine the causes of party voting we find that, with considerable variation, there is a relationship between legislative cohesion and party competition. Further, if we probe deeper, both legislative cohesion and party competition are related to the industrialization and urbanization of a state. Accordingly, it is best to treat economic and political variables as components in a single system, rather than as independent or dependent variables.

The following table describes the American states in terms of three *political* variables:[25] strength of interest groups, strength of political parties, and legislative cohesion.*

*Because of certain methodological problems, the classification is subject to criticism. In deciding whether a state is characterized by strong, moderate, or weak pressure groups, questionnaires were sent to political scientists in each state. The limitations of this method are apparent. However, there is reason to assume that these evaluations are relatively accurate in view of the consistent patterns which appear in the economic and political factors associated with the three groups of states. The measure of legislative cohesion is taken from the same study but is not subject to the same criticism since objective evaluations of cohesion do exist. The extent of party competition, taken from Austin Ranney's classification, is appropriate since it relies only on state elections. One modification has been made in Ranney's classification. Modified one-party Democratic and modified one-party Republican are merged into a single category since the direction of the partisanship is of no concern.

Table 5

THE STRENGTH OF PRESSURE GROUPS IN VARYING POLITICAL AND ECONOMIC SITUATIONS

SOCIAL CONDITIONS	TYPES OF PRESSURE SYSTEM[a]		
	STRONG[b]	MODERATE[c]	WEAK[d]
Party Competition	*(24 states)*	*(14 states)*	*(7 states)*
One-party	33.3%	0%	0%
Modified One-Party	37.5%	42.8%	0%
Two-Party	29.1%	57.1%	100.0%
Cohesion of Parties in Legislature			
Weak Cohesion	75.0%	14.2%	0%
Moderate Cohesion	12.5%	35.7%	14.2%
Strong Cohesion	12.5%	50.0%	85.7%
Socio-Economic Variables			
Urban	58.6%	65.1%	73.3%
Per Capita Income	$1900	$2335	$2450
Industrialization Index	88.8	92.8	94.0

a. Alaska, Hawaii, Idaho, New Hampshire, and North Dakota are not classified or included.

b. Alabama, Arizona, Arkansas, California, Florida, Georgia, Iowa, Kentucky, Louisiana, Maine, Michigan, Minnesota, Mississippi, Montana, Nebraska, New Mexico, North Carolina, Oklahoma, Oregon, South Carolina, Tennessee, Texas, Washington, Wisconsin.

c. Delaware, Illinois, Kansas, Maryland, Massachusetts, Nevada, New York, Ohio, Pennsylvania, South Dakota, Utah, Vermont, Virginia, West Virginia.

d. Colorado, Connecticut, Indiana, Missouri, New Jersey, Rhode Island, Wyoming.

The table also links these factors with three *economic* variables, urban population, per capita income, and percentage of the population employed in occupations other than agriculture, forestry, and fishing (industrialization). Taken together, these economic factors indicate the existence or absence of a heterogeneous society with its corresponding increase or decrease in group tensions. Thus, a state that has a high per capita income, a high percentage of its population employed in industrial occupations, and a high proportion of its population living in urban areas should exhibit a strong and active group life, but not necessarily a strong pressure group system. This idea becomes clear if we examine the table. With regard to political variables, pressure groups are strongest when political parties and legislative cohesion are weakest. Concerning the economic variables, we see that pressure groups are strongest in states with a relatively backward economy. Combining both types of variables, there are two patterns which emerge. The first pattern consists of strong pressure groups, weak parties (both electorally and legislatively), low urban population, low per capita income, larger proportion of the population engaged in non-industrial occupations. The second pattern consists of moderate or strong pressure groups, competitive parties, an urban, industrial economy. In short, there is a clear relation between pressure politics, party politics, and socio-economic structure.

There are, of course, notable exceptions. For example, California and Michigan are hardly non-industrial, non-urban states, yet they have strong pressure groups. Nevertheless, it can be argued that the pattern is sufficiently clear and that the deviant states do not destroy the pattern. In the strong pressure group category we find every state in the South, the very states where the economy is less developed and organizational memberships are the fewest. What is it about these states that produces a strong pressure group system? If we follow the theory developed so far, we would maintain that it is not the non-industrial nature of the economy per se which is a fundamental cause, but rather that such economies are normally *non-diverse*. That is to say, the economies of such states tend to be dominated by a single type of enterprise. Industrial economies tend to be less keyed to a particular set of businesses and are less likely to be monopolized.

The hypothesis of this section — that urbanism and industrialism increase group membership but decrease group effectiveness — is contradictory to a recently published examination of state legislatures, *The Legislative System,* by Wahlke, Eulau, Buchanan, and Ferguson.[26] These authors consider the impact of interest groups in California, New Jersey, Ohio, and Tennessee. The selection of these states for analysis is fortunate for our purposes because it enables us to consider industrial, urban, politically competitive states in comparison to Tennessee which is well behind the others economically and is classified as modified one-party Democratic by Ranney. With regard to the importance of pressure politics, every test performed indicated that pressure politics were of greatest importance in California and of least importance in Tennessee (note that Tennessee is classified as having strong pressure groups in our table). It is not the fact that Tennessee is given a different classification in this chapter from that in *The Legislative System* which necessitates this explanation. Rather, it is because the reasons given for the weakness of pressure groups in Tennessee are directly opposed to our argument. The authors of *The Legislative System* maintain that the group life of Tennessee is less diverse and complex than any of the more industrial states which they examined. Since Tennessee is less pluralistic than the other states, it is not surprising that interviews with Tennessee legislators revealed that these legislators were *less aware* of specific organizations or interests than was true of legislators in the other states. Also, Tennessee legislators are most likely to resent the activities of pressure groups and be suspicious of their motives. Since the Tennessee legislators are more likely to resist or resent group activity and since Tennessee has a comparatively less developed character of pluralistic group life, the authors conclude that a less diverse group life contributes to a weak pressure system. They thus would maintain that group competition does not reduce effectiveness nor does the absence of such competition increase the potentiality for strong pressure groups. It is true that Tennessee's political party system is less developed than that of the other states, a fact which should contribute to strong pressure groups. However, judging by the response of the legislators, such is not the case. According to the arguments of this chapter, Tennessee should have a very strong pressure system for the same reasons that the authors of *The Legislative System* claim that it has a weak pressure system.

There are two points which should be made here. First, if Tennessee in fact has a weak pressure system then it is the only Southern, non-industrial state to be so classified. Since it is clearly atypical, there should be some explanation as to why this is the case, but there is nothing especially unusual about Tennessee. Second, while the hostility of Tennessee legislators toward group activity and their blurred perceptions of specific organizations is clearly established, does this necessarily retard pressure politics? For example, the excellent study of the Vermont legislature by Garceau and Silverman reveals the fact that Vermont legislators had a very low level of recognition of interest group activity.[27] Yet it appears that pressure groups played a major role in the formation of legislative policy. Garceau and Silverman describe the process whereby the Associated Industries of Vermont, an organization with membership employing about half the payroll of the state, negotiated with legislators and other organizations such as the C.I.O. and Farm Bureau (believed to be, in the words of the authors, "the most powerful organized group in the state"), in an effort to determine the content of an occupational disease bill. Clearly, the major actors in this particular legislative episode were pressure groups, but more than a third of the legislators had never heard of the Associated Industries of Vermont. The low visibility of pressure group activity is explained by Duane Lockard: "The amateur legislators of Vermont are often led by unseen operators who, unknown to the legislators, maneuver legislation through to ultimate approval."[28] It could be presumed that the "amateurs" were not aware of the fact that the Associated Industries of Vermont was "directly influential in the appointments of chairmen and members of the committees considered of probable concern to the business group."[29]

The use of the word "amateur" by Lockard brings up another possibility. The typical state legislator has not had much experience. Lockard notes that in Vermont — as is true of the approximately 7,660 state legislators in office at any particular time — about half are serving their first term. It would seem that these first-term legislators would be generally less likely to be aware of what is actually taking place. Thus, Wahlke, Eulau, Buchanan, and Ferguson found that there were more Facilitators (those having a friendly attitude toward pressure groups and knowledge of the extent of group activity) among the legislators with the most legislative service. They also found that there were fewer Facilitators in Tennessee than in Ohio, California, or New Jersey. It is of interest to note that the Tennessee legislators had considerably less previous experience than had those of the other states. In the Tennessee house, the median previous years' experience is 2.2 years, compared to 3.5 years in New Jersey, 4.8 in Ohio, and 5.2 in California. In the Tennessee senate the median previous years' experience is 4.6 years, compared to 5.0 years in New Jersey, 8.0 years in Ohio, and 8.4 years in California.

It may be possible that the Tennessee legislators, like those of Vermont, are not the best judges of the strength of pressure groups since they are inexperienced and not attuned to the subtleties of the legislative process and know least about pressure groups.

EMERGING PATTERNS OF GROUP CONFLICT. The fact that interest groups thrive in non-industrial states does not mean that there is a *single* pattern of group activity. There are, in fact, four distinct patterns which emerge from the strong pressure group category of states. First, there is the "typical" strong pressure group pattern consisting of a non-diversified economy, relatively non-competitive party politics, and weak legislative cohesion. This pattern is descriptive of the Southern states and of non-Southern states with similar economic and political systems, such as Maine. In these states the strength of interest groups is achieved by means of an *alliance of dominant groups*. Next, there is a pattern with an equally non-diversified economy but with two-party politics and moderate legislative cohesion, such as in Montana. Here we find that a *single dominant interest* strengthens the pressure system. Thirdly, we find a pattern consisting of a non-diversified industrial economy, two-party politics, and strong legislative cohesion. The best example of this pattern is Michigan where there is a *conflict between two dominant groups*. Finally, California is an example of a diverse economy, two-party politics, and weak legislative cohesion. A classic case of the free play of interest groups in a legislature unencumbered by demands originating from political parties, California is best described as the *triumph of many interests*. Note that these patterns have one of two characteristics in common. Either the economic structure of the state is non-diverse or the party system is weak. To understand how each of these systems operates, we shall explore them in some detail.

ALLIANCE OF DOMINANT GROUPS. A good sample of this pattern is Maine, of which Lockard writes: "In few American states are the reins of government more openly or completely in the hands of a few leaders of economic interest groups than in Maine."[30] Specifically, power, timber, and manufacturing — the "Big Three" — have proven to be the catalysts for much of the political controversy in the state. While other interests occasionally voice demands, the Big Three clearly outdistance any rivals in political activity and power. Certainly, the key position of these interests in the economy of the state contributes to their crucial position in the decision-making process of the state. Over three-fourths of the state is woodland and most of this land is owned by a handful of timber companies and paper manufacturers. These interests, combined with power companies and textile and shoe manufacturers, are able — insofar as their well-being is directly involved — to "control" Maine politics.

Maine, as is the case in other states with similar economic structure, went through a phase during which the dominant economic interests engaged in rather flamboyant lobbying techniques. More restrained today, the Big Three still are able to make certain that the content of public policy is to their liking. As examples of this ability, Lockard notes that, while Governor Muskie met with success in securing the passage of most of his legislative program, the largest portion of his defeats came on matters opposed by the Big Three. He was unable to establish an intrastate minimum wage; he could not establish a state labor relations commission; proposals to establish a state income tax and corporate franchise tax were also defeated. Perhaps most indicative of the power of economic interests in Maine was the defeat of a proposed water pollution law in 1955. In this case, in spite of a determined effort to convince the legislature that the prohibition of water pollution would not harm industry, the bill was defeated easily. Lockard concludes that the "predominant authority" of the Big Three is rarely challenged with any significant degree of organization or sustained effort.

Since non-diversified economics, weak parties, and strong pressure groups are a "normal" combination, it is not surprising that the political processes of Maine and that of the Southern states — most of which display this particular combination — are quite similar. V. O. Key, Jr., for example, describes the politics of Alabama: "The Extension Service — big farmer amalgam, which covers the entire state but is most potent in the black belt, usually teams up with the big money interests. . . . The 'big mules' probably exert their strength far more effectively in the politics of legislation than in gubernatorial campaigns. And it is mainly in the legislature that questions of concern for them are settled: measures of taxation and regulation."[31] At the time this was written, Alabama had an urban population of 30.2 per cent. Today, with an urban population of 54.8 per cent, Alabama is not quite so non-competitive a field of combat for the large farmer — "big mule" interests and labor organizations, for example, are becoming more active.

Increasing urbanization and industrialization do seem to contribute to a countervailance of interests against formerly dominant economic power groups. For example, organizations lobbying in favor of state right-to-work laws have generally been successful in Southern or Midwestern states where union membership is low and union political organization weak. Right-to-work laws have been easily defeated in states with strong and active unions, such as California and Illinois, and have never been a serious issue in other heavily unionized states, such as New York and New Jersey.[32] The pressure for the enactment of such legislation in states without right-to-work laws currently on the books is concentrated in such states as Maine, New Hampshire, New Mexico, Vermont, Idaho, Kansas and Delaware, few of which boast any appreciable union membership.[33] Also, in those states currently having right-to-work laws, there is some evidence of a counter-revolution as urbanization and industrialization increase. In Georgia, for example, labor leaders who remember the days when to speak favorably of organized labor on the floor of the General Assembly was to invite informal but severe censure have seen strong legislative support for improved workmen's compensation laws develop and have adopted the repeal of the state's right-to-work law as a long-range, but feasible, goal. One such leader writes: "Things were different at the State Capitol this year. The atmosphere has changed. Labor was treated in a much different manner. Labor was respected . . . we have our head in the door."[34]

A SINGLE DOMINANT INTEREST. In the case of Montana, the economy has become somewhat more diversified and the urban population has increased, but the dominant role of the Anaconda Company has been diminished by self-restraint in addition to competition. In a state in which the extraction of minerals is the major non-agricultural source of personal income, Anaconda is the largest employer. While "the company," as it is known in Montana, began its operations in mining for copper, it now owns mills, aluminum companies, railroads, fabricating plants and forests. The enormity of the Anaconda empire is described by Thomas Paine: "Its strength rests not only in its wealth and resources, but also in its elaborate network of relationships with key citizens, banks, legal firms, and business organizations throughout the state. Rare is that unit of local government — county, city, or school district — that does not have among its official family an associate, in some capacity, of the Anaconda Company."[35] In addition, Anaconda controlled, until 1959, a chain of newspapers with a combined circulation greater than that of all the other daily papers in the state.

In the turbulent frontier atmosphere of the West, Anaconda played the classic role of economic royalist. Its forays into the electoral process were frequent and extravagant. Indeed, politicians such as Burton K. Wheeler became legendary as courageous foes of the Company in much the same manner that Senator Borah built a political career upon the crusade against the trusts. Indeed, much of Montana's political history seems to reflect a basic division of the population: either you were for the Company, or (in the case of the unions and Farmer's Union) against it. In Wheeler's autobiography, the major theme running through the portions dealing with his career prior to becoming a Senator is the struggle against Anaconda. The conflict in the state seemed to be structured around the Company rather than the political parties. Wheeler writes: "In the 1911–1912 legislature the Democrats controlled the House, the Republicans controlled the Senate, and the Company controlled the leaders of both."[36]

The mainstream of public policy in Montana reflects the power of Anaconda, although it is hard to imagine an elite as invulnerable as the Company when described by its enemies. Montana politics is not completely dominated by Anaconda; the Company is a major actor which can claim success in many instances but has been forced to accept defeat under certain circumstances. For instance, its efforts to elect the "right" candidates met with only moderate success. Wheeler was consistently supported by organized labor and enjoyed electoral success in spite of (perhaps because of) the opposition of Anaconda.

The best example of the strength and weakness of Anaconda can be seen in the struggle to increase the taxation of mines. The mining companies had been successful in including an extraordinary clause in the state constitution at the time of Montana's admission to the Union. The clause provided that mining claims could be taxed only "at the price paid the United States therefor" and taxes on "net proceeds" could be levied. In accordance with this constitutional provision, oil production, which grossed only one-sixth as much as mines, paid twice as much in taxes; mines contributed less than 9 per cent to Montana's revenue while farms contributed 32 per cent. As early as 1917 the legislature had become aware of the inequities of such a situation, and in 1918 a faculty member of the University of Montana began a study of the tax system only to be dismissed by the Chancellor. The book based on the research was published, however, and Anaconda's role in its suppression became apparent. In the furor over the author's dismissal, the state board of education reinstated him with back pay.

The next step in the taxation episode took place in 1920 when Wheeler — with his reputation as an enemy of the Company — ran as Democratic candidate for governor against the Republican, Joseph Dixon, who ran with the support of the Company. Wheeler promised tax revision but was defeated by the Republican, who promptly urged the legislature to figure out some way to increase the taxes on mines. However, his proposal for a license tax based on each ton of ore produced was defeated in the legislature with Anaconda lobbyists working vigorously against the man the Company had supported in the election. To overcome his lack of influence with the legislature, the governor submitted the tax revision to the voters in the form of a referendum in the 1924 election. While Dixon, running now as the enemy of the Company, lost the election, the taxing proposal was approved, even though Anaconda maintained that "the mining industry cannot stand any additional tax load."[37]

Defeats such as this convinced the Company that its wisest course of action lay in more moderate demands. In the 1920's the Company press was vitriolic in its treatment of its opponents; in the 1930's the Anaconda-owned papers became less venomous and simply ignored its enemies by not mentioning them or their activities; by the 1940's and early 1950's the papers began to print hostile speeches and their editorials took on a rather neutral flavor; in the late 1950's the Company disposed of its newspapers. As its newspapers reflected a growing concern with its public image, it is not surprising that Anaconda in recent years has tended to remain as quiet as is possible, confining itself to blocking adverse legislation and reducing its efforts to influencing the electoral process.[38]

The experiences of Montana with Anaconda seem roughly parallel to those of other states with a single economic, dominant interest — such as oil in Texas or DuPont in Delaware. In both of these states the reputation for absolute control is widespread. However, it can be suggested that there is a difference between control and the potential for control, just as there is a difference between specific and generalized power. It is no doubt true that Anaconda is capable of protecting or enhancing its interest in areas of specific concern. Success in a specific area leads to assumptions (especially on the part of those who use power as a symbol to be attacked) about generalized power. Thus, we might ask: do the timber, paper, power and manufacturing interests control Maine or do they have the ability to direct partially the course of public policy as it impinges upon their interests? Does Anaconda "control" Montana or is it a significant and frequently decisive determinant of policy in its area of involvement? The same question could be asked of other states in which the dispute over policy is, to varying degrees, bipolarized by reasons of the concentration of economic power.

For instance, the chairman of the Texas Democratic State Executive Committee once said: "It may not be a wholesome thing to say, but the oil industry today is in complete control of state politics and state government."[39] No one needs to be reminded of the loyalty of Texas politicians to the oil depletion allowance in the federal tax structure, but this is a matter of direct and vital concern to the oil producers. A recent case study of the Texas legislature suggests that oil producers are indeed influential but are opposed by influential competitors. In this case, the 1961 session of the Texas legislature, in attempting to pass a tax bill, had to decide between income and sales taxes. The governor, attempting to avoid either solution, presented a program calling for, among other things, an increase in the severance tax on natural gas production. Manufacturing groups, led by the Texas Mid-Continent Oil and Gas Association, countered with the general sales tax proposal. The opposition to the governor was sufficient to insure that the sales tax would be the final solution, but the legislature also supported a tax on the natural gas pipeline companies.[40] Neither side enjoyed total victory; neither group of protagonists could be said to "control" the outcome of this particular issue, much less the sum of the decisions reached by the state government.

The confusion between power and the potentiality for power occurs most frequently in bipolarized states. It is only natural to presume that those who possess resources will choose to maximize them. Yet such is not the case. We have seen how Anaconda restricted its activities. Many other dominant economic interests have found it prudent to follow a similar course of action. In their study of American tariff policy, Raymond A. Bauer, Ithiel de Sola Pool, and Lewis A. Dexter found that large corporations were reluctant to speak openly of their views on foreign trade because of sensitivity about their public image. With so much weight to throw around, the giants were afraid of a public display of strength. In Delaware, for example, DuPont is traditionally protectionist, but none of the elected officials from the state feel that they are under pressure to oppose reciprocal trade. As the authors explain: "A business can be too big to be politically effective along some lines."[41] This is not to say that large companies are always the "good guys." Rather, unless such companies can operate within the processes of government being relatively secure from direct public participation, the fear of the reaction is sufficient to suggest restraint as the wisest course of action. Perhaps this provides a partial explanation as to why right-to-work laws are usually approved by legislatures in non-industrial states. In industrial states most large corporations are reluctant to attack labor unions directly.

CONFLICT BETWEEN TWO DOMINANT GROUPS. The states considered up to this point have had rather underdeveloped economies which, it is maintained, contributes to bipolarization of political conflicts. In Michigan, we have an industrial, urban, competitive state with strong cohesion in legislative parties — a combination of factors sharply deviant from the normal strong pressure group pattern. Michigan is the only state in the strong pressure group category which contains no single characteristic in common with the other states in this category, at least insofar as the variables in Table 5 are concerned. However, Michigan's economy is perhaps less diversified than even that of Montana. The economic life of the state is strongly keyed to the activities of the automotive industry, a fact which has contributed to periodic crises which probably would not have taken place in a more diversified economy. There is no doubt that a progressive diversification of the economy is taking place. In 1949, automotive workers accounted for 19.2 per cent of the non-farm employment of the state, 21.3 per cent of all wage and salary workers, and 44.1 per cent of the manufacturing wage and salary workers; by 1958 these percentages had declined to 12.4, 13.9, and 34.0, respectively.[42] Still, automobile manufacturers are the largest single employer.

Under these circumstances it is not surprising that the conflict between union and management has been a consistent theme running through Michigan politics since industrialization.[43] There are many organized interests in Michigan, as there are in most urban states, and surely the assumptions of a pluralistic theory of power are substantiated by the Michigan experience. However, as is the case in the other states examined so far, when matters of concern to powerful interest groups are raised, these groups become major actors in the formation of public policy. As Joseph LaPalombara concludes: ". . . no major issues of policy (taxation, social legislation, labor legislation, etc.) is *(sic)* likely to be decided in Michigan without the intervention, within their respective parties and before agencies of government, of automotive labor and automotive management."[44]

The major difference between Michigan and the other bipolarized states is the degree to which interest group cleavages have been mirrored and hence institutionalized in the structure of the political parties and the legislature. In Maine, the "Big Three" functioned to some extent within the Republican party, but the loose and sprawling nature of that organization made efforts at control hardly worth the effort since control of the party would not improve the chances of controlling the legislature. In Montana, Anaconda worked first with one party then with another, finally showing slightly more interest in the Republicans. However, in Michigan, LaPalombara speaks of the intervention of unions and management "within their respective parties."[45] This statement merely reflects the fact that the Michigan unions, especially the United Automobile Workers, are deeply involved in the affairs of the Democratic party while the automotive managers are equally involved in the Republican party. It would be an exaggeration to maintain that either of these two interests "controls" the party, but it is surely the case that labor and management are the most active and influential components of "their" parties.[46]

Neither management nor labor makes much of an effort to extend its base of operations beyond the parties, for the cohesion of the legislative parties is strong. On matters of labor legislation, the Michigan legislature reveals parties as cohesive as those of the House of Commons. For example, in the 1954 session of the legislature the indexes of cohesion on partisan roll-calls were seventy-seven for the house Democrats and seventy-five for the senate Democrats. However, on partisan roll-calls involving labor legislation the index of cohesion for house and senate Democrats was ninety-seven.[47]

It would seem, then, that the coincidence of cleavage contributes to an intensification of group conflict in Michigan. Rather than serving as moderators of group conflict — as the national parties do — the Michigan parties communicate interest group values to the electorate and to the governmental officeholders.[48] Still, the vigor of pressure groups does not mean that the Michigan parties function as auxiliaries; if anything, the reverse is true. Neither unions nor management are so cohesive as to avoid the periodic squabbles which allow other interests to compete more effectively. Further, if unions and management are the single largest contributors to their respective parties, it is these parties which maintain the machinery necessary for the contesting of elections. It would be hard to imagine the United Automobile Workers deciding to withdraw support from the Democratic party.[49] Key's description of the pressure group as a "junior partner" in the alliance with a party holds true even in Michigan.[50] The unions must remain Democratic in order to maintain a viable bargaining position. If the pressure group has little choice but to support party candidates, the party usually assumes a position of dominance.

A comparison might be made with the behavior of interest groups in Washington (two-party) and Massachusetts (two-party). In Washington, the degree of affiliation between pressure groups and parties is as close as in Michigan, but there is no basic economic cleavage contributing to bipolarized conflict. Pressure group leaders are frequently party officers, and voluntary associations play a significant role both in the financial support of candidates and the writing of party platforms. Such close association in the electoral process leads individual legislators frequently to use interest group personnel for staff assistants.[51] In this case, while the relation between interest groups and parties is as close as is the case in Michigan, there is no counterpart of the United Automobile Workers or automobile manufacturers. Candidates, with a much less centralized party apparatus than that of Michigan, are on their own during political campaigns and are obliged to create their own personal organization and draw upon the resources of interest groups.

In Massachusetts the relation between interest groups and parties may be described as falling between the two extremes of Washington and Michigan. Here the parties are as centralized and competitive as in Washington, but the economy of the state is more diversified. While labor is firmly aligned with the Democrats and business with the Republicans, the primacy of the party is firmly established: "In Massachusetts . . . the party organizations sit astride the channels through which all legislation must flow, a fact to which the pressure group must accommodate itself."[52] Of course, both labor and business have easy access to the leaders of their respective parties and, at least in the case of labor, the role of interest groups in campaigns seems equally as vital as in Michigan. Also, as in Michigan, more time is spent lobbying within the party than in direct contacting of legislators. Still, even with these similar features, the role of interest groups in the formation of policy is more significant in Michigan than in Massachusetts.

These examples bring home again the notion that interest groups are most powerful where parties are weak or the economy undiversified. Of course, a lesson to be learned from the situations in Massachusetts, Michigan, and Washington is that strong parties do not necessarily mean a reduction of interest group strength but rather a channeling of the *direction* of the pressure toward the party.

THE TRIUMPH OF MANY INTERESTS. The economic structure of California is more diversified than that of any state considered in this analysis. Raw materials, which were primarily derived from forest land in Maine, for example, are abundant and of considerable variety in California. Manufacturing enterprises run the gamut from cement to motion pictures, and agriculture is far from a single crop activity. Under these circumstances, while the economic basis for strong pressures is apparent, the structure of economic activity leads to a fragmentation of interest group activity. Indeed, the diversification of the economy and the attendant competitiveness of the political game make it difficult to comprehend the strength that interest groups have been able to develop in California.

At one point in the history of California, a single interest — the railroads, especially the Southern Pacific — did dominate both parties and the legislature.[53] However, the national reaction against the "trusts" which arose in the early years of the 20th century contributed to a wave of reformism in California. This reformism weakened the parties and, ironically, paved the way for pressure groups which, even when the most lurid and sensational exposés are discounted, were perhaps more powerful than those at any other state legislature. One feature of party-weakening reform was the system of cross-filing in elections. From 1917 until 1954 the election laws of California provided that a person could contest both the Democratic and Republican nominations without his party affiliation appearing on either ballot. In 1952 party labels were required, and in 1959 the system was abolished. The system of cross-filing seriously weakened the ability of the party to assume any significance in the consciousness of the legislator. Further, the lack of any effective party organization left candidates to the state legislature on their own as they sought adequate funds for campaigning. As in the Southern one-party states, the interest groups of California were willing and anxious to meet this need for capital.

The spectacular nature of California politics and lobbying attracted reporters and resulted in some extravagant statements concerning the nature and source of interest group strength in California.[54] Recently, California politics has come under the scrutiny of more systematic observers. The superb study of the California legislature by William Buchanan takes a careful look at interest groups in California and concludes that the sensationalism of journalism should not obscure the fact that, especially during the "lobby era" of 1942–1953, the initiation of public policy was largely the responsibility of organized groups.[55]

During the administration of Governor Earl Warren, the practice of cross-filing became quite common and the viability of parties diminished. Buchanan notes that: "The advantage went to the candidate who best could obscure his party affiliation, attract or pay for attention in the press, and wrangle endorsements from editors and the local units for pressure groups." Very few legislators could afford to meet the costs of such requirements and very few could resist the temptation of easy money from interest groups. The interest-dominated environment of California is well illustrated by the perceptions of legislators of their career patterns. Nine per cent of the California legislators referred to interest groups as sponsors of their careers as compared to 1 per cent in New Jersey and 2 per cent in Ohio. Only in Tennessee, with parties less competitive than those in California, did legislators (16 per cent) refer to interest groups as sponsors more frequently.[56]

In one sense, the interest groups of California actually resembled political parties in organization. The most famous of the lobbyists, Artie Samish, expended a great amount of money and energy in the electoral process. Samish began his career as a lobbyist for bus companies in the 1930's but soon began to expand his operations to include a host of other interests, including the California State Brewers' Institute, railroads, horse racing, gambling, motion pictures, and many others.[57] It is not unusual in the state legislatures for lobbyists to represent more than one client. Moreover, Samish was a successful agent for his numerous clients. In most cases legislators see relatively little of multi-group lobbyists because they are frequently responsible for a series of explicit and limited interests which are concerned with a small portion of the legislative output. There is little doubt, however, that Samish's influence with the California legislature was considerable. Buchanan maintains that Samish's influence was developed not from the fact that his clients were affluent but because he welded the diverse interests he represented into an organization which performed the function of a political party in the individualized environment of California politics. The common denominator of these interests was that they were all industries new to the state when Samish began to recruit his organization in the 1930's. The main thrust of Samish's efforts was the prevention of state taxation of these enterprises. Other constellations of interest groups functioned simultaneously with the Samish organization but not necessarily in competition with it. For example, a "conservative lobby" of insurance companies, large farmers, and utilities were interested in preventing any departure from an anti-tax philosophy and found cooperation with the Samish organization useful. This collection of interest groups, essentially non-ideological like a typical American political party, selected candidates to run for office and supplied them with the funds for effective campaigning. When campaign costs were high and parties unwilling to pull their share of the load, the Samish organization was the single cohesive factor in the life-style of the legislator. Of this situation, Buchanan writes:

> In the absence of adequate party machinery at the local level they (interest groups) took over what is ordinarily the party's function of financing and managing campaigns. Thus they came to restrict the potential candidate's route of access to legislative power. It is not difficult then to snatch from the limp hands of the party the privilege of organizing the legislative chambers. Once influential in legislative organization, lobbyists could make attractive offers of exchange of power inside the legislature.[58]

The California experience is somewhat special due to the unusual legal restrictions on partisan activity. However, it affords us an opportunity to speculate on the relationship of parties and pressure groups in a period of flux. The addition of party labels to the ballot in 1952 coincided with structural reforms in the legislature which gave political parties a part in organization of that body. During the same period the legislature, stung by national publicity surrounding the activities of lobbyists, passed a lobby control act. An embryonic partisanship — expressed first in the form of factional alignments — indicated that the legislature was moving away from lobby dominance and toward active participation by parties. In 1957, the year the California legislators were interviewed in connection with the preparation of *The Legislative System,* partisanship still had not developed to a degree comparable with other urban, competitive states. Three out of five legislators believed parties played little or no part in the legislative process, a proportion nearly as high as that of Tennessee, a weak minority party state. It is significant, however, in this unsettled situation that the Democratic party was judged to be more influential than the Republican party. While legislators did not *perceive* parties as influential, roll-call analysis indicates that party membership accounted for more divisions in voting than any other characteristic of the members. Hence, party influence was growing and was more important than the members themselves believed.

Did emerging partisanship reduce the influence of interest groups? We should be cautious not to imply a single cause-effect relationship. After all, legislative salaries had increased to the point where it was possible to survive in Sacramento without the largess of lobbyists, and the exposés of Artie Samish had reduced the legitimacy of lobbying to some extent. Further, lobbying by the Samish organization had developed during the 1930's, a period which, by California standards, was partisan. Nevertheless, there does appear to be some inverse relationship between the strength of parties and interest groups. As the parties began to play some role, however small, in the legislative process they also began to meet campaign costs, reducing the necessity of interest groups. In terms of legislative output, the challenge to the interest groups by parties resulted in the first significant increase in beer taxes in 1959, despite the prediction of the brewers (once the heart of the Samish organization) that the tax could be defeated.

CONTRASTING PATTERNS: STATES WITHOUT A DOMINANT PRESSURE SYSTEM. A strong party system contributes to a balancing of the power between parties and interest groups or, in some cases, to a clear dominance of the parties. If the strength of parties produces a more balanced distribution of power, we can expect to find that interest groups are vigorous and active, but clearly dependent upon parties for access to governmental decision-makers. Contributions are channeled to the candidate through the party organization, and it is to the party that the fealty of the candidate is owed. Further, there is a tendency for each party to develop its own constellation of interests from which support can be expected. These interests rarely attempt to persuade individual legislators to cast a favorable vote on a specific issue but rather devote their attention exclusively to party leaders. In these situations it is clear that the party is in control. In Connecticut, for example, parties are able to punish an interest group if its demands become intolerable.

In contrast to this pattern of cooperation, Missouri is an example of a genuinely low pressure system. Salisbury has described the pressure system of Missouri as one of *ad hoc* rather than permanent alliances. He finds that broad coalitions of groups in conflict with rival combinations do exist, but are a rare phenomenon.[59] The shifting, temporary issue-oriented alliances in Missouri cannot compete with the stable and competitive party system. Lacking a major economic cleavage, interest groups have not developed either the ability to work closely with a party as in Michigan or the power to circumvent and dominate the parties as in Maine or California. In fact, Missouri and California have similarly diverse economies. It is probable that, had California not undergone its unique historical development, its pressure system would have been as weak as Missouri's. Diffusion and fragmentation of power, a pluralistic situation endemic to most industrial, urban states, provides parties with the opportunity to function without severe competition from interest groups.

LOBBYING AS A COMMUNICATIONS PROCESS

In order to achieve success in state politics, the interest group must have access to key decision-makers. Up to this point, factors within the political and socio-economic system over which interest groups have no control have been described in terms of their impact upon the performance of groups. It is true that such factors structure and limit the activities of interest groups and that success or failure is probably more dependent upon the nature of the society than upon the skills or techniques of lobbyists. Nevertheless, it is within the power of interest groups to maximize whatever advantages accrue to them because of their place within a social system. A high status manufacturers' organization might sacrifice its initial advantage by lobbying techniques which offend the sensibilities of legislators or make it difficult for them to vote the way the organization would prefer. If, for example, such an organization publicly threatens to defeat all legislators who vote the "wrong" way, it may be necessary for these legislators to establish their independence by voting against the wishes of the organization. Access, then, does depend to some extent upon skills. In lobbying, as in any other profession, such skills are acquired by experience and practice. A pertinent question is: how experienced are state lobbyists?

THE CHARACTERISTICS OF STATE LOBBYISTS. The available information does not present a picture of *most* state lobbyists as more professional at their job than the legislators are at theirs. In fact, the proportion of newcomers to the lobbying ranks seems to be about the same as the proportion of newcomers to the legislature. Patterson found that about 47 per cent of his sample of forty-three Oklahoma lobbyists were registered for their first term at the time of the interview.[60] An examination of the lobbying records of the states which make such information available indicate that Oklahoma is typical in lobbyist turnover.

There are, without doubt, many experienced lobbyists just as there are experienced legislators. However, to lament the amateurism of the legislator is to forget that the lobbyist, mythology to the contrary, is not any more of a professional. Walter DeVries' study of lobbying in Michigan, for example, points out that the majority of lobbyists are not very frequent visitors to Lansing; only a core of regulars are really familiar with the vagaries of the legislative process. Of equal significance is that not very many lobbyists spend their full time in lobbying during the session. Patterson found that over 60 per cent of the Oklahoma lobbyists spend half their time or less engaged in lobbying. In North Carolina, 59 per cent of the lobbyists interviewed indicated that they spend no more than half their time in lobbying.[61]

Finally, there should be some mention of lobbying specialization. If it is to be argued that legislators do not have the time to become fully informed about specific areas of public policy and, therefore, look to representatives of the interested organizations to supply information (this is, in fact, a basic function of lobbying), then what can we say of the lobbyists who are on retainer from several organizations — in some cases dozens — to handle a

particular problem? Approximately one-fourth of the lobbyists registering in
the states represent more than one client. Judging from what little evidence
can be gathered from the various changes in registration, most of the lobbyists with multiple clients change clients as the issues being debated before the
legislature change. Thus, in one session lobbyists for brewers and bankers
might return for the next session as lobbyists for bakers and butchers. Of
course, such lobbyists would make only sporadic appearances. In fact, the
number of registered lobbyists at any given session is not a very reliable guide
to the intensity of group activity because the majority of lobbyists are not to
be seen more than once or twice during a session. It is likely that the full-time
lobbyists are not those retained for a specific assignment by a number of
clients. Like legislative skills, lobbying skills develop with experience and
practice; like state legislators, such experience is possessed by relatively few
lobbyists.

What kinds of backgrounds do state lobbyists have? One striking difference between the backgrounds of state and national lobbyists is the relative
absence of lawyers among the ranks of the state lobbyists. Milbrath found
that most Washington lobbyists were lawyers, but in none of the states for
which we have information is the proportion of lawyers this high. In Oklahoma, only four out of a sample of forty-three indicated law as their occupation. Twelve per cent of the Michigan lobbyists were lawyers; however, in
Virginia and North Carolina the respective percentages were 46 and 41.[62]
Whether the higher proportion of lawyers as lobbyists in Southern states is
coincidence or reflective of the cultural or political structure of the South
cannot be ascertained from so few cases. The largest single occupational
category in both Oklahoma and North Carolina is that of full-time executive
or employee of an association engaged in lobbying; in Virginia, association
executives are second to lawyers. Beyond this category, there is little pattern
in the occupational background of lobbyists. At any rate, it is certainly
worthy of attention to note the absence of lawyers, because of the popularly
held assumption that legal experience contributes to political effectiveness.
The only study which explicitly tests the relationship between occupation
and effectiveness is DeVries' study of Michigan which found no statistically
significant relationship. Lobbyists who were lawyers were no more effective
than lobbyists who were not.

It would seem that interest groups would be anxious to employ people
who had such knowledge, and that ex-legislators would be eagerly sought
after. This may be the case, but relatively few ex-legislators ever become
lobbyists. Zeller, Patterson, Epstein, and DeVries have called attention to
the absence of ex-legislators among lobbyists before state legislatures; North
Carolina conforms to the pattern.[63] This does not mean that ex-legislators
are not useful as lobbyists. Indeed, DeVries' study suggests that there is a

significant relationship between any amount of legislative experience and lobbying effectiveness. Thus, while a group employing an ex-legislator may have an advantage, very few groups are so fortunate. On the other hand, quite a few lobbyists have had some form of governmental or political experience. This experience may be at the executive level or perhaps at the local level. While evidence sufficient for a firm generalization is lacking, it is probable that, of those lobbyists with governmental experience, most come from non-legislative, governmental careers. DeVries found no significant relationship between non-legislative experience and lobbying effectiveness, confirming that legislative service provides the most desirable background. Moreover, there is a significant relationship between *length* of government service and effectiveness: the longer the experience, the greater the effectiveness. The same sort of relationship exists with regard to experience in a political party. Milbrath noted that the Washington lobbyists find it useful to avoid partisan activity and that "the party with which a man identifies appears to be relatively unimportant in lobbying."[64] The competitive nature of Congress would make open partisanship hazardous, but in states in which one party can be relied upon to control the legislature the risks are less and the advantages considerable. Although Patterson found that few Oklahoma lobbyists had held party positions, this condition did not hold for Michigan and North Carolina where more than half the lobbyists had been active in party affairs. Membership in the dominant legislative party (the Democrats in North Carolina and Republicans in Michigan) is an asset to the lobbyists who can use party ties as a means of access to legislators. Thus, in Michigan, the lobbyists with a considerable number of years in the Republican party were more effective than those lacking such experience. Certainly this would be the case in a state in which the party played a major role in the determination of public policy. A strong party system does not necessarily mean the diminution of the influence of interest groups but may mean a channeling of pressure toward holders of party office rather than toward the party rank and file. This is the case in Michigan and Massachusetts, for example, where labor organizations serve frequently as auxiliaries to the parties.

MONEY: HOW NECESSARY FOR ACCESS IS IT? In establishing a satisfactory relationship with a group of legislators, the use of money cannot be ignored but can be put in proper perspective. In the first place, it is relatively easy for journalists to nod knowingly at the magic power of money and assume that merely by uttering the word they have offered the insider's explanation of how legislation is enacted. What does money buy? How is money spent? These are questions frequently left unanswered. Consider for example the case of entertainment. Reports on various states such as Wisconsin, Florida, and Michigan suggest that lobbyists at the state level do more entertaining than do lobbyists in Washington.[65] However, it does not appear that lobbyists rate entertaining as high as other techniques and that its role is exaggerated by popular accounts. Also the style of entertaining is probably more circumspect than might be expected. While some lobbyists maintain an open bar for legislators, most entertaining seems to fall into the category of lunches for small groups or annual dinners for the entire legislature. It is likely that such affairs are more in the nature of creating access than in the discussion of explicit legislation. A lobbyist who relied upon entertaining exclusively would not be very successful; however, at least in Michigan, the more effective lobbyists spend more time entertaining than the less effective ones.

We can exclude overt bribery from our consideration of state lobbying because it is either extremely rare or impossible to substantiate. On the other hand, contributions to political campaigns can be an important part of group strategy. Realistically speaking, money does not win elections. If it did, Republicans would win more than they do. However, money can create a relationship of gratitude and trust. Politicians seeking public office have basic campaign costs to meet, and those organizations willing to meet some or all of these costs certainly can be assured of at least formal access to decision-makers. The Artie Samish organization in California was perhaps the prototype of the interest using money for this purpose. More recent examples are equally useful because we can compare the use of campaign contributions in states with competitive and non-competitive party systems. The basic difference seems to be that in the competitive systems the contributions are channeled to candidates through the party organization, while in one-party systems the contact between candidate and organization is not marred by an intermediary. Within the competitive systems, a distinction can be made between groups which contribute with a specific goal in mind and groups which make contributions because of general agreement with a political party. Turning to the first example, Andrew Hacker's study of the conflict between railroads and truckers in Pennsylvania is instructive. The truckers, undertaking a long and arduous campaign to repeal a state law limiting the weight of trucks to 45,000 pounds, contributed heavily to the campaigns of state legislators. The specific goal was the repeal of the law; the partisan sympathies of the trucking companies were of no concern. Therefore the $76,000 collected by the Pennsylvania Motor Truck Association was divided almost equally between the parties. It is clear that the organization expected to recoup this expenditure by revenue gained from a more favorable weight law, a point made by Hacker: "Many of the men who voted for S.615 (to increase the permissible weight of trucks) knew that they were doing so to repay a campaign debt or in anticipation of future contributions . . . they consciously made a bargain to limit their freedom in return for a payment."[66]

Such an unequivocal exchange is unlikely to take place in situations where groups with more continuing and long-range goals are giving the money. The best example is, of course, organized labor. Labor contributions usually flow through the offices of the Democratic party on a more or less permanent arrangement. Labor organizations are — because of their relatively large membership — also anxious to offer their services in the mobilization of voters for the Democratic party. Alexander Heard points out that the financial resources and potential voting strength of unions are concentrated in seventeen* states where the percentage of union members among persons of voting age equalled or exceeded the national percentage and in which the percentage of non-agricultural employees was thirty or more.[67] In such states as Massachusetts and Michigan, the collaboration between the unions and the Democratic party is complete to the point where the unions serve as auxiliary parties and assume many of the responsibilities of the formal party organization. We have already touched upon the situation in Michigan; of Massachusetts, Lockard writes, "In some areas the Democratic party . . . will leave to labor almost the whole job of campaigning for state candidates, and in many campaigns the money labor gives is a very crucial factor in the Democratic effort."[68] In other states of the seventeen mentioned by Heard, the collaboration is less formal. In Washington, for example, the unions are friendly to the Democratic party but have not infiltrated to the extent of those in Michigan and Massachusetts. The point is that these contributions are probably not accompanied by explicit expectations. Also, it is likely that, at least in Michigan and Massachusetts, less money filters down to candidates to the state legislature and more ends up in the coffers of gubernatorial candidates.

In one-party states, the exchange between candidate and interest groups is more explicit in the absence of a party organization. Joseph Bernd's investigation of contributions in Georgia shows that about 50 per cent of the money received by major candidates for governor came from liquor dealers and highway contractors, both of which have clear and narrowly defined expectations.[69] Here, again, the money flows past the legislature to the place where it is thought it can do the most good.

While campaign contributions do form part of the strategy of those groups in state politics able to afford it, it would hardly be accurate to assume that it plays a more important role at the state than the national level. Certainly in terms of the total amount of money spent, the state political process would come off a poor second. However, it may be suggested that a little money goes a longer way at the state level, where candidates are personally

*The states are: New York, Pennsylvania, California, Illinois, Ohio, Michigan, New Jersey, Indiana, Massachusetts, Missouri, Wisconsin, Washington, Minnesota, West Virginia, Oregon, Montana, and Nevada.

less well-off and of lower general social status than are candidates to the national legislature.[70]

Money may also be used in public relations campaigns but, with a few notable exceptions, state interest groups are not as concerned with the "new lobby" technique of mass persuasion. Examples of the use of public relations campaigns usually appear where the state interest groups have an affiliation with a national organization which provides much of the propaganda. For instance, the struggle over right-to-work laws has attracted national organizations which supply state units or sympathetic, but unaffiliated, organizations with literature, arrange for public meetings, and the like. The same set of circumstances seems to apply to the perennial conflict between trucking companies and railroads in which the representatives of the respective national associations have displayed an understandable interest. The relatively slight use of public relations at the state level is not difficult to understand. The indirect communication of the mass media, for example, is not presumed to be as persuasive as personal communication. Since the state legislators are generally more accessible than their national counterparts, the use of indirect methods to create a favorable climate of opinion is not really necessary. Daily attendance at the state capitol, the cultivation of key legislators, the establishment of feelings of respect and confidence on the part of those legislators who have authority in the area of interest to the lobbyist and his organization — these are the preferred techniques of experienced lobbyists.

THE ADVANTAGE OF THE DEFENSE. Groups whose basic goal is defensive and who are satisfied with the status quo and concern themselves primarily with maintaining it have a better chance of success than those who try to alter the existing distribution of values. In Michigan, high-status groups such as manufacturers or professional associations have been able to play the role of policeman with considerable success, while groups such as labor unions which are struggling for social change feel they are at a disadvantage. The coexistence of high-status groups and defensive posture is not coincidental, but does not necessarily mean that labor unions will usually be on the attack in the state legislatures. In Massachusetts, for example, the unions spend practically all their time in a consciously defensive set of maneuvers to prevent the opposition from *weakening* existing labor laws. Of course, labor's most consistent defensive position has been against right-to-work laws. In states listed by Heard as being those with the greatest concentration of union membership, the union lobbyists can play the role of policeman while it is the job of the business groups to induce the legislature to change the status quo. An excellent description of the policeman's role is given by the following account:

One morning in late January the four-man legislative team of the Oregon A.F.L.-C.I.O. in Portland was scanning the batch of bills dropped into the hopper of the newly-convened legislature the previous day.

This was a daily routine for the labor watchdog committee. An important part of the job was to read every bill introduced in the two branches of the legislature as a safeguard against reactionary attacks on the rights of working people in the state.[71]

The author of this statement goes on to relate how the labor lobbyists discovered a "backdoor" right-to-work law hidden in legislation which seemed on the surface to be unrelated to labor-management relations. A civil rights bill introduced by a Republican legisator would have amended the Oregon Fair Employment Practices Act to provide that no person should be denied a job because of race, religion, color, or "membership or non-membership in any organization of any kind." The quoted words were the extent of the proposed amendment. The discovery of this "sleeper" by the labor lobbyists and the subsequent death of the amendment in committee illustrate not only the value of the defense but also the necessity for full-time, rather than amateur, lobbyists.

LOBBYING TECHNIQUES: THE COMMUNICATION OF INFORMATION. Turning now to the specific techniques of influence, a word of caution should be offered. We cannot assume that, merely because the more experienced lobbyists are more successful, their experience includes knowledge of the ways to manipulate legislators, to guide unpopular legislation through a series of hostile entrapments and, in general, to utilize "pressuring." In practice, the role of the skilled lobbyist is far less dramatic. Generally, his job can be little more than that of an agent serving to *communicate* the position of a group on a given issue to someone who he believes will have some control over the outcome.[72] Of course, it is also part of the lobbyist's job to communicate the notion of group power, but this is largely a matter determined without the intervention of lobbying skills. Actually, when we say that the job of the lobbyist is communication, we have given him quite an assignment, for it does not follow that his role is merely the automatic transmission of information. To whom should communications be addressed? When is the proper time to approach a legislator? How should the argument be phrased? Such questions are not answered the same way for every situation.

Recent studies of Washington lobbying all have a similar thrust: lobbying is very rarely directed at legislators who have taken a position in opposition to the desired goals of the group employing the lobbyist. Most contact between lobbyist and legislator is typically that of two partisans reinforcing agreement.[73] In this context, "pressure" is not a very useful concept. In the legislature, as with the general public, "pressure" is a tactic only opponents engage in. If the legislator and lobbyist have similar goals, communication is likely to be perceived as the legitimate expression of a sound point of view. Consequently, the feeling that the legislature is under considerable pressure (if the legislators feel this to be the case) probably indicates either that the lobbyists are talking to the wrong people or the legislator "has heard" of great pressure (on the part of his opponents). In addition to the evidence gathered about the national legislative process, a study of the Indiana legislature is in conformity with these suggestions. The study records the correlation between the occupational affiliation of the legislator with attitudes toward specific interest groups. It finds that the clearest relationship is that of sympathetic identification between legislators and lobbyists from the same occupational category. Thus, legislators whose occupation is farming rank the Farm Bureau first in order of agreement with organizational goals; businessmen agreed with the goals of business groups, etc. Naturally, there is a relationship between the attitudes of the legislator and his ranking of the legislative efficiency of the various groups. Legislators who agreed generally with the goals of a particular organization rank that organization somewhat higher in effectiveness than those groups with which they disagree. Democrats ranked the A.F.L.-C.I.O. higher than the Farm Bureau, while the order is reversed for the Republicans.[74] However, the question which elicited this response was phrased so as to equate effectiveness with the group's skill in presenting its case to the legislature, a judgment which would be colored by the values of the legislator. A rural Republican would hardly credit labor with much skill in presentation. Yet when the question was phrased to include the word "powerful" a different set of responses was obtained. In this case, legislators who disagreed with the policies of the group were more likely to name that group as powerful. The evidence of occupational sympathies in Indiana demonstrates again the amateur status of state legislators. Since serving in the state legislature is in many cases a part-time job, legislators retain active ties with their businesses or professions. The possibility of "built in" access exists because state legislatures are likely to contain more people without the perspective of a career politician and more people engaged in private business on an active basis than in the national legislature. Given interest group members who are actually an official part of the legislative process, the job of lobbying is eased considerably.

CHOICES OF STRATEGIES. In establishing a contact with a friendly legislator to transmit the position of his organization, the lobbyist has a choice of strategies. He can elect to operate primarily through the official channels of the legislature. Testimony at committee hearings is the most usually em-

ployed device of this type. The lobbyist can also try to develop a personal relationship with as many legislators as possible so that they will look upon him
as reliable and dependable. If he is successful, the formal testimony of the
hearing room can be supplemented with informal conversation. If he represents a wealthy organization the establishment of a personal relationship
might be undertaken by means of entertainment — the "social lobby." Other
methods of communication are more indirect. The lobbyist can urge members of his organization to write or contact a legislator personally, or his
organization can engage in a long-range public relations campaign intended
to impress both members and non-members in the hopes that some of these
people will feel inclined to take action. Organizations may hope to establish
communication through gratitude and invest funds in the campaigns of legislators. Needless to say, methods of establishing communication channels
like the last mentioned are reserved to those few organizations affluent enough
to undertake such activities on a continuing basis. Of course, an organization
may try any combination of these methods but usually there is a distinct
preference for one, depending both on the nature of the organization and
the particular characteristics of the situation. It is also true that lobbying
techniques depend to some extent upon the political system in which the
lobbying takes place. For example, interest groups have been able to establish
a more permanent web of interaction with administrative agencies than they
have with the legislature because of the inherently monopolistic tendencies
of administrative politics. At the state level, each agency will have responsibility for a narrowly defined set of operations and will come into almost daily
contact with a clientele whose interests are affected by the agency's operations.
Thrown into constant association with a specific clientele, administrators see
very little of a more general public and gradually tend to identify their values
with those of their clientele. The establishment of a set of mutually shared
values between agency and clientele can be useful not only in turning legislative defeat into administrative victory but also in the pursuit of group goals
through legislation. A combination of private interest group and public agency
is a valuable one in the event that a group without access to the administrative
agency tries to change the structure of power through the legislature.[75]

Because of the more unstructured nature of state legislatures, more time
is devoted to the cultivation of valuable personal relationships. Consequently,
the full-time, experienced lobbyists prefer to operate as what Patterson calls
"contact men." In his article on Oklahoma, Patterson describes the contact
man as one who:

> . . . conceives of his job as primarily that of making contacts, personal
> acquaintanceships and friendships with various legislators, and of main-
> taining these contacts. The Contact Man provides a direct communica-
> tions link between the interest group and the individual member of

the legislature. When faced with a legislative problem for his group, the lobbyist with a Contact Man orientation is likely to propose as the solution the personal contacting of as many members of the legislative body as possible, directly presenting the interest group's case to them.[76]

Patterson found that more than half the Oklahoma lobbyists were contact men but, more important, a substantially greater portion of the contact men were on the job more than half the time. Similar findings appear in DeVries' study of Michigan. The lobbyists who were in the top portions of the effectiveness scale were more likely to rely on personal presentation of arguments than those at the bottom of the scale, and less likely to rely on formal presentation at committee hearings than those at the bottom of the scale. In North Carolina, the same pattern prevailed; formal presentation was regarded as a less effective method than personal presentation. Of course, most organizations do arrange for formal testimony but the impression prevails that this is more for the sake of form — for showing the required amount of interest and enthusiasm — than for the sake of persuasion. There is an interesting comparison that can be made with the national legislative process on the question of preferred lobbying techniques. Milbrath discovered that, while the Washington lobbyists feel direct personal communication to be their most effective method, they spend little of their time in direct conversations with legislators.[77] Thus it may well be that the state legislative process, because of its relative informality, facilitates the direct approach.

While it may be true that the state legislative process presents more opportunities for direct access to legislators, the contact men must be in a position to use this access to best advantage. Stated simply, there must be a sufficient amount of trust between legislator and lobbyist so that the legislator will feel that the statements of the lobbyist can be relied upon for their accuracy. Pressure groups are most readily accepted by legislators if they avoid a mere assertion of demands and provide information useful to legislators as they try to develop an accurate picture of the situation. Lobbyists who have established a reputation for reliability are more likely to be effective contact men than lobbyists whose reputation is for pressuring or threatening. An interesting example of how *not* to be a successful lobbyist comes from Colorado. In this case the Colorado Motor Carriers Association, in trying to defeat a gross ton-mile tax, relied upon the "old style lobby" techniques. Lavish entertainment, threats to defeat legislators at the polls, and even, it is said, threats to persuade bankers to call in overdue notes owed by legislators favoring the tax were prominent in this campaign. Legislators apparently were unimpressed by these efforts and they doubted the authenticity of the technical information supplied by the truckers' association. Threats to call a strike of truckers, to move trucking concerns out of the state, and to refuse to pay the new tax contributed further to a deterioration of the relationship between the interest group and the legislature. At any rate, the lobbyist responsible for the drive against the tax was dismissed.[78]

THE FLOW OF COMMUNICATION. The question of whom to contact is answered to some extent by the structure of the legislature and the role of the political party in determining legislative policy. Needless to say, lobbyists do not spend much time talking to legislators whom they regard as unimportant; they want to communicate with party leaders in states with strong party discipline and cohesion, and with the chairmen of standing committees in states with a tradition of committee dominance like that of Congress. In states where the parties and their satellite interest groups exist in a well defined system of interaction, the problem of access does not exist. Business groups can talk with Republicans and labor unions can talk with Democrats with confidence that their views will be taken seriously. It is in the legislatures without the control of a party organization that the job of locating and impressing the key decision-makers becomes acute. Jewell has noted that standing committees in state legislatures rarely exercise the independence typical of those of Congress. Most of the important bills are guided to a few committees dominated by a few legislators, usually party or faction leaders.[79] To establish and maintain access to these committees becomes a major goal of the state lobbyist and it is here that competition is keenest. In the frantic atmosphere of a legislature which meets only for a few months every other year, the rush of legislation makes the task of the lobbyist difficult. The simple question of time may become quite important. Consequently, the patient cultivation of good will can make the difference between talking to a legislator or waiting all day without so much as a glimpse: "The harassed member will give his ear to those advocates he knows and likes in preference to persons he knows only distantly."[80]

LIMITS ON THE EFFECTIVENESS OF TECHNIQUES. This discussion of the techniques of the lobbyist should not obscure one fundamental point. The techniques of lobbying as practiced by a representative of an interest group are less important than the group itself in contributing to any given legislative outcome. In the words of the authors of *The Legislative System,* ". . . reasons connected with a group's claim to be represented or with its general political power appear . . . to be more significant than reasons associated with its lobbying activities in the legislative arena itself."[81] General political power is, of course, difficult to define and is probably best understood as a subjective definition on the part of the individual legislator. Groups will rarely (if they are represented by experienced lobbyists) threaten a legislator with electoral defeat and they will rarely flaunt economic power openly. On the other hand, wealth or potential electoral strength are credited by legislators as being critical factors in the effectiveness of groups. One plausible explanation is that political power and representative quality in an organization are frequently perceived as being synonymous by legislators. For example, the Florida Dairy Products Association, an organization representing practically all the milk distributors in Florida, had a virtual monopoly on access to the house Public Health Committee which would never report out a bill opposed by the organization. Those who sought alterations in the laws governing the sale of milk in Florida did not go to the legislature or to one of its committees. They went first to the Florida Dairy Products Association. Why was this the case? Of course, the large milk distributors such as Sealtest, Borden's, and Foremost are economically powerful, but it is difficult to believe that the control of the legislative committee was due exclusively to wealth. The strength of the association was certainly not due to its voting strength. Rather, it is more likely that its influence was due to the willingness of the legislative committee to accord it, because of its representative quality, the role of legitimate spokesman for an economic interest.[82]

If we use the idea of the legislative acknowledgment of legitimacy as a source of influence, we can return once again to the idea of power as relative to the situation. An excellent illustration of this idea is provided by Wilder Crane's study of bankers and the Wisconsin legislature. In this case, the issue was whether to allow banks to establish paying or receiving stations on parking lots within 1,000 feet of the bank. The Wisconsin Bankers Association opposed the bill and most of the larger Milwaukee banks hired their own lobbyists to voice their opposition. The bill was defeated and Crane's subsequent investigation led him to conclude that the activities of bankers formed the crucial factor in its defeat. Only 6 per cent of the legislators voted against what they believed to be the dominant pressure from bankers in their district. Further, many legislators took the initiative away from the lobbyists by contacting the bankers themselves to find out where they stood. This bill was perceived as being an issue on which bankers had a legitimate right to be heard. Other factors, such as rural-urban conflict or party loyalty, were not present in the situation and most of the conflict came from within the banking community. Since labor did not take a position, Democrats contacted bankers about as frequently as Republicans.[83] It can easily be seen that the power of the bankers was keyed to the particular situation and cannot be described as generalized power. When the legislature considers banking legislation it calls upon bankers. This simple explanation is most useful in understanding the play of groups upon the legislature. Given another set of circumstances — for example, the entrance of a competitive group of equal status into the competition, or another definition of the situation by the legislature — the position of the bankers may have been less prominent. Also, there are some issues on which no pressure group has very much to say. For example, questions of legislative reapportionment do not permit groups to play as significant a role as they might at other times.[84]

CONCLUSIONS

Just as the strength of political parties varies from state to state, the significance of interest groups is greater or less, depending (partially) upon a series of circumstances, as outlined in this chapter. A major variable is the political and social structure of the state. There is some validity in the long assumed notion that pressure groups do not thrive in states characterized by cohesive political parties, but in many cases peaceful coexistence and mutually beneficial cooperation are possible. Political parties as cohesive agencies serve to channel the direction of pressure away from the individual legislator and perhaps reduce the salience of pressure politics for the rank and file. Within any given politico-economic structure, the importance of pressure groups varies with the peculiarities of the situation. Groups powerful in some situations are powerless in others. Even in states characterized by strong and active groups, it is likely that a pluralistic rather than monolithic structure of power exists. Interest groups may be conceptualized as one of a series of actors in the political process with influence that increases or diminishes in relation to other actors. Organized groups form a portion of the total matrix of pressures flowing in a certain direction. To assign to them a major or minor role is a job that can be undertaken only with consideration of both long term factors and more immediate, situational factors.

Considering the more immediate factors first, a basic conclusion is that lobbying skills are not as important as the legitimate claim of the group to represent a public that has a stake in the outcome of a given decision. Techniques can maximize the advantage gained from the according of legitimacy to a group, but cannot *create* this legitimacy. Hence, even in the short run, success or failure may be a function of forces beyond the control of the interest group.

In the long run, the strength of interest groups is governed by developments in other components of the system. We have described interest groups as part of a political and social system. A system consists of a set of interrelated parts. A change in one of the parts brings about a change in the others, or there is no system. Since we have concluded that the strength of interest groups varies with the strength of parties and the degree of industrialization and urbanization of a state, we can offer a prediction based upon changes in the other parts of the system. States are becoming more industrialized and urban. As the socio-political structure of the states changes, changes in the political structure will follow. Thus, political parties are becoming more competitive. The areas of one-party domination are becoming fewer. Consequently, we can say that it is probable that the independent influence of interest groups will *decline* in the future. As states without effective party organizations gradually develop party competition, part of the vacuum formerly filled by interest groups will be filled by political parties. In the South, where all states have strong interest groups, this process is underway. Pressure groups, like other systems of human endeavor, will continue to adjust to a change in environment.

NOTES

1. Arthur Bentley, *The Process of Government* (San Antonio: Principia Press of Trinity University, 1949) p. 176.
2. For a critique of group theory literature, see Robert T. Golembiewski, " 'The Group Basis of Politics': Notes on Analysis and Development," *American Political Science Review LIV* (1960) 962.
3. See Harmon Zeigler, *Interest Groups in American Society* (Englewood Cliffs, N.J.: Prentice-Hall, 1964) pp. 33–37 for a discussion of distrust of interest groups.
4. The data and tabulations utilized in this section were made available by the Inter-University Consortium for Political Research. The data were originally collected by Gabriel Almond and Sidney Verba and published as *The Civic Culture* (Princeton: Princeton University Press, 1963). Tables 3, 4, 5, and untabulated material related to these tables were taken from the United States sample of the five-nation study undertaken by Almond and Verba. Neither the originators nor the Consortium bear any responsibility for the analyses or interpretations presented here.
5. David Truman, *The Governmental Process* (New York: Alfred A. Knopf, 1951) p. 30.
6. Lester Milbrath, *The Washington Lobbyists* (Chicago: Rand McNally & Co., 1963) pp. 241–282.
7. Robert Engler, *The Politics of Oil* (New York: Macmillan Co., 1961) p. 380.
8. Milbrath, pp. 302–303.
9. Voluntary association memberships in the other countries included in the study are: Great Britain, 47 per cent; Germany, 44 per cent; Italy, 29 per cent; Mexico, 25 per cent.
10. Robert E. Lane, *The Regulation of Businessmen* (New Haven: Yale University Press, 1954) pp. 53–54.
11. See Robert E. Lane, *Political Life* (New York: Free Press of Glencoe, 1959) pp. 76–79, for a summary of the evidence for this statement. See also Charles R. Wright and Herbert H. Hyman, "Voluntary Association Membership of American Adults: Evidence from National Sample Surveys," *American Sociological Review XXIII* (1958) 284–294. For a discussion of the implications of the data on organizational membership for group theory, see William C. Mitchell, "Interest Group Theory and 'Overlapping Memberships' " (Paper presented to the 1963 meeting of the American Political Science Association).
12. Quoted in Eugene V. Price, "Organized Labor in Idaho Politics," M.A. thesis, University of Utah, 1952, p. 139.
13. Diane Phillips, "Access to Governmental Machinery as It Is Perceived by Negro Leaders" (unpublished ms.) p. 6.
14. Walter Murphy, "The South Counterattacks: The Anti-NAACP Laws," *Western Political Quarterly XII* (1959) 372.
15. Stuart S. Nagel, "Off the Bench Judicial Attitudes," in Glendon Schubert (ed.),

Judicial Decision-Making (New York: Free Press of Glencoe, 1963) pp. 29–53. See also Nagel, "Judicial Attitudes and Those of Legislators and Administrators" (Paper presented to the 1962 meeting of the American Political Science Association).

16. Kenneth N. Vines, "Southern State Supreme Courts and Race Relations," *Western Political Quarterly XVIII* (1965).

17. Engler, pp. 381–384; House Select Committee on Lobbying Activities, *Hearings, Housing Lobby,* 81st Cong., 2d. sess., 1950, pp. 681–682; Andrew Hacker, "Pressure Politics in Pennsylvania: The Truckers vs. the Railroads," in Alan F. Westin (ed.), *The Uses of Power* (New York: Harcourt, Brace & World, 1963) p. 355; Wayne Goodwin, "An Investigation of Pressure Group Activity of the Colorado Trucking Industry," M.A. thesis, University of Colorado, 1954, p. 46.

18. Joseph C. Palamountain, *The Politics of Distribution* (Cambridge: Harvard University Press, 1955) p. 163.

19. Proceedings of the A.F.L.–C.I.O. 4th Annual Convention, pp. 176–180.

20. The following people were helpful in locating lobbying lists which were not immediately available: Ethan P. Allen, University of Kansas; James R. Bell, Sacramento State College; Alan L. Clem, University of South Dakota; Elmer E. Cornwell, Jr., Brown University; J. C. Davies, Bowdoin College; Wayne Francis, Syracuse University; Malcolm E. Jewell, University of Kentucky; Robert G. Scigliano, Michigan State University; R. D. Sloan, Jr., University of Nebraska.

21. For Ohio, California, Tennessee, and New Jersey, see John C. Wahlke, *et al., The Legislative System* (New York: John Wiley and Sons, 1962) p. 315. The Michigan research is reported in Walter DeVries, *The Michigan Lobbyist: A Study in the Bases and Perceptions of Effectiveness,* Ph.D. dissertation, Michigan State University, 1960. The North Carolina findings are based on interviews with lobbyists rather than legislators. The interviews were conducted under the auspices of the Political Studies Program of the University of North Carolina. They were made available through the courtesy of Professor William J. Crotty, Department of Political Science, University of Georgia. The Political Studies Program is under the direction of Professor Donald R. Matthews.

22. E. E. Schattschneider, *The Semi-Sovereign People* (New York: Holt, Rinehart & Winston, 1960) p. 31. Lester Milbrath, *The Washington Lobbyists* (Chicago: Rand McNally & Co., 1963) pp. 30–31. Schattschneider examined the listings of *National Associations of the United States* while Milbrath interviewed a sample of lobbyists.

23. P. W. Cherington and R. L. Gillen, *The Business Representative in Washington* (Washington: The Brookings Institution, 1962). See also Harmon Zeigler, *The Politics of Small Business* (Washington: Public Affairs Press, 1961).

24. E. E. Schattschneider, p. 35.

25. The classification of states according to strength of interest groups and legislative cohesion is taken from Belle Zeller (ed.), *American State Legislatures* (New York: Thomas Y. Crowell Co., 1954) pp. 190–191.

26. Wahlke, *et al.,* pp. 317, 323, 327.

27. Oliver Garceau and Corinne Silverman, "A Pressure Group and the Pressured: A Case Report," *American Political Science Review XLVIII* (1954) 672–691.

28. Duane Lockard, *New England State Politics* (Princeton: Princeton University Press, 1959) p. 42.

29. Garceau and Silverman, p. 673.

30. Lockard, p. 79.

31. V. O. Key, Jr., *Southern Politics in State and Nation* (New York: Alfred A. Knopf, 1949) p. 56.

32. Hywell Evans, *Governmental Regulation of Industrial Relations* (Ithaca: New York State School of Industrial and Labor Relations at Cornell, 1961) pp. 92–93. States having right-to-work laws are Alabama, Arizona, Arkansas, Florida, Georgia, Indiana, Iowa, Kansas, Louisiana, Mississippi, Nebraska, Nevada, North Carolina, North Dakota, South Carolina, South Dakota, Tennessee, Texas, Utah, Virginia, and Wyoming.

33. *Proceedings of the A.F.L.–C.I.O. 4th Constitutional Convention,* Vol. II (1961) pp. 176–180.

34. Quoted in Joseph R. Gladden, Jr., "A Modern Revolution in Georgia: Organized Labor and the General Assembly," Senior Honors thesis, Emory University, 1963, p. 28.

35. Thomas Payne, "Under the Copper Dome: Politics in Montana," in Frank H. Jonas (ed.), *Western Politics* (Salt Lake City: University of Utah Press, 1961) pp. 197–198.

36. Burton K. Wheeler with Paul Healy, *Yankee from the West* (Garden City, N.Y.: Doubleday and Co., 1962) p. 84.

37. Joseph Kinsey Howard, *Montana: High, Wide and Handsome* (New Haven: Yale University Press, 1943) p. 249.

38. Richard T. Ruetten, "Anaconda Journalism: The End of an Era," *Journalism Quarterly XXXVII* (1960) 3–12. See also John M. Schlitz, "Montana's Captive Press," *Montana Opinion* (1956) 1–11.

39. Quoted in Engler, p. 354.

40. Clifton McClesky, *The Government and Politics of Texas* (Boston: Little, Brown, 1963) pp. 136–150.

41. Raymond A. Bauer, Ithiel de Sola Pool, and Lewis Anthony Dexter, *American Business and Public Policy* (New York: Atherton Press, 1963) p. 266.

42. William Haber, Eugene C. McKean, and Harold C. Taylor, *The Michigan Economy: Its Potentials and Its Problems* (Kalamazoo, Mich.: The W. E. Upjohn Institute for Employment Research, 1959) p. 105.

43. Stephen B. and Vera H. Sarasohn, *Political Party Patterns in Michigan* (Detroit: Wayne State University Press, 1957).

44. Joseph LaPalombara, *Guide to Michigan Politics* (East Lansing: Michigan State University, Bureau of Social and Political Research, 1960) p. 104.

45. *Ibid.*

46. See John P. White and John R. Owens, *Parties, Group Interests and Campaign Finance: Michigan '56* (Princeton: Citizens' Research Foundation) for a careful analysis of the role of labor unions and automobile manufacturers in party finance.

47. Robert Lee Sawyer, Jr., *The Democratic State Central Committee in Michigan, The Rise of the New Politics and the New Political Leadership* (Ann Arbor: University of Michigan, Institute of Public Administration, 1960) p. 261.

48. See Austin Ranney and Willmoore Kendall, *Democracy and the American Party System* (New York: Harcourt, Brace and Co., 1956) pp. 459–533 for a discussion of national parties as moderators of group conflict.

49. Nicholas A. Masters, "Organized Labor as a Base of Support for the Democratic Party," *Law and Contemporary Problems XXVII* (1962) 255.

50. V. O. Key, Jr., *Public Opinion and American Democracy* (New York: Alfred A Knopf, 1961) p. 524.

51. Daniel M. Ogden, Jr., "Relations Between Pressure Groups and Political Parties in

the State of Washington," *Western Political Quarterly XI* (1958) 711–713. See also Daniel M. Ogden, Jr., and Hugh A. Bone, *Washington Politics* (New York: New York University Press, 1960) pp. 54–63.

52. Lockard, p. 162.
53. Joseph P. Harris and Leonard Rowe, *California Politics* (2nd ed.; Stanford: Stanford University Press, 1959) p. 20. The dominance of railroads has been noted in other states. See Dayton David McKean, *Pressures on the Legislature of New Jersey* (New York: Columbia University Press, 1938); and Andrew Hacker, "Pressure Politics in Pennsylvania: The Truckers vs. the Railroads," p. 326.
54. See, for example, Lester Velie, "The Secret Boss of California," *Colliers,* August 14 and 20, 1949.
55. William Buchanan, *Legislative Partisanship: The Deviant Case of California,* University of California Publications in Political Science, Vol. XIII (Berkeley and Los Angeles: University of California Press, 1963).
56. Wahlke, *et al.,* p. 100.
57. Edwin N. Atherson and Associates, *Legislative Investigative Report* (Sacramento: Premier Publications, 1949). This is a reprint of the report prepared by H. R. Philbrick and printed in the *Senate Journal,* April 4, 1939, and subsequently removed from the record.
58. Buchanan, p. 143.
59. Nicholas A. Masters, Robert H. Salisbury, and Thomas H. Eliot, *State Politics and the Public Schools* (New York: Alfred A. Knopf, 1964) pp. 37–38.
60. Samuel C. Patterson, "The Role of the Lobbyist: The Case of Oklahoma," *Journal of Politics XXV* (1963) 79.
61. DeVries, p. 36. See also John P. Hackett, "Lobbying in Rhode Island," *Providence Sunday Journal,* August 11, 1963.
62. DeVries, p. 63; North Carolina Political Studies Program; Thomas J. Moore, "An Analytical Study of Lobbying during the 1962 Session of the General Assembly of Virginia" (unpublished) p. 36. The last source was made available through the courtesy of Professor Spencer Albright of the University of Richmond.
63. Belle Zeller, p. 249. Patterson, p. 76. DeVries, p. 78. Leon Epstein, *Politics in Wisconsin* (Madison: University of Wisconsin Press, 1958) pp. 118–119.
64. Milbrath, p. 77.
65. Epstein, p. 103. DeVries, p. 177. William C. Havard and Loren P. Beth, *The Politics of Misrepresentation* (Baton Rouge: Louisiana State University Press, 1962) pp. 235–236.
66. Hacker, p. 333.
67. Alexander Heard, *The Costs of Democracy* (Chapel Hill: University of North Carolina Press, 1960) p. 175.
68. Lockard, p. 163. See also Joseph LeVow Steinberg, "Labor in Massachusetts Politics: The Internal Organization of the C.I.O. and A.F.L. for Political Action, 1948–1955," Senior Honors thesis, Harvard University, 1956.
69. Joseph L. Bernd, *The Role of Campaign Funds in Georgia Primary Elections, 1936–1958* (Macon: The Georgia Journal, 1958) p. 3. Another good example of the explicit expectations which accompany contributions is the case of Ellis Arnall and an oil investor group. The investors agreed to provide strong backing for Arnall in his 1942 gubernatorial race against Eugene Talmadge because Talmadge failed to support statutory authorization for a pipeline project. See Bernd, pp. 4–5.
70. See chapter 5 in this volume for a more complete discussion of the social status of state legislators.

71. Andrew J. Biemiller, "R-T-W Forces Try 'Back Door,'" *American Federationist LXVIII* (1961) 5.
72. Bauer, de Sola Pool, and Dexter, pp. 422–433. See also Donald R. Matthews, *U.S. Senators and Their World* (Chapel Hill: University of North Carolina Press, 1960) pp. 177–178.
73. Frank Bonilla, "When is Petition 'Pressure'?" *Public Opinion Quarterly XX* (1956) 46–48.
74. Kenneth Janda, Henry Teune, Melvin Kahn, and Wayne Francis, *Legislative Politics in Indiana* (Indiana University: Bureau of Government Research, n.d.) pp. 18–19. See also Henry Teune, "Occupational Affiliation and Attitudes Towards Interest Groups" (Paper presented to the 1962 meeting of the American Political Science Association).
75. J. Leiper Freeman, *The Political Process: Executive Bureau–Legislative Committee Relations* (Garden City, N.Y.: Doubleday and Co., 1955). On state administrative politics see the following: Harmon Zeigler, *The Florida Milk Commission Changes Minimum Prices* (New York: The Inter-University Case Program, 1963); Donald G. Balmer, *Interest Groups in Action: A Case Study of Oregon Milk Control, 1933–1954*, Ph.D. dissertation, University of Washington, 1956; William W. Boyer, "Policy-Making by Government Agencies," *Midwest Journal of Political Science IV* (1960) 267–288; James W. Fesler, "Independence of State Regulatory Agencies," *American Political Science Review XXXIV* (1940) 935–947.
76. Patterson, p. 83. See also Patterson, "The Role of the Labor Lobbyist" (Paper presented to the 1962 meeting of the American Political Science Association).
77. Milbrath, p. 215.
78. Goodwin, *loc. cit.*
79. Malcolm E. Jewell, *The State Legislature* (New York: Random House, 1962) p. 93.
80. Buchanan, p. 102.
81. Wahlke, *et al.*, p. 334.
82. Harmon Zeigler, *The Florida Milk Commission Changes Minimum Prices* reprinted in Edwin A. Bock (ed.), *State and Local Government: A Case Book* (University of Alabama Press, 1963) pp. 395–428.
83. Wilder Crane, Jr., "A Test of the Effectiveness of Interest Group Pressures on Legislators," *Southwestern Social Science Quarterly XLI* (1960) 335–340.
84. Malcolm E. Jewell (ed.), *The Politics of Reapportionment* (New York: Atherton Press, 1962) pp. 32–34. Gilbert Y. Steiner and Samuel P. Gove, *Legislative Politics in Illinois* (Urbana: University of Illinois Press, 1960) p. 116. See also Gordon Baker, *The Politics of Reapportionment in Washington State* (Eagleton Institute Cases in Practical Politics: New York: Holt, Rinehart & Winston, 1960).

SELECTED BIBLIOGRAPHY

Buchanan, William. *Legislative Partisanship: The Deviant Case of California.* University of California Publications in Political Science, Vol. 13, Berkeley and Los Angeles: University of California Press, 1963. A careful evaluation of the changing nature of interest groups in California with particular emphasis upon the relationship between interest groups and political parties.

Crane, Wilder, Jr. "A Test of the Effectiveness of Interest Group Pressures on Legislators," *Southwestern Social Science Quarterly XLI* (1960) 335–340.

A case study of the influence of banks in Wisconsin based upon legislators' evaluation of demands made upon them.

DeVries, Walter. *The Michigan Lobbyist: A Study in the Bases and Perceptions of Effectiveness.* Ph.D. dissertation, Michigan State University, 1960. The effect of interest groups is estimated by means of a questionnaire administered to lobbyists, legislators, and newspaper reporters.

Garceau, Oliver, and Corinne Silverman. "A Pressure Group and the Pressured: A Case Report," *American Political Science Review XLVIII* (1954) 672–791. An examination of the 1951 session of the Vermont Legislature from the point of view of the Associated Industries of Vermont and the members of the Vermont Legislature.

Hacker, Andrew. "Pressure Politics in Pennsylvania: The Trucker vs. the Railroads," in Alan F. Westin (ed.), *The Uses of Power.* New York: Harcourt, Brace & World, 1962, pp. 324–376. An analysis of the role of public relations firms in the development of group strategy.

Lockard, Duane. *New England State Politics.* Princeton: Princeton University Press, 1959. The politics of six New England states are described by a former member of the Connecticut senate. States with strong and weak pressure groups are contrasted.

Masters, Nicholas A., Robert H. Salisbury and Thomas H. Eliot. *State Politics and the Public Schools.* New York: Alfred A. Knopf, 1964. A discussion of the activities of educational associations in Illinois, Michigan, and Missouri.

Patterson, Samuel C. "The Role of the Lobbyist: The Case of Oklahoma," *Journal of Politics XXV* (1963) 72–92. The backgrounds of lobbyists and their perceptions of their roles are described and interpreted by means of a mail questionnaire.

Wahlke, John C., Heinz Eulau, William Buchanan and Leroy C. Ferguson. *The Legislative System.* New York: John Wiley and Sons, 1962. Chapter 14 contains an analysis of legislators' role orientations toward interest groups in California, New Jersey, Ohio, and Tennessee.

PART THREE

THE POLICY-MAKING ARENAS

POLITICAL ACTIVITY is usually directed at a governmental agency in order to influence the formulation of policies or programs. Some people want new legislation; some want to influence the manner in which a law is administered; others want a judicial interpretation.

Each of the states has a legislature, an executive branch, and a judiciary, but although the institutions bear similar names, they do not operate in an identical manner. Their formal and informal rules of decision-making change from state to state. The participants who are active in each of the institutions vary. The policy decisions made in these arenas differ.

STATE
LEGISLATIVE
POLITICS

CHAPTER 5
by
THOMAS R. DYE

GENERALIZING ABOUT AMERICAN STATE LEGISLATURES IS DIFFICULT as
there are fifty of them to consider and all are different. Some are important political bodies which make the crucial decisions about public policy
in their respective states. Others simply "rubber stamp" the decisions of
a strong governor, influential party leaders, or powerful interest groups.
Some legislatures are completely dominated by a single party and there
is little likelihood of the minority party's ever capturing control; in other
states a more competitive situation exists and control of the state legislature frequently shifts from one party to the other. In some state legislatures voting is frequently along party lines, while in other states voting is
more affected by factional rivalries or constituency pressures than by
party loyalties. In some the conflict between rural and urban interests
dominates legislative politics, whereas in other states conflict between
regions, between legislature and governor, between liberal and conservative, or between labor and industry may take precedence. Some legislatures have voted generous expenditures for public schools, welfare
programs and higher education; others have been more concerned with
keeping public expenditures at a minimum. In short, state legislatures
can be quite different from one another. The problem facing anyone
who wants to talk about legislative politics in fifty states is not only to
describe these differences from state to state but, more importantly, to
explain these differences. That is the task of this chapter.

THE FUNCTION OF LEGISLATURES

From a legal viewpoint, the function of state legislatures is the enactment of statutory law. If volume of statutory writing and revision were
the criterion upon which state legislatures were judged, it could rightly
be said that legislatures have never functioned so well as they have in
recent years. In the 1950–51 biennium, American state legislatures con-

sidered over 47,000 bills, but by the 1960–61 biennium this figure had grown to over 104,000. The total number of state legislative enactments grew from approximately 15,000 to over 33,000 in that same ten-year period.[1] As a society grows more complex and becomes increasingly urban and industrial the need for formal statutory control seems to grow. While intervening, short-term conditions may obscure this relationship in any single legislative session, Table 1 indicates that in general the states which enacted over 1,000 statutes in 1960–61 were more urban and industrial than the states which enacted fewer than 500.[2]

Table 1

SOCIO-ECONOMIC DEVELOPMENT AND NUMBER OF LAWS
ENACTED BY STATE LEGISLATURES, 1960–61

| NUMBER OF ENACTMENTS | INDICES OF ECONOMIC DEVELOPMENT* (*Figures are mean scores*) | | | |
	Urbanization	*Industrialization*	*Income*	*Education*
Over 1000 (11 states)	72.5%	94.8%	$5595	10.4 yrs.
500–1000 (16 states)	58.7	89.9	4937	10.2
Less than 500 (23 states)	58.6	89.1	5525	10.9

*Indices are as follows: Urbanization: % Urban; Industrialization: 100 — % engaged in agriculture, forestries and fisheries occupations; Income; median family income; Education: median school year completed.

The range of subject matter of bills considered even in a single session is enormous. A legislature may consider the authorization of a billion dollars of state spending, the extension of the hunting season on racoons, participation in the national defense highway system, the designation of an official state flower, an increase in teachers' salaries, and whether or not license plates bearing the inscription, "The Poultry State," would cause the state to be called "chicken." Obviously, these considerations range from the trivial to the vital; yet every bill which comes into a legislature is important to someone. In addition to the enactment of statutory law, legislatures share in the process of state constitutional revision, approve many executive appointments, establish congressional districts, and consider amendments to the U.S. Constitution. But perhaps their single most important legal function is the passage of the appropriations and tax measures in the state budget. No state monies may be spent without a legislative appropriation, and it is difficult to think of any governmental action which does not involve a financial expenditure. Potentially, a legislature can control any activity of the state government through its power over appropriations, but as a practical matter this legal power over fiscal affairs does not amount to political control.

From a political viewpoint, the function of state legislatures is to assist in the formulation of public policy. It is misleading to say merely that "the legislature makes policy," for obviously the legislature is not the only group which shares in this task. The governor, the courts, executive agencies, organized interests, the press, political parties, and many individuals — the interested as well as the apathetic — share in the making of public policy. How then do we distinguish the role of the legislature from that of other groups? For example, do legislatures merely ratify and thereby lend legitimacy to the decisions which are actually made by the governor, or the bureaucrats, or the organized interests? Or are legislatures an important part of the process of proposing, deliberating, and deciding about public policy? If they are an important part of the decisional process, what function do they perform in this process? Does the legislature merely referee the struggles between political interests in the state, recording the terms of surrender, compromises, or conquests in the form of statutes? Or does the legislature exercise independent influence over policy? If the latter is the case, on whose behalf does it exercise this influence — the parties, the constituencies, or particular interests in the state? Are legislatures initiators of public policy or do they merely articulate expressions of public sentiment in favor of, or in opposition to, policies initiated by others? These are the critical questions about the function of legislatures in state policy-making. Much of the rest of this chapter is an attempt to come to grips with these questions.

THE PARTISAN SETTING OF LEGISLATIVE POLITICS

There are ninety-six partisan legislative chambers in the United States; Nebraska and Minnesota legislatures are elected on a non-partisan ballot. In recent years the Democratic party has dominated American state legislative politics. Table 2 shows the number of upper and lower houses in state legislatures controlled by Democrats and Republicans from 1954 to 1962. The Democratic party's control of lower houses is even more pronounced than its control of state senates: Democrats have never controlled fewer than twenty-six lower houses at any one time and have controlled as many as thirty-nine. It might also be noted that in general the Democratic party has fared well in controlling governors' chairs. In that same period Democrats have held between twenty-seven and thirty-five of the fifty governorships.

Table 2 also shows the frequency of divided government, where the governor's chair is held by one party, while one or both chambers are held by the opposition party. Only sixteen states completely avoided divided government during this period; these are the one-party states of the South plus New

Table 2

GOVERNORSHIPS AND STATE LEGISLATIVE CHAMBERS CONTROLLED BY DEMOCRATS AND
REPUBLICANS AND THE FREQUENCY OF DIVIDED GOVERNMENT, 1954–62

| | UPPER HOUSES | | | LOWER HOUSES | | | GOVERNORSHIPS | | DIVIDED |
	Dem.	Rep.	Tie	Dem.	Rep.	Tie	Dem.	Rep.	GOVERNMENT
1962	28	20	0	27	20	1	33	17	15
1960	30	18	0	31	17	0	34	16	17
1958	31	17	0	38	9	1	35	15	22
1956	25	21	2	28	20	0	31	19	18
1954	20	25	1	26	20	0	27	21	15

Source: *Statistical Abstract 1963*, pp. 379–380.

Hampshire and Vermont. All thirty-four states with some semblance of competitive parties have experienced some divided government. Democratic governors are more likely to face hostile legislatures than Republican governors. In all of the instances of divided government from 1954 to 1962, 70 per cent of the governors facing an opposition majority in one or both houses were Democrats, while only 30 per cent were Republicans.[3] Governors who have succeeded only in winning by a small margin are more likely to face opposition legislatures than those elected by wide margins. When Democratic governors are elected in the normally Republican Midwestern and upper New England states, they usually face a Republican legislature. On the other hand, Republican governors elected in the traditionally Democratic border states are generally faced with the Democratic legislatures. Divided government may be expected to appear in the states of the old Confederacy if the rising tide of Republicanism there should result in the capture of any Southern governorships.

What types of states are most likely to experience Democratic or Republican legislative control? State legislatures can be classified according to the proportion of total seats in both houses of the legislature held by each party from 1954 to 1962. Table 3 divides the states into five categories: one-party Democratic (70 per cent or more of the legislative membership of both houses from 1954 to 1962 being Democratic); Democratic dominant (over 50 per cent of the legislative membership of both houses being Democratic); divided (over 50 per cent of the legislative membership of one house Democratic but over 50 per cent of the other house Republican); Republican dominant (over 50 per cent of the legislative membership of both houses being Republican); and one-party Republican (over 70 per cent of the legislative membership of both houses from 1954 to 1962 being Republican). It is clear from Table 3 that socio-economic development does not consistently favor one party or the other. Rather high levels of urbanization, industrialization, income, and education foster party competition for legislative control. Both one-party Republican and one-party Democratic legislatures occur in rural, agricultural states with populations possessing lower income and educational attributes.[4]

Table 3

SOCIO-ECONOMIC DEVELOPMENT AND PARTY CONTROL OF STATE LEGISLATURES, 1954–62

	INDICES OF ECONOMIC DEVELOPMENT[a] *(Figures are mean scores)*			
	Urbanization	Industrialization	Income	Education
One-Party Democratic:				
Over 70% Both Houses Democratic (16 states)[b]	55.2%	90.3%	$4448	9.5 yrs.
Democratic Dominant:				
Over 50% Both Houses Democratic (12 states)[c]	69.3	93.3	6037	11.5
Divided:				
One House Over 50% Democratic, One House Over 50% Republican (4 states)[d]	78.0	96.5	6578	11.5
Republican Dominant:				
Over 50% Both Houses Republican (12 states)[e]	64.5	90.6	5762	10.9
One-Party Republican:				
Over 70% Both Houses Republican (4 states)[f]	44.5	82.1	4840	10.6

a. Indices are the same as Table 1.
b. Alabama, Arkansas, Florida, Georgia, Kentucky, Louisiana, Maryland, Mississippi, New Mexico, North Carolina, Oklahoma, South Carolina, Tennessee, Texas, Virginia, West Virginia.
c. Alaska, Arizona, California, Colorado, Delaware, Hawaii, Massachusetts, Missouri, Montana, Oregon, Rhode Island, Washington.
d. Connecticut, Nevada, New Jersey, Utah.
e. Idaho, Illinois, Indiana, Kansas, Michigan, New Hampshire, New York, Ohio, Pennsylvania, South Dakota, Wisconsin, Wyoming.
f. Iowa, Maine, North Dakota, Vermont.

What difference does it make whether a state *has competitive or noncompetitive* legislative politics? First of all, it is plain that one-party states do not have cohesive party organization with power to hold legislators in line on crucial legislative decisions. In one-party legislatures, divisions over public policy follow constituency, factional, or interest group lines rather than party lines. Parties exercise more influence in legislative decision-making in competitive than in non-competitive states.[5]

It is often argued that competitiveness results in increased benefits for citizens because the parties are forced to bid for votes. This implies that policy choices of competitive legislatures are different from those of non-competitive legislatures. Party competitiveness in legislative politics can be expressed as the majority party's margin of legislative control without regard to which is the majority party. The proportion of seats in each house held by the majority party from 1954 to 1962 is a measure of competition per se. In Table 4 these competition scores are correlated with several measures of public policy.

In the field of education, party competition is associated with higher average salaries for school teachers and higher school expenditures per pupil. In the field of welfare, party competition is associated with more liberal benefits. However, the problem in trying to determine the impact of party competition on specific policies is this: it is always possible that party competition does not itself produce liberal welfare policies or high educational expenditures but, instead, both party competition and these policies are made to occur together because some third intervening variable produces both of these phenomena. Since it is known that competitive and non-competitive states differ in their degree of socio-economic development, it may be that most of the policy differences between competitive and non-competitive states are due to differences in socio-economic development rather than party competition itself.[6]

Table 4

THE RELATIONSHIP BETWEEN PARTY COMPETITION, STATE EDUCATION, AND WELFARE POLICIES

(*Figures are simple correlation coefficients, 48 states*)	PARTY COMPETITION LOWER HOUSES	PARTY COMPETITION UPPER HOUSES
Education (1961–62):		
Average Public Schoolteacher's Salary	.52	.53
Average Expenditure Per Pupil in Average Daily Attendance	.63	.60
Welfare (1962):		
Average Weekly Unemployment Benefit	.68	.68
Average Monthly Old Age Benefit	.65	.62
Average Monthly Payment, Dependent Children	.76	.70
Average Monthly Payment, Aid to Blind	.63	.61

The visibility of parties in a competitive system may produce the most important differences between competitive and non-competitive systems. A party label in a competitive system is a very conspicuous attribute of a candidate for the legislature. One-party states may have important factions of varying durability. Yet in two-party states a party label must be worn on election day and can be seen by every voter. It is not so obscure as a vague alignment with a faction. Most of the students of state party systems feel that it is more difficult to hold factions responsible for policies than it is to hold competitive parties responsible, even though it may be none too easy to accomplish the latter. Factions are fluid and change their personnel and policies much more frequently than parties. Even in Louisiana, which has one of the more durable bi-factional systems among the one-party states, observers have felt that factionalism was "considerably inferior to two-party politics."[7] V. O. Key argues that Southern factional systems obscure politics for most voters and permit conservative interests to manipulate factional groups.[8] A large number of people who have little knowledge about policies and membership in various factions are easily misled. This is not to say that many voters are not confused about the policies of parties in a competitive state, or that competitive parties can always hold their legislators responsible; but it is merely to say that party competition is more likely to clarify things for the voter than factional politics. Even if policy differences between parties are vague, there is at least an "in-party" and an "out-party" which can be identified at election time. Finally, in one-party states and even in states with limited competition, the minority party very often fails to run candidates in many legislative districts. A voter in such a district has no opportunity to exercise discretion in the general election.

THE COMPOSITION OF LEGISLATURES

LEGISLATIVE DISTRICTS. The politics of representation center about the size and composition of legislative districts and who gains and who loses from the variations. Inequality of representation, or "malapportionment," is claimed when there are differing numbers of people in districts which receive the same number of representatives in the legislature. For example, if one legislator represents a district of 10,000 inhabitants and another a district of 40,000, it is said that the right to vote in the smaller district is worth four times what it is in the larger district. Drafters of model plans of representation often suggest that the population of the largest legislative district should not exceed the smallest by more than 50 per cent, or a population ratio of 1.5 to 1. According to this standard, every state legislative chamber in the nation is unrepresentative as are both houses of the U.S. Congress. In 1960 the lowest ratio of largest-to-smallest district was 2.2 to 1 in the Hawaiian house of representatives. Forty-seven of the ninety-nine legislative chambers in the nation (only Nebraska has a unicameral legislature) had ratios in excess of 10 to 1, i.e., the largest district was ten times larger than the smallest. In nine chambers this ratio exceeded 100 to 1.

Thus, malapportionment in the technical sense is widespread. But malapportionment only becomes politically relevant when it operates to discriminate against important political interests in a state. While some persons may object as a matter of principle to any inequality in representation, the important political question is whether or not malapportionment affects policymaking. To date, research in malapportionment has centered about its impact on the conflict between rural and urban interests. The assumption is that urban interests are most likely to be the subject of discrimination.

In order to determine the degree of discrimination against urban areas in American state legislatures, David and Eisenberg[9] compared the "value" of a vote cast for a state legislator in rural and urban areas in every state.*

Table 5 shows national averages of the value of a vote in four categories of counties by population. Clearly, the more populous counties in the nation are underrepresented in American state legislatures. And prior to 1962 it did not seem that the situation was improving with time. Dauer and Kelsay reported that the representativeness of thirty-eight senates and thirty-five lower houses declined from 1937 to 1955.[10]

Table 5

RELATIVE VALUES OF A VOTE FOR STATE LEGISLATORS,
NATIONAL AVERAGES FOR COUNTIES BY SIZE, 1910–60

CATEGORIES OF COUNTIES BY POPULATION SIZE	1910	1930	1950	1960
Under 25,000	1.13	1.31	1.41	1.71
25,000 to 99,999	1.03	1.09	1.14	1.23
100,000 to 499,999	.91	.84	.83	.81
500,000 and Over	.81	.74	.78	.76

Source: David and Eisenberg, *Devaluation of the Urban and Suburban Vote*, p. 8.

*David and Eisenberg first computed the average size of the constituency of a single member in each state. Actual constituencies were then compared to this average constituency; the "value" of a vote was the ratio of a real constituency to the average constituency in the state. For example, in a constituency twice the size of the state average, the value of a vote is .50; in a constituency half the size of the state average, the value of a vote is 2.0. The average value of a vote in rural and urban areas can be compared in this manner both within a single state and between states. See *Devaluation of the Urban and Suburban Vote*, p. 2.

How does urban underrepresentation come about? The task of districting a state generally falls upon the legislature itself. One explanation attributes urban underrepresentation to our rural heritage: districts drawn when our nation was overwhelmingly rural remain because of the rural legislator's distrust of growing city populations. Entrenched rural and small town interests are reluctant to surrender control to city populations with their large blocks of ethnic, laboring, Catholic, and Negro voters. Rural interests are often allied with those urban interests who share this view of the urban electorate. Often revealingly frank defenses of rural overrepresentation are made on the grounds that rural and small town people are "better" or "safer" citizens than big-city voters. In addition, there is always a natural reluctance of legislative bodies to perform major surgery on themselves; to expect a legislature to redistrict itself is to expect legislators to threaten their own incumbency. Therefore, many state legislatures simply refuse to reapportion, or carry out token reapportionment, despite increasing urbanization in their state. In 1961 Tennessee and Alabama had not reapportioned their legislatures in sixty years. In the last few decades only half of the states have reapportioned their legislatures during the ten years following a census.

In many cases, however, urban underrepresentation is a product of political compromises made in constitutional conventions, compromises similar to those made in the Convention of 1787 in which the United States House of Representatives was made representative of population, while the Senate was made representative of the states regardless of their population. Many state constitutions base representation, particularly in the upper chamber, upon some unit of government within the state, usually the county, rather than population. Two recent state apportionments show that these constitutional provisions are not necessarily a hangover from our rural heritage but represent political compromises of a recent vintage. In 1955 Cook County with over half the population of Illinois was given only twenty-four of that state's fifty-eight senators. The new constitution of Hawaii gives Oahu only 40 per cent of the senate although the island contains 80 per cent of the state's population.[11]

Is it possible to explain urban underrepresentation in terms of socioeconomic characteristics? Are the rural agricultural states more likely to underrepresent urban areas than the urban industrial states? Table 6 indicates that there is a slight relationship between urban underrepresentation in state legislatures and the several measures of socio-economic development. The two measures of malapportionment used were Dauer and Kelsay's[12] index of general representativeness,* and David and Eisenberg's measure

---

*This measure is the minimum percentage of the state's population that can elect a majority of each house. Minimum percentages for both houses are combined to give a score for the state legislature as a whole.

of the value of the right to vote in the largest county.[13] Both measures correlate slightly with socio-economic development. While rural states are somewhat more likely to underrepresent their urban areas, factors other than economic development must be looked to for an explanation of most of the differences between states in their approach to the representation question.

Table 6

THE RELATIONSHIP BETWEEN SOCIO-ECONOMIC DEVELOPMENT
AND URBAN UNDERREPRESENTATION IN STATE LEGISLATURES, 1960

| | INDICES OF ECONOMIC DEVELOPMENT | | | |
| | *(Figures are simple correlation coefficients, 50 states)* | | | |
	Urbanization	*Industrialization*	*Income*	*Education*
Index of General Representativeness	.18	.21	.33	.28
Value of Vote in the Largest County	.27	.33	.35	.05

The foregoing description of the extent of malapportionment in the states is subject to rapid change in the months and years ahead. Ever since March of 1962 when the U.S. Supreme Court decided *Baker* vs. *Carr,* reapportionment has been a chief topic of concern for state legislatures in all fifty states. For many years the federal courts avoided the distasteful task of compelling legislative reapportionment by asserting that this was a legislative rather than a judicial function.[14] Underrepresented populations were told by the courts that their remedy was to elect a legislature which would do its duty, a worthless prescription, of course, since electing a legislature was the very thing which underrepresented populations could not do. The position of the courts changed radically, however, after the U.S. Supreme Court decision in *Baker* vs. *Carr.*[15] This case involved the complaint of urban residents in Tennessee that the legislature had failed to apportion itself since 1901 in spite of rapid increases in the population of urban areas. In the Tennessee lower house, the largest district was twenty-three times larger than the smallest district. Petitioners argued that such inequalities in state apportionment laws denied them "equal protection of the laws" guaranteed by the Fourteenth Amendment and that the federal courts should grant relief from these inequalities. The Supreme Court decided: (1) that even though apportionment is a legislative function, the federal courts can accept jurisdiction where a constitutional question is involved; (2) that voters in underrepresented areas are entitled to judicial relief from apportionment laws which violate constitutional mandates; and (3) that discriminatory and arbitrary state apportionment laws can violate the Fourteenth Amendment's prohibition against laws which deny citizens equal protection. The Supreme Court returned the Tennessee case to a lower federal court which ordered reapportionment.

Reaction to the decision was immediate and widespread. Underrepresented voters throughout the nation petitioned federal courts to order state legislative reapportionment on the basis of the equal protection clause of the Fourteenth Amendment. Federal courts found themselves struggling with the mathematics of apportionment. The courts did not decide on any minimum mathematical standard of correct apportionment, holding only that "as nearly as practicable, one man's vote should be equal to another's."[16] State after state was induced to reapportion its legislature under the threat of judicial intervention. Federal courts generally allowed legislatures time to reapportion themselves, but token reapportionment was found unacceptable. The courts threatened to bar legislative elections by districts in states which fail to meet constitutional standards of apportionment. In addition to requiring legislative apportionment on a population basis, the Supreme Court also required population equality in congressional districting by state legislatures,[17] and threw out the county unit system of voting in statewide elections.[18] The philosophy underlying all of these decisions was expressed by the Court: "The conception of political equality from the Declaration of Independence to Lincoln's Gettysburg Address, to the Fourteenth, Fifteenth, Seventeenth, and Nineteenth Amendments can mean only one thing — one person, one vote."[19] The Court made no distinction between malapportionment which was a product of state law or that which was embodied in state constitutions; both forms of malapportionment were declared to be in violation of the Fourteenth Amendment.

It was not until two years after *Baker* vs. *Carr* that the Supreme Court got around to deciding whether representation in the second house of a state legislature also had to be based on population. Most state constitutions based representation in the upper chamber upon some unit of local government, rather than population. The justifications for such an arrangement are rooted deep in American democratic theory. The idea of bi-cameralism was based in part upon the advantages of having two separate systems of representation in a legislature. *The Federalist* papers vigorously defend a second chamber capable of checking the popular majority which was represented in the lower chamber and protecting interests which may be threatened by that majority. Several lower federal court decisions implied that, so long as one chamber was based on population, it would not be arbitrary or discriminatory to base representation in the second chamber upon some basis other than population. However, in 1964 the Supreme Court in *Reynolds* vs. *Sims,* a case involving Alabama's attempt to base representation in its senate on counties, the Court voted that *both* houses of a state legislature must be fairly apportioned according to population.[20] In the words of Chief Justice Earl Warren,[21] writing for the Court: "Legislators represent people, not trees or acres. Legislators are elected by voters, not farms or cities or economic interests. . . . The complexions of societies and civilizations change, often with amazing rapidity. A nation once primarily rural in character becomes predominantly urban. Representation schemes once fair and equitable became archaic and outdated."* The Court dismissed the federal analogy as "irrelevant" because "political subdivisions of states . . . never have been considered as sovereign entities." The court argued that requiring both houses to have the same basis of representation did not make bi-cameralism meaningless, because differences between the houses in numbers, terms of office, and size of constituencies would still remain. So much recent activity in apportionment has been generated by *Baker* vs. *Carr* and *Reynolds* vs. *Sims* that it is impossible to measure yet the full impact of these decisions on state legislators or legislative politics. It is quite clear, however, that malapportionment cannot long remain as a distinguishing characteristic of state legislative politics.

However, all of this concern over urban underrepresentation may not be politically relevant if there are no policy differences between rural and urban legislators. Malapportionment may give rural legislators a potential for power over their urban counterparts, but if they do not vote together with a high degree of unity to oppose urban interests on actual policy questions their advantage is more hypothetical than real. The weight of evidence in the literature on state politics supports the contention that there are important policy differences between urban and rural legislators and that malapportionment grants a real political advantage to the latter. If the perceptions of legislators themselves about conflict are to be accorded any weight, rural-urban conflict is not only discernible but is the most important conflict in American state legislatures. Rural-urban conflict was the only type of conflict rated "important" by over half the legislators interviewed in four separate states.[22] In contrast David Derge relied upon roll call votes rather than the perceptions of legislators in a study of the Illinois and Missouri legislatures.[23] He found that metropolitan and non-metropolitan legislators seldom opposed each other as unified voting blocks. But as Richard Frost pointed out, this finding

*Apparently representational schemes once fair and equitable can grow archaic very rapidly, for it was as late as 1948 that Earl Warren, the Governor of California, wrote: "The agricultural counties of California are far more important in the life of our state than the relationship their population bears to the entire population of the state. It is for this reason that I never have been in favor of redistricting their representation in our state senate on a strictly population basis. It is the same reason that the founding fathers of our country gave balanced representation to the states of the Union, equal representation in one house and proportionate representation based on population in the other." Quoted in *Time*, June 26, 1962, p. 22.

does not weaken the contention about the importance of rural-urban conflict; it merely demonstrates the need to clarify our definition of "urban." The "urban" category is often stretched to include very small towns — the census bureau calls any incorporated place of 2,500 persons "urban."[24] Moreover, within metropolitan areas there are real conflicts of interests between city and suburbs based upon different attributes of persons living in each area. Crowded slum dwellers have different opinions about public policy than inhabitants of suburban split-levels on half-acre lots. On some issues we find a conservative coalition of suburban and rural legislators. Robert S. Friedman has concluded that rural and urban identifications are less useful in explaining state politics than "more detailed interest groupings." However, because legislators still think in terms of rural-urban conflict, such conflict remains an important element in state politics.[25]

Later we shall attempt to describe the "more detailed interest groupings" which affect legislative decision-making, but it is safe to say that legislators from large, central cities and those from rural areas and small towns differ over the following: housing and welfare measures, aid for urban renewal and mass transit, the division of the state's tax dollar, state aids to schools, the location of highways, and the regulatory authority granted cities.[26] In some Southern states, urban legislators represent a "moderate" approach to race relations, while segregationists remain strong in rural areas. Richard Frost demonstrated that the New Jersey lower house, which directly represents population, is more favorably disposed toward "city bills" — labor, housing, city streets, city pork barrel, etc. — than the upper house which greatly over-represents rural areas.[27] According to the President's commission on inter-governmental relations, the unrepresentativeness of state legislatures causes urban areas to take their cause to the federal government where they feel they can obtain a fairer hearing. The rural character of state legislatures results in a by-passing of the states by cities requesting direct federal-to-local grants-in-aid such as the federal public housing and urban renewal programs.[28]

Does urban underrepresentation in the legislature noticeably affect the content of policies adopted by the states? This is a difficult question to come to grips with in a systematic fashion. So many intervening variables besides urban underrepresentation affect the policies of a state that it is difficult to attribute specific policies to any single factor. Table 7 shows the relationship between the two indices of malapportionment and several measures of education and welfare policies. There is some association between urban under-representation and teachers' salaries and per pupil expenditures in public schools: teachers' salaries and per pupil expenditures are somewhat higher in the states which grant better representation to urban areas. However, since we already know that it is the urban industrial states which grant better representation to urban areas, it is possible that higher teachers' salaries and per pupil expenditures are a result of urbanism and industrialization rather than the apportionment system. The same is true with regard to welfare benefits. There is a relationship between better urban representation and higher welfare benefits, but better urban representation probably does not cause higher benefits. Both are more likely a product of socio-economic development. This interpretation is supported where a strong relationship between socio-economic development and public policy is reported.[29] A recent study by Herbert Jacob of the impact of urban underrepresentation on party competition, public health expenditures, and the distribution of state highway funds in the fifty states also failed to establish any direct relationship between malapportionment and specific policy choices of legislatures.[30]

Table 7

**THE RELATIONSHIP BETWEEN URBAN UNDERREPRESENTATION
AND STATE EDUCATION AND WELFARE POLICIES**

(*Figures are simple correlation coefficients, 50 states*)		
	Index of General Representativeness Dauer and Kelsay	*Value of the Vote in the Largest County David and Eisenberg*
Education (1961–62):		
Average Public Schoolteacher's Salary	.42	.29
Average Expenditures Per Pupil in		
Average Daily Attendance	.24	.35
Welfare (1962):		
Average Weekly Unemployment Benefit	.22	.29
Average Monthly Old Age Benefit	.08	.37
Average Monthly Payment, Dependent		
Children	.06	.49
Average Monthly Payment, Aid to Blind	.01	.32

Malapportionment may not only discriminate against urban interests in the state but also against one or another of the political parties. Urban underrepresentation hurts the Democrats in those Northern and Eastern states where Democratic strength is heavily concentrated in urban areas. Michigan has been cited as a clear example of an apportionment system shaping party politics. From 1948 to 1962 Michigan elected Democratic governors to seven consecutive two-year terms, but during this entire period the Democratic party failed to obtain a majority in either house of the state legislature. Democratic voters are concentrated in the largest county, Wayne, which includes the city of Detroit; Wayne County has 40 per cent of the state's population but only seven of its thirty-four senators. Illinois, Ohio, and New Jersey are other examples of urban underrepresentation affecting the Democratic party. However, recently the underrepresentation of Republican suburbs has tended to offset the partisan impact of malapportionment on the Democrats. In New York and Pennsylvania, particularly, it is the Republican suburbs which are the most underrepresented areas of the state. Maryland's three largest suburban counties outside of Washington and Baltimore have substantially more people than the city of Baltimore but together elect only half as many representatives in each house. The apportionment system also works to the disadvantage of Republicans in those Southern, Southwestern, and border states where rural votes traditionally support the Democratic party.[31] In many of these states the Republican party is strongest in the growing urban and suburban areas. In Arizona in 1958 the Republican party captured the governorship but only one seat in the fifty-member senate; Republicans in Florida and Oklahoma also come primarily from underrepresented urban centers. If the Republican party continues to grow in the urban South, Republicans may soon feel frustrations of malapportionment, so long suffered by urban Democrats in the North. In short, reapportionment may have little *net* effect on the parties.

SOCIAL CHARACTERISTICS OF LEGISLATORS. The assumption that a direct association exists between a representative's social background and the behavior which he will manifest in office is open to question. While it is true that in the general population class position correlates with opinion on a variety of public issues, there are always a large number of deviators from the majority opinion on every class level. And, as Peter Rossi explained, it is precisely to these deviators among persons of high status that the popular support of lower status groups may be attracted.[32] Class position, then, may affect decisions of voters but may be a poor predictor of the decisions of elected representatives. In addition, the role of representative involves an incumbent in a whole series of well defined relationships with other individuals and groups, and these relationships may establish criteria for his behavior. The representative must accommodate his constituency, his party, his friends, and a wide variety of significant persons and groups, all of whom may bombard him with information, arguments, persuasion, and coercion. This is not a denial that an individual's personal or social characteristics may affect his performance as a decision-maker. But social characteristics are not related to decision-making in any simple and direct fashion.

Perhaps the real value of studying the social background of legislators is to reveal the nature of the influences to which they will be subjected during their tenure. A legislator's social attributes reflect the values of his constituency. Mosca has observed that decision-makers will usually possess "some attribute real or apparent which is highly esteemed and very influential in the society in which they live."[33] Both the local party and the constituency tend to select representatives who reflect the dominant social values in the district. Of course, a representative need not himself be typical of his constituency in order to fully represent their goals and aspirations. Background data on legislators should tell something of the criteria recruiters have in mind when they go searching for candidates. Recruiters must find a candidate whose personal characteristics endear him to his constituents — a candidate whose social affiliations enable him to win the confidence and support of his neighbors. Later we shall examine directly the influence of constituency on legislative decision-making, but that topic is foreshadowed here by observing the social relationship between legislators and their constituents.

What are the social characteristics to which the constituents demand the conformity of their representative? Evidence indicates the "birthright" characteristics — race, religion, ethnic and national background — tend to be the "givens" in the recruitment formulas to which candidates must conform. In a thorough study of state legislative representation in Pennsylvania, Frank Sorauf found that the religious composition of constituencies had a distinct impact on both Democratic and Republican candidates for the state legislature.[34] Protestant candidates came from Protestant districts and Catholics tended to win in Catholic districts. These religious differences paralleled ethnic differences. The Democratic party in that state, although heavily Catholic, did not run Catholic candidates in the Protestant "Bible-Belt" counties. Nor did the Republican party, although predominantly Protestant, run Lutherans or Presbyterians in the Irish and Italian wards of Philadelphia. Another social characteristic to which the constituencies demand conformity is race. The small number of Negro state legislators in Pennsylvania all came from heavily Negro districts, and predominantly Negro districts still dominated by white political leadership were threatening to end that domination. It is increasingly clear that this situation can be generalized outside Pennsylvania; a predominantly Negro district in Atlanta elected a Negro to the Georgia senate in 1962.

Another important criterion which constituencies establish for their representatives is place of residence. Legislators are far less mobile than the population as a whole; they tend to have deep roots in their constituencies. Sorauf reports that in Pennsylvania, a state with considerable population mobility, the odds against a "newcomer" with only twenty or twenty-five years' residence in a district are prohibitively high.[35] In 1957, 83 per cent of the state legislators of New Jersey had been born in the district they represented or had lived there over thirty years; in Tennessee this figure was 76 per cent and in Ohio it was 88 per cent. Even in California, one of the states with the highest population mobility, 56 per cent of the legislators had been born in their district or had lived there thirty years, and only 10 per cent had lived in their districts less than ten years.[36]

Certain social characteristics, however, escape the constituencies' demand for conformity. The feminine half of our population is seldom represented by more than 5 to 10 per cent of the members of any state legislature. Sorauf reports that the legislative chambers bear the signs of the male club, highly burnished cuspidors, for example; the lady legislator "may be viewed as an intruder in the smoking-room company."[37] More than three-quarters of the nation's state legislators have been exposed to a college education, a striking contrast to the educational level of the total population. Legislators are also concentrated in the occupations with more prestige. A great majority of legislators are either engaged in the professions, or are proprietors, managers, or officials of business concerns. Farmers constitute a sizeable minority of legislators in all but the most urban states. Lawyers are the largest single occupational group.[38]

Since the populations of the fifty states vary in ethnic and religious composition, it can be expected that state chambers will reflect ethnic and religious attributes in varying proportions. Table 8 indicates that the educational and occupational levels of legislators in every state will tend to be higher than the general population in those states. There is, however, a tendency for legislatures to reflect their states in certain characteristics. The Catholic percentage of the population in New Jersey, Pennsylvania, and Wisconsin is higher than the other states, and there are more Catholics in these legislatures. There are very few Catholics in the population or the legislature of Tennessee and Georgia. The farm populations of Tennessee, Georgia, and Wisconsin are larger than those of the other states, and there are correspondingly more farmers in their legislatures.

Social background information on state legislators also indicates that legislators tend to come from the "upwardly mobile" sectors of the population.[39] This places many of them among the "second-rung" elites in the status system rather than the established wealth. Although the sons and grandsons of distinguished old families of great wealth are increasingly entering Presidential and gubernatorial politics in the states, they seldom run for the state legislature. In contrast, state legislators have tended to take up occupations with more prestige than their fathers. Legislators are frequently among the middle or upper-middle status groups for whom politics is an avenue of upward mobility. Constituencies accept higher educated, more "prestigiously" employed candidates in the name of success, status, and the popular conceptions of "qualifications" for the legislative job. In general, constituencies seek gregarious, socially rising men from the prevailing racial, religious, and nationality groups of the district. Candidates should be "respectable" in

Table 8

SOCIAL BACKGROUND OF STATE LEGISLATORS, SELECTED STATES

	PER CENT COLLEGE GRADUATE	PER CENT PROFESSIONAL, MANAGERIAL OR SALES	PER CENT FARMERS AND FARM LABORERS	PER CENT CATHOLIC
California				
Population	10	48	2	22
Legislators (1957)	54	86	13	17
New Jersey				
Population	8	45	1	37
Legislators (1957)	63	92	2	36
Ohio				
Population	7	40	3	18
Legislators (1957)	58	88	10	23
Tennessee				
Population	5	35	10	1
Legislators (1957)	46	84	13	2
Pennsylvania				
Population	6	39	2	27
Legislators (1958)	32	76	5	34
Georgia				
Population	6	35	8	0.9
Legislators (1961)	57	78	22	0.4
Wisconsin				
Population	7	37	11	29
Legislators (1953)	40	68	22	33

Sources: Figures are derived from the following: John C. Wahlke, *et al., The Legislative System,* pp. 486–491; Frank J. Sorauf, *Party and Representation,* pp. 69–71; *The Wisconsin Blue Book 1954; Georgia Official and Statistical Register 1961;* National Council of Churches of Christ, *Churches and Church Membership in the U.S.* (New York: 1956); U.S. Bureau of Census, *U.S. Census of Population 1960,* "United States Summary" PC1 (1)–1C (Washington: U.S. Government Printing Office, 1962).

whatever ways the local mores define that term. The voters seem to want candidates typical of themselves in religion, race, and ethnic background, but with education, occupation, and social status above the average. In short, constituents seem to prefer that their legislators be "local boys made good."[40]

Legislators are also "joiners." Participation in a wide variety of public activity can insure that the candidate has at least a modest circle of acquaintances, that he is a "good mixer," and that he is known for his interest in the community. Religion and sports are particularly good avenues for legislative recruitment. Lay preaching and church ushering, and coaching, sponsoring, or announcing local sports create a favorable local image which can be used as a springboard for office. The record of group activity of most legislators indicates that they have many points of contact with their constituents.

Occupational data also clearly reflect the fact that the state legislator's job is a part-time one with a salary which is not self-supporting. Legislators must come from occupational groups with flexible work responsibility. The lawyer, the farmer, and the business owner can adjust his work to the legislative schedule, but the office manager cannot. The overrepresented occupations are those involving extensive public contact. The lawyer, insurance agent, farm implement dealer, tavern owner, and undertaker establish in their business the wide circle of friends necessary for political success. In short, the legislator's occupation should provide free time, public contacts, and social respectability.

In the urban industrial states, Democratic and Republican legislators differ in their social attributes. Catholic legislators are more likely to be Democrats than Republicans in these states. Legislators with strong ethnic ties are also likely to be Democrats, as are Negro legislators. Sorauf found marked differences in educational levels of Democratic and Republican legislators in Pennsylvania; 39 per cent of the Democratic legislators there did not graduate from high school while only 6 per cent of the Republican legislators were non-high school graduates.[41] Republican legislators in Pennsylvania on the whole were found to hold higher status occupations than Democratic legislators; 26 per cent of the Democratic legislators were in blue collar occupations (craftsmen, foremen, operatives, and laborers), while none of the Republican legislators could be so classified. These differences between the legislators of the two parties in the urban states do not grow out of the parties' expressed preference for specific social types. They are differences which are imposed by the separate constituencies represented by each party in most of the urban states. In these states the Republican and Democratic parties represent separate types of constituencies: urban, low-income, and ethnic constituencies are usually represented by Democrats; rural and high-income urban and suburban districts are usually represented by Republicans. In the more rural states the constituencies of the parties more closely resemble each other in their social composition, and hence Republican and Democratic legislators cannot be clearly differentiated according to their social attributes.

Finally, let us turn from considering the social status of legislators and ask, What is the social status of the office of state legislator? Sorauf reports, "If there is an order of accessibility to public office, the state legislature in Pennsylvania apparently stands just above small city borough and township office, below county and large city office, and greatly inferior to statewide or national office."[42]   Certainly the record of turnover of state legislators indicates that returning to office is not particularly high on their scale of values. Over half of the nation's state legislators are new at each session, the lower chambers having a greater percentage of new members than the upper chambers. This turnover is clearly not a product of competition for the job; only a very small proportion of legislators are turned out of office at the polls. An eight-state survey of legislative turnover from 1925 to 1933 shows that only 15 per cent of legislators who left service during that period were eliminated by electoral defeat.[43]   Most simply do not seek re-election and quit because of dissatisfactions: "Being in the legislature has hurt my law practice and cost me money"; "Any way you look at it the job means a sacrifice to you, your home, and your business"; "A political career is too uncertain and hazardous"; "You have to take a beating"; "It's a nervous life"; "The more service a man has, the more enemies he makes."[44]   Another indication that the turnover is not a product of competition is revealed in the state-by-state breakdown of turnover figures. The urban industrial states with competitive party systems have *less* turnover among legislators than the more rural states.[45]

RECRUITMENT OF LEGISLATORS.   Something has already been said about the recruitment process in the previous section. The constituencies fix broad standards of "social acceptability" of candidates, standards within which specialized recruiting agencies must operate. It is within the broad outlines of constituency expectations that party or non-party recruiters must set more specific criteria and go through the mechanics of recruitment.

Why does a legislator decide to run for office? It is next to impossible to determine the real motivations of office seekers — they seldom know themselves. It is even difficult to establish the real circumstances surrounding their recruitment. We can ask the legislators why they ran for office, who asked or encouraged them to run, and what role the party played in their decision. Yet the story which we are likely to get usually magnifies the legislator's political initiative and independence, describes his motivations in socially acceptable terms, and understates his debt to the party or other nominating groups. The chief rationalization for seeking office seems to be an interest in or a sense of obligation for public affairs: "The reason I was interested was that I felt I could do the community a service"; "I felt it a civic duty to run."[46]   Only seldom are the reasons for candidacy expressed in personal terms: "Oh, I just think it's lots of fun." Seldom will a legislator say that he ran to feed his ego, but occasionally a frank answer relating candidacy to professional or career aspirations is encountered: "It was an opportunity to expand my knowledge of the law and also good during the lean years of practice." Running for office is the classic form of "ethical advertising" for lawyers. The state legislature has occasionally been viewed as an alternative to unemployment: "The only job that was possible for me to get during the depression years was some sort of political one." Gregariousness and the desire to socialize no doubt contribute to the decisions of many office seekers: "I like people and being here you get all kinds." Politics has a special lure all of its own: "It gets into your blood and you like it." The need to feel useful and keep busy after retirement is not an infrequent motive: "You know a man of seventy can't find a $5,000 a year job so easy." Occasionally, a legislator will admit having nothing else to do: "When I came out of the Navy I was wholly free, nothing to do, absolutely nothing." Particular issues may mobilize a political career but idealogical involvement occupies a relatively unimportant place in a candidate's motives. Activity in organizations which are themselves deeply involved in politics often leads to candidacy: "About the time I decided to run I was quite active in the Union." Or candidacy may spring from a desire to contribute to a group interest: "I naturally have a desire to make advances beneficial to my race"; "If I hadn't, we would have lost the Jewish seat, and we never would have been able to get it back." However, despite some amazingly frank reasons for seeking to enter the state legislature, most decisions to run are cloaked in impersonal rationalizations: "I would like to serve the public as guaranteed by the principles as set forth by the constitution . . . ." Attempts to quantify these rationalizations seem fruitless, and it does not appear that the reasons for seeking legislative office are very different from state to state.

Circumstances of a legislator's recruitment are almost as obscure as his motives. Not surprisingly a large number of legislators declare that they were prevailed upon by friends, constituents, backers, or party leaders to seek the office. This expresses the old tradition that the office should seek the man. Few legislators seem willing to perceive their careers as party-sponsored. Genuine self-initiated candidacies are probably far fewer than the interview data indicate. We should expect that in the more competitive party states, legislators would be more likely to see the party as the necessary vehicle for a political career. Sorauf found that "party is obviously the chief stimulus to candidacy in Pennsylvania."[47] He also found the party instrumental in the primary elections; less than 5 per cent of the legislative membership in the 1958 legislative elections in Pennsylvania ran against and defeated party opposition in the primary. Most successful candidates for the legislature enjoyed pre-primary party endorsement; this endorsement not only helped defeat primary opposition but also operated to frighten off potential competition in the primary. The Legislative System studies also found more legislators in the competitive states willing to view their career as party-sponsored than legislators from the non-competitive state, Tennessee.

It also appears that the more competitive the state's party system, the more likely it is for legislators to have had some prior governmental experience, particularly service at the local level of government. The most common pre-legislative service is on city councils, county boards, and school boards. *The Legislative System* studies show the following percentages of legislators having some prior local government experience: New Jersey — 58; Ohio — 43; California — 33; Tennessee — 29.[48] This order in the states seems related to the degree of party competition in each of them. A separate study confirms this relationship between local government experience and party competition by reporting the following percentages of state legislators with experience in locally elected bodies: Wisconsin — 71; Nebraska — 33; West Virginia — 15; South Carolina — 8.[49] Even within a state the stronger the party organization in a constituency, the more likely a legislator is to have had local government experience before election to the legislature.[50] In competitive party systems the party is more likely to participate in the nominating process and state legislative office is likely to be looked upon as a reward for faithful party service at the local level.

How much competition exists for legislative seats? First, let us consider competition in primary elections. In 204 of the 308 legislative primaries in Pennsylvania in 1958 (66 per cent) there was no opposition at all to the single entry in each.[51] Wisconsin in the years 1946 to 1956 had contests in only a few more of the legislative primaries than did Pennsylvania.[52] In both of these states more than half of the legislators were unopposed for their party's nomination. In the non-competitive states, primary competition may occur more frequently in the majority party primaries; competition in the minority party primaries is very unlikely. Of course, competition is not only measured in terms of existence of contestants, but also in terms of the closeness of the races. Many legislators engaged in primary contests face only token opposition. Available evidence suggests that primary competition is greater where the likelihood of victory in the general election is greater. V. O. Key has shown that most primary competition occurs in a party's "sure" districts, some contests occur in "close" districts, and there is a distinct shortage of candidates in districts where the party's chances are poor.[53] The exceptions to this generalization are to be found in areas with strong party organization, where party discipline discourages insurgency even though prospects for success in the general election may be bright. Primary competition has also been hypothesized to be a function of urbanism and incumbency; competition increases in urban areas and whenever incumbents are running.

The culmination of the recruitment process is the general election. Yet so entrenched is one party or the other in many legislative constituencies that the voters have little real choice at the general election. A sampling of legislatures by Malcolm Jewell shows that the proportion of contested seats to total seats in general elections can range from a low of 41 per cent (North

Carolina senate, 1956–1960, New Hampshire house, 1950, Kentucky house, 1947–1957) to 100 per cent (Rhode Island senate and house, 1952–1956, Michigan senate, 1958–1960, New York house and senate, 1958–1962).[54] In most of the legislatures sampled about 80 per cent of the seats were contested in the general election. More seats are contested in states with close, two-party competition. In the Southern and border states where the legislatures are heavily Democratic there is little competition in the general election for legislative seats (of course it is in these states where primary competition in the majority party is frequent). In contrast, party competition in New York is so intense that both parties are given maximum incentive to run full legislative slates throughout the state. Statewide competition is only one of the factors explaining contested elections. Party organization and cohesion is another factor; even a party which obtains frequent statewide victories may experience local problems in organization strength resulting in a failure to run candidates. It takes time and work to build up local party organizations to produce a complete legislative slate. Even in hotly contested Pennsylvania occasionally nominations will go begging owing to a collapse of local party organization. After the Democratic party in Michigan had built itself into a competitive party in the 1930's and even captured majorities in the legislature, they left as many as one-quarter of the seats uncontested.[55] V. O. Key has argued that the direct primary itself weakens local party organizations and increases the percentage of uncontested elections.[56] Until recently California was a clear example of a primary system which inhibited the growth of party organization and fostered uncontested elections. Until 1959, the state permitted candidates to file in the primaries of both parties and until 1954 the primary ballot did not indicate the party of the candidate. For many years the same candidate won both primaries in over half of the California legislative districts.[57]

Competition means more than a name filed under the opposition party label. Generally, a competitive election is one where the winning candidate wins by something less than 2 to 1. Under this more realistic definition of competition, the absence of truly competitive politics in legislative elections is striking. In Pennsylvania, one of the more competitive states, over half of the legislators are elected by margins in excess of 2 to 1.[58] Similar findings are reported for competitive Massachusetts and Michigan.[59] Furthermore, in 47 per cent of the Pennsylvania constituencies in 1958 the voters had *neither* a contested primary nor a competitive general election; whoever recruited the party's candidates in these districts made the only meaningful choice in the entire selection process. Usually legislators from non-competitive districts face the session with little danger of defeat at the next election. It is interesting to note how their behavior in the legislature differs from the behavior of legislators from competitive districts (see page 187).

THE STRUCTURE OF LEGISLATURES

ENVIRONMENT. The pay, prerequisites, and working conditions of legislators vary a great deal from state to state. In general, the more populous urban industrial states provide more comfortable environments for their legislators than the smaller rural states. New York legislators receive an annual salary equivalent to $15,000 and legislators in California, Pennsylvania, Illinois, Massachusetts, New Jersey, and Ohio receive compensation in excess of $10,000 per year.[60] In contrast, New Hampshire pays its legislators $200 for the biennium. It is not surprising that turnover is higher among legislators from rural than from the urban states. However, the larger urban states tend to consider more legislation, remain in session longer, and demand more time of their legislators. This means that their legislators probably devote a smaller proportion of their time to private business and become more dependent on their legislative salary. The following contrasts were observed in the environment of legislators in California, New Jersey, Ohio, and Tennessee:[61]

California — In both demands and compensation the legislator's job is larger than most other states, but he may still suffer because in time and pay it is too much for a part-time job and not enough for a full-time one. The legislature meets five days a week from January to May in odd years and during March in even years, roughly 59 working days per year. Each member gets a modern two-room office suite and a full-time secretary. He can call on a legislative council with a large staff of lawyers and clerks to draft his bills and a large staff of the joint budget committee to review the two-billion-dollar executive budget. Every day he is supplied with copies of every bill with its latest amendments, an up-to-date agenda for both houses, yesterday's journal, and a "history" showing the current progress of all bills.

New Jersey — Legislators are paid well and enjoy a one day a week schedule, which enables them to fit their legislative work into their business with minimum interruption. They meet Mondays only from January to June every year, roughly 22 days a year. They receive only a small allowance for secretarial service which usually goes to their wives. No offices are provided. Ample research and bill drafting service is available.

Ohio — A legislator is paid well for meeting three to five days a week January through May in odd years only. But he must put more time into his job than his counterparts in New Jersey, roughly 49 days per year. His desk on the floor must serve as his office for the session. He must share a secretary with a number of other members. His legislative reference bureau is staffed by part-time students at Ohio State University.

Tennessee — A legislator receives a paltry $600 per year. He meets

4 to 5 days a week January through March in odd years only. He puts in about 28 working days per year. He must work at his desk or hotel room and he can only borrow on occasion a secretary from a state administrative agency. A legislative reference service is available for bill drafting. He can obtain copies only of general bills and the floor proceedings are not published until after the session is over.

RULES AND PROCEDURES. The formal rules and procedures by which a legislature operates are designed primarily to make the legislative process fair and orderly. Without established customs, rules, and procedures, it would be impossible for 50, 100, or 200 men to arrive at collective decisions about the thousands of items submitted to them during a legislative session. Yet the formal rules and procedures of legislatures also lend themselves easily to use by those who would delay or obstruct legislative action. It is a difficult process for a bill to become a law; legislative procedures offer many opportunities to defeat legislation. It is not surprising that a political institution which functions as an arbiter, rather than an initiator, of public policy should be designed to minimize deliberation even at the expense of granting advantage to those who would oppose change.

Legislatures follow a fairly standard pattern in the formal process of making laws. Table 9 provides a brief description of some of the more salient procedural characteristics of legislatures. The table illustrates the deliberative function of legislatures and the consequent advantage given to those who do not want action to be taken.

RULES OF THE GAME. Partly to counteract the impact of formal rules and procedures, legislatures develop a number of informal "rules of the game."[62] These unwritten rules are not merely "quaint and curious folkways." They support the purposes and functions of the legislature by helping to maintain the working consensus among legislators essential to legislative output. Legislators are aware of these rules (only 2 of 474 were unable to perceive any unwritten rules of the legislative game when questioned), and they carry clearly recognized sanctions which can be imposed upon errant members. A great majority of legislators appear to accept the functional utility of "rules of the game," some by stating clearly that observance of the rules contributes to legislative efficiency, others by giving reasons why certain rules are necessary.

Some rules contribute to the legislative function by *promoting group cohesion and solidarity*. In the words of legislators themselves, "Support another member's local bill if it doesn't affect you or your district"; "Don't steal another member's bill"; "Accept the author's amendments to a bill"; "Don't make personal attacks on other members"; "Oppose the bill, not the man"; "Don't be a prima donna, an individualist, an extremist or a publicity

Table 9

SUMMARY OF LEGISLATIVE PROCEDURE FOR BILL PASSAGE

1. *Introduction of Bill* (House or Senate)	One or more members file bill with Clerk or presiding officer who gives it a number and refers it to a committee. This constitutes the first reading.
2. *Committee Hearings*	Important bills may be given public hearings at which all interested persons or groups may testify. Committee may speed or delay hearings.
3. *Committee Report*	Committee meets in executive (closed) session. Bills may be amended or pigeonholed or reported favorably or unfavorably.
4. *Bill Placed on Calendar*	Bills reported by committee are placed on calendar for floor consideration. Urgent or favorite bills may get priority by unanimous consent or informal maneuvering; other bills may be delayed, sometimes indefinitely.
5. *Floor Debate, Amendment, Vote*	The second reading of the bill before the entire chamber is usually accompanied by debate and perhaps amendments from the floor. Often the crucial vote is on an amendment or on second reading.
6. *Third Reading and Passage*	Usually a bill is delayed one calendar day before it is brought to the floor for third reading. On third reading debate is not customary and amendments usually require unanimous consent. After final vote, bill is certified by presiding officer and sent to second house.

hound"; "Don't be overambitious"; "Don't divulge confidential information"; "Defend the legislature and its members against outsiders." Another category of rules *promote predictability of behavior within the system:* "Keep your word"; "Abide by commitments"; "Don't conceal the real purpose of bills or amendments"; "Don't engage in parliamentary chicanery"; "Notify in advance if you can't keep a commitment." Some rules *channel and put limits upon conflict:* "Be willing to compromise"; "Accept half a loaf"; "Go along with the majority of the party"; "Respect the seniority system"; "Respect older members"; "Don't try to accomplish too much too soon"; "Respect committee jurisdiction"; "Don't vote to discharge a committee." Other rules

Table 9, continued

7.	*Referral to Second Chamber*	Bill is sent to second chamber where steps 1 through 6 must be repeated. Bills must pass both chambers in identical form before going to governor.
8.	*Conference Committee*	If there are differences in wording in the bills passed by each house, one or the other house must accept the wording of the other house or request a conference committee. This committee is made up of members of both houses and it arrives at a single wording for the bill.
9.	*Vote on Conference Committee Report*	Both houses must vote to approve conference committee wording of bill. Bills may be shuttled back and forth and eventually die for lack of agreement between both houses.
10.	*Governor's Signature or Veto*	An identical bill passed by both houses becomes law with the governor's signature. It may also become law without his signature after a certain lapse of time (e.g., 10 days) if the legislature is still in session. If the legislature has adjourned during this time, the governor's failure to sign is the same as a veto. A governor may formally veto a bill and return it to the house of origin for reconsideration. An unusual majority is generally required to override a veto.

are designed to *expedite legislative business:* "Don't talk too much"; "Don't fight unnecessarily"; "Don't introduce too many bills and amendments"; "Be punctual and regular"; "Take the job seriously"; "Don't be too political"; "Don't call attention to the absence of a quorum."

A most important, informal device is the granting of unanimous consent for the suspension of the formal rules; this permits a legislature to consider bills not on the calendar, to pass bills immediately without the necessary three readings, to dispense with time-consuming formalities, to permit non-members to speak, and to otherwise alter the formal procedures. Another informal rule is the practice in many states of passing local bills without debate or opposition when the local delegation unanimously supports the measure. Also listed among the rules of the game are personal qualities of legislators which are normally valued highly in any social group: courtesy, sociability, gracefulness in defeat, caution in commitments, self-restraint in goals, integrity, objectivity, and intelligence. These informal rules of the game are recognized to some degree by legislators everywhere.

These rules are enforced by clearly recognized sanctions. Over 89 per cent of the legislators in four states cited specific sanctions for enforcing these unwritten rules. The most frequently mentioned sanction involved obstructing the errant legislator's bills: "Abstain or vote against him"; "Bottle up his bills in committee"; "Amend his bills"; "Pass them only if of major importance to the general welfare." Another sanction is social ostracism: "Give him the silent treatment"; "Subtly reject him personally." Errant legislators may also become the object of mistrust: "Cross-examine him on the floor and in committee"; "Don't put any trust in him." Or they may lose some of their political perquisites and rewards of office: "Take away patronage and good committee assignments." Other sanctions include denial of legislative courtesies and privileges and occasional overt demonstrations of displeasure, such as ridicule, hissing, or laughing. The observance of rules, however, is not obtained through fear of sanction so much as the positive recognition on the part of legislators of the utility of rules in helping the legislature perform its chores.

COMMITTEE SYSTEMS. While it is most convenient to study legislative decision-making by observing floor actions, particularly the division of Ayes and Nays, the floor is not the only locus of important legislative decisions. Many observers and legislators feel that committee work is essential to the legislative process. Here it is that public hearings are held, policies pleaded and debated, legislation amended and compromised, bills rushed to the floor or pigeonholed. The function of the committee system is to reduce legislative work to manageable proportions by providing for a division of labor among legislators. But by so doing the committees themselves often come to exercise considerable influence over the outcome of legislation. Another opportunity is provided for delay and obstruction by less than the majority of legislators, sometimes by a single committee chairman. Duane Lockard reports, "What a new legislator soon finds is that there is no choice but to depend upon his colleagues to inform him about issues assigned to their committees, and, like it or not, he is reduced to following their advice unless he knows the subject well enough to have an opinion. It is a source of surprise to many new members how many issues they are too ignorant to have an opinion about. . . ."[63]

A typical legislative chamber will have between twenty and thirty standing committees which consider all bills in a particular field, such as revenue, appropriations, highways, welfare, education, labor, judiciary, or local government. Many houses operate with a rules committee which governs house proceedings and determines the priority given the bills on the legislative calendar. Committees may prevent the bill from coming to the floor for vote by inaction ("pigeonholing") although twenty states require every committee to report on every bill referred to it either favorably or unfavorably.

The importance of committee systems seems to vary from state to state. Yet Malcolm Jewell argues effectively that state legislative committees do not exercise the independent influence over legislation that Congressional committees enjoy. He offers several reasons "why legislative standing committees are but pale shadows of their Congressional counterparts."[64] Most state legislatures meet only a few months every other year giving committees very little time for any careful review of bills. Committees seldom have any staff assistance, legislative turnover is high, a seniority system is not as prevalent as it is in Congress, and committee members seldom acquire the experience and expertise of their Congressional counterparts. In most state legislatures the rules committee does not have the power to determine what bills will reach the floor as does the rules committee of the U.S. House of Representatives. The committee system, in short, does not offer the state legislator an independent source of power separate from party or factional basis of power. Of course, the fact that legislative committees are not independent sources of power does not mean that they are never used as important instruments of party or factional control.

A study of the 1959 Florida legislature provides an excellent example of a dominant, conservative rural faction using the committee system to perpetuate its control.[65] Thirteen senators of thirty-eight held forty-nine seats including all committee chairmanships on the six most important committees. In Florida a bill unfavorably reported on by a committee requires a two-thirds vote to pass. In contrast, a recent study of the Illinois legislature provides an example of a legislature in which the committee system is relatively unimportant.[66] Committees invariably accede to the urging of a bill's sponsor to bring his bill to the floor and very few bills are ever reported on unfavorably. Furthermore, committees seldom make any important amendments to bills. In New Jersey, parties choose to operate through a caucus system rather than the committee system. The chambers are small enough (fifty in the house and twenty-one in the senate) that the majority caucus can engage in frank and informal discussion. Bills approved by the caucus must technically be recommended by a standing committee, but committee approval is so assured that committees seldom even meet; the chairman merely circulates copies of bills for members' signatures. Committees do not fail to report bills approved by the majority caucus.

These and other studies suggest the following explanations for variations among the several states and the strength of their committee systems: (1) Committees exercise less independent influence over legislation in two-party states where party discipline is high; (2) Committees exercise less influence in two-party states when the governor and the legislature are of the same party, but exercise more influence under divided government; (3) In states where the governor, the party, or a faction exercises strong influence over the legislature, committees are not likely to play an independent role; (4) In contrast, committees are more likely to be influential in one-party states where the governor does not exert strong leadership.

LEGISLATIVE ROLES. Roles are expectations about the kind of behavior people ought to exhibit. Expectations are placed upon legislators by his fellow legislators, his party, the opposition party, the governor, the legislative leadership, his constituents and interest groups, his friends, as well as the expectations he places upon himself. A legislator may change roles as he acts to fulfill different expectations. Some expectations loom so large in the eyes of certain legislators that these men can easily be categorized according to the roles which seem to dominate their behavior.

Perhaps the most important and distinctive roles in the legislative process are those of leadership.[67] The typical legislative chamber has a presiding officer, majority and minority floor leaders, a number of committee chairmen, and a steering committee. The expectations with regard to these officers are rather consistent. Their behavior is subject to the restraints and demands of the membership. The functions of leaders are similar to the functions of rules. First of all, leaders are expected to help make the legislative system stable and predictable. They are expected to maintain order, to know the rules and procedures, to follow the rules, and to show fairness and impartiality. This of course is more true of presiding officers and committee chairmen than party leaders (see Table 10). The leaders are also expected to help focus the issues and resolve conflict. They can do so by presenting issues clearly, narrowing the alternatives, organizing hearings, and promoting the party or administration point of view on bills. The majority leader is supposed to "get the administrative program through" while the minority leader tries to develop criticism, "find party issues," and "develop a constructive opposition." Leaders are also expected to administer the legislature and expedite business. This includes "promoting team work," "helping individuals," "being accessible," "cracking the whip in the interest of time and smooth operation," starting the sessions on time and keeping them on schedule, and distributing the work load. It also involves communication, coordination, and liaison with the governor, with administrative departments, and with the other chamber. Finally, leaders are expected to know what is going on;

this includes knowing the subject matter of bills. Role conflict can occur when differing expectations are placed upon leaders; this is a particularly important problem for presiding officers. They are both referees and partisan leaders. As one legislator explained it: "He should be fair to both sides — except in a real pinch."

Table 10

BEHAVIOR EXPECTED OF LEGISLATIVE OFFICERS IN FOUR STATES

	PRESIDING OFFICERS*	COMMITTEE CHAIRMEN*	PARTY LEADERS*
Promoting a stable, predictable system	72%	49%	15%
Focusing issues and resolving conflict	57	63	63
Administering the system, expediting business, and promoting harmony	56	47	52
Knowing the content of bills	6	22	10

*Percentages represent proportions of all legislators in California, New Jersey, Ohio, and Tennessee, describing the behavior of legislative officers in these terms.

Source: Wahlke, *et al., The Legislative System*, p. 174.

Another set of legislative roles that are commonly encountered and which make important contributions to the legislative process are the "subject matter experts." Unlike leadership roles, the roles of subject matter experts are not embodied in formal offices. However, the existence of subject matter experts is closely associated with the committee system and the practice of recognizing seniority within the committee. The committee system introduces specialization into legislative process and the seniority system places at the head of the committee the majority member longest exposed to information about the subject matter of the committee. Subject matter experts are widely recognized among legislators; they occur in the fields of law, finance, education, agriculture, conservation, local government, labor, transportation, etc. *The Legislative System* study reported that 91 per cent of 471 state legislators interviewed named one or more members they considered specialists in some field, and 83 per cent named fields in which they, themselves, had specialized. Legislators often acquire a reputation for expertise through their occupations. Others become expert through contact with the dominant interest in their constituency. Still others see the acquisition of expertise as a source of influence and personal advancement: "I examined the fields to see what were the most important subjects of statewide interest which each area would see as important for years to come. I was looking for a vehicle to move forward in state politics."[68] There is some evidence to support the contention that experts exercise more influence over bills within their fields than non-experts. A study of California legislators showed that, other things being equal, an expert legislator will be more successful in getting bills passed in his field than a legislator who has no recognized expertise.[69]

Still another way of describing characteristic behaviors is to discover the legislator's orientations toward the expectations of constituents and party. Legislators have been classified as either "trustees" (those who are guided in legislative affairs solely by their personal conscience and judgment), "delegates" (those who are guided by the instructions or wishes of their constituents), or "partisans" (those who look to the party leadership for guidance).[70] Despite the concern of political scientists since Burke with the classic question of whether legislators should represent their party, their constituency, or their conscience, few legislators actually exhibit in their behavior a firm commitment to any of these. The fact that most legislators claim in interview situations to be guided solely by their own conscience is not behaviorally relevant. Most legislators when facing specific issues do not perceive any conflict between the wishes of their constituents, their party, or their own judgment. Even where conflict is perceived, most legislators attempt to balance conflicting demands rather than opt exclusively for one role or the other. One legislator whisked the whole problem away with a little semantic trickery: "A representative's judgment should arise from knowing the needs and wants of his district and state."[71] For most legislators the formal attribution of the role of "trustee" is little more than a verbalism. It reflects the heroic image of the independent and courageous defender of the public interests who acts out of his own personal virtue and conviction regardless of the consequences. However, the way in which legislators actually balance party and constituency in their voting behavior is discussed below. Yet there are a handful of legislators in every chamber who approach the pure type of trustee, delegate, or partisan.

Legislators might also be classified according to the way in which they, themselves, perceive the legislative function — in other words, according to the expectations they place upon their own behavior as legislators. *The Legislative System* study found four discernible types of self-conceptions among legislators — the ritualist, the tribune, the inventor, and the broker.[72] The ritualist sees his job in terms of the mechanics of legislative operations. He is preoccupied with parliamentary rules and routine; their mastery appears to the ritualist as his principal task. Legislative maneuvering becomes an end in itself. Passing a budget is viewed as a necessary routine rather than as an important policy-making act. Committee work is important to the ritualist. The technical perfection of laws seems almost as important to him as their policy implication. Some ritualist orientations were expressed as follows: "Primarily I should acquaint myself with parliamentary procedures and rules and regulations, in finding out where I may avail myself with the necessary information to enable myself to represent my constituency to the highest degree"; "The most important thing which isn't done enough is to watch the type of bills that pass and to watch the language of bills."

The tribune perceives himself "as the discoverer or connoisseur of popular needs, as the defender of popular interests, or as the advocate of popular demand." He sees his principal task as one of understanding local problems, making himself available to the people back home, and keeping track of public opinion: "Well, most important is to keep in close touch with your constituents and find out what they want"; "A legislator has an obligation to protect people's rights — every time you pass a law, you take away from them"; "With me the only reason is to improve things for the ordinary man and the underdog — big business and rich people have attorneys, accountants, and loopholes in the laws but damn few people are interested in the underdog and minorities."

Few legislators opted for the role of inventor. The inventor sees himself as the initiator and creator of public policy. He wants the legislature to take the lead in solving the current major problems in his state — welfare, education, highways, taxes, and so on. He believes the legislature "should be in front of things." The fact that few of the legislators interviewed even claimed to approach their task in a creative manner is evidence that legislators themselves recognize that the function of policy initiation has shifted from the legislatures to the governor, executive agencies, and interest groups. The true inventors in the legislature are probably frustrated men, since seldom does the legislature do anything but respond to the inventiveness of the governor or civil servants or active pressure groups. Only in those two-party states where legislature and executive are controlled by two different parties is it likely that the legislature will attempt to compete with the governor in making public policy. Still, many legislators persist in seeing their task in grand proportions: "Like a doctor, this job is to cure ills. This state has many economic and social problems, and a legislator with lots of background can grasp these problems and introduce legislation to better them. He can cure just like a doctor can."

A central theme in many legislative studies is that the legislature plays the role of the referee or broker in the struggle between interest groups, constituencies, and executive agencies. The broker's task is to balance, to compromise, and to arbitrate between conflicting interests. Although the role of broker is probably a realistic appraisal of the functions of legislatures as a whole, only a minority of legislators will state that this is their personal role.

However, those that do may be the more discerning and efficacious legislators. As one legislator expressed the brokerage role: "It's important to see the other man's point of view. Even if you feel that what you want is the absolute best, give a bit and get the next best thing."

The roles mentioned here by no means exhaust the possibilities.[73] In the words of a former Connecticut state senator:

> It is obvious of course that there is no such thing as the single perspective on the legislature; the member's conception of his own proper role determines how he sees the legislative process, and the illusions that members bring with them to the state capitol are by no means identical. Some see their task in terms of an idealized, if fuzzy, conception of a rational man whose task it is to mediate on all questions, resist all special interest pressures, and decide all issues on their "merits" regardless of the pressures brought to bear by anybody — even including constituents. Others see themselves as the chosen delegates of some special element in the society — farmers, laborers, insurance and real estate businesses, or the party organization — and they fully expect to act accordingly.[74]

DECISION-MAKING IN LEGISLATURES

LEGISLATIVE CONFLICT. Many of the decisions made by state legislatures do not involve conflict. Most bills are enacted into law without a single negative vote. Separate studies of the Pennsylvania legislature in 1951 and 1957 show that roughly 80 per cent of the total roll calls in the senate were unanimous and 70 per cent of the total roll calls in the house were unanimous.[75] Yet this does not mean that legislative chambers are free from conflict; unanimous bills are generally local or minor bills involving decisions which are not deeply devisive.

What are the principal types of conflicts which affect legislative decision-making? If we can rely on the perceptions of legislators themselves about the types of conflicts which consume their energies, then Table 11 is a valuable indicator of the separate types of conflicts which prevail in different states. In California, regional conflicts rank most important, yet such conflicts were not perceived as particularly intense in New Jersey, Ohio, or Tennessee. Conflicts between the legislature and governor appeared important in New Jersey and Tennessee but not in California. Only rural-urban conflicts were rated as important by over half of the legislators in all four states.[76]

PARTY INFLUENCE. The influence of parties in legislative decision-making in the fifty states is by no means uniform. First of all, it is obvious that parties in one-party states do not exercise tight party discipline over the voting of legislators. Five state legislatures have not seated a Republican since Reconstruction Days and ten others have averaged over 70 per cent

Table 11

CONFLICTS PERCEIVED AS IMPORTANT BY STATE LEGISLATORS IN FOUR STATES

| TYPE OF CONFLICT | PER CENT DECLARED "IMPORTANT," HOUSE AND SENATE | | | | | | | |
| | California | | New Jersey | | Ohio | | Tennessee | |
	H	S	H	S	H	S	H	S
Rural-Urban	65	74	53	50	79	65	91	63
Party	26	26	96	85	49	59	23	17
Governor-Legislature	18	24	76	70	36	38	89	96
Liberal-Conservative	58	74	22	25	52	59	29	37
Labor-Management	65	62	18	15	61	55	54	67
Regional	69	44	18	40	17	10	13	20

Source: Wahlke, *et al., The Legislative System*, p. 425.

Democratic in the last ten years. In terms of legislative behavior one-party states are really no-party states. As a Tennessee legislator expressed it: "You never thought about the Democratic party unless the Republicans were trying something — for example reapportionment."[77]

The extent of partisanship in legislative decision-making varies even among the more or less competitive states. One common measure of party influence on voting is the percentage of non-unanimous roll call votes on which a majority of Democrats voted against the majority of Republicans. The compilations by the *Congressional Quarterly* show that the proportion of Congressional roll calls in which the two parties have been in opposition has ranged from 35 to 50 per cent. Table 12 suggests that party voting may be higher in the state legislatures of New York, Pennsylvania, Connecticut, Rhode Island, and Massachusetts than it is in Congress. Party voting is also common in Ohio, Illinois, New Hampshire, Washington, and Kentucky. Parties appear less influential in Colorado, Missouri, and California. Notice that Table 12 excludes unanimous or nearly unanimous votes in determining the influence of parties. Of course since most legislative decisions are unanimous, party votes would represent only a very small proportion of *all* roll call votes. Yet this does not justify the conclusion that parties are insignificant in legislative decision-making. The function of political parties is to offer alternatives where significant conflict exists, and a unanimous or nearly unanimous vote is evidence that no real demand existed for an alternative decision. Thus, the importance of parties is best observed on non-unanimous votes.[78]

A very different approach to party influence has led to similar findings. *The Legislative System* studies attempted to determine the role of parties in legislative decision-making by asking legislators what they thought the role of parties to be. Over 90 per cent of New Jersey's legislators perceived much

Table 12

PARTY VOTING IN SELECTED LEGISLATURES ON NON-UNANIMOUS ROLL CALL VOTES

| | PER CENT OF NON-UNANIMOUS ROLL CALLS WITH PARTY MAJORITIES IN DISAGREEMENT | | |
STATE	*Senate*	*House*	*Years*
Rhode Island	96	96	1931, '37, '51
Connecticut	90	83	1931–51
Massachusetts	82	87	1931, '37, '51*
New York	62	61	1947, '49*
Pennsylvania	64	81	1945*
Pennsylvania	34	43	1951
Pennsylvania	51	43	1957
Ohio	52	40	1949, '55, '57*
Illinois	53	54	1949*
New Hampshire	72	68	1931, '37, '51*
Washington	71	51	1945*
Kentucky	54	41	1944, '46*
Colorado	36	38	1941, '47*
Missouri	23	36	1945, '46*
California	20	32	1947, '49*
California	†	34	1957*
California	31	49	1959*

*In the starred years, percentages are based upon roll calls with at least 10 per cent of the members voting in the minority.
†Data not available.

Source: Malcolm Jewell, *The State Legislature*, p. 52.

or considerable party influence. Ohio legislators were more divided: 51 per cent perceived considerable party influence, while 31 per cent saw little or no party influence. In California and Tennessee 40 and 57 per cent of their legislators felt that parties exercise little or no influence; only 6 and 21 per cent perceived considerable party influence. It was also found that belonging to the majority party strengthens a legislator's feelings of personal effectiveness. Members of the majority parties in all but Tennessee, the state rated lowest in perceived party influence, felt more efficacious in their law-making activities than members of the minority party.[79]

On what types of issues did the parties exercise great influence? Minor bills involving the licensing of water well drillers, beauticians, or barbers do not usually become the subject matter of party votes, and only infrequently will the parties divide over such matters as the designation of an official state bird. In the more urban and industrialized states, parties usually display the greatest cohesion on issues involving taxation and appropriations, welfare, education, and regulation of business and labor — in short, the major social and economic controversies which divide the national parties. Party influence in budgetary matters is particularly apparent since the budget often involves basic issues of social welfare and class interest on which parties in urban states are split. In addition, the budget is clearly identified as the product of the governor and carries the label of the party of the governor. Appeals are made for legislators to support the budget of the governor of their party, while opposition legislators are stimulated to force changes in the budget in order to create issues for coming elections. Another type of bill which is often the subject of party voting is one involving the party as an interest group. Parties often exhibit an interest in bills proposing to transfer powers from an office controlled by one party to an office controlled by the other, or bills proposing to create or abolish non-civil service jobs. Parties display considerable interest in bills affecting the organization of local government, state administration, the civil service, registration and election laws, and legislative procedure. On issues which directly affect the party organization and prestige, the parties react in a fashion characteristic of interest groups.[80]

What factors distinguish those states in which the party substantially influences legislative decision-making from those states in which it does not? First of all, party cohesion is found in the competitive states rather than the non-competitive states. Since the non-competitive states are the rural non-industrial states, party voting appears related to urbanism and economic development if all fifty states are considered. Party voting is more frequent in the legislatures of urban industrial states. However, there are some urban states in which party voting is not a frequent occurrence; California is a notable example. Party cohesion is really strongest in those urban industrial states in which the parties represent separate socio-economic constituencies. Party voting occurs in those competitive states in which Democratic legislators represent central-city, low-income, ethnic and racial constituencies, and Republican legislators represent middle-class, suburban, small town and rural constituencies. Party cohesion is weak in states where party alignments do not coincide with socio-economic divisions of the constituencies.[81]

What then is the basis of party cohesion in the states where it exists? Is party cohesion a product of effective party organization and discipline? Or is it really a result of similarities in the constituencies represented by each party? For example, is Democratic party cohesion in industrial states a result of party organization pressures? Or is it the fact that Democrats typically are elected from metropolitan centers with strong labor groups, many Catholic voters, racial and ethnic minorities, and persons with few skills and poor education, and it is really constituency similarities which hold the Democratic legislators together? Could it be that Republican cohesion in these states is a product of the fact that Republicans typically represent middle-class suburbs, small towns, and rural areas, and these types of constituencies have similar ideas about public policy?

There is some evidence to suggest that party organization and discipline can be independently effective in mustering support on major questions. Duane Lockard reports of his experiences as a Connecticut senator:

> While the parties do not always initiate policies nor do they often frame the bills and proposals made (although they do both in some instances), any wise promoter of a bill will turn first to the leaders of the party and seek their support on the well founded assumption that their support is crucially necessary. It may be possible to defeat the party leadership and recruit the necessary support from the membership of the legislature without regard to party lines, but in states where there is significant party organizational strength no experienced actor would ever fail to seek the support of the party leadership, and if their support is not available he will seek their neutrality as the next best alternative.[82]

Lockard also reports that leaders can discipline members in many subtle ways: by making the non-conformist feel socially ill at ease in the legislature, by refusing to grant legislative time for his pet projects, and by opposing him for higher offices on the state level. Sanctions are rarely used, however, since the knowledge of their existence is a sufficient deterrent to party disloyalty. Moreover, the use of discipline is probably less important than the habit of working together in party groups. If the established ethos in the legislature is to work with the party, the new member easily falls into the prevailing pattern. In contrast, where a tradition of independence exists, party leadership would have great difficulty initiating control, even through the use of sanctions.

CONSTITUENCY INFLUENCE. It is unlikely that party organization and discipline alone is the cause of party voting, for organization and discipline can only be effective under certain conditions. The weight of evidence seems to support the hypothesis that party influence is only effective where the parties represent separate and distinct socio-economic coalitions. Where the constituencies of a state are divided along social and economic lines and where the party division coincides with these constituency divisions, only then will party program and discipline be effective in shaping policy in legislative chambers.

Pennsylvania is an excellent example of a state in which Republican and Democratic legislative districts are clearly differentiated by socio-economic variables. The parties are first divided along rural-urban lines, and within urban areas they are further divided along indices of socio-economic status. Republicans dominate in rural areas and in the wealthier urban areas (upper middle-class suburbs and several "silk stocking" districts in Phila-delphia and Pittsburgh). Democratic districts are found predominantly in the less wealthy, urban areas of the state. A similar pattern emerges if occu-pational, religious, or racial characteristics are considered. Republican districts within urban areas prove to be the districts with greater concentra-tions of professional, managerial, sales, and clerical jobs. Republican candi-dates fare badly among Negro voters; thirteen of fourteen legislative districts with 15 per cent Negro population elected Democratic legislators in 1958. The Democrats dominate the southern and eastern European, Irish, Catholic districts which are frequently the big-city, mining, or mill districts. The Re-publicans draw heavily in the Anglo-Saxon northern and western European, Protestant districts of the state. This same sort of party division of legislative districts has been documented in Massachusetts and Michigan.[83] In short, the Democratic and Republican division of legislative constituencies in these states follows the socio-economic divisions of national party politics.

It is this division of constituencies which is the basis of party cohesion and influence in the legislature. Evidence to support this view is provided if we examine the voting behavior of legislators elected from districts *atypical* of districts which usually elect members of their party. Since rural and high-income urban districts in Pennsylvania generally elect Republicans, and low-income urban districts generally elect Democrats, atypical districts are rural or wealthy urban districts which elect Democrats and low-income urban districts which elect Republicans. Studies in Pennsylvania, Massachusetts, and Michigan of the voting behavior of representatives from these atypical districts show that they tend to cross party lines much more frequently than representatives elected from districts typical of their party.[84] The threat to Democratic party cohesion in these states came from small bands of rural Democrats; insurgency within the Republican party originated from the urban Republican legislators. The fact that party cohesion breaks down among representatives elected by districts atypical of their party indicates that co-hesion may really be a function of constituency similarities rather than party organization and discipline.

One of the more rigorous investigations into the causes of party voting in a state legislature is Thomas A. Flinn's study of party voting in Ohio. Flinn expresses the constituency basis of party cohesion in the following hypothesis: ". . . legislators from similar constituencies will vote together and in opposition to legislators from constituencies with contrasting character-istics. To the extent that parties find their support in contrasting constitu-encies, party responsibility is the consequence."[85] Flinn argues that constituency factors alone do not fully explain party cohesion, since members of the same party representing dissimilar districts show greater cohesion than the membership of the rural and urban blocs. On the other hand, the experience in Ohio does indicate a relationship between constituency and party loyalty. Within each party, members from districts typical of their party in socio-economic attributes support the party position more often than members from districts atypical of the party. Flinn concludes:

> Party responsibility is a consequence of party competition. . . . Various factors may intervene to inhibit or promote party responsibility, but the only important one located with substantial confidence . . . is constituency. Prospects for increased party responsibility depend, therefore, on the spread of party competition and upon a sorting out of legislative constituencies so that the districts represented by the respective parties are more homogeneous.[86]

The effect of constituency on voting behavior can be observed in still another fashion. In the urban states, "close" legislative districts (where the margin of victory is less than two-to-one) are those in which typically Republican socio-economic characteristics balance typically Democratic socio-economic differences. In contrast, "safe" districts (where the margin of victory is greater than two-to-one) are those with a socio-economic imbalance favoring one or the other party. It turns out that legislators elected from "safe" districts generally show greater party loyalty on roll call votes than legislators elected from "close" districts. Legislators with relatively thin margins of victory reflect the socio-economic balance of their districts in their voting and exhibit less party loyalty.[87]

Constituency characteristics, then, help to explain not only the outcome of elections but the behavior of the elected. The constituency basis of party cohesion has been studied in Pennsylvania, Michigan, Massachusetts, Ohio, and Kansas and appears to be operative in New York, Illinois, and many other states.[88] In contrast, Washington presents an example of a state where party lines do not follow constituency differences and, as a consequence, party unity is lower despite a high degree of organization in the legislature.[89] The constituency of each party in Washington includes both rural and urban legislative districts in reasonable, balanced proportions. Democratic party cohesion is broken down by the existence of liberal and conservative wings which roughly follow a rural-urban division. In California, too, the parties do not clearly follow rural-urban divisions within the state, and the result is a lack of party cohesion and influence in the legislature. The California system of apportionment which grants one senate seat to each county regardless of population strengthens the rural wing of the Democratic party in the senate. This contributes to a lower level of party voting in the senate than in the assembly. Of course the tradition of non-partisanship in California has also tended to reduce the influence of party in the legislature. Phrases like "playing at parties" and "captive of your party" from interviewed legislators attest to the persistence of anti-party bias in California.[90] Party voting is also low in Missouri, and there, too, we do not find a clear rural-urban or metropolitan out-state alignment of the parties. Both parties draw their votes from rural and urban constituencies in approximately equal proportions. Salisbury reports that economic and social conflicts are not developed along party lines and that, as a result, Missouri is a "politically bland" state.[91]

If constituency influences operate through the party system in competitive states, it would follow that these influences would operate more directly on voting behavior in one-party states where the party is removed as an important reference group for the legislator. A study of voting behavior in the 1959 Oklahoma house of representatives tends to confirm this line of reasoning.[92] In this study of a one-party legislative chamber (9 Republicans faced 110 Democrats), voting on seven separate categories of subject matter were analyzed in 107 non-unanimous votes. Voting on the governor's legislative program and election regulations was related to the political competitiveness of the constituencies. Voting on education issues was closely related to the socio-economic status of the constituencies, while voting on public morals issues was related to the rural-urban characteristics of the constituencies. A coalition of big-city and rural legislators opposed the legislators from small and medium-sized cities on taxation issues. On labor and welfare issues interest groups working through the committee system seemed most influential; there are few factory or union workers in the Oklahoma work force and little basis of constituency support exists for labor measures. Voting on labor and welfare issues suggested that in the absence of both party and constituency influence, organized interest groups may be more effective.

It is important to note, however, that the constituency characteristics which influenced voting in Oklahoma shifted from one category of issue to another. Permanent voting factions did not exist in this one-party legislature. Malcolm Jewell argues that this is typical of many Southern one-party legislatures. No permanent voting blocs, based upon constituency or any other factor, can be discerned. "Rural, conservative legislators have been able to maintain sufficient identity of interest and harmony within their ranks to prevent the development of clearly defined blocs in the legislature."[93] However, in those Southern states which are rapidly urbanizing, notably Florida, Texas, Georgia, and Louisiana, rural-urban factions are emerging. To date, these voting blocs are forming within the Democratic legislative party. The growth of legislative factions in these states is likely to be intensified by reapportionment.

To say that constituencies make themselves felt in legislative decision-making is not to swallow whole the image of a legislator as an errand boy, a delegate, or a "lackey." In fact, most legislators seem to side with Burke's classic argument that the representative should be guided not by "local purposes" or "local prejudices," but by "his unbiased opinion, his mature judgment, his enlightened conscience." Sixty-three per cent of legislators in four states identified themselves with the Burkean position, rather than subscribe to the role of district delegate or even admit to balancing personal views with those of constituents.[94] It is not surprising that most legislators perceive themselves as unfettered decision-makers drawing their wisdom chiefly, if not completely, from their own virtue, knowledge, and experience.[95] Yet formal protestations of independence in an interview obscure more than they reveal the real influence of the constituencies. Aside from the social incentive to assert their independence, legislators themselves are seldom conscious of the many ways in which their constituency impinges upon their behavior. The classic choice posed by Burke between district demands and personal judgment is an artificial issue to most legislators. They are products of their constituency and they share its goals and values. Conflicts between their district's views and their own are rare. We have seen that legislators have roots deep in their constituencies — many organizational memberships, life-time residency, shared religious and ethnic affiliations, for example. The party with which the legislator identifies is also a creature of the constituency; it accedes to local interests, local political mores, local political style. The legislator is so much "of" his constituency that he needs little direct prompting or supervision. As one discerning legislator commented: "Basically you represent the thinking of the people who have gone through what you have gone through and who are what you are. You vote according to that. In other words, if you come from a suburb you reflect the thinking of people in the suburbs; if you are of depressed people, you reflect that. You represent the sum total of your background."[96]

ORGANIZED GROUP INFLUENCE. The character and influence of organized groups in legislative decision-making varies from state to state. Elsewhere in this volume the reader will find a discussion of interest groups in state politics and an analysis of their relative influence in the fifty states. One way to approach interest group activity in the legislative process is to ask legislators what groups, if any, they perceive as being powerful. This was the approach of the authors of *The Legislative System*. In the course of their interviews, California legislators refer to fifty-six specifically named organizations; New Jersey legislators named thirty-eight formal organizations; Ohio legislators mentioned sixty-eight organizations; and Tennessee lawmakers mentioned forty organizations.[97] Thus, there seems to be little doubt that most legislators are aware of considerable organized interest group activity. There is also considerable agreement among legislators about which types of interest groups were perceived as most powerful. Business interests were named as "most powerful groups" more often than any other interests in all four states. Educational interests rank second in three states and tie for third in the other, and labor interests rank third in all four states. Agricultural interests, government interests (associations of city, township and county governments and government employee associations), ethnic and demographic interests, and religious, charitable, and civic interests were given some mention as powerful interests.

Legislators disagree about the usefulness of interest groups in the legislative process. *The Legislative System* study classified 36 per cent of the legislators interviewed in four states as "facilitators" (those having knowledge of group activity and a friendly attitude toward it); 37 per cent of the interviewees were classified as "resisters" (those having knowledge of group activity but a hostile attitude toward it); 27 per cent were classified as "neutrals" (those having either little knowledge about group activity or no strong favorable or unfavorable attitudes towards it). Facilitators were more ready than neutrals or resisters to attribute importance to the views of interest groups and were more ready to use the aid of lobbyists in drafting bills and lining up support for their own bills. Resisters and neutrals were less likely to feel that the views of interest groups were important in shaping the opinions of legislators. Facilitators and resisters could not be differentiated with regard to income or occupational status or rural-urban residence or age. However, better educated legislators tended more than others to be facilitators. This finding suggests that increased knowledge of the complexity of society is associated with greater realization and acceptance of group activity.[98]

On what kinds of decisions are interest groups most likely to exercise influence? Party and constituency interests are most apparent on broad social and economic issues. On narrower issues parties are less likely to take a stand, and constituents are less likely to have either an interest or an opinion. The legislator is, therefore, freer to respond to the pleas of organized groups on highly specialized topics than he is on major issues of public interest. The absence of both party and constituency influences on certain types of issues contributes to the effectiveness of organized interests. Economic interests seeking to use the law to improve their competitive position are a major source of group pressure on these specialized topics. Of course their arguments are phrased in terms of "the public interest." As Jewell reports in Kentucky:

> Representatives of horse racing interests write that the introduction of dog racing to Kentucky would damage not only them but the state's way of life. The chiropractors are upset by a bill sponsored by the state medical association. Bank presidents wire to protest a bill that would permit small loan companies to loan larger amounts. Florists and nurs-

erymen want licensing laws to limit competition. Local dairies want legislation to guarantee orderly market practices and undercut methods used by chain stores.[99]

Particularly active in lobbying are the businesses subject to extensive government regulation. The truckers, railroads, and liquor interests are consistently found to be among the most highly organized and active lobbyists in state capitals. Organized pressure also comes from associations of governments and associations of government employees. State chapters of the National Education Association are persistent in presenting the demands of educational administrators and occasionally the demands of the dues-paying teachers as well. Lobbying is largely unregulated except for registration requirements established by about half of the states. Duane Lockard summarizes interest group activity from the perspective of the legislator:

> Their pleas are not stated in terms of relative competitive position, yet that is exactly what is involved when large garages attempt to exclude small ones from making major automobile repairs; when liquor stores seek to prevent the sale of liquor in drug stores; when druggists seek to sell liquor at later hours than are permitted the liquor stores; when farmers, dentists, engineers, and countless others get into squabbles over their internal affairs. The arguments are put in terms of public safety, health standards, free enterprise, or fair trade, and the legislator is subjected to a drum fire of telegrams, letters, telephone calls, personal pleading, and propaganda on such bills. Should automobile dealers be allowed to sell insurance on the cars they sell? For some reason — all connected with the highest motive of public welfare naturally — insurance men doubt the ability of auto dealers to advise wisely on insurance and they therefore propose to prohibit the sale of automobile insurance by car dealers. Not only does this bring forth vigorous pleas from the auto dealers and insurance men in the legislator's district, but a legislator who has no particular connection with business soon notices that his colleagues who do have connections frequently become unashamed lobbyists within the legislature. While the incidence of outright bribery and corruption in most American legislatures is nowadays slight, the practice of acting in behalf of one's own economic interests — in the most flagrant disregard of the moral obligation to avoid conflict of interest — is all too common; indeed it is unusual to see a legislator refrain from taking advantage of his inside position.[100]

THE GOVERNOR IN THE LEGISLATURE. The responsibility for the initiation of major statewide legislative programs falls upon the governor and he relies heavily upon his staff and executive personnel to fulfill this responsibility. There is not much incentive for a governor to shirk this responsibility. In the eyes of a large segment of the public the governor is responsible for everything that happens in the state during his term of office, whether he has the authority or capacity to do anything about it or not. There is a general public expectation that every governor will put forward some sort of legislative program, even a governor committed to a "caretaker" role. The governor's programs are presented to the legislature in various governor's messages and in his budget. Through his power of policy initiation alone, the governor's impact on the legislature is considerable. The governor sets the agenda for public decision-making; he largely determines what the business of the legislature will be in any session. Few major state undertakings ever get off the ground without gubernatorial initiation. And in setting the agenda of legislative business he frames the issues, determines their context, and decides their timing. Few would argue that these functions have little to do with the outcome of issues. However, as influential as a governor can be through policy initiation alone, few governors seem content with the role of "initiator" and most act to interject themselves into the role of "arbiter" as well.

A variety of formal and informal powers accrue to governors which enable them to directly involve themselves in legislative decisions.[101] Among the formal powers is the governor's right to call special sessions; by utilizing this power a governor can focus attention on an issue and intensify pressure on the legislature. Another formal power is the veto which every governor has, except in North Carolina; in thirty-five states it requires a two-thirds vote to override a veto rather than a simple majority. The governor has an item veto on appropriations measures in forty-one states. The closing days of any legislative session generally see a flurry of bills passed. A governor can exercise his veto on these measures after the legislature has adjourned and for all practical purposes foreclose the opportunity of being overriden. Overriding vetoes is a difficult process, since a governor is seldom so weak that he cannot count on at least one-third of the legislature to sustain his veto. A 1947 study[102] showed that there were 1,253 vetoes by American state governors (about 5 per cent of the total bills passed) of which only 22 were overridden.* The mere threat of a veto can also operate to change the course of legislative action. The state constitution may limit or strengthen the governor's influence in the legislature by determining his frequency of election and ability to succeed himself. All other things being equal, a governor with a four-year term and an opportunity to succeed himself should be in a stronger position than a governor who faces election every other year or one who cannot serve more than four years.

The governor's informal powers over legislatures center around his role

*Of course national figures conceal wide variations among states; most vetoes and overridden vetoes occur where there are partisan cleavages between governor and legislature.

in the state political system. The governor's office carries prestige in any state; no man becomes governor without considerable political resources of one kind or another. It is natural that a governor will attempt to use his prestige and resourcefulness to influence legislatures. The governor is the most visible state official. His comments are more newsworthy than those of legislators. He is much more sought after for television, radio, and public appearances. As a consequence, he is able to focus public attention on issues which he deems important. There is no assurance that he will always be able to influence public opinion but there is little doubt that he has ample opportunity to be heard. Skillfully used, the power of publicity can be more influential than any formal power. Legislators must respect the governor's greater access to the communication media and hence to the minds of their constituents. Apart from the political advantages of being on the good side of the governor, there are social advantages as well. James Barber reports the following account of a governor's tea rendered by a legislator: "We were very impressed. I mean you couldn't help but be impressed. It's a beautiful home. . . . The state trooper took the car, parked it for me. . . . so we had tea and the governor talked with us. His wife talked with us. And when it came time to leave, we departed. And again — a warm handshake. None of this fishy handshake, but a warm handshake. And ah, they thanked us for coming — whereas normally we should have thanked them for being invited. . . . You couldn't help but be impressed."[103] In addition, the governors of the populous urban states are invariably thrust into prominence in national politics. This added national prestige can also be used to advantage with legislators, many of whom are anxious to rub shoulders with the great and near great on the American political scene.

In addition to the influence inherent in the office of governor, a governor will also be an important figure in his party, perhaps even its dominant figure. In states with competitive two-party systems, the program of the governor is likely to be identified in the public's mind as the program of his party. Legislators know that they will carry that same party label into the next election. In some measure they will share with the governor the responsibility for the success or failure of his program because of their common party label. It may be sufficient for a governor to tell his party leaders in the legislature that he feels that his prestige is at stake on a particular measure and that he expects the support of the party faithful. The governor can thus be instrumental in bringing to bear upon the legislature all of the cohesive forces described earlier which are associated with party. In the urban industrial states, where party lines reflect socio-economic, religious and ethnic affiliation, the governor can exercise great power over legislators in his party by making any issue a party issue, and thereby activating these underlying affiliations. Given the absence of divided government, gubernatorial influence in law-making appears strong in a competitive two-party state. Of course, when a governor in a competitive two-party state faces a legislature controlled by the opposition party, the fact that the governor's program is linked to the fortunes of his party operates to reduce his influence over the legislature rather than strengthen it. The more his program bears a party label, the more likely it is to activate the cohesive forces of the party in opposition to the governor.

In contrast to the situation in competitive two-party states, the governor of a one-party state cannot inspire either intense loyalty or intense opposition by virtue of party identification alone. Legislators run independently of the governor and have no political stake in the success of the governor's program. Since party lines do not reflect class, ethnic, or religious divisions in the constituency, an appeal to party loyalty, unaccompanied by threat of sanctions, will have little meaning. However, in the event that party loyalties do not provide sufficient incentive to support the governor, he can still fall back on certain sanctions available to him by virtue of his office and party position. Sanctions can only be effective against occasional errant legislators; they cannot be used effectively when the governor's opposition is widespread. The ultimate sanction, that of denying the party's renomination to an errant legislator, is usually unavailable to a governor. Party machinery is localized; it responds to constituency demands, not the voice of the governor. So long as the recalcitrant legislator does not violate constituency expectations, his local party will probably renominate him. Even in states with strong party organizations, the basis of organization is the local constituency, not a centralized party hierarchy. Only when the local constituency is offended can a governor pose a threat to the legislator's renomination.

In the one-party states where party appeals in themselves are insufficient, the astute use of patronage and pork is indispensable in securing support for the governor's program. Pork can include construction contracts, roads, parks, hospitals and other institutions, state insurance contracts, and innumerable other items. It is in one-party states, with their rural economies, lower family incomes, and poorly educated work forces, that state jobs look most attractive and local pork is most important. Frank Sorauf reports that patronage jobs in urban industrial economies are insecure and unattractive, at best "short term desperation job alternatives."[104] But in economically depressed states including large parts of the South, state jobs are more highly valued. Robert Highsaw writes about the source of gubernatorial influence in the one-party South: "It is fairly standard practice now for executive leaders to make a careful tabulation of legislative votes on gubernatorial programs and to tell dissenting legislators that if their attitudes and votes are not changed they will get no more jobs for constituents, no more state aid for rural roads in their districts, no more favors done which are the life blood of state legislators. The relationship is not subtle; it is direct, brutal, and it is effective."[105]

It is apparent that the legislative influence of governors varies from state to state and varies over time within states. The problem in describing variations among the states in gubernatorial influence is in finding a suitable method of measuring such influence which could be applied uniformly in all fifty states. To date, no systematic measure has been devised which would permit a precise assessment of gubernatorial influence across state lines. Governors are often compared in terms of their success in getting their legislative program passed. Yet assessing gubernatorial influence in this manner is no simple equation. One governor may not choose to place before the legislature a very far-reaching program or he may tailor his program to what he thinks the legislature will accept prior to submission. Another governor may put forward an extensive legislative program or ask for more than he expects to get in the hope that eventual compromises will still leave him with substantial accomplishments. It is obvious that the legislative batting average will officially show the first governor to have been more successful with his legislature, but the second governor may have really exercised more "influence" over the legislature, that is, causing legislators to do what they otherwise would not have done in the absence of executive action. In the absence of any systematic method of measuring gubernatorial influence in all fifty states, the conditions which have been said to contribute to a governor's influence in the preceding discussion can only be advanced as tentative hypotheses.

LEGISLATIVE DECISIONS. The end product of legislative decision-making is public policy. Public policy can be viewed as the major dependent variable which political science seeks to explain. It is public policy which makes the authoritative allocation of values for a society. Elsewhere in this volume state policies in a number of fields are examined in detail. Therefore, we shall cover only briefly the relationship between public policy and the character of state legislative systems.

Evidence has already been presented to support the view that one of the functions of legislatures is to represent local interests in state policy-making. Constituency influences were viewed as the basis of party voting in competitive states, and they were shown to be major independent determinants of voting in non-competitive states. Constituency characteristics were shown to influence recruiting and the social character of legislators. As we might expect, these same constituency attributes also affect public policy. Table 13 shows the relationship between socio-economic development and several measures of state education and welfare policies. The coefficients in Table 13 leave little doubt that a state's socio-economic development — its degree of urbanization, industrialization, wealth, and education — vitally affects public policy in these areas. The liberality of welfare benefits is closely associated with increases in each of the measures of socio-economic development, particularly family income. Public school expenditures per pupil and average teacher's salaries are also closely related to socio-economic development, particularly family income.

Table 13

THE RELATIONSHIP BETWEEN SOCIO-ECONOMIC DEVELOPMENT
AND STATE EDUCATION AND WELFARE POLICIES

| | INDICES OF SOCIO-ECONOMIC DEVELOPMENT | | | |
| | (*Figures are simple correlation coefficients, 50 states*) | | | |
	Urbani- zation	*Industriali- zation*	*Income*	*Education*
Education (1961–62):				
Average Public School- teacher's Salary	.74	.68	.91	.60
Average Expenditure per pupil in average daily attendance	.55	.38	.85	.63
Welfare (1962):				
Average Weekly Unemploy- ment Benefit	.54	.31	.80	.67
Average Monthly Old Age Benefit	.49	.15	.63	.60
Average Monthly Payment, Dependent Children	.51	.26	.74	.55
Average Monthly Payment, Aid to Blind	.59	.28	.70	.64

The question remains, however, whether specific features of a state's legislative system *independently* affect public policy. Does malapportionment or party competition, for example, actually affect the content of public policies in the states? Or are constituency attributes, particularly urbanization, industrialization, and wealth, so influential in determining legislative outcomes that these outcomes are really unaffected by particular features of a legislative system? This question is difficult to come to grips with because, as we have already seen, socio-economic development not only affects public policy but also affects the character of the legislative system. As a consequence, it is difficult to sort out the effects of system characteristics on public policy from the effects of socio-economic development. Ideally, we would wish to hold the effect of socio-economic development constant and see what differences in public policy would be produced by changes in apportionment or party competition. This is what Dawson and Robinson undertook to do in a study of welfare policies in the fifty states.[106] Although V. O. Key and Duane Lockard had earlier asserted that the degree of party competition affected welfare policies (increased competition was said to lead to more liberal policies),[107] Dawson and Robinson found that constituency attributes, particularly wealth, really accounted for liberal welfare policies. Holding constant for wealth, party competition was found to have little effect on welfare policies.

In short, attributes of statewide constituencies, notably socio-economic development, may have more to do with the content of public policy than specific features of the state legislative system. The data presented in this chapter tend to support this view. The coefficients in Table 13, which measure the closeness of the relationship between socio-economic development and certain public policies, are larger than the coefficients in Tables 4 and 7, which measure the closeness of the relationship between party competition and public policy, and malapportionment and public policy, respectively. This indicates that socio-economic development is more influential in explaining these state policies than either party competition or malapportionment. Differences in the policy choices of state legislatures appear more related to socio-economic attributes of state populations than to party competition or apportionment.

CONCLUSIONS

At least two general propositions about the function of legislatures in state political systems seem to emerge from the discussions in this chapter. First of all, it seems safe to say that most state legislatures function as "arbiters" of public policy rather than as "initiators." Policy initiation is the function of the governor, the bureaucrat, and the interest group. It is principally these elements which develop policy proposals in the first instance; legislatures are placed in the role of responding to the stimulus provided by these groups. The structure of legislatures clearly reflects their deliberative function.

Their rules and procedures and their leadership and committee systems do not lend themselves to policy initiation so much as they lend themselves to deliberation, discussion, and delay. The size and complexity of state government has reached a scale where expert knowledge rather than lay enlightment is the critical ingredient in policy formation. The state budget, for example, perhaps the single most important policy-making document, is drawn up by bureaucrats subordinate to the governor and modified by the governor before submission to the legislature. Legislatures make further modifications but seldom do they undertake to rewrite an executive budget. Legislatures are still critical obstacles through which appropriation and revenue measures must pass; they are still the scenes of bloody battles over the ends for which public money is to be spent. Yet prior to legislative deliberation, the agenda for decision-making has already been drawn up, the framework for conflict has already been established, and the issues have already been placed in particular bills. Sophisticated law-makers are aware of their function as arbiters rather than initiators of public policy. As one of them put it: "We're the policy-making body of the state government, and basically we should give leadership necessary to meet the problems the state faces. But in practice it comes from the executive branch."[108]

A second general proposition about legislatures is that they function to inject into public decision-making a parochial influence. Legislatures function to represent locally organized interests, interests which are manifested in local rather than statewide constituencies. Legislators have deep roots in their local constituencies. They have the religious and ethnic affiliations of their constituents, they have lived among them for most of their lives, and they meet them frequently in their businesses and clubs. The process of recruiting legislators is carried on at the local level. A governor may alienate a particular interest in his state and turn for support to other interests within his heterogeneous constituency. Legislators have no such discretion; their flexibility is limited by a more restricted and specialized constituency. State legislators clearly function to represent local interests in state politics. Precisely because the constituency of the legislature is territorially defined as many small segments of the state, the legislature will exhibit a parochial bias in decision-making. This localistic bias has often been attributed to malapportionment and rural overrepresentation in state legislatures; V. O. Key stated: "A body that is condemned by its constitution to a defense of partial interests in the state becomes, if not a council of censors, something other than a representative body in the conventional sense." While malapportionment may exaggerate this parochial bias, Key's proposition needs reformulation. Any representative body whose members are chosen by partial interests throughout a society represents that society in a manner different from a representative chosen by the society at large. By representing small segments of a state, each legislator represents a more homogeneous constituency than the governor who is chosen by the state at large. The legislator's constituents share a local environment whether it be rich or poor, rural or urban, mining or manufacturing. As a result they are more likely to have roughly similar opinions on policy matters. The constituency influences on legislators are relatively clear, unmixed, and unambiguous. A governor on the other hand must please a wider, more heterogeneous constituency. No single local interest can dominate his judgment; he can balance one interest against another; he is free to represent widely shared interests throughout the state; and he is freer to direct himself to statewide problems and concerns.

NOTES

1. Council of State Governments, *The Book of the States.* Published biennially by the Council of State Governments, Chicago.

2. Indices of socio-economic development used throughout this chapter were derived from U.S. Bureau of the Census, *U.S. Census of Population 1960,* "United States Summary" PC-1 (1)–1C (Washington: U.S. Government Printing Office, 1962). The measure of industrialization used is the percentage of a state's labor force engaged in occupations other than agriculture, forestry, or fishing; the measure of wealth is the state's median family income; the urbanization measure is the proportion of the state's population living in urban rather than rural areas; and the education measure is the median number of school years completed by the population over twenty-five years old.

3. These figures confirm V. O. Key's findings regarding Democratic and Republican legislative control from 1930 to 1950. Key found that "Republican governors in our thirty-two (competitive) states had much less of whatever grief comes from dealing with an opposition legislature than did Democratic chief executives." See V. O. Key, Jr., *American State Politics: An Introduction* (New York: Alfred A. Knopf, 1956) pp. 658–662.

4. Malcolm Jewell used a slightly different formula for classifying state legislatures according to degree of two-party competition (1947–1962), but the resulting grouping of states was not unlike that in Table 3. The relationship between socio-economic development and party competition is also apparent in Jewell's classification of states. See Malcolm Jewell, *The State Legislature* (New York: Random House, 1962) pp. 9–17.

5. See discussion on party influence in legislative decision-making, pp. 184–188.

6. See discussion on legislative decisions, pp. 198–200, and also Richard E. Dawson and James A. Robinson, "Inter-Party Competition, Economic Variables, and Welfare Policies in the American States," *Journal of Politics XXV* (1963) 265–289.

7. Alan P. Sindler, "Bifactional Rivalry as an Alternative to Two-Party Competition in Louisiana," *American Political Science Review XLIX* (1955) 641.

8. V. O. Key, Jr., *Southern Politics in State and Nation* (New York: Alfred A. Knopf, 1949).

9. Paul T. David and Ralph Eisenberg, *Devaluation of the Urban and Suburban Vote* (Charlottesville: Bureau of Public Administration, University of Virginia, 1961).

10. Manning J. Dauer and Robert G. Kelsay, "Unrepresentative States," *National Municipal Review XLIV* (1955) 551–575.

11. See Jewell, pp. 17–24.

12. See Dauer and Kelsay, pp. 571–575.

13. David and Eisenberg, p. 8.

14. *Colegrove* vs. *Green,* 328 U.S. 549 (1946).

15. *Baker* vs. *Carr,* 369 U.S. 186 (1962).

16. *Westberry* vs. *Sanders,* 84 S. Ct. 526 (1964).

17. *Ibid.*

18. *Gray* vs. *Sanders,* 83 S. Ct. 801 (1963).

19. *Ibid.,* p. 809.

20. *Reynolds* vs. *Sims,* 84 S. Ct. 1362 (1964).

21. *Ibid.,* p. 1381.

22. John C. Wahlke, *et al., The Legislative System* (New York: John Wiley and Sons, 1962) p. 425.

23. David Derge, "Metropolitan and Outstate Alignments in the Illinois and Missouri Legislative Delegations," *American Political Science Review LII* (1958) 1052–1065.

24. Richard T. Frost, "On Derge's Metropolitan and Outstate Legislative Delegations," *American Political Science Review LIII* (1959) 792–795.

25. Robert S. Friedman, "The Urban Rural Conflict Revisited," *Western Political Quarterly XIV* (1961) 495.

26. See Jewell, pp. 17–33; William C. Havard and Loren P. Beth, *The Politics of Misrepresentation* (Baton Rouge: Louisiana University Press, 1962); Gordon E. Baker, *Rural Versus Urban Political Power* (New York: Doubleday and Co., 1955).

27. Frost, pp. 792–795.

28. Commission on Intergovernmental Relations, *A Report to the President for Transmittal to the Congress* (Washington: U.S. Government Printing Office, 1955) p. 39.

29. See pp. 159–160.

30. Herbert Jacob, "The Consequences of Malapportionments: A Note of Caution," *Social Forces* (Winter 1964), 256–261.

31. See Malcolm Jewell, "The State Legislatures in Southern Politics," *Journal of Politics XXVI* (1964) 177–196.

32. Peter Rossi, "Community Decision-Making," in Roland Young (ed.), *Approaches to the Study of Politics* (Evanston: Northwestern University Press, 1958).

33. Gaetano Mosca, *The Ruling Class* (New York: McGraw-Hill Book Co., 1939).

34. Frank J. Sorauf, *Party and Representation* (New York: Atherton Press, 1963) pp. 89–94.

35. *Ibid.,* p. 74.

36. Wahlke, *et al.,* p. 488.

37. Sorauf, p. 67.

38. The data on social characteristics of state legislators are voluminous. More useful studies include: Charles S. Hyneman, "Who Makes Our Laws," *Political Science Quarterly LV* (1940) 556–581; Paul Beckett and Celeste Sunderland, "Washington State Lawmakers," *Western Political Quarterly X* (1957) 180–202; Joseph A. Schlesinger, "Lawyers and American Politics," *Midwest Journal of Political Science I* (1957) 26–39; David Derge, "The Lawyer as Decision-Maker in the American State Legislature," *Journal of Politics XXI* (1959) 408–433.

39. Wahlke, *et al.,* pp. 489–490; Sorauf, pp. 75–81.

40. Sorauf, p. 91.

41. *Ibid.,* pp. 75–81.

42. *Ibid.,* p. 83.

43. Charles E. Hyneman, "Tenure and Turnover of Legislative Personnel," *Annals of the American Academy of Social and Political Science CXCV* (1938) 30–31.

44. Quotations from Wahlke, *et al.,* pp. 127–133.

45. Hyneman, pp. 30–31.

46. Quotations from Wahlke, *et al.,* pp. 95–134.

47. Sorauf, p. 103.

48. Wahlke, *et al.,* p. 95.

49. W. J. M. Mackenzie, "Local Government Experience of Legislators," in John C. Wahlke and Heinz Eulau (eds.), *Legislative Behavior* (Glencoe: The Free Press, 1959).

50. Sorauf, p. 84.

51. *Ibid.,* p. 111.

52. Leon D. Epstein, *Politics in Wisconsin* (Madison: University of Wisconsin Press, 1958) p. 131.

53. V. O. Key, Jr., *American State Politics*, pp. 171–181.

54. Jewell, *The State Legislature*, p. 36.

55. Joseph LaPalombara, *Guide to Michigan Politics*, Bureau of Social and Political Research, Michigan State University, 1960, p. 23; also cited by Jewell, *The State Legislature*, p. 39.

56. V. O. Key, Jr., *American State Politics*, pp. 181–196.

57. Jewell, *The State Legislature*, p. 39.

58. Sorauf, p. 117.

59. Duncan MacRae, "The Relations Between Roll-Call Votes and Constituencies in the Massachusetts House of Representatives," *American Political Science Review XLVI* (1952) 1046–1055; Robert W. Becker, *et al.*, "Correlates of Legislative Voting: Michigan House of Representatives, 1954–61," *Midwest Journal of Political Science VI* (1962) 384–396.

60. Daniel R. Grant and H. C. Nixon, *State and Local Government in America* (Boston: Allyn and Bacon, 1963) p. 174.

61. Wahlke, *et al.*, pp. 50–52.

62. This section relies heavily upon *ibid.*, pp. 146–161; quotations are from the same study.

63. Duane Lockard, *The Politics of State and Local Government* (New York: Macmillan Co., 1963) p. 28.

64. Jewell, *The State Legislature*, p. 93.

65. Loren P. Beth and William C. Havard, "Committee Stacking and Political Power in Florida," *Journal of Politics XXIII* (1961) 57–83.

66. Gilbert Y. Steiner and Samuel K. Gove, *Legislative Politics in Illinois* (Urbana: University of Illinois Press, 1960) pp. 12–13.

67. This section relies heavily on Wahlke, *et al.*, pp. 170–190; quotations are from the same study.

68. *Ibid.*, p. 206.

69. William Buchanan, *et al.*, "The Legislator as Specialist," *Western Political Quarterly XIII* (1960) 636–651.

70. Sorauf, pp. 121–146; Wahlke, *et al.*, pp. 281–286.

71. Sorauf, p. 125.

72. The discussion which follows relies upon Wahlke, *et al.*, pp. 245–266; quotations from the same source.

73. Legislators may also be classified according to the way they behave toward organized interest groups; see page 193.

74. Lockard, p. 280.

75. William J. Keefe, "Parties, Partisanship and Public Policy in the Pennsylvania Legislature," *American Political Science Review XLVIII* (1954) 450–464; Thomas R. Dye, "A Comparison of Constituency Influences in the Upper and Lower Chambers of a State Legislature," *Western Political Quarterly XIV* (1961) 473–480.

76. Wahlke, *et al.*, p. 425.

77. *Ibid.*, p. 359.

78. Malcolm Jewell provides useful comparative data on party voting in state legislatures. See *The State Legislature*, p. 52, and "Party Voting in American State Legislatures," *American Political Science Review XLIX* (1955) 773–791. Jewell cites the following published studies as sources of data on roll call votes: Duane Lockard, *New England State Politics* (Princeton: Princeton University Press, 1959); Keefe, *op. cit.*, pp. 450–464; Thomas A. Flinn, "The Outline of Ohio Politics," *Western Political Quarterly XIII* (1960) 702–721; Dean R. Cresap, *Party Politics in the Golden State* (Los Angeles: The Haynes Foundation, 1954).

79. Wahlke, *et al.*, p. 355.
80. Keefe, "Parties, Partisanship and Public Policy," pp. 450–464; William J. Keefe, "Comparative Study of the Role of Political Parties in State Legislatures," *Western Political Quarterly IX* (1956) 726–742; Jewell, "Party Voting in American State Legislatures," pp. 773–791.
81. Jewell, *The State Legislature*, pp. 53–61.
82. Lockard, *The Politics of State and Local Government*, p. 300.
83. MacRae, pp. 1046–1055; Becker, *et al.*, pp. 384–396.
84. MacRae, pp. 1046–1055; Dye, pp. 473–480; Sorauf, pp. 133–146; Becker, *et al.*, pp. 384–396.
85. Thomas A. Flinn, "Party Responsibility in the States: Some Causal Factors," *American Political Science Review LVIII* (1964) 60–71.
86. *Ibid.*, p. 71.
87. MacRae, pp. 1046–1055; Dye, pp. 473–480.
88. For an analysis of the constituency basis of party cohesion in Kansas see John G. Grumm, "A Factor Analysis of Legislative Voting," *Midwest Journal of Political Science VII* (1963) 336–356.
89. Daniel M. Ogden, Jr., and Hugh A. Bone, *Washington Politics* (New York: New York University Press, 1960); also cited by Jewell, p. 55.
90. Wahlke, *et al.*, pp. 351–359.
91. Robert H. Salisbury, *Missouri Politics and State Political Systems;* University of Missouri, Bureau of Governmental Research, 1959; also cited by Jewell, p. 59.
92. Samuel C. Patterson, "Dimensions of Voting Behavior in a One-Party State Legislature," *Public Opinion Quarterly XXVI* (Summer 1962) 185–200. A study of voting in the one-party Florida senate also shows a division of constituencies; the fast growing, and socially and economically changing south Florida constituencies aligned against the relatively unchanging, traditional north Florida constituencies. See Malcolm B. Parsons, "Tensions and Conflict in a One-Party Legislative System," *American Political Science Review LVI* (1962) 605–614.
93. Jewell, "State Legislatures in Southern Politics," p. 187.
94. Wahlke, *et al.*, pp. 267–286.
95. See Sorauf, pp. 147–154.
96. Quotation from Wahlke, *et al.*, p. 253.
97. *Ibid.*, pp. 311–342.
98. *Ibid.*
99. Jewell, p. 70.
100. Lockard, *The Politics of State and Local Government*, pp. 283–284.
101. For a discussion of the governor's legislative powers, see Jewell, *The State Legislature*, pp. 105–127; and Coleman B. Ransone, Jr., *The Office of Governor in the United States* (University, Ala.: University of Alabama Press, 1956).
102. Frank W. Prescott, "The Executive Veto in American States," *Western Political Quarterly III* (1950) 97–111.
103. James D. Barber, *Lawmaker: A Study in Political Adaptation* (New Haven: Yale University Press, forthcoming) p. 75; cited in Grant and Nixon, p. 163.
104. Frank J. Sorauf, "The Silent Revolution in Patronage," *Public Administration Review XXVIII* (1960) 30.
105. Robert B. Highsaw, "The Southern Governor — Challenge to the Strong Executive Theme," *Public Administration Review XIX* (1959) 7.
106. Dawson and Robinson, pp. 265–289.
107. Key, *Southern Politics*, pp. 298–314; Lockard, *New England State Politics*, pp. 320–340.
108. Quotation from Wahlke, *et al.*, p. 255.

SELECTED BIBLIOGRAPHY

Dawson, Richard E., and James A. Robinson. "Inter-Party Competition, Economic Variables, and Welfare Policies in the American States," *Journal of Politics XXV* (1963) 265–289. Correlation analysis reveals that welfare policies are more closely related to the socio-economic characteristics of a state than to its degree of party competition.

Flinn, Thomas A. "Party Responsibility in the States: Some Causal Factors," *American Political Science Review LVIII* (1964) 60–71. A summary and critique of studies of party voting in state legislatures in the light of data derived from an analysis of roll call votes in Ohio.

Jewell, Malcolm. *The State Legislature*. New York: Random House, 1962. Dealing exclusively with state legislative politics, this volume provides an excellent summary of material on the fifty states while extolling the virtues of party competition.

MacRae, Duncan, Jr. "The Relation Between Roll Call Votes and Constituencies in the Massachusetts House of Representatives," *American Political Science Review XLVI* (1952) 1046–1055. A study of roll call votes reveals the complex relationship between party cohesion, constituency influence, and legislative voting.

Sorauf, Frank J. *Party and Representation*. New York: Atherton Press, 1963. On the basis of extensive interviewing, this study examines the many ties legislators in Pennsylvania have with their local constituents and describes the parochialism of legislative politics in that state.

Wahlke, John C., and Heinz Eulau. *Legislative Behavior*. Glencoe: The Free Press, 1959. This reader in legislative politics presents forty-two selected articles analyzing political, sociological, and psychological bases of legislative behavior and includes many of the most important studies of American state legislatures.

Wahlke, John C., Heinz Eulau, William Buchanan, and Leroy C. Ferguson. *The Legislative System*. New York: John Wiley and Sons, 1962. This volume reports the results of comprehensive interviews with legislators in four states focusing on the perceptions legislators have of their jobs.

THE POLITICS
OF THE
CHAPTER 6
EXECUTIVE
by
JOSEPH A. SCHLESINGER*

THE POLITICS OF ADMINISTRATION concerns the relation of political decisions to the business of the state. How do political objectives affect the
manner in which laws are carried out? Does the arrangement of state
agencies and personnel have anything to do with the fate of political
goals? The American states are excellent laboratories in which to study
such questions unencumbered as they are by well ordered bureaucracies.
Students of bureaucracy can often only sense conflicting goals which are
obscured by an orderly hierarchy of authority. But the American states,
for the most part, consist of a variety of agencies whose relations are
either so ill defined that they are uncertain of their jurisdictions or so well
defined that they can act independently of each other. The observer,
therefore, need not probe too deeply to find the impingement of politics
upon administration.

The failure of the states to develop neat administrative hierarchies is
due in large part to the fact that state governments were not created at
once but are the products of the gradual accretion of new functions and
agencies.[1] When a new problem arises, the pressures for action often
force the state to use the simplest administrative solution, the creation of
a new agency. A water pollution control board may be set up outside
the bureau of conservation partly because its existence is a symbol that
the state is doing something about the problem, but also because of a
suspicion that the old bureau would not be interested enough in forceful
execution of the policy. Then too, functions which at first appeared unrelated, such as recreation and conservation, come into conflict — e.g.,
when the growth of population creates a need for coordination which did
not originally exist. Even states which have sought to develop neat administrative hierarchies by establishing functional departments keep facing

*For assistance in gathering data for this chapter I wish to thank Rex Pierce,
Janet Winger, and Lee Weber, as well as the All-University Research Committee
of Michigan State University.

new problems. Thus New York State has constitutionally limited the number of its departments to twenty-one, but it had to use one, the executive department, as a catchall to include such unrelated agencies as that for liquor control and atomic development.[2]

Of primary importance in the study of the politics of state administration is the intermediary and ambiguous role of the state in the American political system. The intermediate position of state government leads to uncertainty about policies and responsibilities and laxity about standards of performance. This does not mean that state government is unimportant, or that it does not deal with matters having a direct impact on the daily lives of its citizens. A state may have an excellent department of public health on which the localities do in fact depend for the prevention of disasters. Its state police may be the principal instrument for crime prevention or for preserving traffic flow in metropolitan areas. A state's tax policy may have something to do with the economic health of its industries. However, a state may avoid solutions to all such problems as long as people can turn either to the cities or nation. Indeed, it is the general failure of states to handle adequately the problems of expanding metropolitan areas which has led increasingly to direct relations between cities and the federal government, for the cities cannot tolerate a breakdown in transportation and health, nor can the federal government, which is politically more receptive to urban problems than many states. For state governments, the consequence of its intermediate character is that a great variety of administrative arrangements are possible, which are never confronted with hard tests. They may or may not be successful. But the costs of failure are not always clear.

ORGANIZATIONAL CONSEQUENCES OF INDETERMINATE GOVERNMENT

POLITICAL PARTIES. The unclear function of state administration, its varied character, and its relative freedom from public reckoning affect the ways in which men organize to achieve political goals at the state level. In most states party organization has generally been weak. Although some American states are reasonably competitive, most states are dominated by one or the other major party.[3] But as a party tends to dominate a state its organization tends to become more fragmentary, although it may contain persistent factions. Even where the states are more or less competitive for the top executive position of governor, lesser executive offices are often much less competitive,[4] reflecting the willingness of the voter to dilute as well as to divide party control of the state executive. More often than not, governor must govern either with executives of the opposite party or with executive of their own party freed of the constraint of having their re-election dependent upon the head of state.

Whether a state is competitive or not, the turnover in the office of gov

Table 1

COMPETITION FOR ELECTIVE OFFICES, 1914–1958 (SOUTHERN STATES EXCLUDED)

	NUMBER OF STATES*	TYPE OF COMPETITION (PER CENT)		
		Competitive†	*Cyclical*†	*One-Party*†
Governor	36	50	6	44
Lieutenant Governor	24	21	25	54
Treasurer	26	15	35	50
Auditor	21	14	34	52
Secretary of State	30	13	30	57
Attorney General	26	11	31	58

*The number of states varies since minor officers are not elected independently in each of them.
†An office is rated as competitive if no party held it for more than 70 per cent of the time during the period 1914-58 and if there was a change of party control in 30 per cent or more of the elections. If the rate of turnover was less than 30 per cent, it is a cyclical office. The office is considered as one-party if one party won over 70 per cent of the elections.
Source: Table is based on Joseph A. Schlesinger, "The Structure of Competition for Office in the American States," *Behavioral Science V* (1960) 200.

ernor is generally high, thus placing further limits on the governor as party leader. In close to three-fourths of the states a governor can expect to hold office for less than five years, and in eighteen states for less than four years. Such high turnover is not simply a product of constitutional restraints on re-election for it occurs even where there are no restraints.

The willingness of the voter to tolerate and even to impose weak party organization at the state level is partly a consequence of the national two-party mold, and partly a result of the nature of state government. National politics can stifle strong state party efforts. Yet state parties often stand in sharp contrast to strong one-party control at the local level. Lincoln Steffens long ago pointed out that there were critical functions which the party "machine" imposed upon local government.[5] The failure of state party machines to develop is one indication of the uncertain political expectations which we have of the states. The brief tenure of the typical governor limits the opportunities to develop a personal political machine which could serve the function of coordinating state government. Brief tenure tends to release from the governor's influence all the non-party officials who know they can outlast him: civil servants, lobbyists, and others with long terms of office.

On the other hand, the role of the governor as political leader in the state administration should not be minimized. Whether rapid turnover in office is cause or effect, it is certain that many governors use their office as a steppingstone to higher positions in the federal government. Some governors are prime candidates for Presidential or Vice-Presidential nomination. Many can hope for a cabinet position or a significant administrative post. A major outlet is the U.S. Senate where 22 per cent have been governors.[6] The flow of personnel from the state to federal government runs below the gubernatorial level. Of all second-level federal political executives from the Roosevelt through the Kennedy administrations, nearly 40 per cent had some form of state or local office experience, the most common being head of a state agency.[7] To the extent then that men are controlled by their ambitions, by their desire for advancement to more important offices, the fact that the governor is a critical link with the federal government adds to his powers. No matter who appoints an official, or to whom he is formally responsible, if he sees that the governor controls or can affect his chances to attain a desired position then the governor gains influence over him. And such influence spreads: those in the governor's coterie also attract followers who hope to advance.[8]

It is important to point out that the advantages which may accrue to a governor from his position of influence within the national structure vary considerably from state to state. All states are not equal in the federal system. For example, in terms of career outlets it is certain that some states are much better ones from which to gain a federal position than others. While this is obvious in terms of the Presidency, the same can be said for lesser positions in the Presidential complex: Cabinet appointments and positions in the Supreme Court. Thus there are some twelve states which between 1900 and 1958 had received no Presidential appointment to the Cabinet or Supreme Court. On the other hand, a few states such as New York and Massachusetts received more than two and three times the number of such positions as their population size warranted.[9]

Such differences in the relative positions of the states in the federal system have a great impact on the states' administrative politics. For one thing, the more closely the state and federal career ladders are joined, the more influence this gives persons outside the state over the state administration. Within the state it gives those who have some say about those promotions more influence over the behavior of administrators. In other words, if we try to assess the relative influence of the governors of two states over their administrations, it is not enough simply to know something of the formal controls available, or even all about the internal politics of the state. The fact that one governor is in an excellent position to gain the Presidency while the other has no prospects is equally important, if not more so, in describing the kinds of things they can do or the prospects they can hold out in attaining their goals within their own state. V. O. Key[10] has pointed out that the party systems of states vary in degree of interdependence with the national system some states are closely bound to national trends and others effectively divorced. The same is true of administrative politics: some states are far more closely bound to the nation by the very ties of personnel and their careers.

In effect, the governor has great freedom in defining his relation to his administration. His leadership is essentially political. He must be concerned whenever conflict arises, as well as whenever scandals emerge. But his relations with day-to-day administration can be very tenuous. It would appear that governors find it more important to maintain their political standing than to influence administration directly through daily oversight. Ransone[11] in surveying the distribution of the governors' time each week found that only 10 per cent was devoted to talking with department heads, while typically governors hold two press conferences a day.

Being head of a state administration does not hold a man close to his desk. He can make extensive out-of-state political forages, since he is restrained primarily by fears of what political conflicts might break out at home while he is away. Writing in 1948 Warren Moscow, the political reporter of *The New York Times,* said that, compared with the task of being mayor of New York City or President of the United States, the job of governor of New York was a:

> . . . soft snap. Save in rare emergencies, the press of work is not so much greater than that of any big-business executive. The physical strain is light enough so that any man of sound mind and sound politics with the ability to pick trustworthy subordinates can function adequately as governor.
>
> The reason for this is simply that the important part of the job of governor lies in the fields of policy-making rather than in the handling of administrative detail. The Governor is not wakened late at night or early in the morning by recurrent crises in international affairs, nor is his executive domain so vast that the number of minutes in the calendar week is insufficient to permit even abbreviated conversations with each of his lieutenants, a difficulty which plagues a modern president.[12]

Yet the governor does not even have to assert policy leadership, for rarely does he face such hard tests of success as a mayor or the President. In the severe governmental crises caused by the race issue, the governor among elective executives has had the greatest choice for involvement. Many governors have involved themselves deeply on one side or the other, while others have chosen to skirt the issue. None has had involvement thrust upon him in the way local race riots and aggressive demonstrations for school desegregation have involved mayors and three Presidents of the United States. Even such a prominent governor as Nelson Rockefeller was able to continue his convalescence after the political battles for the Republican Presidential nomination, while the New York City race riot of July, 1964, brought Mayor Robert Wagner home from vacation in Switzerland and caused President Johnson to assure the public through a press conference that the F.B.I. was supplying him with daily reports on the New York situation.

INTEREST GROUPS. Interest groups[13] are the second principal way in which men organize to influence state government and its administration. While we have no reliable tests of the relative influence of interest groups at various levels of government, it does appear that they are exceptionally important in determining what the states do. Here again the intermediate character of the state is the underlying factor. For one thing, as party organization weakens, it seems reasonable to expect other methods of gaining influence to become stronger. But also when there are no clear expectations about the functions of a unit of government, the way is open for interested organizations to use that government for their own purposes. Thus, it is hard not to conclude that the many state boards regulating a great range of professions and trades including doctors, lawyers, barbers, morticians, architects, cosmetologists, and psychologists were put there to regulate competition among the practitioners as much as to protect the public. This is most evident where the members of the regulatory agencies are drawn primarily from the practitioners themselves. Similarly, we can note the way in which the state government often becomes an extension of local industries — providing tourist councils, and economic development agencies empowered to give preferential tax treatment to new industries and even to build factories. Since the late 1930's Mississippi has had a program to "Balance Agriculture with Industry" (BAWI), and it has been estimated that at least a fourth of the state's industrial payroll comes from plants built by the program through bonds backed by tax revenues.[14] State administration has long been closely entwined with farm organizations through the agricultural extension services and the county agents. Much of the latter relationship has been fostered through the grant programs of the federal government.

Indeed both the federal and local governments act as pressure groups upon the states and may even register as lobbyists. In providing inducements to the states through matching grants, the federal government has not only had a strong impact on the policies of the states, but it has also sought effectively to define the manner of administration of the programs. Merit systems for example, while far from being all-inclusive in state employment, are found everywhere in those agencies dealing directly with federal grant programs. In the day-to-day administration of programs the responsible federal agency is there to be considered. Local governments, because all of their powers and much of their revenue come from the state, exert some of the most persistent pressures on state administration.

As was the case with political parties, there are important variations in the activities of pressure groups from state to state. Powerful economic groups often have their greatest impact upon the governments of the states in which their principal resources are based. Thus the Anaconda Copper Company was almost synonymous with state government in Montana[15] until the federal government during the New Deal became a formidable competitor. Similarly, Ford, General Motors, and the United Auto Workers have had their most direct impact upon state government in Michigan. At the same time, certain states — principally New York and California — are often singled out for special attention by groups whose concerns are nationwide. In 1962 the California highway budget alone was larger than the entire state budget of forty-two other states, and New York spent more on highways than twenty-eight states spent on all of their functions.[16] A highway safety group, by getting New York to require the installations for seat belts in every new car sold there, forced the auto industry to supply them in all new cars and increased the use of belts throughout the remaining forty-nine states.

DOCTRINAL CONSEQUENCES OF INDETERMINATE GOVERNMENT

Thus far we have emphasized the uncertainty which surrounds the states' functions and its varied organizational consequences. People respond differently to uncertainty. Some may simply withdraw. It is evident most people pay little attention to state government. In a survey of one Michigan city, only 2 per cent of the respondents found the problems of state government to be of great interest or importance, while 59 per cent felt national problems to be highly significant.[17] Uncertainty about the future or about the consequences of choices may, on the other hand, lead to the development of a doctrine, or a set of prescriptions, about the "good" state. In other words, those who do take an interest in state government will tend to react less in pragmatic terms than in terms of logic or rhetoric.[18] If a person does not know the consequences of administrative structure — of giving more or less power to the governor, for example — yet feels that it is important, he is forced into making ideological responses. All levels of government have been affected by the arguments about administrative reform as they have developed historically. But it is a measure of the greater indeterminacy of state government that here the arguments have had a high degree of independent strength.

Most of the arguments have served to establish and maintain a non-hierarchic state administration, keeping the governor from having much formal influence over the rest of the state government. The first argument to emerge, stemming from the colonial experience, was "fear of the executive." It remains today and can be heard at every attempt to give more power to the governor. Such characteristics of state government as short terms of office, restrictions on re-election, the election of lesser executives, restraints on the governor's appointive and removal power, and overlapping terms are all expressions of the desire to prevent a governor from gathering too many of the instruments of control into his hands.[19]

A second argument which emerged during the Jacksonian era was that of "popular democracy." This argument asserted that the way to assure popular control of state government was to elect most of the important administrators. It followed logically from the fear of the executive. As an argument it dominated constitution-making throughout the 19th century during the time when the basic format of most of the states was being framed. One of its major results was the establishment of many popularly elected executive officials. Their distribution may be seen in Table 2. But note that it is an argument which has run its course. Those officials who are elective tend to head agencies which were important during the last century. While these are not irrelevant today, the great new functions of health, welfare, and highways tend not to be headed by elective officials, and the great share of state effort is carried on by these agencies. Education, one of the earliest functions of state government, is the only great function which is headed by an elected executive in a large number of states.[20]

Table 2

NUMBER OF STATES (1960) WITH POPULARLY ELECTED OFFICIALS

Governor	50		
Attorney General	42	University Regents	7
State Treasurer	40	Mining Commissioner	5
Secretary of State	39	Tax Commission	3
Lieutenant Governor	38	Highway Commissioner	2
State Auditor	30	Board of Equalization	1
Superintendent of Education	26	Printer	1
Public Utilities Commission	14	Railroad Commission	1
Agriculture Commission	11	Fish and Game Commission	1
Controller	10	Corporation Commission	1
Board of Education	10	Commissioner of Charities	1
Insurance Commissioner	8	Secretary of Internal Affairs	1
Land Commissioner	8	Adjutant and Inspector General	1

Source: Darrah and Poland, *The Fifty State Governments,* Table 2.

The representative character of state government is also reflected in the construction of boards and commissions to head agencies. Collective executives derive their rationale from the assumption that each member may represent a divergent interest. Various groups may be permitted to control the naming of personnel, thus assuring a breadth of access and influence.

In the politics of state administration, "anti-politics" has been one of the most pervasive themes. There is an undeniable distrust on the part of many

Americans of political parties, politicians, and any activity which might be called political. In the late 19th and early 20th centuries this feeling dominated the American states. In electoral politics it had its expression in the movement for the direct primary and for non-partisan offices. In administrative politics the notion of taking politics out of administration arose from the same sentiment. While no one has yet found a way of achieving that feat, some have suggested a "state manager" as a counterpart to the city manager. The anti-politics theme has been most successful in the establishment of civil service systems in place of patronage appointments.

A variation of the same theme is the goal of separating state politics and administration from those of the nation. As an approach to state politics, it rejects the national parties as having any proper relevance to state affairs. The most common way in which this divorce is sought is by timing the election of state officials in the years when there is no Presidential election. Most recent changes in the selection of the governor give him a four-year term elected in that manner. New Jersey, Virginia, and Louisiana elect their governors in odd-numbered years, avoiding any coincidence of federal and state elections.

A fourth theme, "administrative efficiency," emerged in part as the positive side of the anti-politics notion. It was, therefore, also essential to the development of a merit system for the hiring and promotion of personnel. Administrative efficiency, however, has since 1900 developed its own momentum, producing organizations such as the National Municipal League dedicated to the creation of administrative structures more efficient than the non-hierarchic state. Efficiency in the reform rhetoric has become equated with coordinated government, with central responsibility placed in the hands of the governor. The many "little Hoover commission" reports framed after World War II were dominated by this trend, usually advocating a reduction in the number of departments, more functional integration, and more power in the governor's office. As an argument about the proprieties of administration this theme runs counter to the earlier positions. The argument for strengthening the governor has surely not swept all before it, but whenever major changes are made today by conventions or legislation their trend is usually in that direction.[21]

Doctrine and ideology have their independent impact, particularly when little is known about the consequences of particular arrangements. But arguments about efficient arrangements sometimes have their uses for groups which have a very clear notion of what they want from government. For example, the drive for a merit system probably had its roots in a doctrinal concern for efficiency in government and for the establishment of the "neutral competence," which is the hallmark of the best civil service. But the momentum for the adoption of the merit system by the states can be traced as

easily to the rise in the proportion of people directly involved in state government, as to its rational appeal. Despite the appeal of the merit system for the
respectable citizen, its adoption has been slow. The Pendleton Act establishing
a federal civil service was passed in 1883. In the years immediately following,
a few states rushed to develop similar plans. States such as Illinois and New
York which led the administrative reform movement were in this group, as
well as some of the states which at the turn of the century were leaders in the
progressive movement, states such as California and Wisconsin. By 1930,
however, only nine states had adopted this reform. The major additions have
come about since 1930, so that today some thirty-two states (including Alaska
and Hawaii) have a statewide merit system of some kind.[22]

Table 3

MERIT SYSTEMS

STATES THAT HAVE ADOPTED A GENERAL MERIT SYSTEM
AND THE DATES WHEN ADOPTED

Before 1900	Massachusetts, New York
1900–1909	Colorado, Illinois, New Jersey, Wisconsin
1910–1919	California, Ohio
1920–1929	Maryland
1930–1939	Alabama, Connecticut, Maine, Michigan, Minnesota, Rhode Island
1940–1949	Kansas, North Carolina, Oregon, Virginia
1950–1959	Georgia, Louisiana, Nevada, New Hampshire, Vermont, Wyoming
1960–	Kentucky, New Mexico, Oklahoma, Washington, Utah

NUMBER OF FULL-TIME STATE EMPLOYEES PER 10,000 POPULATION
(AS OF OCTOBER 1962) AND THE EXISTENCE OF A MERIT SYSTEM

Number of Employees per 10,000	Number of States with	without
	General Merit System	
120 plus	5*	1
100–119	7	4
80–99	10	5
under 80	8†	8
	30	18

*Four of these adopted a merit system since 1940.
†Five of these adopted a merit system before 1920.

Source: Adoption of merit systems from the Council of State Governments, *The Book
of the States, 1940–1963*. Per capita government employment from U.S. Bureau of
the Census, *Statistical Abstract of the United States: 1963* (Washington: U.S. Government Printing Office, 1963) p. 438.

If we look at the timing of adoption and the states involved we can discern factors other than an ideological drive for more efficiency. Some of the post-1930 adoptions were undoubtedly due to the federal government through the grant-in-aid program. But also we note that many of the states which have come to adopt a merit system in the latter decades have been ones where a relatively high proportion of the state's population have been employed by the state. It is true that the evidence here is only suggestive, and the lack of early data on employment makes it impossible to assert that states adopting a merit system in the early periods were not at that time also states of relatively high per capita state employment. The fact remains that at the present time there is a distinct tendency for those states without a merit system to be also those with a low per capita state employment. Those states which have a merit system, but which have a relatively small proportion of their population working for the state tend to be those which adopted the plan early, before 1920. There, undoubtedly, doctrine had its impact. The more recent adoption of a merit system by states with relatively high state employment more likely reflects the preference of a politically potent group for the kind of job security which is becoming increasingly part of the American economic picture.

Thus we see that the indeterminate character of state government suffuses every aspect of the organization of its administration. For the citizen, the federal government and his local government are the most conspicuous governmental units, those he can most easily approach. Having only the dimmest of notions of what he can or should expect from state government, he accepts a variety of arrangements. For politicians, too, the state is very often a halfway house. For many governors and other state executives state government is but an intermediate point in a career which can lead to federal office. Those who have the clearest and most direct involvement in state government are organized interests or pressure groups and they leave their mark everywhere. But, because political expectations have been vague, vague doctrinal responses have most frequently been made to the problems of state administration.

A COMPARISON OF THE RELATIVE POSITIONS OF GOVERNORS

Since the governor's role is central to administrative-political relations we turn now to an assessment of the relative position of the governors in the several states. We have come to speak of "strong" and "weak" governors. Here we shall examine a number of major organizational devices which define the strength of the governor, rate the governors according to each, and then combine the various ratings to obtain an over-all measure of the relative political impact of the governors upon the administration of the states.

One element which defines the influence of one administrator over others is status. It is, however, a factor difficult to quantify. The organizational chart of a state is largely a definition of the relative status of individuals, departments, and agencies. In part, status may be defined as who appoints whom, but it also derives from the placement of agencies within larger entities. An agency head beneath the governor is expected to consult with him. If an agency is a unit within a larger department, then it is to be expected that its head will consult with others in the same department and will report to the head of the over-all department. An organizational chart is, therefore, a statement of formal communication channels and the influence which derives from control of information.

While the organizational chart is overtly a statement of who has the power to tell others what to do, it is also a chart of the incentive system of the state. We have argued earlier that an official is as much driven by his ambitions as by those forces or individuals which have put him into his present place. The organization of the state is the means whereby those ambitions are defined. A finely graded bureaucracy which constantly holds out the hope of promotion is most capable of controlling the behavior of its members. The more extensively an organization seeks to control the behavior of its members, the more refined must be the status system, as in the case of military organizations.

In most of the states the organizational status system is not very clearly defined, a fact which affects the behavior of administrators. An agency head whose unit is one of many in a large department may temper his devotion to his own agency because he hopes to be promoted to department head. The more independent the agency, the more he is likely to devote himself to internal goals exclusively. No doubt the resistance of agencies and their clientele to the integration of their departments with others rests upon some awareness of its policy consequences.

Status is also defined by pay. The governor outranks all other political executives, except in Maine where other executives, such as the secretary of state, get the same salary. The discrepancy between the governor's pay and that of other executives does vary greatly. One exception to the salary-status system should, however, be noted. In many states the members of administrative boards may be unpaid or may be simply reimbursed for expenses. In Delaware most administrative agencies are headed by such unpaid boards.[23] When the state does not provide the salary incentive for men charged with executing its policies, it is difficult not to conclude that the non-governmental employers of such officials find their influence increased. The existence of such a method of employment is another sign of the extent to which the state governments are not neatly closed systems but are bound up with the group structure of their states. The boundary between the government office structure and society is never so clean that officials are free of external influence. But what is characteristic of the states is the extent to which a customary device for defining the boundaries of an organization from its environment — the use of salaries and wages to define to whom an official is responsible — can also be extended to the larger society and economy.

Let us turn now to some aspects of the governor's administrative position which can be measured.

TENURE POTENTIAL. We have already noted that governors typically enjoy short terms of office which may reduce their influence. When the governor's tenure is compared with the tenure of the other elected executives we can see that he is at a further disadvantage.

Table 4

THE GOVERNOR'S TENURE IN OFFICE COMPARED WITH THAT OF THE SECRETARY OF STATE

AVERAGE TENURE IN YEARS (1914–1958)	DISTRIBUTION OF STATES			
	Governor		*Secretary of State*	
	No.	%	No.	%
Under 3	3	7	0	0
3.0–3.9	15	31	4	10
4.0	12	25	4	10
4.1–4.9	5	10	3	8
5.0–7.9	13	27	8	20
8.0–9.9	0	0	8	20
10.0 plus	0	0	12	32
	48	100	39*	100

*Number of states with an elective Secretary of State.

Source: Turnover figures for governors and secretaries of state derived from state manuals and blue books.

Compared with the secretary of state the governor can expect to be in office only a short time. Whereas in the period from 1914 to 1958 no governor could expect an average of eight or more years in office, over half of the secretaries of state could; and in twelve states the typical secretary's term ran to over ten years. A similar relationship can be found for the other minor executive posts, with the exception of lieutenant governor and attorney general which are also positions of high turnover. Since ambition is probably related to opportunity, the possibility of long tenure for lesser elected officials helps determine the extent to which they can be controlled by a governor or anyone else through their career expectations.

The term of office for governors ranges today from two to four years, although it has been as short as one year. Together, the length of term and the stipulations on re-election state the likelihood of long tenure for governors. In Table 5 the states are ranked according to tenure potential for the governor. Note that all four-year-term states have a higher rating than any two-year-term state, regardless of restraint on re-election, in accord with experience. Much the longest tenure is found in those four-year-term states which permit re-election. It is in these states that we would expect a governor to last long enough in office to put his mark on the state administration.[24]

Table 5

THE GOVERNORS' TENURE POTENTIAL, 1960

Four-year term, no restraint on re-election (5 points) *

California	Illinois	Utah
Colorado	Montana	Washington
Connecticut	Nevada	Wyoming
Idaho	New York	

Four-year term, one re-election permitted (4 points) *

Delaware	Maryland	Ohio
Maine	New Jersey	Oregon

Four-year term, no consecutive re-election permitted (3 points) *

Alabama	Louisiana	Pennsylvania
Florida	Mississippi	South Carolina
Georgia	Missouri	Tennessee
Indiana	North Carolina	Virginia
Kentucky	Oklahoma	West Virginia

Two-year term, no restraint on re-election (2 points) *

Arizona	Michigan	Rhode Island
Arkansas	Minnesota	Texas
Iowa	Nebraska	Vermont
Kansas	New Hampshire	Wisconsin
Massachusetts	North Dakota	

Two-year term, one re-election permitted (1 point) *

New Mexico	South Dakota

*The points are used for the construction of the General Power Index, Table 9.
Source: *The Book of the States, 1960–1961.*

The shortness of the governors' tenure is due to various factors. Most important is the American attitude which rejects long tenure for chief executives. The attitudes which led to the Twenty-Second Amendment of the federal Constitution restricting a President to two terms have produced similar restraints on the terms of governors. Apart from governors, elective state treasurers and auditors frequently have limited terms, which reflects the constitution writers' distrust of those put in charge of the state's monies. Yet lesser officials often overcome the constitutional restraint by the practice of rotation, as in Colorado where the state treasurer and auditor frequently alternate over a series of elections. On the other hand, there are no instances where governors have circumvented the constitutional intent, evidence that the formal restraint upon the chief executive has popular support.

Despite popular support, the consequences of formal restraints upon the governors' tenure are by no means clear. The governor who cannot run for re-election undoubtedly has limited control over the personnel who can hope to outlast him. On the other hand, the governor himself is freed from the control of the gubernatorial electorate and can carry on his administration with greater flexibility. The unexpected behavior of some Southern governors is probably related to the fact that restraints on gubernatorial tenure are characteristically a Southern rule. Therefore, it is not always easy to predict from his campaign how a Southern governor will react to the civil rights crisis. In 1958 S. E. Vandiver, Jr., was elected governor of Georgia on a strong segregationist platform which pledged that no school would be integrated while he was governor.[25] Nevertheless, in 1961 he lent the power of his office to further peaceful integration of the University of Georgia.

Vandiver's subsequent behavior in aiding integration may be interpreted as a result of the need to change his constituency, if he wished to continue his political career. Unable to succeed himself as governor he had no place else to go in Georgia politics. The road to the Senate was effectively blocked. Both of the state's Senators, Russell and Talmadge, were powerful figures and, in any event, Vandiver was related by marriage to the former and had been a campaign manager for the latter. With the election of John Kennedy as President, Vandiver was pushed strongly for Under Secretary of the Army, an appointment civil rights groups managed to block because of his campaign stands. But the experience pointed the way to future national office.[26]

Vandiver's behavior contrasts with that of Orval Faubus of Arkansas, a state which allows its governors re-election. Considered a moderate, Faubus nevertheless in 1956 sparked the first major crisis over school integration. Since then he has been re-elected four times, breaking a two-term tradition.

It is true that in most of the states where a governor may not succeed himself he may run for re-election after an interval. But the politics of such re-elections are a good deal more complex than in the case of an incumbent governor, and they are not a common occurrence. The most prominent examples are James E. "Kissin' Jim" Folsom of Alabama, A. B. "Happy" Chandler of Kentucky, Theodore G. "The Man" Bilbo of Mississippi, Earl

K. Long of Louisiana, and Gifford Pinchot of Pennsylvania. In seeking re-
election to the governorship after an enforced interval, a strong personality
is undoubtedly an essential asset.

THE POWER OF APPOINTMENT. The most widely appreciated means of
controlling officials is the power to name them. Presumably, if a person
can name an official, not only is the official beholden to him, but that person
can also hope to affect the administration by naming someone whose values
are close to those he wishes to implement. A sign of the diffusion of administrative control in the American state is the diversity of ways in which men
are named to offices. As we have seen, many are popularly elected. The
governor, with varying degrees of freedom, may name others. Then, again,
boards or commissions may name the agency head.

We can measure a governor's appointive power by defining the extent
to which he is free to name the heads of the major agencies. Taking sixteen

Table 6

THE APPOINTIVE POWERS OF THE GOVERNOR

STATE RANKINGS					
*5 Points**		*4 Points**		*3 Points**	
79	Tennessee	54	Michigan	49	Iowa
71	New Jersey	54	Vermont	49	New Mexico
68	Pennsylvania	53	Missouri	49	Utah
65	Maryland	53	Ohio	48	Rhode Island
61	New York	52	Oregon	46	California
57	Idaho	51	Minnesota	46	Nebraska
57	Indiana	51	Washington	45	Alabama
57	Virginia	50	Connecticut	45	West Virginia
56	Illinois	50	Kentucky	43	Arizona
				42	Wyoming
*2 Points**			*1 Point**		
41	Nevada	35	Alaska	26	Texas
40	Arkansas	33	Maine	25	South Carolina
39	Kansas	33	Mississippi	23	Delaware
39	Louisiana	31	New Hampshire	20	Oklahoma
39	Montana	29	Massachusetts	18	North Dakota
39	South Dakota	27	Georgia	15	Colorado
38	Wisconsin				
37	Florida				
37	North Carolina				

*The points are used for the construction of the General Power Index, Table 9.

principal functions and offices we can score each according to the relative influence, in formal terms, which the governor has over the appointment of the head of the function. The scale of values runs as follows:

5: the governor appoints alone;
4: governor must obtain approval of one house of the legislature;
3: governor must obtain approval of both houses of the legislature;
2: appointment by a board, of which the governor is a member;
1: appointment by an agency or individual other than the governor;
0: executive is popularly elected.

The range, then, is a statement of the likelihood that the governor can influence the administrator on the basis of formal appointive powers alone.

For each of the sixteen major functions the governors have been rated and the score for each function totalled. Since not all states have each of

Table 6, continued

The figure for each state is based on the governor's powers of appointment in sixteen major† functions and offices. It indicates the degree to which the governor can be assumed to have sole power over the sixteen functions or offices.

For each function, the index is scaled according to the governor's powers of appointment according to the following formula:

$$\text{Index} = \frac{\text{Maximum values of } P_1 + P_2 + P_3 \ldots (100)}{P_1 + P_2 + P_3 + \ldots P_n}$$

where P = 5 if governor appoints;
        4 if governor and one body approves;
        3 if governor and two bodies approve;
        2 if appointed by director with governor's approval,
          or by governor and council;
        1 if appointed by department director, by board,
          by legislature, by civil service;
        0 if elected by popular vote;

and where subscript indicates the chief administrator for each of the sixteen major functions and offices.

†Functions are: Administration and Finance, Agriculture, Attorney General, Auditor, Budget Officer, Conservation, Controller, Education, Health, Highways, Insurance, Labor, Secretary of State, Tax Commissioner, Treasurer, and Welfare.

Source: The table is computed from Darrah and Poland, Table 6.

the sixteen functions, the index has been converted into a percentage of the possible maximum rating in a state. Thus, if a governor rated a 5 for all of the functions in his state, he would get a 100. If, on the average, he rated a 4, i.e., he appointed everyone with the approval of one house of the legislature, then he would rate an 80. A rating of 60 would mean that he appoints on the average with both houses' approval, and so on.

The ranking of the governors shows a great range, going from 79 in Tennessee to a low of 15 in Colorado.[27] States such as New Jersey and New York which, along with Tennessee, have had major state constitutional revisions in the last thirty years also rate highly. States such as Illinois and Virginia which pioneered in administrative reforms in the first part of the century rank highly, too.[28] Thus the rating is a good reflection of the extent of the impact of the dominant trend in management reform on the several states.

A better idea of what the rankings mean can be had from looking at selected states. The reasons why Tennessee ranks as high as it does are: first, the governor (with the exception of three public utilities commissioners) is the only elective officer; second, most of the other positions are filled by him without the need of legislative approval. Even here, however, there are major officers chosen not by the governor but by the legislature itself — the secretary of state, the treasurer, and the controller. At the other extreme, Colorado's governor has weak appointive powers not only because such positions as secretary of state, attorney general, treasurer, and auditor are popularly elected, but also because the major functional departments such as agriculture, labor, health and the like are headed by civil service appointees — a unique condition in state administration. North Dakota's governor has weak appointive powers because, in addition to the usual elective offices, such positions as tax commissioner, and the commissioners of agriculture, labor, and insurance are also elective.

The ratings given here of the governors' appointive powers are necessarily indicative only of gross differences. Not all offices and functions are equal in importance, nor do the values of our point scale have any inherent validity. As we noted earlier there is a historical difference between the older elective offices and the newer functions of great importance which are more often appointive. So it is probably more important for a governor to appoint a welfare director than a state auditor, or even a secretary of state. Of all the older elective offices it is probably the attorney general's which is most important because the judgments and legal advice he is called upon to give may have great political importance. Attorneys general, along with lieutenant governors, are the minor elected executives who have most effectively been able to use their posts to advance to the governorship or the U.S. Senate. In this connection it is interesting to note that the earliest state official resistance to the 1954 desegregation decision of the Supreme

Court was among Southern attorneys general, a fact which Krislov has attributed to their aspirations for local office.[29]

Again, it is well to look at the governor's appointive powers within the total context. While the power to appoint is an obvious means of controlling subordinates, once the appointment is made the influence fades rapidly unless it is backed either by the use of power to remove or preferably by control over future appointments. Even when a governor can remove an official he is constrained by the wrangle which would result. It is a power to be used only as a last resort. Far more effective is control through the hope for reappointment or for advancement. Here lies the significance of political parties in state administration. For, while governors may come and go, a party organization has a memory which enables future governors to reward administrators for past services.

Party organization may modify our ratings in another respect. In our scale we have rated elective positions as those over which the governor is likely to have the least influence. This is true only to the extent that the individual does not owe his nomination and election to the governor. In a competitive state it is not at all unlikely that a governor or candidate for governor will be closely involved in the selection of his party's candidates for lesser state offices, and to the extent that they can ride his coattails they are as dependent on him as any formal appointee. Of course, to the extent that the lesser official develops independent electoral support, as we have already pointed out, the governor's influence is lessened. However, it is also likely that men who run for elective offices are sensitive to political protocol and will conflict with a governor only if they feel it will aid their political ambitions.

CONTROL OVER THE BUDGET. One important control over administrative agencies is the power of the purse. The power to give and withhold operating funds may transcend weaknesses in the appointive power. In general, the power is shared by the governor and the legislature, most states having placed the authority to prepare the budget in the hands of the governor. We can define the governor's strength again on a five-point scale according to the extent to which the budgetary authority originates with him:

5: governor has the responsibility for preparing the budget and shares it only with persons appointed directly by him;

4: governor has the responsibility but shares it either with a civil service appointee or an appointee of someone other than himself;

3: governor shares power with a committee selected by himself, but from a restricted list. (Indiana is the only case, where the appointees are from both parties in the state legislature);

2: governor shares authority with another official whom he does not appoint, the elected state auditor;

1: governor prepares budget only as a member of a group, usually of other elected state officials or members of the legislature.

As may be seen from Table 7, most states today give the main authority for budgetary preparation to the governor. Note also that diffuse control

Table 7

THE GOVERNORS' BUDGET POWERS

*Full Responsibility (5 points)**	*Shares with a Civil Service Appointee or with Person Appointed by Someone Else (4 points)**
Alabama	Colorado
Arkansas	Connecticut
California	Kansas
Georgia	Louisiana
Illinois	Maine
Iowa	New Mexico
Kentucky	North Carolina
Maryland	Rhode Island
Massachusetts	
Michigan	*Shares with a Committee Appointed from a Restricted List (3 points)**
Minnesota	
Missouri	Indiana
Montana	
Nebraska	*Shares with Another Popularly Elected Official (2 points)**
Nevada	
New Hampshire	Arizona
New Jersey	Vermont
New York	
Ohio	*Shares with Several Others with Independent Sources of Strength (1 point)**
Oklahoma	
Oregon	Delaware
Pennsylvania	Florida
South Dakota	Idaho
Tennessee	Mississippi
Utah	North Dakota
Virginia	South Carolina
Washington	Texas
Wisconsin	West Virginia
Wyoming	

*The points are used for the construction of the General Power Index, Table 9.

Source: *The Book of the States, 1960–1961,* pp. 140–143.

Table 8

THE GOVERNORS' VETO POWERS

Very Strong (4 points)*	Strong (3 points)*	Medium (2 points)*	Weak (1 point)*
Alabama	Arizona	Arkansas	Indiana
California	Georgia	Connecticut	North Carolina
Colorado	Idaho	Florida	Rhode Island
Delaware	Illinois	Iowa	Tennessee
Louisiana	Kansas	Kentucky	West Virginia
Massachusetts	Michigan	Maine	
Missouri	Minnesota	Maryland	
Montana	New Mexico	Mississippi	
New Jersey	North Dakota	Nebraska	
New York	Oregon	Nevada	
Oklahoma	South Dakota	New Hampshire	
Pennsylvania	Texas	Ohio	
Virginia	Utah	South Carolina	
	Washington	Vermont	
	Wisconsin		
	Wyoming		

*The points are used for the construction of the General Power Index, Table 9.

Source: F. W. Prescott, "The Executive Veto in the American States."

exists in many states. For example, it is common practice to "earmark" funds for particular purposes, such as gasoline taxes for highways. Then, too, many states finance special projects such as highways, bridges, and power resources through tolls and fees. Such devices provide the agencies concerned with an independent income, further reducing the governor's control.

THE VETO POWER. Finally the governor's formal strength may be defined by his power to veto bills passed by the legislature. While not strictly speaking a control over administration, it is a means by which a governor can prevent administrators from going over his head and obtaining support from the legislature. This is particularly true when the governor has the item veto or the power to veto a particular item of an appropriation without being forced to accept or reject the entire bill.

As in the case of budgetary powers the governors are typically strong with respect to the veto. The accompanying table classifies the states by veto strength according to a four-point scale derived from F. W. Prescott.[30] The governors' veto powers vary in several ways. In one state, North Carolina, the governor has no veto power at all. In others, the veto power is restricted by giving the governor only a short time to consider a bill after it has passed the legislature, by permitting a simple majority of legislative members to override the veto, or by requiring vetoed bills to reappear at the next legislative session. On the other hand, in addition to the item veto, a governor's power is greater the longer he has to consider a measure and the greater the number of votes required to override his veto. Some states permit the governor to go further than the veto and submit his own amendments to legislation.

As in the case of all formal powers, the veto must be considered within the total political context. Despite the fact that he has no veto, the governor of North Carolina does not appear weaker in relation to the legislature than other Southern governors. Most governors can dominate their legislatures on matters of policy because if the governor is weak in formal powers, the state legislatures are still weaker as instruments of policy leadership. Legislatures have only the barest capacity to provide any kind of oversight of the state administration. Frequently the legislative leadership itself is chosen by the governor, as in Tennessee, a fact which makes meaningless the presumed "weakness" of his veto power.[31]

A GENERAL INDEX OF THE GOVERNORS' FORMAL POWERS. To arrive at a general rating of the governors' formal powers we have combined the four measures of each governor's strength already presented: his tenure potential, and his appointive, budgetary, and veto powers. The maximum possible rating is a 19, found only in New York. The lowest rating is 7, found in North Dakota, Texas, Mississippi, and South Carolina. The median score is 13. Although each measure is independent of the others, they appear to go together. Formal powers for the governor are cumulative and their adoption undoubtedly reflects similar, over-all views of the governor's role.

A cursory examination of the general ratings shows that there is a relation between the size of the states and the formal strength of their governors. Texas is the only populous state where the governor's formal strength is low. All of the urban giants — New York, Illinois, California, Pennsylvania, and New Jersey — have ratings at the top. Indeed, the seven states with a formal power index of 17 or more contain over 37 per cent of the total population of the United States. Close to half the population lives in states where the governor has a power index of 16 or better.

Undoubtedly, the many factors which account for the variations in population among the states account for the variations in their formal power index. Factors related to the size of the states relate to the power index in the same manner. Therefore, the higher the proportion of urban population in a state and the smaller the percentage of agricultural employment, the higher the formal power index.

Table 9

A COMBINED INDEX OF THE FORMAL POWERS OF THE GOVERNORS

	BUDGET POWERS	APPOINTIVE POWERS	TENURE POTENTIAL	VETO POWERS	TOTAL INDEX
New York	5	5	5	4	19
Illinois	5	5	5	3	18
New Jersey	5	5	4	4	18
Pennsylvania	5	5	3	4	17
Virginia	5	5	3	4	17
Washington	5	4	5	3	17
California	5	3	5	4	17
Maryland	5	5	4	2	16
Missouri	5	4	3	4	16
Oregon	5	4	4	3	16
Utah	5	3	5	3	16
Wyoming	5	3	5	3	16
Montana	5	2	5	4	16
Alabama	5	3	3	4	15
Connecticut	4	4	5	2	15
Ohio	5	4	4	2	15
Tennessee	5	5	3	1	14
Kentucky	5	4	3	2	14
Michigan	5	4	2	3	14
Minnesota	5	4	2	3	14
Nevada	5	2	5	2	14
Colorado	4	1	5	4	14
Idaho	1	5	5	3	14
Louisiana	4	2	3	4	13
Oklahoma	5	1	3	4	13
Iowa	5	3	2	2	12
Nebraska	5	3	2	2	12
Wisconsin	5	2	2	3	12
Georgia	5	1	3	3	12
Massachusetts	5	1	2	4	12
Indiana	3	5	3	1	12
Arkansas	5	2	2	2	11
South Dakota	5	2	1	3	11
New Mexico	4	3	1	3	11
Kansas	4	2	2	3	11
Maine	4	1	4	2	11
New Hampshire	5	1	2	2	10
Rhode Island	4	3	2	1	10
North Carolina	4	2	3	1	10
Vermont	2	4	2	2	10
Arizona	2	3	2	3	10
Delaware	1	1	4	4	10
West Virginia	1	3	3	1	8
Florida	1	2	3	2	8
Mississippi	1	1	3	2	7
South Carolina	1	1	3	2	7
Texas	1	1	2	3	7
North Dakota	1	1	2	3	7

Table 10

GOVERNORS' POWER INDEX
RELATED TO SELECTED SOCIAL AND POLITICAL CHARACTERISTICS OF THE STATES

(a) *Distribution of total population in U.S., 1960*

Power Index	No. of States	Per Cent of Total Population
16–19	13	43.42
12–15	18	35.42
7–11	17	20.21

(b) *Distribution of states according to size of population by quartiles*

Power Index	1st Quartile (largest states)	2d Quartile	3d Quartile	4th Quartile (smallest states)
16–19	5	4	1	3
12–15	4	7	5	2
7–11	3	1	6	7

(c) *Distribution of states according to percentage urban, 1960*

Power Index	Over 75%	60–74%	45–59%	Under 45%
16–19	4	6	3	0
12–15	2	9	6	1
7–11	2	5	2	8

(d) *Distribution of states according to percentage in agricultural employment, 1940*

Power Index	0–14%	15–29%	30–44%	45% and Over
16–19	7	5	1	0
12–15	4	4	10	0
7–11	4	5	4	4

(e) *Distribution of states according to degree of party competition**

Power Index	1st Quartile (most competitive)	2d Quartile	3d Quartile	4th Quartile (least competitive)
16–19	7	3	2	1
12–15	3	6	4	3
7–11	2	3	6	6

(f) *Distribution of states according to percentage of national leaders coming from them (1900–1958)*

Power Index	2.5% plus	1.0–2.1%	0.42–0.84%	0.0
16–19	6	3	3	1
12–15	6	4	5	3
7–11	1	4	4	8

*The index applies only to forty-six states, as Nebraska and Minnesota have non-partisan elections to the state legislature and Alaska and Hawaii were not states for most of the period.

Sources: Distribution of party competition from Richard E. Dawson and James A. Robinson, "Inter-Party Competition, Economic Variables, and Welfare Policies in the American States," *Journal of Politics XXV* (1963) 275–276; distribution of national leaders based on 238 men receiving major party nominations for President and Vice-President, Cabinet, and Supreme Court appointments in the period from 1900 through 1958.

The fact that the formal strength of the governor is positively associated with the size of the state suggests that, as the complexity of a state increases, the governor's need for explicit means of control over his administration also increases. We have already pointed out that there is not necessarily a relation between the formal devices for administrative control and the influence which the governor wields. Within the context of their own states the governors of Mississippi and North Dakota may have as much, if not more, influence as do the governors of New York and Illinois. A governor trying to oversee the spending of a $2 billion budget has a much harder task than one dealing with a budget of $100 million. The terms "state" and "governor" mask differences in administrative problems not unlike those which separate the small neighborhood dress shop from the large department store.

Apart from differences in the size of the operation the government of the small rural state looms much larger on the economic horizon than that of the industrial state. An industrial, urbanized state has separate and sizable aggregates of wealth and population. The president of a major manufacturing concern, the head of a labor union, and the mayor of a metropolitan center can compete with a governor. On the other hand, in a state with no large cities and only minor industries there is no figure as important as the governor. Thus, if a governor of New York had to work with the administrative apparatus of Mississippi he would be helpless in competition with its varied interests. Yet it is a mistake to infer that the governor of Mississippi is helpless. The minor jobs, the contracts, and the patronage which a Mississippi governor dispenses provide him with the influence over legislators, administrators, and interest groups which his formal powers appear to deny him.[32] For a New York governor such patronage in a vast domain would be a crushing burden; he needs the order which formal, hierarchical controls help provide.[33] However, should the rural state governor obtain these controls he might well have an excess of power. Perhaps this explains the resistance of rural, particularly one-party rural, states to the arguments for administrative reform.

But there are also political factors to be considered. Political indices as well as the factors of size relate to the power index. The more highly competitive states tend to concentrate power in the hands of the governor. There is, too, a direct relation between the extent to which a state contributes to the national leadership corps (defined as Presidential candidates and appointees to the Cabinet and Supreme Court) and the formal power index. These political characteristics are, of course, also related to the size of the state and its degree of urbanism. Yet party competition may be the critical factor — the need for parties to make their mark in a competitive political situation. The principal aberrations from the gradation of power according to size are those states out of line in terms of competition as well. Thus, one-party Texas has a weak governor, while the highly competitive but thinly-populated mountain states of Utah, Montana, and Wyoming have strong governors.

THE POLITICAL IMPACT OF THE STATES' ADMINISTRATIVE ARRANGEMENTS. So far, we have been concerned with the development and the nature of the states' administrative arrangements and particularly with the uncertainty which surrounds them. We should, however, also attempt to search out relationships between administrative structure and policies, while being cautious in attributing cause. Do administrative arrangements affect the distribution of the state's resources among functions? Much of the argument about hierarchy and coordination, about elective and appointive heads, and about budget formation turns on the expectation that a particular arrangement will enable a particular function, e.g., health, education or highways, to get a "fair" or better share of state funds. The variety of structures provided by the states permits us to see if there is any visible relationship.

We have already seen that there are great variations in the way the heads of services are named. Now we should ask, do elective heads do better in garnering funds than those appointed by the governor or by a board? These propositions are best tested by examining education, a service on which a large share of the state's budget is spent and for which there is a diversity of arrangements. Twenty-four states elect their chief educational officer, while in twenty-six he is appointed either by a board or by the governor. As may be seen at the top of Table 11, there are distinct differences in the share of the state budget going to education, ranging from a low of 13 per cent in Massachusetts to a high of 46 per cent in New Mexico (1960). These figures do not necessarily indicate how much money is actually spent within a state on public education for the states differ markedly in their dependence on local taxation for this purpose. Nevertheless, we do see that the smallest proportion of state funds for education was spent in states with board-appointed heads. There is relatively little difference between the states which elect their educational officer and those states where the governor appoints. In both situations rarely was less than 25 per cent of the budget spent on education, whereas almost half of the board-appointed states fell to that low.

It is of course impossible from these figures to assert the method of appointment is the cause of the differences in amount spent on education. It is just as reasonable to conclude that those states where the citizens felt that education was a prime state function were also likely to be the ones which would choose to elect their superintendents of education. But if we take the other functions on which the greater part of state money is spent — health, public welfare and highways — we find similar, if not as conclusive, results.

Elective officials for these functions are rare but a similar trend does

Table 11

THE IMPACT OF ADMINISTRATIVE ARRANGEMENTS
ON STATE EDUCATION, HEALTH, WELFARE, AND HIGHWAY EXPENDITURES

PERCENTAGES OF TOTAL STATE EXPENDITURES

Method of Selecting *Chief Educational Official*	EDUCATION (1960)			*No. of* *States*
	Over *35%*	*25–34%*	*Under* *25%*	
	(Figure is percentage of states)			
Elected	46	50	4	(24)
Appointed by governor	40	60	0	(5)
Appointed by board	24	33	42	(21)

Method of Selecting *Chief Health Officer*	PUBLIC HEALTH (1960)				*No. of* *States*
	Over *10%*	*7–9%*	*5–6%*	*Under* *5%*	
Appointed by governor	16	37	31	16	(32)
Named by council or by civil service	12	33	33	22	(18)

Method of Selecting *Head of Public Welfare*	PUBLIC WELFARE (1960)				*No. of* *States*
	Over *20%*	*15–19%*	*10–14%*	*Under* *10%*	
Appointed by governor	4	19	56	21	(32)
Appointed by board	17	17	22	44	(18)

Method of Selecting *Head of Highways*	HIGHWAYS (1960)			*No. of* *States*
	Over *35%*	*25–34%*	*Under* *25%*	
Appointed by governor	33	45	22	(33)
Elective	0	100	0	(2)
Appointed by board	20	33	47	(15)

Source: Data on state expenditures for various functions is from *Statistical Abstract of the United States, 1962*, pp. 426–427.

exist. In general, states tended to give a larger share of their budgets to agencies or services headed by appointees of the governor than to those headed by board appointees.

It appears then that when a function is divorced from the electoral process its chances of getting state money are reduced. In the contest for money, an elected leader has a mandate or claim for support which carries over to his appointees. But an agency "out of politics" has no claim other than the inherent virtues of its program. When a pressure group seeks to remove an agency "from politics," its goal may be the assurance of professional control. However, the cost can be high: the agency's loss of influence within the state administration.

Of course, as we have already noted, the proportions spent by the states on education, highways, and the like are not necessarily the final figures. In the states, both local and federal governments stand ready to come to the aid of vital functions. Thus federal and local governments reduce the cost of the states' administrative diffusion for interest groups and others concerned with state functions.

It should be pointed out that the increasing demands being made on the states are working to reduce their freedom in administrative affairs. Ten years ago Karl Bosworth[34] in discussing the politics of the state administrative reform movement pointed out that state taxes were so small compared to the federal income tax and local property taxes that arguments about reducing costs had little relevance for state administration. Since then, state costs have risen and the example of the governor whose political fate is tied to a tax battle is becoming more frequent. If the states are becoming more visible arenas of government, then the governor's role must also change. Indeed, one observer claims that the decline in the position of the governors with respect to the Presidential nominations of 1960 and 1964 is due to the fact that more and more they have had to govern and to face responsibilities.[35] State government and governors, then, are perhaps at the point where they can no longer be all things to all men and all interests.

NOTES

1. See A. E. Buck, *The Reorganization of State Governments in the United States* (New York: Columbia University Press, 1938), for a rundown of state problems of organization at the time. A current outline is Earl L. Darrah and Orville F. Poland, *The Fifty State Governments: A Compilation of State Executive Organization Charts* (Berkeley: Bureau of Public Administration, University of California, 1961). Note also the Council of State Governments, *Reorganizing State Government* (Chicago, 1950).

2. *The New York Red Book* (Albany: Williams Press, 1960–61). State manuals contain the most readily available details on administrative structure. For a compilation of the contents of the manuals for each state, see Charles Press and Oliver Williams, *State Manuals, Blue Books and Election Results* (Berkeley: Institute of Governmental Studies, University of California, 1962).

3. V. O. Key, Jr., *American State Politics* (New York: Alfred A. Knopf, 1956) p. 99; Joseph A. Schlesinger, "A Two-Dimensional Scheme for Classifying States According to Degree of Inter-Party Competition," *American Political Science Review XLIX* (1955) pp. 1120–1128.

4. See Table 1.

5. Lincoln Steffens, *Autobiography* (New York: Harcourt, Brace and Co., 1931).

6. Based on unpublished data on the careers of Senators and governors elected be-

tween 1914 and 1958. There is a good deal of stability over a period in such careers. Thus Donald Matthews, *U.S. Senators and Their World* (New York: Vintage Books, 1960) p. 55, finds that 22 per cent of post World War II Senators came from the governor's office.

7. Dean E. Mann, "The Selection of Federal Political Executives," *American Political Science Review LVIII* (1964) p. 97.

8. For a more thorough treatment of the relationship between ambitions for office and party organization, see Joseph A. Schlesinger, "Party Organization," in James G. March (ed.), *Handbook of Organizations* (Chicago: Rand McNally & Co., 1965).

9. Unpublished figures from a study of the structure of political opportunities in the United States.

10. Key, *American State Politics*, chapter 2.

11. Coleman B. Ransone, Jr., *The Office of Governor in the United States* (University, Ala.: University of Alabama Press, 1956) pp. 123 ff.

12. Warren Moscow, *Politics in the Empire State* (New York: Alfred A. Knopf, 1948) pp. 186–187.

13. See chapter 4 of this volume for a fuller treatment of pressure groups in the states.

14. Robert B. Highsaw and Charles N. Fortenberry, *The Government and Administration of Mississippi* (New York: Thomas Y. Crowell Co., 1954) p. 326.

15. On the relations between Anaconda and Montana government, see Joseph K. Howard, *Montana, High, Wide, and Handsome* (New Haven: Yale University Press, 1943).

16. *The Book of the States, 1964–1965* (Chicago: Council of State Governments, 1964) pp. 208–209.

17. Ralph Smuckler and George Belknap, *Leadership and Participation in Urban Political Affairs* (East Lansing: Governmental Research Bureau, Michigan State University, 1956) p. 30.

18. See Anthony Downs, *An Economic Theory of Democracy* (New York: Harper, 1957) pp. 96–113, for an elaboration of the relationship between uncertainty and the development of ideology.

19. On the development of various arguments about administration, see Herbert Kaufman, "Emerging Conflicts in the Doctrines of Public Administration," *American Political Science Review L* (1956) pp. 1057–1073.

20. Samuel K. Gove, "Why Strong Governors?" *National Civic Review LIII* (1964) pp. 131–136.

21. There is a large amount of literature on the subject of administrative reform. For a critical survey see Dwight Waldo, *The Administrative State* (New York: Ronald Press, 1948), as well as *The Study of Public Administration* (New York: Random House, 1955). A good summary with particular reference to the states is in Duane Lockard, *The Politics of State and Local Government* (New York: Macmillan Co., 1963) chapter 12.

22. The development of merit systems is based on the Council of State Governments, *The Book of the States, 1940–1963*.

23. Paul Dolan, *The Government and Administration of Delaware* (New York: Thomas Y. Crowell Co., 1956) pp. 94–95.

24. Note that the trend is to adopt a four-year term. Since 1962 the Minnesota governors have four-year terms, as will the governors of Nebraska and Michigan after November 1966.

25. *The New York Times,* January 11, 1961.

26. For a critical discussion of the effects of limitations on succession, as well as other

aspects of the governor's powers, see Gove, "Why Strong Governors?"; and Rob
ert B. Highsaw, "The Southern Governor — Challenge to the Strong Executive
Theme," *Public Administration Review XIX* (1959).

27. In this and in subsequent rankings the Michigan governor is rated according to the
    constitution in existence prior to the ratification of the new constitution in 1963.
    The new constitution gives the governor greater powers according to the measures
    used here, although in some respects, such as in the power to appoint members of
    the judiciary, the new governor is weaker.

28. Leslie Lipson, *The American Governor, from Figurehead to Leader* (Chicago:
    University of Chicago Press, 1939).

29. Samuel Krislov, "Constituency versus Constitutionalism: The Desegregation Issue
    and Tensions and Aspirations of Southern Attorneys General," *Midwest Journal
    of Political Science III* (1959) pp. 75–92.

30. F. W. Prescott, "The Executive Veto in the American States," *Western Political
    Quarterly III* (1950) 98–112.

31. On the relationship of the governor to the Tennessee legislature, see John Wahlke,
    et al., The Legislative System (New York: John Wiley and Sons, 1962) pp. 56–59.

32. On the Mississippi governor, see Highsaw, p. 9.

33. For a discussion of the difficulties faced by a New York governor in gaining
    control of that state's administration, see Clark D. Ahlberg and Daniel P. Moynihan,
    "Changing Governors — and Policies," *Public Administration Review XX* (1960)
    195–204.

34. Karl Bosworth, "The Politics of Management Improvement in the States," *Ameri-
    can Political Science Review XLVII* (1953) 84–99.

35. Louis Harris, "Why the Odds Are Against a Governor's Becoming President,"
    Public Opinion Quarterly XXIII (1959) 361–370.

SELECTED BIBLIOGRAPHY

Abernethy, Byron R. *Some Persisting Questions Concerning the Constitutional
State Executive.* Lawrence, Kans.: Governmental Research Center, University
of Kansas, 1960. Compilation and discussion of the major questions in the
structure of the state administration.

Buck, A. E. *The Reorganization of State Governments in the United States.* New
York: Columbia University Press, 1938. An early compilation of the achievements of the administrative reform movement.

Council of State Governments. *Reorganizing State Government.* Chicago: 1950.
Similar to the previous reference, but brought up to date as of 1950.

Key, V. O., Jr. *American State Politics.* New York: Alfred A. Knopf, 1956.
Analysis of the electoral conditions surrounding the choice of the governor
and other state executives.

Lipson, Leslie. *The American Governor, from Figurehead to Leader.* Chicago:
University of Chicago Press, 1939. History of the early reform movement.

The Office of Governor. Urbana: Institute of Government and Public Affairs,
University of Illinois, 1963. A good collection of papers dealing primarily
with the office of governor in Illinois.

Ransone, Coleman B., Jr. *The Office of Governor in the South.* University, Ala.:
Bureau of Public Administration, 1951.

————. *The Office of Governor in the United States.* University, Ala.: University of Alabama Press, 1956. Useful surveys of the operations of the governors' office from the orthodox administrative reform point of view.

Schlesinger, Joseph A. *How They Became Governor.* East Lansing: Governmental Research Bureau, Michigan State University, 1957. Analysis of career backgrounds of governors from 1870–1950.

Willbern, York. "Administration in State Governments," in *The Forty-Eight States.* New York: The American Assembly, 1955. A perceptive survey of the problem.

COURTS
AS POLITICAL
AND GOVERNMENTAL
AGENCIES

CHAPTER 7
by
KENNETH N. VINES

OUR THIRD BRANCH OF STATE GOVERNMENT, THE COURTS, intervenes in public policy through the settlement of disputes. Controversies in the courts, for example, may concern almost any activity of the political system — a clash among economic interests, a dispute over an election, a rivalry between two government agencies or an attempt by the government to regulate the economic or social system. Moreover, judicial intervention may come at any phase of the policy process, at the end or near the beginning as interested parties begin their efforts in the courts or turn there as the final step in a long and exhausting controversy.

While judicial decision-making affects the distribution of power in society, much of what the courts do, as in the legislature and the executive, has mainly routine significance. The many divorce and traffic cases heard by the courts have their counterpart in the private pension and government claims bills of the legislatures and in administrative decisions concerning drivers' licenses and hunting and fishing licenses. Such decisions, taken as a whole, are not without public significance but individual decisions are commonly routine and affect the political system in remote ways.

Decision-making in the courts differs from that in other political institutions because special legal factors influence the judicial process as well as the form and outcome of judicial decisions. Except in Louisiana where something of the Civil Law tradition persists, American states adhere to the terminologies and processes of the Common Law imported from England in colonial days. Legal traditions affect the courts, for example, by court requirements that claimants obtain access in case form and present their demands in traditional legal form and language. Furthermore, legal conceptions limit the scope of court decisions; for example, courts cannot make appropriations although they can affect, through the settlement of conflicts, the allocation of wealth and resources; they cannot directly appoint non-court officials although they can designate an important candidate through decisions affecting the recruitment process.

In the political analysis of courts it is necessary to look past the legal structure of the case and to read between the lines for the broader social and political significances that are often not expressed in the decision. Injunctive suits, torts, and breaches of contract often conceal the identity of the claimants and the nature of the demand being made, as well as the outcome of the decision. Lawyers and judges, a former state judge tells us,[1] become skilled in reading between the lines of judicial decisions.

A recent case emanating from the Supreme Court of Pennsylvania illustrates how a judicial decision may affect the political process. The case concerned an important election in Pennsylvania, a primary to determine the Democratic nominee for United States Senator. In a very close race between Michael Musmano, a judge of the Pennsylvania Supreme Court, and Genevieve Blatt, victory in the contest turned on the validity of some 5,000 blank ballots cast. These were ballots on which the voter cast his choice on the wrong line but otherwise indicated a clear choice. Without the blank ballots, Miss Blatt was the narrow winner; with them, Judge Musmano would win by a slight margin. In a three-to-two decision the Supreme Court of Pennsylvania decided that the blank ballots should not be counted, thereby giving the nomination to Miss Blatt. The majority based its decision upon an 1897 case on a similar subject but the two minority justices thought the 19th century precedent did not properly apply and that the voters who cast blank ballots were being improperly disfranchised.[2]

This case tells us several important things about the courts. It shows how courts may affect state politics through intervention into the selection of public officials; it shows how they may influence the distribution of power by favoring one candidate or faction over another; and it indicates that courts are not loath to take a hand in even the most controversial of election disputes. The division of opinion on the court describes both the controversial nature of the situation and the failure of "objective legalism" to lead to a consensus on the court. Both the majority and minority had access to the same precedents of law dealing with elections and ballots; both heard the same arguments by counsel and presumably both sides were trained in competent law schools. Yet, the majority and minority saw the controversy in quite different ways, interpreted the law in a different fashion, and reached opposite conclusions. The decision in the case suggests that, although the controversy was carried on in legal terms, non-legal considerations not accounted for in the legal theory of decision-making were important.

STRUCTURE OF STATE COURTS

POLICY STYLES IN THE COURTS. Perhaps more so than in any other institution of government, decision-making in the judiciary is diffused among a series of layers, branches, and special agencies, many of whom perform quite particular functions and enter into the judicial process in highly specialized ways. Among an array of state courts there are distinct styles of decision-making. Some are highly important and have great impact upon the society; others make routine decisions that affect the society only in quite remote ways.

Table 1

DIFFERENCES IN DISCRETION AND POLITICAL FUNCTIONS OF COURTS
IN STATE JUDICIAL ORGANIZATION

COURT	AMOUNT OF DISCRETION	POLITICAL FUNCTIONS
Appellate (Courts of Last Resort and Intermediate Courts):	Maximal — Settles controversial questions, resolves political and social conflicts where precedents are not clear, but also handles routine cases.	Effects major resolution of conflicts over distribution of social, economic, and political power; a few important positions at stake in elections or appointments.
Trial Courts of General Jurisdiction (district, superior, circuit, etc.):	Medium — Much directed decision-making but some novel and controversial decisions.	Major cases probably will be appealed; much routine work but initial handling of important issues; moderate number of positions at stake in elections or appointments.
Local trial courts of limited jurisdiction (county, justice, magistrates, municipal):	Minimal — Confined to idiosyncratic deviation in decisions and variations in sentencing.	Case impact largely in administration and sentencing patterns. Closely linked to local party structures as a source of patronage.

Table 1 describes the general political functions of various kinds of courts in state judicial systems and suggests that there are distinctive differences among them in the manner in which they affect state politics. Of all courts, state courts of last resort* have the most visible, important political impact upon state politics. There are a number of reasons for the political importance of state supreme courts. Through a process of elimination by appeal, the high courts get the most controversial cases and those with the most at stake, since these are the cases most likely to be appealed all the way to the end of the judicial process. In about half the states there is an appeal

*State courts of last resort go by various names in the states, for example, the Supreme Court of Appeals in Virginia, the Court of Appeals in New York, and the Supreme Judicial Court in Massachusetts. Hereafter, we shall refer to them as supreme courts, their most common name.

as of right to the state supreme court in all cases, thus imposing a burden of as many as five or six hundred cases a year on some high courts and severely limiting the deliberative functions of these courts.[3] Legal reformers have recommended that appeals to the states' highest courts should be limited, and recently Florida, Louisiana, and Virginia have adopted provisions that allow the state supreme court to select the cases it hears, presumably those of greatest public significance.[4]

State supreme courts gain in authority and visibility from the fact that their decisions, unlike those of trial courts, are usually written down, published, and distributed. The decisions of supreme courts are thus publicized and communication facilitated with the public and with the remainder of the political system. In addition, the opportunity for individual political expression exists in the writing of majority opinions, dissenting opinions, and concurring opinions, and a judge may, through his written opinions, call attention to his views on matters of public policy, an opportunity not readily available to trial judges.[5]

In fourteen states, supreme courts share the appellate function with intermediate courts of appeal, and provision is made that cases must first be appealed through these courts before going on to the supreme court. Like the supreme courts, intermediate appellate courts consist of more than one justice, and decisions are made through the processes of conference, agreement, and conflict. Decisions made in these courts are also commonly written and published, and the opportunity exists for expression of political views.[6]

Moreover, supreme courts are the focus of institutional interaction in the judicial system of the states. Conflicts that are initiated and appealed throughout the judicial system may eventually come to the supreme court for final resolution. About one in three of the appellate cases heard by state supreme courts results in a reversal of the decision previously made in a lower court. By serving as the courts of last resort in the state judicial systems, supreme courts can become the ultimate decision-makers in the judicial process and, on occasion, in the state political process.

TRIAL COURTS OF GENERAL JURISDICTION. A feature of judicial organization common to all the states is a statewide trial court of broad jurisdiction. Called by many names in different states — district courts, circuit courts, superior courts, county courts, common pleas courts, or supreme courts (in New York) — these trial courts of general jurisdiction settle civil and criminal cases arising out of the major statutes, common law, and constitutions of the states. While there are only one or two appellate courts within a state, there exist from one (in Connecticut, Maine, New Hampshire, and Rhode Island) to over a hundred (in both Indiana and Texas) of these courts. The numbers of such courts in the other states vary between the two extremes, but there are about 1,500 courts of general jurisdiction in the whole United States.[7]

Sometimes the states supplement trial courts with special courts established to meet special needs. The most common of these are municipal courts established to help care for the volume of litigation produced by urbanization; such courts exist in cities like Chicago, New Orleans, Baltimore, and Detroit and exercise broad jurisdiction along with other general trial courts.[8] In other states the general jurisdiction is divided among more than one court: for example, in New York the county courts have jurisdiction over most criminal and some civil actions, along with the supreme courts. In the four states of Arkansas, Delaware, Mississippi, and Tennessee chancery courts still survive and exercise jurisdiction over equity cases just as in England; in other states equity cases are handled by the major state trial courts.[9]

In emphasizing the importance of appellate courts, we should not overlook the policy-making functions of general trial courts. These courts in interpreting complex statutes and applying the law to changing social and economic conditions necessarily make many important decisions.[10] As the initial agency for many important litigations, they also make the initial decision in a controversy so important that it may finally occupy the attention of the supreme court. In addition, the courts have some appointive powers in selecting minor court officials, such as bailiffs and clerks. They sometimes administer property where there are disputes about its ownership or use and commonly undertake reconciliation measures for certain kinds of civil disputes, such as those involved in divorces.

Although the trial courts are courts of original jurisdiction, they are also, in one sense, courts of last resort for most of the litigants who appear before them. Judge Frank has estimated that not more than 5 per cent of the cases decided in the trial courts are appealed, and one study of trial courts indicated that from 1 to 8 per cent of the cases decided were appealed in various states.[11] Nonetheless, it is probable that most of the controversial cases of major political significance get appealed to the higher courts where they face the possibility of reversal of the decision made in the trial courts.

An example of appellate reversal of an important lower court decision occurred in the controversy between the Reform faction and the William F. Buckley faction in New York City. Mr. Buckley, a congressman defeated for renomination, tried to keep control of the Bronx area by merging several opposition controlled districts and thus keeping control of the county Executive Committee. The Bronx Supreme Court (a court of general jurisdiction) held for the Buckley forces but an appellate court, the Appellate Division of the New York Supreme Court, reversed the decision and held that the Bronx Court erred in holding the merger legal and proper.[12] Although the lower court did not prevail, it did participate in the process of deciding an important political issue.

LOCAL COURTS OF LIMITED JURISDICTION. Last in the hierarchy of policy-making significance are the multitude of local and special courts that exist in the states. Even initially, these courts get few of the major social and political conflicts that are settled in the appellate courts. Their time is spent with the multitude of traffic cases, small claims, petty civil litigation, and misdemeanors that make up so much of the work of the courts at the local level. More representative of the work of these courts than the major controversies deliberated in the collegial atmosphere of the appellate courts are the traffic courts where most offenses are disposed of without trial and the justice courts where that legendary figure of American life, the justice of the peace, fines a a speeding tourist or trespassing hunter.

These grass-roots courts perform much more decision-making than the trial court of general jurisdiction, and the political impact of these courts is felt in the way the work of the court is administered and in the sentencing practices. Individual cases are very rarely of significance beyond the personal concerns of the litigants, but the patterns embodied in the methods of administration and sentencing practices may have public impact in various policy areas. For example, almost every city has a traffic court where the judge is tough on traffic violators in general or on drunken drivers in particular, and this court policy may help keep traffic violators in line or encourage safe driving. On occasion, magistrates in New York City may achieve a reputation as being tough on slum landlords[13] through their attitudes in handling property violations. It is possible that such a policy of judicial enforcement will encourage owners of slum properties to keep their rentals in proper repair.

Possibly the most important political feature of the local courts is their close link with the partisan structure of the states. In many areas, particularly in those states with partisan elective methods of judicial selection or where the judiciary is appointed by the governor, judicial office at the county and municipal level is one of the most important sources of patronage existent for the political parties.[14] A careful study of the selection of judges in Chicago has shown how closely local judges are sometimes joined to the activities of political parties. Chicago judges recognized the need for taking time to maintain good party relations, for securing endorsement of party leaders to secure the judicial nomination, and on occasion for responding to political pressures that were brought to bear when important cases occurred in which party influentials were interested. Often judges campaigned for judicial office and contributed to political campaign funds in order to hold their judgeships.[15] In a recent factional fight in the Democratic party of New York City, one faction punished the rival faction and showed its domination of the party by dictating the nomination of judges for the coming elections.[16]

When we think, therefore, about the political impact of courts upon politics in the states, we single out the supreme courts as loci of particularly strategic decision-making and as those courts likely to make final decisions on controversial matters of social and political import. In the more numerous district and local courts we look for significant patterns of judicial enforcement and sentencing practice that may influence public policy. We recognize, however, that among the millions of private controversies there may occur a case of special importance or may begin a litigation that is not settled before the case is adjudicated somewhere on the appellate level.*

ORGANIZATION OF THE COURTS. The course of justice in the states is affected by the variety and the unusual complexities of the organization of the courts. Although we think of the judicial process as a rational one, there may be more ambiguity and complexity in the jurisdiction and procedures of the judiciary than in either the legislature or the administration.

No two states have similar court organizations[17] and court systems range from the simple to the highly complicated, from highly generalized jurisdictional divisions to extremely complicated jurisdictional schemes where many special interests and philosophies are institutionalized in the courts. Two examples illustrating the extremes in court organization may be seen in the structures of New York and Wyoming as of 1962. Wyoming had a simple court structure with highly generalized jurisdiction located in but three layers of courts; New York, on the other hand, had a highly complex court structure with jurisdiction highly specialized and diffused throughout a number of members. The two contrasting court structures looked like this:

Wyoming	New York
Supreme court	Court of appeals
District courts	Appellate divisions of supreme court
Justice courts	Appellate terms of supreme court
	Supreme courts
	Court of claims
	Surrogates' courts
	Courts of general sessions
	Children's courts
	County courts
	Domestic relations courts
	City courts (continued on page 246)

*We should not overlook that supreme courts also settle many routine cases. For example, in 1961–62 divorce and criminal cases accounted for 21.8 per cent of the total cases in Idaho, 24.2 per cent in Louisiana, and 8.6 per cent in Pennsylvania. Of course, divorce and criminal cases may involve novel and important cases, but it is probable that most are routine.

New York, continued:

                               Municipal courts
                               Magistrates' courts
                               District courts
                               Justice courts
                               Police justice courts
                               Traffic courts
                               Recorder's courts
                               Police courts
                               Courts of special sessions

The structure of court organization, however simple or complex, derives its character from several strands of interested activity in the judiciary. One such course which tends to increase the number of courts is the retention of traditional courts invented in England and kept in the United States when often such courts have lost their useful functions in modern society. Examples are justice courts and magistrates' courts where local justices confront the public, probate courts whose business is with wills, chancery courts which deal only with equity cases, and orphans' courts. A second theme in court organization is the addition of courts that deal with problems raised by the character and problems of a modern industrial and urban society. Such courts are represented by municipal courts which handle cases arising in the cities, juvenile courts that handle cases involving young people supposedly with an understanding of the modern temper concerning the role and responsibilities of children, and domestic relations courts where the problems of family relationship — such as divorce and child care — are considered. A third trend which expands the number of court institutions in the states is a dispersion of jurisdiction among several courts of general jurisdiction, and these cover various geographical areas to pinpoint justice in some local detail. Examples are county courts, city courts, and district or superior courts, as they are variously called. A final addition to court organization is the allocation of appeals to more than one court. In all states there is at least one appeal as of right for all cases, but in fourteen states the process of appeal is a two-step affair that may end in an intermediary court of appeals or go to the court of last resort.

THE POLITICS OF COURT ORGANIZATION. Specific courts are added or taken away from state judicial systems in response to political and social pressures.[18] These pressures are of several varieties. Professional legal pressures operate through state and local bar associations or through judicial councils and usually are concerned with simplifying and rationalizing court organization in order to create a more favorable environment for the practice of law.[19] Often these legal pressures run counter to other pressures which want to retain or expand court service. Traditional legal pressures are found in those groups that favor retention of courts where there are jobs and fees. Included in this group are justices of the peace (those familiar figures of American lore) who garner fees for various legal services and fines from transgressors, probate and surrogate courts which handle wills and other succession problems and often collect fees for probating wills, for serving as guardians, and for receivership services, chancery courts whose separate courts would be abolished if equity functions were integrated with other judicial functions as is usually the case, and orphans' courts whose functions are normally handled by other courts. Finally, there are pressures to expand court organization by locating specific jurisdictions in the court system in separate fashion so that special problems characteristic of modern society can be handled. Courts often added by these pressures include municipal courts, traffic courts, juvenile courts, courts of domestic relations, small claims courts, and tax courts. Clearly, the different pressures often conflict with each other. For example, six states in 1961 (Colorado, Iowa, Illinois, Nebraska, New York, and North Carolina) submitted plans for court reorganization to voters. Typical was Colorado, where the proposal was to abolish justice courts and to reduce the levels of ordinary procedure from four to three, and add a juvenile court for Denver. Here we may assume the opposition of the justices of the peace to this organization change proposed by the Judicial Council, and the promotion by interests in Denver to push the proposal for a juvenile court there. Recently an attempt to rationalize the structure of the Connecticut court system was successfully opposed by the Probate Judges' Association which stymied an attempt to reorganize the state's 123 probate courts.[20] Basically, the politics of court organization and reorganization consists of interacting pressures generated by legal organizations, existing traditional court politicians who depend upon often archaic forms for jobs and sustenance, and social reform organizations and welfare groups who see the courts as a political agency to deal with modern problems engendered by urbanization and industrialization.

Table 2 describes the variations among the court structures in the states by noting the presence of types of courts in the judicial system. The patterns of court organizations thus visible suggest few obvious social and political characteristics with which variations in court structure can be associated. For example, one hypothesis accounting for the continuance of traditional court structures might be the need for judicial offices as patronage in states with strongly competitive party systems; another reason for their continuance in rural states with few urban and industrial developments might be that in these states the traditional structures (such as justice courts) would better serve the needs of a society for which they were originally designed. Table 2 indicates that the states maintaining such court organizations are neither

Table 2

VARIABLE CHARACTERISTICS OF STATE COURT STRUCTURES

Two or more traditional court organizations (probate, surrogate, justice, chancery or orphans)	Two or more modern court organizations (domestic relations, juvenile, municipal, small claims, tax or traffic)	Simplified rational jurisdiction (no more than three layers of general jurisdiction including trial and appellate courts)	Two appellate layers (court of last resort and intermediate appellate court)
Alabama	Colorado	Alabama	Alabama
Arkansas	Delaware	Arizona	California
Delaware	Florida	California	Florida
Idaho	Illinois	Colorado	Georgia
Illinois	Indiana	Hawaii	Illinois
Indiana	Louisiana	Idaho	Indiana
Iowa	Michigan	Iowa	Louisiana
Louisiana	New Jersey	Louisiana	Missouri
Maryland	New York	Maine	New Jersey
Massachusetts	North Carolina	Massachusetts	New York
Michigan	Ohio	Minnesota	Ohio
Minnesota	Oregon	Mississippi	Oklahoma
Mississippi	Utah	Montana	Tennessee
New York	Virginia	Nevada	Texas
North Carolina		New Hampshire	
North Dakota		North Carolina	
Ohio		North Dakota	
Pennsylvania		South Carolina	
Rhode Island		Virginia	
South Carolina		Washington	
Vermont		Wisconsin	
Wisconsin		Wyoming	

Source: *State Court Systems* (Chicago: Council of State Governments, 1962).

predominantly rural nor characterized by competitive party systems. However, Western states seem to be entirely lacking from the groups, suggesting that late establishment of court institutions may facilitate elimination of traditional court structures and that justices of the peace and probate courts are more difficult to reform in those states where they have been established longer. In those states with modern courts, simplified court procedures, and extended appellate levels, no social and political associations are obvious. Sections of the country, levels of party competition, and urbanism-industrialism do not seem to determine which states are included in the groups and which are not.

Because professional legal pressure, the existence of a viable bar association, or judicial council is important in organization, reform and reorganization of court structures, we may speculate that the presence of strong bar associations and judicial council movements is associated with such factors as the reform of traditional courts and the simplification of jurisdiction and appellate procedures, while the existence of social welfare and municipal groups have much to do with adding modern court structure. It should be noted that the retention of archaic organizational forms does not necessarily preclude the adoption of modern specialized courts, for example, in the court systems of Delaware, Illinois, Indiana, Louisiana, Michigan, New York, North Carolina, and Ohio. It is not necessary to eliminate old institutions in order to add new ones, and the result is often an increasingly complicated and disordered court structure.

ACCESS TO STATE COURTS

A key problem in the politics of the judiciary involves communication and presentation of issues before courts — in a word, "access" for interested persons and groups. The special problems of access to the judiciary are derived from the formal rules under which the courts operate and the traditional procedures that govern the functions and procedures of the courts.

For example, the enforcement of laws in the courts is accomplished through the intervention of the state as a party in the litigation, that is, by the prosecution of the laws. To gain access to the courts for the enforcement of laws, it is necessary therefore that the state institute litigation, and this it does through the process of prosecution. In most instances this involves prosecution for violation of the laws, or criminal prosecution.

THE POLITICS OF CRIMINAL PROSECUTION. The process of criminal prosecution is highly political for several reasons.[21] In the first instance, decisions concerning the extent of law enforcement or the degree of enthusiasm with which particular laws should be enforced are often controversial and affect members of the public in different ways. Almost everyone is in favor of vigorous enforcement of some of the major felonies — murder, rape and armed robbery — but differences of opinion arise over the enforcement of gambling laws, Sunday closing laws, or housing codes that affect slum properties. It is in the enforcement of the controversial laws that political pressures make themselves felt. Another reason for the political significance of criminal prosecution is the frequency with which the job of prosecutor leads to other and higher political offices. In general, the task of prosecuting is politically significant because it is the center of diverse intersecting pressures concerned with the effectuation of laws. In a sense, the state prosecutors have much ultimate discretion over the effects and consequences of policies enacted elsewhere in the political system; the legislator and the governor may enact policy, but vigorous prosecution can help secure its effectuation.

The prosecutor — variously called throughout the states: commonwealth attorney, county solicitor, state's attorney, or criminal district attorney — may be initiating a long political career because the job sometimes leads to higher office.[22] The prosecutor, mindful that the office may be a stepping-stone to higher office, may seek publicity to build a reputation as a crusader against vice, or a fighter against the interests. Schlesinger has shown that during the period from 1930–50 thirty-five public attorneys became governors,[23] and of the federal district judges sitting in 1959, sixty-six had once held some office involved in criminal prosecution.[24]

Most of all the political power of the prosecutor rests with the great amount of discretion he exercises in disposing of cases or in initiating prosecution in criminal cases. From arrest to sentencing and afterward, the course of criminal law is not automatic but may take various directions in the enforcement process. It is the prosecutor who gives the process of criminal prosecution direction and character, who makes it an instrument to scourge the law violator, or who allows its functions to lie fallow. Depending upon how he uses the discretion available to him in the process of criminal prosecution, the prosecutor may become known as a crusading D.A. or he may be regarded as a lackadaisical official who allows law violators their way. Usually elective, appointive only in the Eastern states of Connecticut, Delaware, Rhode Island, and New Jersey, the office of prosecutor is perhaps one of the most politically sensitive in the whole political system.

Discretion in the process by which criminals are convicted is designed to insure that the prosecutor may deal with the problems of law enforcement strongly but in flexible fashion. Such possibilities in the variation of prosecution allow the prosecutor more leeway to respond to political and social pressures. For example, Negroes in a Southern city were treated more harshly in criminal prosecutions after the increase of tensions following the decision to desegregate the public schools. However, in those wards where Negro registration was high there was a tendency to be more lenient toward Negroes than in those wards where Negro registration was low.[25]

Justice as ordinarily pictured — involving arrest, indictment, and trial by judge or jury and sentencing or acquittal — is not an accurate representation of the actual disposition of cases in the typical instance of prosecution. For one thing, a great many cases never actually go to trial, but are settled by procedures discretionary with the prosecutor. What are the procedures that enable the prosecutor to exercise such discretion in the disposition of cases? Besides the decision to concentrate on a problem of law enforcement, the technical procedures built into the system by which cases are processed under the criminal law allow great leeway for judgment by the prosecutor.

The important points at which criminal procedures against persons may either be dropped or carried through by the prosecutor begin with actual arrest and the possibility of police discharge after arrest. Next, failure to issue an affidavit showing the cause of arrest may also result in dropping charges. A flexible weapon in the hands of the prosecutor is the device of nolle prosequi, nol-pros, or nolle as it is often called. A case is nol-prossed whenever an arrest has been made and a charge issued but the prosecutor feels that adequate proof is lacking, or for some other reason decides that the case should not be pressed. At any moment after arrest and before the trial begins the prosecutor may decide that a case should be "nolled." In many states the law permits the prosecutor to fulfill the function of the grand jury by indicting through bills of information. Even when a person is indicted for a crime, the consequences of conviction may be considerably mitigated by a decision of the prosecutor to allow a guilty plea, possibly with a lesser charge than the one originally contemplated or on a promise of a lighter sentence. Even if an individual is convicted, the prosecutor may play a role in allowing him to seek bench parole with all the attendant advantages that a respite from conviction may bring.[26]

In the administration of law enforcement the prosecutor shares discretion with other law enforcement officials — the police and the judge. In the determination of the direction of law enforcement, however, responsibility rests largely with the prosecutor who sets the discretion and tone of enforcement policy. Few states put effective obstacles in the way of major discretion by the prosecutor. In three states — Louisiana, Illinois, and West Virginia — the prosecutor enjoys absolute power to dismiss a case. In fourteen states the prosecutor may dismiss only with the court's permission, but it is unlikely that courts systematically withhold permission due to the non-familiarity and lack of involvement of court officials with the business of the prosecutor.[27] The business of criminal prosecution also brings other interests into the picture. Bail bondsmen are an inevitable adjunct to criminal courts with a considerable financial stake in the criminal process and a highly political interest in the definition of conditions for setting and fulfilling bond requirements. Criminal lawyers, expert in the conduct of all phases of criminal prosecution, are also much involved as interested parties in the politics of criminal prosecution. A vigorous district attorney desiring to make a public reputation for himself may attack other participants in the criminal prosecution situation, as District Attorney Garrison of Orleans Parish, Louisiana, did in charging publicly that judges, criminal lawyers, and bail bondsmen exercise improper influence on the process of criminal prosecution and hamper the prosecutor's office in its attempt to maintain law and order.[28]

Table 3 describes some aspects of prosecutor's discretion in two different localities in the states of Louisiana and Pennsylvania. In the case of Philadelphia, we see that there is some variation in the nol-prossing of crimes

Table 3

PROSECUTION DISPOSITION OF CASES IN TWO COUNTIES

NEW ORLEANS, 1954–60 (1864 CASES)		PHILADELPHIA, 1954 (8888 CASES)	
Disposition of Cases	*%* *Cases*	*Offenses*	*%* *Nol-Prossed*
Plead Guilty on Original Charge	39.7	Murder (77)	10.4
Plead Guilty on Reduced Charge	5.2	Frauds (692)	13.3
Plead Innocent and Tried	9.9	Conspiracy (234)	15.0
Dismissed on:		Voluntary Manslaughter	
Nol-Pros	32.7	(103)	40.8
Affidavit Dismissed	11.0	Sex Crimes (535)	10.8
Prescribed	1.5	Rape (50)	4.0
	———	Thefts (1773)	8.2
	100.0	Assault & Battery (2116)	27.3

Sources: Herbert Jacob, "Politics and Criminal Prosecution in New Orleans," in Kenneth N. Vines and Herbert Jacob, *Studies in Judicial Politics,* Tulane Studies in Political Science VIII (New Orleans: 1963) 81; and "Prosecutor's Discretion," *University of Pennsylvania Law Review CIII* (1955) 1082.

in that location depending on the type of crime. Crimes involving thefts, murders, and frauds are nol-prossed less frequently than are those involving assault and battery and voluntary manslaughter.

The gamut of disposition in the criminal process for New Orleans is described in the case of Orleans Parish. Nearly half of all offenses were dismissed by the prosecutor by either nol-prossing, dismissal by affidavit, or through prescription. Of the remaining cases, 5.2 per cent pleaded guilty on reduced charges and less than 10 per cent protested their innocence and thereupon went to trial. About 10 per cent of all those sentenced were put on probation, had sentences suspended, or were paroled.[29] The description of cases nol-prossed in Philadelphia illustrates how cases may vary according to the type of offense involved. Cases involving murder, sex crimes, and crimes against property were dismissed much less frequently than assault and battery and voluntary manslaughter cases. Here we have an instance of judgment on the part of the prosecutor reflecting perceptions about the seriousness of crimes that are proper subjects for dismissal and others that should not be dismissed.[30]

The prosecutors also affect the flow of litigation to the courts. By their zeal and efficiency in prosecuting cases for the state they help determine how much public litigation will go to the courts and what kind. With an eye cocked toward public advancement, they are the most direct and sensitive link of the judicial process to the public.

GENERAL ACCESS. Access other than that in criminal prosecution is taken on the initiative of interested groups and individuals. While communication with the courts in general may be had only by litigation, that is, by initiating a case before the courts, there are other ways in which the eye of the judges can be caught and attention called to fundamental issues involved in the courts. Briefs *amicus curiae* may be presented to the supreme courts, and persons not party to the actual litigation may argue for one side. Articles and notes published in state law reviews are probably noticed by state judges, and this may be a means of attracting their attention to a legal point with policy implications.[31]

The reputation of courts may relate closely to the zeal and frequency with which interests try to use the courts as policy instruments. An excellent case in point is the role of state courts in the South in decision-making in race relations. In their drive to secure favorable policy enactments, Negro groups have used the state courts less frequently than they have the federal courts. Negroes perceive that they have little chance for favorable treatment of civil rights issues in the state courts[32] and on occasion have pleaded this formally in order to avoid appearing before the Southern state courts when they would have preferred federal courts.[33]

It is instructive, in this regard, to examine the appearances of Negroes before state and federal courts. Over 90 per cent of the plaintiffs, the initiators of race relations cases in the federal courts, were Negroes, while in the state courts only 33 per cent of the race relations cases in state supreme courts were initiated by Negroes.[34] It appears that the reputation of Southern state courts had much to do with the failure of Negroes to seek access to the courts, and the frequency with which white groups and state and local governments appeared before state courts to try to undo the process of desegregation in the states concerned. As a matter of fact, Southern state governments overtly attacked Negro interest groups, especially those specializing in litigation, in an effort to reduce the effectiveness of Negroes in the courts.[35]

A special problem facing those who would attain access to the courts is obtaining the services of an intermediary, a lawyer, who communicates with the courts. Lawyers are normally used to present and argue all issues before courts, except where some minor administrative business with the courts is involved or where the conflict is litigated in small claims courts. As we have noted before, the formalistic nature of proceedings in the courts require the services of professionals who are specially trained for the presentation of issues before the courts.

When the services of lawyers cannot be obtained, access to the courts is difficult, if not impossible, and as a consequence proper presentation of the case is greatly handicapped. Recognizing this, the Supreme Court of the

United States recently decided that all indigent defendants were to have legal counsel if they required it. Most states have recognized that indigent persons would lack access to the courts through their inability to hire a lawyer and have provided various solutions. In some, the court can appoint counsel for a defendant: for example, in New Jersey the judge can make the appointment from a list of all lawyers in the county; in other states, a Public Defender, a governmental or private agent who specializes in providing legal services to those who need them, is available.[36]

On occasion, access to the courts may be blocked through congestion and overloading of the judicial dockets. One group of studies by the Institute of Judicial Administration found that in courts of four states — Illinois, New York, Indiana, and Connecticut — a delay of over two years occurred before a case filed could be brought to trial. In sixteen other states the time required to bring a case to trial exceeded a year.[37] If the adage, "justice delayed is justice denied," is to be believed, then delay in the state courts is often a serious problem in hampering access to the judicial process. This problem is perceived by legal groups to be an important one in the judicial process, occurring more frequently perhaps than any other. While others (plaintiffs, individual lawyers and corporations) are interested in the problems of delay, they only rarely devote much attention to the problems concerned with speeding up the judicial process.

Table 4

VOLUME OF CASES HANDLED BY THREE STATE COURT SYSTEMS

STATE	COURT	NO. OF CASES FILED
Arizona	Supreme Court	321
	Superior Courts	40,151
	Justice and Municipal Courts	Not recorded
California	Supreme Court and District Courts of Appeal	3,139
	Superior Courts	352,256
	Justice Courts	820,000
	Municipal Courts	6,933,812
New Jersey	Supreme Courts and Appellate Courts	1,016
	District Courts	189,336
	Municipal Courts and County District Courts	1,614,174
	Juvenile and Domestic Relations Courts	56,940

Sources: *Second Report of the Administrative Director of the Supreme Court of Arizona* (Phoenix: 1962); *1962 Annual Report of the Administrative Office of the California Courts* (Sacramento: Judicial Council of California, 1963); *Annual Report of the Administrative Director of the Courts* (Trenton: Administrative Office of the Courts, 1962).

THE BUSINESS OF THE COURTS

Judged by quantity alone, state courts do a great deal of business. While state and city legislative bodies consider that they have worked hard to pass a few hundred enactments a year, state courts process a yearly output sometimes amounting to millions of cases.

The quantity of cases filed in the courts, illustrated in Table 4, can be put into perspective by a further analysis of the types of cases handled. In both California and New Jersey, automobile cases counted for a large share of the cases filed in municipal courts. In New Jersey municipal courts only 93,000 of the more than one million cases were on non-traffic subjects, while in California the six million cases filed in municipal courts consisted of over three million parking cases, and a large portion of the remainder were traffic cases of other varieties. Justice courts handled a similar large volume of traffic cases, and in California this amounted to 73.8 per cent of all cases handled in those courts. Justice courts handled small numbers of small claims, cases involving misdemeanors, and felony preliminaries; superior and district courts on a higher level handled large numbers of divorce cases — for example, over 5,000 such cases in California — as well as a large number of probate cases involving questions of inheritance and succession, and personal injury and property damage cases.[38]

Fortunately, the business of the courts is less than the amount of filings would indicate. Evidence shows that less than one-half of the cases filed in major trial courts ever come to court. For example, one study of courts in Connecticut indicated that during a twelve-year period only 40 per cent of the cases filed were terminated by court consideration; the rest were settled out of court or were allowed to lapse. In many instances the trial courts merely provide the background against which settlements can be reached out of court.[39]

Clearly, the work done by the lower courts has mainly routine importance when we look at the character of the litigation. The flood of cases stems from the administration and adjudication of state and local laws that affect the daily lives of the public, their traffic habits, personal lives, and small business transactions. These are the daily tasks of the numerous state and local judiciary whose appointive positions are so important as patronage in the states. Their work assumes public significance according to the administration and sentencing patterns they maintain and the consequent impact on public conditions.

In contrast to the many routine settlements made in the lower courts, quite a few of the cases handled by the courts of last resort and many of the appellate cases handled at an intermediate level have broader public significance. Few litigants will be bothered with the great expense and trouble in appealing a case unless the stakes are worthwhile. Even some of the criminal cases and the divorce cases that are heard in the supreme courts are apt to involve novel questions of due process, important social values due for a hearing, or changes in basic disposition of conflicts.[40]

Another characteristic of the business transacted by the state courts is its increase in recent years. Not only are the courts busy but they are doing comparatively more all the time. Measured in gross terms, the amount of civil litigation in the New Jersey courts has increased 91 per cent over a period of ten years, while the population of New Jersey increased by only 25 per cent over the same length of time;[41] over a similar ten-year period, case filings in California increased 57 per cent, while the population of the state was increasing 35 per cent.[42] Another more precise way of measuring increase in the amount of judicial business is by comparison of rates in filing per unit of population. To illustrate this, in the superior courts of California filings per 100,000 population increased from 2,051 in 1950 to 2,221 in 1960; in Iowa filings per 100 population in the district courts increased from 8.5 in 1956 to 9.7 in 1960. The separate increases indicate not only that the total amount of business handled by the courts has grown along with population, but also that the population is filing more cases.[43]

However, in California the appellate courts handled only 3 per cent more cases in 1960-61 than in 1950-51, an increase which did not begin to keep up with the population growth; on the other hand, cases docketed by the Maryland high court of appeals increased from 178 to 344.[44] These differences reflect variations in the manner in which state courts of last resort can control the number of cases they hear. Where the cases appealable of right are restricted and where the practice of certiorari is used to select cases heard, high courts are able to keep business stable or even to cut the number of cases if the load has been excessive; where many cases can be appealed of right and where the courts have no way to select and limit cases they hear, the high courts face the problem of rapidly increasing case loads with less time to hear cases of public interest.

Why has litigation grown to such heights, particularly in the lower courts, even expanding faster than population growth? It is tempting to blame the automobile — to say that the increase in their number and the resultant expansion of mobility has led to an inevitable multiplication of court cases. One state study has shown, however, that automobile negligence cases are increasing no more rapidly than litigation generally.[45] Likewise, divorce and matrimonial cases may be ruled out as the constituent of expansion.

In general, the increase in litigation is due to the development of more complicated social and political conditions. Every major pattern of development, such as the population explosion, the advent of automobiles and other mechanized transportation, the growth of urban communities, the expansion of business and trade systems, and the expanding role of government in social and economic regulation, have all contributed to an increased role of the courts. More specifically, such political programs as workmen's compensation, welfare programs, unemployment compensation, and zoning and urban redevelopment are a continuous source of litigation. The activities of government agencies, bodies such as the Civil Service Commission, utilities commissions, labor relations boards, and milk regulation commissions — all created since 1930 — help create litigation.

These considerations lead us to a theory about the business of the courts. To a large extent courts depend upon other agencies of government to provide them with the legislation and executive acts which, in turn, lead to litigation. The courts react according to a set of cues provided by other political institutions, and one of their important functions is to implement avenues of policy laid down in legislation and other political actions. Courts, also, the character of litigations suggests, are unusually sensitive to social change, political conflict, and economic developments. Social changes often lead to modification of family life, stress in social relationships, or unusual economic difficulties, and are soon reflected in the character of litigation that the courts process. For example, problems in family life and the breakdown of morals have led to an increase of matrimonial cases and juvenile cases in the courts; the Depression brought an avalanche of foreclosure and home ownership cases.

COURT PERSONNEL

THE SELECTION SYSTEMS. Questions about the selection of judicial personnel and their conditions of tenure dominate discussion of the politics of judicial institutions. For one thing, political institutions which normally function in the political process do not play a visible and salient role in the judicial process. Political parties, political factions, and interest groups approach or are involved in the judicial process in special ways. For example, judges are not organized on the basis of membership in political parties as they are in the legislature, and the processes by which party cohesion and support in the legislature are secured remain unknown in the courtrooms. The methods by which interest groups establish communication with the legislature — the professional lobbyist who makes a career out of proper contact, the office of communication situated near the legislative scene of action, and the arranged campaign of letters from constituencies and telegrams from influential constituents — are either unknown with regard to the courts or regarded as so improper that their use would be met by indifference or shocked surprise.

True, parties and interest groups achieve access to the courts through lobbying by litigation,[46] but representation before the courts in this fashion is cloaked by the forms and symbols of the law and is only possible by being a party to a litigation.

An exception occurs in the professional legal activity of court personnel. Through judicial conferences, participation in the bar association activities, and other legal activities ostensibly having to do with the promotion of justice, lawyers enter into familiar contact with judges and join them in pursuit of "legal" policy objectives. These policy objectives are severely limited by the nature of the legal culture and are pursued primarily within the framework of bar and bench activities.

Since judges are not organized into party organizations or represented as members of factions or interest groups, the individual court actor looms large in the political system. This fact leads to great emphasis on methods of judicial selection and upon choosing judges in such a way as to take them out of politics. Taking judges out of politics is usually defined as having them recommended by a committee of the bar and laiety, appointed by the governor, and then run on their record rather than against an opponent or a representative of a political party.[47]

Five different methods of judicial selection are used among the states. Although each method has distinctive characteristics, all involve some combination of appointive and elective procedures. The five methods are: *partisan election* in which judges are chosen by election with participation by political parties in their nominations by primaries or conventions; *non-partisan election* where judges are popularly elected but with restrictions on partisan designation of candidates and participation of parties in the campaign for judicial election; *election by the legislature; appointment* which puts the selection of judges in the hands of the governor who may choose them according to whatever criteria he wishes; and *the Missouri Plan* which has the governor select judges from among those recommended by a special commission and in which judges thus chosen must run against their records when the electorate says in a referendum whether it wishes to retain the incumbent judges. In California where the system of appointment-referendum selection was first adopted in 1934, the governor appoints without committee recommendation, but his appointments must be confirmed by a commission.

Table 5 shows the various ways in which judges are selected in the states. Thirty-four of the states elect some judges by a form of popular election, about half by partisan election, and half by non-partisan election in which party designations are presumably barred. In twelve states, judges are chosen by government agencies, in five, by their legislatures, and in seven, they are appointed by the governor. Six states choose some of their judiciary by the Missouri Plan which is really a variant of the appointive system in which the governors consult the recommendations of a committee and the judges then run against their record in a referendum.[48]

Table 5

METHODS OF JUDICIAL SELECTION IN THE STATES

Partisan Election	Election by Legislature	Non-Partisan Election	Appointment	Missouri Plan*
Alabama	Connecticut†	Alaska	Delaware	Alaska
Arkansas	Rhode Island	Arizona	Hawaii	California
Colorado	South Carolina	California	Maine	Iowa
Florida	Vermont	Idaho	Maryland	Kansas
Georgia	Virginia	Michigan	Massachusetts	Missouri
Illinois		Minnesota	New Hampshire	Nebraska
Indiana		Montana	New Jersey	
Iowa		Nebraska		
Kansas		Nevada		
Kentucky		North Carolina		
Louisiana		Ohio		
Mississippi		Oregon		
Missouri		South Dakota		
New Mexico		Tennessee		
New York		Utah		
North Carolina		Washington		
Oklahoma		Wisconsin		
Pennsylvania		Wyoming		
Texas				
West Virginia				

*Several Missouri Plan states select some judges according to the Missouri Plan, other judges by election.

†Formally by legislature, actually by nomination of the governor.

Source: *State Court Systems* (Chicago: Council of State Governments, 1962).

The variations in state selections of judicial personnel are deeply rooted in tradition on the one hand, and subject to constant pressures from the legal profession on the other hand to take the judiciary out of politics by changing the method of selection. Several surmises do not seem to explain the variations among the states. We might expect that states in which political parties are most competitive and where there is most partisan activity would select their judges by partisan election in accord with the prevailing political culture or in response to the partisan demands. However, a glance at a group of the twelve most competitive party states in state elections — Delaware, Montana, Massachusetts, Illinois, Utah, Idaho, Pennsylvania, Rhode Island, Washington, Connecticut, California, and New York — indicates that these states have all types of selection systems and that no single system predominates. We might expect states in which there is little party competition (one-party states or modified one-party states) would choose by non-partisan methods since parties there would be less important and the pressures for party selection of political personnel would be weaker. Non-competitive party states are found, however, throughout the range of selection systems — appointive and elective.

Despite the agitation carried on by professional legal interests for change, few states have altered their methods of selection. The six Missouri Plan states represent the only victories for judicial reform. Judicial election has, indeed, been remarkably resistant to changes during the last century. History records that the last political movement to have an impact was the Jacksonian movement when many state appointive systems were swept away in the enthusiasm for choosing political officials by popular election and the supposition that popular election would bring surcease from control by the interests and the forces of oligarchical corruption.[49]

There are pronounced sectional differences in the distribution of states' selection systems, but these geographical differences also involve adherence to different political traditions. The thirteen original colonies all choose their judiciary by appointive systems, legislative or executive, save two — Georgia and New York. These eleven have had appointive systems from the beginning of their statehood and never changed. Only Hawaii of all the appointive states was not a member of the original Union. States admitted to the Union later either had partisan selection systems from the beginning, or switched during the Jacksonian period, or were caught up later in the spreading enthusiasm for election of public officials by non-partisan methods. Fourteen of the sixteen states that use the non-partisan method of selection may be grouped as part of the regional response to the Progressive Movement in the Northwest and the West. Only Ohio and Tennessee stand out as states not a part of the Progressive regional pattern.

Systems of judicial selection demonstrate the importance of traditional habits in defining institutional practices in state politics and illustrate how resistant such practices are to movements of reform. States' resistance to revision of judicial selection may be due to the sloganeering of legal reform groups in keying their efforts to "take judges out of politics." As one state judge put it, "There is no harm in turning a politician into a judge — the curse of the elective system is that it turns almost every elective judge into a politician."[50]

The argument of removing judges from politics needs more careful examination.[51] In fact, taking the judge from party politics does not remove him from politics; it puts the selection of judges in different hands . . . in the hands of professional legal leaders and organizations and in the hands of the governor. Rarely examined in the argument is whether it is better to have judges with known partisan directions or only those with known legal skills; we could argue that a partisan selected judge might be more sensitive to the social problems and changes of the time, the kind of political issues that are the stock-in-trade of political parties. A bar committee or gubernatorial selectee might be unaware or ill-equipped to deal sensitively with social and political problems since the practice of law is capable of insulating its practitioners from the social problems of the time. Would a substitution of the Missouri system in all the states recruit judges better fitted for the adjudication of important social and economic conflicts? The problem has rarely been discussed in these terms by the reformers.

THE EFFECTS OF SELECTION SYSTEMS. Given the differences among the selection systems, we may still ask: Does the method of recruitment make a difference in the kinds of judges who are selected? Even in partisan election systems, the legal groups may still exercise influence through endorsement of candidates, through the announcement of referenda on candidates, and by the personal intervention of prominent members of the bar. The precise influence of bar polls and endorsement in the states remains to be measured and

Table 6

EDUCATION AND LOCALISM OF TRIAL AND APPELLATE JUDGES

SELECTED ACCORDING TO DIFFERENT SYSTEMS IN TWELVE STATES
(N = 924)

	Partisan Elected (N = 335) %	Non-Partisan Elected (N = 348) %	Appointed (N = 162) %	Legislative Elected (N = 56) %	Missouri Plan (N = 23) %
Localism					
Born in district the judge serves:	52.5	8.9	35.2	16.1	17.4
Attended law school in state of court:	63.3	55.2	31.5	48.2	87.0
Education					
Prior college degree:	46.9	52.6	32.7	67.9	56.5
Law school honors:	7.5	8.6	9.9	14.3	26.1
Attended substandard law school:	20.0	2.3	26.5	1.8	30.4
Political Experience					
Held prior public or party office:	31.3	54.9	59.9	94.6	30.4
Held prior judgeship:	24.4	17.3	24.1	57.1	21.7

Source: The author is indebted to Professor Herbert Jacob for making available the data on which this table and the following discussion are based. Data are based on a tabulation of background experiences of trial and appellate judges in 12 states. The states chosen to represent different systems of judicial selection are: California, Connecticut, Illinois, Maine, Massachusetts, Missouri, New Jersey, Pennsylvania, South Carolina, Vermont, Washington, and Wisconsin.

fully documented[52] but its presence is often a part of normal state judicial elections. If the Missouri Plan systems work as supposed, they would lead to the selection of judges with certain qualifications — judges more able as measured by social, political, and personal qualifications. In addition, judges appointed under approved, non-partisan plans would behave differently, be less susceptible to partisan pressures, and be more independent of judgment. While analysis of judicial decision-making under different selection systems must await further research, we are able to compare the personal and social characteristics and experiences of judges chosen under the different systems. Table 6 makes this comparison by looking at the judges of twelve states representing the different ways in which judicial personnel are chosen.

The presumptions in favor of the appointive and Missouri plans are that the appointive committees and agents will be free to choose persons of higher qualifications. These "higher" qualifications might include better education and legal training, experience in public life, an absence of localism, and judicial experience. These expectations are in part fulfilled; in part they are not. While partisan elected judges surpass all others in attachment to their districts, non-partisan elected judges are the least localistic in this respect (born in district only 8.9 per cent of the time). And while legislative and appointive judges have attended out-of-state law schools more than the popularly elective judges, Missouri Plan judges are the most parochial of all in this respect (87 per cent went to law school in the state). Judged by the quality of the law school attended, appointive judges and Missouri Plan judges do not come up to expectations, but legislative judges and those elected under non-partisan systems get high marks.

As regards political experience, the elective judges have had less than the other judges and we are not surprised to learn that those chosen by legislatures and governors have been legislators quite frequently. The legislature could be expected to choose one of their own for judicial office, and the governor, when he appoints to judicial office, often selects a legislator whom he may have known in the course of activities in state politics. The prior judicial experiences of the groups are not significantly different, except that Missouri Plan judges have been judges before appointment a little more frequently than the others.

We conclude, then, that different systems of selection do tend to sort out judges with different social and political backgrounds.[53] Approved systems (the appointive and Missouri Plan), however, by no means monopolize all favorable characteristics. Non-partisan elective judges rank higher on education and localism indices than do appointive and Missouri Plan judges. Since non-partisan judges are usually elected in those states with a background of Progressivism in their political history, a good guess is that in these states there may be traditions that tend to militate for the selection of superior political personnel.

INTERACTION OF ELECTIVE AND APPOINTIVE PROCEDURES. It is a mistake to think of elective and appointive procedures in selecting the judiciary as entirely separate, with no overlapping and no interaction. In fact, we assume that the governor or committee in deciding on selection responds to pressures in the political environment of the state. After all, the governor, if he is not the leader of one of the state's parties, is certainly one of its most prominent and active partisans. A governor may see the appointment of a judge as a way to gain strength in some section of the state or to compensate for weaknesses with a particular wing of the party. Pressures may be brought to bear upon the governor at the time of judicial selection that represent the partisan system in microcosm. Diverse partisan pressures may be brought to bear upon the governor at the time of appointment and the appointment may become an important tool in reconciling one faction, rewarding another, or simply choosing between several equally strong factions in the state, each of which has a candidate to offer for appointment.[54]

The elective system is also influenced by the practice of judicial appointment. Direct entrance of the governor into the selection process in elective states is gained by his power to make interim appointments. In this manner the governor can make appointments in all those instances where the judgeship is vacant because of the retirement or death of the incumbent between elections. True, the interim-appointed incumbent must seek election at the next regular election but, in the meantime, he has assumed the valuable status of incumbent judge and then can run on a plea to retain the incumbent and thus promote the independence and stability of the judiciary. In the normal run of events the governor would have the opportunity to make few interim appointments if he appointed only those posts in which the incumbent died before the election (presumably the incumbent would retire at the end of his term and just before the election). If we hypothesize that members of the judiciary might wish the governor to make appointments and would retire between elections to make this possible, the appointive power of the governor would be greatly increased. Indeed, the governor might come to make most of the initial selections even though, formally, judges were elected in the particular state. The evidence on this possibility is summarized in Table 7.

A considerable number of judges in states with elective systems are appointed by the governor as Table 7 indicates. While there is wide variation among the states, over half of the judges of courts of last resort are initially appointed and a significant proportion of trial judges as well. A great disparity exists among different states — for example, two states have appointed no judges to the high court, while in three states 80 per cent or more of the judges were initially appointed.

An initial hypothesis that might account for the differences would concern the nature of the state's partisan system. Where the system is avowedly

Table 7

APPOINTMENT AS A MEANS OF INITIAL ACCESSION TO ELECTIVE STATE COURTS

STATES AND COURTS	% OF JUDGES APPOINTED
All Elective Courts of Last Resort (1948–57)	55.8 (N = 434)*
Florida Supreme Court (1945–51)	75.0 (N = 12)
Louisiana Trial and Appellate Judges (1945–62)	20.2 (N = 133)
Kansas Supreme Court (1908–56)	40.0 (N = 30)
Texas Trial and Appellate Judges (1952–62)	66.0†

*Number of judges.
†Number of judges not given in source.

JUDGES APPOINTED TO ELECTIVE SUPREME COURTS, SITTING 1957

% APPOINTED	NO. OF STATES
100.0	0
80 — 99.9	3
60 — 79.9	4
40 — 59.9	10
20 — 39.9	9
10 — 19.9	8
0	2

Sources: Group elective courts of last resort: James Herndon, "Appointment as a Means of Initial Accession to Elective Courts of Last Resort," *North Dakota Law Review XXXVIII* (1962) 60–73;
Florida: Emmett W. Bashful, *The Florida Supreme Court: A Study in Judicial Selection* (Tallahassee: Bureau of Governmental Research and Service, 1958);
Louisiana: Kenneth N. Vines, "The Selection of Judges in Louisiana," in Kenneth N. Vines and Herbert Jacob, *Studies in Judicial Politics,* pp. 99–119;
Kansas: *Selection of Judges* (Topeka: Kansas Legislative Council, 1956);
Texas: Bancroft Henderson and T. C. Sinclair, *Judicial Selection in Texas, An Exploratory Study* (Houston: University of Houston Public Affairs Research Center, 1964).

non-partisan or where the state's partisan system is stable and non-competitive we would expect more of the judges to be appointed. In the non-partisan and non-competitive states, there might well be less pressure to let the judgeship come to election since there is less competition and since contenders for political office are less concerned with the elective system as a means of gaining public office. This proves to be the case since in partisan states 51.0 per cent of the judges are appointed, while the percentage for semi- and non-partisan states is 66.3 per cent. In addition, those states in which there have been more competitive parties, as evidenced by frequent alternation in office, appoint fewer judges than those states which have quieter partisan political histories.[55]

JUDICIAL ELECTIONS. The movement to elect judges by the people rather than have a state executive appoint them had its impulse in the Jacksonian feeling that the mass electorate could choose aspiring candidates; a further assumption was that there would be no shortage of candidates in the competition for office. Yet studies of legislative elections have shown that incumbent officeholders are often unopposed and that when they do have competition the vote is often not close enough to be called competitive.[56] Some indication of the nature of competition for elective judgeships is shown in Table 8.

Table 8

SOME MEASURES OF COMPETITION FOR JUDGESHIPS IN SELECTED STATES

COURTS	% UNOPPOSED
Kansas (Primaries and General Elections)	
573 Trial Judges, 1908–56	54.0
Louisiana (Primaries)	
237 Trial and Appellate Judges, 1945–62	66.2
Tennessee (General Elections)	
194 Trial and Appellate Judges, 1926–58	77.8
Texas — All Trial Judges for 1956	86.0
Wisconsin (General Elections)	
184 Trial and Appellate Judges, 1945–62	58.2

COURTS	% DEFEATED
Kansas — 560 Trial and Appellate Judges, 1908–56	10.2
Louisiana — 82 Trial and Appellate Judges, 1945–62	8.5
Tennessee — 73 Trial and Appellate Judges, 1926–58	2.1
Texas — Trial and Appellate Judges, 1952–62	6.6
Wisconsin — 80 Trial and Appellate Judges, 1945–62	4.3

Sources: Louisiana, Kansas, Texas: Same as Table 7;
Tennessee: Unpublished data from the files of Kenneth N. Vines;
Wisconsin: Same as Table 6.

In contrast to legislative elections, competition is even less institutionalized in judicial elections than the theory of competitive elections would predict. While there is variation among the states and the data available are not complete, indications are that most judicial incumbents do not face opposition during their tenure. The tendency of judicial incumbents to win through lack of opposition gives added power to those interim appointments made by the governor in states where elective systems are normally in force. What this means is that interim appointments turn into regular appointments, given the good chance that incumbents have to hold onto their offices.

Adding to the stability of judicial office is the low rate of turnover due to elections, the rarity with which incumbents are actually replaced in office due to defeat, and the long terms of office. As Table 8 shows, incumbents in judicial elections meet defeat in not more than one out of ten elections and often less frequently. There are several reasons that would account for the difficulty opponents face in unseating a judicial incumbent. Foremost is the little perceived salience of policy issues emanating from the judiciary. Except for the actions of the prosecutor, decisions from the judiciary rarely come to the attention of the public, and newspapers seldom devote systematic attention to the coverage of court activities in the same way that the activities of legislative sessions are covered, analyzed, and editorialized. The unknown importance of judicial activity is due also to the fact that the language and symbols of the law make it difficult to read between the lines and extrapolate the social and political significance of judicial decisions. Judges, themselves, seldom spell out the larger significance of their actions. Contributing to the low political awareness of court decisions is the traditional secrecy and recondite behavior of the courts as institutions in which judges do not seek publicity and direct links with partisan influences, mass media, or other social communication systems; we see and hear judges less than other public officials and they tend to remain largely hidden from public view. It is difficult, therefore, for a judge to run on his record, for opponents to attack the records of judges, and for substantive policy judgments to be made of judicial actors in the political system. The means of information which would make the public aware of judicial policy activities are either lacking or well insulated.[57]

The lack of public records of performance to assess the judicial officeholder leads to a criticism heard frequently of that feature of the Missouri Plan which would have a judge run on his record: that the Missouri Plan fails to provide any special mechanism to document and publicize judicial performances and one criticism, therefore, is that appointment under the plan is appointment for life, despite the referendum aspect of the selection process. The criticism continues: "You can't beat somebody with nobody" and, given the difficulties in producing public records for judges, running under the referendum feature of the Missouri Plan is equivalent to being unopposed. The record seems to support this criticism, as no judges in California have been defeated in over twenty years' operation of the plan, and only one judge has been beaten in Missouri since the plan went into operation in 1940.[58] We could argue that the plan has produced such excellent judges in California and Missouri that they deserved to be continued in office, but such an argument assumes a great deal of the judges appointed in these states.

Judicial elections have been studied less than other elections, but the available evidence indicates that the results of such elections follow the prevailing patterns at a given election, are in tune with partisan shifts within the states, and reflect partisan structures at a given moment. In West Virginia, for example, the Democratic vote for circuit judges correlated .78 with the Democratic vote for secretary of state in judicial districts, and the Democratic vote for all state officers was generally close to that of the judiciary, the Democratic vote for the judiciary rising and falling very closely as the state Democratic vote fluctuated.[59] In Kansas, a predominantly one-party Republican state, Republican judges were usually elected to the judiciary with Democrats gaining only occasional victories.[60]

In general, partisan influences operate in the non-partisan selection of judges just as non-partisan influences tend to structure non-partisan elections for other officials. In Minnesota's non-partisan elections, incumbent judges ran and campaigned as a bloc, irrespective of party affiliations, and political parties frequently endorsed individual judges. The Minnesota Supreme Court ruled there was nothing illegal in partisan endorsement of judges, although the court commented that such endorsement seemed a bit improper for non-partisan elections. When the Farmer-Labor party dominated Minnesota politics in the early 1930's, the party also entered into competition for judicial posts and, as a result, incumbent judges were opposed more frequently than usual. Although the Farmer-Labor party had some success in electing its judges, they were not elected as often as their candidates for other state offices.[61]

THE POLITICS OF DECISION-MAKING

Concern for the politics of decision-making — the actual content of court decisions — generally ranks below other institutional issues in the perceptions of reformers and professional judicial administrators. Questions concerning how judges ought to be selected and how the docket can be cleared and delay in the courts avoided dominate the legal periodicals and judicial reports; only very rarely is any attention paid to the question of the content of the decisions.[62] The result is that state courts are seldom perceived in the light of the politics of their decision-making; instead it is assumed that a correctly selected court or one whose docket is clear will somehow engage in correct decision-making — whatever that may mean.

During the Progressive era some Western states were concerned about the conservative effects of court decisions and the way in which state court decisions often favored the "interests" . . . the railroad, mining, and grain processing companies. Following a suggestion by Theodore Roosevelt, Colorado tried a unique experiment, the popular recall of state court decisions. The experiment was short-lived, however, for the Colorado Supreme Court, in a gesture of exasperation, declared the recall law unconstitutional and the judgment held.[63]

Previously we have shown that courts are linked to partisan structures and to political officials and are open to access for political and social interests. In the following pages the patterns of decision-making in state courts and their relation to features of the political system will be examined.

CONFLICT AND CONSENSUS. An important theme in the study of the national Supreme Court has been the discovery that members of the Court can be described by the blocs and coalitions they form in voting for and against certain policies. The implication of this line of analysis is that judges behave consistently with regard to policy problems and that particular decisions are influenced by these consistent attitudes toward public policy. It has been suggested that this same analysis can also be applied to state courts and that a consistency of attitudes and behavior determines decisions of the state supreme courts.

The method of structuring blocs by plotting judges who dissented together is described by Schubert who takes the Michigan courts as an example.[64] In the Michigan court, highly cohesive blocs defined as left and right positions were in evidence. These blocs followed partisan lines within the state, the left bloc composed of G. Mennen Williams' Democrats who were liberal on workmen's compensation and other policy questions, and the right bloc composed of Republicans plus an "old-line" Democrat who were conservative on similar questions. Voting in the Michigan court is clearly influenced by policy blocs responding to major socio-economic issues.

Dissension in the Supreme Courts of Idaho, Louisiana, and Pennsylvania is described in Table 9.[65] Only Pennsylvania has a sufficient number of dissents to tell us much about the nature of interaction in that court. By a reading of the relevant opinions we suspect that Smith of the Idaho Court and Hamiter of the Louisiana Court are liberal dissenters from conservative decisions but the number of opinions involved, two and five respectively, is not large enough for us to be sure. On the Pennsylvania Court a great deal of solitary dissenting occurred, with Musmano dissenting alone twenty-two times, Cohen nineteen times, and Bell in twenty-one decisions. Less frequently judges dissent together: Jones with Bell nine times in conservative coalition, and Musmano with Eagen in four cases in a liberal pair. Judge Musmano's dissents were most often those of a liberal protesting the conservative direction of a decision, as those of Cohen were liberal particularly in civil rights cases, while Bell was the perennial conservative protesting what he regarded as the too liberal constructions of the majority of the court.

Compared with the rate of dissent on the United States Supreme Court which exceeds 50 per cent, state judges dissent on few cases. To understand the low rate of dissent of state courts it is useful to ask what the function of opinion writing is in the courts and what effect writing a dissenting opinion might produce. On rare occasions a dissenting opinion may catch the eye

Table 9

DISSENTING BLOCS ON THE SUPREME COURTS OF IDAHO,
LOUISIANA, AND PENNSYLVANIA, 1962–63

	IDAHO SUPREME COURT				
	Knudsen	*McQuade*	*McFadden*	*Taylor*	*Smith*
Knudsen	(1)	0	0	0	0*
McQuade	0	(1)	0	0	0
McFadden	0	0	(0)	0	0
Taylor	0	0	0	(0)	1
Smith	0	0	0	1	(2)

Total no. of dissents (6 of 101 cases)

	LOUISIANA SUPREME COURT						
	Fournet	*Hamiter*	*Hamlin*	*Hawthorne*	*McCaleb*	*Sanders*	*Summers*
Fournet	(1)	0	0	0	2	0	0*
Hamiter	0	(5)	2	0	0	0	1
Hamlin	0	2	(0)	0	0	0	1
Hawthorne	0	0	0	(1)	0	1	1
McCaleb	2	0	0	0	(0)	0	1
Sanders	0	0	0	1	0	(1)	1
Summers	0	1	1	1	1	1	(1)

Total no. of dissents (17 of 33 cases)

	PENNSYLVANIA SUPREME COURT						
	Musmano	*Cohen*	*Eagen*	*O'Brien*	*Bok*	*Jones*	*Bell*
Musmano	(22)	2	4	0	0	1	3*
Cohen	2	(19)	0	0	2	6	4
Eagen	4	0	(4)	0	0	2	0
O'Brien	0	0	0	(0)	0	0	2
Bok	0	2	0	0	(2)	0	1
Jones	1	6	2	0	0	(1)	9
Bell	3	4	0	2	1	9	(21)

Total no. of dissents (111 of 332 cases)

*Numbers refer to paired dissents except those in parentheses which refer to solitary dissents.

Source: See footnote 65.

of a legislator or some other political official and lead to reform or correction of conditions. There is a tradition in the national Supreme Court that dissenting opinions can keep alive a point of view or even serve as the basis for the adoption of the point of view by later, more enlightened courts. Perhaps a little of that conception is present in the writing of dissents in the state courts.[66]

To explore the point further, we may ask for whom do judges write opinions. Opinions may be written for other justices, for the newspapers, or even for partisan companions. Justice Musmano, for example, has become a well known liberal political figure in Pennsylvania and his frequently solitary dissents for liberal points of view have undoubtedly contributed to this reputation. His candidacy for the Democratic nomination for the United States Senate indicated that he had political ambition and was trying to use the judiciary as a stepping-stone to national political office and to escape the confining milieu of the Pennsylvania court.

Judgments on the propriety of dissents range from Justice William Douglas' idea that "dissent is a safeguard of Democracy" to the notion that the great majority of dissents are useless and "do not fare well." There are good reasons, however, why state judges should not express public disagreement with majority points of view in their court through written dissents. There may be little need to express a disagreement because a paragraph in the opinion or an interpretation of the main theme may take care of the divergence of opinion and allow complete unanimity. Even if a judge disagrees with the majority, political reasons may cause hesitation in expressing opposite points of view in writing. Viewed from the legal viewpoint, dissents tend to destroy the illusion of absolute certainty in the law and judicial infallibility; perhaps judges feel that lack of unanimity is damaging to judicial prestige.

On elective courts it is possible that judges feel, despite the long terms, that dissent would single them out and give them political identity when they might wish to run for re-election as non-political judicial incumbents. It is hard to imagine, for example, that Southern judges would write strong opinions for civil rights cases because to do so would single out the judges for political difficulties in the next campaign for re-election. With the majority, on the other hand, there is safety with the team and a disagreeing judge may wonder if the formal dissent is worth the trouble.

While dissent is comparatively rare in state supreme courts, there is variation among the states as to amount, as described in Table 10. More than half the courts listed had dissents in less than one out of twenty cases. In only five states was the rate of dissent more than 15 per cent. Of the states with the largest degree of dissension, four — Indiana, Michigan, Pennsylvania, and California — are competitive party states where judges of both parties can expect to be represented on the court, even when appointed as in California. The fifth, Louisiana, though a one-party state has had strong factionalism in its history between the Long and anti-Long elements of the Democratic party, and at times these disagreements have been expressed on the court. Not all competitive partisan states have high rates of dissent in their courts. Massachusetts, Idaho, Montana, and Connecticut although highly competitive have low rates of dissent. In general, partisan competition seems to be slightly related to rates of dissent in state supreme courts, but there are clearly some other unidentified influences at work also.

Table 10

PERCENTAGE OF DISSENTS IN TOTAL NUMBER OF CASES
HEARD IN SELECTED STATE SUPREME COURTS, 1961

% OF DISSENTS	STATE
0–4.99	Alaska, Arizona, Connecticut, Delaware, Georgia, Idaho, Illinois, Iowa, Maine, Massachusetts, Montana, Nebraska, Nevada, New Hampshire, North Carolina, Tennessee, Texas, Virginia, Wisconsin, Wyoming
5.0–9.99	Colorado, Kansas, Minnesota, Oregon, Rhode Island, Utah, Washington
10.0–14.99	Arkansas, Hawaii, New York, Vermont, West Virginia
15.0–19.99	Indiana, Louisiana, Michigan, Pennsylvania
Over 20.0	California

Source: *Workload of State Courts of Last Resort* (Chicago: Council of State Governments, 1962).

Taken as a whole, analysis of dissenting blocs in the state courts seems to be less useful in understanding their operation than interpreting the national Supreme Court's. The most important reason is that there is simply less dissent in the state courts and the minute amounts often can tell us nothing about the politics of the courts. From what we know about dissension in the state courts we conclude that party affiliations are more often the cause of dissent than is true on the national Supreme Court where party boundaries are often crossed. Bloc analysis also assumes that judicial behavior maintains a high degree of consistency, over a period of time. But some recent findings tend to challenge that notion. Alignments in a court system may change over a span of time because all judges may shift policy positions, or because some may remain consistent while others may change abruptly as courts adjust to changing conditions in social and political life.[67]

INTERESTS BEFORE STATE COURTS. The legal terminology of cases hardly describes the claims and demands that are made of the judiciary in its function as a political institution, for in legal terms the courts do such things as settle tort claims, hear injunctive suits, and consider intrusion into office suits. Yet, access to the courts is available to all sectors of the political system — to partisan groups, to political officials, and to social and economic interests — once these groups make their claims in the formal case manner required.

Looking first at the economic interests represented before the courts, we find that in three states — Idaho, Louisiana and Pennsylvania — from 37 per cent (in Louisiana) to 45.5 per cent (in Idaho) of the total number of cases handled by the courts are concerned with the interplay of economic

Table 11

ECONOMIC INTERESTS IN THE IDAHO, LOUISIANA, AND
PENNSYLVANIA SUPREME COURTS, 1962–63

INTEREST	NUMBER OF CASES		
	Idaho	*Louisiana*	*Pennsylvania*
Gas and oil	1	5	6
Insurance	11	8	14
Labor	0	0	11
Small retail businesses	15	3	59
Real estate	2	2	5
Lumber and mining	8	2	3
Transportation	3	6	21
Taxation cases (other than above)	0	0	17
Utilities	3	0	2
Workmen's compensation	17	0	4
Other business	0	1	8
% Cases involved with economic interests	59.4	37.0	45.2
	(60 of 101)	(27 of 73)	(150 of 332)

Source: See footnote 65.

interests. The identity and number of cases involving economic interests are described in Table 11.

The different interests litigated in the courts tend to reflect the dominant resources and activities of the states concerned. For example, Louisiana and Pennsylvania have had more gas and oil cases, while Idaho has had more lumber and mining. Pennsylvania, reflecting its industrial nature, has experienced more transportation and labor litigation. Insurance and small retail businesses seem to be equally important objects of litigation in all three states.

The oportunities for economic interest litigation are due to several important features of state government. The most important of these factors concerns the ways in which states regulate, channel, and allocate economic resources in their borders. Almost all states regulate utilities, defining the conditions under which transportation, water, and electrical companies shall operate. For example, the Louisiana Supreme Court received a case in which the Railway Express Agency appealed an order from the Louisiana Public Service Commission refusing to permit the agency to close three offices in the state, and thus cut off service for the three areas. The court reversed the Commission order and Railway Express was allowed to proceed with its plans.[68] The Idaho Supreme Court received a case that concerned the allocation of natural gas distribution rights. One company was awarded the distribution rights and another company appealed the decision of the Idaho Public Utilities Commission.[69] In Pennsylvania a racing corporation appealed an order of the State Harness Racing Commission to the Supreme Court which gave another company a license to engage in harness racing but denied one to the appellant.[70]

Other state activities that attract economic interests to the courts are zoning restrictions, labor regulations, licensing operations, and state activities which concern such activities as highway building, irrigation, and condemnation proceedings. Economic rivalries and disputes are also fought out in the courts, using legal concepts or state statutes as conceptual weapons. Illustrations of these cases are: a farmer sues a frozen foods company for refusing to pay for a crop of peas promised under a verbal contract;[71] the New Orleans Opera Guild sues the musicians' union for keeping the Guild on its "unfair list";[72] or a beverage company sues a union to stop its harassment of the company after the union failed in its bid for election as bargaining representative.[73]

Another important category of cases includes those we classify as political controversies because they involve disputes over elections, appointments to government positions in the states, or disputes between different government agencies over jurisdiction, power, or money. Such conflicts are quite directly political because they involve selection of government personnel or allocation of power within the state government. One detailed study of political cases in the Louisiana Supreme Court provides us with a case study of the frequency and importance of such cases.[74] Over a period of sixteen years representing different periods of recent political history, there were 204 cases that dealt with political questions as we have defined them. There were 76 election cases, 48 involving intergovernment disputes, and 80 concerned with controversies over the appointment of political personnel.

Significantly, the Louisiana court rarely refused to hear cases of political import on the ground that the conflict involved a "political question," a strategem that the United States Supreme Court often has invoked when it has refused to hear political cases.

A spectacular instance of the Louisiana court's influence in state politics occurred during the Huey Long era. Faced with an anti-Long court upon his domination of the state's political system, the Louisiana boss overcame this problem by packing the court. When a vacancy occurred as a result of the death of one of the anti-Long justices, the Long faction succeeded in getting John B. Fournet chosen for the vacancy despite the fact that another candidate had already won the election. Fournet had helped crush the removal proceedings against Governor Long when Fournet was Speaker of the House of Representatives. Fournet became chief justice. A little later the Long-dominated court decided a case by which Long was able to dictate his choice for succession to the governorship after he had resigned that position to run for the United States Senate.[75]

Table 12

DISTRIBUTION OF POLITICAL CASES IN IDAHO, LOUISIANA, AND PENNSYLVANIA, 1961–62

| | NUMBER OF TYPES OF CASES | | |
State	*Elections*	*Appointments*	*Intergovernment Disputes*
Idaho	0	0	2
Louisiana	3	1	3
Pennsylvania	6	10	10

Source: See footnote 65.

The number of political cases in Idaho, Louisiana, and Pennsylvania is described in Table 12. We note that the Pennsylvania Supreme Court handled more political cases than the other courts, and that in Idaho there were only two such cases. Remembering that Idaho handled a great number of interest group cases we suppose that the clash of interests is more frequently contested all the way to the judiciary than elections, appointments, or intergovernment disputes. Politics in Pennsylvania more frequently involves protestations about political contests that result in further attempts at winning an entrance into the judiciary when all else fails.

A pair of Pennsylvania cases demonstrates how intensely partisan political cases can become in the courts and how deeply the courts can become involved in the political life of the states. At issue were the attempts of a group of Philadelphia citizens spearheaded by the Republican Alliance to have the courts of Pennsylvania convene a special grand jury and appoint a special prosecutor to look into alleged graft and scandals in the Democratic municipal administration of Philadelphia. At first, the courts refused on the grounds that the petitioners did not have proper standing as a party to the controversy. Chief Justice Bell, the arch conservative of the Supreme Court, disagreed in a dissent, commenting that the investigation was "imperatively" needed and that the ordinary processes of the law had already proved to be inadequate.[76]

By means of intricate maneuvering and timing the Republicans managed to get the case before Judge Alessandroni who was sympathetic to their cause and he authorized the convention of a special grand jury and the appointment of a special prosecutor. The authorization was appealed to the Supreme Court and Judge Musmano, later candidate for Senator in the Democratic primary, reversed the order commenting poetically on Judge Alessandroni's decision as something that happens when:

> . . . regular form and procedures are not followed and a judge embarks on independent ventures, sailing in ships without sails of authority, using engines devoid of constitutional power and employing a compass lacking decisional direction.

Chief Justice Bell in his dissent charged, "A Grand Jury investigation of alleged sale of legislation by members of City Council — and by members of the Democratic City Committee . . . is imperatively required . . . to ferret out crimes and the criminals."[77]

PARTY INFLUENCES. Political parties are linked to the courts in several ways. Where judges are appointed, the governor ordinarily selects men of his own political persuasion more frequently than he appoints members of opposition parties. If judges are elected in partisan contests, they are generally identified with the partisan patterns of particular states; in normal times Kansas judges will be Republicans, while Louisiana judges will be Democrats. As we have seen, elections for the judiciary tend to follow the partisan tides of the state's politics and we may expect that when a state shifts parties in power the judicial offices involved in the election will follow suit. In non-partisan states judges are not allowed to run as party candidates but this may not mean that the judge lacks party identification.

Table 13

PARTY IDENTIFICATION OF JUDGES
SELECTED UNDER DIFFERENT SYSTEMS IN TWELVE STATES

SYSTEM OF SELECTION	DEM.	REP.	IND.	OTHER	DON'T KNOW
Appointive	20.4%	49.4%	1.9%		28.3%
Partisan Election	24.8	44.2	.3	9.9%	20.8
Missouri Plan	17.4	8.7	0	0	73.9
Legislative	44.6	48.2	0	0	7.2
Non-partisan Election	13.2	36.5	3.2	1.4	45.7

Source: See Table 6.

Table 13 compares the party identification of judges chosen under different selection systems. A greater number of judges selected under non-partisan and Missouri Plan systems identify themselves as having no party affiliation, while under the other systems a majority of the judges show an identification with some party. About half of the non-partisan judges refuse to identify with a party as do nearly three-fourths of the Missouri Plan judges. Clearly the systems advertised as non-political do recruit more judges unwilling to identify themselves with political parties.

Yet it would be a mistake to think that the judiciary is a mirror of the state's partisan structure. Long overlapping terms of office in both the trial and appellate courts are often the rule in state courts. Of the elective states, nine — Colorado, Louisiana, Maryland, New York, North Dakota, Pennsylvania, Utah, West Virginia and Wisconsin — allocate terms of ten years or more to appellate judges; the remainder of the states give terms of from six

Table 14

POLITICAL PARTY REPRESENTATION ON THE SUPREME COURT
IN THE FIFTEEN MOST COMPETITIVE STATES, THE FIFTEEN LEAST COMPETITIVE STATES,
AND IN SEVEN APPOINTIVE STATES

RANK IN PARTY COMPETITION	STATE	% DEMOCRATIC JUDGES ON THE SUPREME COURT
1	Delaware	33
2	Montana	67
3	Massachusetts	29
4	Illinois	29
5	Utah	75
6	Idaho	25
7	Pennsylvania	29
8	Rhode Island	60
9.5	Connecticut	60
9.5	Washington	0
11	California	50
12	New York	71
13.5	Indiana	0
13.5	Wyoming	0
15	Colorado	43
46	Mississippi	100
45	South Carolina	100
44	Louisiana	100
43	Georgia	100
42	Texas	100
41	Alabama	100
40	Arkansas	100
39	Florida	100
38	Virginia	100
37	North Carolina	100
36	Tennessee	100
35	North Dakota	25
34	Oklahoma	100
33	Arizona	100
32	Vermont	0
SEVEN APPOINTIVE STATES		
	California	50
	Delaware	33
	Maine	17
	Massachusetts	29
	Missouri	67
	New Hampshire	40
	New Jersey	60

Source: See footnote 79.

to ten years to appellate judges. Only a few states — New York, Delaware and Maryland — give trial judges more than ten-year terms; trial judges normally are selected for terms of from four to eight years at the district and circuit court levels.[78] This means that appellate courts in particular lag behind other political institutions in expressing partisan change in the states because judicial elections do not occur frequently enough to catch many year-to-year developments.

The partisan representation in the supreme court of the fifteen most competitive states and the fifteen least competitive states[79] is described in Table 14. In general, party representation on the courts tends to follow over-all party balances in the partisan structure of the state, as measured by indices of state party competition. In one-party states, judges from the minority party are excluded entirely except in the case of North Dakota which has slight Democratic representation among the Republican majority. On the other hand, in the competitive states where the party battle is comparatively even, the parties are represented somewhat more equally. However, there are three competitive states — Washington, Indiana, and Wyoming — that have no Democrats on the bench. From the evidence in Table 14 it appears that balanced representation on the high courts tends to follow competition in the states.

Party representation on the courts is tied to party fortunes in the states where judges are elected; where the judges are appointed, the governor could, if he wished, maintain a balanced partisan court. Among the states with appointive courts, party representation is somewhat more evenly distributed than in the remainder of the states. Particularly notable are Missouri and New Hampshire which are one-party states where the minority party is represented on the court by a proportion of more than one in three. But in other appointive courts, Maine's one-party Republican dominance is reflected in the membership of the court, and in Massachusetts the Democrats have been discriminated against by the governor despite the fact that Massachusetts is generally a highly competitive state in elections.

What differences do party affiliations make in the courts? General evidence from studies of political behavior indicates that partisan attachments influence political behavior. On the other hand, the myth of judicial objectivity holds that decisions in the judiciary are made by reference to authoritative norms in relevant precedents and through reasoning by means of a series of logico-legal interpretative propositions.[80]

The theory of legal decision-making probably presents a relatively true description of proceedings in the lower trial courts for the great majority of cases. There, conflicts often involve more personalized litigation, with few social and political implications. Civil actions and criminal violation cases are much alike and present little variation. In such instances there is no reason why the theory of judicial objectivity should not work for decision-making much of the time. Appellate courts are a different matter. They present, as we have seen, much more important conflicts whose social and political implications are often obvious. Precedents may not be clear in these disputes, or there may be a choice to be made among several lines of precedents, so complicated are the cases. Feelings may run high in the course of the litigation, and there may be at stake considerable amounts of money, political power, the role of the state in public policy, or settlement of conflict between contending factions in the state's political system. It is highly probable that appellate court judges are well aware of the issues in such conflicts and sensitive to their values. Political parties are one way in which political feelings are expressed and organized, and we would expect, therefore, political parties would play an important role in the decision of cases in appellate courts.

One study of the relation of party affiliation to decision-making in state courts has been made by Nagel.[81] Using non-unanimous decisions of state supreme courts, he compared the direction of decisions made with the party affiliation of judges sitting on the courts. Democratic judges differed from Republican judges significantly by deciding cases more frequently:

1. For the defense in criminal cases;
2. For the administrative agency in business regulation cases;
3. For the claimant in unemployment compensation cases;
4. For finding a constitutional violation in criminal cases;
5. For the government in tax cases;
6. For the tenant in landlord-tenant cases;
7. For the consumer in sales of goods cases;
8. For the injured in motor vehicle accident cases;
9. For the employee in employee injury cases.

The decisions made by Democratic judges indicate sympathy for the consumer and working man, for regulation of business and utilities, and for the defendant in criminal cases. These are attitudes we might predict that Democrats would express, and this finding is evidence that political party affiliations are relevant to decision-making in the state courts. The Ohio court was a case in point, and illustrates the disparity between Republican-Democratic attitudes on the supreme court in business regulation cases. In two cases, one involving regulation of a telephone company and the other zoning a power company facility, the court held for regulation, but the only dissenter in the telephone company case was a Republican and all three dissenters against zoning the power company were Republicans.[82]

The attitude of the Michigan Supreme Court on unemployment compensation cases indicates some of the complexities that may be involved in the response of judges of different partisan backgrounds to important economic and social questions. Governor Williams' domination of Michigan only gradually included the supreme court. When elected initially in 1948 the Governor had no supporter on the supreme court, but by 1957 he had controlled the election of four of the nine members and by 1958 had a majority of five. As the Williams' Democrats increased in the supreme court, the court began to decide increasingly for the defendant in workmen's compensation and contributory negligence cases, both types involving attitudes toward labor. But, not all the Democrats on the court supported the labor position. One "old-Democrat" not sympathetic to the Williams' movement voted with Republicans, and not all Republicans always voted against the position of the claimant. The Michigan example tells us that factions within a single party may differ on fundamental policy attitudes and may express this attitude in the way in which they reach decisions on the courts.[83]

INSTITUTIONAL CONSERVATISM OF STATE COURTS. The general reputation of courts as conservative institutions is due, no doubt, to a combination of their characteristics. The reliance on precedents and other usages of the past, the recruitment of lawyers as official participants in the judicial process, and the relative insulation of courts from social change — all contribute to this condition. Attitudes of general conservatism, quite apart from party affiliations, training, and legal attitudes, are significant if they affect judicial decisions.

One method of obtaining information on judicial propensities is to study off-the-bench attitudes of judges. Information on attitudes can be garnered from the decisions of the judiciary and represent official statements of value, but a more direct way to examine judicial attitudes is to look at those expressed in an unofficial capacity.

In one study of off-the-bench attitudes of state judges, they proved to be quite conservative.[84] State judges were more conservative than members of the British Conservative party on marital problems, family planning, criminal rehabilitation, collectivism, and faith in democracy, while they were more liberal on matters concerning international peace movements, sex equality, ethnic equality, and religion. When political parties were held constant, conservatives — whether Democratic or Republican — responded in their decisions in similar fashion. That is, conservative Democrats and conservative Republicans were alike, while liberal Democrats and liberal Republicans decided cases in similar fashion.

When conservative judges were compared with those having liberal attitudes, the two groups differed significantly in their treatment of different groups of decisions. Judges having higher liberal scores decided cases more frequently:

1. For the defense in criminal cases;
2. For the administrative agency in business regulation cases;
3. For the injured party in motor vehicle accident cases;
4. For the employee in employee injury cases.[85]

These differences are consistent with general expectations that the liberal judges are more apt to favor government regulation, favor the claimant in tort cases, and the defendant in criminal cases. We suppose, then, that conservatism does make a difference and that the institutional conservatism of state courts is one of their significant characteristics.

Other evidence that state supreme courts have conservative leanings may be inferred from the activities of the Conferences of Chief Justices. This conference is an annual meeting of chief judges of state supreme courts and is reminiscent in some respects of the Conference of State Governors. The resolutions passed at the Conferences of Chief Justices reveal a pronounced conservatism in their attitudes. An especially strong statement of conservatism was embodied in the Report of the 1958 Conference. The Report emanated from the Committee on Federal-State Relationships as Affected by Judicial Decisions and was adopted by a vote of thirty-six to eight of the chief justices present. Accusing the national Supreme Court of acting without proper judicial restraint and exercising powers primarily legislative, the Report indicted the Supreme Court of the United States for improperly undercutting the rights of the states and upsetting the constitutional balance of the federal system.[86] Since the decisions to which the report presumably referred were decisions in favor of extending national power to social and economic problems and checking the excesses of the state in denying civil rights, the substance of the criticism was undeniably conservative. Although couched in legal terms and objecting to many of the procedures of the Supreme Court, the report was not unlike typical states' rights statements from other conservative political officials in the states. Its approval by such a large majority of the chief justices indicates a rather widespread conservatism in the state courts. We do not know whether the chief justices are typical of the other judicial personnel of the courts, but the prestige of the office of the chief justice makes their criticism an important one.

SOCIAL AND ECONOMIC FACTORS. To explain some of the propensities of judicial behavior the cliché is sometimes offered that judges are human. What this rather useless statement means to say is that judges are identifiable by personal, social, and economic characteristics and belong to a culture in the same way as other actors in American politics — the American voter, the state legislator, or the American Congressman.

State judges are recruited, as are other political officials, from certain dominant social groups. State judges also belong to high economic and social groups because of the prestige of their office and their relatively high salaries. Protestant religious groups and Anglo-Saxon ethnic groups are represented disproportionately among state judges. Studies of political behavior have found that these social and economic factors tend to affect differentially the behavior of persons in voting or in decision-making in the legislature. Do these characteristics also make a difference in the behavior of judges? Nagel's study of decision-making in the non-unanimous cases decided by state judges seems to indicate that they do.[87] For example, judges with non-Anglo-Saxon ethnic backgrounds decided cases more frequently than judges with Anglo-Saxon backgrounds:

1. For the defense in criminal cases;
2. For finding a violation in criminal-constitutional cases;
3. For the wife in divorce cases.

While the two groups of judges were especially far apart in these cases, judges with British ancestry were also more conservative on eleven additional categories of cases.

Differences were also discovered between Catholic and non-Catholic judges. Catholic judges tended to decide:

1. For the defense in criminal cases;
2. For the administrative agency in business regulation cases;
3. For the wife in divorce settlement cases;
4. For the debtor in creditor-debtor cases;
5. For the employee in employee injury cases.

Less significant but still discernible differences were observed between Catholic and non-Catholic judges in categories of cases involving other policy areas. Judges in these instances are following well-known behavioral patterns that indicate the effects of social economic backgrounds in engendering attitudes toward public policies.[88]

Certain social characteristics of long standing and deep social and political significance tend to produce strongly patterned behavior of long duration. Such behavior, like that of Southern reactions particularly in the field of civil rights, we call political culture. We know that Southern voters, legislators and other political officials tend to follow behavior patterns influenced by the content of Southern political culture.

Table 15 describes the decisions made by Southern state supreme court judges in the field of race relations, perhaps the most salient area of political concern in the South.[89]

The disposition of cases in Southern supreme courts is divided into the deep South and border states and averages of each given. It is instructive

Table 15

DISPOSITION OF RACE RELATIONS CASES BY SOUTHERN STATE SUPREME COURTS, 1954–63

STATES	% OF CASES FAVORABLE TO NEGROES
Alabama	7.7
Arkansas	33.3
Georgia	54.5
Louisiana	29.1
Mississippi	23.8
South Carolina	28.6
Average of Deep South States	29.3
Florida	9.5
North Carolina	46.6
Tennessee	40.0
Texas	40.0
Virginia	50.0
Average of Peripheral Southern States	37.2
Average of All Southern States	32.3

Source: Kenneth N. Vines, "Southern State Supreme Courts and Race Relations," *Western Political Quarterly XVIII* (1965).

to compare the decisions of Southern courts with those in national courts and other Southern political institutions. While supreme courts in the South favored Negroes in race relations cases much less frequently than did the federal district courts in the same category of cases, the courts were more favorable to Negroes than other institutions of Southern political life. Both the legislatures and the executives very rarely made decisions that could be interpreted as favorable to Negroes, but the high court decided nearly one out of every three cases for Negroes. While the courts were more liberal on civil rights than other Southern political institutions, they were much more conservative than Southern federal judges.

The influence of Southern environment can be illustrated by comparison of two groups of states that represent different Southern regions. The border states, those on the periphery of the deep South, were more favorable toward Negroes in race relations decisions than were the states of the deep South. A reading of the individual state records indicates variation among the states and within regions. For example, Florida, a border state, rarely decided cases for Negroes, while Georgia in the deep South had a much more favorable record. Still, despite state variations, the difference between the two sub-regions remains significant.

The conservatism on race relations seems to be part of a general conservatism on the part of Southern judges. Compared to non-Southern judges, Southern judges were significantly more conservative on a measure of off-the-bench attitudes. Comments in decisions by Southern judges sometimes indicated a fully developed philosophy of white supremacy which is articulated in race relations cases. For example, a Florida judge in writing the opinion for a school desegregation case before the state supreme court commented on the races:

> To replace it [referring to the system of segregation] with antithetical doctrine will take years of skillful nurture in a soil that must be made congenial to the change. The ratio of Negro to White population makes the way to change difficult. . . . To homogenize Topsy, Little Red Riding Hood and Mary who carried her lamb to school will be difficult.[90]

CONCLUSIONS

We have examined the decision-making activities of courts and have found that the politics of the judiciary is similar in many ways to politics elsewhere in the political system. Our investigation has shown that courts are involved in partisan activities and are responsive to interest demands; that although much of what they do is routine, they are sometimes involved in political controversies of great passion; and that judges interact in patterns of conflict and consensus and are influenced by many of the same social and economic forces that move other political actors. Moreover, the organization and staffing of the courts reflect long-standing political traditions or else serve various political needs.

The evidence seems to say the legal theory that judges make decisions according to objective principles of legal rationalism is not a correct description of judicial decision-making. This does not mean, however, that the legal theory is without influence. Believed, in all probability, by a number of judges, lawyers, and a sector of the public, this theory influences the way in which the public thinks about the courts, its institutional problems, and practices. The problems of the selection of judicial personnel and the responsibilities of judges in court are often discussed as if the legal myth were correct.

No doubt these myths serve important social purposes, but a realistic view of the political functions of the courts better informs us of the nature of the courts and their problems.

NOTES

1. Robert Leflar, "Some Observations Concerning Judicial Opinions," *Columbia Law Review LXI* (1961) 817.
2. *The New York Times,* July 28, 1964, p. 9.
3. Arthur Vanderbilt, *Minimum Standards of Judicial Administration* (New York: Law Center of New York University, 1949) p. 396.

4. For a discussion of the change in the Florida Supreme Court see Daniel Jones, "Certiorari Power of the Florida Supreme Court to Review Decisions of the District Courts of Appeal," *University of Miami Law Review XV* (1960–61) 258–268.

5. For a description of this aspect of the supreme courts' work see *Workload of State Courts of Last Resort* (Chicago: Council of State Governments, 1962) pp. 1–2.

6. *State Court Systems* (Chicago: Council of State Governments, 1962) unpaged, and *Workload of State Courts of Last Resort.*

7. *Trial Courts of General Jurisdiction in the Forty-Eight States* (Chicago: Council of State Governments, 1951) pp. 18–19.

8. *Ibid.,* p. 14.

9. *Ibid.*

10. *Ibid.,* p. 5.

11. *Ibid.,* p. 6.

12. *The New York Times,* July 1, 1964, p. 1.

13. *Ibid.,* January 9, 1960, p. 15.

14. See for example, Wallace S. Sayre and Herbert Kaufman, *Governing New York City: Politics in the Metropolis* (New York: Russell Sage Foundation, 1960) 538 ff.

15. Edward W. Martin, *The Role of the Bar in Electing the Bench in Chicago* (Chicago: University of Chicago Press, 1936) chapter 23.

16. *The New York Times,* July 29, 1964, p. 42.

17. Court organizational systems are summarized in *State Court Systems.*

18. For an excellent case study in Illinois see Gilbert Steiner and Samuel Gove, *Legislative Politics in Illinois* (Urbana: University of Illinois Press, 1960) chapter 7.

19. See especially the opinions and proceedings of the American Judicature Society as reported in its Journal.

20. Murray Bloom, "Your Unknown Heirs," *Harper's Magazine,* August 1961, p. 33.

21. A standard work on the subject is Raymond Moley, *Politics and Criminal Prosecution* (New York: Minton, Balch & Co., 1929).

22. But Professor Jacob finds that in Wisconsin many prosecutors do not use the position for political advancement, *Justice in America* (Boston: Little, Brown, 1965).

23. Joseph A. Schlesinger, *How They Became Governor* (East Lansing: Michigan State University, 1957) p. 94.

24. Unpublished data from the files of Kenneth N. Vines on political careers and backgrounds of federal judges collected by Kenneth Casanova.

25. Herbert Jacob, "Politics and Criminal Prosecution in New Orleans," in Kenneth N. Vines and Herbert Jacob, *Studies in Judicial Politics,* Tulane Studies in Political Science VIII (New Orleans: 1963) 82–83.

26. Jacob, *Justice in America,* chapter 9.

27. "Prosecutor's Discretion," *University of Pennsylvania Law Review CIII* (1955) 1057–1081.

28. *New Orleans Times-Picayune,* October 20, 1964, p. 15.

29. Jacob, "Politics and Criminal Prosecution in New Orleans," p. 81.

30. *University of Pennsylvania Law Review CIII.*

31. See Clement Vose, "Litigation as a Form of Pressure Group Activity," *Annals of the American Academy of Political and Social Science CCCXIX* (1958) 20–31.

32. Dianne Jennings, "Access to Governmental Machinery as It Is Perceived by Negro Leaders," Tulane University, 1962, unpublished paper.

33. *N.A.A.C.P.* vs. *Gallion,* 290 F 2d 337.

34. Kenneth N. Vines, "Southern State Supreme Courts and Race Relations," *Western Political Quarterly XVIII* (1965).

35. Walter Murphy, "The South Counterattacks: the anti-N.A.A.C.P. Laws," *Western Political Quarterly XII* (1959) 371–390.
36. For development of this problem see Jacob, *Justice in America,* chapter 4.
37. Hans Zeisel, Harry Kalven, Jr., and Bernard Buchholz, *Delay in the Court* (Boston: Little, Brown, 1959) p. xxi.
38. *Annual Report of the Administrative Director of the Courts* (Trenton: Administrative Office of the Courts, 1961–62), and *1962 Annual Report of the Administrative Office of the California Courts* (Sacramento: Judicial Council of California, 1963).
39. *Trial Courts of General Jurisdiction in the Forty-Eight States,* p. 6.
40. For illustrations as to how traditional legal concepts may change through judicial interpretation see Edward H. Levi, *An Introduction to Legal Reasoning* (Chicago: University of Chicago Press, 1948).
41. *Annual Report of the Administrative Director of the Courts.*
42. *1962 Annual Report of the Administrative Office of the California Courts.*
43. *Ibid.*
44. *Ibid.*
45. *Annual Report of the Administrative Director of the Courts.*
46. See Vose.
47. A summation of the arguments may be found in Rondal G. Downing, Frederick G. Spiegel, and Richard A. Watson, "Judicial Selection Under the Missouri Plan," paper delivered at the Midwest Conference of Political Scientists, 1964.
48. *State Court Systems.*
49. William S. Carpenter, *Judicial Tenure in the United States* (New Haven: Yale University Press, 1918) pp. 1–50.
50. Quoted in *Selection of Judges* (Topeka: Research Department Kansas Legislative Council, 1956) p. 4.
51. This is done in Downing, *et al.*
52. A pioneering attempt is made in Martin.
53. Professor Jacob reaches similar conclusions in his article, "The Effect of Institutional Differences in the Recruitment Process: The Case of States Judges," *Journal of Public Law XIII* (1964) 104–119.
54. John E. Crow, "Subterranean Politics: A Judge is Chosen," *Journal of Public Law XII* (1963) 275–290.
55. James Herndon, "Appointment as a Means of Initial Accession to Elective Courts of Last Resort," *North Dakota Law Review XXXVIII* (1962) 60–73.
56. Julius Turner, "Primary Elections as the Alternative to Party Competition in 'Safe' Districts," *Journal of Politics XV* (1953) 197–210.
57. On judicial campaigns see Claude J. Davis, *Judicial Selection in West Virginia* (Morgantown: Bureau for Government Research, West Virginia University, 1959).
58. *Selection of Judges,* p. 7.
59. Davis, p. 28.
60. *Selection of Judges,* pp. 15–21.
61. Malcolm Moos, "Judicial Elections and Partisan Endorsements of Judicial Candidates in Minnesota," *American Political Science Review XXXV* (1941) 69–75.
62. Sayre and Kaufman note a similar tendency in New York in *Governing New York City.*
63. J. Patrick White, "Progressivism and the Judiciary: A Study of the Movement for Judicial Reform, 1901–17," unpublished dissertation, University of Michigan, 1957.

64. Glendon Schubert, *Quantitative Analysis of Judicial Behavior* (Glencoe: The Free Press, 1959).

65. Data and following analysis on the supreme courts of Idaho, Louisiana, and Pennsylvania are derived from a systematic tabulation of decisions for the years 1962–63. To obtain a representative year, a 50 per cent sample, taking every other case, was used for the two years. The author wishes to acknowledge the help of Henry Glick and Richard Bath in the tabulation.

66. For observations on the functions of dissents in state courts by a former state supreme court judge see "The Voices of Dissent," *Columbia Law Review LXII* (1962) 923–929.

67. Albert Somit, Joseph Tanenhaus, and Walter Wilke, "Aspects of Judicial Sentencing Behavior," *University of Pittsburgh Law Review XXI* (1959–60) 607–620.

68. *Railway Express Agency* vs. *Louisiana Public Service Commission,* 243 La 518 (1962).

69. *Washington Water Power Company* vs. *Idaho Public Utilities Commission,* 372 P2d 409 (1962).

70. *Keystone Raceway Corporation* vs. *State Harness Racing Commission,* 173 A2d 97 (1963).

71. *Anderson* vs. *Smith Frozen Foods of Idaho,* 365 P2d 965 (1962).

72. *New Orleans Opera Guild, Inc.* vs. *Local 174 Musicians Mutual Protective Union,* 242 La 134 (1962).

73. *Terrizi Beverage Co.* vs. *Local Union No. 830 Brewery and Beer Distributors Drivers,* 184 A2d 243 (1962).

74. Kenneth N. Vines, "Political Functions of a State Supreme Court" in Vines and Jacob, *Studies in Judicial Politics,* pp. 51–77.

75. *Ibid.,* pp. 66-69.

76. Appeal of Hamilton, 180 A2d 797.

77. *Smith* vs. *Gallagher,* 185 A2d 135.

78. *State Court Systems.*

79. All data on party competition are taken from Richard E. Dawson and James A. Robinson, "Inter-Party Competition, Economic Variables, and Welfare Policies in the American States," *Journal of Politics XXV* (May 1963) 265–289. Data on party affiliation of supreme court judges are taken from Stuart Nagel, "Unequal Party Representation on the State Supreme Courts," *Journal of the American Judicature Society XLIV* (1961) 62–65.

80. For commentary on this point, see Levi.

81. Stuart Nagel, "Political Party Affiliation and Judges' Decisions," *American Political Science Review LV* (1961) 843–851.

82. *Ibid.,* p. 845.

83. Sidney Ulmer, "The Political Party Variable on the Michigan Supreme Court," *Journal of Public Law XI* (1962) 352–362.

84. Stuart Nagel, "Off-the-Bench Judicial Attitudes," in Glendon Schubert (ed.), *Judicial Decision-Making* (Glencoe: The Free Press, 1963) pp. 29–55.

85. *Ibid.*

86. *Proceedings Tenth Annual Meeting of the Conference of Chief Justices* (Chicago: Council of State Governments, 1958). For other conservative attitudes, see also the Proceedings of the Thirteenth (1961), Fourteenth (1962), and Fifteenth (1963) Conferences.

87. Stuart Nagel, "Ethnic Affiliation and Judicial Propensities," *Journal of Politics XXIV* (1962) 92–110.

88. *Ibid.*
89. Vines, "Southern State Supreme Courts and Race Relations."
90. *Manatu* vs. *Florida Board of Public Instruction, 75* SE2d 691 (1954).

SELECTED BIBLIOGRAPHY

Jacob, Herbert. "The Effect of Institutional Differences in the Recruitment Process: The Case of State Judges," *Journal of Public Law XIII* (1964) 104–119. A comparative study of the differences in judicial recruitment among twelve states representing different systems of selection.

――――. *Justice in America.* Boston: Little, Brown, 1965. A systematic and politically aware treatment of the whole judicial process in the United States, bringing together the diverse elements into an integrated description.

Nagel, Stuart. "Political Party Affiliation and Judges' Decisions," *American Political Science Review LV* (1961) 843–851. An inquiry into the influence of political party preferences on judicial decision-making.

Trial Courts of General Jurisdiction in the Forty-Eight States. Chicago: Council of State Governments, 1951. A useful tabulation and description of the structure and function of trial courts in the states.

Ulmer, Sidney. "The Political Party Variable on the Michigan Supreme Court," *Journal of Public Law XI* (1962) 352–362. An analysis of the dynamics of party influences on decision-making in the Michigan Supreme Court.

Vines, Kenneth N. "Southern State Supreme Courts and Race Relations," *Western Political Quarterly XVIII* (March 1965). An analysis of decision-making in the Southern supreme courts in the area of race relations.

―――― and Herbert Jacob. *Studies in Judicial Politics.* New Orleans: *Tulane Studies in Political Science,* 1962. Exploratory studies into several aspects of local judicial politics including politics and criminal prosecution, judicial selection, and political functions of courts.

PART FOUR

POLICIES AND PROGRAMS

PEOPLE PARTICIPATE IN POLITICS for many reasons. Most, however, enter politics in order to advance particular policies or programs.

State political systems have an especially large voice in the formulation of policies for taxation, education, welfare, and highway programs. Each of these areas is important to most state citizens. Moreover, each of them involves large sums of money. All states must deal with the problems concerning these items but no two states solve their problems in an identical fashion. Taken together, these policy areas constitute much of the substance of politics at the state level.

THE
POLITICS
OF
TAXATION

CHAPTER 8
by
CLARA PENNIMAN

ALTHOUGH RELATED, TAXES AND EXPENDITURES of states are not merely opposite sides of the same coin. First, they do not balance neatly in the fashion a careful bookkeeper might wish. Even a firm intention to balance may go astray as neither revenue nor expenditure estimating is such an exact science. States, moreover, have revenues apart from taxes, through federal grants in aid, income from governmental enterprises, fees and special charges, occasional gifts, and loans.

Secondly, economic analysis shows government spending and government taxing have quite different effects on the economy. Among other differences, well-conceived taxes that hold down an inflation may add to the difficulties of a depression, whereas government expenditures that check a depression may spread inflation. Even though much of the manipulation of governmental taxes and expenditures is likely to be done at the national level (the states are too economically interdependent and have too limited borrowing ability for a major role), the states may well accept the obligation not to operate at cross purposes.

Most importantly for this discussion, the politics of taxation often appears fairly distinct from the politics of expenditures. Legislators and governors have regularly found that their constituents respond more favorably to increased spending than to new taxes. Not individual irrationality, but different desires and perspectives among citizens may lead to such conduct. Voter A believes in good schools but is willing to do without four-lane highways in various sections of the state. If his desires were generally shared, increased and improved education might be bought with no increase in taxes. Voter B, however, demands many four-lane highways as a convenience for his personal travel and as a requisite for his business. To satisfy the expenditure demands of both A and B, new and increased taxes are needed, yet A and B, who view expenditure priorities differently, may pool their resources politically to oppose the tax increases.

Activists, whether office-holders or not, organize to increase particular expenditures or to oppose additional taxes but seldom manage to find great strength to oppose expenditures or to support tax increases.

Which decision is made first, to tax or to spend? Do taxes follow expenditures or are expenditures simply fitted to tax revenues? Since political alignments on these issues vary, the order of decision may determine the magnitude of both. If expenditures are more popular than taxes, then making the decision to spend *before* deciding *what taxes* could finance the expenditure should produce larger budgets than if the decisions were made in reverse order. Or to state it another way, where governors and legislators emphasize programs rather than how to finance them, expenditures will be higher. Such a hypothesis requires modification. No institutional arrangements to look at expenditures or revenues first and then match the other insures separation. Protagonists within and without the government know the probable magnitudes of present revenues and hence the margin at which further expenditures will demand further taxes. Or conversely, looking initially at taxes may blur but will not obliterate all of the expenditure demands.

If tax decisions are not independent of expenditure decisions, neither are they independent of the past nor of the whole complex of attitudes and preferences that fix the political and governmental climate of each state. Significant differences appear among the states in the height of taxes, in the selection of particular taxes, in the degree of emphasis on particular taxes, and in the administration of taxes. This chapter will attempt first to provide something of the setting for state taxation in general, then to identify the choices the states have made in taxes selected and the "mix" that has been chosen. Finally, we shall undertake analysis of some of the factors that have contributed to the making of the tax choices identified.

STATE PATTERNS

THE CONSTITUTIONAL CONTEXT. Our federal system of government has affected taxation as it has most other institutions and practices of government. The national Constitution in Article I, Section 8 provides that the Congress "have power to lay and collect taxes, duties, imposts, and excises," but in Section 9 prohibited "capitation, or other direct, tax . . . unless in proportion to the census. . . ." (The Sixteenth Amendment, 1913, assured that this provision would not prevent personal and corporate income taxes.) Both the states and the national government were prohibited from laying any tax or duty on exports from the states or among the states. In practice, the national Constitution has prevented state taxation only if it were a tax on interstate commerce or it were found to be a violation of due process under the Fourteenth Amendment. Not a part of the Constitution but by Congressional action in certain grants-in-aid legislation, most notably the Hayden-Cartwright

Act, the states are required to segregate particular taxes for specified use. Thus, the Hayden-Cartwright Act (1934) requires (with a few exceptions) that the states place gasoline tax revenues in special funds for highway purposes only.

Faced with few restrictions by the national Constitution, the states, nevertheless, have placed limitations on their own taxing powers and especially on those of their local governments. Almost every state constitution continues to ignore the admonition of the National Municipal League that: "Ideally, a (state) constitution should be silent on the subject of taxation and finance, thus permitting the legislature and the governor freedom to develop fiscal policies for the States to meet the requirements of their time."[1] Fear of future legislative extravagance or legislative favoritism led some states early to limit borrowing; to prohibit in their constitutions the raising of taxes for specific purposes; and to include statements requiring the uniformity and universality of taxes (actually with reference to the property tax, but often not so identified) that provided the base for later restrictive state court decisions.

The single rate of the sales tax has normally led state courts to approve it, while denying the constitutionality of income taxes under the older property tax "universality" and "uniformity" clauses. Even today most of the present states without an income tax could only adopt such taxes after passage of appropriate constitutional amendments. The 1962 Michigan constitution prohibits the levying of a *progressive* income tax. Nevada would have to amend its constitution to levy an estate or inheritance tax.

State constitutions may also limit the total permissible height of taxes. These latter restrictions, where they exist, often apply to local governments only. Finally, by statute or constitutional provision, particular taxes may be set aside for only one type of expenditure. Most states have not only accepted the restrictions on taxes imposed by some grant-in-aid legislation, but have restricted the uses of other taxes in addition. Whether such action helps or hinders the particular program is debated.[2]

Constitutions — national, state, or local — can be amended, but it takes time and unusual majorities. Where constitutional change is required, any new tax, increase in tax, or other change in taxing faces barriers that are lifted only under great pressure.

More limiting perhaps than formal constitutional barriers and, in fact, helping to bring about constitutional restrictions, is the concern for "what the other fellow does." Federation allows opportunities for freedom and experimentation, but its members often seek the solace of uniformity. States constantly test their tax policies against those of their sister states and question whether unilateral passage of particular tax legislation will place them at a competitive economic disadvantage. Florida in 1924 repealed its inheritance-

Figure 1

INCOME AND TAXES OVER SELECTED YEARS

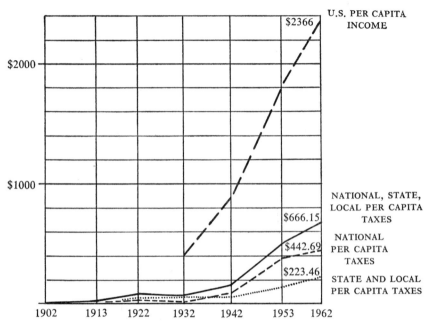

Sources: Per capita taxes from same sources as Table 1, see page 297. Per capita income from same sources as Table 3; see page 309.

estate law in an overt appeal to the wealthy of the nation to end their days where fine physical and tax climates would be combined. Nevada followed with similar constitutional action in 1925. Only Congressional passage of the 1926 law to permit crediting state inheritance-estate taxes against federal probably prevented a rush of other states from copying the Florida tax action. (Neither the wishes nor actions of other state legislators could reproduce the physical climate.)

Although the national Constitution did not establish separate tax paths for the national government and for the state and local governments, 19th century practices differed almost as if separate roads had been prescribed. Until the 20th century, with brief exceptions, the national government depended on customs and excises. The state and local governments utilized the general property tax. In 1902, the states and local governments raised $860 million from taxes, 82 per cent of which was raised by the property tax. Actually, the towns, villages, and cities spent the bulk of the $860 million, or a total of $704 million. In the same year, national governmental taxes totalled only $513 million. The national government subsequently has had to meet recurring crises of war, depression, war, and threats of war.

These, together with increasing demands in a changing and ever more inter-dependent economic and social system, have magnified the height and choice of taxes by the national government. Sixty years after 1902, the national government collected $82,262 million in taxes, with 81 per cent of this amount coming from individual and corporate income taxes unknown in 1902.*

The state and local governments also had forged new patterns of expenditures and taxes by 1962. In that year, the fifty states collected $20,561 millions in taxes, and their local governments collected another $20,962 millions. Although local governments still raised most of their taxes through property levies, the states had shifted to special and general sales taxes, corporate and personal income taxes, and inheritance-estate taxes. In contrast to 1900, when the states generally required the local governments to add a further mill rate to their property tax collections to be turned over to the state, the states with expanded tax choices not only raised their own revenue but also levied substantial taxes to be turned back to their local governments in shared taxes and state aids. Property taxes now represented only 46 per cent of state and local taxes.

It is true that both the nation and the states have increased their governmental activity relative to local governments, but the great change is the increase in taxes at all levels. Equally, or more startling, to the citizen of 1900 would be the affluence of most individuals today *after* taxes. Our economy so far has produced an increasing abundance that has made it possible for citizens to choose to have government do more and still have more left to spend personally than in earlier periods. Chart I shows the trends of governmental taxes by decades from 1902 to 1962. It also shows the estimated personal income for the years 1932, 1942, 1953, and 1962.

TAX LEVELS. As a first step in our analysis we need to examine the comparative height of taxes in the states, the difference between the highest taxing and lowest taxing states, and the stability of tax levels in the 20th century.

Comparative Height. To compare the height of taxes among the states, some refinements to gross, over-all tax dollars collected must be introduced. Comparisons over time require adjustment for price level. Population affects both the cost of government and the burden of taxes. The density of population affects the cost of government. Total income and its distribution affect the burden of taxes and, no doubt, the cost of government. Regional salary levels may affect the cost of government and the burden of taxes. As im-

*The national government, as well as the Confederate, raised war funds through income taxes in the 1860's. The federal government let its income tax lapse subsequently. When the Supreme Court held a new national income tax act unconstitutional in 1894, efforts were shortly made to secure a Constitutional amendment. The Sixteenth Amendment, 1913, opened the door to the national income taxes of this century.

Table 1

STATES IN UPPER AND LOWER QUARTILES
FOR PER CAPITA STATE AND LOCAL TAXES IN SELECTED YEARS

UPPER QUARTILE	1962* (a)	1953 (b)	1942 (c)	1932 (c)	1922 (d)	1913 (c)	1902 (e)
State	N.Y.**	Nev.	N.Y.	N.Y.	Nev.	Calif.	Calif.
Taxes	$309.05	$196.27	$116.68	$81.15	$82.09	$31.34	$23.40
State	CALIF.	Calif.	N.J.	Nev.	Ore.	Nev.	Mass.
Taxes	303.68	191.05	104.24	80.80	61.45	30.18	22.57
State	NEV.	N.Y.	Calif.	N.J.	Calif.	N.Y.	Colo.
Taxes	272.99	188.06	97.61	72.91	59.96	27.25	22.51
State	MASS.	Mass.	Nev.	Mass.	N.Y.	Mass.	Nev.
Taxes	270.62	166.24	96.09	72.67	57.55	25.42	21.90
State	CONN.	Wash.	Conn.	Calif.	Ariz.	Ore.	Mont.
Taxes	257.10	156.69	93.91	72.48	56.63	23.19	21.74
State	COLO.	Wis.	Mass.	Conn.	Wash.	Wash.	N.Y.
Taxes	255.15	155.29	93.67	65.41	55.23	22.22	21.67
State	WASH.	Colo.	R.I.	N.H.	Mass.	Mont.	Wash.
Taxes	252.54	154.77	91.34	64.38	53.63	21.79	18.69
State	Hawaii	Wyo.	Ill.	Mich.	Minn.	Ariz.	R.I.
Taxes	250.75	154.61	85.70	64.24	53.40	21.74	16.46
State	Minn.	N.H.	Mont.	Del.	Iowa	R.I.	Ariz.
Taxes	250.51	154.04	81.37	63.89	52.50	18.03	14.94
State	WYO.	Minn.	Mich.	Ore.	Mich.	Colo.	N.J.
Taxes	246.45	152.76	81.05	62.72	51.44	17.31	14.60
State	WIS.	Ore.	Wis.	Wis.	Colo.	Conn.	Conn.
Taxes	243.70	151.13	79.13	60.25	50.22	17.21	14.49
State	Ill.	Mich.	Wash.	Ariz.	S.Dak.	N.J.	Wyo.
Taxes	241.74	149.52	78.51	57.96	50.03	17.01	14.55

a. U.S. Department of Commerce, Bureau of the Census, *Governmental Finances in 1962* (Washington: U.S. Government Printing Office, October 1963) Table 20, p. 42.
b. U.S. Department of Commerce, Bureau of the Census, *State and Local Government Revenue in 1953,* State and Local Government Special Studies, No. 37 (Washington: U.S. Government Printing Office, 1954) Table 3, pp. 14–16.
c. U.S. Department of Commerce, Bureau of the Census, *Historical Review of State and Local Government Finances,* State and Local Government Special Studies, No. 25 (Washington: U.S. Government Printing Office, June 1948) Table 22, pp. 31–32.
d. U.S. Department of Commerce, Bureau of the Census, *Wealth, Public Debt, and Taxation: 1922, Taxes Collected* (Washington: U.S. Government Printing Office, 1924) Table 1, pp. 12–16. Data include some amount of non-tax revenues and are not pre-

Table 1, continued

LOWER QUARTILE	1962 (a)	1953 (b)	1942 (c)	1932 (c)	1922 (d)	1913 (c)	1902 (e)
State	Neb.	Tex.	N.M.	La.	W.Va.	Tex.	Ky.
Taxes	$184.24	$104.94	$50.52	$33.44	$28.75	$7.86	$7.42
State	**TEX.**	Mo.	Vt.	N.M.	Okla.	Va.	N.M.
Taxes	183.42	103.35	49.03	32.18	26.10	7.51	7.18
State	**W.VA.**	S.C.	Tex.	Okla.	Tex.	N.M.	W.Va.
Taxes	170.68	101.29	45.71	32.09	22.76	7.36	6.97
State	**N.C.**	Ga.	N.C.	N.C.	Miss.	Okla.	Tex.
Taxes	157.23	96.03	43.45	30.00	20.99	7.29	6.59
State	**GA.**	N.C.	Va.	Va.	Va.	Tenn.	Va.
Taxes	152.43	95.22	40.30	29.92	19.77	7.25	5.57
State	**KY.**	Va.	Tenn.	Tenn.	Ky.	Ga.	Ga.
Taxes	150.21	90.14	40.27	25.34	19.40	6.99	5.32
State	**VA.**	Tenn.	Ky.	Ky.	Tenn.	W.Va.	Ark.
Taxes	146.70	88.19	39.13	25.33	18.46	6.52	5.17
State	**TENN.**	W.Va.	S.C.	Miss.	N.C.	Miss.	Tenn.
Taxes	144.29	88.04	39.12	23.90	17.94	5.48	4.79
State	**MISS.**	Miss.	Ga.	S.C.	Ga.	Ala.	Ala.
Taxes	140.07	80.89	34.99	22.83	14.39	5.34	4.17
State	**ARK.**	Ky.	Miss.	Ga.	S.C.	Ark.	Miss.
Taxes	139.77	79.54	33.84	22.14	14.13	5.05	3.94
State	**S.C.**	Ark.	Ala.	Ala.	Ark.	N.C.	S.C.
Taxes	136.26	76.13	32.35	19.57	13.87	4.55	3.37
State	**ALA.**	Ala.	Ark.	Ark.	Ala.	S.C.	N.C.
Taxes	131.66	75.28	31.39	18.58	12.68	4.45	3.24

cisely comparable with other years. There is no evidence, however, that the discrepancies throw off relative relationships.

e. U.S. Department of Commerce and Labor, Special Reports of the Census Office, *Wealth, Debt, and Taxation* (Washington: U.S. Government Printing Office, 1907) Table 4, p. 966.

*Decade years from 1902 to 1962 have been selected wherever comprehensive Bureau of the Census data in local as well as state finances are available. In 1913 and 1953, it was necessary to use the following year. Even then there are occasional gaps.

**States printed in bold type are those which ranked high in four of the seven years or low in four of the seven years.

portant as any of these are the variations in the ways states have chosen to divide program and revenue raising responsibilities between themselves and their local governments. In a state with low taxes, the municipalities may have disproportionately high taxes or a high tax state may have low municipal taxes.

Table 1 initially attempts to improve the comparisons of the level of taxes among the states with only two refinements: state and local taxes are combined, and combined on a per capita basis. Moreover, we have abstracted for the table lists of only those states appearing in the upper and lower quartiles of per capita state and local taxes. We then find New York, in 1962, had the highest taxes with $309.05. Alabama was lowest with $131.66, or less than one-half those of New York. This analysis says nothing about tax burden or tax effort in the states. Since the low tax states are primarily in the South and lower income levels have tended to prevail there, we can reasonably believe that many of these states have a higher *burden* of taxation (taxes paid as a per cent of income received) than some of the states with higher absolute tax levies. The question of tax burden will be temporarily postponed.

Gap between High and Low. Comparisons over the years from 1902 to 1962 show that the gap between the lowest and highest tax states has significantly narrowed. (Although New York and Alabama did not have the highest and lowest tax rates in 1902, both were in the upper and lower quartiles — New York, sixth highest, and Alabama, fourth lowest.) In 1902 and 1913, the highest taxing states were collecting approximately seven times the revenue of the lowest taxing states. In 1922, the margin was almost ten-to-one. With the Depression year of 1932, the difference had dropped to approximately four-to-one; and, as we have already noted, 1962 showed a high of only slightly more than twice the lowest per capita state and local tax collections.

How real is the observable narrowing margin? First, the reliability of the percentage margin as an index of narrowing differences among the states assumes that factors influencing cost have not changed in this century or, more realistically, that they have changed in the same direction and in the same proportion for all states. We don't have enough data to establish whether base factors, such as "real cost of living" variations, increasing urbanism, shifts in population density, corruption or efficiency in government operation, have changed relatively in the same degree. Apart from statistics for some factors, we have general impressions for others. For example, we know that a number of states turned the proverbial corner in the first and second decades of the century in adopting measures to improve the efficiency of their governments and to reduce or eliminate the usual sources of corruption. Other states have not yet taken some of these steps, but still may have improved on both counts.

That there has been change in common factors accounting for taxes and that the change across the nation has been in the same direction seem certain. Impressionistically, it appears that the broad influences across the country of increased populations, increasing urbanism, and increasing affluence are more important than the differential details. Nevertheless, caution is required in interpretation of this narrowing gap. Beyond and above this trend may be the fact that the absolute difference between high and low taxing states in 1962 was substantially greater than the difference between high and low taxing states in 1902. Whether political and economic factors in 1962 are more or less congenial to broad general agreement among the states than they were in 1902 is a major question both for policy purposes and for our understanding of the political process.

Stability and Tax Levels. Table 1 suggests strongly that state and local governments do not readily change their levels of taxation. Nine states (California, Colorado, Connecticut, Massachusetts, New Jersey, Nevada, New York, Washington, and Wisconsin) were in the upper quartile of twelve with the highest per capita state and local levies at least four of seven years under review. California, Massachusetts, Nevada, and New York were in the upper quartile all seven years. Washington was there in six of the seven years. Consistency is even stronger on the low tax side than on the high tax side. Eleven states (Alabama, Arkansas, Georgia, Kentucky, Mississippi, North Carolina, South Carolina, Tennessee, Texas, Virginia, and West Virginia) were in the lower quartile of twelve with the lowest per capita state and local levies at least four of the seven years under review. Eight of the eleven appear seven times, while Tennessee and Texas appear six times and West Virginia appears five times.*

TAX CHOICES. Having identified the unusually high tax and low tax states, the next question concerns any possible relation between high taxes or low taxes and the particular taxes emphasized by the state. Do the states that spend the most depend largely on income taxes or on sales taxes or on both? What are the patterns of emphasis in taxes chosen today? What were the patterns at the beginning of the century?

In the 19th century, the states as well as their local governments used property taxes almost exclusively. Both the range of types of taxes and the distribution of tax burden would have been narrow as one state was compared with another. Then from the second through the fourth or fifth decades of this century, there were at least three patterns of taxing with differential

*This analysis does not establish that the repeating states in the seven-year statistics were also in the upper quartile or lower quartile all or most years in between. A quick check of the available census data (and the census does not provide information on local revenues for all of the intervening years) suggests a strong presumption that the same states have been high or low most of the 20th century.

tax burden distribution. States appeared to have dug in their heels either for an income or a sales tax as their major revenue source with a small minority of states having neither. Today's states still show important differences in the combination of taxes used, but the divergencies may be narrowing again. For example, twenty-six states use both income and general sales tax and all states supplement their major revenue source or sources with gasoline taxes and liquor taxes.

Property Taxes. The general property tax reigned in the 19th century among state and local governments, supplemented by special bank taxes, a few excise taxes, and a few poorly drawn and poorly enforced income taxes. The "classic" general property tax was uniform and universal. It was also impersonal in the sense that it was property that was taxed, not individuals. The total property the individual owned had no meaning to the tax law. Presumably all property, whether personal or real, whether tangible or intangible, was assessed at market value and a single rate determined by the taxing unit. On the assumption of market value assessments by municipalities within the county, the county determined its tax needs and apportioned its revenue requirements among the municipalities. The state also determined its expenditures and apportioned the required levies among counties. Thus, all property of similar market value would bear the same state property tax rate, but county and municipal rates would vary depending on the value of property within their jurisdictions and voter decisions as to governmental activities and expenditure levels.

In practice, the situation was less simple. Most states exempted from taxation at least some property — for example, property owned by religious institutions. By the end of the century, a few states classified property and applied differential rates. All states found that their municipalities assessed some or all property at other than "market" or "true" value. Some assessors were more diligent than others in locating property, just as some taxpayers were more forthright than others in declaring the existence and value of personal and intangible property not easily known to the assessor. States, in other words, employed rather different versions of the same general property tax.

New Taxes. From almost exclusive reliance on the property tax at the beginning of the century, most of the states (although not their local governments) had moved away from the general property tax by the beginning of World War II. Whereas, as late as 1932, the states drew over 17 per cent of their revenue from property taxes, in 1962 they drew only 3 per cent and most of this consisted of special types of property taxes. General sales taxes now occupied first place, providing almost 25 per cent of state revenues. Personal and corporate income taxes provided almost another 20 per cent

Most local governments have continued to depend on the property tax so that the "mix" of property versus other taxes usually depends on the "overall mix" of tax and expenditure decisions between the state and its local governments. If the state assumes roughly one-half or two-thirds of the responsibility, then the property tax dependence for state and local governments will be roughly one-half or one-third. A few major exceptions exist, such as New York City's use of the sales tax and the use of income taxes by cities in Ohio and Pennsylvania, but these exceptions are still drowned in the general dependence on the property tax.

Wisconsin in 1911 initiated a modern, enforceable *income tax* that thirty-eight more states adopted in the succeeding decades — most adopted both the personal and corporate income taxes, but a few adopted only one or the other. All of the eleven states that did not adopt an income tax, except Nebraska, chose general retail sales taxes. Mississippi adopted the first modern general sales tax in 1932. Under the pressure of revenue needs in the Great Depression, other states quickly followed. By 1937, half had retail sales taxes. Since World War II, thirteen more have joined the list of sales tax states. Gasoline taxes — an excise or special sales tax — became popular in the 1920's with the spreading ownership of automobiles and the feverish demand for improved highways. From the first adoption in 1919, all states had gasoline taxes within ten years. The national government adopted the tax in 1930.

Another widely used, but not highly productive, tax is the estate tax (often technically both an estate and inheritance tax). A number of states had used the estate tax for decades before adoption by the national government in 1916. The displeasure of states that regarded the estate tax as a state preserve and the threat to interstate competition enunciated by Florida in its constitutional amendment to eliminate all estate taxes there led Congress in 1926 to take special action. Under the legislation adopted at that time, an estate may offset up to 80 per cent of its federal tax by payments of such amount in inheritance and estate taxes to the state government. All states were thus encouraged to adopt inheritance or estate tax statutes since they could gain revenue at the expense of the national government and with almost no additional cost to their own citizens.* Only Nevada failed to adopt such a tax.

Tax Emphasis. The unanimous decision of the states to eliminate or reduce

*The national credit provision has not been changed since 1926 despite the increase in federal estate tax rates. Hence, the advantage to the states rests in terms of the much lower federal rates of 1926. Florida first raised the question of unconstitutionality of the Federal Act of 1926, and then, after it lost this battle in the U.S. Supreme Court, immediately amended its own constitution.

Table 2

STATE TAX COLLECTIONS, BY SOURCE AND BY STATES: 1962

State	Amount (in Millions)	Individual Income	Corporation Income	General Sales or Gross Receipts	Motor Fuels	Alcoholic Beverages	Tobacco	Motor Vehicle & Operators' Licenses	Property	Inheritance & Gift	Other
		(in per cent of total taxes)									
I. INCOME TAX STATES[a]											
Alaska	$ 36.5	33.4%	4.9%	....%	15.1%	6.8%	5.2%	7.4%	0.3%	0.3%	26.6%
Colorado	234.4	26.8	6.3	23.7	17.2	3.0	....	7.9	3.1	2.6	9.4
Delaware	91.2	37.9	8.0	....	11.3	2.2	3.7	5.3	3.8	3.7	24.1
Idaho	71.9	30.0	7.2	....	20.6	2.5	4.5	15.6	4.6	1.2	13.8
Maryland	404.0	24.6	4.9	22.5	15.0	2.4	5.6	7.4	3.7	1.6	12.0
Massachusetts	549.7	32.4	6.0	....	14.9	5.1	7.7	4.5	0.1	3.8	25.5
Minnesota	403.4	30.4	8.7	....	14.8	4.9	6.2	11.2	6.1	2.2	15.5
Montana	71.8	19.8	6.3	....	25.2	5.6	8.6	6.4	9.6	2.9	15.6
New York	2,328.6	42.5	12.8	....	10.0	2.6	5.4	6.5	0.2	3.5	16.5
North Carolina	539.1	17.7	10.5	24.3	20.0	3.9	....	6.4	2.5	1.5	13.2
Oregon	212.7	42.5	10.1	....	18.2	0.7	....	15.6	....	3.8	9.1
Vermont	49.7	25.8	5.0	....	18.7	8.9	7.4	16.3	0.8	2.4	14.2
Virginia	359.6	25.5	8.4	....	26.1	6.2	4.1	7.1	4.3	1.4	16.9
Wisconsin	459.7	31.4	11.7	3.0	16.5	3.4	5.6	9.7	7.9	3.3	7.5
II. SALES TAX STATES[b]											
Alabama	295.7	9.3	3.3	31.9	25.4	5.5	5.3	2.2	5.0	0.6	11.5
Arizona	186.9	7.8	3.0	40.6	15.2	2.2	2.1	5.9	15.2	0.5	7.6
Arkansas	177.3	6.9	5.8	34.2	23.7	3.6	5.6	9.4	0.2	0.4	10.2
California	2,369.4	12.6	12.3	31.9	15.4	2.4	2.7	6.1	5.8	3.2	7.6
Connecticut	309.9	....	12.4	30.0	15.8	4.8	6.1	5.4	....	7.4	18.1
Florida	563.6	....	....	32.2	23.4	8.8	1.8	11.3	3.9	1.1	17.5

State	Amount (in Millions)	Individual Income	Corporation Income	General Sales or Gross Receipts	Motor Fuels	Alcoholic Beverages	Tobacco	Motor Vehicle & Operators' Licenses	Property	Inheritance & Gift	Other
		(in per cent of total taxes)									
Georgia	$ 402.9	10.8%	6.2%	39.0%	22.2%	5.6%	5.3%	5.0%	0.3%	0.4%	5.2%
Hawaii	132.3	23.0	5.5	49.8	9.0	2.7	1.8	...	...	0.8	7.4
Illinois	980.4	...	...	47.6	15.3	4.2	5.6	11.3	0.1	3.2	12.7
Indiana	420.1	15.1	...	48.7	25.1	3.4	4.2	9.5	1.6	1.7	5.8
Iowa	276.5	15.1	1.6	30.2	21.6	1.2	4.3	16.9	1.5	3.0	4.5
Kansas	228.3	11.9	3.9	35.0	18.7	2.6	4.2	15.2	4.1	2.3	2.1
Kentucky	309.3	12.0	6.8	31.3	21.0	5.5	2.8	4.4	5.3	1.9	9.0
Maine	93.4	...	...	31.6	25.1	3.5	8.7	10.9	2.1	4.0	14.1
Michigan	1,007.5	...	...	45.7	15.1	1.4	5.1	7.6	5.7	1.4	18.0
Mississippi	204.6	4.0	6.4	37.0	23.8	2.5	5.8	4.0	2.1	0.6	13.8
Missouri	395.3	18.2	3.0	32.5	16.6	2.2	5.5	10.9	1.4	1.7	8.0
Nevada	53.1	...	...	28.6	18.3	4.1	4.1	13.9	4.0	...	27.0
New Mexico	138.1	9.3	...	27.1	18.5	1.6	5.1	8.8	7.0	0.4	22.2
Ohio	891.7	...	...	29.5	24.7	4.2	7.1	11.2	4.5	1.3	17.5
Pennsylvania	1,321.6	...	11.6	31.7	19.3	4.0	6.9	7.2	0.1	4.6	14.6
Rhode Island	96.8	...	9.8	27.6	18.5	3.5	7.5	10.1	...	3.1	19.9
South Carolina	243.6	11.2	7.4	30.3	21.9	7.4	5.0	4.2	0.5	0.7	11.4
South Dakota	56.8	...	0.9	30.5	27.6	5.1	6.3	10.6	...	1.8	17.2
Tennessee	329.1	2.0	6.5	34.2	24.5	2.8	5.9	9.1	...	2.0	13.0
Utah	115.9	14.6	6.1	31.8	19.0	0.9	2.1	6.6	8.8	1.2	8.9
Washington	522.6	...	...	55.0	14.4	3.7	4.1	5.2	7.0	2.0	8.6
West Virginia	212.7	9.9	...	45.9	16.7	1.5	5.5	6.6	0.1	1.3	12.5
Wyoming	44.0	...	...	28.2	18.9	1.4	4.0	18.2	18.4	0.9	10.0

Table 2, continued

Table 2, continued

State	Amount (in Millions)	Individual Income	Corporation Income	General Sales or Gross Receipts	Motor Fuels	Alcoholic Beverages	Tobacco	Motor Vehicle & Operators' Licenses	Property	Inheritance & Gift	Other
	(in per cent of total taxes)										
III. STATES NOT HEAVILY EMPLOYING EITHER INCOME OR SALES TAXES[a]											
Louisiana	$485.3	3.9%	4.8%	18.6%	13.7%	4.3%	5.7%	2.8%	3.3%	1.0%	41.9%
Nebraska	94.8	....	....	....	41.7	3.4	6.9	8.2	30.2	0.4	9.2
New Hampshire	46.3	3.7	....	....	30.7	2.4	9.9	16.0	3.9	6.0	27.4
New Jersey	431.2	1.5	5.9	....	28.4	5.3	13.7	18.1	0.6	5.6	20.9
North Dakota	64.1	10.1	2.8	23.1	19.0	5.3	5.8	17.3	4.1	0.6	11.9
Oklahoma	307.9	9.5	4.7	19.6	20.3	3.9	6.6	13.4	....	2.4	19.6
Texas	941.3	....	....	11.0	20.9	4.1	10.1	10.3	4.3	1.8	37.5

a. All states that raised 25 per cent or more of their state tax revenues in 1962 from individual and corporate income taxes. California and Hawaii qualify in both divisions I and II but, since their dependence on sales taxes was greater, we have included them in Section II.

b. All states that raised 25 per cent or more of their state revenue in 1962 from general sales or gross receipts taxes.

c. Louisiana, Oklahoma, and Texas derive substantial revenues from taxes on oil; Nebraska heavily uses the property tax; New Jersey has used corporation and railroad property taxes extensively; New Hampshire has used property taxes and has now adopted a lottery for state revenues.

Source: U.S. Department of Commerce, Bureau of the Census, *State Tax Collections in 1962* (Washington: U.S. Government Printing Office, August 1962) Table 3, p. 5. Because percentages were rounded off, their sum is not always exactly 100 per cent.

their use of the general property tax in the 20th century has not resulted in agreement on a single substitute. Table 2 identifies the choices states have made in emphasizing particular taxes. Nebraska alone seeks important revenues from the property tax (about one-third) and has neither an income nor general sales tax. The highly productive gasoline tax, used by all of the states, seldom is available for anything but highway purposes. Estate or inheritance taxes typically produce less than 5 per cent of total state revenues, 2.6 per cent as an average in 1962. Severance taxes on natural resources provided more than 10 per cent of state taxes for Louisiana, New Mexico, Oklahoma, and Texas. These four states alone accounted for 88 per cent of all state severance taxes levied in the nation in 1962. A few states have resolutely held out against either the income tax or the sales tax. Of the eleven states without any income tax, a constitutional change appears necessary before legislative adoption in several. As noted earlier, Michigan is restrictive as to type of permissible income tax. Oregon has adopted the most purist attitude on sales taxes by refusing up to the present even to adopt a special sales tax on tobacco products, although it does tax gasoline and liquor sales.

Delaware, Massachusetts, Minnesota, New York, Oregon and Wisconsin for decades have given income taxes (personal and corporate) the leading role in their tax structures by frequently drawing 40 per cent or more of their state revenue from this source alone. Ten other states raised at least a fourth of their state tax revenue from income taxes in 1962. (California with its 24.9 per cent plus has been included in the ten.) Of these last ten, California and Hawaii still drew even more from general sales taxes. Twenty-nine more states derived at least a fourth of their state tax revenues from general sales taxes in 1962. And Arizona, Hawaii, Illinois, Indiana, Michigan, Washington, and West Virginia drew 40 per cent or more tax revenue from this source alone in 1962. In terms of percentage emphasis then, Delaware, Massachusetts, Minnesota, New York, Oregon, and Wisconsin are the strong income tax states with only Wisconsin levying any general sales taxes. In contrast, Arizona, Hawaii, Illinois, Indiana, Michigan, Washington, and West Virginia have been identified as the strong sales tax states. Of these, Arizona, Hawaii, and West Virginia also levy state income taxes. (Indiana adopted a low rate proportional income tax in 1963.)

All of the high income tax states were also high per capita taxing states except Delaware and Minnesota. Only Washington of the strong sales tax states was also a high per capita taxing state. None of the high income or sales tax states, however, were low per capita taxing states.* Since whether

*High and low are defined in terms of whether the state was in the high or low quartile of per capita state and local taxes four or more of the seven selected years. It will be found later that others of the high sales tax states were low tax states when income, rather than per capita measures, is the test.

a state was a high income or sales tax state depended on its own relative emphasis on this form of taxation and not its total tax take, there was no necessary reason why the relationships noted should be true.

Further analysis of the "mix" of tax ingredients shows that Oregon makes unusually heavy use of the income tax even among income tax states. A recent study showed that the average yield of individual income taxes employed by state and local governments represented 1.21 per cent of the adjusted gross income of the states employing them.[3] Oregon, however, showed a rate of 3.20. Delaware had a rate of 2.86; New York, 2.13; Wisconsin, 2.21. California placed much heavier emphasis on general sales tax than on its income tax, with the result that its income tax rate was only .78 per cent or less than one-fourth of neighboring Oregon's.* California had an "effective" general sales tax rate in 1960 of 5.19 (average effective rate among states 3.72), exceeded only by a few states — notably Washington with 8.70 and Hawaii with 13.48.[4]

Even among states that have chosen the income tax (or the sales tax) there may be wide differences in impact. These differences in part reflect choices on issues already noted in the property tax. The income tax in one state may be more inclusive, with higher maximum rates and steeper progression. Income exempt from taxation or the deductions permitted may be generous. Where states closely follow the federal pattern of deductions, exemptions, and special provisions and further allow deduction of the federal income tax, the net impact of the income tax is likely to be low. Thus, California, where we have noted that the actual effective rate is low, has relatively low rates and low progression and frequently follows the federal pattern of exemptions and deductions. Additionally, some states strictly enforce their income tax laws, while others "save" by allotting limited funds for enforcement.

Even a "general" sales tax may include or exclude food or clothing from the tax base. Professional or other services, medicines, and many special items may be within or outside the tax base. "General" sales tax rates vary from 2 per cent to 5 per cent. And, as in the case of the income tax, enforcement ranges from good to haphazard. This again affects productivity and burden.

TAX BURDEN. The tax burden concept attempts to relate taxes to income. Thus, tax burden normally has reference to the amount of taxes paid as a per cent of income. The concept may have reference to taxes as a per cent of

*Despite year-to-year variations, analysis would show few changes in relationships so long as the states reviewed maintained their present tax systems and had no radical local economic distortions. Both conditions have held constant for California and Oregon for the last quarter century at least.

an individual's or a family's income, or taxes as a per cent of income by income classes, or as a relation of total taxes to total income in a state.

The per capita, over-all height of taxes in a state in relation to per capita, over-all personal income is usually identified as the *total* tax burden (Table 3). Thus, over a span of time (at least three out of four listed decades), Colorado, Louisiana, Minnesota, Mississippi, Montana, North Dakota, South Dakota, and Wisconsin showed a relatively high burden of taxes in relation to personal income, whereas Connecticut, Delaware, Illinois, Maryland, Missouri, and Virginia repeatedly ranked with a low burden of taxes.*

The relation of the *mix* of tax ingredients to the *distribution* of income in the states indicates tax burden in a more refined sense by income groups. Neither the total tax, nor the total income, nor their distribution in the states is constant, so that the precise tax burden varies from year to year. Moreover, there are no centrally gathered statistics that tell us with certainty what the distribution of income is, nor do we know without question who finally pays a particular tax.† The burden of some taxes may be almost totally exported by the levying state to users in other states. Thus, Minnesota's taxes on its iron mines are paid by iron and steel users throughout the nation. Other states with major natural resources may similarly succeed in reducing their own tax burdens.

Despite the difficulties, scholars from time to time have attempted to make the needed estimates and to analyze the distribution of state and local tax burdens by income groups. (No study makes the distribution state by state.) Although economic assumptions, changes in state and local tax laws, and changes in the economy will affect the detailed findings, the general conclusion that state and local tax systems are regressive has been found in every study covering the fifty (or forty-eight) states. In Table 4 are estimates of

*These rankings and the more refined ones that follow require caution in interpretation. Tax "burden" is a defined term, and the word, "burden," high or low, should not produce a simple emotional reaction. A high tax burden may mean a high level of governmental services and a general good standard of living, whereas a low tax burden may mean the reverse. Or it may mean simply that incomes are low in the first instance and high in the second instance, and a similar tax system and level of services is present on both occasions. Or the categorization may result from some other combination of decisions and circumstances. Here, as in other instances, value judgments and preferences should include considerations of economic trends.

†Some economic assumptions relative to shifting and incidence are accepted almost universally by economists, but other assumptions would be widely disputed. It is usually assumed that personal income taxes are paid by the individual. In the case of rental property, it is usually assumed that the renter pays the property taxes through the increased rentals levied by the landlord. Most retail sales taxes are assumed to be paid by the purchaser of the item. Not only are there refinements even to these assumptions but, in the case of corporation income tax, the assumption divides the taxes among profits, wages, and prices, depending on the precise competitive position of the corporation.

Table 3

GROSS TAX BURDEN, SELECTED YEARS

	PER CENT STATE AND LOCAL TAXES OF PER CAPITA INCOME[a]			
	1962	1953	1942	1932
Vermont	11.5	9.6	6.4	14.6
LOUISIANA[b]	11.3	10.4	8.9	13.9
Wyoming	11.3	8.3	6.6	14.9
MINNESOTA[b]	11.2	9.3	9.4	15.5
Maine	11.0	9.0	8.0	13.9
MISSISSIPPI[b]	10.9	9.0	7.6	18.9
COLORADO[b]	10.7	8.9	8.6	14.7
Arizona	10.6	8.8	6.9	18.4
Kansas	10.6	8.7	7.1	19.1
WISCONSIN[b]	10.6	8.7	9.0	16.5
Iowa	10.5	9.5	7.9	16.7
MONTANA[b]	10.5	7.8	9.0	16.3
New York	10.5	8.7	9.9	11.9
California	10.4	8.7	7.6	12.6
Hawaii	10.4	——	——	——
New Mexico	10.2	8.8	8.0	15.3
Utah	10.2	8.4	7.6	13.9
Washington	10.1	7.9	6.5	13.6
SOUTH DAKOTA[b]	10.0	10.4	11.0	28.3
Idaho	9.8	8.9	6.7	19.9
Oregon	9.8	8.4	6.6	16.3
Massachusetts	9.7	8.4	8.7	11.6
Michigan	9.7	7.1	7.7	16.3
Oklahoma	9.7	8.5	9.4	14.8
Florida	9.6	9.1	7.4	15.6
NORTH DAKOTA[b]	9.5	11.6	10.5	25.2
West Virginia	9.4	6.9	8.4	14.2
Arkansas	9.2	7.7	6.6	11.9
Rhode Island	9.1	5.6	8.0	9.4
Texas	9.1	6.7	6.4	13.2
New Hampshire	9.0	9.8	9.1	14.9

the over-all distribution by income classes of state and local taxes raised in the United States in 1958. The table shows a clear regressive pattern — taxes falling hardest on the lowest income level and in descending order on incomes as they increased.*

Tax burden studies require statistics beyond any normally gathered. Even well-directed and financed studies require estimates and assumptions

---

*Standard tax terminology defines *regressive* taxes as taxes that decrease as a ratio of income with increases in income; *progressive* taxes increase as a ratio of income with increases in income; *proportional* taxes show a constant ratio without regard to changes in income. Both a tax and a tax system may be classified on this basis.

Table 3, continued

	PER CENT STATE AND LOCAL TAXES OF PER CAPITA INCOME[a]			
	1962	1953	1942	1932
North Carolina	9.0	8.1	7.5	16.0
South Carolina	8.8	8.9	7.2	14.5
Kentucky	8.7	6.5	7.3	12.0
Pennsylvania	8.7	5.9	8.1	10.9
Georgia	8.6	7.7	6.1	16.0
Indiana	8.6	6.8	7.1	16.8
Illinois[c]	8.5	6.2	8.2	10.8
Alabama	8.4	6.9	6.2	12.1
Tennessee	8.4	7.2	7.2	12.8
Connecticut[c]	8.3	5.9	6.3	10.5
Nevada	8.3	8.3	6.2	14.9
Ohio	8.3	5.8	7.1	12.7
Maryland[c]	8.2	6.1	5.4	9.0
Nebraska	8.1	7.6	6.7	14.5
New Jersey	8.1	6.4	8.9	12.3
Alaska	8.0	——	——	——
Missouri[c]	7.8	6.0	6.5	10.0
Delaware[c]	7.7	4.2	5.3	10.8
Virginia[c]	7.2	6.1	5.1	10.6

a. Per capita taxes (see Table 1 for sources) divided by per capita personal income
drawn from the following sources:
U.S. Department of Commerce, Office of Business Economics, *Personal Income by
States Since 1929,* A Supplement to the Survey of Current Business (Washington:
U.S. Government Printing Office, 1956) Table 2, pp. 142–143.
———, *Survey of Current Business, August, 1963* (Washington: U.S. Government
Printing Office, 1963) Table 2, p. 9.
b. States in capital letters are those that show *high* taxes in relation to personal income
three or more times in the four decades.
c. States printed in italics show *low* taxes in relation to personal income three or more
times in the four decades.

based at best on limited samples. The economic interdependence of the
states brings especially difficult problems into assumptions of tax shifting and
incidence. Hence, national aggregate studies usually give the best obtainable
view subject to modification by particular state patterns. If the over-all national finding is one of regressive state and local tax systems, we can assume
a similar finding in a state that has (1) an average income level and distribution, and (2) a tax system that depends largely on the usual ingredients —
a general sales tax, low or no income taxes, gasoline, tobacco, and liquor
excise taxes, motorist and motor vehicle licenses, and (locally) the property tax. Deviations from average in either income distribution or tax system

Table 4

STATE AND LOCAL TAXES AS A PERCENTAGE OF TOTAL INCOME
BY INCOME CLASS, CALENDAR YEAR 1958

SOURCE	FAMILY PERSONAL-INCOME CLASS							TOTAL
	Under $2,000	$2,000– 3,999	$4,000– 5,999	$6,000– 7,999	$8,000– 9,999	$10,000– 14,999	$15,000 *& Over*	
Individual income	0.5	0.8	0.6	0.2	0.2	0.3	0.7	0.5
Corporation income	.2	.2	.1	.1	.2	.2	.4	.2
Excises and sales	4.8	3.9	3.7	3.6	3.5	3.2	2.1	3.3
Estate and gift	…	…	…	…	…	…	.5	.1
Property	5.9	4.6	4.1	3.7	3.4	2.8	2.1	3.5
Total, excluding social insurance	11.4	9.5	8.5	7.6	7.3	6.5	5.8	7.6

Source: George A. Bishop, "Tax Burden by Income Class," *National Tax Journal* (March 1961) p. 54, quoted in staff report of the Advisory Commission on Intergovernmental Relations, *Measures of State and Local Fiscal Capacity and Tax Effort* (October 1962) p. 23. (Incorrect totals in Bishop's article have been corrected here.)

Table 5

EFFECTIVE TAX RATES FOR WISCONSIN'S STATE AND LOCAL TAX STRUCTURE, 1956

INCOME CLASS	CASE II-B* ADJUSTED GROSS INCOME REVISED
$0 – under 1,000	29.83%
1,000–1,999	14.94
2,000–2,999	11.10
3,000–3,999	9.67
4,000–4,999	8.87
5,000–5,999	8.46
6,000–7,499	8.34
7,500–9,999	8.31
10,000 and over	10.88
All Classes	9.76

*"Case II-B" refers to specific assumptions as to shifting and incidence.

Source: Adapted from Table 8, p. 55, University of Wisconsin Tax Study Committee Report, *Wisconsin State and Local Tax Burden* (Madison: 1959).

would modify the findings. For example, in 1956 when Wisconsin had no general sales tax, an analysis of the distribution of its tax burden suggested regression at the lowest end of the income scale, approximate proportionality in the middle, and slight progression at the high end of the income scale.

Some of the differences in the national aggregate findings and the Wisconsin findings (comparing last line of Table 4 with column of Table 5) are the result of differing assumptions especially in the case of large differentials in tax rates at the lowest end of the income scale, but broadly the results are as expected. Wisconsin in 1956 depended heavily on personal and corporate income taxes and traditionally has taxed somewhat higher than the average among the states. With all the reservations already stated, it is clearly not easy to compare state tax systems on a regressive-progressive tax burden scale with any of the degree of the earlier certainty when we were merely comparing reported collections with personal income.

If we exclude property taxes and special excise taxes as having fairly similar importance and impact across the country (a not fully accurate but still not wholly unreasonable assumption in gross terms), the two major ingredients left are general sales and income taxes. A general sales tax that includes food purchases is classified as regressive. A progressive individual income tax adds almost the only progressive element in state-local tax structures. Heavy and consistent use of the sales tax or the progressive income tax gives us a fair standard with which to identify the distribution of tax burden among states. With this broad and unrefined measure, we can identify tentatively the states that would probably belong in the upper and lowei quartiles of a progressive-regressive comparison. Table 6 represents our judgment of the extremes in the progressive-regressive continuum among the

Table 6

PROGRESSIVE-REGRESSIVE STATE TAXES*

Most Progressive State Tax Systems	Most Regressive State Tax Systems
Alaska	Arizona
Delaware	Arkansas
Idaho	Hawaii
Massachusetts	Illinois
Minnesota	Indiana †
New York	Michigan
Oregon	Mississippi
Vermont	Tennessee
Virginia	Washington
Wisconsin	West Virginia

*As the text indicates, this table necessarily is judgmental. The largest difference in judgment would come with pattern of local taxes. New York, for example, is included with its high state income tax (individual and corporate) and no sales tax; but the City of New York draws substantial revenues from the city sales tax.
†Indiana in the future may not belong since its 1963 adoption of a flat rate income tax and major reduction of its gross receipts tax.

states. Nevertheless, even the high income tax states (when property taxes and special excise taxes are considered) tax their *lowest income* citizens proportionally higher than their highest income citizens, but in the middle income ranges the tax burden is likely to be proportional or slightly progressive. Texas now has a sales tax and both it and Nebraska (with no income tax and heavy reliance on the property tax) may qualify in the highly regressive class.

FISCAL CAPACITY AND TAX EFFORT. How extensively a state uses its resources to produce tax revenues represents both a different set of choices and a different context for choices than the decisions it makes on tax burden. At least temporarily a state presumably has a set of more or less fixed resources to draw on for tax revenues. The political choice in tax effort is how much to tax what is present. All of the intellectual problems of measuring tax burden continue, aggravated somewhat by devising an index of resources whether taxed or not.

The best study of fiscal capacity and tax effort is the recent one by the staff of the Intergovernmental Relations Commission.[5] Briefly, they have identified by state three measures of income — personal income, income produced, and composite income — and have related current tax collections by states to each measure. As a fourth index, they have applied a carefully adjusted "representative tax system" (an average rate structure of total state tax systems) to the taxable resources of each state as a measure of comparative effort.*

Some states appear as high tax effort states no matter which of the four indices is applied. "High" is defined as tax effort of 10 percentage points above the norm of 100 per cent if the states were exactly average. Nine states rank as making a high tax effort on all indices: Hawaii, New York, Vermont, Maine, Mississippi, Massachusetts, Washington, Oregon, and Wisconsin. California is high on all of the income indices and just misses inclusion (109) under the "representative tax system." Arizona, Colorado, Louisiana, and Minnesota qualify as "high" by the income indices and rank between 100 and 110 under the "representative tax system." Michigan, on the other hand, has the 110 ranking for "high" on the "representative" tax scale, but only rates between 100 and 110 on the income effort scales.

In contrast to the high tax effort states, a few states show consistently low effort (10 percentage points or more below 100). By all four measures, Illinois, Kentucky, Missouri, and Virginia are low. Ohio is low on all of the income indices but misses (91) inclusion in the "low" group under the "representative" tax measure. Pennsylvania qualified as "low" by the income measures, but again misses (96) inclusion as "low" under the "representative tax system." Indiana, Nebraska, and Texas measure above 90 in effort on *one* of the income scales, but otherwise are consistently low in tax effort. Pennsylvania, Ohio, Indiana, Illinois, Kentucky, Missouri, and Nebraska turn out to be neighbors (Virginia almost borders), forming a large fragment of the mid-center of the nation. Only Texas of the low tax effort states is geographically widely separated.

MAJOR TAX DECISIONS. As a summary to this section covering major characteristics of the tax systems of the states in this century, we can identify those states that have taken the more critical choices. We include as "major" characteristics: (1) whether the state has been rather consistently a high or low taxing state per capita; (2) whether the state is making a high or low tax "effort" on the basis of income measures and on the basis of a "representative tax system." Table 7 summarizes the findings.

*Again, as was the case for tax burden, the term "tax effort" should be understood with its technical meaning and not in a pejorative sense. The states showing low tax effort may have such wealth that they do not "need" more governmental services either to satisfy their citizens or to provide a level above other states. Only analysis of expenditures could establish the relationship of low tax effort states and "inadequate" service states. Similarly, high tax effort states may still not supply a satisfactory level of services.

Table 7

"CRITICAL" TAX CHOICES AND STATES MOST IDENTIFIED WITH EACH

High per Capita Tax States	High Tax States re: Income Measures*	High Tax States re: Representative System*	High on Two or More Indices	Low per Capita Tax States	Low Tax States re: Income Measures*	Low Tax States re: Representative System*	Low on Two or More Indices
		Alaska			Alaska		
				Alabama			
	Arizona			Arkansas		Arkansas	Arkansas
California	California		California			Delaware	
Colorado	Colorado		Colorado			Idaho	
Connecticut				Georgia			
	Hawaii	Hawaii	Hawaii		Illinois	Illinois	Illinois
	Kansas				Indiana	Indiana	Indiana
	Louisiana			Kentucky	Kentucky	Kentucky	Kentucky
	Maine	Maine	Maine	Mississippi			
Massachusetts	Massachusetts	Massachusetts	Massachusetts				
		Michigan					
					Missouri	Missouri	Missouri
						Montana	
	Minnesota					Nebraska	
	Mississippi	Mississippi	Mississippi			New Mexico	
	Montana				Nebraska		Nebraska
				North Carolina			
Nevada					Ohio		
New Jersey							
New York	New York	New York	New York	South Carolina	Pennsylvania		
	North Dakota			Tennessee			
	Oregon	Oregon	Oregon	Texas	Texas	Texas	Texas
		Rhode Island		Virginia	Virginia	Virginia	Virginia
	South Dakota			West Virginia			
	Vermont	Vermont	Vermont				
Washington	Washington	Washington	Washington			Wyoming	
Wisconsin	Wisconsin	Wisconsin	Wisconsin				

*Source: The Advisory Commission on Intergovernmental Relations, *A Staff Report: Measures of State and Local Fiscal Capacity*

A significant feature of Table 7 is the number of states omitted and the fact that these by most observations belong in a broad group where deviation from the average is relatively small and where, by slightly different measures, states may slip back and forth across a mythical average. If we were to develop a map with shadings from black to white that allowed a tolerance level on the composite characteristics previously indicated, we would find the large majority of states coming within some shade of gray. Occasionally one of these "gray" states might still show up as an exception on an individual characteristic but would then fade back into the general gray.

A few states, however, would show as black or white (a matter of identification, not a moral symbol) consistently or in apparently decisive particulars. Examining Table 7 in a little more detail, we can classify twelve states by at least two of the measures as "high": California, Colorado, Hawaii, Maine, *Massachusetts,* Mississippi, *New York, Oregon, Vermont,* Washington, and *Wisconsin.* The five italicized states emphasize the income tax. Maine and Washington use sales taxes and exclude income taxes. The remaining four states use both probably to neutralize any significant deviation from the broad regressive pattern of state-local taxes.

The "low" tax states by at least two of the measures in Table 7 include eight: Arkansas, Illinois, Indiana, Kentucky, Missouri, Nebraska, Texas, and Virginia. Only Virginia is an important income tax state. Illinois, Indiana, Nebraska, and Texas exclude income taxes and all except Nebraska emphasize a general sales tax. Arkansas, Kentucky, and Missouri employ both income and sales taxes.

POLITICS AND TAX CHOICES

The fifty states in the Union operate under the common bonds of a federal system that has lasted for almost two centuries. The founders expected and desired diversity. And no amount of generalization about the states should obscure the fact that differences exist. We have already found strong evidence of a number of states consistently "going their own way" in taxes. Economic and demographic analyses assist in identifying general trends within the federal system, but do not fully explain why particular states are consistently at the extremes.

For political scientists, the important questions include: "Why have certain states chosen to tax their citizens more heavily than have other states? Why have other states chosen to tax their citizens much more lightly than have other states?" A simple, important, but only partial, answer is tradition. Clearly, once levels of services and taxes are established, they are cumulative. Economists discussing national trends in western nations find customary levels of taxes continue until dislodged by crisis. They do not find the meaning of "crisis" consistent and can identify it looking backward more easily than in looking forward. The Depression appears to have been a "crisis" for the United States but not for England. Wars have been "crises" for both.[6]

Can we identify "crises" in state governments that would indicate the points at which a tradition to tax heavily or lightly is made? Is there, for example, a point of balance in agricultural, labor, and industrial interests that is critical for decisions? At such a time does the degree of party competition, the presence of a particular leader, the distribution of income that may affect the degree of voter participation, the manner of legislative apportionment, or other similar characteristics determine the direction of the decision?

Answers to other related questions may contribute to our understanding. (1) Does a highly productive tax favor the search for expenditures, whereas a lean tax increase the search for economy? The casual critic of the bureaucrat would answer "yes" without thinking. His response may well be true but in a more subtle fashion than he recognizes. A state that has chosen, deliberately or not, a tax that proves highly productive in a given period may learn to enjoy a higher level of services that becomes itself the leverage for securing higher taxes in the future. (2) Another question that we explore shortly in this chapter concerns the degree of consistency in policy that individual states exhibit over time. Are high taxes present with "liberal" legislation, and low taxes with "conservative" legislation? Care is needed to separate policies of state origin and policies brought about by federal grants-in-aid. (3) Another analysis might involve further pursuit of the hypothesis suggested by Sachs and Harris that high state grants to local governments are positively related to high state and local taxes.[7]

Most of the studies directed at the political explanations for policy decisions have examined *present* characteristics. They have not seen the decisions as cumulative; they have not attempted to find a "beginning"; and so they have not identified characteristics that might have been present at such "beginning." The following pages progress only slightly beyond previous studies, but the questions and suggestions above warrant serious consideration.

COMMON FACTORS. In many respects the states share a common environment. The federal system and certain economic and demographic factors are prominent among the common factors influencing the politics of tax choices.

Federalism. The states in the 20th century have made their tax choices within the context of many common conditions. They are all members of a federal union with unfettered economic exchange. Despite two wars, the Great Depression, and several recessions, we have had increasing affluence, not necessarily equally shared but still general. We have continued to develop as an industrialized, urban nation. Our population has rapidly expanded. The increase in the role of the national government and its vastly changed, relative role in expenditures and taxes have affected all. Such political decisions of the national government affect all of the states, and all of the states have shared in directing the national government forward in this expansion.

In the fields of welfare and highways especially, the states, and this has been with near unanimity again, have in effect asked the national government to extend its program as a means of further development of state programs. We noted earlier that there has been a percentage reduction in the gap between high and low taxing states. The turning point seems to have been the Depression, at least the figures (Table 1) indicate an abrupt reversal of the widening percentage gap from 1913 and 1922 over 1902, to a percentage gap in 1962 apparently as narrow or narrower than any point in the 20th century. In these same years, the national government significantly increased its grants-in-aid to the states, often with conditions that required very little new from the high taxing states but additional effort from the low tax states.

Increasing economic interdependence among the states and great mobility of peoples bring pressures for uniformity. Voters of low service, low tax states may increase governmental demands; the movement of industry, into the South for example, has inevitably brought added governmental demands. The old fears of interstate competition may hold down expansion in government in the high taxing states, thus adding to the movement toward the center.

Interstate competition is a constant touchstone for tax decisions in height and type. What the neighboring states are doing in taxes is almost a beginning and ending point of discussions in political campaigns, in state legislatures, and among many voters. If neighbor A has a sales tax, that is an argument for state B to adopt it. If neighbor C has low per capita taxes, many in state B will argue theirs should be at least as low — but without affecting state services!

Volumes of economic analysis and empirical evidence to the contrary have not eliminated the argument in tax discussions that "high" taxes drive out business and scare new industry away.* We already noted that Congress wrote the 80 per cent state credit against national estate taxes in 1926 at the insistence of states which otherwise might have felt compelled to follow Florida and Nevada in repeal of existing estate taxes. The unemployment compensa-

---

*When pressed, the more knowledgeable tax discussant agrees that taxes are important only on the margins when all other desired conditions, i.e., transportation, raw materials, labor force, etc., are equal. The fact that most locational decisions can more readily be explained in these terms than at the margins has not lessened political use of the argument.

tion tax was enacted nationally in part on the argument that only thereby would most states dare enact the program.

Federalism also makes copyists out of the states. Once a pioneer breaks the old pattern, others may do likewise. The break-through in state income taxation by Wisconsin in 1911 brought a rapid succession of adoptions within a few years. Even somewhat peculiar local technical provisions (such as the Wisconsin method of providing for deduction of dependency exemption by a fixed dollar figure from the calculated tax total that has the effect of increasing progressiveness) reappeared in the Kentucky and Arizona statutes. Adoption of sales taxes also shows a bunched pattern. The creativity of one or two states brought adaptation from many others under the common pressure of the Depression.

Economic and Democratic Factors. A series of studies by economists have identified factors, present to a greater or lesser degree in all the states, to explain the direction and rate of growth in expenditures.[8]

These economists have emphasized, with some dissents in relative emphasis, per capita income, population density, and per cent urban. More recently, Sachs and Harris have added national grants to the states, and state grants to local governments as having a positive relation to increased expenditures. Fisher has suggested that the *proportion* of low income individuals and families may be important in its negative relation to increased expenditures. Each study has stressed that the height of income explains the largest portion of the height of taxes in the several states.†

Understanding of services and their costs lends credence, even without the depth analyses made, to the fact that certain service costs — such as police, fire, health, and certain welfare items — increase with urbanization. Other per capita costs, such as highway and higher education, tend to increase with low population densities. High per capita income and high per capita expenditures, no doubt, tend to relate positively, partly as a reflection of higher "costs of living" and of decisions to improve certain services, such as

*Not only is information transmitted through newspapers and mail correspondence, but it is exchanged at professional meetings of tax economists and tax administrators. Moreover, states from time to time pay for individuals to go and get a first-hand impression. In the case above, an Arizona tax administrator came to Wisconsin and generally liked what he saw. Once the political decision to adopt an income tax was made in Arizona, he was asked to fill in the details and he followed the patterns he had come to know. This is an important political influence not always recognized.
†Economic tests have usually shown a high correlation between industrialization and income. By using "value added by manufacturing" as an index, degree of industrialization was cross checked with high and low tax states. The agreement was no greater than on the income index. Consistently for most years since 1890, New York, California, Ohio, Illinois, Pennsylvania, Michigan, Indiana, Massachusetts, New Jersey, and Wisconsin have been in the top quartile. Both high and low tax states are in this group.

education or highways. However, both federal grants-in-aid and state-local grants appear to be of a different magnitude than the other factors listed. On the one hand, as Fisher states, federal grants perhaps have more often promoted uniformity rather than disparity. On the other hand, state grants to local governments (shared taxes or aids) are a state political decision in a way per capita income, urbanization, and density of population are not. Any relation of aids and shared taxes to the level of taxes may well be dependent on the same conditions that then require explaining.

The economic analysis gives us broad underlying factors that explain moderate diversity within a federal system that has strong pressures for uniformity. The analysis does not explain the extremes where the economic factors are in agreement.

FACTORS OF DIFFERENCE. Under similar general conditions and with intense pressures for uniformity, the fascinating question then arises as to why some states have fairly consistently differed, quite apart from economic characteristics. New York is a highly urbanized, highly industrial state with high per capita income. It has also been a high tax state with general emphasis at the state level on progressive income taxes. Illinois, with all of the same general characteristics, has tended to be a low tax state with emphasis on general sales taxes.

General Political Indexes. The most usual, general political indicators — degree of party competition and which party is in control — are not a good means of distinguishing the highest and lowest tax states. We find the same confusion of political characteristics as of economic factors among these extremes. Of the high tax states, Mississippi is one-party (Democratic); Maine, Vermont, and Wisconsin are modified one-party (Republican); California, Colorado, Massachusetts, New York, Oregon, and Washington are two-party states. Diversity of party competition also characterizes the low tax states. Arkansas and Texas are one-party (Democratic); Kentucky and Virginia are modified-one-party (Democratic); Illinois, Indiana, Missouri, and Nebraska are two-party.[9] The absence of a modified one-party Republican state among the low tax states has seemingly little significance.

Nationally, the Democratic party is more often identified with higher levels of governmental services, hence higher taxes, and with taxes based on ability to pay, thus progressive income taxes.[10] The deviations in state party political philosophies from national do not permit such easy generalizations. And again our high tax states are not predominantly Democratic, nor our low tax states predominantly Republican. Neither do income and sales tax emphasis in state tax systems translate into Democratic and Republican states.

Recognizing tax decisions as political decisions does not restrict us to two broad political indexes. Other facets of political action deserve attention.

First, it seems desirable to brush away a few fairly simple points of tax politics. Taxing units normally do not wish to kill the goose that laid the golden egg. Or in more behavioral terms, major economic interests usually have the political strength to influence legislators to withstand proposals of heavy taxation. Obvious examples come to mind to illustrate the point whichever way it is stated. Wisconsin has been notoriously lenient in taxing the beer industry and in taxing cigar-wrapping tobacco, of which it raises a considerable quantity. The Southeastern states where most of the tobacco is produced tax cigarettes less than the national average. North Carolina does not tax tobacco, and Virginia taxes tobacco at less than one-tenth the national average. California and New York look kindly on their vineyards. The big oil-producing states secure large revenues from this natural resource but not at great disadvantage to the industry. These examples, and they could be multiplied, are seldom party issues within the states. Many votes are involved, and "too high" taxes (one cannot give precision to "too high" in this context) might hurt the industry.

Second, allowing for the ability of special state interests to keep their own taxes down, some states still may have access to substantial tax resources not available generally. Oil, natural gas, iron, timber represent the peculiar taxable possessions of certain states only. Even at low rates, the possessing states may obtain substantial revenue and with the bargain that much of the tax burden is shifted through need by citizens in the other forty-nine states for these same natural resources.

Timing. Since citizens and politicians prefer to avoid taxes whenever possible, governing bodies postpone tax decisions until pressures build up either through heavy expenditure demands or through intense dissatisfaction with current taxes. In fact, heavy expenditure demands may create intense dissatisfaction with particular taxes. States in the first forty years of the 20th century reacted to the combined pressures of demands for expanded state services and disenchantment with the property tax as an equitable state tax in an industrial economy.

The timing of major tax decisions influences the tax choice. It may also be true that a tax consensus is delayed until the time permits a particular choice. All of the major income tax states made the decision to use the income tax before World War II, three before 1920, and the others early in the Depression. Usually adoption of the tax represented victory for tax equity "reform" and expanded state services. The Depression spawned sales taxes in states innocent of Keynesian economics. The states needed revenues. States without income taxes saw here a broad-based, low-rate tax that seemed to have revenue dependability. Even a number of states with income taxes added sales taxes to give stability to tumbling revenues.

Whatever the individual state tax choices, they proved more than sufficiently productive in the war years when tax revenues increased with the expanding economy and war-time controls prevented state and local governments from attacking backlogs of building and highway needs. As the income tax had faltered in the Depression, it now responded handsomely to prosperity, and income tax states especially found it possible to develop financial reserves. Often the major state tax actions in this era centered around modifications of state income tax statutes to accord with federal. A number of states removed or reduced the older privilege of state taxpayers to deduct federal income taxes — with the new high federal rates, deductibility would drain off much of the largesse of good times. Only in the 1950's and 1960's have expenditure needs again pressed tax revenue systems and required either higher rates for old taxes or additional taxes. In this last popularity contest, the sales tax has normally won.

In the early state adoption of income taxes, support came from articulate labor groups and populist, liberal reform elements. Although business opposition was general, income tax supporters could often bring combinations together. Before World War II, farmers frequently supported state income taxes. The Colorado Depression income tax was said to be the result of the coalition of the railroads and the farmers who wanted out from the property tax and often had no income to be taxed. Since World War II, the continuing height of national income tax rates and perhaps the general affluence have helped to dim the older appeals to equity of progressive state taxation.*

Sales tax support came largely from the opponents of income taxes, but again timing affected the coalitions. Typically in all periods, retail merchants who bear half or more of the "nuisance" of sales taxes strongly opposed adoption at least until they were guaranteed a percentage (usually 1 or 2) of their collections as recompense. Farm groups with more income

*Proof that affluence loses income tax adherents is difficult to establish. Conforming to many of our assumptions, a recent Wisconsin study indicated decreasing support, with increase in income, for an income tax as the major revenue source. The same finding held true where the question concerned tax preference for raising additional state revenue. The shift came at the $8,000–$10,000 family income bracket. [Leon D. Epstein, *Voters and Taxes* (Madison: University of Wisconsin Press, 1964) Table 33, p. 59.] The fact that the steep progressive rates of many state income tax programs have been amended very little, if at all, from their original enactment to reflect the changing concepts of low, middle, and high incomes (and as a result apply the top rate at the $10,000–$15,000 level) may have aggravated the tendency.

after the Depression could sometimes be brought to support a sales tax or at least to remain neutral if many farm purchases, such as machinery and feed grains, were exempt.

States then that made early choices of major new taxes chose the income tax, while states choosing during the Depression and even more since World War II have more often turned to the sales tax as their major revenue source. Once the decision is made, there is seldom a reversal. Most of our major political decisions do not get reargued every new legislative session — rather decisions are cumulative. The choice of major tax dependence is by any standard an important political decision, often one that is debated through several gubernatorial and legislative campaigns before a consensus is developed. Sniping, simply in the form of oratory or more concretely in attempted or successful modification of particular provisions, may subsequently occur, but repeal of the tax work of a carefully constructed legislative majority almost never develops. Even rate structures and exemptions become sacred. Supporters and opponents adjust to the new taxes and later may regard them as the only acceptable way.*

TAX CHOICES AND OTHER POLICY DECISIONS. If tax choices are major policy decisions, we should expect some consistency between the type of tax choice made and other policies adopted. If levying high taxes is a "liberal" policy decision, have these states adopted other "liberal" programs? Conversely, if levying "low" taxes is a conservative policy decision, have these states adopted other "conservative" programs?†

Relation of Tax Choices to Policies. At least until recent years, most laymen would have labelled the income tax as "liberal" legislation and the sales tax as "conservative." Similarly, a "high" tax state would be presumed to be "liberal" and a "low" tax state "conservative."

In attempting to classify other legislative actions as "liberal" or "conservative" and in turn to compare such actions with tax decisions, leadership in early adoptions and in some cases "liberal" provisions of such measures are emphasized. Also included are some "conservative" items together with a few items that would not easily classify as either. The selection omits (1)

---

*Such behavior may have a degree of economic rationality, as economists see the economy so absorbing many taxes over a period of time that eventually "no one" and "everyone" pays them. Again this is less true of individual income and retail sales taxes.

†It is recognized that scholars and laymen are not agreed on a general classification of "liberal" and "conservative" policies. Consequently, each of the items which follows is classified separately as "liberal" or "conservative" in the manner that most writers have dealt with the policy under discussion.

functions and programs where federal aid may influence the adoption and direction, and (2) the large program generators of expenditures — education, highways, and welfare.

Tax Policies. We begin by noting there is some consistency in liberal or conservative tax decisions, since nine of the eleven high tax states levy income taxes and five of these high tax states are also five of the high income tax states. Of the eight consistently low tax states, six levy sales taxes and four would be classified as having particularly regressive tax systems. Not all states are consistent in these terms: The high tax states of Washington and Maine depend heavily on the sales tax and have no income tax, and the low tax state of Virginia has no sales tax and depends heavily on the income tax.

Labor Legislation. Massachusetts led the states in the 19th century with the earliest legislation to protect the health and welfare of industrial workers, especially children. The concern for working conditions in the second decade of the 20th century brought forty-two states to adopt workmen's compensation legislation within a span of nine years. Yet the progress of the states in the field did not match the developing national pressures, and the Depression witnessed the general transfer of much of the leadership to the national government. Distinctions among the states today lie largely in the liberality of provisions and coverage of workmen's compensation and unemployment compensation provisions, special provisions covering hours and working conditions for women and children, the existence and coverage of state minimum wage legislation, and whether or not the state has adopted "right-to-work" legislation. Comparisons of detailed provisions offer complexities not yet measured on a satisfactory comparative scale. Detail for high and low tax states has been presented here on only two labor items: minimum wage and right-to-work laws.

Of the high tax states, all but Mississippi have enacted minimum wage legislation, much of it going back to 1913 or earlier. Among the fifty states in 1961, 38.5 per cent of employed workers (excluding domestics) were not covered by minimum wages either of the federal government or the states. In the high tax states, eight of the twelve states show as much or greater coverage than this average. In Massachusetts, only 10.9 per cent of private employees were not covered by state and federal legislation; Oregon was precisely average with 38.5 per cent; but California, Colorado, and Mississippi were above average, with Mississippi showing 58.2 per cent of private employees not covered by federal legislation and with no state protection.

In contrast, all of the low tax states were above average in the proportion of employees not covered by minimum wage legislation, and only Arkansas and Kentucky had any minimum wage statutes.

Table 8

HIGH AND LOW TAX STATES AND OTHER POLITICAL DECISIONS, 1962

States	Emphasis (a)	TAXES Year of Adoption	Quality of Administration (b)	MINIMUM WAGE Year of Adoption (c)	% Not Covered by U.S. of State (d)	DATES OF ADOPTION OF SELECTED LEGISLATION				
						Right-to-Work Legislation (e)	Public Accommodations (f)	Fair Employment Practices (g)	Open Occupancy (f)	General Merit (h)
TOTAL STATES				(27)	(38.5)	(19)	(27)	(25)	(9)	(32)
"HIGH" TAX STATES										
Calif.	3	Income 1935 / Sales 1933	10	1913	40.3		1897	1959		1913
Colo.	2	Income 1937 / Sales 1935	30	1913	45.1		1885	1957		1907
Hawaii	3	Income 1901 / Sales 1933	(no eval.)	1955	22.1			1963		1960
Me.	3	Sales 1951	20	1939	15.4			....		1937
Mass.	1	Income 1916	20	1912	10.9		1865	1946	1957	1885
Miss.	2	Income 1912 / Sales 1932	30	....	58.2	1954	....	....	....	....
N.Y.	1	Income 1919	10	1933	22.3		1874	1945	1955	1883
Ore.	1	Income 1913	10	1913	38.5		1953	1949	1957	1940
Vt.	1	Income 1931	10	1957	25.8		1957	1963		1939
Wash.	4	Sales 1935	20	1913	17.6		1890	1949		1960
Wis.*	1	Income 1911 / Sales 1962	10	1913	26.5		1895	1957		1905
"LOW" TAX STATES										
Ark.	2	Income 1929 / Sales 1935	20	1915	61.9	1944–47	....	....	....	....

| State | TAXES | | | MINIMUM WAGE | | DATES OF ADOPTION OF SELECTED LEGISLATION | | | | |
	Emphasis (a)	Year of Adoption	Quality of Administration (b)	Year of Adoption (c)	% Not Covered by U.S. of State (d)	Right-to-Work Legislation (e)	Public Accommodations (f)	Fair Employment Practices (g)	Open Occupancy (f)	General Merit (h)
Ill.	4	Sales 1933	20	....	46.8		1885	1961		1905
Ind.*	4	Sales 1934	(no eval.)	....	41.7	1957	1885	1963	....	....
Ky.	2	Income 1936	30	1938	47.8					1960
		Sales 1960	(no eval.)							
Mo.	2	Income 1917	30		50.1			1961		
		Sales 1934	(no eval.)							
Nebr.		....	..	....	59.0	1947	1885			
Tex.	4	Sales 1961	(no eval.)		55.7	1947				
Va.	1	Income 1916	30		52.3	1947				1942

a. A judgment, see Table 6 for comment. 1 = progressive (high income tax use); 2 = neutral, leaning toward progressive; 3 = neutral, leaning toward regressive; 4 = regressive (high sales tax use).

b. Clara Penniman and Walter W. Heller, State Income Tax Administration (Chicago: Public Administration Service, 1959) Table 1, p. 3. And John F. Due, State Sales Tax Administration (Chicago: Public Administration Service, 1963) Table 1, p. 3. The ratings — 10 = high, 20 = middle, 30 = lowest quality of administration based on a judgment made from research on the income tax and evaluation of Due's appraisals, pp. 127–130.

c. State Minimum Wage Laws and Orders, Women's Bureau Bulletin 267, Revised January 1, 1963, Part II: "Analysis of Rates and Coverage," U.S. Department of Labor, Women's Bureau (Washington: U.S. Government Printing Office, 1963) pp. 1–107.

d. Congressional Quarterly, Week ending March 31, 1961, p. 518.

e. U.S. Department of Labor, Bureau of Labor Standards, Bulletin No. 204, May 1959, p. 4, and The Book of the States.

f. Theodore Leskes, "State Law Against Discrimination," in Milton R. Konvitz, A Century of Civil Rights (New York: Columbia University Press, 1961) pp. 155–159, 197–203, 225–230, 236–240.

g. The Book of the States, 1964-65, fn. 3, p. 523.

h. The Book of the States, 1964-65, pp. 178-181.

*Wisconsin adopted a limited sales tax in 1962 and Indiana adopted a flat rate income tax in 1963. These actions may subsequently affect the degrees of progressive-regressive characteristics of each state's tax system.

Right-to-work statutes, in effect prohibiting the closed union shop and considered by labor as anti-union, came up for action in many states following World War II. Mississippi alone of the high tax states has adopted right-to-work legislation, whereas five of the low tax states have adopted right-to-work laws. Although Southern states are prominent in right-to-work legislative adoptions, Indiana and Nebraska have also done so. In the nation as a whole, a number of other Northern and Western states have passed right-to-work statutes.

Human Rights Legislation. Following the Civil War, many Northern states continued to express their sympathy with Negroes by adopting public accommodations statutes to assure equality of services in hotels, restaurants, and other businesses. Enforcement varied and sometimes was non-existent but, in the post-World War II period, these old statutes have often been revived as the basis for further civil rights action. Also since World War II more than two dozen states have adopted fair employment legislation with some enforcement provisions, and a few states have adopted open occupancy statutes to assist in equalizing housing opportunities.

As we would expect, the Southern states, whether among high or low tax states, have not adopted any of these human rights measures. The high tax states, however, represent a third or more of all the states in the Union that have adopted human rights legislation in the three areas. Three low tax states have public accommodation statutes, and three have fair employment laws.

State Administration. The quality of tax administration and the existence of statewide merit systems do not qualify as either liberal or conservative. It is, nevertheless, of interest to find that the high tax states include a large proportion of the well-administered tax systems and the established merit systems. This should remove any suspicion, if it existed, that high tax states are high due to unusual administrative "inefficiencies." A slight relationship seems to exist between low taxes and lower quality administration, at least for the measures used here.

This policy analysis indicates that, "in general," the states tend to be consistently liberal or conservative in tax policies and in the labor and human rights fields. Further analysis of details of policies and their enforcement might tighten classifications and increase the agreement. Further analysis might also find that the hypothesis needs modification to account for special circumstances that may offset the general pattern. For example, Illinois may be a low tax state as a result of decisions made years ago, but no party could stay in power in such an industrial state without some attention to measures sought by laborers.

CONCLUSIONS

Federalism provides a framework and pressures for such similar political and economic conditions among the states that the large majority make fairly similar tax decisions, both as to level of taxation and choice of taxes. Most differences among this large majority of states presumably can be explained, as several economists have done, in terms of differences in levels of income and, to a lesser extent, by such factors as urbanization and population density.

We have concentrated our attention on the high and low tax states at the extremes — where differences persist that the economic analysis does not seem adequate to explain fully. We found:

1. The relative standing of states as high, low, or moderate appears to persist even though the absolute amount of taxes has changed significantly over the century. This confirms repeated assertions that citizens accept customary levels of taxation.[11]

2. Although the trend in taxes has been steadily upward, particular periods have shown strong upward pressures amounting to steps. This again confirms other studies that the customary tax levels will be shifted only with major crises.[12]

3. The broad political factors of degree of party competition and which political party is in control do not distinguish high and low tax states appreciably better than the economic factors. We recognized that individual states will have particular tax provisions (or tax leniency) as a result of major, influential economic interests different from those present in other states.

4. High tax states are more likely to depend on the income tax exclusively or extensively than the low tax states. The low tax states normally depend exclusively on the sales tax. But exceptions persist.

5. The attempt to relate high taxes with selected liberal legislation and low taxes with conservative legislation met with only limited agreement. Further refinements, including detailed analysis of provisions, administration of other labor legislation, and perhaps of additional areas, such as public utility regulation, are needed to establish whether or not a relationship exists.

6. Finally, the timing of tax decisions may constitute a critical point in our political analysis that requires extended study. We need thorough analysis of the political and economic conditions existing in the states when these critical decisions were made and the differentiating circumstances that delayed or prevented similar decisions in other states.

NOTES

1. National Municipal League, *Salient Issues of Constitutional Revision* (1961) p. 136, quoted by Advisory Commission on Intergovernmental Relations, *State Constitutional and Statutory Restrictions on Local Taxing Powers* (1962) p. 7.
2. The assumption both of scholars and interest groups has been generally that "segregated," "dedicated," or "earmarked" funds advantaged the program. An important modification is suggested by James M. Buchanan, "The Economics of Ear-Marked Taxes," *Journal of Political Economy,"* Vol. LXXI (October 1963).
3. Taken from Table 45, pp. 138–139, the Advisory Commission on Intergovernmental Relations, *A Staff Report: Measures of State and Local Fiscal Capacity and Tax Effort* (Washington: U.S. Government Printing Office, October 1962). The fact that these figures include local income taxes would have almost no effect on relationships in view of the very low local government income taxes.
4. See Table 43, pp. 133–134, *supra.*
5. The Advisory Commission on Intergovernmental Relations, *Measures of State and Local Fiscal Capacity and Tax Effort.* See especially chapter 5, pp. 73–85.
6. Alan T. Peacock and Jack Wiseman, *The Growth of Public Expenditures in the United Kingdom* (Princeton: Princeton University Press, 1961); see especially chapter 2, pp. 12–34.
7. Seymour Sachs and Robert Harris, "The Determinants of State and Local Government Expenditures and Intergovernmental Flows of Funds," *National Tax Journal,* Vol. XVII, No. 1.
8. See especially Solomon Fabricant, *The Trend of Government Activity in the United States Since 1900* (New York: National Bureau of Economic Research, Inc., 1952); Glenn W. Fisher, "Interstate Variation in State and Local Government Expenditure"; and Sachs and Harris, *op. cit.,* both articles in *National Tax Journal,* Vol. XVII, No. 1.
9. See Table 1, chapter 3, of this book.
10. Herbert McClosky, Paul J. Hoffman, and Rosemary O'Hara, "Issue Conflict and Consensus Among Party Leaders and Followers," *American Political Science Review LIV* (June 1960) especially 414.
11. Peacock and Wiseman, *loc. cit.*
12. *Ibid.*

SELECTED BIBLIOGRAPHY

Advisory Commission on Intergovernmental Relations. *A Staff Report: Measures of State and Local Fiscal Capacity and Tax Effort.* Washington: U.S. Government Printing Office, October 1962. An excellent analysis of tax systems among the states and the relative use states make of various taxes of their own resources.

Burkhead, Jesse. *State and Local Taxes for Public Education.* Syracuse: Syracuse University Press, 1963. Although the focus is on all sources of taxes for education, the main emphasis is an analysis of the property tax and its use over a period of time.

Due, John F. *State Sales Tax Administration.* Chicago: Public Administration Service, 1963. Provides a general historical and economic setting for sales taxes in the states as well as detailed analysis of administration.

Fabricant, Solomon. *The Trend of Government Activity in the United States Since 1900.* New York: National Bureau of Economic Research, Inc., 1952. This is the "classic" in the area of economic analysis of state and local, as well as national, expenditures in this country.

National Bureau of Economic Research, a report. *Public Finances: Needs, Sources, and Utilization.* Princeton: Princeton University Press, 1961. This is a fairly technical, economic analysis of expenditure and tax policy at all levels of American government by a number of leading economists.

Peacock, Alan T., and Jack Wiseman. *The Growth of Public Expenditures in the United Kingdom.* Princeton: Princeton University Press, 1961. This is the British companion to the Fabricant United States' analysis. Both are worthwhile for insights and methodology, as well as for findings.

Penniman, Clara, and Walter W. Heller. *State Income Tax Administration.* Chicago: Public Administration Service, 1959. Provides a general historical and economic setting for income taxes in the states, as well as detailed analysis of administration.

STATE
POLITICS
AND EDUCATION

CHAPTER 9
by
ROBERT H. SALISBURY

IN 1961 STATE AND LOCAL GOVERNMENTS SPENT 5 per cent of the personal income of their citizens on education. Thirty-six and six-tenths per cent of the total expenditures of state and local governments was devoted to public education. The sum of $112.40 was spent on schools for each person in the nation, and $432.00 was spent for each pupil in average daily attendance in public school.[1] These figures suggest the magnitude of the education function performed by state and local governments. Only 3.2 per cent of the revenue (1962–63) for elementary and secondary schools comes from the federal government. Education not only involves vast expenditures of money but it also involves many of the major social and political controversies of the mid–20th century. Whether the issue is the international competition between the U.S.S.R. and the United States, racial segregation, church-state relations, or "Why Johnny Can't Read," the school system is at the center of the discussion.

We cannot hope to deal with all the important issues which impinge on education or are affected by the school system in the course of a single chapter. We shall focus on only a few of the most central questions. Particularly, we shall concentrate on an examination of which states spend more and which states spend less on their schools, and we shall try to explain why. To do so requires us to look at the historical background of today's school systems, the group interests and pressures that operate, as well as interstate variations in expenditure. We must remember that education is a function of both state and local authority, and one question of continuing importance concerns the balance between state and local authority, and the conditions under which it changes.

We shall examine public higher education and identify interstate variations in this field which, in terms of interests and political processes, is largely separate from the elementary and secondary school issues. Finally, we shall look briefly at some of the major social issues which, though in a sense tangential, are intertwined with the politics of public education.

THE RISE OF THE PUBLIC SCHOOL

The educational system has been the object of important political con troversy almost since the first settlers landed on the shores of North America. The extent to which governmental authority should be invoked to requir education, make public money available for it, or indoctrinate through th schools is among the oldest American political questions. In 1642, for ex ample, the Massachusetts General Court directed parents to see to it tha their children received a basic education, and in 1647 Massachusetts town were required to establish schools. These initial steps were, in time, followe by other colonies — with important differences among them — until, by th early days of the Republic, every state constitution included some recognitio that education was a responsibility of the state.

The notion that education was a public matter was originally founded o the conception that among the state's primary duties was the maintenance o religious orthodoxy. Each colony tended to be religiously homogenous, an it was not difficult to accept the view that compulsory public education, unde suitable auspices, could reinforce the training received in the church. Th result would be a literate population better able to develop the opportunitie of colonial life and also more articulate and learned in their faith.

This view had much to do with the initial structures established fo school systems. In much of the South the Church of England was dominar and was regarded as the institution primarily responsible for both secula and religious education. School *systems* were organized for the whole of colony relying on the episcopal structure of the church for the units of organ ization, rather than on secular entities like the county. Southern *civil* autho ities were regarded as responsible only for educating orphans or apprentice or other young people unable to utilize the private schools run by the Churc of England. In New England, on the other hand, the congregational struc ture of the dominant religious group lacked any centralized authority throug which to establish schools, and so governmental authority was invoked t implement the educational goals of the Puritan ideal.

Despite the early recognition of the principle of state responsibilit however, during the 17th and 18th centuries local bodies came more an more into effective control of their own educational destinies. In the 18 century, especially during the Great Awakening of the 1740's, the growt of religious heterodoxy throughout the colonies undercut the original reaso for having publicly supported schools, the propagation of the true faith. there were several competing denominations in a colony, then the only a ceptable form of public education was local control of schools according locally predominant sentiment. The result was that colonial or state autho ity was extensively delegated to county (in the South), town, or distri agencies to establish and maintain schools as they chose. Where state monies were provided for local schools they were turned over to local bodies, often even to religious groups, to run the schools according to whatever the prevailing local conditions might require.

Needless to say, the result of such extreme decentralization was that school "systems" varied enormously in quality. Southern *public* schools were generally less well supported than those in New England since they were primarily designed as charity institutions. By no means everyone outside the South was agreed on the desirability of public education, however. As a rudimentary class structure began to differentiate those with greater wealth from those with less, the potential impact of public education upon the social structure became a matter of controversy. Groups argued that general public education would destroy the structure of privilege and open opportunity to all or, alternatively, that it would undercut the roots of wisdom which higher status provided and thereby threaten the stability of the social order. Thus, where the school system had been an object of religious controversy, during the first half of the 19th century it also became embroiled in the socio-economic conflicts of the day.

Implicit in both types of controversy was the assumption that education was not a neutral force but one that would benefit some groups at the expense of others. A dominant religious denomination could reinforce its position through public education. A dominant social class might protect its position by resisting public education. In a state with diverse interests — religious and social — public education might languish as each minority feared that schools would threaten their position. It required the growth of new ideas: that a broadly democratic society could allow all groups to pursue their interests; that education could provide skills essential for this pursuit; that schools could be instruments of secular instruction which need not affect directly the articles of religious or group faith; in short, that general public education was possible and desirable in a society of diverse and conflicting interests — for public schools to become a *fully* accepted part of the American scene.

These articles of public belief were, of course, part of the Jacksonian creed which came to prominence, indeed dominance, in the decades prior to the Civil War. Jacksonian Democracy took root more easily, in regard to schools as well as other issues, in the trans-Appalachian west. The growth of genuinely public schools, supported by public money, controlled by public officials, and open to everyone, found relatively easy acceptance in the West. Especially was this true in the Northwest Territory where the Northwest Ordinance of 1787 provided that one-sixteenth of one section of each township be set aside for support of public schools. Similar provisions were included in other federal grants of land in the new states. But frontier life also frequently bred an "anti-book-larnin" spirit. Furthermore, the social and political complexion of the various parts of the new West reflected in many ways the origins of the settlers. Identification with a political party, attitudes toward slavery, inclinations toward religious denomination and constitutional theory, and, not the least, attitudes toward schools reflected the divergent conceptions and institutions of New England and the Southern states.

Considerable variety had already developed among the older states, as we have seen. Public education was more firmly and widely established in New England than in the South. Moreover, the local school district had been widely adopted to provide for and control New England schools, while the county remained the Southern unit of administration. Generally, until the Civil War, publicly financed education in the South — with North Carolina a partial exception — was primarily charity for the poor.

In the North we find Massachusetts enunciating the principle of general tax support for schools in 1789; Connecticut establishing a school money fund from the proceeds of the sales of public land in 1795; New York providing state funds to match local money in 1812. These early efforts, however, fell far short of achieving completely free common schools, and another half-century of effort was required before schools entirely supported by public money were available even to the children of New York.

THE EMERGENCE OF STATE CONTROL. The task was not simply to establish the principle of free public education but also to create mechanisms which would make the principle effective. The problem of quality in education began to rear its head along with the related problem of equality among districts within a state. Extreme decentralization of the educational function had led to a bewildering variety of pattern and achievement. This was partly a result of the great variations among religious, nationality and private academy groups that controlled the schools in particular localities. Partly it was a result of inequalities of resources and commitments to education among various sections of each state. Partly, too, it was a result of the lack of centralized leadership and focus. The key developments of the pre-Civil War era in public education in one way or another all attacked these problems.

The assertion of public control by placing the schools in the hands of public agencies supported by public money was one side of the development. This, in turn, led to a neutralizing of the curriculum by removing its theological elements and underplaying controversial political and social themes. If the schools were to be a public function they had to function on the common ground of social consensus. Further, public control was sooner or later to mean establishing minimum standards of competence in educational offering. Otherwise, public money would be spent without any standards of achievement to guide the decisions. The effort to raise and equalize standards led to the establishment of state agencies to provide leadership and stimulation. None of these changes occurred easily or without opposition, but by about 1850 all Northern and Western states had accomplished them, and a few of the states in the Old South had moved part way along the path.

New York led the way in the formal creation of state agencies for educational leadership. The Board of Regents of the University of the State of New York was established in 1784, and in 1812 New York established the first state superintendent of schools. In terms of effective, standard-setting state leadership, Massachusetts under Horace Mann and Connecticut under Henry Barnard were in the vanguard. The Massachusetts Board of Education was established in 1837 and Mann was named as the first secretary. Barnard accepted a similar assignment in Connecticut in 1839. For twelve years Mann used all the devices available to him to raise standards throughout the state. He organized teacher institutes, held public meetings to stimulate lay support, argued his case in annual reports to the legislature, and published the biweekly *Common School Journal*. Although there was much opposition to Mann's work — often labeled "Prussianization" of the schools at the expense of local control — Mann and Barnard did succeed in establishing and legitimizing an active role in education for state authority.

In the post-Civil War era the vital decisions affecting both quality and quantity of public education were made increasingly by the states. Although the extent of financial support, the hiring and firing of teachers, and details of the curriculum continued to be decided largely at the local level, more and more educational standards were set by state authorities.

In the post-bellum South it was difficult to legislate at all in order to raise educational quality. The Southern states had a much weaker tradition of public education and they were now confronted by two further inhibiting factors, dire poverty and the race problem. Not until nearly the end of the century was segregation firmly established, deferring indefinitely the fears of Southerners who equated public schools with integration. By 1900 various philanthropic agencies, particularly the Rockefeller-sponsored General Education Board, began their efforts to upgrade Southern education, but by this time an enormous gap had been opened between most Southern school systems and those elsewhere in the country.

Outside the South, rapid strides were being made. Compulsory school attendance laws were passed as early as 1852 in Massachusetts and thirty-two states had them by 1900. Compulsory attendance presaged many other changes, of course, one of which was the enlargement of the public school systems to include high schools and universities. The high school grew rapidly in the 1870's and 1880's, coming to displace the older private academies

but also to serve the ever-growing school population of all social levels, instead of only the college preparatory students. This same period, roughly
1865–1900, is also the period of rapid growth of parochial schools.

The great growth in school attendance of the post-Civil War era required further development of the mechanisms of leadership and control. By
1880 all thirty-eight states had established a position of chief state educational officer, and all these officers found that their functions were increasing.
School consolidation as a means of increasing the quality of education was
specifically permitted by Massachusetts in 1869, and by 1910 a majority of
the states had permissive consolidation statutes. In some, indeed, substantial
consolidation of districts had been achieved. By 1911, a majority of the
states had laws relating to teacher certification, and in many states *only* the
state could certify a teacher.

An important assist in providing for over-all state control of standards
was given by the state universities. Beginning with the University of Michigan
in 1870 and spreading rapidly to other states, students graduating from public schools accredited by the state university were automatically admitted to
the university. Thus, the state school officials and the state universities could
work together to establish and enforce minimum standards of teacher training
and curriculum which local school authorities were bound to accept.

The ultimate lever for setting standards, of course, was money. In 1890
as now, state patterns of school support varied widely. Generally, in the
South the states provided a larger portion and the local units a smaller proportion of the total expenditures than in other parts of the country. The
over-all level of expenditures, however, was much higher in those states with
longer and stronger public school traditions: New England, New York, and
the upper middle west. In addition, the states where Progressivism was strong
expressed that ethos through generous support for schools. But the growth
of large urban centers within many of these states led to new sources of variation and complexity in educational systems and new sources of conflict over
the kind of program and the means of support to be used.

We shall examine the present patterns of state support for schools later
in the chapter. Suffice it to say for the moment that the imprint of the historical development we have described is still clearly visible today.

THE STRUCTURE OF STATE SCHOOL DECISIONS

From 1787 to the present the federal government has played a role in
public education. Periodically, direct support from federal money or land
has been given to the states for schools. In the 20th century a series of programs has been adopted providing support for specialized educational functions, such as vocational education or foreign language training. Though no
legislation providing broad grants to public schools has to date become law

such legislation has been seriously proposed more or less regularly since the Civil War.[3] No federal program or authority, moreover, has provided American education with common administrative structures, standardized curricula, or uniform systems of financial support. Each state has made these decisions on its own authority. Yet it is remarkable that out of the welter of state and local experiences a high degree of consistency has developed in these matters.

THE STATE BOARD. All states except Michigan, Illinois, and Wisconsin have state boards of education with general supervisory authority over the administration of the states' educational programs.[4] In some states a variety of boards may deal with specialized fragments of the program, but by far the most common arrangement is to have one board with broad responsibility. Until recently, almost all boards were appointed, usually by the governor. During the past decade, however, the number of popularly elected boards has tripled, from three to nine. As of 1961, in twenty-three states the board appoints the chief state school officer, more than twice as many as in 1947. The tendency seems to be, therefore, to vest increasing responsibility for over-all direction of state educational affairs in a board which will be directly responsive to the electorate.

Some boards are important in the decision-making process. The New York Board of Regents, for example, is the oldest state board of education, is probably the most powerful, and certainly has the most prestige. Its members are chosen by the legislature for thirteen-year terms! The result is substantial autonomy and substantial power over school administration in New York.

Yet it is unusual for the state board to "run" the schools of a state. As Bailey, *et al.,* point out, state boards:

> . . . are less independent forces in their own right than sympathetic responders to the executive and administrative officials they oversee.
> . . . strong commissioners of education, exercising forceful professional leadership, have a ready sounding-board and supporting officialdom in their state boards.[5]

The Board may serve as an ultimate court of appeals for contending groups or as a device for recruiting lay spokesmen for education interests. But it rarely exercises power to match its authority.

THE STATE SCHOOL OFFICER. The operating head of the state system is the chief state school officer, who may be called commissioner or superintendent or something similar. The authority of this officer varies, of course, from state to state, but generally he and his department perform two types of functions: first, the provision of specialized technical service, advice, and information to local school officials; and second, the establishment and en-forcement of minimum local school standards with regard to curriculum, teacher certification, school construction, and other aspects of school admin-istration. The former category of service is difficult for all but the largest and wealthiest local districts to provide for themselves, and gradually through the years local districts have come to rely on the state department for help in accounting methods, building plans, personnel programs, and a variety of other matters ancillary to the primary concern of education. Of course, the department also provides guidance on curriculum, teaching aids, testing methods, and a host of other matters. In many state departments research of various kinds is carried on to assist the development of educational tech-niques. It may be noted that the districts most in need of this kind of help and least able to provide for it themselves are the rural or outstate districts, and it is generally these which develop the closest working relationships with the state departments.

The standard-setting functions of the state department involve substan-tially greater exercise of power and hence more conflict. Much of the author-ity of the state department derives from the fact that it is the agency which disburses money to the local districts. Programs of federal aid and state aid both, whether categorical aid like vocational education or N.D.E.A., or gen-eral assistance like the state foundation programs, are administered by the state departments. They set many of the standards by which the money is to be given out, and to get the money the local district must meet the stan-dards. As a result, disputes over how many hours of education courses a prospective teacher must take in order to receive a certificate usually revolve around the state department and chief state school officer. They are rarely legislative issues.

The state departments of education are thus arenas of significant con-flict or potential conflict. There are strong tendencies, however, to repress much of this conflict and preserve the appearance of non-political administra-tion, devoted only to elevating the professional standards of education. With state money as the lever, state educational administrators have come to domi-nate the local districts with respect to standards for recruitment and promo-tion of personnel and, in the process, have exercised great influence over the training programs for teachers. Recent critics of American education have charged that the result has been to create an "interlocking directorate of educationists" who eliminate intellectual substance from teacher training in favor of trivial courses in teaching methods.[6] Yet the rationale behind standard-setting is the desire to raise minimum preparation, to eliminate the untrained teacher, to assure the technical competence to organize courses and control classes, etc. Moreover, by requiring technical teacher training as necessary for certification (and certified teachers as necessary for a school to receive state money), more uniformity of experience and identification can be achieved among teachers and this, in turn, can lead to greater professionalism among them.[7] In any case, the institutional heart of the system is the state department of education.

The educational administrators in the state departments do not work in a vacuum, of course. They act on behalf of or with reference to "the educational establishment" — the teachers, the teachers of teachers, the school administrators, the school boards, and other groups more or less deeply involved in the issues of public education. We shall examine these interests in greater detail, but here we should note that state departments and chief school officers are invariably recruited from the ranks of the professional educators. Generally, they come from professional backgrounds that make them sensitive to the needs of the less developed parts of the state school system — the rural areas rather than the metropolitan centers, for example. Insofar as public school educators are in substantial agreement among themselves, the state department may act vigorously and with confidence that its clientele supports its action. Where the clientele is split, the state department may often reflect the split by its own inaction. To understand the administrative politics of education, therefore, it is necessary to look at its clientele.

In concluding this brief discussion of the structure of the decision-making, we should note the role of the legislature and the governor. They are ultimately the authoritative decision-makers on all matters, of course, but, in effect and often explicitly, they have delegated considerable authority to the state boards and/or departments. The ultimate issue, however, in education as in so many matters, is finance — how much money will be available, how is it to be raised and, broadly, who will get it. These are questions that governors and legislators cannot delegate. Accordingly, these agencies are the sites of regular conflicts among educational groups and between them and other interests over money.

MONEY AND SCHOOLS, THE FOUNDATION PROGRAM

The overriding issue in public education is money. Other questions and conflicts may often be present, too, but nearly all of them are shaped by the consideration of finance. Is there a rural-urban split? This takes the form of disputing how much state aid should go to the cities as against the rural areas. Is there opposition to school district consolidation? This is likely to be expressed as sentiment pro or con some state aid formula. Does the religious question intrude? This is manifested mainly in arguments over aid to parochial schools, parents, or students. Money provides the leverage for upgrading teacher preparation, for improving curricula, and for reorganizing the structure of education.

As we have seen, the historical growth of state responsibility for public education was accomplished largely by the use of money — state money dispensed to local schools. By 1900 every state provided significant aid to local schools, but most did so with bewildering varieties of techniques and programs. Through the years each state had tended to work out ways of either giving special assistance to poor districts or providing incentives to greater local effort, or both. Not until 1905, however, with the publication of Ellwood Cubberley's study, *School Funds and Their Apportionment*,[8] were these common denominators brought into focus. Cubberley conveyed intellectual order to the diverse practices then in existence, and during the next two decades professional educators labored hard to explore further the possibility of articulating general principles to govern state aid to schools. Many of these efforts centered around the faculty of Columbia University's Teachers College as its members assisted state after state in studying present practice and recommending future direction. Men like George Strayer, Robert Haig, and Paul Mort were especially influential, and out of their efforts was developed the conception of the *foundation program* which continues to dominate the discussion of state aid today.[9]

Essentially, a foundation program is a formula which sets forth the particular pattern of support the state proposes to give its local schools. The formula of one state may vary greatly from that in a neighboring state, but when adopted into law the foundation formula provides a continuing basis for allocating state money. It sets a minimum total amount and prescribes the bases for dividing the total among local districts.

The formulae embodied in a foundation program generally have one feature in common — a stress on equalization. Clearly expressed by Strayer and Haig, the equalization principle calls upon the state to assure a satisfactory minimum program in every district. The local district would raise as much of the cost as its resources permit and a wealthy district might finance its entire program. State aid would go to all the districts that were below the top in resources. Equalization does not provide incentive to encourage districts to make more than the minimum effort, and many foundation programs include a good deal more than equalization. Nevertheless, the concept of equalization leading toward a minimum educational program throughout the state has been central in developing foundation systems.

The advantages of having a foundation formula are substantial. First, it brings system and order, though often of a very complex kind, to the business of state aid to local schools. The rationale underlying the state programs is made explicit, the relationship of state to local programs is clearly set forth, and, in the process, a very large part of the discussion of educational policy is converted, by formula, into dollar values. That is, with a foundation program, it is possible to set a figure of, say, $300 per pupil in average daily attendance as the desired minimum, compare this with other states, assess the revenue requirements necessary to meet the figure, evaluate local district support, and, in short, make concrete and tangible a host of thorny policy questions.

The second great advantage of the foundation concept is that once a formula is written into state law, further discussion can be centered on the simpler issue of more or less aid, rather than ranging over all the possible combinations of support programs that might be possible. The foundation program concept has greatly simplified the agenda of state policy-making for the public schools. In so doing, the political struggles over state aid to schools have likewise been made simpler and more manageable. To those groups with the greatest active interest in the issue, the professional educators, this is a great advantage indeed.

Having said this, however, it is necessary to repeat that states vary considerably in the particulars of the programs they have adopted. Mort, et al., concluded that eleven states rely almost wholly on flat grants with virtually no equalization included.[10] Nine states provide little except equalization. The other states range between these two extremes. These two elements, equalization and flat grants, are the basic ingredients of state aid regardless of the formula used, and much of the formula will then be devoted to indicating how much there will be of each and how the dollar amounts are to be computed. The flat grant may be one of several kinds. It may take the form of a minimum payment made by the state to every district regardless of other considerations. Many states adopted such provisions when their foundation programs went into operation in order to avoid a net loss to any district as compared with earlier patterns of state aid. In other cases, the flat grant may be provided in order to assure that wealthy districts receive some state money, thereby persuading their legislative representatives to support equalization money for the poorer parts of the state. A third aspect of flat grant payments, or at least of payments not based on equalization needs, is the payment for incentive or as reward. A variety of such payments exist to encourage the local district to undertake more than a minimum program by adding state money to the additional local money raised. Generally speaking, the poorer parts of a state desire that the foundation program emphasize equalization while the wealthier sections, which usually include the metropolitan areas, seek larger flat grants and incentive payments. Once a balance is struck, however, and a program is passed, there are strong pressures to maintain the basic formula intact. This leads us to examine the nature of these pressures.

GROUPS AND INTERESTS

It has been fashionable for critics of contemporary American education to blame the shortcomings of the system on an interlocking directorate of professional educational groups and interests, often labeled the "education-ists."[11] The educationists are said to dominate the colleges of education where teachers are trained. Their ideas command the allegiance of practicing teachers and administrators and shape public policy decisions. The educationists determine who shall teach and what shall be taught. The critics often go on to allege that this tightly knit group is incompetent to wield this massive power in the public interest. These assertions make it clear that we must look at the question of power and its distribution among education interests.

The first point to be made is that the amount and concentration of power over public policy possessed by professional educators varies considerably from state to state. As with most conspiracy theories of politics, that employed by the critics of education fails to do justice to the complexity and variety of educational interests. At the same time, there are kernels of truth in the argument also. There is considerable uniformity of policy demands among the fifty states growing out of a widely-shared set of values that were shaped by a few intellectual pioneers and that are sustained, at least in part, through an organizational framework encompassing the whole country.

THE INNOVATORS. In the northeastern states it is widely acknowledged that George Strayer, Paul Mort and others from Columbia University's Teachers College and Alfred Simpson from Harvard were responsible for much of the content of state actions affecting education.[12] Over the past half-century these men directed research to lay bare what was happening in education and to establish empirical bases for alternatives. They articulated formulae for new policy proposals, including the whole idea of the foundation program. Not the least contribution, they trained scores of professional educators who moved into academic posts in other universities and into state administrative posts, and from both kinds of positions the disciples spread the doctrines. In many states, of course, the Columbia or Harvard men were not directly involved, though it is remarkable how many states they did serve in an official advisory capacity. But it is fair to say that the intellectual shape of educational policy throughout the country was given in outline by these innovators. From them came the ideas of equalization aid and the guaranteed minimum program which are the bases of the foundation approach. These same forceful leaders were among the principal spokesmen for the movement to upgrade teacher preparation, and, again, the people they trained carried this gospel throughout the land. Nor can one forget the enormous impact of John Dewey upon the curriculum.

A recognition of the influence of these innovators, however, does not commit us to the position that today Columbia Teachers College dominates

the American educational scene. In most states we hear neither direct nor indirect reference to the intellectual roots of the policy disputes. Indeed, the
innovators of the 1960's — those who advocate significant changes of direction in educational policy — are largely from outside the "educational establishment." Interestingly, in the published studies dealing directly with state
politics and education we find few references to James Conant, Arthur Bestor,
Hyman Rickover, or the other intellectual gadflies of American education.
The ferment, which they along with innovators in the teaching of mathematics and science have helped create, conditions the atmosphere within
which state governments make their decisions about schools. The decisions
themselves rarely have to do with curriculum, and on the matter of finance
or reorganization the "lay" critics have been much less vocal. Conant's
recent work on teacher education does go to the heart of an important state-
determined policy area — certification. It may therefore find its way into
the hands of legislators, but if so it will be exceptional.

THE TEACHERS ASSOCIATIONS. Most of the continuing efforts to gain
and exercise influence over state educational policy are made by organized
groups. Foremost among these groups and active in nearly every state is the
state affiliate of the National Education Association. State affiliates go by
various names but invariably they are the largest and most active group dealing specifically with questions of public school policy. Nearly two-thirds of
the people professionally employed in elementary and secondary school work
belong to one or another of the state teachers associations. Membership is
much greater proportionately in outstate areas than in cities, however. In
seven of the largest cities, for example, only 13 per cent of the school people
belong to the state association.[13]

The state associations usually speak for both classroom teachers and
school administrators, though in some states the latter have their own organization. Many teachers hope to become administrators eventually and refuse to see a sharp distinction between the two roles. Generally the state
teachers' associations have reflected this view, as does the N.E.A. Rather
than conceiving of teachers as workers and superintendents or school boards
as bosses, the N.E.A. position is that the educator is a professional person
with a special commitment to his function in society — educating the young.[14]
This conception has policy consequences. Many state teachers associations
have been relatively inactive in seeking teacher welfare legislation, such as
tenure protection or fringe benefits. Partly for this reason the state associations have lost members in many large cities to local chapters of the American
Federation of Teachers (A.F.L.-C.I.O.). The latter tend to take a trade
union view of the teacher, bargain hard for economic benefits and job security, and use the traditional weapons of the union including the strike.

In the state political arena the A.F.T. groups have so far demonstrated little except an ability to needle the N.E.A. group into going farther on teacher welfare than it might otherwise have done. If the union continues to grow, however, it will represent a real threat to the "spokesman-for-education" role presently held by the state teachers' groups.

THE OTHER "SCHOOLMEN." In many states a continuing effort is made by "the schoolmen" to achieve a united front. Much of their ability to shape the content of public policy rests on their status as experts in the field. For a group representative to be able to claim expert status, he must not be challenged by opponents with equally professional credentials. Later on we shall examine some of the mechanisms for securing agreement among school interests, but we should note here that this partly accounts for the tendency of school interests and groups to pool their resources, often under teachers association leadership. We have mentioned the tendency of administrators to merge with teachers in a single group. Where administrators have operated separately, as in Michigan, for example, the teachers association has moved sharply in the direction of making greater demands for teacher welfare. In Michigan, indeed, the broad conflict over education issues is both intensified by and stimulating to the divisions among educators.

In most states the school boards have separate organizations, and often these organizations have distinct interests to pursue in the state legislative arena. The boards are likely to be concerned with matters involving the structure of school government, for example, which are of little interest to the teachers. Potentially, the boards and the teachers are opponents in what amounts to a labor-management controversy. Again, Michigan offers an example of considerable direct conflict between the two groups. In many states, however, the school boards and the teachers join forces in behalf of one policy objective which both desire, increasing state aid to schools. In states where more or less formal machinery has been developed to help unify the schoolmen, the school boards are included. Illinois, New York, and New Jersey provide examples. In Missouri the coordination is more informal, with the Missouri State Teachers Association taking the leading role as spokesman and the school boards interest playing a supporting role.

Still further removed from the center of activity are the P.T.A.'s or their equivalents. They are sometimes given formal representation on coordinating committees, as in New York and New Jersey, but their role seems generally confined to providing the appearance of lay support in large numbers for the professionals' recommendations.

Other school groups are visible in some states but participate on a more specialized basis. For example, in Michigan the county superintendents constitute a separately organized group devoted primarily to defending the functions of, or finding new duties for, the county superintendents. In many other states these officials are active in matters of reorganization, and frequently they are significant members of county political groups. Thus, they are often influential with legislators on the specific questions related to their self-interest.

Another specialized education interest, though often with little influence in the state arena, is the big-city school system. Many of these systems are largely autonomous in their governmental structure, separate both from other school systems in the state and from the political system in the city. Therefore the city's legislators are often relatively indifferent to the desires of the city's schoolmen. The problems of the latter are often special, unlike those of non-metropolitan schools. The spokesmen for education at the state level are leaders of groups with little strength in the large city. The result is that the big city schools get a less sympathetic hearing in many states than do the outstate schools. Again, coordinating mechanisms in New York and Illinois include the city schools as a separate interest entitled to separate representation. Generally, however, the big-city school interests, to the extent that they are dependent on increased state aid for meeting their problems, are in a weaker bargaining position than other schoolmen.

ASSOCIATED INTERESTS. The politics of education encompasses a broad range of specific questions and frequently these may involve the direct interests of groups not primarily associated with education itself. For example, a bill to provide special counseling for delinquent children in the schools may draw its principal support from social workers. A bill to loosen the requirements for auditing school accounts may be opposed by the association of certified public accountants. And a bill to provide state aid to bring symphony concerts to the public schools may be introduced at the instigation of a metropolitan symphony society seeking a way out of its perpetual financial crisis. While all these groups may participate in disputes over particular bills, they are not part of the continuing process of decision-making whereby the major shares of state resources are assigned.

We should not conclude, however, that no non-educational groups are directly involved in school issues. Business, labor, and farm associations are relevant in most states to a wide range of the major issues. Certainly they are a part of the process of making public school decisions. Their involvement varies from state to state, both in the extent of impact and the mode of participation. For the most part, these groups become active because the issue of the state's role in education is so largely a question of finance. How much tax money is to be made available to schools and how is it to be raised? Schoolmen are generally inclined to say, "We'll take any live program." Any tax proposal with a reasonable chance of passage is likely to get their support. But labor groups may oppose increased sales taxes or cigarette taxes, while business groups may oppose programs which depend on the income tax for financial support. Farm associations are often major spokesmen for non-metropolitan interests of various kinds. They are likely to oppose any program which may increase the tax burden on real property. They may also take an interest in school consolidation, working to slow down the rate at which small rural schools are abandoned in favor of a larger unit.

None of these groups would allow itself to be put in the position of seeming to oppose schools per se. Schoolmen would always insist that these groups were all friends of the schools, and that any disagreements were minor squabbles over the means to achieve ends that all desired. Nevertheless, decisions to be made are always about means, and the disagreements are often significant barriers to what the schoolmen want. The rhetoric with which the schoolmen advance their cause stresses the consensus among all the interests about the value of education, but they cannot escape the necessity of striking a specific bargain in each state with the interests active in that state's political system.

In cataloguing interests we must note, finally, groups which have so far played only a small role in most states but whose presence is often noted and frequently reacted to by persons with authority to decide school questions. One such group is the Catholics. Bailey and his colleagues concluded that "there is no evidence whatsoever to suggest that the Roman Catholic Church has been a depressant upon state aid to public education,"[15] although, they felt, the Church might have had some such impact at the federal and the local levels. There have been efforts by Catholics, the Citizens for Educational Freedom being one organized group involved, to secure certain kinds of state aid for transportation, books, and the like for children attending parochial schools. These efforts have been sporadic and have had varying degrees of success. What must be recognized, however, is that schoolmen in many states believe that the religious schools and the families whose children attend them pose a *potential* problem of great seriousness. In Illinois, for example, it was found: "The real controversial questions — those dealing with religion, race, federal aid, etc. — are just never brought up. . . . They are too controversial and would divide us."[16]

The sense that these questions are too hot to handle can be translated into some specific strategies for dealing with educational issues. The major one is the strategy of letting the big city schools work out their own problems apart from the rest of the state. Most Negroes and a large proportion of the Catholics are inside the big cities, and by granting local autonomy the state schoolmen may also avoid the divisive issues of race and religion. In turn, by avoiding divisive issues the schoolmen improve their chances of maintaining the united front they need to support their claim of disinterested expertise.

A further aspect of this issue is that in many states the schoolmen are strengthened in their commitment to the non-metropolitan part of the state by this fear of the divisive potential of the social composition of the big cities. The fear may be reinforced by a suspicion of organized labor and occasional conflict with the unions over, for example, a proposed increase in the sales tax. When the teachers' union is strong there is a further basis for schoolmen, meaning usually the N.E.A. affiliate, to regard the cities with suspicion.

Bailey and his colleagues are probably correct, not only for the Northeast but for states in general, in saying that the parochial school issue has not held down state spending for public schools. Neither has the race issue, as such, had a direct impact in non-Southern areas.* But in a variety of subtle and often unspoken ways these issues are an integral part of the process by which state decisions about schools are made. Most observers would agree that they are coming closer and closer to the surface.[17]

BASES OF POWER AND THE QUEST FOR UNITY. The groups we have identified in the preceding discussion all have some degree of influence over the decisions made by the state officials concerning the public schools. On the basis of the studies made of particular states it is possible to specify a number of factors which help account for this influence. Particularly, we are interested in the bases of power of the most influential groups, the schoolmen themselves.

The state education associations derive a very substantial portion of their effectiveness from the classic source of influence in a democratic society, strategically placed numbers. There are thousands of teachers and other school people in each state, located in every town in every county in every legislative district. The school people are relatively well-educated; they have considerable prestige, especially when the school board members are included; they are part of an organizational structure which alerts them to legislative prospects and does so more effectively than most interest groups because the teachers are easily located in the school itself and, being teachers, are responsive to the written communication of a newsletter. All of these elements combine to produce a group which is alert to its interests and well-situated to contact legislators. We must recognize, however, that the access is only potential until skillful leadership transforms strategically placed numbers into genuine power. Leadership is notoriously difficult to identify, much less to measure. Thus it is difficult to speak confidently about the school

*It must be remembered that we are discussing *state* action, not local. In the latter arena, of course, the race issue is at the forefront of school affairs.

leaders, comparing them with other group spokesmen or contrasting one state with another. What is clear, however, is that in some states the school leaders are regarded as extremely skillful. This perception is held by legislators whose positive estimate may partly be based on the tendency of the school spokesmen to adapt their demands to what they think the legislators will accept.[18] In other states the school leaders might be less adaptive and more inclined to insist upon the virtue of their claims regardless of the larger political context in which the claims are pressed. When schoolmen are adaptive they and the legislators believe that they achieve all that is possible. Their adaptation is partly a matter of tailoring their demands to fit the larger political context of the moment and partly a matter of personal style. A rural-dominated legislature is more readily influenced by a schoolman whose background and accent are similar to those of the legislators.

Legislators are likely to respond favorably to groups whose claims on state resources are made in tangible terms. That is, a claim made in behalf of excellence is all very well but has no specific content applicable to a legislator's frame of reference. A claim for an additional allotment of dollars for school districts in a legislative constituency or a demand for more money to be used to raise the salaries of teacher-constituents is concrete. Moreover, it has the ring of respectable self-interest. Partly for that reason, schoolmen may get a more sympathetic hearing than, say, social workers or mental health advocates.[19]

Finally, we may note an interlocked set of variables that vary significantly from state to state. The central factor is that of cohesion among the schoolmen — the extent to which they speak with one voice. This factor is often cited in connection with interest group strength. With education interests, however, there is a complicating factor rooted in the drive among educators for professional standing. If schoolmen are to gain recognition as professionals they must behave with the restraint and unity of purpose which characterizes a professional group. To achieve unity among the disparate elements which make up the schoolmen — classroom teachers, administrators, board members, etc. — may often require sacrifice or compromise on goals. As we have noted in discussing the teachers' union movement, compromise on teacher interests may reduce the enthusiasm of teachers for their organizational spokesmen, and the whole structure of consensus among the schoolmen may break apart as a result.

Maintaining maximum agreement among schoolmen is a central objective of both the political and professional activity of school leaders. If there are many competing "experts" advising the legislature, the legislators are likely to trust none of them. The desire for professional standing leads logically to the quest for unity. So does the notion so widely articulated among educators that education issues are or should be "non-political," i.e., beyond conflict. Moreover, schoolmen believe that in unity there is strength, and that the public schools will receive more state aid when schoolmen are unified.

Not least among the factors facilitating unity among the schoolmen is the view frequently expressed by legislators that there is little political advantage to be gained from school issues. In the past decade or so legislative wariness regarding school matters has been a matter not just of indifference but of "avoiding the heat." Many, perhaps most, legislators represent areas where changes in the population and in its expectations have produced pressures on the local schools. Some of these pressures are felt in the state house, and as individuals the legislators can do little to satisfy the demands. If a legislator can turn to a united and presumptively expert group, he may channel the pressure away from himself in a constructive way. In a number of states there has been created machinery to try to achieve greater agreement among those with a real stake in state decisions affecting the schools.

Missouri provides an example of the simplest kind of integrative mechanism. The Missouri State Teachers Association has very successfully preempted the field as spokesman for the public schools and has managed to keep the various elements of its constituency — teachers, administrators, etc. — reasonably harmonious. M.S.T.A. representatives work closely with legislative leaders, and while they are thoroughly in tune with the norms and folkways of Missouri state politics, M.S.T.A. leaders feel that they succeed in getting all the state aid that the Missouri political system is likely to provide. To get very much more would require a striking change in the whole state's scheme of things.

Illinois also achieves substantial unity among the various school interests but employs a highly institutionalized mechanism for doing it. There the School Problems Commission, formally established in 1949, serves as the principal agency to screen and evaluate major school proposals before they are sent to the legislature. The S.P.C. includes in its membership state legislators who, usually, bring a special interest in education to the Commission and take a highly developed expertise back to the legislature. Members appointed by the Governor have regularly included representatives of the Illinois Education Association, the Illinois Agriculture Association, the State Association of School Boards, the Chicago Board of Education, and often the Illinois Chamber of Commerce. The S.P.C. members have developed a deep commitment to achieving unity among themselves. They tend to avoid the most controversial questions when they can, and try hard to go to the governor and the legislature with unanimous recommendations. For the most part the S.P.C. has been successful in achieving unity, and almost invariably the legislature accepts the Commission's recommendations.

Neither Missouri nor Illinois, however, ranks high in the proportion of personal income devoted to public education. Certainly part of the reason is that the whole political system in these states makes it difficult to pass high-spending programs. In part, however, it may be that unity among schoolmen carries a price in terms of the level of state aid attainable.

Michigan is an example of a state where the school interests are divided both organizationally and ideologically. Efforts to achieve a "consensus program" by creating a broadly inclusive Education Council have broken down completely. Yet Michigan spends a higher share of its income per capita on schools than do Illinois or Missouri. Obviously the factors affecting the level of state support for the schools are more numerous and complicated than the simple issue of unity vs. disunity among the schoolmen, and we shall need to examine these factors further.

Nevertheless, the drive of school groups to achieve not only unity but some predictability in the process of making school decisions — a quest for regularity and normalization — does seem characteristic, even though it may not pay off immediately in getting more state money for the schools. In part, this desire may be linked to the myth that education and politics have nothing in common. To the extent that school groups are unified they may be able to perpetuate this myth, since little overt conflict will arise over state educational policy. The vigor of the myth will, in turn, reinforce the position of professional educators as prime movers on matters of public school policy.

Bailey and his colleagues found that in all the states of the Northeast there was at least some evidence of "the urge to coalesce." In Massachusetts there was only a short-lived, *ad hoc* group. In Rhode Island and New Hampshire the state department of education sparked the formation of a broader grouping. In New York and New Jersey more durable and effective organizations have been established. The "Princeton Group" in New Jersey brings together in relatively informal coordinating or clearing-house meetings representatives of the state Department of Education, the teachers' association, the P.T.A., the school boards, and the superintendents. In New York the New York State Educational Conference Board was created in 1937, modeled after a comparable conference board of farm organizations. Though some nine school groups are formally members, the dominant elements seem to come from the state department, the teachers' association, and the school boards' association.

HOW THE PUBLIC DECISIONS ARE MADE. Education policy finally must be determined by the state legislature, often acting on recommendations of the governor, and is therefore caught up in much the same policy-making processes as other major areas of state concern. The generic state decision-making processes are discussed elsewhere in this volume, so we shall note here only those aspects of legislative and executive behavior regarding education which are distinctive.

It is often impossible to separate the governor's impact on public school policy from his general leadership. Much of his control in this area comes as a by-product of his fiscal and budgetary leadership. Thus governors have been known to set a flat ceiling figure for state aid and force the schoolmen to work out a formula for allocating that size of pie. When the governor seeks to increase taxes he may try to gain broad public support for the increase by promising a part of it to the schools. Generally, however, the governors are not likely to become involved in the details of state school policy. Except as school issues are entwined in finance, the state executive is likely to pay them only sporadic attention.

The legislature is a far more significant arena for determining the specifics of education policy. The myriad of local school decisions are made here, and usually the governor plays no role whatever on these items. Bills affecting reorganization or even state aid may be hotly controversial in the legislature without invoking the governor's participation. The result is that education is a major item on the legislative agenda with important consequences for the ultimate policy product.

Educational interests, we have seen, attempt to maintain the maximum unity in order to sustain their reputation as experts. Within the legislature also, education questions tend to become the domain of experts. Wahlke, et al., found education to be the third most frequently named area of specialization among the legislators of four states.[20] They also found that legislative experts authored more successful bills than non-experts.[21] Masters, et al., found that in Missouri the sponsorship of the crucial education bills — those most desired by the schoolmen — was usually placed in the hands of one or two legislators who combined experience and sympathy for school interests with status and prestige among fellow legislators. Moreover, the relationship tended to be quite durable over time. In Illinois the most advanced stage of specialization could be observed as the legislative members of the School Problems Commission tended to dominate the legislature's consideration of school issues almost completely. The greater the controversy, the more difficult it is for the legislative experts to dominate the discussion; as a consequence, education groups and their specialized legislative friends are agreed that intense controversy on school questions is undesirable. Therefore, they attempt to minimize controversy even though it may cost something in short run achievements.

MONEY AND SCHOOLS: WHO SPENDS WHAT

We discussed earlier the growth of public school systems and pointed out the early origins of regional differences among them. In organizational structure and in strength of public financial support the Southern states were quite different from New England, while Middle Atlantic and trans-Appalachian states also developed along distinctive lines. Today, a surprisingly large residue of these early differences can still be observed. Reinforced by economic and social factors of more recent growth, the states tend to support public education in patterns that exhibit inter-regional variations and intra-regional similarities. Let us examine the evidence in detail.

Analysis of *state* support of the public schools is complicated by reporting and measurement problems. The criteria for determining how much a state spends on education are fuzzier than we might expect. Many reports show the amount of dollars spent in the state per pupil in average daily attendance (A.D.A.) in public school. This is a calculation which is well understood and highly standardized since it is used as a main basis for calculating state aid under a foundation program. Also, it is a highly relevant figure in terms of the quality of support given public education in the states.[22] Money spent per pupil is more indicative than money spent per adult when talking about education. Money spent per pupil in A.D.A. leaves out the parochial school children, and this results in striking differences in the relative ranking of many states. New Jersey, for example, ranks second in expenditures per pupil in A.D.A. but twenty-second in school expenditures on a per capita basis.

Expenditures per pupil can only be used for some of the comparisons we wish to make, however, since the recent available reports do not distinguish between the support per pupil in A.D.A. which the state government provides and the support given by local governments in the state. Clearly, if we are to assess the role of the state, we must differentiate between state and local effort, but to do this we must employ data on per capita expenditures rather than per pupil expenditures since it is only the former which are available in appropriate form.*

A possible further complication might be introduced if, in comparing states in expenditures for schools, we accidentally hit on a year in which were displayed particularly eccentric patterns. Any given year might show this effect, and we have no way of knowing which year, if any, is "normal." The level of school expenditures in all states has risen rapidly, nearly 300 per cent between 1952–53 and 1960–61, with states and local governments increasing their spending at about the same rate. These increases not only accommodated the growing population but permitted the average expenditure per pupil to rise from $228 to $390. These increases have come unevenly, however; one state moving ahead strongly one year, another state catching

*Per capita state and local expenditures for local schools (1961) and per pupil expenditures (1962–63) show a rank-order correlation of .74. While this is quite high, there are some striking variations in rank for particular states. These will be noted in the discussion below.

up two years later. To examine any single year, therefore, might lead to mis-interpretation based on short-run fluctuations. This analysis rests primarily on 1960–62 data. The above-mentioned strictures apply to these years as to others, but state and local expenditures per pupil in A.D.A. during 1961–62 were discovered to be highly related to expenditures in 1937–38.* At least between those two academic years the variation in relative position of the states was slight, and this reflects a tendency for short-run fluctuations in school spending to be cancelled out in the long run. States retain their relative rankings because the rankings are consequences of certain durable long-run characteristics of the states.

The most striking finding with respect to support of public education is its dependence upon wealth.[23] The richer the state the more it spends on schools,† and this is particularly the case in the less urbanized states.‡ If we control for income, on the other hand, neither urbanization nor party competition seems to affect the level of expenditure.§ This confirms the findings of Dawson and Robinson.[24] The only point we may add to their analysis is that in the highly urbanized states even income does not seem to predict expenditure. This may mean that the highly urban states, which are also the wealthiest states, reach a high plateau in school spending. The plateau is a goal to be striven for in less well-to-do states, but once affluence permits its realization, efforts to climb still higher depend on factors such as educational leadership or group activity, rather than broad socio-economic conditions.

Table 1 shows the twenty-seven states which spend money on schools in some rough proportion to their income. Eleven states spend more than might be expected from their income and ten states spend less.

Nine of the eleven high-spending states are upper Midwest and Western with a tradition of Progressivism that is associated with a strong commitment to education. We shall also take note of this tradition in connection with the rise of the state university since several of these states were also prominently among the leaders in developing public higher education. The low

---

*The rank-order correlation coefficient is .91.

†The rank-order correlation coefficient is .89. The relationship between wealth and per capita expenditure yields a rank-order correlation coefficient of .65.

‡On the basis of per capita expenditures in the sixteen most urban states, the correlation of income and expenditures is .19. In the middle sixteen and lowest sixteen, the correlations are .71 and .77, respectively.

§Party competition (using Dawson and Robinson's average ranking, *loc. cit. infra,* n. 24, pp. 275–276) shows a correlation with per capita expenditures of .52. Controlling for income by breaking the states into high income, middle income, and low income categories, the correlations are −.16, .26, and .32, respectively. Following the same procedure for urbanization, the correlations are −.34, .01, and .04.

Table 1

PER PUPIL EXPENDITURES FOR SCHOOLS IN RELATION TO PER CAPITA INCOME, 1961

Expenditures High in Relation to Income (11 States)	Expenditures Proportionate to Income (27 States)	Expenditures Low in Relation to Income (10 States)
Minnesota*	California*	Colorado
Oregon*	Connecticut*	Massachusetts
Rhode Island*	Delaware*	Nevada
Wisconsin*	Illinois*	Ohio
Wyoming*	Maryland*	Indiana
Arizona	New Jersey*	Missouri
New Mexico	New York*	Nebraska
Iowa	Washington*	New Hampshire
Montana	Kansas	Maine†
Louisiana	Michigan	Virginia†
North Dakota	Pennsylvania	
	Florida	
	Oklahoma	
	South Dakota	
	Texas	
	Utah	
	Vermont	
	Alabama†	
	Arkansas†	
	Georgia†	
	Idaho†	
	Kentucky†	
	West Virginia†	
	Mississippi†	
	North Carolina†	
	South Carolina†	
	Tennessee†	

*Denotes highest school spenders.
†Denotes lowest school spenders.

Source: National Education Association, *Rankings of the States, 1963.* Alaska and Hawaii are omitted.

spenders have no such geographical bonds, and we must look elsewhere for whatever characteristics may account for their relative reluctance to support public education.

One possibility would be that the low-spending states are generally conservative in public expenditures and that low school spending is simply one aspect of this conservative ethos. The rank-order correlation of school expenditure and total expenditure is .67, so there is a fairly strong connection between the two. As Table 2 shows, twenty-seven states spend on schools

Table 2

PER PUPIL SCHOOL EXPENDITURE IN RELATION TO TOTAL STATE
AND LOCAL GOVERNMENT EXPENDITURE, 1962

School Expenditure High in Relation to Total Government Expenditure (11 States)	*School Expenditure Proportionate to Total Government Expenditure* (27 States)	*School Expenditure Low in Relation to Total Government Expenditure* (10 States)
Connecticut*	California*	Colorado
Illinois*	Delaware*	Montana
Wisconsin*	Minnesota*	Nevada
Maryland*	New York*	North Dakota
New Jersey*	Oregon*	Vermont
Rhode Island*	Washington*	Louisiana
Indiana	Wyoming*	South Dakota
Ohio	Arizona	Utah
Pennsylvania	Iowa	Idaho†
Missouri	Kansas	Maine†
Texas	Massachusetts	
	Michigan	
	New Mexico	
	Florida	
	Nebraska	
	New Hampshire	
	Oklahoma	
	Alabama†	
	Arkansas†	
	Georgia†	
	Kentucky†	
	Mississippi†	
	North Carolina†	
	South Carolina†	
	Tennessee†	
	Virginia†	
	West Virginia†	

*Denotes highest school spenders.
†Denotes lowest school spenders.

Source: National Education Association, *Rankings of the States, 1963,* and Council of State Governments, *The Book of the States, 1962–63.* Alaska and Hawaii are omitted.

about what we might expect, judging from total state-local expenditure. Eleven states spent more than might be expected; ten spent less. If we combine the material summarized in Tables 1 and 2, several types of relationships emerge, and we may group them in the following way:

1. *School spending highly related to income:* Alabama, Arkansas, California, Georgia, Iowa, Kansas, Kentucky, Maine, Michigan, New Hampshire, New York, South Carolina, Tennessee, Washington and West Virginia (fif-

teen). This group includes most of the Southern and low-income states plus several of the most wealthy. Perhaps it may be said that in these states a "normal" proportion of the state wealth is spent on schools.

2. *School spending high in association with generally high expenditures:* Arizona, Minnesota, Oregon, Rhode Island, Wisconsin (five). These states all provide a generally high level of public services, ranking higher in spending than in income. Education fully participates in the results.

3. *School spending high in relation to income, low in relation to expenditures:* Louisiana, Montana, New Mexico, North Dakota, South Dakota, Wyoming (six). In these states most public services are generously provided for. Some of this generosity spills over to benefit the schools, but schools trail other functions in money received. The Great Plains concentration in this category is patent.

4. *School spending low in relation to income, high in relation to expenditures:* Massachusetts, Missouri, Ohio, Virginia (four). These states are generally rather conservative in fiscal affairs, significantly less so with regard to their schools than in other areas, but low spenders for schools, nevertheless.

5. *School spending a function of income, high in relation to expenditures:* Illinois, Indiana, Maryland, New Jersey, North Carolina, Pennsylvania, Texas (seven). These states are conservative in non-education functions but support public schools in rough proportion to their respective incomes.

6. *School spending a function of income, low in relation to expenditures:* Connecticut, Idaho, Mississippi, Oklahoma, Vermont (five). These states are high spenders in some areas but neither high nor low in education.

7. *School spending low in relation to income, consistent with expenditures:* Delaware (one). Although Delaware falls in the highest quartile of the states in expenditures, it ranks several places lower in spending than it does in income.

8. *School spending low in relation both to income and to expenditures:* Colorado, Florida, Nebraska, Nevada, Utah (five). These states seem to single out education for particularly penurious treatment. Utah, however, has a very high proportion of school-age residents and on a per capita basis its school expenditures rank third rather than thirty-fourth! Nevada jumps from nineteenth to fourth when looking at per capita expenditure, and Colorado's position also improves. Florida and Nebraska are low spenders by either measure.

These eight categories continue to display certain regional patterns. In the South, the upper Midwest and Plains, and the far West considerable homogeneity is apparent. Yet the differences are striking within, as well as between, regions. The groupings are too numerous and each is too small to permit useful statistical tests to determine what common factors, if any, may bind each group together.

We must make still another breakdown of states in order to determine in which states the local governments provide the bulk of the school money and where it is the state authority which bears the larger share. To a considerable extent, state expenditure and local expenditure are inversely related.* We would expect to find this since expanded state aid has been predicated on "foundation" assumptions and has sought to equalize educational opportunities in the state at an acceptable minimum level. The less the local units spend, the more the state must help.

Generally speaking, in the wealthier and more urbanized states, the local governments provide much the larger share of the school money. Income correlates with per capita local expenditures for local schools at .5, with state expenditures for local schools at −.02. Moreover, in the sixteen least urban states, income correlates with local expenditures at .86, with state expenditure at −.73. This is broadly true within each state as well, and we may recall the point made earlier in the chapter that "the schoolmen" tend to speak primarily in behalf of the "outstate" parts of the state. In part, however, these relationships may be the result of another kind of regional-historical factor. The strength and longevity of local school support in New England is great. We noted its early origins and connections with the growth of religious diversity. This tradition grew hardly at all in the ante-bellum South, and after "The War" extreme poverty delayed the expansion of local school systems still more. Public education did not really come to maturity there until substantial state-aid programs had begun to supplement local efforts in other parts of the country. Naturally, the state's role was proportionately larger. In states like those in the upper Midwest the New England pattern of strong schools, locally supported, was given early and continuing support by successive generations of settlers.

Table 3 shows the contemporary pattern of state-local relations. This pattern, moreover, is remarkably durable over time. Mort, *et al.,* found that between 1890 and 1956 the proportion of local school money coming from the state increased in most states; eighteen states provided 30 per cent or more of the money in 1890, while thirty-one states provided that proportion in 1956. Only a few states changed their support relative to other states, however, and Mort concludes that "the posture of the several states in regard to state support had already become fairly well fixed by 1890."[25]

The factors associated with relative changes in state aid as against local school support are not entirely clear, but some tendencies can be identified. The historical picture shows state aid increasing in relative contribution most strikingly during economic recession. Thus, total state and local expenditures

---

*The rank-order correlation is −.47, using per capita expenditures rather than expenditures per pupil.

Table 3

PER CAPITA SCHOOL EXPENDITURES BY STATE GOVERNMENTS IN RELATION TO
SCHOOL EXPENDITURES BY LOCAL GOVERNMENTS, 1961

State Expenditures High in Relation to Local Expenditures (22 States)	*State Expenditures Proportionate to Local Expenditures* (6 States)	*State Expenditures Low in Relation to Local Expenditures* (20 States)
Minnesota	California*	Arizona*
Nevada	Michigan	Oregon
New York	Connecticut	Colorado*
Utah	Idaho	Montana*
Wyoming	Rhode Island	North Dakota*
New Mexico	Virginia	Indiana
Washington		Maryland
Alabama†		Utah†
Delaware†		Iowa*
Georgia†		Wisconsin*
Louisiana†		Nebraska*
Oklahoma		New Jersey*
Pennsylvania		South Dakota*
Texas		Kansas*
Florida†		Illinois
West Virginia†		Massachusetts
North Carolina†		Ohio
Mississippi†		Maine
South Carolina†		Missouri
Tennessee†		New Hampshire
Arkansas†		
Kentucky†		

*Denotes highest local school expenditures.
†Denotes lowest local school expenditures.

Source: National Education Association, *Rankings of the States, 1963.* Alaska and Hawaii are omitted.

for schools increased about 10 per cent between 1930 and 1940, but local support decreased. We observed earlier that state aid is proportionately high in the poor Southern states. Conversely, in periods of prosperity, past and present, state aid increases but local support for local schools increases faster. Thus the state's role with respect to education tends to be that of supplementer; it is strongest in poor states or in general economic recession. Again, this is true not only between states but within each one, as the state program tends, albeit imperfectly, to give primary attention to raising up the poorest districts.

There are individual state exceptions to this broad pattern, of course. Delaware, for example, has provided almost all of its school money from the state, virtually treating the entire state as a single district. Nebraska, on the other hand, has a strong tradition against state expenditure and provides well over 90 per cent of its school money locally.

In summary, we may say that the most important factor in determining state spending for local schools is income, but historical tradition, manifested in regional groupings of states, also plays an important role in conditioning the perspective with which state decision-makers view the school needs of their state. Finally, the special circumstances of each state's political system affect education issues as they affect all the decisions made in the political arena.

PUBLIC HIGHER EDUCATION

The role of the state in higher education followed a cycle similar to that regarding the common schools.[26] In colonial times it was common for the government to appropriate funds for privately established colleges. Harvard, for example, received public money on more than one hundred occasions before 1789. Williams College received as much from the state between 1793 and 1823 as from private sources. Indeed, in many Eastern states, the legislatures continued to support private colleges well into the 20th century. A convenient date to divide this intermixture of public and private money and authority from the later growth of exclusively public institutions is 1819. In that year the U.S. Supreme Court held that the state of New Hampshire could not alter the terms of the charter of Dartmouth College.[27] The state, therefore, could not take over private institutions and convert them to public facilities.

> The Dartmouth College decision, by encouraging college-founding and by discouraging public support for higher education, probably helped to check the development of state universities for half a century.[28]

Following the Dartmouth decision there was a great wave of private college founding, particularly under the auspices of the various religious denominations. Sectarian colleges could not be given state aid without inviting conflicts among all the rival denominations. The more secular institutions, like Harvard, lost their claim to state support as they sought to broaden their geographical coverage by attracting students from other parts of the country. As a result, public higher education languished. In 1834, for example, the Missouri legislature petitioned Congress to be allowed to use money earmarked for universities in the common schools. By the Civil War era the concept of public support of higher education, especially of private universities, was regarded as an insidious threat to the American way. Opposing the creation of a tax-supported national university, President Charles Eliot of Harvard said, in 1873, that "our ancestors well understand the principle that to make a people free and self-reliant, it is necessary to let them take care of themselves, even if they do not take quite as good care of themselves as a superior power might."[29]

In pre-Civil War America, therefore, the college had become a private, often sectarian institution and, moreover, by maintaining a relatively rigid classical curriculum, had become largely alienated from the Jacksonian temper of public opinion. It was primarily in the South that the state university achieved a firm footing in the ante-bellum years. There the colleges served as centers of cultural adornment, buttressing the social status quo. Accordingly, state-supported universities could exist as minor luxuries of a distinctive socio-economic system. But, while they existed, they did not grow or serve a broad audience. And in the post-war era the universal poverty of the South afflicted its colleges as it did the rest of Southern educational institutions.

In the West conflicting forces were at work. Land grants had long been used to support higher education, the culmination being the Morrill Act of 1862. In the East most states were slow to respond to the stimulus to create or expand public higher educational facilities. West of the Alleghenies, however, the Jacksonian spirit was stronger, and many dirt farmers looked askance at universities. The prospect of college-trained or "fancy" farmers and mechanics produced by state universities supported by Morrill Act funds was by no means regarded as an unmixed blessing. Middle-class reformers sponsored technical institutes both for farmers and for urban dwellers but met with an indifferent response. It was not until "practical science" research began to pay off in the immediate post-Civil War period that broad popular approval was achieved. The heirs of the Jeffersonian ideal of public higher education for large numbers of people, men like James B. Angell of Michigan, were successful in articulating and selling the notion of state-supported higher education. Under their leadership:

> . . . the growth of a body of applied agricultural science, the experiment stations, farmer approval, and federal and state assistance all fed upon one another, helping to develop the land-grant colleges into a significant educational movement.[30]

As we have noted, it was the state universities that led the way in creating public secondary schools. For a time most of the universities relied on college preparatory programs which they themselves operated to bridge the gap between the common school and college. Beginning with Michigan in 1870 the university's accreditation of state public schools so stimulated the expansion of public high schools that the preparatory school became largely unnecessary.

It was also the state university that led the way toward introducing "modern" subjects into the college curriculum and broadening the curriculum of the high school as well. By 1910, for example, the University of California accepted thirty different subjects for admission credit while Yale and Princeton accepted only thirteen.

In the 20th century, of course, the state university systems expanded enormously, especially in recent years. Even in this burgeoning, however, we can still observe the regional differences which emerged nearly a century ago. The Midwestern states were in the vanguard of the state university movement. In Michigan, Wisconsin, and generally throughout the Great Plains service-oriented higher education came to be one facet of the Progressive spirit. The states of the West likewise reflected this ethos. The South lagged behind for its own special historical reasons, poverty and the race problem combining to slow down the growth of all public educational institutions. In the Eastern states the numerous strong private universities perhaps made state institutions less necessary than in the West. Many Eastern universities received mixed public and private support — some like Cornell and Pennsylvania still do. The result was that the concept of strictly public institutions of higher learning grew much more slowly in the seaboard states, and state support was consequently modest. Only in the last decade has New York, for example, begun to operate a full set of state universities. The regional differences may gradually disappear but they and their historical roots remain visible today.

HIGHER EDUCATION EXPENDITURES. In this field the historical patterns which have emerged run parallel to the patterns of support for local schools, i.e., the states have tended to develop a kind of state perspective regarding education which conditions the level of support given to both higher education and the public schools. The result is that on a per capita basis there is a .68 correlation in rank orders among the states on the two types of expenditures. But expenditures for higher education bear a much lower relation to local support for local schools (.39) or state support for local schools (.28). Moreover, higher education spending is unrelated to income (.03), although in the least urbanized states there is a greater association (.49). Higher education expenditure is unaffected by party competition (.03) though again in the less urban states there is some relationship (.54). Urbanization bears a somewhat negative relation to spending for higher education (−.34). Yet all of these relationships seem to be largely the result of the strong regional variations in the traditional strength of public higher education which we noted in tracing the growth of publicly supported colleges and universities.

The foregoing discussion of state expenditures for higher education may tend to imply that state appropriations constitute the sole source of income for state colleges and universities and that, consequently, the comparative

Table 4

PER CAPITA EXPENDITURES FOR HIGHER EDUCATION IN RELATION TO
PER PUPIL EXPENDITURE FOR PUBLIC SCHOOLS, 1961–62

Expenditures for Colleges High in Relation to Public School Expenditures (20 States)	*Expenditures for Colleges Proportionate to Public School Expenditures* (14 States)	*Expenditures for Colleges Low in Relation to Public School Expenditures* (14 States)
Colorado	California*	Delaware
Kansas*	Washington*	Minnesota
Michigan*	Wyoming*	Wisconsin
New Mexico*	Oregon*	Illinois
Montana*	Nevada	Maryland
Utah*	Arizona	Ohio
Vermont*	Iowa	Connecticut †
North Dakota*	Nebraska	New Jersey †
Indiana	New Hampshire	New York †
Oklahoma	Texas	Rhode Island †
South Dakota	Maine †	Massachusetts †
Louisiana	South Carolina †	Pennsylvania †
West Virginia	Tennessee †	Missouri †
Virginia †	Georgia †	Florida †
Alabama		
Arkansas		
Idaho		
Kentucky		
North Carolina		
Mississippi		

*Denotes highest college expenditures.
†Denotes lowest college expenditures.

Source: National Education Association, *Rankings of the States, 1963.* Alaska and Hawaii are omitted.

quality of the states' schools may be measured rather directly by examining the spending figures. Actually, only about one-half of the money for publicly controlled institutions comes from the state governments, the rest being derived from student fees, research contracts, endowments, football tickets, and other sources. Various federal programs are of growing importance, providing nearly one-fourth of the income of publicly controlled institutions. In recent years a number of states have departed from the traditional paths of direct appropriation, finding other means to give aid to public higher education. Many states have chosen to issue bonds for capital improvements in colleges and universities rather than paying for them as they were built. The results of these efforts, of course, are to channel more state resources into higher education than the short-run expenditures would seem to report.

THE POLITICS OF HIGHER EDUCATION. Public higher education bears little political relationship to elementary and secondary schools. In organizational structure, in methods of financing, and in the pressures and politics of decision-making, state colleges and universities are part of a different system from the schools. We noted the impact of the state universities on the high schools with regard first to establishment and then to development. Publicly supported colleges have both trained the teachers and provided the critics who denounce teacher training. Much of the intellectual innovation in education comes from the universities' scholars, and the public and private universities are intellectually indistinguishable from one another. Thus, functionally the two kinds of educational enterprise are closely linked. But politically the differences are major, indeed.

The governing structures of public colleges and universities vary widely from state to state, but in virtually every case these structures are separate from the state departments of education and the chief state school officers.[31] In some states the governing authority of the universities is vested in trustees who are popularly elected, but the more common pattern is to have appointed boards. In the past there were separate boards for each institution in the state, but in one state after another the enormous expansion of public higher education has made it necessary to establish coordinating boards or councils. California has proceeded the farthest in developing a complex but highly integrated system of colleges and universities in which each institution fits into a broad pattern. As the costs of education rise, however, other states are moving in this direction in order to achieve the greatly expanded services required of higher education in the face of rising enrollments at manageable cost levels.[32]

In many states, however, a unified system on the California model is far from realization, and the task of getting appropriations from the legislature is one which is pursued through the traditional processes of political negotiation and bargaining. Although board members have prestige and influence, the chief spokesmen of the universities and colleges are their presidents. Whereas the public schoolmen work largely through associations, pressing their claims through a mass membership, the demands of higher education are more often expressed by prominent individuals occupying the highly political roles of public university presidents.

The ability of a university, through its president, to command public funds often depended in the past on the specific services rendered by the university to the state and its legislative representatives. A state teachers college, for example, might get money primarily on the ground that it trained teachers for a specific region of the state. Representatives from the several regions could trade off in logrolling fashion, either by having the college representatives get together beforehand to develop a package to present to the governor and the legislature, or they could negotiate in the legislature itself. The university served through its service-oriented research, analyzing the mineral resources of the state, developing crop strains suitable for the state's climate, or advising local governments of the state on their personnel practices. Other university functions were appreciated too: admission or special treatment of marginal student-constituents might be of service to a legislator; a winning football team or a fancy marching band stimulated legislative enthusiasm which, in turn, would support research on medieval poetry.

All these considerations are still part of the political foundation of public education. Unquestionably, too, the traditional posture in the state toward education — the value placed on good schools — provides a context within which legislators operate and that context has much to do with the level of appropriations. California, Kansas, and Michigan are simply more generous toward public higher education than Missouri or Connecticut, and variations in the quality of their football teams will not explain the difference.

Support for higher education has changed in recent years, however. First-rate universities have come to be regarded as a positive asset of a state. Their research facilities and their intellectual resources may attract new industry and professional people to locate there. Government contracts for space research may be forthcoming. Moreover, the sharp increase in broad public demands for higher education for everyone requires greatly enlarged facilities. The cultural norms have shifted to require both excellence and universality of public higher education, and legislators have had to respond with vastly increased appropriations.

The politics have changed, too. The tendency toward coordinating boards has already been noted. In many states, however, the inter-university competition is greater rather than less. Many erstwhile teachers colleges have become universities, for example, and begun to compete for funds directly with the older land-grant institutions. In this competition educational quality is not only a goal but also a persuasive argument for more money. Alumni may be organized, pride in a section of the state appealed to, and both Rose Bowl and College Bowl victories celebrated — all in an effort to get a larger slice of the rapidly growing appropriations pie. Such open competition may be short-lived, however, for the pie cannot always grow, and coordinating mechanisms are emerging to help bring order and system to each state's system of public institutions of higher education.*

THE JUNIOR COLLEGE. We may conclude our discussion of public higher education by noting the dramatic increase in the number of junior colleges. Publicly supported two-year institutions of higher education have

*In 1957 some seventeen states created formal agencies to coordinate higher education. A number of others have done so since then, bringing the total to about twenty-five.

existed since the turn of the century. Only in the last decade or so, however, have they come to perform such an important role in the educational system. Most of the nearly four hundred such colleges derive much of their support from the local communities which are their primary service areas. The state then supplements this support with state money. The result is that for a growing portion of the system of public higher education the state-local relations are similar to those regarding elementary and secondary schools. Junior colleges, of course, are designed to help meet the great increase in college enrollments. As college training becomes more and more universal it may be that a still greater similarity will develop between public school politics and the politics of higher education.

CONCLUSION

We conclude this chapter with a brief mention of some important questions regarding the politics of education which have hardly been mentioned in the foregoing pages. Some of these are major social issues which involve the schools since the schools are basically social institutions. Foremost among these issues is that of race.

It is not possible to separate the controversies over race relations from those over education. The historic *Brown* vs. *Board of Education*[33] decision involved the public schools as have a large portion of the related cases providing basic interpretations of individual rights to equal protection of the laws. More recently the militant protests of Negroes, seeking to implement their *de jure* rights with more thorough *de facto* integration, have focused much attention on the schools. Indeed, almost every question of education, in the metropolitan centers at least, has become partially a race question too. That this intertwining will become increasingly relevant to the state politics of education is obvious. We have not examined it here because in the Northern states its impact on *state* decisions is still primarily in the future. In the South, of course, race and education have been intimately bound up for a century, and that fact helps account for the distinctive patterns of Southern behavior we have observed earlier.

A second area we have neglected includes more strictly educational issues of intense controversy. Debates over the proper function of the public schools have been carried on seriously for generations and never more vigorously than today. Questions of what a curriculum should include, what facilities a school should have, and how its teachers should be prepared are constantly argued in local communities across the nation. Teacher certification is primarily under state control and thus is involved in the state political system. We alluded earlier to the administrative politics involved in certification and related matters and noted that it was relatively rare for these questions to descend on the legislature for resolution. Money for schools must be provided in competition with all other public functions. Certification and curriculum questions do not involve conflict with non-educational groups, and their resolution largely follows the relative strength of contending interests within the professional education world.* The issues are important, but they are only marginal to the central processes of state politics.

We said little about reorganization of school districts. The justification for omitting this question is that it is so largely accomplished. During the past thirty years the number of school districts has been reduced from 127,422 to 36,880. Consolidation is continuing but in most states without very much controversy. The defense of "the little red school house" once aroused deeply felt emotions, but seldom does it do so now.[34]

Last in our list of omissions is the matter of federal aid to education. The federal government already provides a noticeable portion of the total public school budget. Vocational education has long been supported with federal funds. The school lunch program is unchallengeable. The National Defense Education Act of 1958 provided federal help for science, language, and mathematics programs. Substantial sums of money are provided to assist the schools in areas where large federal installations have swollen the public school population. The Impacted Area program, as it is called, provides a sizable portion of the federal money, which in Alaska, Arizona, and Georgia amounts to more than 10 per cent of the total expenditure on public schools.

Existing federal aid programs are significant. Prospective programs expanding federal aid would be even more important. Yet it is most unlikely that any federal programs will relieve the states of the need to provide increasing sums of money for schools. This being so, the connections between *state* politics and education will continue to be important subjects of public concern.

NOTES

1. These statistics are taken from the extremely useful compendium, *Rankings of the States, 1963*, Research Report 1963-R1 (Washington: Research Division, National Education Association, 1963).

2. The history of American education is treated in detail by a number of authors. Especially relied upon are: R. Freeman Butts and Lawrence A. Cremin, *A History of Education in the United States* (New York: Henry Holt and Co., 1953); and H. G. Good, *A History of American Education* (New York: Macmillan Co., 1956).

3. For a convenient discussion of the politics of federal aid to education, past and present, see Frank J. Munger and Richard F. Fenno, *National Politics and Federal Aid to Education* (Syracuse: Syracuse University Press, 1962).

*We should not entirely overlook the attacks of strongly conservative groups on school administrators in various communities. For the most part, these controversies have been confined to particular school systems, but in California the issue became state-wide in the 1962 election campaign for State Superintendent of Public Instruction.

4. *The Book of the States* (Chicago: Council of State Governments, biennial) contains useful data summarizing state governmental structures affecting education.

5. Stephen K. Bailey, Richard T. Frost, Paul E. Marsh, and Robert C. Wood, *Schoolmen and Politics: A Study of State Aid to Education in the Northeast* (Syracuse: Syracuse University Press, 1962) p. 27.

6. See, for example, Arthur E. Bestor, *Educational Wastelands* (Urbana: University of Illinois Press, 1953).

7. A recent and judicious discussion of the pros and cons of present certification practices is in James B. Conant, *The Education of American Teachers* (New York: McGraw-Hill Book Co., 1963). See also James D. Koerner, *The Miseducation of American Teachers* (Boston: Houghton Mifflin Co., 1963).

8. New York: Teachers College, Columbia University, 1905.

9. The most important statements are contained in George Strayer and Robert Haig, *The Financing of Education in the State of New York* (New York: Macmillan Co., 1923); and Paul Mort, *State Support for Public Schools* (New York: Teachers College, Columbia University, 1926).

10. Paul Mort, Walter Reusser, and John Polby, *Public School Finance,* (3rd ed.; New York: McGraw-Hill Book Co., 1960) p. 218.

11. A pioneering discussion of group interests in education is Thomas H. Eliot, "Toward an Understanding of Public School Politics," *American Political Science Review LIII* (1959) 1032–1052. For expressions of the "educationist" argument, see Arthur E. Bestor, *The Restoration of Learning* (New York: Alfred A. Knopf, 1955), and *Educational Wastelands;* Hyman Rickover, *Education and Freedom* (New York: E. P. Dutton & Co., 1959).

12. Bailey, *et al.,* pp. 23–26. Much of the discussion which follows is drawn from the Bailey study and from Nicholas A. Masters, Robert H. Salisbury, and Thomas H. Eliot, *State Politics and the Public Schools* (New York: Alfred A. Knopf, 1964).

13. See *N.E.A. Handbook,* 1963–64 (Washington: National Education Association, 1963) pp. 347–350.

14. For a convenient summary of the development of the N.E.A., see Edgar B. Wesley, *N.E.A.: The First Hundred Years* (New York: Harper and Bros., 1957).

15. Bailey, *et al.,* p. 46.

16. Masters, *et al.,* p. 141, n.2.

17. The issues involved in race and education are examined in Albert Blaustein and Clarence Ferguson, *Desegregation and the Law* (New Brunswick: Rutgers University Press, 1957); Don Schoemaker (ed.), *With All Deliberate Speed* (New York: Harper and Bros., 1957); and the annual reports of the U.S. Civil Rights Commission. A summary of several of these can be found in Wallace Mendelson, *Discrimination* (Englewood Cliffs, N.J.: Prentice-Hall, 1962). The most comprehensive work on religion and the public schools is Leo Pfeffer, *Church, State, and Freedom* (Boston: Beacon Press, 1953). Also see David Fellman, *The Supreme Court and Education* (New York: Teachers College, Columbia University, 1960); and Theodore Powell, *The School Bus Law* (Middleton: Wesleyan University Press, 1960).

18. See, for example, the discussion of Missouri in Masters, *et al.,* pp. 12–99. Less adaptive school leaders apparently were found by John Wahlke, Heinz Eulau, William Buchanan, and Leroy Ferguson in their study of state legislators in Tennessee, Ohio, California, and New Jersey; see *The Legislative System* (New York: John Wiley and Sons, 1962) especially p. 335.

19. Wahlke, *et al., p.* 337, found that among major types of interest groups education associations were least likely to be regarded as unselfish or public spirited but most able to mobilize votes to affect the outcome of elections.
20. *Ibid.,* p. 200.
21. *Ibid.,* pp. 212–213.
22. Mort, *et al.,* pp. 80–87, report a number of studies which have attempted to correlate the educational outputs, measured in terms of both educational achievement and kind of school program, with expenditure levels. The findings are quite consistent for different periods of time and different school systems, showing a correlation of about .6.
23. Charles S. Benson reports that per pupil spending and per capita income showed a correlation of .79 in 1929–30, and .84 in 1959–60, suggesting the durability of the relationship. *The Economics of Public Education* (Boston: Houghton Mifflin Co., 1961) pp. 62–63.
24. Richard E. Dawson and James A. Robinson, "Inter-Party Competition, Economic Variables, and Welfare Policies in the American States," *Journal of Politics XXV* (1963) pp. 286–289.
25. *Public School Finance,* p. 197.
26. Much of the following discussion is based upon Frederick Rudolph, *The American College and University* (New York: Alfred A. Knopf, 1962).
27. *The Dartmouth College Case,* 4 Wheaton 518.
28. Rudolph, p. 211.
29. *Ibid.,* p. 185.
30. *Ibid.,* pp. 261–262.
31. No single summary of the formal governmental structures affecting higher education is presently available. Even if it were, it would soon be out of date for the systems are changing rapidly in many states. Recent works which discuss the questions of governmental structure include Malcolm Moos and Francis Rourke, *The Campus and the State* (Baltimore: The Johns Hopkins Press, 1959); Lyman A. Glenny, *Autonomy of Public Colleges* (New York: McGraw-Hill Book Co., 1959); John J. Corson, *Governance of Colleges and Universities* (New York: McGraw-Hill Book Co., 1960); and T. R. McConnell, *A General Pattern for American Public Higher Education* (New York: McGraw-Hill Book Co., 1962).
32. Glenny's book is a particularly thorough discussion of the problems of coordination as well as an illustration of the variety now existing in institutional forms
33. 347 U.S. 483 (1954).
34. A summary of reorganization developments may be found in C. O. Fitzwater, *School District Reorganization* (Washington: U.S. Department of Health, Education, and Welfare, 1957).

SELECTED BIBLIOGRAPHY

Bailey, Stephen K., Richard T. Frost, Paul E. Marsh, and Robert C. Wood. *Schoolmen and Politics: A Study of State Aid to Education in the Northeast.* Syracuse: Syracuse University Press, 1962. One of two major studies of the politics of state decisions affecting education.

Benson, Charles S. *The Economics of Public Education.* Boston: Houghton Mifflin Co., 1961. A broad examination of economic relationships in this field.

Butts, R. Freeman, and Lawrence A. Cremin. *A History of Education in the*

United States. New York: Henry Holt and Co., 1953. A thorough general survey by two leading scholars in the history of American education.

Glenny, Lyman A. *Autonomy of Public Colleges.* New York: McGraw-Hill Book Co., 1959. One of a series of studies of American higher education centered at the University of California.

Masters, Nicholas A., Robert H. Salisbury, and Thomas H. Eliot. *State Politics and the Public Schools.* New York: Alfred A. Knopf, 1964. Provides detailed material on a subject which has received little attention from political scientists — covers Missouri, Illinois, and Michigan.

Moos, Malcolm, and Francis Rourke. *The Campus and the State.* Baltimore: The Johns Hopkins Press, 1959. Survey of the governing arrangements for public higher education.

Mort, Paul, Walter Reusser, and John Polby. *Public School Finance.* 3rd ed. New York: McGraw-Hill Book Co., 1960. Useful survey and guide to more detailed literature. The senior author was a leading innovator in state aid issues a generation ago.

Munger, Frank J., and Richard F. Fenno. *National Politics and Federal Aid to Education.* Syracuse: Syracuse University Press, 1962. An excellent short review of the history and the contemporary struggle over this thorny question.

Rudolph, Frederick. *The American College and University.* New York: Alfred A. Knopf, 1962. An excellent study of the growth and development of the American system of higher education.

The Economics and Politics of Public Education Series, published by the Syracuse University Press, contains ten other titles in addition to the works by Bailey, *et al.,* and by Munger and Fenno listed above. Any or all of these may be of interest to the reader, even though they are not specifically noted in the present discussion.

THE POLITICS
OF
WELFARE

CHAPTER 10

by

RICHARD E. DAWSON and JAMES A. ROBINSON*

STATE POLITICS, LIKE POLITICS EVERYWHERE, revolves around decisions about "who gets what, when, and how," to borrow the pungent epigram of Harold D. Lasswell. State governments make "authoritative allocation(s) of values," which David Easton identifies as the distinguishing characteristic of political activity. From such generic characterizations of politics come some of the continuing questions for political analysis:

Why do state governments adopt programs to affect some values and not others?

Why do state governments favor the values of some groups above those of others?

Does the decision-making process of state governments make any difference for the content of governmental programs, i.e., for decisions about what values of which groups governments will try to affect?

Are the economic resources available to state governments more important than the decision-making process of government in determining governmental activity?[1]

One of the values about which governments make decisions is "welfare." Values mean the goals, events, objectives, or preferences that people would like to realize and maintain. Welfare values refer to those events or objects that pertain to the maintenance of the physical activity of the individual person. Representative welfare values include *wellbeing* (the health and safety of the person), *wealth* (income received from goods and services), *skill* (proficiency in work or occupation), and *enlightenment* (knowledge and education).[2] Other chapters in this book cover state governmental activity with respect to wealth (e.g., tax

*The authors acknowledge the National Center for Education in Politics for its support of their research from which this chapter is drawn, and Norman H. Nie and John Paul Dubinsky, who helped collect and analyze data.

policies) and with respect to skill and enlightenment (e.g., educational policies). This chapter is a comparative analysis of state policies that affect well-being.

We shall concentrate on only a few of the many state welfare programs, especially those devoted to the well-being of dependent children, the elderly, the blind, the totally and permanently disabled, and the unemployed. To understand American state policies toward these sets of persons, we trace the development of public welfare programs from their English origins; describe the setting in which contemporary American welfare policies are decided, with special attention to the participation of the federal government; compare efforts among the states; and analyze socio-economic and political factors that determine the extent of state welfare efforts.

The development of public welfare policies in the United States parallels the development of other governmental policies. The number of welfare activities performed by government has continually — if irregularly — grown, and the responsibility for initiating and executing them has gradually shifted to higher levels of governmental authority. Today the formulation, financing, and implementation of welfare programs is a joint responsibility of local, state, and federal governments. Although the basic responsibility for public welfare rests upon state governments, the federal government largely finances most of the important welfare programs, and local governments administer and implement the policies jointly formulated by state and federal governments. Contemporary welfare programs include wholly federal programs, federal-state programs, federal-state-local programs, wholly state programs, state-local programs, and wholly local programs.

Wayne Vasey classifies these programs according to (1) their clientele; (2) the kind of services they render; or (3) the arrangements among the different levels of government that participate in them.[3] The clientele of current welfare programs include the aged, the unemployed, dependent or neglected children, the physically handicapped, the mentally retarded, the mentally ill, the delinquent, emotionally disturbed children, veterans, criminals, and, in some instances, simply "needy persons."

Most of the programs provide income maintenance either through social insurance or through public assistance. Others attempt to meet such needs as health services, rehabilitation, job retraining, and institutional care.

Governmental participation includes local, state, and federal levels. As of 1958 Vasey listed and categorized governmental welfare programs as follows:[4]

Federally-administered programs
  Old-age, survivors', and disability insurance
  Railroad workers' insurance

Services to veterans
Services to wards of government
Federal probation and parole
Administration of federal prisons

Federal-State Programs
Old-age assistance
Aid to the blind
Aid to dependent children
Aid to the disabled
Unemployment compensation
Vocational rehabilitation
Mental health services
Crippled children's services
Child welfare services
Maternal and child health

State, State-Local, and Local Programs
Workmen's compensation
Disability insurance
General assistance
Local probation
Parole
State and local prisons and reformatories

This is, of course, not an exhaustive list. New programs, such as the Kerr-Mills medical aid program, have been added in the federal-state category since 1958. Other programs, such as public health services, might also be included. A discussion of all these programs is beyond the scope of this chapter. We shall confine our consideration to six programs. These include four categorical assistance programs operating with both federal and state participation, one social insurance program (unemployment compensation), which is also a joint federal-state program, and general assistance, which is a wholly state program. The old-age, survivors', and disability insurance program will be excluded because it is a wholly federal program. Although not inclusive of all state programs affecting well-being, these six are the most important, as measured both by the amount of money spent and by the number of persons receiving aid.

DEVELOPMENT OF PUBLIC WELFARE POLICIES AND PROGRAMS

EARLY PRACTICES: THE ENGLISH EXPERIENCE AND ITS TRANSFER TO THE UNITED STATES. The sources of this complex array of programs are found in the origins and development of American political, social, and economic practices in general, as well as in the history and traditions of specific welfare values and policies. Like many other American developments, public welfare policies originated in early English practices that were brought to colonial America. To understand how and why public welfare policies and practices developed, especially during the earlier periods, we must know something about the English heritage. Governmental policy toward the care of the destitute evolved during the disintegration of certain feudal and religious institutions of the Middle Ages. The earliest secular concerns were with the regulation of begging and the control of the movement of laboring classes.[5] As early as 1572, Parliament recognized the principle of public provision for the destitute and put the responsibility for raising funds for poor relief upon local governments. It was, however, the Poor Relief Act of 1601, the Elizabethan Poor Law, that formally established the nature and techniques of governmental responsibility for the care of the poor. This act codified earlier legislation and influenced subsequent policies of relief to the poor in both England and the United States for three and a half centuries. The Poor Relief Act acknowledged governmental responsibility for the care of the destitute and delegated the provisions of such aid to the smallest unit of local government, the parish.

The 1601 Act also established other precedents. It allowed for tax funds to support poor relief and to establish workhouses and almshouses. It recognized the principle that relatives have legal responsibility to support impoverished members of their families. It established residence or "settlement" requirements to discourage indigent travelers. These early laws reflected the sentiment that poverty is a personal disgrace caused by individual laziness, moral weaknesses, or other individual and personal shortcomings.[6] These basic welfare principles, although amended and extended from time to time, constituted the basis for public welfare policy in England and the United States from the 17th into the 20th centuries.

When the English colonists settled the North American continent during the 17th century, they brought with them many English institutions and practices. Among the customs first introduced to the New World was the English method of caring for the destitute. The colonial governments emulated the principles of the Elizabethan poor laws soon after settlement. The statutes of the Plymouth Colony, for example, as early as 1642 stipulated that:

> Every township shall make competent provisions for the mainte-
> nance of their poor according as they shall find most convenient and
> suitable for themselves by an order and general agreement in public
> town meeting. And notwithstanding the permission that all such person
> and persons as are now resident and inhabitant and within the said towns
> shall be maintained and provided for by them.[7]

The principles that government bears responsibility for the care of the poor and that this responsibility rests with local units of government were embodied in public policy quite early. New England colonies designated the town as the governmental unit to administer poor relief. Southern colonies delegated relief first to the parish and later to the county. Middle Atlantic states assigned responsibility either to township or county governments.

THE DEVELOPMENT OF PUBLIC WELFARE IN THE UNITED STATES: THE GROWTH AND TRANSFERENCE OF GOVERNMENTAL RESPONSIBILITY. By the time the United States attained independence, a system of poor relief was in operation. Its most important political features were those that assumed public responsibility, no matter how slight the actual effort, and relied upon local governments to establish, support, and administer welfare programs. These features were carried westward as new territories and states were formed. The statutes of the Northwest Territory in 1790 and of the Missouri Territory in 1815 contained the principle of local responsibility. The states formed from these territories adhered to this principle in establishing their poor laws.[8] State legislation to care for the poor was enacted from time to time, but these laws merely delegated responsibility or permissiveness to local governments. This pattern of almost total reliance upon local government existed throughout the nation until the Great Depression of the 1930's. Most states devolved responsibility for poor relief upon the county, as shown in Table 1.

Table 1

POLITICAL UNIT RESPONSIBLE FOR POOR RELIEF, 1934

NUMBER OF STATES	UNIT
24	Counties
7	Counties, townships, and cities
6	Counties and cities
5	Towns (all 5 in New England)
3	Counties, townships, cities, and villages
2	Counties and townships
1	Towns and cities (Rhode Island)

Source: Lucy W. Brown, "Poor Relief Laws: A Digest," American Public Welfare Association, 1934; taken from Josephine C. Brown, *Public Relief: 1929–1939* (New York: Henry Holt and Co., 1940).

Certain specialized state programs developed — notably during the latter part of the 19th century and the early part of the 20th — for aid to the poor. The earliest direct state responsibility for the care of the destitute provided relief for the unsettled poor or for those poor or needy persons not classified as residents of any local community. State laws and court decisions as far back as the colonial period assumed state responsibility for these persons. Connecticut stipulated that the poor and defective who belonged to no town or place in the colony were to be cared for at the expense of the colony.[9] State governments also adopted programs for disaster relief and for assistance to military veterans. By 1910 all save six states provided for relief of veterans of the Civil War and some for veterans of other wars and military conflicts.[10]

Another set of persons who early received aid from state governments were dependent persons, such as children without parental support, the deaf, dumb, and blind, the feebleminded, and the insane. Aid for these persons came through special state institutions, asylums, and "homes." The number of state institutions for the care of these several categories of needy persons grew steadily throughout the 19th century. The creation of these institutions marked the first assumption of direct state responsibility for welfare, as distinguished from delegating responsibility to local governments.[11]

The next stage in history of state welfare activity was the formation of state boards to supervise institutions and programs. The first state supervisory agency was the Massachusetts Board of Charities established in 1863. New York followed in 1867 with the creation of a Board of State Commissioners of Public Charities. Other states acted similarly during the following seventy years, and by 1931 all but five states had a department concerned with general public welfare problems.[12] The jurisdiction of these boards varied from state to state, but usually they inspected and supervised the administration of state and local institutions. Only in a few instances did jurisdiction extend to non-institutional welfare activities.

In the early 20th century a new type of state welfare program evolved — that of granting aid to needy individuals without placing them in institutions. These new policies included direct aid to categories of individuals such as the blind, the aged, and dependent children. Wisconsin passed the first state law for aid to the blind in 1907; Illinois adopted the first program of aid for dependent children in 1911; and Montana and Nevada enacted the first for the aged in 1923.[13] Because these programs granted aid to specified types of individuals, they became known as categorical assistance programs. The enactment of these assistance programs, however, proceeded slowly. By 1934, prior to the enactment of the national Social Security Act, only twenty-four of the states aided the blind, twenty-eight states helped the elderly, and forty-two states assisted mothers and dependent children. Some of these programs were not available in all counties.[14] Even in states in which these categorical assistance programs had been adopted, they were only partially operative and, on the whole, not very effective.[15]

Despite limitations on their effectiveness, these state programs constituted significant developments in basic welfare policies — both in terms of the types of assistance extended and in the level of governmental responsibility. The categorical relief programs radically changed the concepts and methods of public assistance that had prevailed since the Elizabethan poor laws. Basic changes were made in the criteria by which aid was granted, in the form in which the aid was given to the recipients, in the administrative procedures involved, and in the kind and extent of participation of state governments. These early 20th century developments are also significant because they form the foundation upon which contemporary state welfare policies have been based.

The Great Depression of the 1930's marked a major watershed in the development of public welfare policies, as it did for many other public policies. The Depression contributed both to the extension of the types of and the amounts of public welfare programs and the expansion of state responsibility and participation. As a result of the Depression the federal government initiated large-scale participation in welfare policies, especially in financing programs. The significant changes that occurred in the level of governmental participation in financing public aid during the 1930's are demonstrated in Table 2. The total amount expended for public assistance increased greatly,

Table 2

SOURCES OF PUBLIC EXPENDITURES FOR ASSISTANCE AND WORK PROGRAMS, 1930-1941

YEAR	TOTAL AMOUNT (IN THOUSANDS OF DOLLARS)	PER CENT FEDERAL	PER CENT STATE	PER CENT LOCAL
1930	98,024	0.0	8.7	91.3
1931	217,043	0.0	18.0	82.0
1932	421,370	17.5	21.9	60.6
1933	1,059,675	63.9	11.7	24.4
1934	1,779,313	75.8	10.0	14.2
1935	1,871,315	73.3	13.1	13.6
1936	2,505,580	77.4	13.4	9.2
1937	2,173,580	71.0	18.2	10.8
1938	2,827,300	72.9	17.5	9.6
1939	2,638,869	69.4	20.1	10.5
1940	2,309,068	68.6	20.7	10.7
1941	1,950,269	66.5	22.6	10.9

Source: "Trends in Financing Public Aid, 1930–1941," in *Public Assistance 1941*, The Federal Security Agency, Social Security Board, Bureau of Public Assistance, No. 4.

and financing shifted from local to state governments and, especially, to the federal government. During the next decades the trend toward larger welfare expenditures continued. Following a decline in the mid-1940's, the expenditures of all levels of government for public aid programs rose to $3 billion in 1955 and to more than $4 billion in 1960. The relationship between federal and state-local expenditures for public aid programs has leveled off; the federal government now pays about half, and state and local governments pay half.[16]

The impact of large-scale unemployment and widespread poverty that accompanied the Great Depression proved far too great for the patchwork system of local and state welfare programs to meet. The always insufficient funds and the limited revenue sources for these programs dwindled rapidly. The collapse of the locally based system, coupled with unprecedented economic needs, led both to the involvement of the federal government and to more active participation by state governments. In the earliest years of the Depression, many states supplemented their local welfare activities through greater state aid and state participation. In 1931 New York, the first state to adopt a relatively long-term program of financial aid for the unemployed, created a Temporary Emergency Relief Administration to distribute money to local relief agencies. A majority of the states followed with programs of their own.[17] Even in the midst of the economic crisis, however, states maintained the tradition that welfare or public aid was a local responsibility.

Active federal participation began in mid-1932 with the enactment of the Emergency Relief and Reconstruction Act, which, although small in scope, represented the first major departure from the traditional non-participation of the federal government in welfare programs. The Act authorized loans with 3 per cent interest to states as advances on future federal grants for highway construction. The evolution of federal welfare activity during the 1930's occurred in two stages. In the first stage, during the Hoover Administration, the federal government adopted emergency relief programs and public works projects. With the new Roosevelt Administration in Washington in 1933, one less opposed to federal participation in welfare programs, a more extensive relief measure was enacted in May, 1933 — the Federal Emergency Relief Act. This legislation appropriated funds for unemployment relief to the states in the form of grants rather than loans and created a Federal Emergency Relief Administration to supervise the disbursement of these federal funds by the states. The federal government enacted other emergency relief and public works programs during 1933 — in March, the Civilian Conservation Corps; in June, the Federal Emergency Administration of Public Works; in October, the Federal Surplus Relief Corporation; and in November, the Civil Works Administration.[18] These were, however, intended to be emergency and temporary measures against an immediate and, hopefully, short-term crisis.

The second stage came in the mid-1930's. By that time a permanent federal-state social insurance and public assistance program had aroused considerable interest. In 1934, President Roosevelt created the Committee on

Economic Security to study the problems of economic insecurity and want, and to present proposals to deal with them on a more permanent basis. This Committee submitted its report to the President on January 17, 1935, and on the basis of its findings the President made recommendations to Congress. These proposals, modified by Congress, became the Social Security Act in August, 1935. The Social Security Act has served as the basic framework for public welfare policies in nearly all fields and for all levels of governmental activity. It includes both programs administered and financed entirely by the federal government and programs administered and financed jointly by the states and the federal government. Although the Act authorized extensive federal participation, especially through financial assistance and minimum standards, it placed basic responsibility for all of the programs, except the old-age insurance program, on the state governments. Congress amended the Act several times later, but its essential features have remained the same. It includes three basic types of programs: old-age and unemployment insurance, public assistance, and children's services. The original legislation included a federally administered program of old-age and survivors' insurance. Through the imposition of a payroll tax on employers of eight or more persons, it induced the states to enact unemployment insurance legislation. Its public assistance provisions included categorical aid programs for the aged, the blind, and dependent children. In 1950, Congress extended aid to the totally and permanently disabled. Under the children's services provisions, lump sum grants were made to the states for aid for maternal and child health, for services to crippled children, and for child welfare services in rural areas.

The Social Security Act was a hybrid of welfare approaches. It replaced the traditional poor laws and changed the basic philosophy of public welfare. Before its enactment a small amount of aid was granted to a small number of needy persons; now a comprehensive system was established to cover large segments of the population. The Act induced greater participation in welfare programs by state and local governments, but required centralization at the state level. It introduced new and broader methods of financing public welfare with programs of social insurance and with extensive grants-in-aid from the federal government and, in some instances, grants from the state governments to the local units. Perhaps most importantly, it initiated a new approach in intergovernmental relations among federal, state, and local units. Although the widespread financial participation of the federal government in welfare programs constituted the most significant political innovation of the Act, the vastly increased participation it established for states in defining, financing, and administering the programs should not be underrated.

CONTEMPORARY PUBLIC WELFARE—GOALS, STRUCTURE, AND POLICY

Public welfare policies result from many factors. They emerge from particular social-economic conditions, from public attitudes toward social problems, and from the ways in which political decisions are made. In the preceding section we traced the most important steps in the evolution of state welfare policies that exist today. We noted the important participation of the federal government in contemporary welfare programs. As much as for any other state program, welfare has been influenced by decisions made at the national level. This is primarily a consequence of the time and conditions under which governments at all levels undertook new and expanded welfare activities. Although from their earliest periods the American states have had some form of welfare policies, programs that were slowly expanding during the 19th and early 20th centuries, the whole system of welfare assistance underwent change in only a few years during the 1930's. This rapid change occurred primarily as a response to extraordinarily adverse economic conditions. The federal government adopted a variety of measures that both directly and indirectly affected the development of welfare policies at the state and local levels. Consequently, state and local policies now operate within the framework of a national program. Federal policy, through grants-in-aid and other economic enticements, largely defines the types of welfare measures that will be adopted and sets minimum standards for eligibility and administration of the state programs.

To say that the federal government establishes major guidelines for welfare programs at the state and local level, however, is not to say that the states do not participate significantly in the formulation and implementation of policies. Within the broad outlines of federal policy, room remains for state-by-state differences in the extensiveness of programs, the amount of money that will be allocated, and the means by which the programs will be administered.

The welfare expenditures and efforts of the states differ greatly. For example, in 1960 the per capita expenditures for public welfare of state and local governments ranged from $55.17 in Oklahoma and $48.52 in Colorado, to $8.57 in Virginia and $11.01 in Maryland. Likewise, the percentage of the state's budget allocated to welfare varied from a high of 29.27 per cent in Oklahoma to a low of 4.69 per cent in Wyoming. Per recipient payments for programs also differ widely among the states. The average weekly payment for persons receiving unemployment insurance varied between $21.24 in North Carolina, to $42.32 in Ohio in 1960. The source of money to finance the programs, even when the participation of the federal government is discounted, also varies among the states. As of 1960, local governments in Arkansas, Louisiana, Pennsylvania, Utah, and Washington paid none of the cost of the several public assistance programs; in contrast local governments contributed 35.7 per cent of the cost in Minnesota and 33.0 per cent in New Jersey. All states do not participate in all federally supported programs. As late as 1960, Arizona, Indiana, and Nevada di not participate in the federal program of aid to the permanently and totally disabled.

GOALS AND OBJECTIVES OF AMERICAN WELFARE POLICIES. Public policy is initiated and enacted in the pursuit of goals. Goals may involve the improvement of a small group of individuals at the expense of the larger society, or the improvement of larger groups at the expense of the few. It is, however, often difficult to specify concretely the objectives of public policies. This is true of public welfare policy. In the broadest sense, the objectives of welfare measures have been to establish a basic standard of living for individuals unable to provide for themselves. The principle that taxpayers should provide life's necessities for destitute individuals has long been accepted in western societies and has been the underlying goal of welfare policies and programs. This idea has been part of the Anglo-American common law for several centuries. In the *Commentaries on the Laws of England,* written in the late 18th century, Blackstone states the major objective of law in providing minimum standards:

> The law not only regards life and member and protects every man in the enjoyment of them, but also furnishes him with everything necessary for their support. For there is no man so indigent or wretched, but he may demand a supply sufficient for all the necessaries of life from the more opulent part of the community, by means of the several statutes enacted for the relief of the poor.[19]

Some welfare programs, such as aid to the blind and aid to dependent children, provide for the well-being of special categories of individual needs. Others, such as general assistance, care for cases of destitution not otherwise provided for. The objective of still other welfare policies, such as unemployment insurance, is to contribute some income to employable persons who are temporarily out of work. Others offer economic security for individuals who are no longer able to support themselves because of age or physical disability. The programs of old-age and survivors' insurance aim to supply the needs of the former, and aid to the permanently and totally disabled, those of the latter.

Welfare programs have other consequences. They reallocate financial resources among the general population. Social insurance programs reallocate a person's money from one time period to another. Public assistance programs reallocate money from those persons who have "adequate" income to those who do not. In the social insurance programs, the individual contributes a portion of his income while he is able to work to accumulate some income for periods when he is unable to work.

In addition to these goals, federal welfare policy has been designed to achieve several more specific objectives. Through the inducement of grants-in-aid in the Social Security Act of 1935, Congress encouraged the states to adopt certain types of categorical assistance programs and programs of unemployment insurance. Through requirements for participation in the federally aided programs, it also sought to achieve minimum standards of payments, financial contributions from the states, more liberalized eligibility, and some form of statewide administrative machinery. The formulae to determine the amount of federal aid to be granted also sought to equalize welfare aid in the states in the face of different levels of need and state ability to finance welfare programs.

Table 3

PER CENT OF FUNDS FOR ALL PROGRAMS PROVIDED
BY FEDERAL, STATE, AND LOCAL GOVERNMENTS, 1961

STATES BY REGION	PER CENT FEDERAL	PER CENT STATE	PER CENT LOCAL
Northeast			
Connecticut	34.0	58.4	7.6
Maine	62.0	27.9	10.1
Massachusetts	40.1	36.2	23.7
New Hampshire	50.3	24.0	25.7
New Jersey	37.8	29.2	33.0
New York	37.6	32.0	30.4
Pennsylvania	45.1	54.9	0.0
Rhode Island	44.2	50.6	5.2
Vermont	66.0	23.5	10.5
North Central			
Indiana	52.1	17.2	30.7
Iowa	52.6	31.6	15.8
Kansas	53.3	24.7	22.0
Illinois	37.4	55.8	6.8
Michigan	36.7	36.2	27.1
Minnesota	43.1	21.2	35.7
Missouri	64.0	35.8	0.2
Nebraska	60.9	27.6	11.5
North Dakota	51.4	35.8	12.8
Ohio	42.4	49.5	8.1
South Dakota	61.9	25.8	12.3
Wisconsin	42.7	24.8	32.5
South			
Alabama	74.0	25.9	0.1
Arkansas	73.2	26.8	0.0
Delaware	46.8	33.1	20.1
Florida	68.6	26.9	4.5

SOME CHARACTERISTICS OF WELFARE PROGRAMS: STATE AND LOCAL PARTICIPATION. As we have indicated, the political and administrative structure of contemporary American public welfare policies entails the joint efforts of state, federal, and local governments. The major responsibility, however, devolves upon the states. Despite huge financial contributions of the federal government, the states retain the legal right to determine whether they will participate in federal programs. Within the broad provisions of the federal regulations, the states determine the amount of aid to be allocated each recipient, the requirements of eligibility, and how the programs are administered. The states also decide to what extent the programs will be financed and administered by local governments.

Table 3, continued

STATES BY REGION	PER CENT FEDERAL	PER CENT STATE	PER CENT LOCAL
Georgia	72.8	22.0	5.2
Kentucky	73.3	25.3	1.4
Louisiana	64.9	35.1	0.0
Maryland	59.1	26.3	14.6
Mississippi	76.9	22.4	0.7
North Carolina	71.1	11.9	17.0
Oklahoma	60.9	38.4	0.7
South Carolina	73.5	25.6	0.9
Tennessee	74.9	20.0	5.1
Texas	70.9	27.5	1.6
Virginia	69.1	15.7	15.2
West Virginia	73.3	24.6	2.1
West			
Arizona	67.0	32.9	0.1
California	42.1	38.0	19.9
Colorado	42.7	48.6	8.7
Idaho	62.6	37.1	0.3
Montana	45.9	21.7	32.4
Nevada	42.6	25.2	32.2
New Mexico	67.9	31.7	0.4
Oregon	45.5	40.1	14.4
Utah	55.0	45.0	0.0
Washington	39.9	60.1	0.0
Wyoming	47.9	19.7	32.4

Source: Data taken from *Social Security Bulletin: Annual Statistical Supplement; 1959–61,* The Social Security Administration, U.S. Department of Health, Education, and Welfare (Washington: U.S. Government Printing Office, 1961) p. 104. Alaska and Hawaii are omitted.

The participation of local governments in financing and administering social welfare programs varies from state to state. The Social Security Act required that participating states create an administrative board and that the programs operate in all subdivisions of the state, but the Act left open other questions of state and local participation. In some states the programs are entirely state-financed and state-administered. In others the local units — counties, towns, or townships — participate with varying degrees of control and financial contributions. The financial contributions of different governmental levels for public aid programs in 1961 are shown in Table 3. The most important pattern observable in these data is a geographic one. The New England, Middle Atlantic, and Midwestern states tend to rely on the local governmental units for money, the Southern states rely very little upon local governmental units, and the Western states rely less on local government than the East and Midwest, but more than the South.

FEDERAL INTERVENTION. Federal standards apply to the administration of the programs, the form of payments, and the requirements for eligibility. The programs must apply to all parts of the state, and although some aspects of administration and financing may be left to the local governments, centralized state administration of the programs must be established. Appeal procedures must be available to applicants or recipients who feel that their cases have not been treated fairly or adequately. Federal provisions require that aid be distributed in money rather than in voucher relief or in the direct distribution of goods and services. This provision constitutes an important departure from the old poor laws. Eligibility requirements center around rules restricting the length of residence and requiring citizenship. To receive federal funds, the states must meet federal standards, but within this broad framework the states have discretion in determining the amount of money to be paid and to whom it will be paid.

VARIATIONS IN FINANCING: GRANTS. Federal contributions to the categorical assistance programs take the form of grants-in-aid that pay a specified proportion of the amount of money paid per recipient. When the programs were first enacted in 1935, the federal payments matched state contributions, with one dollar for each dollar that the state paid per recipient. Since then this formula has been amended with the result that the federal government pays a larger share of the cost and grants more money to states with higher needs and less wealth. Congress adopted these changes in an attempt to equalize welfare efforts among the states. Under the new formulae the federal government pays a large share of the first part of a grant and a lesser share of the remainder up to a maximum amount, above which it pays no part.[20]

The same principle is followed with respect to aid to dependent children. The federal government also pays half the cost of the administration of the assistance programs.

The objective of the formula was to help the poorer states meet greater welfare needs despite their limited fiscal capacities to carry the burden of welfare. However, because the formula means that the federal government pays for a higher portion of lower payments, the programs reward states for low payments per recipient. The way for a state to get the most aid from the federal government is to pay small amounts of money to a large number of people. This is what appears to happen in the poorer states, especially in the South. This helps explain the differences in the percentage of public assistance funds coming from the federal government, as shown in Table 3. The proportions paid by the federal government ranged from 34.0 per cent in Connecticut to 76.9 per cent in Mississippi in 1961.

FEDERALLY FINANCED INSURANCE PROGRAMS: TAXES. The other major federal-state welfare program that concerns us is unemployment compensation, which is financed through a withholding tax on income. Like the public assistance programs, Congress enacted it as part of the Social Security Act in 1935. Also like the categorical assistance programs, it is basically a state-adopted and state-administered program with financial incentives from and general standards set by the federal government. The Social Security Act requires the collection of an unemployment insurance tax on payrolls. Ninety percent of the revenue from this tax is to be used as a tax credit for states that enact unemployment insurance programs. The other 10 per cent of the tax money is given to the states to help them pay the administration of their programs. The federal government collects the money and returns a specified amount to the states. The Act was an incentive to the states to adopt unemployment insurance programs. Within a few years all states adopted such programs.

The standards imposed by the federal government are not extensive, and the states exercise considerable discretion in designing their programs. A statewide system with appeal machinery must be established. Federal regulations specify that employees cannot be denied benefits for refusing to work at jobs available because of labor disputes or at jobs whose wage rates are substantially below prevailing rates for similar work. Decisions concerning the amount of benefits, eligibility, and the length of time for which unemployment insurance can be drawn are left primarily to the states.

ASSISTANCE PROGRAMS: STATE FINANCING. The general assistance program is entirely state-financed and state-administered. It is best conceived as a residual relief program to cover those needy individuals who, for one reason or another, are not covered under any of the other welfare programs. It is the contemporary program most like the earlier poor relief programs. Without federal participation these programs differ even more radically from state to state than the others. The criteria for eligibility, the amount of and even the type of payments, and the financing and administration of these programs are handled quite differently throughout the states. In some, the general assistance programs are administered entirely by counties or townships. Payments in food orders or rent orders are often given under general relief instead of in cash, as required by the categorical assistance programs. Payments are usually much smaller than those of the other public assistance programs, and the criteria for granting payments are often vague. Nevertheless, general relief remains an important social welfare program, and it sustains several hundred thousand persons each month. Its use gradually declines as an increasing proportion of elderly people receive old-age and survivors' insurance.[21]

DESCRIPTIONS AND COMPARISONS OF STATE WELFARE EFFORTS

The cost and coverage of welfare programs differ considerably from state to state. This is evident from even a cursory look at almost any aspect of state welfare policies, but a precise measurement and description of state welfare efforts is not simple. Any single indicator, such as the amount of payment per recipient for a specified program, presents only a partial picture of any state's welfare activity. Therefore, it is desirable to start with a number of different indicators of state welfare efforts in order to have a full picture. If several indices of welfare output yield similar descriptions, we shall be inclined to accept the total portrait with greater assurance than if we have only a single indicator, or if different indicators produce different descriptions.

We shall use four principal indices of state welfare effort:

1. The amount of payment per recipient for several programs;
2. The percentage of program funds coming from state and local government;
3. & 4. The per capita expenditure for welfare, including both the per capita expenditure from state and local governments and the total amount spent per capita with federal contributions included.

Although we are mainly interested in welfare policies as they existed in 1961, we also consider state policies at two other stages, extending throughout a period of twenty years. Comparable data on programs are available for 1941, the first year in which all states participated in most of the federal-state public assistance and unemployment programs. Therefore, we collected and analyzed data from three different years spanning this twenty-year period — 1941, 1950 and 1961. The comparative indices of state welfare efforts for these three dates not only permit us to make comparisons of state welfare efforts at different times, but allow us to compare developments within the same state during this time span.

The first index is *the average payment received per recipient under each of these six programs.* Each program involves a cash payment to a specified set of needy individuals. Table 4 reports the average payments per recipient together with the comparative ranking of the states for 1961. The state paying the highest average payment for each program is ranked first, and the one with the lowest average payment is ranked last.

As Table 4 indicates, great differences exist between the states in the average payments per recipient for these six programs. The differences between the average payment of the highest paying state and the lowest paying state range from about three-fold in old-age assistance to nine-fold in general assistance. Similar differences occur at each of the three time points. Although all states have substantially increased their payments per recipient, differences between the highest paying states and the lowest paying states have remained quite large. In fact, the gap between the highest paying state and the lowest paying state has sometimes increased. For example, in the program of aid to dependent children the ranges between the lowest and the highest paying states for the three different years were as follows: from $13.33 to $57.70 in 1941; from $18.28 to $124.10 in 1950; and from $36.38 to $178.57 in 1961.

The comparative rankings of the states for these programs have remained remarkably stable during the twenty-year period. The rankings of the states, according to payments per recipient, for the three categorical assistance programs that have been in operation throughout the three time periods are shown in Table 5. In relatively few instances have the states substantially changed their ranks. Arizona, Connecticut, Ohio, Pennsylvania, and Utah dropped a bit relative to the other states. Iowa, Minnesota, New Jersey, and Oklahoma, on the other hand, rose. With these exceptions the comparative rankings throughout the whole period show relative stability.

The rankings of the states according to *the per cent of money spent for welfare programs that comes from their own resources* are quite close to those of the payments per recipient. This relationship results in large part from the formula for federal contributions. As we pointed out earlier, in all of the categorical assistance programs involving federal participation the federal government pays a high per cent of the payment up to a certain small amount of money, a lower per cent of the amount paid from that figure up to a higher figure, and no part of the payment above the second figure. This means that the less a state pays per recipient, the greater the proportion of its total payment that comes from federal funds. Consequently, the higher

Table 4

AVERAGE PAYMENTS PER RECIPIENT FOR SIX STATE WELFARE PROGRAMS, 1961

State	Aid to Dependent Children		Old Age Assistance		Aid to the Blind		Aid to the Permanently and Totally Disabled		General Assistance		Unemployment Insurance	
	Amount	Rank	Amount	Rank	Amount	Rank	Amount	Rank	Amount	Rank	Amount	Rank
Connecticut	$178.57	1	$64.95	30	$79.14	21	$93.47	11	$74.36	6	$37.30	7
New York	172.67	2	81.58	13	96.39	7	107.40	3	70.94	9	36.79	10
Illinois	171.67	3	78.13	19	86.23	14	75.62	12	91.36	3	34.40	15
New Jersey	167.98	4	92.44	5	88.35	12	95.32	9	110.76	1	32.73	19
California	167.56	5	91.50	6	106.92	2	99.90	8	61.27	17	40.99	2
Washington	167.21	6	94.96	2	103.95	4	100.08	7	73.49	7	32.82	17
Wisconsin	162.91	7	89.12	7	94.35	8	110.84	2	86.84	4	39.86	4
Minnesota	160.61	8	94.50	3	106.65	3	61.51	33	72.27	8	29.71	27
New Hampshire	160.58	9	85.33	9	86.50	13	100.63	5	60.19	18	27.34	36
Idaho	153.31	10	82.65	12	72.38	28	81.89	18	a	a	35.18	12
Massachusetts	152.39	11	81.14	15	126.45	1	132.90	1	63.88	14	37.05	8
North Dakota	151.25	12	94.23	4	70.96	29	100.23	6	55.16	20	28.87	32
Oregon	146.15	13	84.08	10	93.16	9	93.67	10	56.17	19	35.76	11
Rhode Island	143.79	14	80.89	16	79.94	20	86.88	14	53.04	22	30.20	25
Wyoming	141.01	15	75.44	22	84.69	16	76.66	17	63.18	15	40.65	3
Kansas	140.59	16	83.06	11	85.79	15	87.47	13	67.77	10	34.42	14
Utah	135.89	17	70.67	25	78.01	22	79.71	16	61.43	16	33.69	16
Michigan	131.59	18	79.63	17	80.62	18	102.41	4	102.75	2	37.03	9
Colorado	129.95	19	96.51	1	80.41	19	71.17	23	42.05	28	38.48	5
New Mexico	126.50	20	67.42	27	59.88	37	70.67	24	41.59	29	29.54	29
Maryland	126.35	21	63.80	33	65.00	32.5	65.00	30	65.77	12	31.06	21
Iowa	126.31	22	88.46	8	98.53	6	75.52	19	38.64	32	30.07	26
Montana	125.99	23	64.22	31	72.76	26	72.41	22	53.00	23	27.73	35
Oklahoma	122.76	24	81.34	14	89.15	11	80.13	15	13.78	42	26.61	37

	Amount	Rank	Amount	Rank	Amount	Rank	Amount	Rank	Amount	Rank	Amount	Rank
Ohio	$122.75	25	$77.50	20	$77.67	23	$75.41	20	$76.15	5	$42.32	1
Arizona	121.66	26	60.82	35	72.54	27	b	b	45.78	26	30.81	22
Pennsylvania	120.62	27	66.95	28	73.33	25	58.64	34	54.96	21	32.80	18
Nebraska	118.89	28	76.44	21	92.59	10	73.94	21	52.25	24	30.31	24
South Dakota	114.12	29	64.03	32	62.55	36	65.22	28	29.05	38	29.29	30
Vermont	110.15	30	71.44	23	62.67	35	65.17	29	a	a	28.73	33
Indiana	106.07	31	66.10	29	76.36	24	b	b	34.88	34	31.88	20
Virginia	98.15	32	55.05	37	59.78	38	61.94	32	45.69	27	24.94	39
West Virginia	97.92	33	40.98	47	44.21	46	43.81	42	30.49	37	23.43	43
Louisiana	96.17	34	71.43	24	80.79	17	56.40	35	50.88	25	30.41	23
Nevada	95.24	35	78.35	18	100.87	5	b	b	38.38	33	37.56	6
Missouri	93.48	36	61.73	34	65.00	32.5	64.04	31	66.67	11	29.03	31
Maine	92.59	37	67.64	26	65.27	31	69.19	25	40.86	30	22.24	47
Delaware	87.71	38	49.72	42	70.79	30	66.70	26	64.46	13	34.67	13
Georgia	86.95	39	47.07	43	52.67	43	51.52	38	30.91	36	26.46	38
Kentucky	86.78	40	50.18	41	53.07	42	54.92	36	39.28	31	29.63	28
North Carolina	79.93	41	45.08	45	55.49	41	50.90	39	18.92	40	21.24	48
Texas	76.99	42	52.78	39	58.41	39	54.37	37	a	a	24.25	40
Tennessee	70.13	43	44.03	46	47.45	45	46.07	41	19.97	39	24.12	41
Arkansas	61.66	44	52.46	40	58.18	40	41.86	43	13.77	43	22.55	45
Florida	61.37	45	60.36	36	62.84	34	65.45	27	a	a	28.05	34
South Carolina	61.25	46	45.84	44	49.75	44	50.38	40	31.44	35	22.36	46
Alabama	41.05	47	53.92	38	42.01	47	37.55	44	12.89	44	23.38	44
Mississippi	36.38	48	35.40	48	38.43	48	34.85	45	15.24	41	23.71	42
U.S. Average	$116.68		$67.85		$73.36		$68.19		$65.13		$33.84	
High State	178.57		96.51		126.45		132.90		110.76		42.32	
Low State	36.38		35.40		38.43		34.85		12.89		21.24	

a. Data not reported in The Book of the States.   b. State not participating in this program.

Source: Data on the per recipient payments for these programs are taken from The Book of the States: 1962–63 (Chicago: Council of State Governments, 1963) pp. 392–398, 530. Alaska and Hawaii are omitted.

Table 5

COMPARATIVE RANKINGS OF THE STATES FOR PER RECIPIENT PAYMENTS
FOR THREE WELFARE PROGRAMS

STATE	AID TO DEPENDENT CHILDREN			OLD-AGE ASSISTANCE			AID TO THE BLIND		
	1961	1950	1941	1961	1950	1941	1961	1950	1941
Connecticut	1	3	6	30	5	7	21	5	8
New York	2	6	3	13	7	9	7	6	9
Illinois	3	12	31	19	25	11	14	23	6
New Jersey	4	13	22	5	15	17	12	15	16
California	5	4	2	6	2	2	2	1	1
Washington	6	1	11	2	3	4	4	2	2
Wisconsin	7	11	13	7	29	13	8	22	17
Minnesota	8	17	15	3	16	19	3	10	11
New Hampshire	9	5	5	9	19	16	13	20	19
Idaho	10	7	25	12	17	14	28	16	21
Massachusetts	11	2	1	15	4	5	1	3	18
North Dakota	12	9	24	4	12	31	29	17	26
Oregon	13	10	7	10	10	18	9	4	13
Rhode Island	14	18	4	16	23	21	20	14	31
Wyoming	15	8	18	22	6	10	16	13	12
Kansas	16	22	20	11	14	20	15	19	24
Utah	17	14	8	25	24	8	22	21	10
Michigan	18	20	9	17	21	32	18	18	14
Colorado	19	16	26	1	1	1	19	9	3
New Mexico	20	31	34	27	33	35	37	38	34
Maryland	21	26	21	33	34	29	32.5	30	27
Iowa	22	24	42	8	13	22	6	12	15
Montana	23	23	28	31	11	23	26	11	23
Oklahoma	24	35	43	14	22	30	11	24	33
Ohio	25	25	12	20	20	12	23	25	32
Arizona	26	15	16	35	8	3	27	7	4
Pennsylvania	27	19	14	28	32	15	25	32	7
Nebraska	28	21	23	21	26	25	10	8	29

the per recipient payment, the greater the contribution or effort of the state. Higher payments require higher per recipient efforts by the states. The statistical correlation between payments per recipient and the per cent of the funds coming from state and local funds is above .9 for the programs of aid to dependent children, the aged, the blind, and the disabled.

The next index of welfare effort is the *per capita expenditure* of the states for welfare programs. This is an index of how much money is paid out for welfare in the state. It is best to consider this variable in two ways. First, we shall look at the total per capita expenditures for welfare within the states. This measures how much is expended for welfare programs per

Table 5, continued

STATE	AID TO DEPENDENT CHILDREN			OLD-AGE ASSISTANCE			AID TO THE BLIND		
	1961	1950	1941	1961	1950	1941	1961	1950	1941
South Dakota	29	29	32	32	30	26	36	37	36
Vermont	30	33	19	23	36	33	35	33	25
Indiana	31	30	29	29	35	28	24	34	30
Virginia	32	38	40	37	45	42	38	42	39
West Virginia	33	32	30	47	40	34	46	40	28
Louisiana	34	37	33	24	18	37	17	28	35
Nevada	35	b	35	18	9	6	5	b	5
Missouri	36	34	27	34	27	38	32.5	31	a
Maine	37	27	10	26	28	24	31	26	22
Delaware	38	28	17	42	39	39	30	27	a
Georgia	39	40	37	43	43	47	43	43	41
Kentucky	40	45	a	41	47	44	42	46	a
North Carolina	41	41	44	45	44	41	41	39	37
Texas	42	42	39	39	37	27	39	36	20
Tennessee	43	39	41	46	38	40	45	35	40
Arkansas	44	44	47	40	41	48	40	41	45
Florida	45	36	36	36	31	36	34	29	38
South Carolina	46	45	45	44	42	45	44	44	42
Alabama	47	46	46	38	46	43	47	47	44
Mississippi	48	47	38	48	48	46	48	45	43

a. Data not reported in *The Book of the States*.
b. Less than 50 cases, and data not computed.

Sources: Data for 1941 from *Social Security Bulletin XIV* (December 1941) 38–41.
Data for 1950 from *The Book of the States: 1952–53* (Chicago: Council of State Governments, 1953) pp. 321–329. Data for 1961 from *The Book of the States: 1962–63* (Chicago: Council of State Governments, 1963) pp. 392–398. Alaska and Hawaii are omitted.

capita, regardless of whether the funds come from within the state or from the federal government. Then, we want to know the amount of effort the state expends from its own resources. Thus, we have two indices: (1) the total per capita expenditures for welfare; and (2) the state per capita expenditures for welfare. Because of the extensive role of the federal government in financing the public assistance programs and because of the formula for federal contributions, the relationships between the total per capita expenditures and the state per capita expenditures are not always close. The amounts of expenditure per capita and the ranks of the states for these two indices are given in Table 6.

Table 6

PER CAPITA EXPENDITURES FOR WELFARE PROGRAMS, 1961

STATE	TOTAL PER CAPITA EXPENDITURES		STATE PER CAPITA EXPENDITURES	
	AMOUNT	RANK	AMOUNT	RANK
Oklahoma	$55.17	1	$21.57	3
Louisiana	49.94	2	17.53	6
Colorado	48.52	3	27.80	1
Washington	36.71	4	22.06	2
California	35.05	5	20.30	5
Massachusetts	34.33	6	20.57	4
Missouri	33.13	7	11.93	17
Rhode Island	28.59	8	15.95	9
Minnesota	28.05	9	15.96	8
New Mexico	27.14	10	8.71	27
New York	26.71	11	16.67	7
Arkansas	26.23	12	7.03	33
Maine	25.26	13	9.57	24
Vermont	25.06	14	8.55	29
Alabama	25.05	15	6.54	35
Oregon	24.59	16	13.40	13
Illinois	24.39	17	15.29	10
Mississippi	24.36	18	5.62	40
Iowa	24.09	19	11.44	18
Kansas	23.97	20	11.19	21
Georgia	23.85	21	6.49	36
North Dakota	23.19	22	11.27	19
Connecticut	22.61	23	14.92	11
Ohio	22.57	24	13.00	14
Michigan	22.35	25.5	14.15	12
West Virginia	22.35	25.5	5.97	39
Montana	22.12	27	11.97	16

Those states in which the rank on total per capita expenditures is substantially higher than that on the state per capita expenditure — states in
which a larger proportion of the total is financed by the federal government — are also the states in which the highest numbers of recipients
are receiving aid and the lowest amount of aid per recipient is paid. These,
then, are states that pay relatively small amounts to a relatively large number of persons. Owing to the formula of federal participation, these are the
states that receive the largest amount of money from the federal government.

For the comprehensive description of state welfare efforts, we shall use
four indicators: (1) the average rank payment per recipient for the various
public assistance programs and unemployment insurance (six programs in

Table 6, continued

STATE	TOTAL PER CAPITA EXPENDITURES		STATE PER CAPITA EXPENDITURES	
	AMOUNT	RANK	AMOUNT	RANK
Wisconsin	21.75	28	12.46	15
South Dakota	21.70	29	9.24	31
Utah	20.98	30	9.44	25
Pennsylvania	20.83	31	11.23	20
Kentucky	20.58	32	5.49	43
New Hampshire	20.03	33	9.95	23
Arizona	19.42	34	6.41	37
Idaho	19.37	35	7.24	32
Texas	19.25	36	5.60	42
Nevada	18.06	37	10.37	22
Florida	17.94	38	5.63	41
Nebraska	17.89	39	6.99	34
Delaware	17.59	40	9.34	26
Tennessee	17.52	41	4.40	46
Wyoming	16.27	42	8.48	30
North Carolina	15.76	43	4.55	44
New Jersey	13.95	44	8.68	28
South Carolina	13.29	45	3.52	47
Indiana	13.28	46	6.36	38
Maryland	11.01	47	4.51	45
Virginia	8.57	48	2.66	48

Source: Data for the total per capita expenditure index are taken from *The Book of the States: 1962–63* (Chicago: Council of State Governments, 1963) p. 218. The data for the state per capita expenditures are arrived at by taking the total per capita expenditure figure for each state and multiplying it by the per cent of funds for public welfare that comes from the state and its local subdivisions. Alaska and Hawaii are omitted.

1961); (2) the percentage of the money for these state programs that comes from the state and local governmental units; (3) the state payments per capita for welfare; and (4) the total per capita expenditures for welfare in the states. The first index, average rank payment per recipient, is constructed by averaging the ranks of the state for each of the measures reported in Table 3, and re-ranking the states according to this average rank. The second index is a composite measure of the percentage of the state's welfare budget that is financed by state and local funds. The latter two indices were discussed earlier. The comparative rankings for forty-eight states on these four indicators are given in Table 7. In all instances, the lower rank (i.e., 1, 2, 3 . . .) represents the higher level of effort, and the higher rank (. . . 46, 47, 48) represents the lesser welfare effort.

The Politics of Welfare

Table 7

FOUR MEASURES OF STATE WELFARE EFFORTS, 1961

State	Average Rank Payment Per Recipient[a]	Percentage of Money From State – Local[b]	Per Capita Expenditures, States[c]	Per Capita Expenditures, Total[d]
	Rank	Rank	Rank	Rank
Wisconsin	1	11.5	15	28
California	2	8	5	5
Washington	3	6	2	4
New York	4	4	7	11
Massachusetts	5.5	7	4	6
New Jersey	5.5	5	28	44
Illinois	7	3	10	17
Michigan	8	2	12	25.5
Oregon	9	16	13	16
Connecticut	10	1	11	23
Kansas	11	24	21	20
Minnesota	12	13	8	9
Wyoming	13	19	30	42
New Hampshire	14	20	23	33
Ohio	15	9	14	24
Colorado	16	11.5	1	3
Idaho	17	31	32	35
North Dakota	18	22	19	22
Rhode Island	19	14	9	8
Iowa	20.5	23	18	19
Utah	20.5	25	25	30
Nevada	22	10	22	37
Nebraska	23	27.5	34	39
Oklahoma	24	27.5	3	1
Maryland	25.5	26	45	47
Pennsylvania	25.5	15	20	31
Louisiana	27	33	6	2
Montana	28	17	16	27

As Table 7 indicates, the rankings of the states on the first three indices — average rank payment per recipient, per cent of money coming from state and local sources, and state per capita expenditures for welfare — are similar. Considerably more differences, however, occur between the total per capita expenditures and those three indices. The greatest differences occur in some of the Southern states that rank low in payment per recipient and per cent of money from state and local government, slightly higher in state per

Table 7, continued

State	Average Rank Payment Per Recipient[a]	Percentage of Money From State – Local[b]	Per Capita Expenditures, States[c]	Per Capita Expenditures, Total[d]
	Rank	Rank	Rank	Rank
Arizona	29.5	35	37	34
Delaware	29.5	18	26	40
Indiana	31	21	38	46
New Mexico	32	36	27	10
Missouri	33	32	17	7
Vermont	34	34	29	14
South Dakota	35	29	31	29
Maine	36	30	24	13
Virginia	37	38	48	48
Florida	38	37	41	38
Kentucky	39	42.5	43	32
Texas	40	39	42	36
Georgia	41	41	36	21
West Virginia	42	44	39	25.5
North Carolina	43	40	44	43
South Carolina	44	45	47	45
Arkansas	45.5	42.5	33	12
Tennessee	45.5	47	46	41
Alabama	47	46	35	15
Mississippi	48	48	40	18

a. Computed by averaging the ranks of the states on the six state welfare programs and then ranking the averages. For data on which the averages are based, see Table 4.
b. Based on the percentage of money for all the welfare programs that comes from state and local governments. For the raw data on which these ranks are based, see Table 3.
c. See Table 6 for data on which this index is based.
d. Computed by multiplying the per cent of money coming from state and local units times the total per capita expenditure. See Table 6 for raw data.

capita expenditure, but notably higher in total per capita expenditure. These differences reflect the influence of federal participation in the welfare programs.

We computed rank-order correlations among these four indices for the three different points in time. Similar indices were used for the two earlier periods, although fewer welfare programs were operative in 1941.

The correlations between average rank payments per recipient and the proportion of welfare funds coming from state and local rather than federal sources were moderate to strong.* States in which welfare clients received relatively large average payments contributed much of the money themselves. This was true throughout the twenty-year period, but more so for 1950 and 1961 ($r = .90$) than for 1941 ($r = .70$).

Weaker relations were found between these two variables (average rank payment and the proportion of funds from state and local sources) and the state per capita expenditures for welfare. A notable difference appears between per cent of money from state and local governments and per capita state expenditures during the twenty-year period. The relationship is greater for 1950 and 1961 ($r = .76$) than for 1941 ($r = .57$).

The relationships among the first three variables, which represent direct state expenditures, and the variable total per capita expenditures, however, show a different trend during the three time periods. For each of the three years, the total per capita expenditure tends to be less closely related to the other three variables. The most marked drop-off in association among these factors occurs for the relation between average rank payment per recipient and the total per capita welfare expenditure. The correlation coefficients decline from .74 in 1941, to .46 in 1950, to .27 in 1961. The decline in the other two relations is in the same direction, although not so great. The correlation between per cent of money from state-local sources and total per capita expenditure changes from .41 to .40 to .23; between per capita state expenditure and total per capita expenditure from .97 to .92 to .76.

These relationships and their changes through time reflect the impact of increased federal participation in welfare programs. They particularly demonstrate the change in the formula by which the federal government appropriates welfare money to the states. Whereas in 1941 the federal government appropriated funds to the states on a fifty-fifty matching basis, in the 1950's and 1960's the federal government allocated money on the basis

*In the discussion of the statistical tables, correlations (r) of .80 or larger have been arbitrarily referred to as strong; .60–.79 as moderate; less than .60 as weak. This represents a self-discipline to be consistent in interpreting data and to resist occasional temptations to read stronger relationships than the data justify. No known convention prescribes such an interpretation of correlations. However, Arthur S. Banks and Robert B. Textor introduce a somewhat similar usage in *A Cross-Polity Survey* (Cambridge: M.I.T. Press, 1963) pp. 38–39.

Moreover, we have not used statistical tests of significance. Tests of significance are invoked to decide whether a relationship among two variables in a sample drawn from a universe of data might be a chance phenomenon, rather than a uniform pattern distributed throughout the universe. (This implication may be found in Sidney Siegel, *Nonparametric Statistics for the Behavioral Sciences* [New York: McGraw-Hill Book Co., 1956] chapters 1–3, 9, *passim*.) Because the data exhaust the universe and, therefore, are not a sample, the view adhered to is that tests of significance would be inappropriate here.

of how much the state paid per recipient. This later formula guarantees that states spending less per recipient receive a higher proportion of the total payment from federal funds. Thus, the Southern states that paid out small amounts to relatively large numbers of recipients receive substantially more from the federal government than the states that paid out larger amounts to smaller numbers of recipients. Consequently, increasingly greater differences have resulted between both the average payments per recipient and per cent of funds from state and local governments and the total per capita amounts expended for welfare. This indicates that one of the objectives of federal participation — greater equality among the states in welfare efforts — has been achieved in at least one respect — the total amount of money expended for welfare. However, inequality of payments per recipient remains. In fact, the provisions of the federal programs could be said to promote inequality. The state that wants to obtain the most federal money for the least expenditure of its own resources can do so by maintaining its per recipient payment at a very low level.

The comparative rankings of the states along three of these dimensions remain relatively constant throughout the twenty years. In spite of increases in the average payments per recipient and in the per capita expenditure for welfare from the states' own resources, in spite of the decrease in the per cent of welfare money coming from state and local sources for all of the states, the states maintain the same or similar ranks vis-à-vis the other states. In order to measure the strength of the relationship between the comparative rankings of states in 1941 and 1961 for the four composite measures of state welfare efforts, we computed rank-order correlations between the rankings of the states in 1941 and 1961 and each index.

The correlations between the average rank payment per recipient, per cent of money coming from state and local sources, and the per capita payment from state sources indices are moderately close. The correlation between the 1941 and the 1961 average rank payment indices was .84; between the 1941 and 1961 per cent of money from state and local governments was .76; between the 1941 and 1961 per capita state expenditure was .79. The relationship between the 1941 and 1961 rankings on total per capita expenditure, however, is substantially less; the correlation was .46. This is a further indication of the impact of federal financial contributions.

SOCIO-ECONOMIC CORRELATES OF STATE WELFARE EFFORTS

Welfare expenditures vary considerably among the states regardless of which index we use to measure them. The reasons for these variations are not obvious. One possibility is that they are associated with the social, economic, and political conditions of the states. We can demonstrate that variations in socio-economic and political factors are associated with variations in the extent of state welfare policies. Public welfare policies are the factors to be explained by economic and political variables. As we have already noted, the states expend different amounts of effort on public welfare programs. The important question is why some states spend more on public welfare than others. This is a political question; it involves the allocation or reallocation of values and resources by the political system. The decisions on how much money is to be spent on welfare programs, who is eligible to receive welfare benefits, and how the programs are to be financed are made by state legislatures and state executives in conjunction, especially in their implementation, with state and local administrative agencies. Some of the decisions about financing and the types of programs to be used are also made by Congress and federal administrative agencies. Our objectives are to identify important factors that affect these political decisions and to indicate their relative influence.

We use four sets of variables to explain differences in the extent of state welfare efforts. First, we consider a set of socio-economic characteristics, namely *urbanization, industrialization,* and *ethnic group origin* (or ethnicity). Second, we consider several indicators of *objective welfare needs* in the states. Thirdly, we consider the ability of the state to pay for welfare measures or the wealth of the state in terms of *per capita income*. Finally, in the next section, we look at two political characteristics — *inter-party competition* and *electoral participation*. We give major attention to conditions in 1961 but, as in the previous section, we also analyze trends from 1941 to 1961.

SOCIAL-ECONOMIC CONDITIONS AND THE ADOPTION OF WELFARE POLI-CIES. Students of politics have long been interested in the relationship between socio-economic conditions and the operation of political systems or the formation of public policy. Aristotle stressed relations between the distribution of wealth in a society and the form of its government. Marx interpreted political development in terms of the development of socio-economic classes, and more recently Lipset has argued that economic development is requisite to stable democratic governments in western Europe, the English-speaking democracies, and Latin America.[22] We shall look at the relationship between urbanization, industrialization, and per cent of population foreign born or with one or more foreign-born parents and the adoption of welfare policies. Our expectation is that *the more urbanized the state, the more industrialized the state, and the larger the proportion of its population that is foreign born or the children of foreign born, the more extensive its welfare efforts.* The modern welfare state, or the complex of modern welfare programs, is the product of the industrialization and urbanization of western society. Consequently, we expect the more highly urban and more highly industrialized states to expend greater efforts on welfare. The impact of the foreign born upon the development of welfare programs is more difficult to predict. In part, their impact comes from the fact that the ethnic groups have principally resided in and been a major part of the urban and industrial complex. It is also plausible that the members of certain ethnic groups, because of their peculiar life experiences and their special positions within the larger society, have developed different social, economic, and political values and needs, which have caused them to view governmental welfare activities more favorably than the older Americans. Samuel Lubell argues that the changes that occurred in governmental activity and welfare policies during the 1930's resulted not only from the Depression or the impact of Franklin D. Roosevelt, but also from the increasing political participation of large numbers of the ethnic minorities in urban areas. These persons were raised in an environment quite different from the farm or small-town, Protestant, traditional American one, and consequently the demands they made upon the political system when they became important political participants were different.[23]

We used the census definition of urban population as the index of urbanization; the per cent of workers engaged in occupations other than agriculture, forestry, and fishing as the index of industrialization; and the per cent of population in the various states with one or more foreign born parents as the measure of ethnicity. We ranked the states according to these factors and computed Spearman rank-order correlations between them and the four composite measures of state welfare efforts. The results are reported in Table 8.

Table 8 indicates for 1961 moderately close relations between two of these socio-economic factors and welfare efforts, but not for the total per capita welfare expenditures. The relationships between industrialization and the welfare efforts are weak, although consistent with our prediction. By far the closer relationships, however, are found with the foreign born measure.

These relationships also hold for the years 1941 and 1950. As Table 8 demonstrates, the relationship between the socio-economic indices and the four indices of welfare efforts are usually closer for those periods. Moderate to strong relations exist between urbanization and ethnicity, on the one hand, and welfare efforts, on the other, but ethnicity is consistently more closely related to welfare output. Note, however, the important difference in the relationships between the socio-economic indices and the total per capita welfare expenditures. The correlation between total per capita welfare expenditure and ethnicity, for example, drops from .61 in 1941, to .31 in 1950, to .19 in 1961. A similar trend exists with respect to the relation of urbanization to welfare. This suggests that the relationships between the socio-economic factors and welfare efforts hold for the direct state effort. When the

Table 8

RANK-ORDER CORRELATIONS BETWEEN THREE SOCIO-ECONOMIC FACTORS
AND FOUR INDICES OF STATE WELFARE EFFORTS

Socio-Economic Factors	Average Rank Payment Per Recipient			Percentage of Welfare Money from State–Local			Per Capita Welfare Expenditure State			Per Capita Welfare Expenditure Total		
	1941	1950	1961	1941	1950	1961	1941	1950	1961	1941	1950	1961
Percentage of Population Urban	.75	.63	.62	.76	.76	.68	.61	.49	.52	.52	.30	.19
Percentage of Population Industrial	*	*	.39	*	*	.51	*	*	.33	*	*	.05
Percentage of Population Foreign born†	.84	.81	.75	.79	.81	.79	.72	.54	.60	.61	.31	.19

*The measurement of industrialization is not used for 1941 and 1950 because we were unable to obtain data for both periods that were comparable with 1961.

†Percentage foreign born is used here instead of percentage with one or more foreign born parents because the latter measure was not used in census reports prior to 1960.

Interpretation: The more urban, the more industrially populated, and the more ethnic a state, the more extensive its welfare effort.

Sources: Data for 1941 are taken from Bureau of the Census, *Sixteenth Census of the United States: 1940, Vol. II* (Washington: U.S. Government Printing Office, 1943); for 1950 from Bureau of the Census, *Census of Population: 1950, Vol. II* (Washington: U.S. Government Printing Office, 1952); for 1961 from Bureau of the Census, *Census of the Population: 1960, Vol. II* (Washington: U.S. Government Printing Office, 1962). The entries in the table are Spearman rank-order correlations.

impact of federal funds is taken into account, however, the relationships become weaker. In this respect, at least, the federal government has been partially successful in its efforts to equalize welfare programs among states with great differences in social and economic conditions.

It should also be pointed out that, although all of the states have become dramatically more urban and industrial, their comparative levels of urbanization and ethnicity have remained virtually constant. That is, the ranks among the states on indices of urbanization and per cent foreign born have changed very little. The rank-order correlation between the 1941 and 1960 indices of urbanization is .89 and that between the two indices of per cent foreign born or per cent with one or more foreign-born parents is .97. This is consistent with the lack of change among the ranks of the states for the various welfare indices during the same period (Table 5).

COMPARATIVE NEED AND STATE WELFARE EFFORTS. Another type of socio-economic condition particularly relevant to state welfare efforts is the need for more governmental effort as related to conditions of social welfare. Because one of the major objectives of welfare policies is to provide a minimum level of economic necessities for those otherwise unable to provide for themselves, we would expect to find a positive relation between the extent of need and the amount of effort expended for welfare programs. At least three indicators of economic and social need are available: (1) infant mortality (i.e., the number of children per thousand who were born alive but died within a year); (2) children without both parents; and (3) the per cent of children between eighteen and twenty-five without a high school education.[24] Each of these indicators reflects social and economic deprivation. Infant mortality is usually a good indicator of a low state of economic development and a low level of economic resources. A child without both parents often becomes a direct welfare charge handled through aid to dependent children. A low level of education is increasingly related to difficulty in getting and keeping a job, as well as to family stability, acquisition of further knowledge, and skills, and to the enjoyment of health, sanitation, and well-being.

Extensive differences exist between the states in welfare needs. For example, the per cent of youths not finishing school is nearly three times as high in South Carolina as it is in Nebraska and Minnesota. Mississippi has more than three times as many children under eighteen not living with both parents as does North Dakota. Our concern, however, is whether these needs for welfare make any difference for actual state welfare efforts. More specifically, the question is: *Does greater need lead to more welfare effort?* Table 9 presents the rank-order correlations between these three indices of need and the four indices of state welfare efforts. If the indices are measur-

Table 9

RANK-ORDER CORRELATIONS BETWEEN THREE INDICES OF NEED AND FOUR INDICES OF STATE WELFARE EFFORTS

	Average Rank Payment Per Recipient			Percentage of Welfare Money from State–Local			Per Capita Welfare Expenditure State			Per Capita Welfare Expenditure Total		
	1941	1950	1961	1941	1950	1961	1941	1950	1961	1941	1950	1961
Infant Mortality	−.60	−.57	−.63	−.62	−.60	−.56	−.53	−.34	−.28	−.48	−.20	−.17
Children without both parents		−.60				−.53			−.44			−.03
Youths not Finishing High School		−.60				−.43			−.54			−.03

Interpretation: The extensiveness of welfare programs varies inversely with objective need.

ing what we presume they are, the answer is emphatically negative. In regard to the first three measures, which more directly reflect state effort, we find strong negative relations. That is, the greater the need, the less effort put out by the state to meet the needs.

The relationship between needs and the total per capita expenditures for welfare is less clearly an inverse one; it is almost at the zero point, which indicates no relationship. This is further evidence that federal participation adds something to the extent to which a state's welfare efforts are more strongly related to the needs and less strongly to its wealth and political conditions. Nevertheless, the relationship is neutral to slightly negative, instead of positive. The influence of federal participation is made even clearer when the relationship is explored throughout the three time periods. The relationship between the need variables, as represented by infant mortality, and the four welfare efforts measures are also given in Table 9. Again we find strongly negative relationships between need and the welfare effort. However, there is an important difference with regard to total per capita expenditure. In 1941, the correlation between this index and need was −.48, almost as negative as the other three welfare indicators. By 1950, this relationship had changed to −.20 and by 1961 to −.17. These changes indicate that the changes in the extent of federal participation and in the formula for federal contributions have aided the states in meeting more extensively their welfare needs.

COMPARATIVE STATE WEALTH AND STATE WELFARE EFFORTS. The last socio-economic factor we consider is wealth, or the capacity of the state to finance welfare programs. Because welfare payments are inversely related to economic and social need, and because need is inversely related to financial resources, we would expect to find that wealth is positively correlated with state welfare efforts. That is, *the more wealthy the state, the more extensive its welfare efforts.* To investigate this hypothesis we use per capita income as the index of state wealth. That is, *the higher the state's per capita income, the more extensive its welfare efforts.* As was the case with the several socio-economic variables discussed above, changes in comparative per capita income ranks over the twenty-year period have been quite small. The correlation between the rankings of the states according to per capita income in 1941 and 1950 is .96. The relationships between per capita income and the various indicators of state welfare efforts are given in Table 10.

Table 10 indicates moderate to strong relationships between per capita income and state welfare efforts, especially with those indices most directly related to state efforts. We find the same pattern as with other variables in regard to the total per capita welfare expenditures — a continually weakening relationship with per capita income, from .50 in 1941 to .03 in 1961.

Table 10

RANK-ORDER CORRELATIONS BETWEEN PER CAPITA INCOME
AND FOUR INDICES OF STATE WELFARE EFFORTS

Per Capita Income	Average Rank Payment Per Recipient	Percentage of Welfare Money from State–Local	Per Capita Welfare Expenditure State	Per Capita Welfare Expenditure Total
1941	.80	.75	.62	.50
1950	.77	.81	.49	.24
1960	.75	.83	.55	.03

Interpretation: The higher the per capita income of a state,
the more extensive its welfare efforts.

Source: The data for the rankings of the states for per capita income are taken from
Bureau of the Census, *Statistical Abstract of the United States: 1962* (Washington:
U.S. Government Printing Office, 1962) p. 319.

Again, we may observe the effects of increasing federal participation. Federal participation with its present formula helps overcome the influence of wealth in the welfare efforts of the states, although only to a limited degree.

POLITICAL CORRELATES OF STATE WELFARE EFFORTS

Next we examine the relationships between two political factors and the extent of welfare policies in the states. In the preceding section we analyzed the relationships between a series of socio-economic factors and welfare efforts and found several patterns. Wealth, ethnicity, urbanization and industrialization positively correlate with state welfare efforts. Social-economic need, however, correlates negatively with welfare activity. Because we are considering welfare policies as examples of public policies or political outputs, we would expect that the extent to which the state governments expend their resources for welfare purposes is positively related to the political structure and processes within the states.

Many of the formal characteristics of state political systems are quite similar, as other chapters of this book make clear. All states have constitutions with authority divided among legislative, judicial, and executive branches. All have elected officials with specified terms of office. All have a bill of rights similar to that of the United States Constitution. All, at least nominally, have the same two political parties. Thus, we can assume that the basic institutions of the states are similar. These similarities allow us to treat these aspects of the political system as constants and to study other political factors as "variables." The variables that we consider here are *inter-party competition* and *political participation*.

Several recent studies relate the level of competitiveness between political parties and policy outcomes in American states. V. O. Key, Jr., for example, found that the Southern states with loose multifactional systems, in which the coherence and continuity of competition is less, pursue more conservative policies, i.e., policies favorable to the interests of upper socio-economic groups or the "haves." In states with regular competition between two cohesive and enduring factions, more liberal policies are adopted, i.e., policies more responsive to the interests, needs and/or desires of the "have nots."[25] Duane Lockard draws the same conclusions about New England politics.[26] A similar, if less conclusive, relationship was found between inter-party competition and nine welfare policies in forty-six states.[27]

The theory that predicts these relations contends that high inter-party competition causes the competing parties to appeal to the lower socio-economic groups for electoral support and, thus, to advocate public policies more consistent with the demands of those segments of the population. Lockard articulates the theory as follows: "In the two-party states the anxiety over the next election pushes political leaders into serving the interests of the have-less elements of society, thereby putting the party into the countervailing power operation."[28] Key theorizes somewhat differently: "A loose factional system lacks the power to carry out sustained programs of action, which almost always are thought by the better elements to be contrary to its immediate interests. This negative weakness thus redounds to the benefit of the upper brackets."[29] Because welfare policies and programs are of obvious benefit to the lower socio-economic groups, we would expect to find this relationship between inter-party competition and policy outputs holds for the public welfare policies. *That is, the more competitive the state's party system, the more extensive its welfare efforts.*

In order to investigate this hypothesis, we ranked the states according to the competitiveness of their parties and computed rank-order correlations between this index and the four indices of state welfare efforts. The results of these computations are shown in Table 11.

Table 11 suggests mostly moderate relationships between inter-party competition and the welfare efforts of the states, especially in 1961. Although the correlations are less close than they were for most of the socio-economic variables, they follow the same pattern — highest with percentage of welfare money from state and local governments, next highest for average rank payment per recipient, slightly less strong for per capita welfare expenditure state, and much weaker for per capita welfare expenditure total. Again we find that the relationships with total per capita welfare expenditure become weaker from one time period to the next. The relationships with the other measures of welfare efforts, however, become somewhat stronger between 1941 and 1961.

We also expect to find the level of political participation within a state

Table 11

RANK-ORDER CORRELATIONS BETWEEN INTER-PARTY COMPETITION
AND FOUR INDICES OF STATE WELFARE EFFORTS

Inter-Party Competition	Average Rank Payment Per Recipient	Percentage of Welfare Money from State–Local	Per Capita Welfare Expenditure State	Per Capita Welfare Expenditure Total
1960[a]	.60	.75	.57	.06
1950[b]	.53	.53	.39	.24
1941[b]	.47	.51	.45	.44

a. As the measure of inter-party competition for the 1960 period we have used the index from "Inter-Party Competition, Economic Variables, and Welfare Policies in the American States," pp. 275–276. This is a composite measure based upon an average of the average number of seats the major party has held in both houses of the state legislature and the average percentage of the vote received by the major party over a twenty-one year period, from 1938–58. It omits two states, Minnesota and Nebraska, because they have non-partisan legislatures. Alaska and Hawaii were omitted because they were not states during this period. The correlations were then computed for forty-six states.

b. The 1941 and 1950 measures of inter-party competition are based solely upon the percentage of the vote for governor received by the major party for two twelve-year periods. The 1941 measure is based upon the years 1928 to 1940, and the 1950 measure upon the years 1938 to 1950. The membership in the state legislatures was not included because of the difficulty of obtaining the necessary data. The composite index used in 1960 is probably the better measure but, as is pointed out in "Inter-Party Competition, Economic Variables, and Welfare Policies in the American States," p. 276, for the 1938–1958 period the correlation between the average vote for governor and the composite measure was high ($r = .85$).

Interpretation: The more competitive a state's political parties, the more extensive its welfare efforts.

to be positively related to the extent of state welfare efforts. That is, *the higher the level of political participation (measured here by voter turnout), the greater the welfare effort.* Greater participation, at least in the United States, usually means more participation by the lower socio-economic sets of the population. Members of these sets ordinarily exhibit less interest in politics and have lower voting rates. Historically, they were also the last segment of society to obtain the right to vote and to participate in other types of political activity. Today, with the exception of Negroes in some areas of the South, nearly all citizens have the right to vote in most elections. Consequently, non-participation more often than not results from a lack of interest in politics or a low sense of political efficacy. A low voting turnout, therefore, usually means that people at the lower socio-economic levels have not participated. Presumably, they do not find political participation to be particularly relevant and consequently they do not have much influence upon the formation of public policy. When the lower socio-economic sets participate in politics, they exercise some influence upon what types of campaign issues will be articulated and what types of public policies will be adopted by the political system. Public welfare policy is of peculiar concern to the lower socio-economic segments. The advocacy, adoption, and implementation of welfare policies would, therefore, seem to be one means of bringing the lower socio-economic classes into political participation and of keeping them interested and satisfied. Consequently, we would expect the extensiveness of welfare policies to be related to the size of voting turnout and other types of political participation in the American states.

To investigate the relationship between electoral participation and welfare efforts, we ranged the states according to the percentage of persons of voting age who voted in the Presidential elections of 1940, 1948, and 1960. These three elections coincide with the three periods in which we measured welfare efforts. The state with the highest percentage of persons voting is considered to have the highest level of political participation. The rank-order correlations between the participation in these three elections and the four indices of state welfare efforts are shown in Table 12.

Table 12 indicates a less than moderate tendency for higher levels of voting turnout to be associated with greater welfare efforts. The association

Table 12

RANK-ORDER CORRELATIONS BETWEEN POLITICAL PARTICIPATION
AND FOUR INDICES OF STATE WELFARE EFFORTS

Political Participation	Average Rank Payment Per Recipient	Percentage of Welfare Money from State–Local	Per Capita Welfare Expenditure State	Per Capita Welfare Expenditure Total
1960	.53	.55	.39	.08
1950	.51	.53	.33	.14
1941	.43	.56	.54	.50

Interpretation: The more political participation in a state, the more extensive its welfare efforts.

is not as strong as that found between state welfare efforts and the other political and socio-economic factors we have considered. The correlation coefficients signify a relatively weak relationship between participation and welfare policies.

CONCLUSIONS

We have "stayed close to the data" in reporting the statistical analysis of the relations between socio-economic factors and welfare policies and between political factors and welfare policies. Let us summarize the associations we have identified. We observe that both socio-economic and political factors are positively correlated with the extensiveness of state welfare programs. Evidence favors the propositions that the more foreign born people in a state's population, the more extensive its welfare program; that the higher the per capita income in the state, the more extensive its activities on behalf of well-being; and that the more competitive the two major political parties, the larger the state's undertakings in the interest of the well-being of its residents. Among these findings, it should be noted that some socio-economic factors correlate higher with welfare output than do political factors.

Table 13

RANK-ORDER CORRELATIONS BETWEEN CERTAIN SOCIO-ECONOMIC VARIABLES AND WELFARE POLICIES AND BETWEEN INTER-PARTY COMPETITION AND WELFARE POLICIES, HOLDING ONE VARIABLE CONSTANT AND VARYING THE OTHERS

| | HOLDING PER CAPITA INCOME CONSTANT | |
	Foreign Born Population with Average Payment	Inter-Party Competition with Average Payment
Lower 1/3 Income	.80	.46
Middle 1/3 Income	.44	.51
Upper 1/3 Income	.69	−.05

| | HOLDING PER CENT FOREIGN BORN CONSTANT | |
	Per Capita Income with Average Payment	Inter-Party Competition with Average Payment
Lower 1/3 Foreign Born	.77	.41
Middle 1/3 Foreign Born	.26	.48
Upper 1/3 Foreign Born	.64	.33

| | HOLDING INTER-PARTY COMPETITION CONSTANT | |
	Per Capita Income with Average Payment	Foreign Born with Average Payment
Lower 1/3 Competition	.72	.79
Middle 1/3 Competition	.59	.65
Upper 1/3 Competition	.45	.45

Interpretation: Ethnicity and per capita income are more strongly related than inter-party competition to the extensiveness of a state's welfare efforts.

To sift out the relative strength of the economic and political factors we can, statistically speaking, "hold one constant and vary the other." This is what was done in order to obtain the correlations displayed in Table 13. This analysis concentrated on average payment per recipient as the best index of welfare output. When we hold per capita income constant, the relationship between percentage of population that is foreign born and average payment is closer than between inter-party competition and average payment. Likewise, when we hold percentage foreign born constant, we observe that the relationship between per capita income and average payment is closer than the relationship between inter-party competition and average payment. Furthermore, when we hold inter-party competition constant, the relatively high correlations between the economic factors and welfare outputs remain relatively high.

Thus, we conclude that political variables make a difference for policies about well-being, but socio-economic factors make a greater difference. To understand why state governments have the kinds of welfare programs they have, we must take account of economic demand and capacity as well as characteristics of the political process. We have done just that and shown the relative contributions of both sets of variables.

NOTES

1. Harold D. Lasswell, *Politics: Who Gets What, When, and How* (Chicago: University of Chicago Press, 1936); David Easton, *The Political System* (New York: Alfred A. Knopf, 1954); James A. Robinson, "The Major Problems of Political Science," in Lynton K. Caldwell (ed.), *New Viewpoints on Politics and Public Affairs* (Bloomington, Ind.: Institute of Training for Public Service, 1962) pp. 161–188.
2. Harold D. Lasswell and Abraham Kaplan, *Power and Society* (New Haven: Yale University Press, 1950) pp. 55–56; Richard E. Dawson and James A. Robinson, "Inter-Party Competition, Economic Variables, and Welfare Policies in the American States," *Journal of Politics XXV* (May 1963) 265–289.
3. Wayne Vasey, *Government and Social Welfare: Roles of Federal, State, and Local Governments in Administering Welfare Services* (New York: Henry Holt and Co., 1958).
4. *Ibid.*
5. Hilary M. Leyendecker, *Problems and Policy in Public Assistance* (New York: Harper and Bros., 1955) pp. 21–23.
6. Josephine Chapin Brown, *Public Relief: 1929–1939* (New York: Henry Holt and Co., 1940) p. 3.
7. Leyendecker, p. 30.
8. Josephine Brown, pp. 5–6.
9. Lucy W. Brown, "Poor Relief Laws: A Digest," *American Public Welfare Association*, 1934, taken from *ibid.*, p. 18.
10. *Ibid.*, p. 20.
11. Leyendecker, p. 42.
12. Josephine Brown, p. 23.
13. *Ibid.*, p. 26.
14. Leyendecker, p. 54.
15. Josephine Brown, p. 27.
16. Data are from *Statistical Abstracts of the United States: 1962*, U.S. Department of Commerce, Bureau of the Census (Washington: U.S. Government Printing Office, 1962).
17. Leyendecker, p. 67.
18. *Ibid.*, pp. 69–70.

19. Blackstone, *Commentaries on the Laws of England* (12th ed.; London, 1793) Book I, chapter i, p. 131, quoted in Edith Abbott, *Public Assistance, I* (Chicago: University of Chicago Press, 1940) 3–4.
20. Vasey, pp. 281–282.
21. *Ibid.,* p. 169.
22. Seymour M. Lipset, *Political Man* (Garden City, N.Y.: Doubleday & Co., 1958) pp. 54–60.
23. Samuel Lubell, *The Future of American Politics* (Garden City, N.Y.: Doubleday Anchor Books, 1955) pp. 29–85.
24. For a discussion of social-economic need in the United States and data for these indicators see Leonore A. Epstein, "Unmet Need in a Land of Abundance," *Social Security Bulletin XXVI* (May 1963) 3–11.
25. V. O. Key, Jr., *Southern Politics in State and Nation* (New York: Alfred A. Knopf, 1949) especially pp. 298–314.
26. Duane Lockard, *New England State Politics* (Princeton: Princeton University Press, 1959) pp. 320–340.
27. Dawson and Robinson, pp. 265–289.
28. Lockard, p. 337.
29. Key, p. 308.

SELECTED BIBLIOGRAPHY

Dawson, Richard E., and James A. Robinson. "Inter-Party Competition, Economic Variables, and Welfare Policies in the American States," *Journal of Politics XXV* (May 1963) 265–289. Places welfare politics in the context of the political process and analyzes the influence of several political and economic factors on the extent of nine state welfare programs.

Leyendecker, Hilary M. *Problems and Policy in Public Administration.* New York: Harper and Bros., 1955. A useful introduction to political and administrative aspects of important welfare programs.

Lockard, Duane. *New England State Politics.* Princeton: Princeton University Press, 1959, pp. 320–340. Illustrates how state political processes and welfare policies can be studied in a small number of states.

Lubell, Samuel. *The Future of American Politics.* Garden City, N.Y.: Doubleday Anchor Books, 1955. Contains many interesting hypotheses about how social and political changes have affected welfare activities of government.

Social Security Bulletin. Published annually by the Social Security Administration, U.S. Department of Health, Education, and Welfare. A storehouse of basic data for comparative analysis, it may be obtained from the Government Printing Office, Washington, D.C.

Vasey, Wayne. *Government and Social Welfare: Roles of Federal, State, and Local Governments in Administering Welfare Services.* New York: Henry Holt and Co., 1958. Describes government programs and their development, and analyzes contemporary roles of government in welfare activities.

STATE POLITICS
AND
CHAPTER 11   # HIGHWAYS
by
ROBERT S. FRIEDMAN

STATE POLITICS IN RECENT YEARS has witnessed consistent victories by supporters of expanded expressways and freeways at the expense of the advocates of other modes of transportation. It has also recorded the controversies associated with financing highways, resolving differences over highway location, awarding of contracts, and classification of existing highways for determination of the financial burden of maintaining them. Decisions concerning highway policy and administration have aroused such diverse interest groups as neighborhood improvement associations, school boards, the Portland Cement Association, the American Association of Railroads, labor unions, and even occasionally mental health associations. These decisions have also provided patronage to maintain political organizations and in some instances they have led to charges of scandal.[1] In short, highway decision-making is close to the nerve center of American politics and this is especially true in the arena of state government.

In this chapter, we shall examine state highway systems, their needs, specifications, and sources of finance, as well as the impact of federal highway programs and highway organization on the systems. We shall also describe the conflicts which arise, the competitors in them, and their outcome. Finally, we shall explain the factors that have encouraged the differences in state highway construction and maintenance activity in the United States, by examining the statistical relationship between highway expenditures and a number of political and economic variables.

GROWTH AND DEVELOPMENT OF HIGHWAYS

Any discussion of state highway politics must begin with the extraordinary expansion of the highway system in the 20th century. By way of illustration, in 1900 there were only 128,500 miles of surfaced roads in the entire United States. In 1961 Texas alone had over 150,000 miles of surfaced roads and the national total exceeded 2,500,000. In 1900 there were only 8,000 motor vehicle registrations, while in 1961 there were over 75,000,000.[2] As a consequence, governmental expenditures in 1900 for highway construction and maintenance were miniscule except at the municipal level. At the present time all levels of government are significantly involved. In fact, in approximately half of the states total state and local expenditures for highway purposes range from one-fifth to one-third of all governmental expenditures, and in no state is the figure under one-eighth. When we consider the magnitude of political activity undertaken on behalf of governmental participation in the fields of education, health, welfare, public safety, recreation, etc., the successes scored by the supporters of an ever-expanding highway system are all the more impressive.

The general growth in highways and highway use in all fifty states has been fairly uniform and is closely associated with a steady increase in motor vehicles of all kinds. Under these conditions, the same categories of highway demands are found throughout the states. Construction specifications, with allowances for peculiarities in terrain and climate within each of these categories, tend to be similar. Variations exist in the financing of highways, but here again similarities outweigh differences. The political game of highway building and maintenance has similar categories of players; and the arenas, structure of the arenas, and rules of the game have only modest variation from state to state.

Nevertheless, these uniformities tend to obscure numerous differences. When one highway official was asked about the comparative quality of highway systems among the states, he had little difficulty in distinguishing what he regarded to be the very best highway systems from the very worst.[3] When expenditures are compared, there is no doubt that in some states a substantially larger segment of the budget is earmarked for highways than in others.*

HIGHWAY SYSTEMS

HIGHWAY NEEDS. The need for new highways is often described by highway engineers in terms of optimum traffic flow, based on safe speeds in urban and rural areas. Underlying these need patterns are differences in demands by various classes of highway users. In effect, these users compete in the political market place for scarce dollars to construct and maintain particular kinds of roads necessary to their social and economic ends. Retail merchants in the core city demand expressways in the heart of the city to compete with growing suburban shopping centers. Rural school administrators urge improvement of rural roads to enable school buses to complete their daily

---

*Because of the difficulty in distinguishing local from state expenditure, for comparative purposes our discussion of expenditures includes both state and local expenditure.

rounds. The interstate trucking industry supports improved, primary inter-city roads. Operators of highway motels and restaurants and gas stations press for more access roads to interstate highways. Farmers demand paved roads from farm to market. And residents of suburban subdivisions insist upon paved neighborhood streets.

Until World War II, the major controversies involved in these demands concerned the question of which would be met.[4] From the advent of the automobile until World War II, emphasis was on construction of rural roads — both primary and secondary. Cities had created street networks that were able to service motor vehicle needs reasonably well, especially with the continued vitality of street railway systems. Road conditions in rural America were so poor that even the railroads joined in support of improved farm-to-market roads in order to guarantee access to railroad terminals.[5] As a result, state after state created highway departments charged with the task of constructing primary rural highways, and schemes were devised whereby state aid was granted to local units of government, other than cities, to relieve the problem of inadequate farm-to-market roads.

HIGHWAY CLASSIFICATION. Since World War II, the domination of motor vehicles in the field of surface transportation has engendered great demand for highway construction activity in both urban and rural areas. In general, the response to the demands for all categories of highways has been extremely favorable. The areas of conflict have not included whether highways should be built, but have been over the allocation of costs and over issues, such as location and specifications for highways.

The burden of cost is a knotty problem since it encompasses not only the tax system but also the distribution of state aid to local government units and the scheme of highway classification.[6] A system of highway classification has been devised in many states to provide orderly development and a scheme of responsibility for state and local roads. Categories vary, but a typical classification system includes:

A. Rural:

1. Primary state highway system — the network of major state traffic routes comprising the state-designated system.

2. Secondary highway system — the web of traffic channels distributing traffic between the state primary system and land service roads.

3. Land service road system — roads, the principal function of which is to provide direct access to farms and rural homes.

B.   Urban:

1. Primary street system — the network of main traffic arteries furnishing interconnection between the major sections of a city.

2. Secondary street system — the web of minor traffic channels (the sub-arteries) which distribute traffic within a given urban district, and serve as routes intermediate between the primary street system and local streets.

3. Local street system — streets, the principal function of which is to provide direct access to adjacent residences, business establishments, recreational facilities, and the like.[7]

Designation of roads in these categories has an impact on policy decisions, for it determines the level of government — state, county or city — charged with construction and/or maintenance. It also settles the source of funds for construction or maintenance — state taxes, local taxes, or special assessments on abutting property owners.[8]

The criterion for inclusion in the state system which is most often adopted is the stipulation that "the primary system shall connect all counties or county seats." In the view of one observer this system "strongly favors rural interests in that it allocates equal weight to each area of the state regardless of the sparsity or density of its population."[9] Another frequently used criterion to define the state primary system is "roads which connect population and market centers." Although this kind of provision permits considerable discretion, it is undoubtedly more favorable to the more concentrated population centers. Other stipulations include development of natural resources, development of business, industry, and agriculture, traffic needs, public welfare, provision for an integrated system, and the financial capacity of the state. All permit wide leeway and considerable political flexibility.

A leading student of highway financial policy has argued that while in theory highway classification is designed to differentiate arteries of statewide from local importance for purposes of establishing revenue and expenditure policy, in practice it serves as an additional form of state aid. His argument is based on the fact that in many states pressure is exerted with considerable success by local interests to transfer roads from classification as locally maintained roads to state highways. The purpose of this pressure is to relieve the burden upon local revenue sources and also to obtain higher quality road service.[10]

There are great variations among the states in the percentage of rural roads incorporated into the state system, ranging from a low of 7.1 per cent in New Jersey and 8.8 per cent in North Dakota to 100 per cent in Delaware,

North Carolina, and West Virginia.[11] Variations among the fifty states conform neither to regional lines nor to differences in urbanization or intensity of party competition. There also does not seem to be a relationship between the percentage of local roads under state control and the independence of the highway department from control of the governor.

Whatever distribution of responsibility and control is agreed upon within the state political system, the categories of highways outlined earlier are found to some extent in all states. In Michigan, for example, with its highly concentrated industrial population, in 1960 there were 3,028 miles described as principal trunkline routes, 1,044 miles described as "other major routes," and 5,406 miles of secondary state roads. County roads subdivided again into primary and local totalled 85,825, and city streets subdivided into major and local accounted for another 14,411 miles, for a grand total of 109,714 miles.[12] In contrast to less urban states, Michigan has a higher concentration of primary roads of interstate quality or bordering on interstate quality.

COST VARIATIONS. Differences in costs of highways result not only from differences in population but also from a number of other conditions.[13] Variations in soil and terrain lead to considerable differentiation in highway cost. It is relatively cheap to construct highways on desert sands, but expensive in rocky terrain. Similarly, the prairie lands of the Midwest present few obstacles as compared with mountainous regions of the Rockies or even West Virginia. Climatic conditions also add to the cost of highways in some regions. The needs for repairs due to damage by deep winter frost and for snow removal both represent expenses not found in the South. On the other hand, excessive rainfall adds to highway costs in some areas. In short, within the general uniformities in highway needs there are variations resulting from natural factors which are not a product of the vicissitudes of the political system.

HIGHWAY LOCATION. Highway engineers and economists have developed technical standards for highway location, rights-of-way, construction practices and use of highways.* Nevertheless, each of these has served as a source of political conflict in some states. A picture of the extent to which this has happened may be obtained from statements by policy-makers in a state highway department in a large industrial state.[14] These officials were asked to list individuals and interest groups most directly affected by the services performed by the department. They were also asked to identify groups which, they thought, felt benefited and those which felt they were harmed. To a

---

*The Highway Research Board of the National Academy of Sciences — National Research Council — is perhaps the leader in this field. The highway construction industry has itself been active in research and development.

large degree, when administrators mentioned groups harmed they mentioned only those affected by "technical aspects" of highway building. The head of the department, for example, in citing such groups, identified owners of roadside services on highways which had been relocated and persons whose property had been purchased for highway rights-of-way. Only after further questioning did he mention the competitive facets of highways and the railroad and airline industries. The department's director of administration in response to the same question identified local communities by-passed by primary trunklines, people whose homesteads are in the path of highways, railroads which are required to resolve the grade crossing problem, and the road building industry which is compelled to meet high specification standards. A similar reaction was echoed by the department's public information officer.

In effect, therefore, emphasis on technical aspects of highway policy-making may tend to obscure controversy, but controversy, nevertheless, occurs frequently in such matters. We may illustrate this by examining a number of problem areas. Decisions on highway location enhance property values for some and diminish values for others. Such actions encourage commercial and industrial development nearby and discourage activity along abandoned or downgraded routes.[15] In some instances, conflicts occur between the builders of highways and those displaced from their homes or those opposed to tampering with historical sites or areas of scenic beauty.[16] Some of the dislocation conflicts have been alleviated by the Federal Highway Act of 1962 which authorizes states to enact legislation to reimburse property owners dislocated by highway building.[17]

RIGHTS-OF-WAY. The entire process of purchase and disposition of rights-of-way for highway purposes is a delicate one in which public officials are compelled to participate in real estate transactions. Despite fairly elaborate rules of conduct, discretion abounds permitting manipulation which can be used to the economic advantage of some, and the political advantage of others. Because of the flexibility essential in this kind of activity it is not surprising that charges of impropriety are made from time to time. Congressional hearings conducted by a House of Representatives subcommittee, chaired by Representative Blatnik of Minnesota, disclosed conduct thought by the committee to be of questionable nature in several states, but especially in Massachusetts and Florida.[18] In its report on land purchase and disposition in Florida the committee pointed to the sharp differences in costs between the land-boom states of Florida and California. It found that despite similar land value increases, California highway officials were purchasing land at a far lower cost than their counterparts in Florida.[19]

CONSTRUCTION POLICIES. In highway construction uniformities prevail partly as a result of federal program specifications and partly because of developments in highway engineering practices. Nevertheless, the range of discretion has encouraged activities which have occasionally raised the spectre of scandal. In Massachusetts allegations were made that a testimonial dinner was held by grateful highway contractors for a highway official who was rewarded with the net proceeds of the dinner in return for services rendered. In the same state the Public Works Department, which builds the highways, was charged with dividing contracts into pieces of less than $1000 so that competitive bidding could be waived and "deserving" contractors rewarded.[20]

More commonly, highway politics leads to disputes like the one in Minnesota which began in the late 1930's and was not settled for a decade. A local manufacturer of natural cement requested that the highway department be required to use a blend of Portland and natural cements which he argued would prevent scaling caused by winter weather and also would aid local industry. Highway department officials rejected the request on the ground that the claims made for the blend were not substantiated by research. As a result the blend would have to compete in bidding with Portland cement. Since the latter was less expensive, the effect was to remove the blend from competition. The struggle which ultimately led to this decision involved not only the highway department and the affected industries, but also the legislature, the governor, and the U.S. Bureau of Public Roads.[21]

WEIGHT LIMITS. Undoubtedly the technical problem about which most controversy has revolved is that of the use, or "wear and tear," on highways. Highway use by different classes of motor vehicles has varying physical effects on the highway.* Particularly significant is the extent to which heavy motor vehicles destroy highways. Because of the generally accepted notion that heavy trucks have a deleterious effect on highways, many states have placed limitations upon truck weight. Some states have been more zealous in this endeavor than others, and this has been the product of the relative political strength of trucking groups and competing transportation facilities.

A classic example of this occurred in Pennsylvania. Pennsylvania is a key state for the transportation industry not only because it is a populous industrial state, but also because it bridges the Eastern seaboard and the Midwest, and the North Atlantic and South Atlantic regions. In addition, the home office of one of the nation's largest railroads, the Pennsylvania, is situated in the state.

In 1943 the over-all weight limit for trucks in Pennsylvania was fixed at 45,000 pounds.[22] This figure was the lowest (except for Kentucky) of any

*One element of the problem concerns differentials in benefit derived from highway use and therefore raises concomitantly the question of inequities in the incidence of the financial burden. This is discussed in connection with highway revenue sources on pp. 425–426.

state in the United States. Neighboring states had load limits of 60,000–70,000 pounds. The railroads hoped that trucks would have to unload before entering Pennsylvania and some shippers might be frustrated enough to ship via the railroads. In addition, the heavily taxed railroads felt that a relaxation in the weight limit would give truckers an unfair competitive advantage. The trucking industry launched a counteroffensive in the 1950's which led to passage of a law supported by Democratic Governor Leader that increased the weight limit to 60,000 pounds. Although Republican Governor Fine, Leader's predecessor, had earlier vetoed a similar measure, the conflict was not primarily partisan. In fact, party lines were sharply broken on both sides of the legislative aisle. The division involved an intense campaign between the two directly affected interests, each of which created coalitions with numerous other groups that either had an indirect interest or owed some allegiance to one or the other of the protagonists. The struggle may have been more heated in Pennsylvania than elsewhere, but similar issues have arisen in numerous states.

In summary, the politics of highway construction and maintenance is to a large degree centered around conflicts concerning mundane technical issues. The focal point for dealing with these controversies is the state highway department, although in exceptional circumstances the governor, legislature, courts, and other agencies of government may enter the picture before a settlement is reached.

FEDERAL HIGHWAY AID PROGRAMS

EARLY LEGISLATION. Perhaps the most important factor in providing conformity in state highway programs has been the role of the federal government. Since 1916 the federal government, through the Bureau of Public Roads, has provided funds for highway construction under terms which have insured standards of organization and procedure established at the national level. In order for a state to participate in the program initiated by the Federal Aid Road Act of 1916, it was required to have a highway department.[23] Plans for highway construction under the program were to be drawn up by individual highway departments but submitted to federal highway authorities for approval. Plans were required to show locations of roads to be constructed, specifications, and cost estimates. Money was only available for construction purposes and was limited to the intercity road system. An amendment enacted in 1921 stated that aid was to be limited to a maximum of 7 per cent of the total road mileage of the state. Federal appropriations were made from the general fund and allocated on the basis of one-third according to area, one-third according to population, and one-third on the basis of total mileage of rural delivery and star routes* in the state. States were required to match federal grants dollar for dollar.[24]

Two changes of lasting significance were instituted during the Depression period. The National Industrial Recovery Act provided that at least one-fourth of the federal aid funds allocated to the states be used on extensions of federal aid highways into or through incorporated municipalities. In addition, up to one-fourth of the funds could be used for secondary or feeder roads. These changes were predicated upon work relief policies rather than highway policies, but their adoption gave added support to the advocates of highway aid for purely urban and rural needs in later years.[25] The highway act of 1944 specifically incorporated these policies into the permanent highway program. Under the act, appropriations were made specifically for primary roads, urban extensions of primary roads, and secondary roads. A mileage limitation was continued on aid to the primary system, but none was placed on either of the other two programs. Three separate allocation formulae were used. The primary system continued to receive aid on the formula of one-third area, one-third population, and one-third mail route mileage. The secondary system allocation was similar, except that only rural population was used. Urban area funds were apportioned on the basis of population in urban places, with 5,000 being used as the minimum for a place to meet the test of an urban area.[26]

LATER INNOVATIONS. The Federal Highway Acts of 1944 and 1956 have had a significant impact on state highway politics because they have created for the first time a single network of primary highways with uniform minimum standards. The result of these enactments has been to increase the role of the U.S. Bureau of Public Roads in decision-making in matters previously left entirely to state and local authorities.

The 1944 act created for the first time a system of interstate highways limited to 40,000 miles (later increased to 41,000) and designed to connect the principal metropolitan areas, cities, and industrial centers by as direct a route as possible. State highway departments were required to cooperate with departments in adjoining states to determine routes, subject to federal approval. No specially designated funds, however, were earmarked for these roads until 1952.[27] The net effect of the act was to shift federal highway activity from a predominantly rural focus to a largely urban focus.

The 1956 act shifted the emphasis even more to urban needs and also

*The post office department is authorized to contract for the transportation of mail over a post road other than a railroad, and such contract may include collection and delivery service to patrons of the postal service. Such roads are designated star routes. 39 USCA 6401.

provided the Bureau of Public Roads with meaningful supervisory tools which guaranteed for it a major role in decision-making in construction of primary roads. Specifically, the Bureau was granted an important part in highway classification and route selection. In the latter case, although theoretically route selection continued to be initiated by the states, in practice real influence resided in the Bureau of Public Roads. Under the 1956 act each state was awarded a certain number of the 41,000 miles of interstate highways. However, if a state did not designate the artery desired by the Bureau of Public Roads, the mileage and money could be given to another state. In fact, the Bureau has even occasionally recommended major modifications of route alignment or recommended selection of entirely different routes.[28]

A number of other features of the act have enhanced the role of the Bureau of Public Roads and have assured uniformity among the states. One of these is the requirement that all interstate highways be controlled access roads. Another provision discouraged signs and billboards along highway rights-of-way. Any state regulating such signs on rights-of-way acquired after 1956 was granted a .5 per cent reduction in its share of the cost of the program. Finally, the act froze maximum size and weight limits at their 1956 level.[29] To some extent the Bureau of Public Roads has administered these provisions so that flexibility has been permitted, but a significant amount of control has remained in its hands. This control was assured largely by the formula whereby the federal government's portion of the cost of the program was increased from a 50-50 matching of funds to a 90-10 arrangement.

One other aspect of the federal program is important to an understanding of state highway politics. Distribution of funds for the first several years of the interstate program was based one-half on population and one-half on the primary road system formula developed in 1916. Since then, distribution has been based on need for completion of the program. Determination of need has been left largely to the states with only minimum specifications set by the Bureau of Public Roads. This has benefited states which had ignored their interstate roads during the period before 1956 in favor of construction of other roads. States, particularly in the congested Northeast and the Pacific Coast, which had used federal and state money earlier for their interstate highways were simply "out of luck."[30]

ORGANIZATION OF STATE HIGHWAY DEPARTMENTS

One of the ironies of highway politics is that, despite the highly charged conflicts which prevail, strong endorsement is found in many states for a highway organization which is superficially removed from the mainstream of partisan political decision-making. For example, during the 1961–62 Michigan constitutional convention, highway groups such as the Michigan Road Builders Association, the Associated Petroleum Industries of Michigan, the Oil and

Gas Association of Michigan, and the Good Roads Federation all argued for retention of an independently elected highway commissioner. They argued that highway building needed to be removed from regular political channels, using the following rationale:

> Michigan's economy depends on highways, and highway construction and maintenance are something apart from other functions. The governor's views might control elsewhere but not with respect to highways. Michigan has an outstanding system and this is due to two factors, a highway commissioner separately elected and a system of earmarking revenues for highway needs.[31]

RELATIONSHIP TO THE GOVERNOR. What consequences do differences in organization and relationships of the highway department with the governor have for highway politics? It has been suggested that the extent to which the governor can exercise control over highway policy determines, to a degree at least, the competitive position of highway building and maintenance vis-à-vis other programs. This proposition is based on the assumption that if the highway department is under the wing of the governor, it will have to compete with other functions for support. Where the department is independent its supporters and staff are freer to plead their own cause. Because of the visibility of highways and their tangible quality, only vigorous action by a governor is likely to restrain legislatures from pouring money into highways, rather than mental health and similar programs. Even a vigorous governor operates with a handicap in states in which the highway department is independent.

Before examining the validity of this proposition, it is essential to describe the differences between a highway department which is organizationally independent and one which is dependent upon the governor or the executive branch in general. At the outset it should be noted that, as with other complex organizations, formal structural arrangements do not entirely describe the decision-making patterns. In Louisiana, for example, a multi-membered board appointed by the governor for staggered terms exceeding that of the governor serves as the governing body of the highway department. It appoints and removes the highway director. In actuality, however, recent governors upon taking office have "arranged" to have the legislature remove "undesirable" commissioners by a device known as "addressing out of office."[32] Through this technique any governor so desiring may name his own highway director and exercise strong gubernatorial control over the department. In some states, formal structural arrangements probably do reflect actual practice.

A number of criteria may be used to measure the independence of highway departments from governors or their dependence upon them. These include plural versus single-headed governing authority, independent

election or prescriptive gubernatorial selection versus unrestricted gubernatorial selection, legislative confirmation versus no confirmation, term
of office exceeding that of the governor versus coincidence of term of office,
and removal only for cause versus service at the pleasure of the governor. A
dependent highway department would be one in which a governor was free
to name his own department head without restrictions regarding partisanship
or professional background and without veto by legislative failure to confirm.
The highway director would serve at the pleasure of the governor. An independent department would be governed by a multi-membered board chosen
by the governor, but with prescriptions neutralizing partisanship and perhaps
guaranteeing occupational and regional representation. Legislative confirmation would be required and the term of office would exceed that of the governor. Removal would be for cause only. In addition, control over the appointment of the highway director would be entirely within the purview of the
board, and usually professional qualifications would be written into the
system.

There are very few states in which either of the model types is operative.[33] However, using these, we have classified formal structure of state highway departments under three heads: independent, partially dependent, and
dependent. Table 1 lists the distribution of these structural arrangements
among American states. This classification was used to test the hypothesis
described above and no evidence was found that highway programs in states
in which independence prevails are more favored than in states in which the
governor has significant control over the department. This will be discussed
in greater detail when we have put into place other aspects of the system.

A second hypothesis that suggests itself is that in states with low party
competition, or more specifically in one-party states, highway interests ought
to fare better than in competitive states.[34] Highway builder and user groups
are among the largest contributors to political campaigns at the state level.[35]
In a two-party situation the money goes into the party coffers and is less
identifiable. Therefore, it is more difficult for highway groups to commit
candidates to specific programs. In contrast, in one-party states campaigns
and campaign finances are individualized. As a result this enables highway
groups to deal directly with the candidate.[36] However, when comparison is
made among the states in terms of percentage of all governmental expenditures devoted to highways, no greater proportion is spent in one-party states
than in competitive two-party states.

BOARD REPRESENTATION. A number of other features of highway organization are relevant to this discussion. The first of these is the stipulation
in a number of states employing highway commissions that commissioners
represent geographical districts rather than the state at large. The usual

Table 1

RELATIONSHIP OF HIGHWAY DEPARTMENT TO GOVERNOR

INDEPENDENT	PARTIALLY DEPENDENT	DEPENDENT
Arizona	California	Alabama
Arkansas	Connecticut	Alaska
Colorado	Kansas	Hawaii
Delaware	Louisiana	Illinois
Florida	Maryland	Kentucky
Georgia	Minnesota	Nebraska
Idaho	Nevada	New Jersey
Indiana	Oklahoma	New York
Iowa	Oregon	North Dakota
Maine	South Dakota	Ohio
Massachusetts	Vermont	Pennsylvania
Michigan	Virginia	Rhode Island
Mississippi	West Virginia	Tennessee
Missouri		
Montana		
New Hampshire		
New Mexico		
North Carolina		
South Carolina		
Texas		
Utah		
Washington		
Wisconsin		
Wyoming		

Source: See footnote 33.

rationale for such provision is that problems vary from place to place and the district highway commissioner is able to convey this to the highway department. Variations of this device are in use in approximately half of the states. Commission members in these states are usually appointed from particular geographical districts, such as counties, highway districts, supreme court districts, judicial districts, congressional districts, and in some instances from particular cities.[37] Proponents of coordinated highway planning for the state highway network frown on this device as a deterrent to the accomplishment of their ends and charge that localism results from it.[38] It would be difficult to measure the validity of the charges. However, it is probable that the impact of the interstate highway program has been to diminish the probability of localism in state highway affairs, regardless of the presence or absence of a district system for appointing highway commissioners.

In organizing some governmental functions, commissions have been created with occupational or professional requirements designed to represent either affected economic interests or professional standards. There are no cases in which legislation requires that highway commissions represent particular occupations. However, there may be informal recognition in some cases of particular occupations. In one state in which the highway director is required by law to appoint an advisory committee, conscious effort is made to represent "affected" industries. The highway director in question was very prompt in pointing out that the committee does not make policy and serves at most as a sounding board. Professional qualifications are seldom required of commissions. However, in Michigan and West Virginia which have single executive heads, the department head must meet technical qualifications.[39] This is also frequently the case for highway directors in commission states.

STATE-LOCAL RELATIONS. Although the focus of our attention is on state highway politics, the political and administrative relationship between state and local highway systems is so close that mention should be made of the impact of the state highway department on local road affairs. Customarily, highway construction and maintenance of local roads — urban and rural — have been local responsibilities. Local road systems were in operation long before state highway networks were on the drawing board. In recent years, local governments have had to rely more on state funds for their local road programs. This has led to increased supervision by state highway departments and greater state control of local roads. Reference has already been made to the great variation among states in the percentage of local roads under state control. Equally varied is the amount of influence accruing to the state from control of the purse strings. Influence in some instances appears potentially great, but only minimal in practice. In instances in which local road organizations are popularly elected or chosen politically, freedom to defy state edicts is maximized. Nevertheless, dependence upon state revenue will tend to determine the extent to which local officials will flex their muscles.

City highway organizations are far freer from state supervision than their rural counterparts. To a large extent, this is not of their own making. They have participated in state aid programs in relatively few states. Where no money is dispensed, little control is exercised. With the advent of the federal program for urban roads, the pattern has changed. In some states, however, even after the mandate, the inability of city forces to marshal legislative strength meant little state aid. In Louisiana, for example, in the late 1940's and early 1950's the cities of New Orleans and Baton Rouge, which had city-county consolidations, did well because of their eligibility for parish (county) road funds. So did towns having under 5,000 population in which urban extensions of primary state roads represented the main street of the city. Cities of intermediate size were receiving nothing. State legislation in

1955 and the interstate program have altered this substantially.[40] In general, however, except for coordination and general street planning, city highway departments remain independent of the state system.

HIGHWAY FINANCES

REVENUE SOURCES. The heart of the highway political game centers around who is going to benefit from highway construction or what money is expended for, and who is going to pay for it.[41] Prior to the use of the automobile as a major means of transportation, highway expenditures were derived from the general fund and revenue came mostly from property taxes. Automobile travel has changed highway finance substantially and has led to an increasing reliance upon highway-user revenue sources based on the benefit principle. The earliest of these devices was the motor vehicle registration fee which was initiated for purposes of identification, but which has been used increasingly for revenue purposes. Shortly after World War I, sales levies were begun on gasoline. Again, the theory behind the tax was that those who benefit from highways ought to pay for them. This point of view was supported most vigorously by the railroads which argued that since use of the highway is free of charge, failure to charge the user in a more direct way represents unfair competition with the railroads.

At present, approximately 50 per cent of all highway receipts are derived from the gasoline tax. Prior to the vast state highway building programs begun in the 1950's, considerable variation existed in the size of the gasoline levy. Southern states often had levies ranging up to seven cents per gallon even during Depression years, in contrast to two or three cents in the Northeast. Gasoline taxes began inching up around 1950 and now all states levy gasoline taxes from five to seven cents. In most states an exemption from the motor fuel tax is made for consumption by vehicles not using highways. This proves extremely beneficial to farmers.

The second most important state revenue source for highway purposes is the motor vehicle registration fee. In some states, particularly in the South, this source continues to be used almost exclusively as a regulatory device, and fees are pegged very low. Louisiana charges only $3.00 for regular passenger cars. More than half of the states increase the fee for heavier weight vehicles, with Oklahoma's $70.57 for heavy-weight cars the highest in the country. In general, trucks and buses pay even higher fees on the ground that they tend to inflict greater damage on highways than motor cars do. Again many states provide reductions for farm vehicles which, it is argued, do not use highways as extensively as other vehicles of the same size.

In a number of states in recent years, the so-called third structure taxes have been levied. These taxes combine heavy vehicle weight and high level travel. In other words, heavy trucks and buses carrying greater weight and traveling more miles are taxed at a higher rate. The technique is strongly supported by railroad interests and equally strongly opposed by truckers and bus companies. Thus far, it has been a very small revenue producer.

Because of the backlog of highway needs which had accrued by the end of World War II, many states resorted to bond issues to finance highway construction. This approach to the problem spreads out the time in which payment is to be made and in some cases transfers the incidence of the ultimate burden exclusively from the highway user to the population in general.

The use of toll roads has gained support in a number of states, particularly in the Northeast. The burden, of course, is placed directly on the highway user. Railroads have frequently endorsed this approach, but automobile clubs, truckers, and bus companies complain that they are facing double taxation on the grounds that they have already been compelled to pay motor vehicle and motor fuel taxes. In practice, the toll road is a most useful device for states which handle a great deal of through traffic beginning in other states and destined for still other states. It is not surprising that over half of all toll receipts are collected in the states of New York, New Jersey and Pennsylvania.

EARMARKING FUNDS. In a few states general revenues are used for highway purposes, but the huge revenue derived from highway levies has reduced these totals to negligible proportions. In fact, what is most significant about highway financing at the state level is the extent of earmarking of funds raised from highway sources for highway expenditure. Pressed by highway groups, more than half of the states have adopted constitutional provisions forbidding or restricting diversion of highway revenues from highway purposes to other expenditures. Other states have adopted similar provisions by statute or administrative practice. The device guarantees road-building funds even in circumstances in which legislative politics might otherwise favor reduction in activity. In effect, highways are given preferential treatment. In Michigan's notorious cash crisis of 1959 when the general fund was depleted, no financial problem existed for the highway building agency.

What is most interesting about the anti-diversion concept is that there is a definite relationship between permissibility and actual diversion on the one hand and the amount of highway spending in the states in relation to other activities. In 1959 nine states diverted in excess of 10 per cent of highway revenues from highway purposes; another ten states diverted from 2 to 10 per cent. Not one of these states was in the first quartile of states in terms of the percentage of highway expenditures to all other expenditures in the period 1958–62, and eight were in the last quartile. Quite a number of the states involved were highly urbanized states; yet even when urbanization is held constant there is a significant relationship between diversion and high-

way expenditures. Of the twenty-four most rural states in the United States,*
sixteen had no (or negligible) diversion. Of these states only one did not
rank in the top half of the states in terms of ratio of highway to other expenditures, and eleven were ranked in the top quartile. Of the eight rural states
with some or substantial diversion, only one ranked in the top quartile in
expenditures and three ranked in the lower half. Earmarking and anti-diversion provisions are symptomatic, therefore, of the success scored by supporters
of highway expenditures.

FEDERAL AND LOCAL REVENUE. Federal and locally raised revenues are
also vital to state highway finance because of their basic interrelationship
with state taxes. Historically, local highway work was paid for by taxes on
property and by special assessments on abutting property owners. These still
remain the major locally raised revenue sources. Because of traffic congestion
and the financial burden upon central cities, in recent years parking meters
and "wheel taxes" on vehicles using city streets have provided an increasing
amount of funds in many places.

During World War I the federal government entered the field of highway
taxation by levying a tax on motor vehicles and parts. These expired at the
end of the war. The federal government re-entered the field in 1932 by instituting a one cent per gallon tax on gasoline and taxing new automobiles and
auto accessories. With the expansion of federal expenditures, the gasoline
tax has been increased to four cents and the tax on new vehicles to 10 per
cent. In the first twenty years of the vehicle tax, trucks and buses were taxed
at a somewhat lower rate than autos, and some observers have concluded that
this gave the two industries an advantage that they have never relinquished.
In addition to these revenue sources, diesel fuel has been taxed since 1951
and a tonnage weight levy has been put on trucks since 1956. The petroleum
industry and other groups have tended to oppose the expanding role of the
federal government in the area of highway taxation, but the very extensive
revenue derived directly from these taxes has neutralized this opposition. This
is especially true in states which have benefited most, particularly the rural
South and West.

EXPENDITURES. In addition to looking at total highway expenditures,
it is also important to examine the distribution of expenditures within states
and differences in level of expenditures between states. By way of introduc-

*For purposes of analysis, percentage of population in standard metropolitan statistical
areas has been used to measure state urbanization. The choice of this measure rather
than the simple percentage of people in urban places is based on the fact that for
highway purposes it is largely urban concentrations that distinguish urban and rural
needs.

Table 2

HIGHWAY USER REVENUE DIVERSION AND HIGHWAY EXPENDITURES

STATE	PER CENT DIVERTED 1959	RANK ACCORDING TO PERCENTAGE OF HIGHWAY EXPENDITURE TO ALL STATE AND LOCAL EXPENDITURE 1958–62
New Jersey	28.2	47
Florida	27.4	37
Rhode Island	27.2	41
Georgia	26.8	34
New York	22.3	46
Texas	21.0	16
Washington	20.2	42
California	16.5	48
Oklahoma	14.2	29
Delaware	10.0	32
South Carolina	9.5	23
Tennessee	7.1	12
New Mexico	6.5	20
Wisconsin	5.6	18
Arkansas	3.6	15
North Carolina	3.1	38
Connecticut	2.9	24
Colorado	2.1	43
Oregon	2.1	26
Minnesota	1.5	27
Indiana	0.8	40
Kentucky	0.8	13
Illinois	0.7	30
Kansas	0.7	11
Alabama	0.6	19
Massachusetts	0.6	45

tion it should be pointed out that one of the most difficult aspects of highway systems to measure is over-all quality and its relationship to political strength. Nevertheless, over-all highway expenditures do provide a rough measure of the extent to which the supporters and users of the highway system have achieved their ends.[42] Therefore, it should be remembered that the state expending the greatest ratio of its budget for highways need not be the state with the best system, but it is probably the state in which supporters of the system are strongest politically.

Highway engineers might expect the division of funds for various categories to be determined primarily on the basis of highway use. In practice this has tended not to be the case. In most states, until the impact of the interstate system began to be felt, rural secondary roads used by farmers and

Table 2, continued

STATE	PER CENT DIVERTED 1959	RANK ACCORDING TO PERCENTAGE OF HIGHWAY EXPENDITURE TO ALL STATE AND LOCAL EXPENDITURE 1958–62
Wyoming	0.6	3
Utah	0.5	31
Mississippi	0.1	14
New Hampshire	0.1	4
Arizona	0	36
Idaho	0	8
Iowa	0	6
Louisiana	0	28
Maine	0	10
Maryland	0	35
Michigan	0	39
Missouri	0	33
Montana	0	7
Nebraska	0	9
Nevada	0	21
North Dakota	0	5
Ohio	0	25
Pennsylvania	0	44
South Dakota	0	1
Vermont	0	2
Virginia	0	17
West Virginia	0	22

Sources: Philip H. Burch, Jr., *Highway Revenue and Expenditure Policy in the United States,* p. 65; U.S. Bureau of Public Roads, *Highway Statistics, 1959,* pp. 37–38; and U.S. Bureau of the Census, *Governmental Finances in the United States, 1958–1962.*

small town dwellers tended to be favored above rural primary and urban roads. Burch found in sixteen selected states that in every case the percentage of the total state expenditure devoted to secondary rural highways exceeded the estimated percentage of secondary to total rural travel on state highways. In Alabama, Florida, South Carolina, and Virginia the percentage was more than double. By 1959, in all instances the percentage expenditure on these roads had declined and in some it had declined to a point beneath the figure for percentage traveled.[43]

Expenditures in urban areas are even more out of line. In only a handful of states do cities receive state highway expenditures commensurate with use. Add to this the fact that cities receive relatively little financial help from state aid to localities and the picture is made complete. One of the most frequent explanations made for this is the underrepresentation of urban areas in the legislature.[44] In order to examine the validity of this, the percentage of "fair share" which urban areas were receiving from state expenditures as developed by Burch was compared with the David-Eisenberg index of representativeness.[45] In using the technique of rank-order correlations, no relationship was found, either positive or negative. In short, the answer must be sought elsewhere. There was a modest, positive relationship between states responding most favorably to urban needs and the degree of urbanization of the state. In other words, states like Rhode Island, Illinois, New Jersey, Connecticut, California, Massachusetts, and Ohio ranked in the top ten in terms of "best" ratio of actual to "proper" expenditures for urban areas. Similarly, the bottom ten states in terms of "poorest" effort in providing aid to urban areas were predominately rural. It seems apparent, therefore, that malapportionment has not been a factor of consequence in determining state aid to cities. In states with large metropolitan concentrations aid has been forthcoming. Where urban dwellers are a relatively small force, even when adequately represented, they have not had the influence to obtain state highway expenditures.

The most important change in recent years, of course, has been the increased activity in urban areas resulting from the Interstate Highway Program. The visibility of this activity has not been lost on rural officials. A series of interviews was conducted in 1960 with parish (county) officials in Louisiana in which officials were asked to comment on whether state aid to local government gave adequate consideration to urban needs. The response from rural respondents was invariably that the larger cities were doing extremely well under the Interstate Program and that this more than compensated for lack of state aid to these cities.[46]

STATE AID TO LOCALITIES. State financial aid to local highway systems bulks large in the local highway operation in most states. Justification for such aid has been based on arguments that there is a need for minimum highways throughout a state, that inadequate resources are available at the local level to support a highway system, that inadequate technical skills are available at the local level, and that there is a desire to guarantee to less wealthy areas at least a minimum highway program. The range of possibilities for determining a distribution of funds would place at one end some sort of need formula and at the other the ability of local political leaders to negotiate for funds. The difficulties associated with each of these approaches has led to a number of fairly fixed formulae which most states use either singly or in combination. Some of the yardsticks used are road mileage, vehicle miles traveled, gasoline consumption, population, motor vehicle registrations, area, and equal amounts for each subdivision. Formulae such as vehicle miles traveled, gasoline consumption, population, and registrations are more favorable to urban areas; and road mileage, area, and equal dollar distribution are devices conducive to more favorable treatment for rural areas.

Increasing influence of urban centers among legislative bodies in recent years has brought a somewhat more satisfactory response from legislatures. An interesting example of this was the revision of the highway aid formula in Louisiana in 1955. Louisiana is a state which by the time of the 1950 census had approximately half of its population situated in metropolitan areas. A need study had been done by the Automotive Safety Foundation in the early 1950's which found substantial road deficiencies in the state. A larger proportion of these deficiencies was found in parishes with high urbanization than in rural ones. The 1955 legislation granted parishes highway aid on the basis of a need formula with a minimum built in so as to guarantee some aid to all areas. In addition, older programs were continued under a gasoline consumption formula and a flat sum grant. A "sop" was thrown to municipalities with assurances of state assumption of the main cost of urban extensions of state highways. Finally, a classification system in state highways was written into law which included a primary, secondary, and farm-to-market system. The net result was to bring about action to remove highway deficiencies, particularly in urban parishes, without alienating rural constituencies.[47] However, since parish highway departments were forbidden to work within city limits, the needs of central cities, in some cases, remained unfulfilled.

In general, aid formulae have been geared to counties and sometimes town or township needs but seldom to the needs of municipalities. Approximately fifteen states, largely in the Northeast and the South, give no direct assistance to local highway needs in municipalities, and most of the rest give very limited assistance. Furthermore, in some states county road agencies do not provide either construction or maintenance services within city limits. In Louisiana, for example, where a gasoline consumption formula has provided a substantial sum of money at the parish level and has included gasoline consumed in municipalities, none of the money may be used within city limits except in New Orleans and Baton Rouge which have consolidated city-county government. Interviews with local highway officials brought out many more feelings of discrimination against cities because of this restriction than feelings of discrimination because of inadequate aid to urban areas under the general state formulae.[48] In summary, it is possible that patterns of aid distribution are changing to the advantage of urban counties, but limitations on the activity of county highway units within municipalities in some states has continued the lag with respect to many municipalities.

Table 3

COMPARATIVE STATE AND LOCAL HIGHWAY EXPENDITURES

State*	Rank According to Ratio of Highway Expenditures to All Governmental Expenditures	Per Cent Highway Expenditures of All State and Local Expenditures 1958–62 Average	Rank According to Per Capita Highway Expenditures	Per Capita Highway Expenditures 1958–62 Average	Rank According to Per Vehicle Highway Expenditures	Per Vehicle Highway Expenditures
South Dakota	1	33.24	3	$ 99.52	5	$199
Vermont	2	32.54	2	107.95	1	313
Wyoming	3	32.42	1	144.59	2	229
New Hampshire	4	30.60	7	84.17	3	219
North Dakota	5	28.64	4	98.80	6	196
Iowa	6	27.22	8	79.40	13	173
Montana	7	27.10	6	89.29	12	176
Idaho	8	27.00	10	75.10	22.5	148
Nebraska	9	26.64	14	69.25	18	155
Maine	10	26.56	16	67.93	7	189
Kansas	11	25.40	9	76.14	25	146
Tennessee	12	24.36	31	52.01	28.5	143
Kentucky	13	24.26	32	51.68	40.5	123
Mississippi	14	23.76	29.5	52.32	8	187
Arkansas	15	23.02	40	45.71	30	141
Texas	16	22.96	24	56.58	31	136
Virginia	17	22.80	36	49.95	37	127
Wisconsin	18	22.74	15	68.02	26	145
Alabama	19	22.42	39	47.84	17	157
New Mexico	20	22.00	12	69.43	14	169
Nevada	21	21.98	5	94.68	33.5	132
West Virginia	22	21.48	41	45.62	11	183
South Carolina	23	20.86	48	32.15	38.5	124

State*	Rank According to Ratio of Highway Expenditures to All Governmental Expenditures	Per Cent Highway Expenditures of All State and Local Expenditures 1958–62 Average	Rank According to Per Capita Highway Expenditures	Per Capita Highway Expenditures 1958–62 Average	Rank According to Per Vehicle Highway Expenditures	Per Vehicle Highway Expenditures
Oregon	26	20.24	13	$69.30	19	$154
Minnesota	27	20.10	29.5	52.32	22.5	148
Louisiana	28	19.76	19	63.47	4	204
Oklahoma	29	19.68	25	56.03	47	105
Illinois	30	19.44	26	55.54	16	158
Utah	31	19.40	20	59.24	35	130
Delaware	32	19.38	18	63.81	9.5	185
Missouri	33	19.10	42	45.55	33.5	132
Georgia	34	18.70	44	42.98	38.5	124
Maryland	35	18.28	35	50.41	20.5	150
Arizona	36	17.92	23	57.51	20.5	150
Florida	37	17.86	37	48.98	32	134
North Carolina	38	17.82	46	35.19	45	108
Michigan	39	17.36	28	53.90	27	144
Indiana	40	17.28	17	66.51	43	116
Rhode Island	41	17.04	43	44.91	40.5	123
Washington	42	17.02	21	59.22	36	128
Colorado	43	16.76	22	57.52	44	109
Pennsylvania	44	16.48	45	40.44	42	118
Massachusetts	45	15.88	38	48.49	15	162
New York	46	13.92	33	51.47	9.5	185
New Jersey	47	13.00	47	34.60	46	107
California	48	12.82	34	50.49	48	100

*Alaska and Hawaii are excluded because they were not states during the entire period covered.
Sources: U.S. Bureau of the Census, *Governmental Finances in the United States, 1958–1962*; and U.S. Bureau of Public Roads, *Highway Statistics, 1963*.

EXPENDITURE VARIATIONS. A final aspect of state highway expenditures involves the question of which states tend to spend more on highways and which spend less. The explanation of these differences is reserved for the concluding section, and at this point we shall simply describe the differences. Even such a limited description is fraught with hazards. Total dollars spent is a meaningless figure. Dollars spent per capita has limitations because of area difference, terrain problems, population concentration and sparsity factors, and a host of other drawbacks. Dollars per vehicle has some merit but has many limitations similar to those of per capita expenditure. The figure that we have chosen to rely upon is the percentage which highway expenditures represent of all government spending. This approach has the limitation that it makes "low effort" states on other programs which spend proportionately more on highways appear to be big spenders while making those which put a great deal of money into schools, health, welfare, etc., appear to be niggardly on highways. Nevertheless, it provides an index of where highways stand in total government activity. Table 3 lists the states in rank order according to this dimension; it also lists per capita and per vehicle expenditure and rank.

The most striking feature of the table is the high ranking of rural states and the very low ranking of the nation's most urban states.[49] These factors are somewhat less noticeable when the per capita and per vehicle dimensions are used. This may be explained partly by the lower ranking of the rural South where expenditures for all government activity are at a substantially lower level.

POLITICAL CONFLICTS

Earlier discussion has provided numerous examples of conflict in highway policy-making. These areas of conflict need to be brought into focus. Primarily, conflict in highway affairs can be classified under four major headings: (1) conflicts among transportation media for a share of the transportation market; (2) conflicts among economic interests which are dependent in varying degrees upon highways; (3) conflicts among producers of highway materials and building contractors; and (4) conflicts over partisan and constituency service needs in which contestants are only incidentally concerned with highways. Each of these conflict areas will be described so as to illustrate the kinds of contestants, the kinds of struggles about which conflict occurs, and the universality of these struggles throughout the United States.

TRANSPORTATION INDUSTRY. Conflicts within the transportation industry are directly related to economic competition. This includes competition for freight between truckers and railroads, competition for long distance passengers between buses and, indirectly, automobile users and manufacturers on the one hand, and railroads and, to a lesser extent, airlines on the other, and competition for urban passenger transport between the automobile on the one hand and transit facilities on the other. Each of these competitors has allies but, for purposes of simplicity, only the primary protagonists are listed. Issues about which conflicts occur include level of highway expenditure, classification of highways for which expenditures are made, impact and incidence of the revenue systems, and limitations on weight carried by motor vehicles traversing highways.

Railroads have been in the forefront of all of these conflict areas for a great many years. In the late 19th century, curiously enough, the railroad industry participated prominently in the good roads movement.[50] At the time, the main thrust of this movement was in support of highways from farm to town. This, of course, was encouraged by railroads because it expedited transportation from farm to train depot. When the good roads movement extended its interest to primary roads and eventually to urban streets, the posture of the railroad industry changed, for a threat to its own survival seemed to be rising. At the present time, railroads are avoiding endorsement or opposition to the construction of various classes of highways. Instead they have centered their attack on the incidence of taxation and the truck weight limit issue.[51] In general, they have supported the principle that highway users should pay for highways in proportion to the use and "damage" done to the highways. Specifically, this has led to support for the use of revenue bonds, rather than general obligation bonds for long term indebtedness in order to avoid transfer of the incidence of the cost from highway users to the general taxpayers. They have argued for fuel taxes, including those on diesel fuel, which reflect the added use given to roads by heavy vehicles. On toll roads, railroad people have urged the maintenance of a toll structure under which commercial vehicles will pay on the basis of weight. They have also recommended weight limitations on heavy motor vehicles and penalties for violations which are stringent enough to discourage further violations.

It is axiomatic that the point of view of the railroads is challenged strongly by truckers and to a lesser extent by other highway users. In general, all components of the automotive transportation industry have joined in this effort. In Michigan, for example, the Good Roads Federation has included officers from such diverse organizations as the Associated Petroleum Industries of Michigan, Chrysler Corporation, Corregated Metal Pipe Association, County Road Association of Michigan, Ford Motor Company, General Motors Corporation, Michigan Asphalt Paving Association, Michigan Bell Telephone Company, Michigan Construction Equipment Dealers Association, Michigan Farm Bureau, Michigan Municipal League, Michigan Road Builders Association, Michigan Sand and Gravel Producers, Michigan State Highway Department, Michigan State Grange, Michigan State Police, Michigan Trucking Association, Oil and Gas Association of Michigan, Portland Cement Association, and Allied Chemical Corporation. Auto transport groups have urged maximal highway spending. With respect to financing highway programs, they have opposed toll roads and encouraged anti-diversion provisions in connection with the use of funds derived from highway user taxes. They have also supported general purpose bonds as opposed to revenue bonds, and the truckers have opposed third structure taxes, taxes on motor vehicle accessories, diesel fuel, etc. The trucking industry has been especially hostile to weight limitation and particularly differentiations from state to state which they regard as harassment.

To a great extent, the good roads movement in general and the trucking industry in particular have emerged victorious. A portion of this victory was scored in the Interstate Highway Program with its encouragement of highway spending and its discouragement of further toll road building. Victories have also been scored at the state level with monotonous regularity. Certainly the victory won by the truckers in allegedly railroad-dominated Pennsylvania on the truck weight issue seems to support this.

OTHER ECONOMIC INTERESTS. The second category of conflict involves groups with secondary interests or those involved in single struggles. These groups include economic and other interests which are not as dependent upon highways as truckers but whose welfare is affected in some measure by highway decisions. It also includes groups of people who experience property loss or gain from highway decisions. A list of such groups would include the following:

1. Utility companies interested in highways for purposes of industrial attraction.

2. Motel, restaurant, and gasoline operators concerned not only with construction of more highways but also with their location in terms of existing enterprises.

3. Downtown business groups, both in large cities and small towns, fearful of the loss of business resulting from suburban shopping centers which have superior highway access.

4. Neighborhood and downtown theater owners threatened by competition from highway drive-in theaters.

5. Farmers interested in farm-to-market roads.

6. School administrators concerned with satisfactory roads for school buses.

7. Groups concerned with an adequate network of national and civil defense highways.

8. Nature lovers and others concerned with preservation of scenic beauty spots and natural resources.

9. Neighborhood groups disturbed by threats to property values resulting from highway location.

10. Property owners displaced by highway building needs. (In this case not only are some individuals forced to abandon property against their wishes, but some are beneficiaries of large profits from speculation in right-of-way purchases.)[52]

The above list is only suggestive and by no means exhaustive, but it does provide some idea of the range of issues about which disputes occur and variations that might exist in their outcome. The major issues in dispute among these groups include highway classification and emphasis on expenditure within classes, decisions regarding highway location, right-of-way purchase, and the problem of displacement and abandonment of existing property use in favor of highways. These issues have not been resolved in a similar manner in all states. Possible explanations for these differences may stem from high and low population concentrations, highly competitive two-party systems and less competitive systems, heavy industrial concentration and agricultural concentration, etc. The relative significance of each of these factors will be discussed in the concluding section of this chapter.

Patterns of conduct among the states on issues other than expenditures are less clearly discernible because of the absence of systematic data, but there are variations which could be determined by constructing a continuum in which state highway procedures are ranked on the basis of emphasis upon engineering considerations at one end and political considerations at the other. It is probable that with respect to highway location issues, for example, a vast majority of states would be found in the middle of the continuum. However, on matters of right-of-way purchase, compensation for property expropriation, and related issues differences among them would be far greater.

HIGHWAY BUILDERS. Competition among various industries supplying material and labor for highway construction and maintenance represent a third source of conflict. The most heated controversies occur over which materials should be used, the maintenance of competitive bidding, and the like. Because of very strict regulations in many states, resulting in part from federal programs, much of the discretion has been removed from matters of highway construction. When industries urge their products upon highway departments because they help solve problems of terrain, freezing, excess moisture, etc., conflicts arise over granting preferential treatment. Occasionally, preferential treatment is defended on the ground that a "home industry" ought to be protected against underpricing by out-of-state bidders.

A matter of major importance politically is the distribution of maintenance equipment contracts. Maintenance expenditures are generally rather small in terms of individual outlays. As a result contracts can be broken up in such a way that a system of favoritism and patronage is possible because outlays are smaller than the minimum required for competitive bidding.[53] Highway maintenance crews are also susceptible to patronage manipulation because they consist of much unskilled labor, and regulations in some states are extremely flexible in employing highway labor.[54] Related to this is union hostility to the use of convict labor on highway crews.[55] No convenient measurements are available to facilitate explanation of differences among states in construction and maintenance practices.[56] As a result, it would be an over-simplification to characterize this as a function of the party system.

PARTISAN AND LOCAL REPRESENTATIONAL INTERESTS. The last of the four conflict areas involves partisan needs and local service needs. In the American political system with its loose partisan ties, a political party cannot depend upon membership dues as its main source of revenue in conducting campaigns. Therefore, it is essential to solicit money from large donors. What better source can be found than industries and organizations which benefit directly from government activity? In this respect, highway contractors are an especially fruitful source of funds. Presumably, however, donors expect some favor in return. As was stated earlier, it is possible to hypothesize that states with one-party, highly personalized politics are more susceptible to favoritism in exchange for contributions from the highway industry than two-party states in which other factors tend to downgrade the importance of these contributions. Bernd reports on contributions in Georgia as follows:

> Figures on receipts by major candidates in recent years (1946–54) indicate that at least 50 per cent of the money handled by central headquarters and auxiliary groups came from highway contractors and liquor dealers. The inordinate contractor position in Georgia stems from the new governor's dominance of the highway board and the legislature, which nominally elects the board, and from the negotiated non-competitive contract, frequently let by the individual county. Rewarding his faithful backers is the quintessence of the governor's loyalty code and he has the power to pay his political debts.[57]

The assumption, however, that the need of officeholders to "pay off" highway builders stems simply from their desire to repay them for their campaign contributions understates the role of highway building in the fulfillment of partisan and representational needs. Public works projects are a splendid device for the attainment of public recognition without arousing hostilities. Construction of buildings and roads may elicit considerable popular support from the direct beneficiaries, while the opposition from non-beneficiaries remains minimal. Subsequently, public officials and political parties of whatever point of view, in both one-party states and two-party states, find highway building far more efficacious in attaining partisan ends than support for controversial programs in the health, education, or welfare field. Huey Long built his political dynasty very largely in this way.[58]

This phenomenon, however, not only crosses political party lines and party systems but also serves legislators and elected executives equally well. As a result, there is a never-ending struggle between a governor and state highway officials who tend to opt for primary statewide highways and the many legislators, whether urban or rural, who are anxious to deliver public works projects for the benefit of their own constituents. In most states, prior to the passage of the Federal Interstate Highway Act in 1956, localism was victorious. The Interstate Program, however, has reversed that pattern to a considerable degree. Nevertheless, even on interstate highways successful entreaties are made for exits to local communities with minimal traffic demands, for advertisements of local roadside facilities, and construction of additional access routes in urbanized areas. In short, therefore, the fulfillment of partisan and constituency needs by elected officeholders is likely to follow paths of little resistance. Relatively few people see themselves as harmed by new or improved highways and, even if a new highway program helps the other fellow more, everyone can be rewarded with something.

VARIATIONS

Highway politics may be examined in a number of ways for purposes of comparison, including the form and process by which decisions are made, and the successes and failures of contestants in terms of the quantity and kinds of highways constructed and maintained. Comparison of the form and process of decision-making has much to commend it, but unfortunately data are too sketchy to do more than provide impressionistic observations. We can best use, therefore, quantitative devices for our comparative purpose.

As stated earlier, even quantitative measures of highway construction raise serious problems. What weight should be given to numbers of people, numbers of vehicles, area, topographic differences, climatic variations, and the rest? A solution to the problem is to avoid weighting and simply to measure the relative standing of highway expenditures to all other expenditures in the states of the Union. In other words, we are measuring not the absolute success and failure of the highway supporters, but their success in relation to other competitors for the governmental dollar. To be sure, some states put considerably more into government activity on a per capita basis and no direct comparison is made of this. In addition, as our earlier discussion has pointed out, the definitions of what is a state highway and what is a local road vary. To avoid this pitfall we have lumped all state and local spending.

Spending was compared to several political variables, namely the independence of the highway department from the remainder of the executive branch, the extent of diversion of highway user revenues to other functions, the competitiveness of the political party system, and legislative malapportionment measured by population. Other factors examined were urbanization in terms of percentage of population living in standard metropolitan statistical areas, per capita value added by manufacture, per capita agricultural production, and per capita income.

There seems to be no relationship between the formal organization of the highway department and comparative success in obtaining support for highway programs. This can be explained in part by saying that formal independence from the governor is not critical to highway supporters. In effect, while it may be desirable in maximizing highway expenditures, similar results may be achieved in other ways. The same cannot be said for the issue of diversion and earmarking highway revenues. A very distinct relationship exists between the states which permit diversion of highway user funds and those which spend relatively little for highways. In short, antidiversionary practices are a benchmark of success for highway supporters.

Our attention next turns to a number of aspects of the political and economic structure of the states which might help to explain why support for highway expenditures has been greater in some states than in others. With respect to party competition we earlier referred to the proposition that two-party competitive states would be likely to spend less for highways since these are the states in which the electorate is divided along ideological or partisan lines so that such functions as welfare are maximized. Furthermore, a number of writers have suggested that access to highway decision-makers is minimized in two-party states because the handling of campaign funds centrally by the party minimizes the direct reward relationship with the victorious candidate. The data provide no support for this hypothesis. The correlation between party competition and percentage of state and local highway expenditures is negligible.[59]

In order to discover what factors were in fact related to highway expenditures, multiple regression correlations were calculated for a series of independent variables, with percentage of highway expenditure to total state and local expenditure as the dependent variable. Included in the analysis were per cent of population in metropolitan areas, per capita income, per capita value added by manufacturing, party competitiveness, an index of legislative representativeness,[60] per capita value added by agriculture, and persons per registered motor vehicle.[61] In using simple rank-order correlations, some significance was found on four of these dimensions. Per cent of population in metropolitan areas, per capita income, and per capita value added by manufacturing showed a negative relationship to large highway expenditures, and per capita value added by agriculture showed a positive relationship. When partial correlations were obtained, it was discovered that the only variable that was significant was percentage of population in metropolitan areas. In effect, when the economic measures were held constant, urbanization still displayed a significant relationship to highway expenditure, but when urbanization was held constant, the others ceased to make any difference.

Table 4

CORRELATIONS BETWEEN PERCENTAGE OF HIGHWAY EXPENDITURE AND TOTAL STATE AND LOCAL EXPENDITURE AND SOCIAL, POLITICAL, AND ECONOMIC CHARACTERISTICS OF THE STATES

SOCIAL, POLITICAL, AND ECONOMIC CHARACTERISTIC	CORRELATION	
	Rank Order	*Partial**
Percentage of Population Living in Standard Metropolitan Statistical Areas	−.823	−.704
Per Capita Income	−.419	.256
Per Capita Value Added by Manufacture	−.476	.006
Per Capita Value Added by Agriculture	.640	.159
People per Registered Motor Vehicle	−.325	−.050
Party Competition Index	−.183	−.105
Representativeness Index	.086	−.063

*A partial correlation coefficient is used to analyze the relationship of several variables to the phenomenon under examination. It indicates the degree of relationship between one variable and the phenomenon *when all the other variables in the analysis are held constant.* It is a far more sophisticated and accurate index than the rank-order correlation coefficient, but cannot be used on some kinds of data.

What seems to be the case is that comparative support for highway expenditure is neither the product of the peculiarities of the political system nor that of the economic system of the states. What remains is a condition in which the smaller the percentage of people living in metropolitan areas within a state, the more likely that state is to spend its money on highways. That this is in no way a function of urban underrepresentation is made evident by the fact that there was no relationship between the David-Eisenberg representativeness index and highway expenditure.

An explanation for this somewhat surprising result is not readily available, but speculation may suggest some possible factors which are relevant to an explanation. Clearly, support for highway expenditures is widespread. In fact, it matters little whether a state is urban or rural, conservative or liberal, one-party or two-party, wealthy or poor—its people will endorse highway building. This is abetted by the growth of federal expenditures which had their origins in 1916 and which have displayed some partiality to sparsely populated areas inasmuch as the formula includes mileage and area factors. In states with large population concentrations, highway expenditures must compete with state expenditures for education, welfare, health, etc., and local expenditures for an array of urban services. Highways fare reasonably well, but in percentage terms the other functions do comparatively better than in states with little urban concentration. There is a pervasively felt need for highways, irrespective of political ideology or urbanization, which does not exist universally for the other major programs of state and local government. As a result, variations in percentage of highway expenditures occur not so much because some states have wanted to do much more or much less in the highway field, but because other functions have been either emphasized or neglected.

CONCLUSIONS

An extremely rapid expansion of highway systems has taken place in the United States in the 20th century. This development may be attributed to a number of things including an affluent society and a political system friendly to the automotive transportation industry. Of particular importance in the latter connection has been the shift in the location of highway construction and maintenance decision-making from local government to agencies of the state and national governments. The increased role of the federal government, as a result of highway legislation enacted in 1944, has been a prime consideration in the development of a reasonably uniform system of primary highways throughout the United States.

The decision-making process and the issues about which decisions have been made have, also, developed reasonably uniformly. Generally, controversies in highway politics may be listed under four headings:

1. Disputes involving competition between automotive transportation and other forms of transportation;
2. Disputes involving other interests aided or hindered by the construction or abandonment of particular roads;
3. Disputes involving producers of highway materials and equipment and builders of highways;
4. Disputes concerning partisan and local needs.

Clashes involving each of these categories have occurred in all states from time to time with similar results. In general, the automotive industry has emerged victorious over its adversaries. Rural roads have been given priority over urban ones, but the pattern is changing to some extent under the Interstate Program. Highway location, purchase of rights-of-way, purchase of equipment and materials, and construction contracts have been subjected to increasingly rigorous standards, although continued flexibility in several aspects of the construction and maintenance process permits favoritism and, perhaps, corruption in some instances.

Despite these uniformities among the states, considerable variation exists in terms of the total allocation of state and local resources for highway purposes. In several states one-third of all state and local expenditures is devoted to highways, whereas in others less than one-seventh is earmarked for this purpose. There is no evidence that the political party system or the institutional structure for decision-making has any relationship to the expenditure variation. There is also no evidence of a relationship between the wealth of the people of the states or the nature of the economy of the states and emphasis on highway expenditure. There is, however, a significant relationship between highway expenditures and urbanization in which the more urban states devote a smaller proportion of state and local expenditures to highways. Apparently, this results from support for governmental services other than highways in urban states not present to the same degree in rural states.

NOTES

1. See Anthony Lewis in *The New York Times,* June 19–21, 1961; and Charles L. Whipple, "Dirty Money in Boston," *Atlantic Monthly CCVII* (March 1961) p. 241. Both of these authors describe highway scandals in Massachusetts.
2. U.S. Department of Commerce, Bureau of the Census, *Historical Statistics of the United States, 1785–1945* (Washington: U.S. Government Printing Office, 1949) pp. 220–223; and U.S. Department of Commerce, Bureau of Public Roads, *Highway Statistics 1961* (Washington: U.S. Government Printing Office, 1963) p. 108.
3. The highway director in a large industrial state was asked confidentially to list the very best and very worst highway systems in the United States in terms of technical quality and quality of administration. He answered without equivocation.
4. For background on the development of American highways prior to World War II, see Charles L. Dearing, *American Highway Policy* (Washington: The Brookings Institution, 1941).
5. *Ibid.,* pp. 226–227.
6. The first two of these are discussed separately on pp. 424–425 and 425–427.
7. David Levin, "The Highway and Land Use," in Jean Labatut and Wheaton J. Lane (eds.), *Highways in Our National Life* (Princeton: Princeton University Press, 1960) p. 268.
8. Much of the discussion of the politics of highway classification is based on Philip H. Burch, *Highway Revenue and Expenditure Policy in the United States* (New Brunswick: Rutgers University Press, 1962) pp. 140–160.
9. *Ibid.,* p. 140.
10. *Ibid.,* p. 144.
11. *Ibid.,* p. 146.
12. *Michigan's Highways 1960–1980 Needs* (Lansing: Michigan State Highway Department, 1962) pp. 5–6.
13. Burch, pp. 20–33.
14. This is part of a larger study being conducted by Robert S. Friedman and Bernard W. Klein of the University of Michigan concerning perception by administrators of their role as representatives.
15. "Pressures in the Process of Administrative Decision: A Study of Highway Location," *University of Pennsylvania Law Review CVIII* (1960) p. 534 ff.

16. See, for example, *The New York Times,* April 29, 1962, Section 4, p. 8.
17. *Ibid.,* July 28, 1963, p. 55.
18. See particularly Eighty-Seventh Congress, *House Reports* No. 363, 364, 1246, 1285, 1819, and Eighty-Eighth Congress, *House Report* No. 617.
19. Eighty-Seventh Congress, *House Report* No. 1285, pp. 65–66.
20. Anthony Lewis in *The New York Times,* June 19, 1961, p. 1.
21. Paul Ylvasaker, "The Natural Cement Issues," in Harold Stein (ed.), *Public Administration and Policy Development: A Case Book* (New York: Harcourt, Brace and Co., 1952) pp. 107–141.
22. The material regarding this conflict is taken from Andrew Hacker, "Pressure Politics in Pennsylvania," in Alan Westin (ed.), *The Uses of Power* (New York: Harcourt, Brace and World, 1962) pp. 324–370.
23. For a discussion of the early federal aid programs, see Dearing, pp. 78–99, and Burch, pp. 211–242.
24. Federal Aid Road Act of 1916, 39 Stat. 355 (1916).
25. Dearing, p. 89.
26. Federal Aid Highway Act of 1944, 58 Stat. 838 (1944).
27. Glenn Fisher, *The Federal Highway Program* (unpublished manuscript, Institute of Public Administration, University of Michigan, 1961) p. 7.
28. Burch, pp. 243–244.
29. The Federal Aid Highway Act of 1956, 70 Stat. 374 (1956).
30. Burch, pp. 250–251.
31. Robert S. Friedman, *The Michigan Constitutional Convention and Administrative Organization: A Case Study in the Politics of Constitution-Making* (Ann Arbor: Institute of Public Administration, University of Michigan, 1963) p. 52.
32. Edward L. Pinney and Robert S. Friedman, *Political Leadership and the School Desegregation Crisis in Louisiana* (Eagleton Institute: Cases in Practical Politics, No. 31) p. 6.
33. Data on formal highway administrative organizations were derived from Highway Research Board, National Academy of Sciences — National Research Council, *State Highway Administrative Organizations: An Analysis,* Special Report 51 (Washington: 1959).
34. For further discussion of this hypothesis, see chapter 4 of this volume.
35. Alexander Heard, *The Costs of Democracy* (Chapel Hill: University of North Carolina Press, 1960) p. 144; and Joseph L. Bernd, *The Role of Campaign Funds in Georgia Primary Elections, 1936–1958* (Macon: The Georgia Journal, 1958) p. 3.
36. Burch, p. 189.
37. Highway Research Board, p. 20.
38. Luther Hodges has described vividly his efforts to create an at-large highway commission while serving as governor of North Carolina in *Businessman in the Statehouse* (Chapel Hill: University of North Carolina Press, 1962) pp. 126–149.
39. Highway Research Board, p. 22. Under Michigan's 1963 constitution, the highway department is governed by a four-member board, effective in 1965.
40. Robert S. Friedman, *State and Local Relations in Highway Finance in Louisiana* (Baton Rouge: Bureau of Public Administration, Louisiana State University, 1962).
41. This section relies heavily upon Burch's book.
42. Data on highway expenditures are derived from the annual U.S. Department of Commerce, Bureau of the Census, *Governmental Finances in the United States.*
43. Burch, pp. 161–163.

44. See, for example, Burch, p. 127.
45. Paul T. David and Ralph Eisenberg, *Devaluation of the Urban and Suburban Vote* (Charlottesville: Bureau of Public Administration, University of Virginia, 1961) p. 5.
46. Friedman, *State and Local Relations in Highway Finance in Louisiana,* pp. 48–60.
47. *Ibid.,* pp. 24–30.
48. *Ibid.,* pp. 75–76.
49. For a more complete explanation of the extent of highway expenditures see pp. 427–431 *supra.*
50. Dearing, pp. 226–228.
51. For a general treatment of the railroad position on highway policy, see American Association of Railroads, *Highways* (Washington: 1955).
52. An excellent discussion of group interests in highway politics may be found in Daniel P. Moynihan, "New Roads and Urban Chaos," *The Reporter XXII,* April 14, 1960. See also generally Burch; Murray Levin, *The Compleat Politician* (Indianapolis: Bobbs-Merrill, 1962); Rosendo A. Gomez, *Intergovernmental Relations in Highways* (Minneapolis: University of Minnesota Press, 1950) pp. 63–65; and Robert S. Allen (ed.), *Our Sovereign State* (New York: Vanguard Press, 1949) pp. 100–101.
53. Anthony Lewis in *The New York Times,* June 19, 1961, p. 1.
54. Frank J. Sorauf, "State Patronage in a Rural County," *American Political Science Review L* (December 1956) 1046–1056.
55. Gomez, p. 64.
56. See especially Eighty-Seventh Congress, *House Reports* Nos. 363, 364, 1246, 1285, 1819, and Eighty-Eighth Congress, *House Report* No. 617.
57. Bernd, p. 3.
58. Allan P. Sindler, *Huey Long's Louisiana: State Politics, 1920–1952* (Baltimore: The Johns Hopkins Press, 1956).
59. Used for this purpose was an index of party competitiveness developed by Richard E. Dawson and James A. Robinson in their "Inter-Party Competition, Economic Variables, and Welfare Policies in the American States," *Journal of Politics XXV* (May 1963) 265–289.
60. David and Eisenberg.
61. Highway expenditures used in the analysis covered the period 1958–62 and other data were for comparable years. All data were derived from the U.S. Bureau of Public Roads, *Highway Statistics,* or U.S. Bureau of the Census, *Governmental Finances.* Forty-five states are used in the analysis. Hawaii and Alaska are deleted because figures for highway expenditures are not available for the entire period of our study. Nebraska and Minnesota are eliminated because they have non-partisan legislatures and are not included in the index of party competitiveness. Arizona is left out because it is not included in the index of representativeness.

SELECTED BIBLIOGRAPHY

Burch, Philip H., Jr. *Highway Revenue and Expenditure Policy in the United States.* New Brunswick: Rutgers University Press, 1962. A description of federal, state, and local fiscal policy placed in its political and administrative setting.

Dearing, Charles L. *American Highway Policy.* Washington: The Brookings

Institution, 1941. A description of highway policy in the United States from its inception to 1940.

Friedman, Robert S. *State and Local Relations in Highway Finance in Louisiana.* Baton Rouge: Bureau of Public Administration, Louisiana State University, 1962. A study of the extent of urban-rural and city-county conflict in state aid to localities in Louisiana.

Highway Research Board, National Academy of Sciences — National Research Council. *State Highway Administrative Organizations: An Analysis,* Special Report 51. Washington: National Academy of Sciences, 1959. A survey of the organization and representational character of highway department governing bodies.

Hodges, Luther H. *Businessman in the Statehouse.* Chapel Hill: University of North Carolina Press, 1962, pp. 126–149. A discussion by a governor of his relationships with a state highway department and his efforts to reorganize its governing board.

Labatut, Jean and Wheaton J. Lane, eds. *Highways in Our National Life.* Princeton: Princeton University Press, 1950. A collection of essays dealing with the history of the development of highways and with sociological, political, economic, and engineering problems related to highways.

Moynihan, Daniel P. "New Roads and Urban Chaos," *The Reporter XXII,* April 14, 1960, 13–20. A discussion of the impact of the first four years of the Interstate Highway Program on the group interests concerned with highway construction.

U.S. Bureau of Public Roads. *Highway Statistics,* annual. Washington: U.S. Government Printing Office. A comprehensive compendium of federal, state, and local highway statistics, including motor fuel use, motor vehicle registration, highway finance, road mileage, and federal aid.

U.S. Congress, House of Representatives, Special Subcommittee on the Federal Aid Highway Program to the Committee on Public Works, *House Reports* Nos. 363, 364, 1246, 1285, and 1819, Eighty-Seventh Congress, and *House Report* No. 617, Eighty-Eighth Congress (Washington: U.S. Government Printing Office, 1961–63). A series of reports based on hearings of a special house subcommittee on the seamier side of the Interstate Highway Program in Oklahoma, Florida, New Mexico, and Massachusetts.

Westin, Alan F., ed. *The Uses of Power: Seven Cases in American Politics.* New York: Harcourt, Brace & World, 1962, pp. 323–376. A case study in this anthology, "Pressure Politics in Pennsylvania: The Truckers vs. the Railroads," by Andrew Hacker describes a conflict over limitation on weight carried by trucks in all of its broad ramifications.

PART FIVE

THE BOUNDS
OF STATE POLITICS

THE STATES ARE ONLY ONE OF SEVERAL governmental levels operating in the United States. The national government, on the one hand, and the localities, on the other, impinge on the operations of state governments and define the boundaries of state political systems.

The manner in which states view the federal government and the impact of local governments on state political systems vary from state to state. We do not have much information about state-by-state variations of these relationships. An examination of the general problems involved, however, will provide us with some of the basic insights needed to understand the boundaries which limit state political systems.

THE STATES
AND
THE NATION

CHAPTER 12
by
DANIEL J. ELAZAR

THE STATES, STANDING AS THEY DO in the center of the American federal structure — between the powerful federal government and the burgeoning metropolitan communities — are the keystones of the American governmental arch. This was the case when the Constitution was adopted in 1789 and remains true despite the great changes that have taken place in the intervening years. One student of contemporary American government has said, "As far as domestic civilian public affairs are concerned, the state and local governments are yet dominant in our governmental life, with every prospect that they will continue to be so."[1] This assertion runs counter to most contemporary perceptions of American government which place the federal government at the center of everything. If it were based upon an analysis of the formalistic Constitutional place of the states alone, there would be great difficulty in substantiating it. It is the political position of the states within the federal Union, protected by formal Constitutional guarantees but transcending formal limits, that gives them their central role. Unlike the more or less visible Constitutional status of the states, their political position is generally of low visibility, not only to the public at large, but often even to those people involved in the day-to-day operations of government. This chapter is devoted to an exploration of the way in which the states function as political keystones, serving (or not serving) their municipal subdivisions and supporting (or not supporting) the over-all structure of national government.

THE STATES AS AUTONOMOUS POLITICAL SYSTEMS

Federalism — national unification without elimination of subnational political systems — is a very familiar aspect of American government. The American federal system is different from a unitary political system where the central authority can centralize as well as decentralize.* In a unitary system, a power allowed the local authorities at one time may be taken away by the central government at another. In the United States, there are Constitutional limits imposed on either course of action. No matter how much the federal government may expand, it cannot take away the rights of the states to act in most areas of domestic concern.[2] American federalism is also different from a confederation of essentially separate political systems where the center is continually weak. In the United States, the federal government is indeed powerful.

It has been rightly said that without the states there could be no such political body as the United States. It is as much a concern of the United States Constitution to preserve the states and their political systems, as it is to preserve the Union and the national political system. To put the matter more formally, "The Constitution, in all of its provisions, looks to an indestructible Union, composed of indestructible States."[3] This means that political issues in the United States must be considered with two questions in mind, viz.: *What kinds of issues are raised in American politics because the states (and their cities) exist as they do,* and *how are issues developed and resolved in the American political system because of the existence of the states (and their cities) in their present form?*

The relationship of the states to the federal system is not a mere "structural" question — it is essentially a "political" question. This is particularly evident in a matter like the civil rights issue. Despite constant reaffirmations by the federal courts in the past two decades that Negro rights are protected under the United States Constitution and despite Presidential willingness to intervene with force in places where certain states have allowed these rights to be publicly suppressed by force, the entire question of Negro rights remains greatly dependent on the willingness of the states to aid in their maintenance, or at least to comply with national policy in this matter.

Accordingly, the immediate problems of overcoming discrimination in the United States are linked to the enduring problems of the federal-state relationship. Discussion of these problems as political issues revolves around such issues as the limits of federal jurisdiction under the Constitution, "states'

*The very word "decentralization" implies the legal investment of power in a central government which may or may not choose to devolve those powers on local governments, as it wills. The desires and interests of the local governments can be made effective only insofar as they can be effectively expressed by local representatives in the councils of the central government. In any unitary system, even a decentralized one, the ultimate power — including the power to alter or abolish all subnational governments — rests with the central government. The American system can be more appropriately termed "non-centralized" because there is no central government with absolute authority over the states in a unitary sense, but, instead, a strong national government coupled with strong state governments in which authority and power are shared, legally and practically.

rights" as a means of promoting or hindering the protection of individual rights, and the proper role of the United States Supreme Court. Progress in overcoming discrimination is measured state by state and pressure to make progress is applied on the same basis.

The Negro rights problem, in many respects, represents the hardest possible case for demonstrating the non-centralizing influence of federalism and the role of the states as civil societies. Here is a problem in which the moral issue is paramount. Even if the Constitution did not offer the guarantee it does, there would be great pressure on the federal government and the states to secure full rights of citizenship for Negroes. Moreover, less than one-fifth of the states are resisting national demands on this issue, coming into direct conflict not only with the national government but with a large majority of their sister states as well.

However, with explicit Constitutional guarantees, *plus* court rulings, *plus* federal executive and legislative actions in the past decade to enforce those guarantees, *plus* the legislative and executive action of some thirty-five states to extend civil rights beyond existing federal law, we might expect the minority of recalcitrant Southern states to succumb to the overwhelming influence and power of the nation as a whole. Indeed, if Southern resistance were only a matter of localities directly opposing the concentrated might of a central government, overt resistance would undoubtedly have been overcome some time ago by directly limiting the power of the local governments to act in areas which involved discrimination. A central legislature representing a majority of four to one could have ordered local compliance directly under the threat of ordering the appropriate central administrative agencies to assume direct control of such functions as education, welfare, and the management of elections. It was in this way that the Northern and Western states eliminated legal discrimination.[4]

Federalism, as it functions in the United States, changes not only the terms in which the issue is considered but also the manner of its resolution. Under the American federal system, the actual implementation of Constitutional provisions, be they "separate but equal" or "equal and not separate," lies primarily with the states. Although the national Constitution may set the standard (and the national Supreme Court may set the guidelines), the state governments are left to apply those guidelines within their own boundaries in a manner consonant with their respective political systems. Only in those cases where it has been clearly demonstrated that the states cannot or will not implement the Constitution as interpreted does it become possible for the federal authorities to intervene. Even then their power to intervene is limited and in no case can intervention be more than temporary.

School integration, the first target of recent efforts to desegregate the Southern states, is a particularly revealing case. Though federal efforts have led to some school desegregation in all of the segregationist states since 1954,

Table 1

FEDERAL PRESSURE AND SCHOOL DESEGREGATION IN SOUTHERN STATES

	PERCENTAGE OF NEGROES ATTENDING DESEGREGATED SCHOOLS		
State	June 1963	December 1963	May 1964

1. States complying with Supreme Court rulings with state and local public support; federal pressure confined to occasional court rulings:

Delaware	55.9	55.4	56.5
Kentucky	54.1	54.8	54.4
Maryland	45.1	48.3	47.8
Missouri	38.8	42.1	42.1
Oklahoma	23.6	28.1	28.0
West Virginia	61.4	87.9	58.2

2. States reluctantly complying with federal court rulings as issued to avoid showdown; federal pressure confined to regular court rulings and spot intervention by the Justice Department, usually in cooperation with state authorities:

Florida	.67	1.53	1.53
Georgia	.01	.05	.05
North Carolina[a]	.26	.54	.54
South Carolina	.00	.004	.004
Tennessee[a]	1.10	2.71	2.72
Texas[a]	2.30	4.29	5.52

3. States attempting massive resistance but abandoning it for reluctant compliance; federal pressure has involved the use of troops or marshals or heavy legal pressure:

Arkansas[b]	.21	.97	.33
Louisiana[b]	.04	.60	.60
Virginia	.53	1.57	1.63

4. States resisting desegregation massively through agencies of state and local government; federal pressure involves regular use of troops and/or U.S. marshals.

Alabama	.000	.004	.007
Mississippi	.000	.000	.000

a. Violent local resistance to state's decision to comply reduced by state intervention.
b. State compliance modified by state-sanctioned local resistance.
Source: *Southern School News*, June 1964.

ten years after the Supreme Court's school desegregation decision of that year only 9 per cent of the school children in the border states and less than 1 per cent in the states of the deep South were attending integrated schools.

Table 1 shows that there is no simple relationship between the extent of federal pressure and the degree of school desegregation achieved in any particular state. The clearest relationship is an inverse one — the more open pressure, the less desegregation. This is not a cause and effect association, but is symptomatic of the power of the states to maintain previously established positions even in the face of federal power. It is clear that desegregation has gone farther in those states whose leadership decided to comply with the Supreme Court ruling without additional federal pressure. Furthermore, regardless of the kind of federal pressure applied, state governments often have been able to restore segregated conditions after the federal intervention has spent itself or, in any case, have been able to confine integration to a token level. Indeed, those states which have chosen nominal compliance from the first generally have been able to maintain their own "timetables," slow as they may be.

POLITICS AND THE CONSTITUTIONAL SYSTEM

NATIONAL INTERVENTION AND STATE AUTONOMY. Considering the continuous involvement of the states and the federal government with similar public concerns, we can ask two important questions: What are some of the ways in which the constitutional and political systems operate to bring order out of the uncertainty that comes from dealing with nationwide concerns in an interlocking system of states and national governments? How do those ways serve to strengthen the viability of the states as political systems?

One thing is clear: interests unable to gain satisfaction at one level of government can turn to another in an effort to better their fortunes. We know how states when their citizens stand together, as in the desegregation issue, can function even in opposition to national demands. We have also noted that few issues confronting the American people have so great an impact on the states as to unite their people in a common front. In most cases, people unable to gain the ends they seek from their state governments directly will turn to outside assistance from whatever source available. This sometimes means an appeal to local government but more frequently means turning to the federal government. If the issue and the hour are right, this appeal will be answered, often redounding upon the states with great force to alter the internal balance of political forces within them.

This situation is most likely to occur when substantial majorities within most states advocate or accept the necessity for a particular program or course of action which their state governments will not adopt or cannot adopt alone. Where there are popular majorities in most of the states and the state governments do not act, it usually means they cannot. The state governments, no matter how willing, are simply unable to cope with certain problems without federal assistance, and in these cases when federal assistance comes it almost invariably acts to strengthen the states.[5] Regulation of interstate commerce is a case in point. The state governments, no matter how willing, could not regulate the great interstate railroads alone, nor could they deal with the great interstate industrial combines. Federal intervention in both cases actually strengthened the abilities of the states to deal with the problems generated by these enterprises within their boundaries. On a different level, most states would have never been able to finance the great water resource projects undertaken within their limits even if they were the principal beneficiaries; federal "intervention" helped to construct them. Or, in yet another kind of problem, until the federal government made it advantageous for all the states to adopt unemployment compensation programs, those which wished to do so were handicapped by threats of major employers to move elsewhere.

There are times, however, when minorities within the states turn to the federal government for assistance. Minority appeals "outward" occur most frequently in states divided between dominant and minority political subcultures, but also happen in any state divided into two or more camps on matters of policy. The possibility for this kind of appeal makes it diffcult for the states to maintain autonomous *politics* unaffected by national currents in their "domestic" decisions even as they maintain reasonably autonomous *political systems*. The autonomy of their political systems may allow the states to bend in the face of blows from the outside and to recover more or less intact after their initial impact (a phenomenon not to be minimized), but it does not necessarily enable them to prevent outside blows in the first place.

The example of the public welfare reformers is, perhaps, classic in this respect. During the first decades of the 20th century, reform groups working within the states sought to enlarge drastically the public welfare programs of the states and their local subdivisions in order to cope with the dislocations incident to an industrial society. After some initial successes in the regulatory field, they were generally rebuffed in their efforts to secure positive programs partly because their proposed programs were expensive and state legislatures did not wish to raise taxes and partly because the interests generally dominant in the states (and in the nation as a whole) opposed such programs. After repeated failures, the reformers began to intensify their efforts to gain federal assistance for their programs without abandoning their efforts at the state level. With the coming of the Great Depression, they were given a tremendous boost by the change in economic conditions and their programs were enacted into law. A system of federal grants to the states was introduced to stimulate the creation of five basic welfare programs in every state under minimal national standards. Given this federal assistance, the welfare reformers were able to gain control over their programs in most of the states, excluding only those states in which (a) the political organizations were too strong, and (b) where there were really no significant indigenous groups of welfare reformers ready to take over. Federal grants replaced "bread and coal basket politics" and a major instrument of party organization and, at least temporarily, weakened traditional political machines, opening the way for reform groups to act on a number of fronts. Federal merit system requirements broke the back of state patronage in welfare departments, opening the door for professional welfare workers to assume basic responsibility for the operation of even general relief programs. The increased funds available to each state opened the door to greater administrative complexity in political systems long noted for resistance to bureaucracy. These and other changes meant that state politics had to be readjusted so that the state political systems could assimilate the new demands placed upon them.[6]

Today urban reformers interested in reconstructing America's cities are following much the same course of action, turning to Washington for aid unobtainable from most of the states in the hope that through Washington they will become powerful in their respective state capitals as well. The reaction of even the ostensibly conservative big city press to the recent court decisions on reapportionment reveals their hope in this regard. These decisions are not only supported but are endorsed on the grounds that more equitable urban representation in the state legislatures will prevent further "drift" of power toward Washington.

While many of the urban reformers may not care whether the federal government seeks to involve the states in federally-aided programs or not, the existence of the Constitution demands state participation. At the very least, the states must pass enabling legislation before any of their cities can participate in federal aid programs or take federal funds. In most cases, the federal legislation is so drawn — by men who respect the Constitution — as to either require state participation or at least give the states the option to participate or not. Thus, the impetus for political change which is no respecter of institutions is brought to heel by the Constitution, to the great benefit of the states as political systems.[7]

THE CONSTITUTIONAL PLACE OF THE STATES. The constitutional place of the states in the federal system is determined by four sets of material: the provisions in the federal and state constitutions that either limit or guarantee the powers of the states vis-à-vis the federal government; the provisions in those constitutions which give the states a role in the composition of the national government; the subsequent interpretations of both sets of provisions by the courts (particularly by the United States Supreme Court); and the unwritten constitutional traditions which have evolved informally and have only later been formally recognized.

The precise federal Constitutional provisions outlining the general position of the states must always be taken into consideration by those who govern even if they are to be transcended through politics. Figure 1 shows the specific limitations and guarantees of state powers. These limitations

Figure 1

FEDERAL CONSTITUTIONAL PROVISIONS SPECIFICALLY LIMITING
OR GUARANTEEING STATE POWERS

GUARANTEES	LIMITS
A. STATE INTEGRITY AND SOVEREIGNTY	
No division or consolidation of states without state legislative consent (IV–2)[a]	States cannot enter into treaties, alliances, or confederations (I–10)
Republican form of government (IV–2)	No separate coinage (I–10)
Protection against invasion (IV–2)	No grants of titles of nobility (I–10)
Protection against domestic violence on application of proper state authorities (IV–2)	No interstate or foreign compacts without Congressional consent (I–10)
Powers not delegated to the U.S. by the Constitution, nor prohibited by it to the states, are reserved to the states (Amendment X)	U.S. Constitution, all laws and treaties made under it to be supreme law of the land, binding on every state (VI)
	Slavery forbidden (Amendment XIII)
States cannot be sued by citizens of another state or a foreign nation (Amendment XI)	All state legislative, executive, and judicial officers, and state Representatives in Congress to be bound by U.S. Constitution (VI)
	No abridgement of privileges and immunities of the U.S. Citizens (Amendment XIV)
	Reduction of representation in U.S. House of Representatives for denial of franchise to citizens (Amendment XIV)
	No payment of debts incurred in aid of insurrection or rebellion against U.S. or for emancipation of slaves (Amendment XIV)
	No abridgement of right to vote on account of race, color, or previous condition of servitude (Amendment XV)
	Popular election of Senators (Amendment XVII)
	No abridgement of right to vote on account of sex (Amendment XIX)
	No poll taxes in federal elections (Amendment XXIV)

a. Numbers in parentheses refer to the Article and Section of the Constitution containing the provision.

Figure 1, continued

GUARANTEES	LIMITS
B. MILITARY AFFAIRS AND DEFENSE	
Power to maintain militia and appoint militia officers (I–8, Amendment II)	No letters of marque and reprisal (I–10)
	No maintenance of standing military forces in peacetime without Congress's consent (I–10)
	No engaging in war without Congress's consent, except to repel invasion (I–10)
C. COMMERCE AND TAXATION	
Equal apportionment of federal direct taxes (I–2, 9)	No levying of duties on vessels of sister states (I–9)
No federal export duties (I–9)	No legal tender other than gold or silver (I–10)
No preferential treatment for ports of one state (I–9)	No impairment of obligations of contracts (I–10)
Reciprocal full faith and credit among states for public acts, records, and judicial proceedings (IV–1)	No levying of import or export duties without consent of Congress except reasonable inspection fees (I–10)
Reciprocal privileges and immunities for citizens of the several states (IV–2)	No tonnage duties without Congress's consent (I–10)
Intoxicating liquor may not be imported into states where its sale or use is prohibited (Amendment XXI–2)	
D. ADMINISTRATION OF JUSTICE	
Federal criminal trials to be held in state where crime was committed (III–2)[b]	No bills of attainder (I–10)
Extradition for crimes (IV–2)	No ex post facto laws (I–10)
Federal criminal juries to be chosen from states and district in which crime was committed (Amendment VI)[b]	U.S. Supreme Court has original jurisdiction over all cases in which a state shall be a party (III–2)
Federal judicial power to extend to controversies between two or more states, a state or citizens of another state when state is plaintiff, and between foreign nation or its citizens with original jurisdiction vested in the Supreme Court (III–2)	Judges in every state bounded by U.S. Constitution and all laws and treaties made under it, notwithstanding the constitutions or laws of any state (VI)
	No denial of life, liberty, or property without due process of law (Amendment XIV)
	No denial of equal protection of state laws to persons within its limits (Amendment XIV)

b. This provision insures the integrity of the state's common law in federal cases.

Figure 2

FEDERAL CONSTITUTIONAL PROVISIONS SPECIFICALLY GIVING THE STATES A ROLE
IN THE COMPOSITION OF THE NATIONAL GOVERNMENT

GUARANTEES	LIMITS

A. NATIONAL LEGISLATURE

GUARANTEES	LIMITS
Members of House of Representatives chosen by people of several states based on those qualified to vote for most numerous house of state legislature (I–2)	Representatives must be 25 years old and citizens of the U.S. for 7 years (I–2)
Representatives must be inhabitants of states from which they are elected at time of election (I–2)	Senators must be 30 years old and citizens of the U.S. for 9 years (I–3)
Representatives to be apportioned among the states according to population every ten years (I–2)	Congress may make or alter regulations as to the times, places, and manner of holding elections for Senators and Representatives (I–4)
State executive has authority to fill vacancies (I–2)	Each House shall be the judge of the elections, returns, and qualifications of its own members, punish its members for disorderly behavior and expel a member by two-thirds vote (I–5)
Each state shall have at least one Representative (I–2)	
Senate shall be composed of two Senators from each state (I–3) chosen by the people qualified to vote for the most numerous house of the state legislature (Amendment XVII) with vacancies to be filled as prescribed by state legislation (Amendment XVII)	Basis for apportionment of representation in House of Representatives may be reduced proportionate to state deprivation of the right to vote of otherwise qualified citizens (Amendment XIV–2)
Senators must be inhabitants of the states from which they are chosen at time of election (I–3)	States cannot be represented by persons who have taken an oath to support Constitution and since engaged in insurrection, without express consent of two-thirds of Congress (Amendment XIV–3)
Times, places, and manner of holding elections for Senators and Representatives shall be prescribed for each state by its legislature (I–4)	
No state to be deprived of equal representation in the Senate without its consent (V)	

Figure 2, continued

GUARANTEES	LIMITS

B. NATIONAL EXECUTIVE

To be selected by the electors of the several states with each state allotted a number of electors equal to the total number of its Senators and Representatives (II–1)

Each state to have one vote if Presidential election is decided in House of Representatives (II–1)

Approval of Presidential appointees by the Senate as Congress shall prescribe (II–2)

Congress may determine the time of choosing electors and a uniform day on which they shall cast their votes (II–1)

C. AMENDMENT OF CONSTITUTION

Amendments must be ratified by three-fourths of the states (V)

Amendments must be proposed by two-thirds of the states (V)

D. VOTING RIGHTS

Cannot be denied or abridged on grounds of race, color, or previous condition of servitude (Amendment XV–1)

Cannot be denied or abridged on account of sex (Amendment XIX–1)

No poll tax may be levied as requirement to vote in federal elections (Amendment XXIV)

E. FOREIGN AFFAIRS

Treaties must be ratified by two-thirds of Senate (II–2)

Appointment of foreign service officers subjected to Senate confirmation (II–2)

Treaties binding on states as supreme law of the land (VI)

F. MILITARY AFFAIRS AND DEFENSE

Power to appoint the officers of and train the militia when not in federal service reserved to the states (I–8)

Congress may provide for organizing, arming, and disciplining the militia when it is not in federal service and for governing it when it is (I–8) and guarantees fall into four basic categories — a general concern with the integrity of the states as well as their subordination to the Union; some brief provisions insuring the states a role in the common defense; a delineation of the role of the states in the management of commerce and raising of revenues; and a description of state responsibilities in the administration of justice. Figure 2 outlines the role that must be played by the states if the federal government is to function and clarifies the Constitutional limits of that role.

The state constitutions are generally silent about federal-state relations. Where they speak at all, it is essentially to ratify the requirements of the federal Constitution by making them applicable to specific local situations. Most state constitutions formally delineate their inviolable borders. In the constitutions of the public land states (created under the tutelage of the federal government after the adoption of the United States Constitution) provisions governing the commitment of federal land grants for specific public purposes serve as a formal acknowledgement of the federal-state partnership which had become important as early as 1802 when Ohio, the first state of this group, adopted its first constitution.[8] The constitutions of the reconstructed Southern states were required to include specific acknowledgements of federal supremacy and adjurations of the "right" of secession.

THE POLITICAL PROCESS AND INTERGOVERNMENTAL COLLABORATION. American federalism is delineated, maintained, and made functional only partly by Constitutional devices. While the role of such devices should not be minimized, the way in which the institutions and purposes of federalism are maintained through the political process is more important.

The party system has become the organizing principle around which national and state politics (and federalism itself) have been able to develop. American political parties rarely centralize power at all. Characteristically they do the reverse, serving as a canopy under which special and local interests are represented with little regard for anything that can be called a party program. Moreover, party operations produce through Congress the basic division of functions between the federal government, on the one hand, and state and local governments, on the other. The operation of parties transforms the Supreme Court's well-known permissiveness with respect to the expansion of national powers into legislation that characteristically provides important roles for state and local governments.[9]

The major effect of the expansion of the role of politics as a means of modifying the Constitution has been to increase the level of intergovernmental collaboration. It has provided means for interests to make demands on the federal government successfully while, at the same time, insuring that the federal response be guided by a solicitude for the position of the states.

This solicitude has meant that federal action usually reinforces the actions of the states and, at the very least, provides for their participation in some way.

Such collaboration, long dominant in American federalism, has been progressively expanded to include virtually every governmental function. From public welfare to public recreation, from national defense to local police protection, the system of sharing has become so pervasive that it is often difficult for the uninformed bystander to tell just who is doing what under which hat.[10] The federal-state mixture of responsibility and activity in serving the nation's "great constituencies" — Agriculture, Business, and Labor — illustrates this situation clearly, as indicated in Figure 3.

This system of sharing or partnership has become tripartite over the years, with the localities carving out a role for themselves as a third level of government. Because they are protected by the same political diffusion of power that protects the position of the states vis-à-vis the federal government, local communities have been able to use their political power to secure a measure of autonomy not formally theirs under Constitutional law. This has given them a measure of control over all government activities within their limits regardless of the level of government formally responsible for them.[11]

THE PARTNERSHIP SYSTEM IN ACTION. The Constitution itself requires federal-state cooperation in some areas (administration of elections, for example) and makes cooperation in other areas possible by giving both governments broad concurrent powers. Since 1790, the courts, Congress, and custom have virtually eliminated all possible restrictions on joint federal-state action, even while generally reaffirming the necessity for institutional dualism. Where concurrent jurisdiction was clearly Constitutional it has been sustained, and where the issue was in doubt concurrent powers have been extended.[12]

This trend has often been viewed as a simple expansion of federal power at the expense of the states. In reality, it has meant an expansion of the realm of activities of both federal and state governments to generate an increase in the velocity of government (that is, the amount of governmental activity in relation to the total activity of society) in the nation as a whole. Thus, the acts of Congress have tended to neutralize centralizing Supreme Court decisions by providing the states with a firm share in virtually all federal domestic programs, including several in which the federal government is apparently given the right to claim exclusive jurisdiction in the words of the Constitution itself. For example, the improvement of navigable waters is a federal responsibility under the written Constitution. In reality, it has become a joint responsibility involving the federal government, the states, and their local subdivisions in cooperative projects. By the same token, po-

Figure 3

THE MIXTURE OF FEDERAL-STATE ACTIVITY IN SERVING THE GREAT CONSTITUENCIES

I. BUSINESS

A. *Establishing Favorable Conditions*
  1. Protection of private property rights
  2. Establishment of organizational forms for business and enterprise

  States have primary responsibility; federal government has limited role

  3. Establishing rules of bankruptcy and business reorganization

  Shared responsibility

  4. Granting of patent rights
  5. Maintaining a monetary system

  Federal responsibility

B. *Direct Aids*
  1. Tariffs
  2. Price supports

  Federal aid

  3. Industrial subsidies
  4. Data gathering and economic studies
  5. Money or credit lending

  Shared aid (federal share generally larger)

C. *Regulation*
  1. Maintenance of competition
  2. Transportation regulation
  3. Atomic energy regulation
  4. Regulating banking, bank credit, bank deposits
  5. Protecting investors

  Shared: federal role largest

  6. Licensing of ordinary business

  State responsibility

  7. Utility regulation

  Shared

  8. Regulation of communications

  Federal responsibility; states have minor role

II. LABOR

A. *Protection against Exploitation*
  1. Limiting child labor
  2. Protecting women workers
  3. Limiting hours of work
  4. Establishing minimum wages

  Shared responsibility with federal share larger

  5. Preventing racial and religious discrimination
  6. Protecting migratory labor

  Primarily state responsibility with federal share growing

  7. Compensation for injuries on-the-job

  State responsibility supported by federal action

Figure 3, continued

II.   LABOR (continued)

B. Protection of Right to Organize and Bargain Collectively

   1. Protecting right to organize

   2. Protecting right to strike   Shared responsibility;

   3. Providing mechanisms for settling   federal share larger
       labor-management disputes

C. Assistance in Finding and Keeping Jobs

   1. Providing employment offices

   2. Stimulating employment opportunities   Shared responsibility;

   3. Assisting in manpower retraining   states have primary role,

   4. Providing unemployment   federal government in
       compensation   supporting role

III.   AGRICULTURE

A. Increasing Productivity

   1. Managing research

   2. Diffusing knowledge   Shared; states have primary

   3. Providing technical assistance   role with federal support

   4. Developing field projects   Shared equally

B. Maintaining Commodity Prices

   1. Insuring parity and supporting prices

   2. Regulating production   Largely federal with state support

   3. Acquiring and storing surpluses

C. Regulating Quality of Produce

   1. Sanitary inspection

   2. Health inspection   Shared

   3. Grading and quality inspection

D. Developing Agricultural Markets

   1. Securing tariff concessions   Federal responsibility

   2. Disposing of the stored agricultural
       surplus   Primarily federal

   3. Promoting produce use   Primarily state

   4. Opening new markets   Shared

licing the waters, originally a state and local responsibility, has come to involve the United States Coast Guard as well.

In some cases, Congress has even "overruled" the Court and turned functions given it by judicial interpretation over to the states. Ownership of the off-shore oil lands, regulation of the insurance business, and pre-emptive powers in the field of labor legislation are cases in point. In all three cases, the Supreme Court ruled that federal authority was pre-eminent, and in all three Congress ceded that authority in all or in part back to the states.[18]

Part of the reason for the development of this kind of sharing as a means to maintain the position of the states and their localities lies in the very real supremacy of the federal government in matters of taxing and spending. Though the power to tax and spend is Constitutionally concurrent, the federal government has been, over the years, clearly in a better position to use its share of the power. Rather than resist this trend, the states and localities have developed means to capitalize on it in a manner calculated to maximize their ability to control the expenditure of funds passing through their hands, no matter what their source. The states have actually used such funds to extend their control over their own local subdivisions.

Political pressures generated in the states and localities to gain federal financial assistance for governmental services, coupled with an increasing interest in those services on the part of federal officials (particularly professionals in the various functional fields), have led to the development of an elaborate system of federal transfers of payments to the states and localities for a wide variety of activities. Since the early 19th century, it has been clear that Congress may use its taxing (and other revenue-raising) powers to support federal-state cooperative programs, attaching such conditions to its grants as it deems proper and providing for the revocation of such grants as it deems necessary. In the years since the establishment of the Republic, a highly institutionalized system of federal-state cooperation has developed which has really become part of the nation's Constitutional tradition. Under this cooperative system, the federal government, the states, and the localities share the burden for the great domestic programs by making the larger governments primarily responsible for raising revenue and setting standards and the smaller ones primarily responsible for administration of the programs.

If the federal system had been predicated on a clean separation of functions as well as structure (i.e., dual federalism), then centralization would probably have been inevitable as it became necessary for the federal government to intervene in problems that, by their very nature, transcended state lines. In actuality, federal intervention can be supplementary and stimulatory rather than pre-emptive because of the possibilities for intergovernmental collaboration. When and where federal action was considered necessary, it could be used to stimulate state action as well, and federal-state cooperation could be so structured as to vest the greatest amount of operating responsibility in the local community.

Since federal involvement in any given program rarely came after substantial state involvement, there are few cases of federal expansion at the expense of ongoing state operations. On the contrary, federal involvement has usually stimulated a great expansion of state activity in the same field and an over-all enlargement of the scope of the state governmental operations. Such expansion has meant not only greater state expenditure of funds but also an increase in the number and quality of the personnel involved in carrying out the state's operations. This, in turn, has led to an increase in the states' ability to make policy for the internal operation of cooperative programs and to make their policy decisions "stick" even in the face of federal opposition.

Take the great federal-state welfare programs which were considered to be such radical attempts at centralization in the 1930's. We commonly think of those grant programs as Federal (meaning national out-of-Washington) programs. Yet in reality they are federal (meaning shared-by-Washington-and-the-states) programs with the emphasis for shaping them increasingly placed on the states. While Washington sets certain basic standards for each welfare program, it is actually the province of the states not only to administer those programs which their legislatures have authorized but also to determine a major share of the policy they will follow. Within certain limits, the states determine the size of welfare payments and the eligibility for different forms of assistance while Congress guarantees to match the state expenditures according to a pre-set formula (approximately but not exactly fifty-fifty, depending on the program) no matter how large they may be. Indeed, if Congress has not appropriated enough money to cover the federal share, it must, by law, make the necessary deficiency appropriations. The federal administrators oversee the transfer of funds and audit their use but do little to interfere with the operations of state welfare programs.[14]

It is misleading, however, to think of the shared aspects of these programs as reflective of a residual state-local obstructionism based on existing political alignments powerful enough to defeat the upwardly-striving federal administrators. Unfortunately, the more spectacular examples of the power of the states within the cooperative framework tend to reflect obstructionism (or something akin to it). The Negro rights problem is clearly a case in point, and even the Illinois welfare case has such overtones. In the less-publicized problems of highway construction, public health, conservation, and the like, and in the routines of day-to-day collaboration common to every program, there is generally little conflict between levels of government as such. When such conflict does erupt, the power of the states and localities is as frequently used to advance projects commonly considered to be in the public interest against what might be called federal "obscurantism." Governor Rockefeller has related one good example of this aspect of the federal-state relationship involving New York. His state wished to acquire certain surplus military lands for park purposes. Private developers who wished to acquire the lands for subdivision put pressure on the federal General Services Administration which put a high price tag on the land, primarily to gain greater return for the federal treasury. The state officials, who felt that the lands should be made available to New York at reduced cost since a public purpose was involved saw to it that the lands were zoned (a power reserved to the states and their subdivisions) in such a way as to prevent their subdivision. The subdividers then had no further use for the property, withdrew their bids, and the G.S.A. had to allow the state to take possession, under the law.[15]

In some cases, the states use their powers to advance clearly national interests. During the late 1950's when the testing of nuclear weapons in the atmosphere was raising levels of radiation to new peaks to the dismay of many scientists and medical experts, the federal Atomic Energy Commission repeatedly ignored any efforts on the part of the public to ascertain the exact amounts of radioactive fallout and contamination reaching the American people. At that point, several of the states on their own initiative — through their own legislation and the activities of their own public health departments — began collecting samples of the atmosphere, the soil, and their local crops, tested these, and made their findings public. The states not only reported their findings but, in some cases, began to take steps to control potential sources of public contamination.

The states could do this despite Atomic Energy Commission recalcitrance and even in the face of A.E.C. opposition because they had independent agencies with independent sources of power. Though these agencies used federal funds for some of their activities, in the last analysis they remained beholden to their states. And even though their officials undoubtedly saw eye to eye with their federal counterparts on most matters, they could take public issue with a federal agency with impunity when they felt it necessary to do so.

SHARING REVENUES. Though the most characteristic element in the partnership system is the cash grant-in-aid (federal-state, state-local, or federal-local), the system actually operates through several devices, among them:

1. Grants-in-aid (both cash and land grants);
2. Shared revenues (examples: timber and mineral royalties, shared license fees);

3. Direct payments to individuals (examples: federal payments for agricultural programs and veterans' pensions, state higher education scholarships, local general assistance aid);

4. Payments to states and localities for discharging federal responsibilities (example: housing federal prisoners);

5. Services-in-aid (the provision of technical assistance through lending or assigning personnel by one level of government to another);

6. Grants and contracts awarded on similar terms to public and private applicants (example: federal research grants to universities);

7. Grants-in-kind (surplus commodities, obsolete military equipment, etc.).

Each of these devices has a long history extending back at least into the 19th century, and each has been sanctioned through different modes of Constitutional interpretation. Furthermore, each has its own "politics," a variation on the over-all theme of the partnership.

Perhaps the most outstanding characteristic of the federal grants and shared revenues in the context of internal state politics is that the political struggle over the use and distribution of the money is essentially an intra-state matter. In practically all the major programs channeled through the states, the federal funds are so mixed with state funds after their transfer that the local beneficiaries have no idea whose money they are receiving. Their efforts to obtain funds are essentially directed toward the state house, not toward the national Capitol.[16]

There are three exceptions to this rule. Occasionally the localities must struggle with the state legislature to gain state participation in a federal program that might benefit them or state authorization for them to participate if it is a direct federal-local program (as in the case of urban renewal). Such conflicts are particularly frequent in states that are in transition from a rural orientation to dominance by larger cities. The rural interests, endeavoring to hang on to a passing era, tend to resist virtually all the demands of the state's burgeoning cities. Such was the case in Iowa until 1961. The rural-oriented legislature refused to allow the state's cities to participate in federal aid urban renewal programs until that year.[17]

A second exception occurs in some of the smaller federal-state programs where the amount of federal funds allocated to each state is too little to satisfy local demands. Local communities then enter into competition at the state level to gain a share of the allocated funds for their own projects. While this competition is also intra-state in character, it is initiated for specific federally-aided projects known to the localities. In certain situations, the localities are even able to call upon federal personnel stationed within them to assist them in advancing their claims.[18]

Finally, in recent years the "pilot project" has become a new way for local communities to get additional federal aid. In many of these cases, the localities must compete with other local communities in Washington for special grants. In most of these cases, they are supported by legislative and administrative representatives of their states, but the burden of the struggle still remains on their shoulders.

The greatest impact of federal spending within the United States comes not from transfers of payments but from defense-related expenditures and direct payments to private individuals, primarily farmers and veterans. The latter, including government grants to institutions for civilian research, average out to approximately one-third of the total amount transferred to the states through federal grants each year. Defense contracts represent the great bulk of the direct federal expenditures within the states. In fiscal 1962 alone, new contracts worth $27,800,400,000 were awarded, approximately four times the total amount distributed through federal grants that same year.[19]

When the state-by-state distribution of federal defense contract expenditures is considered, it is apparent that the old adage, "Them that has, gets," applies. Those states "tooled up" for defense production are repeatedly favored. This is not just a matter of objective efficiency. Part of the "having" is having well-developed methods for influencing the allocation of contracts. Local industries seeking contracts and local communities seeking defense installations work closely in hand with state Congressional delegations and state and local political officials lobbying in Washington. In some cases, states and the larger cities have established "Washington offices," virtually embassies, to work with their Congressional delegations. Massachusetts has been particularly active in this regard for two decades, its Washington office having been opened in 1941. The gains registered by that state since 1961 were not simply a matter of having a Kennedy in the White House, but represented the fruition of hard work by the state's "man in Washington" beginning in 1956 when Governor Foster Furcolo reorganized the office and formalized its relationships with the Massachusetts Congressional delegation.[20]

In fact, states in different sections of the country are favored differently by different kinds of federal aid. To cite some examples: Southern and smaller Western states are favored with a higher per capita return of federal grant funds as part of the ostensibly equalizing aspects of federal grants-in-aid programs. Southern states have been favored with military installations since the Spanish-American War; their Congressmen and chambers of commerce have become specially adept at securing and maintaining such installations. The states of the Southwest and far West have been particularly successful in gaining military contracts which have led to the creation of whole new industries which, in turn, have enabled those states to maintain or enlarge their "boom" conditions. They have been particularly successful in acquiring a virtual monopoly over the nation's aerospace programs, offering climate as an inducement to those interested in year-round testing operations and year-round "outdoor living." The New England states have had a measure of success in attracting federal funds for research and development by capitalizing on their already excellent research and educational facilities and by developing channels of influence in Washington.

The two kinds of federal transfers of payments serve to divide the political struggle over funds into two parts — the intra-state struggle for funds to be used for public services and the interstate struggle for federal defense expenditures. It appears that there is little interstate struggle for the public service dollar. By now Washington has the formula system down pat, and all that must be done is to arrive at an agreement on what kind of formula to use when new programs are inaugurated or old ones revised. Since it has become clear that the margin of allowable gain within the formula structure is limited and the representatives of the states generally recognize the virtues of some measure of redistribution of wealth through federal grants, Congress spends relatively little effort in fighting over it.

By the same token, there is little intra-state conflict over defense funds. This is not only because defense funds represent direct federal expenditures which do not pass through state hands. There is a gentleman's agreement in most states that, while localities are free to submit their own bids up to a point, once the federal authorities have indicated any preferences the entire state will concentrate its efforts on behalf of the favored community.

The federal government also provides some direct aid to localities. Contrary to the general impression, the federal government has been supplying direct aid to local communities since the early 19th century, then as now, primarily in the field of internal improvements.[21] In recent years, however, great metropolitan centers have emerged which face problems of urban reconstruction of unprecedented magnitude. These great cities are politically able to make their influence felt in Washington and are organizationally strong enough to handle the complexities of administering cooperative programs. They have been active in securing the right to develop direct city-federal relationships in certain aspects of the airport construction, urban renewal, and housing fields. Even in these cases, the states retain the right to involve themselves in the relationship if they choose to do so.

PROTECTING STATE INTEGRITY. The Constitutional document binding the federal government and the states clearly provides for federal supremacy and gives the federal authorities the power to maintain that supremacy. At the same time, the Constitutional traditions which have grown up around the document have tempered its use by inducing a policy of federal self-restraint and providing political means for the maintenance of that policy.

The states are best able to protect themselves and to induce federal self-restraint when the problems which confront them are handled through regular political channels and are least able to do so when the problems are not, Constitutional guarantees notwithstanding. For example, the United States Supreme Court has recently taken it upon itself, as the ultimate arbiter of the basis of legislative representation, the drawing of electoral districts for choosing of state and national legislators. The Court has seen fit to do this despite clear Constitutional provisions granting Congress the power to regulate Congressional elections and a history of Congressional legislation in the field, as well as the not quite so clear reservation that the states apportion their own legislatures. The consequences of the Court's entrance into the political thicket of apportionment are not yet clear. What is clear is that in this case, as in so many others, accepted prerogatives of the states are being challenged by the one institution that is least subject to control through the normal channels of politics.[22] Perhaps the influence of the political process will lead to a smoothing out of the "either-or" decision of the Court.* Perhaps the states will resort to amendment of the Constitution to protect themselves. Perhaps the Court's intervention here will lead to a greater change in the relations between the states and their local subdivisions than in the relationship between the states and Washington.

Even with the entrance of the Supreme Court into the apportionment question and the increasing concern of all three branches of the federal government with protecting the rights of Negroes to vote in the Southern states, voting in all elections — federal, state, and local — remains a state-regulated activity. This provides the states with a *de facto* bulwark against overassertion of federal authority subject only to the explicit restrictions placed on it by the Fifteenth, Nineteenth, and Twenty-Fourth Amendments, and the relatively few acts of Congress and Court decisions enforcing these Amendments. Congress actually exercised more control over federal elections a century ago than it does today. In any case, the total number, times, and places of elections are set by the states, as are the age and residence requirements for voters.[23]

The representation of the states in Congress provides another very im-

---

*To say the courts are least influenced by politics is not to say that they are uninfluenced. On the contrary, the standard pattern of recruiting judges from among active politicians has helped make the courts more sensitive to the nuances of the political process than might otherwise be thought to be the case. Indeed, at the lower court levels, the sensitivity of judges often works in the states' favor, neutralizing less sensitive high court decisions.

portant way for them to maintain their integrity and internal autonomy — through a highly institutionalized system of Congressional interference into executive actions. In order to understand this system, it is necessary to look briefly at the growth of administrative rule-making powers.

The discretionary rule-making power of federal administrative agencies has been substantially increased to the point where their rule-making activities have nearly as much effect on state-federal relations as formal legislation and judicial interpretation. The sheer mass of federal business has made this necessary. Congress can, at best, set forth the general guidelines for the implementation of federal-state programs, the awarding of contracts, or the administration of federal programs that touch upon the individual directly (such as the major agricultural and veterans' programs). Once these guidelines are established, however, federal administrators must make the specific rules and then apply them. The individual states, in turn, have found that they must have some means of recourse to influence the way in which those rules will affect them, short of trying to alter the general legislation.

The Representatives of the states have found such a recourse in the institutionalization of "interference" (the term is used in a neutral sense). The tradition of such interference is well developed, dating back to the beginning of the Republic. There are two kinds of interference. Best known is the formal system of legislative oversight with its tradition of insuring a place on key committees for Representatives of states and even localities most seriously affected by the actions of those committees. This has given the states an important line of access to national policy-making through the powers of the committees to review proposed legislation and investigate ongoing programs and through the powers of committee members to demand consideration for their constituents and constituencies as the price for supporting the administration. Considering the important role of the committees, this institution has indeed become a crucial one in the perpetuation of the non-centralized traditions of American federalism.[24]

The states and localities not only possess virtual representation on committees, their interests are also represented by their Congressmen acting singly. Very early in the history of the Republic, Congressmen and their constituents interpreted the right of petition as the right to interfere in administrative affairs on behalf of their constituents — private or public — establishing the right of Congressional interference as part of the nation's unwritten constitution. With the increasing bureaucracy of the federal executive branch, this interference, or "case-work" as it has come to be called, has only the barest connection with the original Constitutional right of petition. It is basically a political device rooted in the power of local groups and the desire of Congressmen to build up credit with potential supporters. Considering only its effects on the relations between the states and localities and the federal government, it is a most useful device for gaining administrative consideration for state and local needs *after* legislation has been enacted and at the point where administrative discretion in statutory interpretation becomes important.[25] Congressional staffs, which have grown in size primarily because of this responsibility, handle their case-work with great care, knowing that their Congressman's performance in that area is likely to influence more voters than his actions on national issues. Administrative agencies also go to great lengths to serve Congressional interests and, by indirection, the interests of the individuals, groups, states, and localities the Congressmen represent because they know that future Congressional support is often dependent on this kind of service. While the great majority of the cases which lead to Congressional interference do not involve other governments, they are nonetheless important to the maintenance of the position of the states and localities. Because the states are political systems, the actions and requests of ostensibly private parties are often highly meaningful for the maintenance of state and local authority or for the development of state and local public policy. For example, a request by a chamber of commerce for the expansion of a local military installation, or a private manufacturer's petition to state and local leaders — if not governments — to promote the development of their "little" economies. Although this form of subnational governmental influence is as yet barely recognized, it is an important adjunct to the maintenance of the position of the states.

The extent to which any state takes advantage of Congressional interference does not appear to follow any recognizable pattern. In one sense, every Congressman is so involved in case-work that the differences among the states are marginal. In another sense, some states organize more actively than others to handle state problems in Washington. The Congressional delegations of several states meet together regularly (often once a week) to plan ways and means to serve the interests of their states. While this kind of cooperation is easier in one-party states and is most prevalent among the Southern delegations whose members are past masters in serving their states through interference, states with very competitive two-party systems — such as California, Massachusetts, and Colorado — also unite in Washington without regard for party lines in matters of state interest. For many states, internal political fights stop at the state line and are replaced by a "bipartisan foreign policy" vis-à-vis Washington.

Even when there is cooperation between partisans, many Northern and Western states are hampered in their efforts to gain access to Washington because the very competitiveness of their internal politics leads to a high turnover in their Congressional delegations. One constant in the measurement of influence on Capitol Hill is seniority. All other things being equal, the greater a Representative's seniority, the greater his ability to serve his state and his constituents. Those states which rarely re-elect men long enough to enable them to acquire seniority are invariably handicapped in their efforts.

Perhaps paradoxically, administrative rule-making often has a decentralizing effect that extends the powers of the states even beyond those allowed by Congressional legislation and interference. The decisions of the professional administrators in the federal service who are charged with overseeing specific programs are shaped by many factors, including the personalities of the men involved, the character of their commitment to the program they are administering, and the influence of the professional "guild" to which they belong. This latter factor is of prime importance since many of the ostensibly "Federal" rules are really "federal" in origin — shaped by the associations of professionals serving the states and localities, as well as the federal government whose responsibility it is to implement the very same programs. Frequently, the "Federal" standards governing the construction of interstate highways are products of the American Association of State Highway Officials working in cooperation with the Bureau of Public Roads. Similarly, the National Education Association and the American Association of State Universities have major roles in shaping the rules for implementing the National Defense Education Act. The same situation prevails in most of the major cooperative programs.

When the professional qualifications of the state and local personnel involved in a given program are established, their federal counterparts are apt to regard their views as equally valid and respectable and to give them great leeway in managing even the federal funds granted for their programs. If the federal administrators are also sympathetic to the idea of non-centralized government, they are more likely to minimize use of the powers they are entitled to exercise. When federal and state administrators are in general agreement as to the "right" way to implement particular programs, the states are most likely to be given a free hand. But even when federal administrators "go by the book," their state counterparts are frequently able to avoid further investigation by submitting the requisite formal documents applying for funds and accounting for their use in the approved manner and thus "buy" freedom from real supervision. As a general rule, the better established a program is, the less likely it is that federal administrators will exercise the supervisory powers legally theirs.[26]

GUARANTEES OF STATE "REPUBLICANISM." While the political process has been put to hard use to find ways to guarantee state political integrity against the pressures of centralization, virtually nothing has been added to the Constitutional guarantees that allow federal authority to be used to maintain representative government within the states. Congress has the exclusive authority to decide whether or not a state has "a republican form of government" by accepting or refusing to seat the state's elected Representatives. It is clear that Congress will rarely exercise its powers in this regard. Though not couched in these terms, the recent federal Supreme Court decisions in the realm of reapportionment may possibly be viewed as an effort to establish criteria or "republicanism" and to enforce them through federal intervention.

The greatest opportunity for federal action to give these guarantees meaning came a century ago during the Civil War; yet no significant reliance was placed upon them at that time, either to restore the Union or to reconstruct the seceding states. The various cases of federal military intervention within the states have rarely, if ever, been justified under any of those guarantees. In the one or two cases when states have apparently abandoned representative government in spirit, they have retained the forms of republicanism, and no effort has been made to invoke federal power or even to exclude the states' Representatives from Congress.

In reality then, such guarantees as exist stem from outside the written Constitution, having their source in the nationwide party system and the penetration of national political concerns into the states. While these may appear to be imperfect, short-range guarantees, in the long run they have proven quite effective in breaking or at least lessening the grip of autocracies and oligarchies which, from time to time, have assumed power in various states to frustrate the spirit of republicanism. The universality of political concerns in the United States and the use of the party system to develop nationwide responses to those concerns has meant that the internal political systems of every state have at least had to assimilate certain nationally approved devices for meeting those concerns. The grant programs, for example, have been adopted by every state, from welfare-conscious New York to oligarchical Virginia to racist Mississippi to middle-class oriented Minnesota. In the process, a level of "republicanism" is introduced into each of those states.

The one major addition to the written Constitution which has had profound effects on the position of the states in the Union is the package of Civil War Amendments — Thirteenth, Fourteenth and Fifteenth. That package formally ratified the supremacy of the national government along the lines set forth in Federalist political theory as embraced by the Yankee North.* It provided the Constitutional basis for the expanded federal supervision of state actions in the field of civil and political rights of recent decades.

*Briefly, most Northerners had always held the views that the national government emerged at the same time as the state governments — during the Revolution; that the Union was permanent unless all parties agreed to its dissolution; and that, under the Constitution, the national government was supreme. By the same token, most Southerners had always believed that the states antedated the national government, which they had created; that the Union was held together by a compact, dissolvable by any of the parties to it; and that sovereignty ultimately resided in the states. Both theories

Even these three wartime Amendments, passed in a period of national crisis with the express purpose of asserting federal supremacy, were ultimately cut down to size through the political process. As Reconstruction ended, the restoration of Southern representation in Congress and the emergence of the "Solid South" made it possible for the ex-Confederates virtually to eliminate Congressional or executive action to enforce many of the provisions of these Amendments. Faced with the potentialities for federal action inherent in the War Amendments, the Southerners devised ways to keep these potentials from being translated into action. Control over the choice of Presidential candidates by the Democratic party through the two-thirds rule, the development of the seniority system in Congress, and the use of the filibuster in the Senate gave the Southern states what John C. Calhoun had advocated a generation earlier — the right to demand concurrent majority decisions in all matters affecting their vital interests (particularly the race issue) and the power to exercise a veto under the concurrent majority system. They maintained this right for nearly a century.

While the Southerners were able to frustrate use of these Amendments for the protection of individual liberties, from the 1880's to the 1930's the Fourteenth Amendment was used to restrict state power to regulate private corporations. Today, this means of limiting the power of the states has been substantially overruled and the states again have wide latitude in the use of their regulatory powers. Instead, the Amendments have been used by the Supreme Court to extend its role as arbiter of the standards of fundamental liberty and criminal justice over state as well as federal law-enforcement agencies.[27]

Though the first impression left by the recent use of these Amendments is that they have increased federal dominion over the states, the Court has in fact acted less to extend federal governmental authority than to establish its own position as an umpire interested in raising the standards of justice applicable at all levels of government. Even so, in virtually every case, the Court's decisions have come only after three-fifths of the states have individually adopted positions, and in no important case except those involving reapportionment have less than half of the states been on the same side as the court. This unwritten (and perhaps unconscious) "three-fifths rule" can be seen to be operative in the whole range of desegregation cases, in the Court's decision to disallow the use of illegally obtained evidence in state courts, in the recently established requirement that counsel be provided in all criminal cases, and in the prohibition of mandatory prayers and Bible reading in the schools.

are of equal age and status in the history of American political thought. See Ralph H. Gabriel, *The Course of American Democratic Thought* (2nd ed.; New York: Ronald Press Co., 1956).

Paradoxically, the three Civil War Amendments have had a dual effect. They have formally clarified federal supremacy in the written Constitution and have provided the Court with the means to make that supremacy "stick" in areas previously immune from federal intervention. Yet they also have become the catalysts for the introduction of a modified version of the concurrent majority system into the unwritten constitution for use by both Congress and the Court.

CONCLUSIONS

Politically speaking, the present system of federal-state relations appears to be maintaining itself despite its many public critics who denounce particular cooperative actions such as infringements upon "states-rights" and "local self-government" and who oppose giving the states a share in federal programs on the grounds that the states are "centers of reaction." The system is popular because it provides most of the competing interests in this country — even those groups who rail against it — with enough satisfactions to convince them that it works. And it provides those satisfactions because it is amenable to political influence in the deepest sense.[28]

Perhaps there was a time when it may have been possible to generalize casually about specific interests being satisfied by different levels of government and to establish a precarious balance between the federal government, the states, and the localities by virtue of these different sources of satisfaction. There appear to have been grounds to support this view a generation ago. Today, it is no longer true about any significant interest. Every interest now tries to develop ties with every level of government and will utilize those ties to varying degrees depending upon the specific issue confronting it. This is no doubt a natural concomitant of the growing complexity of the cooperative system and the increasing involvement of all levels of government in handling the same programs.

In the last analysis, the states remain viable entities in a federal system that has every tendency toward centralization, present in all strong governments. States remain viable because they exist with political systems of their own. They maintain that existence because the American political tradition and the Constitution which embodies it give the states an important place in the over-all fabric of American civil society. The tradition and the Constitution remain viable because neither Capitol Hill nor the fifty statehouses have been able to serve all the variegated interests that compete on the American scene equally well without one another. The American people are known to appreciate the tradition and the Constitution. Most important, they seem to appreciate the partnership, too, and have learned to use all its elements to satisfy their claims on government.

NOTES

1. Carey C. Thompson in *Public Affairs Comment,* Institute of Public Affairs, University of Texas, September 1959. Others have echoed this statement in recent years, particularly as the evidence from studies of American federalism has come in. One of the most authoritative recent statements to this effect was that of (the then) Senator Hubert Humphrey in his speech before the National Association of County Officials, July 1964.
2. For further discussion of these distinctions, see the articles on "Decentralization," "Federalism," and "Federation" in *Encyclopedia of the Social Sciences* (New York and London: Macmillan Co., 1931).
3. This summary paraphrases the words of Chief Justice Salmon P. Chase in *Texas* vs. *White,* 7 Wallace 700 (1869), whose description of the Constitutional position of the states remains classic.
4. For some examples of state action of this sort before the turn of the century, see Gilbert T. Stephenson, *Race Distinctions in American Law* (New York and London: D. Appleton and Co., 1910).
5. William Anderson discusses this at length in *The Nation and the States, Rivals or Partners?* (Minneapolis: University of Minnesota Press, 1955).
6. For a good history of the reformers' activities at the state and national level in this period, see Arthur Schlesinger, Jr.'s trilogy, "The Age of Roosevelt," particularly Volumes I and II, *The Crisis of the Old Order* (Boston: Houghton Mifflin Co., 1957) and *The Coming of the New Deal* (Boston: Houghton Mifflin Co., 1959).
7. Morton Grodzins describes this procedure in "American Political Parties and the American System," *Western Political Quarterly XIII* (December 1960).
8. See Daniel J. Elazar, *The American Partnership* (Chicago: University of Chicago Press, 1962) Part II.
9. See Grodzins.
10. For a description of the involved nature of intergovernmental collaboration, see Morton Grodzins, "The Federal System," in *Goals for Americans* (Englewood Cliffs, N.J.: Prentice-Hall, 1960) chapter 12.
11. *Ibid.*
12. See Carl B. Swisher, *The Growth of Constitutional Power in the United States* (rev. ed.; Chicago: University of Chicago Press, 1963).
13. The tidelands oil case is particularly interesting as it generated a tremendous amount of controversy, with states lining up on both sides. For a history of the case, see Ernest R. Bartley, *The Tidelands Oil Controversy: A Legal and Historical Analysis* (Austin: University of Texas Press, 1953).
14. A description of this relationship is available in the report on *Twenty-Five Grant-in-Aid Programs* submitted to the Commission on Intergovernmental Relations (Washington: U.S. Government Printing Office, 1955). See also discussion in chapter 9 in this volume.
15. This incident is described in Nelson A. Rockefeller, *The Future of Federalism* (Cambridge: Harvard University Press, 1962).
16. This is true in the twenty-five states studied in Governmental Affairs Institute, *A Survey Report on the Impact of Federal Grants-in-Aid on the Structure and Functions of State and Local Governments,* submitted to the Commission on Intergovernmental Relations (Washington: U.S. Government Printing Office, 1956). The

writer has confirmed the statement in three additional states (Georgia, Minnesota, and Wisconsin) through field research.

17. Field research, Davenport and Des Moines, Iowa, 1960, and *General Laws of Iowa,* 1961.

18. The writer has evidence of extensive use of federal personnel stationed locally to lobby for community development projects requiring federal aid in Arkansas, Georgia, Illinois, Wisconsin, and Colorado from his field work in those states in 1958, 1960, 1961, and 1962. Evidence of this in other states is available in the files of the Workshop in American Federalism (formerly of the University of Chicago).

19. Tax Foundation, *Facts and Figures on Government Finances, 1962–1963* (Englewood Cliffs, N.J.: Prentice-Hall, 1963).

20. Interview with Lewis Dexter (formerly affiliated with Governor Furcolo on this project), September 9, 1957.

21. See Elazar, Part II.

22. See Jack W. Peltason, *Federal Courts in the Political Process* (New York: Random House, 1955); and John R. Schmidhauser, *The Supreme Court: Its Politics, Personalities, and Procedures* (New York: Holt-Rinehart-Winston, 1960).

23. See V. O. Key, Jr., *Politics, Parties, and Pressure Groups* (4th ed.; New York: Thomas Y. Crowell Co., 1958) chapter 22.

24. See J. Leiper Freeman, *The Political Process: Executive-Legislative Relations* (New York: Random House, 1955) for further discussion of the role of the committee system.

25. Kenneth E. Gray has made a thorough study of "case-work" which is summarized in "Congressional Interference in Administration," a paper presented at the 1962 Annual Meeting of the American Political Science Association, Washington, D.C. This section draws heavily on his work.

26. *The Impact of Federal Grants.*

27. For a study of the Court's changing role, see John R. Schmidhauser, *The Supreme Court as Final Arbiter in Federal-State Relations, 1789–1957* (Chapel Hill: University of North Carolina Press, 1958).

28. Grodzins refers to the extent of these satisfactions in "The Federal System."

SELECTED BIBLIOGRAPHY

BOOKS AND MONOGRAPHS

Anderson, William. *The Nation and the States, Rivals or Partners?* Minneapolis: University of Minnesota Press, 1955. Anderson's minority report for the (Kestnbaum) Commission on Intergovernmental Relations setting forth his views on the legitimacy and strength of cooperative federalism.

————, and Edward Weidner. *Intergovernmental Relations in Minnesota.* Minneapolis: University of Minnesota Press, 1948–1962. 10 Vols. A series of individually authored reports studying various aspects of the federal-state-local relationship in Minnesota, including fiscal affairs, functional aspects of government, specific programs, and specific local problems.

Elazar, Daniel J. *The American Partnership.* Chicago: University of Chicago Press, 1962. A study of the evolution of cooperative federalism before 1913, stressing federal-state sharing of program administration and financing from the early days of the Republic and the politics behind the evolution of sharing.

Goldwin, Robert, ed. *A Nation of States*. Chicago: Rand McNally & Co., 1962. A collection of articles on various aspects of American federalism that provides both a view of the system as it operates and a view of the arguments about how it should operate.

Grodzins, Morton. "The Federal System," *Goals for Americans*. Englewood Cliffs, N.J.: Prentice-Hall, 1960. "American Political Parties and the American System," *Western Political Quarterly XIII* (December 1960). Two important articles by the leading contemporary student of American federalism describing the workings of the federal system from the "cooperative" point of view.

MacMahon, Arthur W., ed. *Federalism: Mature and Emergent*. An excellent collection of articles on various aspects of federalism by leading specialists in their fields. Primarily devoted to analyzing American federalism, it also deals with federal experiences in other countries and prospects for the use of federalism to unify Europe and the developing nations.

GOVERNMENT REPORTS

Reports of the Advisory Commission on Intergovernmental Relations. This is the permanent body created at the end of the Eisenhower administration to provide a continuing review of federal-state-local relations and to promote action to make the federal system function more smoothly. It includes representatives from all levels of government, has a permanent staff, and issues several reports each year, dealing with many aspects of federal-state-local relations, including state-local relations and metropolitan area problems.

Report of the Commission on Intergovernmental Relations, 1955. 16 vols. This is the well-known Kestnbaum Commission, appointed by President Eisenhower to undertake the first complete study of American federalism by an official body. Its report and the accompanying task force studies form the basis for much of the contemporary research in the field of American federalism.

Reports of the Joint Committee on Intergovernmental Relations, 1958 and 1959. This is the second Eisenhower-appointed body to study problems of federalism. Its purpose was to determine how to turn functions back to the states and which functions to return. Its two reports are most interesting for their limited recommendations and the discussion which explains why they were so limited.

Reports of the Subcommittee on Intergovernmental Relations, House Committee on Government Operations. This is the Fountain Subcommittee which has been studying intergovernmental relations since 1956. The published transcripts of its hearings and the reports based on questionnaires sent to those involved in intergovernmental programs are full of important data on the operations of the federal system.

Reports of the Subcommittee on Intergovernmental Relations, Senate Committee on Government Operations. This is the Muskie Subcommittee which began to function in 1961. Its work parallels that of the Fountain Subcommittee and recently the two have begun to hold joint hearings in various parts of the country.

U.S. Department of Commerce, Bureau of the Census. *Census of Governments, 1962.* This multi-volume report is an invaluable compendium of data on governments at all levels in the United States and is particularly important for those studying state and local governments. Similar censuses were taken in 1957, 1952, and 1941.

ABOUT
THE AUTHORS

RICHARD E. DAWSON is Assistant Professor of Political Science at Washington University of St. Louis. He has co-authored an article on welfare politics in the *Journal of Politics* and contributed a paper on simulation to a symposium. He is co-author of a forthcoming book on political socialization.

THOMAS R. DYE is Assistant Professor of Political Science at the University of Georgia. He was previously a member of the research staff of the Fels Institute at the University of Pennsylvania and on the staff of the Bureau of Government, University of Wisconsin. He is the co-author of *Suburban Differences and Metropolitan Policies* (1965), and has written a number of articles on legislative politics and local politics which have appeared in professional journals.

DANIEL J. ELAZAR is Associate Professor of Political Science at Temple University. Prior to this, he was on the staff of the Institute of Government and Public Affairs at the University of Illinois and he has taught at the University of Minnesota. Professor Elazar is the author of *The American Partnership* (1962), has been a contributor to several books, and has published articles in several professional journals.

ROBERT S. FRIEDMAN is Associate Professor and Associate Chairman of the Department of Political Science at the University of Michigan. He has been on the faculties of Louisiana State University and the University of Maryland. Publications he has authored are: *The Michigan Constitutional Convention and Administrative Organization: A Case Study in the Politics of Constitution-Making* (1963), *State and Local Relations in Highway Finance in Louisiana* (1961), and *The Maryland County Unit*

System and Urban-Rural Politics. He is co-author of *Local Government in Maryland* (1958), *Government in Metropolitan New Orleans* (1960), and *Political Leadership and the School Desegregation Crisis in New Orleans* (1963). In addition, he has contributed to numerous professional journals.

HERBERT JACOB is Associate Professor of Political Science at the University of Wisconsin. Earlier, he instructed at Tulane University. He is author of *German Administration Since Bismarck* (1963), and *Justice in America* (1965), and has co-authored *Studies in Judicial Politics* (1963). In addition, he has written articles for several professional journals and symposia.

LESTER W. MILBRATH is Associate Professor of Political Science at Northwestern University. Before this, he taught at Duke University. He wrote *The Washington Lobbyists* (1963), and *Political Participation* (1965), and has contributed to a number of professional journals.

CLARA PENNIMAN is Professor of Political Science at the University of Wisconsin and Chairman of the department. She is the author of *Science and State Government in Wisconsin* (1956), and *Wisconsin's State and Local Tax Burden* (1959); she co-authored *The Minnesota Department of Taxation* (1955), *State Income Tax Administration* (1959), and *Government in the Fifty States* (1960). In addition she has published many articles on taxation in professional journals.

AUSTIN RANNEY is Professor of Political Science at the University of Wisconsin. His published works include *The Doctrine of Responsible Party Government* (1954), *The Governing of Men* (1958), and *Illinois Politics* (1960), and he has a forthcoming volume on the selection of British Parliamentary candidates. He is also co-author of *Democracy and the American Party System* (1956), and editor of *Essays on the Behavioral Study of Politics* (1962). He has also been a contributor of numerous articles to professional journals.

JAMES A. ROBINSON is Professor of Political Science at The Ohio State University. He wrote *Anti-Sedition Legislation and Loyalty Investigations in Oklahoma* (1956), *The Monroney Resolution: Congressional Initiative in Foreign Policy Making* (1959), and *The House Rules Committee* (1963). Professor Robinson co-authored *National and International Decision-Making* (1961), and has written many articles for professional journals.

ROBERT H. SALISBURY is Associate Professor of Political Science at Washington University of St. Louis. He is co-author of *American Govern-*

ment: Readings and Problems for Analysis (1959), *Democracy in the Mid-Twentieth Century* (1960), and *State Politics and the Public Schools* (1963). He has also contributed papers to professional journals and symposia.

JOSEPH A. SCHLESINGER is Professor of Political Science at Michigan State University. He also has served on the faculties of Boston University, Wesleyan University, and the University of California (Berkeley). In addition to *How They Became Governor* (1957), he has written many articles for professional journals.

KENNETH N. VINES is Associate Professor of Political Science at Tulane University. He is the author of *Republicanism in New Orleans* (1956) and *Two Parties for Shreveport* (1958), and co-authored *Theory and Practice of American Foreign Policy* (1955) and *Studies in Judicial Politics* (1963). Besides these, he has written numerous articles on judicial politics for professional journals and symposia.

HARMON ZEIGLER is Associate Professor of Political Science at the University of Oregon. Previously he taught at Florida State University, Emory University, and the University of Georgia. He wrote *Interest Groups in American Society* (1964), is co-author of *Voting Patterns in a Local Election* (1964), and has contributed to professional journals.

INDEX